THE OBLIGATION TO EXTRADITE OR PROSECUTE

The Obligation to Extradite or Prosecute

KRIANGSAK KITTICHAISAREE

OXFORD
UNIVERSITY PRESS

OXFORD
UNIVERSITY PRESS

Great Clarendon Street, Oxford, OX2 6DP,
United Kingdom

Oxford University Press is a department of the University of Oxford.
It furthers the University's objective of excellence in research, scholarship,
and education by publishing worldwide. Oxford is a registered trade mark of
Oxford University Press in the UK and in certain other countries

First Edition published in 2018
Impression: 1

Published in the United States of America by Oxford University Press
198 Madison Avenue, New York, NY 10016, United States of America

British Library Cataloguing in Publication Data
Data available

Library of Congress Control Number: 2017957343

ISBN 978–0–19–882329–2

Printed and bound by
CPI Group (UK) Ltd, Croydon, CR0 4YY

Preface

With the establishment of the International Criminal Court (ICC) in 2002, there was widespread optimism that the new dawn of international criminal justice had arrived, and that international criminal law had come of age. The existence of a permanent ICC would logically dispense with the further need for the United Nations to set up ad hoc international criminal tribunals like the International Criminal Tribunal for the former Yugoslavia, and the need for special courts such as the Special Court for Sierra Leone. However, prosecution before the ICC has been few and far between. Perpetrators of mass atrocities as well as their potential copycats appear undeterred by examples or threats of punishments meted out at the international level. Human rights violations on a heinous scale continue largely unabated in several corners across the globe. A question may be asked: has international criminal law, which has come of age, not continued to mature but instead gone straight into retirement and demise, having fallen into disuse?

There are ongoing efforts by States to supplement supranational justice with the adoption of a new international instrument on mutual legal assistance and extradition concerning the effective national investigation and prosecution of perpetrators of all the major international crimes. Unfortunately, those States unable or unwilling to cooperate with the ICC will not join such initiatives anyway. Hope thus rests with the obligation to extradite or prosecute under international law, the subject of this book.

In 2012, I succeeded the legendary Alain Pellet as chairman of the United Nations International Law Commission's Working Group on the Obligation to Extradite or Prosecute (*aut dedere aut judicare*). The International Law Commission (ILC) submitted its 27-page Final Report on this topic to the United Nations General Assembly in 2014, with numerous important issues, especially the customary international law status of the obligation, unanswered. The ILC's work on the topic provides an excellent starting point for a comprehensive monographic analysis of the concept '*aut dedere aut judicare*' to help ensure that there be no impunity for perpetrators of serious crimes of international concern.

In addition to aiming to be an authoritative guide to the ILC's work on the obligation to extradite or prosecute, this book will provide a comprehensive analysis of the subject, including issues not settled by the ILC, proffering my own legal assessment thereof, and proposing practical solutions to the daunting challenges facing international efforts to bring to account perpetrators of serious atrocities that shock humankind. It is hoped that this book will be useful to States, law enforcement officers, prosecutors, judges, international lawyers, students of international law, and the civil society entrusted with human rights protection.

I would like to express my appreciation to the following persons whose research assistance has made this book possible: Dharshini Prasad, Trevor Pascal Chimimba, Shinyi Mak, David Koh, Isha Mehmood, Margaux V Roussel, and Francesca Dal

Poggetto. I am also most grateful to the invaluable guidance and efficient editorial service of Merel Alstein, James Baird, Natasha Flemming, and their team at the Oxford University Press.

K.K.

Geneva/Moscow/Hamburg
23 November 2017

Contents

Table of Cases

Table of Treaties and Conventions

Table of National Legislation

Table of International Instruments

Table of Statutes of International Tribunals

Abbreviations

ACJHR	African Court of Justice and Human Rights
AFLA	Africa Legal Aid
AJIL	American Journal of International Law
All ER	All England Law Reports
Ann Dig	Annual Digest and Reports of Public International Law Cases, vols 1–16 (1932–55)
App Ch	Appeals Chamber
ASEAN	Association of South East Asian Nations
ASPA	American Servicemembers' Protection Act
AU	African Union
CAR	Central African Republic
CCPCJ	United Nations Commission on Crime Prevention and Criminal Justice
CDPC	European Committee on Crime Problems
CETS	Council of Europe Treaty Series
ch	chapter
CRA	Compensation and Reparation Authority
CRF	Compensation and Reparation Fund
Ct App	Court of Appeal
CTRH	Commission for Truth, Reconciliation and Healing
DGHL	Directorate General of Human Rights Affairs
Dis Op	Dissenting Opinion
Doc	Document
EAC	Extraordinary African Chambers
ECHR	Reports of Judgments and Decisions of the European Court of Human Rights
ECOSOC	Economic and Social Council
ECOWAS	Economic Community of West African States
EHRR	European Human Rights Reports
EJIL	European Journal of International Law
ETS	European Treaty Series
EU	European Union
F 2d	Federal Reporter, Second Series (United States)
F Supp	Federal Supplement (United States)
FARC	Fuerzas Armadas Revolucionarias de Colombia
GCC	Gulf Cooperation Council
HCSS	Hybrid Court for South Sudan

ICC	International Criminal Court
ICC Statute	Rome Statute of the International Criminal Court 1998
ICCPR	International Covenant on Civil and Political Rights 1966
ICJ	International Court of Justice
ICJ Rep	International Court of Justice Reports: Judgments, Advisory Opinions, and Orders
ICLQ	International and Comparative Law Quarterly
ICRC	International Committee of the Red Cross
ICTR	International Criminal Tribunal for the Prosecution of Persons Responsible for Genocide and Other Serious Violations of International Humanitarian Law Committed in the Territory of Rwanda and Rwandan Citizens Responsible for Genocide and Other Such Violations Committed in the Territory of Neighbouring States, between 1 January 1994 and 31 December 1994
ICTY	International Criminal Tribunal for the Prosecution of Persons Responsible for Genocide and Other Serious Violations of International Humanitarian Law Committed in the Territory of the Former Yugoslavia since 1991
IHL	International humanitarian law
IIIM	International Impartial and Independent Mechanism
ILA	International Law Association
ILA's Statement of Principles	International Law Association's *Statement of Principles Applicable to the Formation of General Customary International Law* (2000)
ILC	International Law Commission of the United Nations
ILM	International Legal Materials
ILR	International Law Reports, vols 17– (1956–) [Previously published as Ann Dig]
IMoLIN	International Money Laundering Information Network
IOM	International Organization for Migration
ISIL	Islamic State of Iraq and the Levant
JIL	Journal of International Law
L & Comp Prob	Law and Contemporary Problems
L Rev	Law Review
LNTS	League of Nations Treaty Series
NAM	Non-Aligned Movement
Nuremberg Charter	Charter of the Military Tribunal at Nuremberg annexed to the Agreement for the Prosecution and Punishment of Major War Criminals of the European Axis, London, 8 August 1945
Nuremberg Tribunal	International Military Tribunal Sitting at Nuremberg, Germany
OAS	Organization of American States
OIC	Organization of Islamic Cooperation
PCIJ	Permanent Court of International Justice

PCNICC	Preparatory Commission for the International Criminal Court, 1999–2002
PC-OC	Council of Europe Committee of Experts on the Operation of European Conventions on Co-operation in Criminal Matters
RAA	Reports of International Arbitral Awards
Rep	Report(s)
SAARC	South Asian Association for Regional Cooperation
SALC	Southern African Human Rights Litigation Centre
SAPS	South African Police Service
SCC	Special Criminal Court
Sep Op	Separate Opinion
Ser	Series
SOFA	Status of Forces Agreement
Stat	United States Statutes at Large
Sup Ct	Supreme Court
Supp	Supplement
Secretariat's Survey	International Law Commission Secretariat, *Survey of multilateral conventions which may be of relevance for the work of the International Law Commission on the topic 'The obligation to extradite or prosecute (*aut dedere aut judicare*)'*, 18 June 2010
T Ch	Trial Chamber
TGoNU	Transitional Government of National Unity
Tokyo Charter	Charter of the International Military Tribunal for the Far East, approved by the Supreme Commander of the Allied Powers on 19 January 1946, and amended by General Order No 20 of the Supreme Commander, General Headquarters, APO 500, 26 April 1946
Tokyo Tribunal	International Military Tribunal for the Far East Sitting at Tokyo, Japan
UDHR	Universal Declaration of Human Rights 1948
UJ	universal jurisdiction
UN	United Nations
UN GAOR	UN General Assembly Official Records
UNGA	UN General Assembly
UNHCR	UN High Commission for Refugees
UNODC	UN Office on Drugs and Crime
UNSC	UN Security Council
UNTS	UN Treaty Series
US	Reports of the Supreme Court of the United States
USC	United States Code
YB	Yearbook
YBILC	Yearbook of the International Law Commission

PART I

PROLOGUE

1

General Introduction

I. The Concept of *aut dedere aut judicare*

The obligation to extradite or prosecute is the obligation assumed by a State having custody of an alleged offender to extradite that person to stand trial in another State or, failing that, to prosecute the person in the custodial State itself. Its underlying rationale is to close any gap and eliminate any safe haven that would allow perpetrators to remain unpunished for serious crimes they have committed.

A succinct historical account of this obligation and its logic is explained by President Guillaume of the International Court of Justice (ICJ) in his Separate Opinion in the *Arrest Warrant* case:

The primary aim of the criminal law is to enable punishment in each country of offences committed in the national territory. That territory is where evidence of the offence can most often be gathered. That is where the offence generally produces its effects. Finally, that is where the punishment imposed can most naturally serve as an example. . . .

The question has, however, always remained open whether States other than the territorial State have concurrent jurisdiction to prosecute offenders. A wide debate on this subject began as early as the foundation in Europe of the major modern States. Some writers, like Covarruvias and Grotius, pointed out that the presence on the territory of a State of a foreign criminal peacefully enjoying the fruits of his crimes was intolerable. They therefore maintained that it should be possible to prosecute perpetrators of certain particularly serious crimes not only in the State on whose territory the crime was committed but also in the country where they sought refuge. In their view, that country was under an obligation to arrest, followed by extradition or prosecution, in accordance with the maxim *aut dedere aut judicare* (Covarruvias, *Practicarum quaestionum*, Chap. II, No. 7; Grotius, *De jure belli ac pacis*, Book II, Chap. XXI. para 4; see also Book I, Chap. V).

Beginning in the eighteenth century however, this school of thought favouring universal punishment was challenged by another body of opinion, one opposed to such punishment and exemplified notably by Montesquieu, Voltaire and Jean-Jacques Rousseau (Montesquieu, *L'esprit des lois*, Book 26, Chaps. 16 and 21; Voltaire, *Dictionnaire Philosophique*, heading 'Crimes et délits de temps et de lieu'; Rousseau, *Du contrat social*, Book II, Chap. 12, and Book III, Chap. 18.). Their views found expression in terms of criminal law in the works of Beccaria, who stated in 1764 that 'judges are not the avengers of humankind in general . . . A crime is punishable only in the country where it was committed' (Beccaria. *Traité des délits et des peines*, para 21).

Enlightenment philosophy inspired the lawmakers of the Revolution and nineteenth-century law. Some went so far as to push the underlying logic to its conclusion, and in 1831 Martens could assert that 'the lawmaker's power [extends] over all persons and property present in the State' and that 'the law does not extend over other States and their subject' (GF de Martens. *Précis du droit des gens modernes de l'Europe fondé sur les traités et l'usage*, 1831, Vol I, paras 85 and 86 (see also para 100)).[1]

Judge Guillaume proceeds to cite Arbitrator Max Huber's pronouncement in the *Island of Palmas* arbitration in 1928 that sovereignty in the relations between States signifies independence in the sense of the exclusive competence of the State in regard to its own territory.[2] In fact, Huber reiterates the decision of the Permanent Court of International Justice (PCIJ) in the *Lotus* case between France and Turkey, decided a year earlier and of which he was President, where the PCIJ held that criminal jurisdiction was primarily territorial.[3] Conversely, the PCIJ also ruled that a State may exercise its jurisdiction within its territory in respect of any case that relates to acts that occurred abroad even if there is no specific rule of international law permitting it to do so, and such exercise is only limited by the *prohibitive rules of international law*.[4] The PCIJ found no rule of international law that prohibited Turkey in that case 'to take into consideration the fact that the offence produced its effects on the Turkish vessel and consequently in a place assimilated to Turkish territory in which the application of Turkish criminal law [could not] be challenged, even in regard to offences committed there by foreigners'.[5] The PCIJ cited the practice of national courts of many States, including France, that 'interpret[ed] criminal law in the sense that offences, the authors of which at the moment of commission [were] in the territory of another State, [were] nevertheless to be regarded as having been committed in the national territory, if one of the constituent elements of the offence, and more especially its effects, [had] taken place there'.[6] Turkey thus had criminal jurisdiction over the French national in the case at bar.

Today, it has become acceptable for a State to exercise jurisdiction based on passive personality, active personality, and protective principles. Under the active personality principle of jurisdiction, a State may exercise jurisdiction over the offender on the basis that the offender is a national of that State. Several States have also asserted

[1] §4, Sep Op of Judge Guillaume, *Arrest Warrant of 11 April 2000 (DR Congo v Belgium)* [2002] ICJ Rep 3. Cf also Stoyan Minkov Panov, 'The Obligation *Aut Dedere Aut Judicare* ("Extradite or Prosecute") in International Law: Scope, Content, Sources and Applicability of the Obligation "Extradite or Prosecute"', PhD thesis (Birmingham 2016) 10–23.

[2] *Island of Palmas (Netherlands/United States of America)* (1928) 2 RIAA 829, 838.

[3] 'International law governs relations between independent States. *The rules of law binding upon States therefore emanate from their own free will as expressed in conventions or by usages generally accepted as expressing principles of law* and established in order to regulate the relations between these co-existing independent communities or with a view to the achievement of common aims. *Restrictions upon the independence of States cannot therefore be presumed.*

Now the first and foremost restriction imposed by international law upon a State is that—*failing the existence of a permissive rule to the contrary*—it may not exercise its power in any form in the territory of another State. In this sense jurisdiction is certainly territorial; it cannot be exercised by a State outside its territory except by virtue of a *permissive rule derived from international custom or from a convention*' (*Case of the SS Lotus (France v Turkey)* 1927 PCIJ Rep Series A/ No 10, 18–19, emphasis added).

[4] ibid 19. Emphasis added. [5] ibid 23. [6] ibid.

jurisdiction over the offender on the basis that the offender's victim is a national of that State (that is, the passive personality principle of jurisdiction). A State may, based on the protective principle, exercise jurisdiction over the offender whose conduct abroad threatens that State's security or interferes with the operation of its government functions. The most controversial base of jurisdiction is universal jurisdiction, whereby a State asserts jurisdiction over a crime that has no connection (*nexus*) with that State at all; in other words, the crime is committed outside its territory, does not have any effect therein, and neither the perpetrator nor the victim is its national.

When a person committed a crime of concern to the international community of nations, an ad hoc tribunal might be set up to dispense justice, instead of extraditing the perpetrator to a State willing and able to prosecute him. The trial and punishment of Peter von Hagenbach in 1474 was a case in point. He was a Dutch mercenary in the employment of the Duke of Burgundy, the then French Head of State, to ransack, pillage, commit mass rape in, and burn the city of Breisach in Germany. He was convicted and sentenced to death for murder, rape, and other crimes 'against the laws of God and man' by a tribunal composed of twenty-eight judges from the allied States of the Holy Roman Empire.[7] After the end of the First World War, it was found necessary to set up the Nuremberg and Tokyo Tribunals to try persons who had perpetrated crimes of international concern before and during the Second World War. Starting from 1994, with the establishment of the International Criminal Tribunal for the former Yugoslavia (ICTY) and that for Rwanda (ICTR), culminating in the establishment of the International Criminal Court (ICC) in July 2002, States can surrender to these tribunals the persons accused of committing serious crimes within the jurisdiction of the respective tribunals, and such surrender has become a 'third alternative' to extradition or prosecution of such persons by domestic criminal courts.

Nevertheless, the 'third alternative' is not always available, as, for example, in two high profile cases.

Adolf Eichmann, an Austrian national who was responsible for the implementation of the Final Solution to the Jewish Question during the Nazi rule in Europe, was kidnapped in Argentina in 1960 by a group of Israeli secret agents and brought to stand trial in Israel for crimes against the Jewish people, war crimes, and crimes against humanity. A request for his extradition from Argentina would have been futile since the military regime in power in Argentina at that time seemed to be shielding Eichmann from those wanting to bring him to account for his crimes against the Jews in Europe. The District Court of Jerusalem[8] held, inter alia, that the crimes in question were not only crimes under Israeli law, but also crimes that offended the whole of mankind and shocked the conscience of nations, being grave offences against the law of nations itself (*delicta juris gentium*). It continued:

> 12. . . . [I]n the absence of an International Court, the international law is in need of the judicial and legislative authorities of every country, to give effect to its penal injunctions

[7] M Cherif Bassiouni, 'Perspectives on International Criminal Justice' (2010) 50 Va JIL 269, 298.

[8] *Attorney-General of the Govt of Israel v Eichmann*, Criminal Case No 40/61 (11 Dec 1961) (1962) 56 AJIL 805.

and to bring criminals to trial. The jurisdiction to try crimes under international law is universal.

13. This universal authority, namely the authority of the '*forum deprehensionis*' (the court of the country in which the accused is actually held in custody) was already mentioned in the *Corpus Juris Civilis* (see: C. 3, 15, 'ubi de criminibus agi oportet'), and the towns of northern Italy had already in the Middle Ages taken to trying specific types of dangerous criminals ('banniti, vagabundi, assassini') who happened to be within their area of jurisdiction, without regard to the place in which the crimes in question were committed (see Donnedieu de Vabres, *Les Principes Modernes du Droit Penal International*, 1928, p. 136). Maritime nations have also since time immemorial enforced the principle of universal jurisdiction in dealing with pirates, whose crime is known in English law as 'piracy *jure gentium*.' See Blackstone, *Commentaries on the Laws of England*, Book IV, Chap. 5 'Of Offences against the Law of Nations,' p. 68: . . . . .

The Court ruled that the State of Israel's 'right to punish' the accused derived from two cumulative sources: a universal source (pertaining to the whole of mankind), which vested the right to prosecute and punish crimes of this order in every State within the family of nations; and a specific or national source (the 'protective principle'), which gave the victim nation the right to try any who assaulted its existence.[9] Although the State of Israel did not exist at the time of the accused's commission of the crimes, it was a nascent State for the Jewish people in Europe and elsewhere whose survival was in peril due to the accused's acts; only when the State of Israel attained sovereignty could the State prosecute the accused before its courts.[10] The Court alluded to the UN Security Council Resolution declaring that the kidnapping of Eichmann from Argentina which affected the sovereignty of Argentina causing international friction might, if repeated, endanger international peace and security, and requesting Israel to make appropriate reparation to Argentina.[11] The Court held:

41. It is an established rule of law that a person standing trial for an offence against the laws of a State may not oppose his being tried by reason of the illegality of his arrest, or of the means whereby he was brought to the area of jurisdiction of the State. The courts in England, the United States and Israel have ruled continuously that the circumstances of the arrest and the mode of bringing of the accused into the area of the State have no relevance to his trial, and they consistently refused in all cases to enter into an examination of these circumstances.

The principle was first established in *Ex parte Susanna Scott* (1829) 9 B. & C. 446; 109 E.R. 106.

The Supreme Court of Israel upheld the judgment of the District Court of Jerusalem.[12] It rejected the contentions that the State seeking to exercise universal jurisdiction over such crimes must first offer to extradite the suspect to his own State,

[9] ibid §30. [10] ibid §38.
[11] UNSC Res 138 (23 June 1960) UN Doc S/RES/138.
[12] *Attorney-General of the Govt of Israel v Eichmann* (Israel Sup Ct 1962) (1968) 36 ILR 277 (English translation).

which could lead to endless delays,[13] and that the territorial State where the crimes were committed had priority over other States in prosecuting the suspect.[14]

The other case concerned *Klaus Barbie*, a member of the German SS and head of the Gestapo in Lyon, Occupied France, in 1942, who was wanted by the French authorities for charges of crimes against humanity committed during the Second World War. France submitted a request for his extradition from Bolivia in 1972, but to no avail. Only after a change in the government in Bolivia in late 1982 did his capture by France become possible. In January 1983, he was convicted by a Bolivian court of a thirteen-year-old fraud charge, for which he paid a US$10,000 fine, and was expelled as an undesirable alien. After arriving at an airport in French Guyana, he was arrested and brought back to France for prosecution.[15]

One of the legal questions for French courts was whether Barbie's expulsion from Bolivia and subsequent arrest by France amounted to an illegal, disguised extradition that would nullify the criminal proceedings against him. The French Supreme Court (Criminal Law Chamber) ruled[16] that where there was no extradition proceeding in progress and the alleged acts were not excluded from extradition by French law, there was no obstacle to the exercise of public prosecution in France against the person expelled from a foreign State, provided that the full due process was ensured before the French investigating and trial court.[17] The Supreme Court also ruled that, pursuant to the London Agreement and Charter of the International Military Tribunal of 8 August 1945 (Nuremberg Charter) setting up the Nuremberg Tribunal to try major war criminals of the European Axis,[18] and as recommended by the UN General Assembly Resolution on the Extradition and Punishment of War Criminals of 13 February 1946,[19] persons suspected of committing crimes against humanity must be returned to the States where such crimes were committed, to be tried there, without necessarily using the extradition procedure. These provisions were held to be in conformity with the 'general principles of law recognized by all nations', referred to in the 1966 International Covenant on Civil and Political Rights[20] and the 1950 European Convention on Human Rights and Fundamental Freedoms[21] binding on France, and were regularly incorporated into the domestic

[13] ibid 302.

[14] ibid 303. See also Amnesty International, *Eichmann Supreme Court Judgment: 50 Years On, Its Significance Today* (Amnesty International 2012).

[15] 'Klaus Barbie, 77, Lyons Gestapo Chief', *New York Times* (26 Sept 1991).

[16] Cour de Cassation [Cass] [supreme court for judicial matters] crim, 6 Oct 1983, Bull crim No 83-93194 (Fr).

[17] 2) EXTRADITION—Expulsion par un état étranger—Arrestation et poursuites en France—Application de l'article 23 de la loi du 10 mars 1927 (non).

Dans la mesure où aucune procédure d'extradition n'est en cours et où les faits poursuivis ne sont pas exclus du domaine extraditionnel par la loi du 10 mars 1927, les articles 23 et 25 de cette loi ne peuvent trouver application à l'expulsion ordonnée par un État étranger, et il n'existe aucun obstacle à l'exercice de l'action publique en France contre la personne expulsée, dès lors que la plénitude des droits de la défense lui est assurée devant les juridictions d'instruction et de jugement (2).

[18] 251 UNTS 279.

[19] UNGA Res 3(I) (13 Feb 1946) UN Doc A/RES/3(I).

[20] 999 UNTS 171.

[21] Council of Europe, *European Convention for the Protection of Human Rights and Fundamental Freedoms, as amended by Protocols Nos. 11 and 14*, 4 Nov 1950, ETS 5.

legal order where they enjoyed a higher authority than that of laws, pursuant to Article 55 of the French Constitution.[22] That Article of the French Constitution provides that duly ratified or approved treaties or agreements shall, upon publication, prevail over Acts of Parliament, subject, with respect to each agreement or treaty, to its application by the other party.

The first prong of the ruling of the French Supreme Court echoes the stance of the Israeli courts in *Eichmann* and is in line with the practice of some other nations. For example, the US Supreme Court held in *Alvarez-Machain* that the fact that a suspected person was forcibly abducted from a foreign State does not prohibit his trial in a US court for violations of US criminal laws.[23] This follows a well-established jurisprudence that personal jurisdiction is not affected by claims of abuse in the process by which the defendant is brought before the court, provided that once in the USA he receives protection under the due process of law.[24] However, basing its reasoning on the recommendation of UN General Assembly Resolution 3(I) of 1946,[25] the French Supreme Court in *Barbie* was at variance with the Supreme Court of Israel regarding the priority or absence of a priority for the territorial State to try the offender. The French Supreme Court's recognition of the obligation to return the offender to the State where his crime against humanity was committed as a general principle of law recognized by all nations is of great interest, and will be analysed further in Chapter 6.

Both *Eichmann* and *Barbie* concern the prosecution of perpetrators of 'grave offences against the law of nations (*delicta juris gentium*)', whose extradition from or prosecution by the States where they were present was not possible. Had these States felt bound by international law to extradite or prosecute the offenders, neither Israel nor France would have taken steps outside the process of extradition to bring these offenders to justice. The establishment of the necessary jurisdiction over perpetrators as part of the obligation to extradite or prosecute as well the question of the priority between the States with concurrent jurisdiction over crimes subject to the obligation to extradite or prosecute will be dealt with in Section II of this chapter as well as in the appropriate parts of Chapters 2–6.

[22] 4) CRIMES CONTRE L'HUMANITÉ—Application des règles du droit pénal international—Dérogation au droit commun de l'extradition.

Selon l'accord de Londres et le statut du tribunal militaire international du 8 août 1945, et comme le recommande la résolution des Nations-Unies du 13 février 1946, les personnes soupçonnées d'être les auteurs de crimes contre l'humanité doivent être renvoyées dans les pays où ces crimes ont été commis, pour y être jugées, sans que soit nécessairement utilisée la procédure de l'extradition; ces dispositions sont conformes aux principes généraux de droit reconnus par l'ensemble des nations, auxquels se réfèrent le Pacte international relatif aux droits civils et politiques ainsi que la convention européenne des droits de l'homme et des libertés fondamentales, et elles sont régulièrement intégrées à l'ordre juridique interne où elles bénéficient d'une autorité supérieure à celle des lois, en vertu de l'article 55 de la Constitution (3).

[23] *United States v Alvarez-Machain* 504 US 655 (1992).

[24] *Frisbie v Collins* 342 US 519 (1952).

[25] The pertinent paragraph of the Resolution recommends UN Member States 'to take all the necessary measures to cause the arrest of those war criminals who have been responsible for or have taken a consenting part in [war crimes, crimes against peace and against humanity contained in the Nuremberg Charter], and to cause them to be sent back to the countries in which their abominable deeds were done, in order that they may be judged and punished according to the laws of those countries'.

II. 1996 Draft Code of Crimes against the Peace and Security of Mankind

The topic 'Obligation to extradite or prosecute (*aut dedere aut judicare*)', on the active agenda of the International Law Commission of the United Nations from 2006 to 2014, had a long history in the Commission's work.

The International Law Commission (ILC or Commission) has been set up by the UN General Assembly since 1947 pursuant to Article 13(1)(a) of the UN Charter, stipulating that the UN General Assembly 'shall initiate studies and make recommendations for the purpose of . . . encouraging the progressive development of international law and its codification'.[26] This purpose is reflected in Article 1(1) of the ILC Statute. Article 15 of the Statute distinguishes, 'for convenience', between progressive development as signifying 'the preparation of draft conventions on subjects which have not been regulated by international law or in regard to which the law has not yet been sufficiently developed in the practice of States', on the one hand, and codification as meaning 'the more precise formulation and systematization of rules of international law in the fields where there has already been extensive State practice, precedent and doctrine', on the other hand.

The ILC meets annually for nine to twelve weeks, mostly in Geneva, Switzerland. The first session was held in 1949. The ILC now comprises thirty-four international lawyers from all geographical regions of the world, elected by the UN General Assembly to serve in their individual capacity for a five-year term and may be re-elected.

The topic of jurisdiction with regard to crimes committed outside national territory and that of extradition were included in the list of topics suggested by the ILC Secretariat for consideration of the ILC at its first session in 1949. The former, but not the latter, topic was included in the provisional list of fourteen topics selected by the ILC in 1949 for codification.[27]

The UN General Assembly, by its resolution 177(II) of 21 November 1947, directed the ILC to: (i) formulate the principles of international law on crimes under international law recognized in the Charter of the post-Second World War Nürnberg Tribunal and in the Judgment of that Tribunal; and (ii) prepare a draft code of offences against the peace and security of mankind, indicating clearly the place to be accorded to the principles mentioned in (i).[28]

[26] United Nations, *The Work of the International Law Commission*, vol 1 (8th edn, United Nations 2012) 4–6.

[27] ILC, 'Report of the International Law Commission on the work of its 1st Session', 12 Apr 1949, Official Records of the General Assembly, 4th Session, Supp 10 vol I, A/CN.4/13 and Corr 1–3 §§15–16.

[28] UNGA Res 177(II) (21 Nov 1947) GAOR 2nd Session, UN Doc A/RES/177(II).

The ILC finished its work on (i) in 1950. The seven Principles, which have lasting effects on the development of international criminal law as well as on the obligation to extradite or prosecute, need to be quoted in full. They read:

Principle I

Any person who commits an act which constitutes a crime under international law is responsible therefor and liable to punishment.

Principle II

The fact that internal law does not impose a penalty for an act which constitutes a crime under international law does not relieve the person who committed the act from responsibility under international law.

Principle III

The fact that a person who committed an act which constitutes a crime under international law acted as Head of State or responsible Government official does not relieve him from responsibility under international law.

Principle IV

The fact that a person acted pursuant to order of his Government or of a superior does not relieve him from responsibility under international law, provided a moral choice was in fact possible to him.

Principle V

Any person charged with a crime under international law has the right to a fair trial on the facts and law.

Principle VI

The crimes hereinafter set out are punishable as crimes under international law:

(a) Crimes against peace:
   (i) Planning, preparation, initiation or waging of a war of aggression or a war in violation of international treaties, agreements or assurances;
   (ii) Participation in a common plan or conspiracy for the accomplishment of any of the acts mentioned under (i).

(b) War crimes:
   Violations of the laws or customs of war which include, but are not limited to, murder, ill-treatment or deportation to slave-labour or for any other purpose of civilian population of or in occupied territory, murder or ill-treatment of prisoners of war, of persons on the seas, killing of hostages, plunder of public or private property, wanton destruction of cities, towns, or villages, or devastation not justified by military necessity.

(c) Crimes against humanity:
   Murder, extermination, enslavement, deportation and other inhuman acts done against any civilian population, or persecutions on political, racial or religious grounds, when such acts are done or such persecutions are carried on in execution of or in connection with any crime against peace or any war crime.

Principle VII

Complicity in the commission of a crime against peace, a war crime, or a crime against humanity as set forth in Principle VI is a crime under international law.[29]

In parallel, in December 1948 the UN General Assembly invited the ILC to study the feasibility and desirability of setting up an international judicial organ to try persons charged with genocide and other crimes over which jurisdiction would be conferred on that organ by international conventions, including the possibility of setting up a Criminal Chamber of the ICJ.[30] The disagreement of the international community on the definition of aggression hindered any progress in relation to the possibility of the establishment of such organ and the adoption of the Draft Code of Offences against the Peace and Security of Mankind as it stood in 1954, which included the crime of aggression therein. In December 1981, the UN General Assembly invited the ILC to resume its work on the Draft Code, the title of which was changed by the ILC in 1987 to the 'Draft Code of Crimes against the Peace and Security of Mankind'.[31]

The 'obligation to extradite or punish' first appears in the report of the Special Rapporteur on the Draft Code in 1987, relying on national courts to enforce the Code without ruling out the possibility of enforcement by an international criminal court at a later stage. It reads:

Article 4. ***Aut dedere aut punire***

1. Every State has the duty to try or extradite any perpetrator of an offence against the peace and security of mankind arrested in its territory.
2. The provision in paragraph 1 above does not prejudge the establishment of an international criminal jurisdiction.[32]

In 1988, the ILC provisionally adopted Draft Article 4, as amended, to read:

Article 4. Obligation to try or extradite

1. Any State in whose territory an individual alleged to have committed a crime against the peace and security of mankind is present shall either try or extradite him.
2. If extradition is requested by several States, special consideration shall be given to the request of the State in whose territory the crime was committed.
3. The provisions of paragraphs 1 and 2 of this article do not prejudge the establishment and the jurisdiction of an international criminal court.* [*This paragraph will be deleted if an international criminal court is established.]

The accompanying commentary to the said Draft Article explains that several possibilities were open to the ILC for ensuring the punishment of the crimes covered in the Draft Code: first, to give jurisdiction to an international criminal court; secondly, to make national courts competent for the prosecution of such crimes; thirdly, to have an international court coexist with national courts; and

29 (1950) ii YBILC 374–78.
30 UNGA Res 260(III) (9 Dec 1948) GAOR 3rd Session, UN Doc A/RES/260(III) Part B.
31 UN, *The Work of the ILC* 97–107.
32 (1987) ii YBILC (Part One) 5; UN, *The Work of the ILC* 108.

fourthly, to enforce the Code through national courts to which would be added a judge from the jurisdiction of the accused and/or one or more judge from jurisdictions whose jurisprudence differed from that of both the accused and the national court in question. Without ruling out any of these solutions, which might be considered at a later stage, the ILC opted for national courts. It also decided that Article 4 would relate only to the general principles of jurisdiction and extradition, leaving the formulation of more specific rules for the actual implementation of the Code which would be included in an appropriate part of the Draft Code to a later stage.

Paragraph 1 establishes the general principle that any State in whose territory an individual alleged to have committed a crime under the Draft Code is present shall either try or extradite him, drawing on the relevant provisions of the 1970 Convention for the Suppression of Unlawful Seizure of Aircraft[33] (Art 7); 1973 Convention on the Prevention and Punishment of Crimes against Internationally Protected Persons, including Diplomatic Agents[34] (Art 7); 1971 Organization of American States' Convention to Prevent and Punish Acts of Terrorism Taking the Form of Crimes against Persons and Related Extortion that Are of International Significance[35] (Art 5); 1977 European Convention on the Suppression of Terrorism[36] (Art 7); and 1979 International Convention against the Taking of Hostages[37] (Art 8(1)). The commentary points out that one member of the ILC reserved his position on Article 4 as a whole, whereas some members could not accept the general applicability of universal jurisdiction to the Draft Code.[38]

The ILC accomplished its work on the Draft Code in 1996.[39] Articles 8, 9, and 10 of the 1996 Draft Code are of direct relevance to the obligation to extradite or prosecute. They read:

Article 8. Establishment of jurisdiction

Without prejudice to the jurisdiction of an international criminal court, each State Party shall take such measures as may be necessary to establish its jurisdiction over the crimes set out in articles 17 [genocide], 18 [crimes against humanity], 19 [crimes against United Nations and associated personnel] and 20 [war crimes], irrespective of where or by whom those crimes were committed. Jurisdiction over the crime set out in article 16 [aggression] shall rest with an international criminal court. However, a State referred to in article 16 is not precluded from trying its nationals for the crime set out in that article.

Article 9. Obligation to extradite or prosecute

Without prejudice to the jurisdiction of an international criminal court, the State Party in the territory of which an individual alleged to have committed a crime set out in article 17, 18, 19 or 20 is found shall extradite or prosecute that individual.

[33] 860 UNTS 105. [34] 1035 UNTS 167. [35] OAS Treaty Series No 37.
[36] ETS No 90. [37] 1316 UNTS 205. [38] (1988) ii YBILC (Part Two) 67–68.
[39] (1996) ii YBILC (Part Two) 17.

Article 10. Extradition of alleged offenders

1. To the extent that the crimes set out in articles 17, 18, 19 and 20 are not extraditable offences in any extradition treaty existing between States Parties, they shall be deemed to be included as such therein. States Parties undertake to include those crimes as extraditable offences in every extradition treaty to be concluded between them.
2. If a State Party which makes extradition conditional on the existence of a treaty receives a request for extradition from another State Party with which it has no extradition treaty, it may at its option consider the present Code as the legal basis for extradition in respect of those crimes. Extradition shall be subject to the conditions provided in the law of the requested State.
3. States Parties which do not make extradition conditional on the existence of a treaty shall recognize those crimes as extraditable offences between themselves subject to the conditions provided in the law of the requested State.
4. Each of those crimes shall be treated, for the purpose of extradition between States Parties, as if it had been committed not only in the place in which it occurred but also in the territory of any other State Party.

Article 8 envisages the establishment of two separate jurisdictional regimes for the crimes under the Draft Code. In the first instance, the national courts of States Parties would be entitled to exercise the broadest possible jurisdiction under the principle of universal jurisdiction. In addition, an international criminal court would be entitled to exercise concurrent jurisdiction over those crimes in accordance with its statute. In the second instance, an international criminal court would have exclusive jurisdiction over the crime of aggression with the singular exception of the national court jurisdiction of the State which committed the aggression.

The obligation to extradite or prosecute is reflected in several conventions, especially those against international terrorism, the fundamental purpose of which is to ensure that individuals who are responsible for particularly serious crimes are brought to justice by providing for the effective prosecution and punishment of such individuals by a competent jurisdiction. Article 9 establishes the general obligation that any State in whose territory an individual alleged to have committed a crime under the Draft Code except for aggression is bound to extradite or prosecute the alleged offender. Article 9 permits, but not obliges, each State Party to decide whether to provide for the jurisdiction of its national courts with respect to the crime of aggression and whether to include this crime in its bilateral or multilateral agreements with other States.

The obligation to prosecute or extradite is imposed on the custodial State in whose territory an alleged offender is present, whereby the custodial State shall take action to ensure that such an individual is prosecuted either by the national authorities of that State or by another State willing to prosecute the case by requesting extradition. The custodial State is in a 'unique position' to ensure the implementation of the Draft Code by virtue of the presence of the alleged offender in its territory and, thus, shall take the necessary and reasonable steps to apprehend an alleged offender and to ensure the prosecution and trial of such an individual by a competent jurisdiction. Any State Party in whose territory an alleged offender is present is competent to try the case regardless of where the crime occurred or the nationality of the offender or the victim, the physical presence of the alleged offender being a sufficient basis for the exercise of jurisdiction by the custodial State. This exceptional basis for the exercise of jurisdiction is often referred to as 'the principle of universality' or 'universal jurisdiction'.

The custodial State usually has a choice between two alternative courses of action either of which is intended to result in the prosecution of the alleged offender: namely, granting a request for the extradition of an alleged offender made by any other State *or* prosecuting that individual in its national courts. Article 9 does not give priority to either alternative course of action, but gives the custodial State discretion to decide. The custodial State may fulfil its obligation under the first alternative by granting a request received for extradition and thereby transferring to the requesting State the responsibility for the prosecution of the case. The ILC clarifies that the custodial State is not required to give priority to a request for extradition made by a particular State if the custodial State receives a plurality of requests from more than one State. While the then Draft Article adopted on first reading recommended that particular consideration should be given to a request from the State in whose territory the crime was committed and the Special Rapporteur of the Draft Code himself proposed on second reading that consideration be given to the inclusion of the priority of the request of the territorial State, the Drafting Committee considered that this question was not ripe for codification. The discretion of the custodial State in this respect is considered by the ILC to be consistent with the Model Treaty on Extradition (Art 16).[40]

Although Article 9 does not specifically address the transfer of an individual who committed any crime under the Draft Code to an international criminal court or the extradition of an individual with respect to the crime of aggression to the State which committed aggression, the commentary to Article 9 recognizes that the custodial State can transfer the alleged offender to a competent international criminal court for prosecution.

In the absence of a request for extradition to another State or transfer to a competent international criminal court, the custodial State would have 'no choice' but to submit the case to its national authorities for prosecution. This 'residual obligation' is intended to ensure that alleged offenders will be prosecuted by the custodial State, in the absence of an alternative national or international jurisdiction.

'An individual alleged to have committed a crime' means 'a person who is singled out, not on the basis of unsubstantiated allegations but on the basis of pertinent factual information'. The ILC recognizes that the national laws of various States differ on the sufficiency of evidence required to initiate a criminal prosecution or to grant a request for extradition. In this regard, the custodial State shall prosecute an alleged offender in its territory when there is sufficient evidence for doing so as a matter of national law unless it decides to grant an extradition request by another State. The element of prosecutorial discretion under which an alleged offender may be granted immunity from prosecution in exchange for giving evidence or assisting with the

[40] UNGA Res 45/116 (14 Dec 1990) UN Doc A/RES/45/116, Annex.

prosecution of another individual whose criminal conduct is considered to be more serious, as recognized in some legal systems, is precluded with respect to the crimes covered by the Draft Code, which are serious crimes of concern to the international community.

The sufficiency of evidence required to grant an extradition request is addressed in the various bilateral and multilateral treaties. The UN Model Treaty on Extradition (Art 5(2)(b)) requires as a minimum 'a statement of the offence for which extradition is requested and a description of the acts or omissions constituting the alleged offence, including an indication of the time and place of its commission'. The relevant provision common to the four Geneva Conventions of 12 August 1949 relating to the protection of victims of armed conflict refers to the notion of a prima facie case.

The obligation to extradite or prosecute an alleged offender under Article 9 is further addressed in Articles 8 and 10 in order to facilitate and ensure the effective implementation of either option.[41]

The 1996 Draft Code of Crimes against the Peace and Security of Mankind, in effect, laid down the groundwork for the ILC's work on the topic 'Obligation to extradite or prosecute (*aut dedere aut judicare*)' in 2006–14.

III. The Treaty Obligation to Extradite or Prosecute for the Most Serious Crimes

The crimes prosecuted by the Nuremberg Tribunal after the Second World War were the crimes against peace (now known as aggression), crimes against humanity, and war crimes. What is now known as genocide was prosecuted by that Tribunal under the heading of crimes against humanity.[42] Of these crimes, only genocide and war crimes are currently regulated by treaties that require their States Parties to prosecute perpetrators of such crimes before domestic courts.

The 1948 Convention for the Prevention and Punishment of the Crime of Genocide[43] does not have any provision on the obligation to extradite or prosecute. Article VI of the Convention merely subjects the person who committed any offence under the Convention to trial by 'a competent tribunal of the State in the territory of which the act was committed, or by such international penal tribunal as may have jurisdiction with respect to those Contracting Parties which shall have accepted its jurisdiction'.

The provision on penal sanctions under each of the four Geneva Conventions of 12 August 1949 is of relevance to the obligation to extradite or prosecute. The High Contracting Parties to the respective Conventions undertake to enact any legislation necessary to provide effective penal sanctions for persons committing, or ordering to be committed, any of the 'grave breaches' of the Conventions. Each High Contracting Party shall 'search for persons alleged to have committed, or to

[41] (1996) ii YBILC (Part Two) 31–32.
[42] See Kriangsak Kittichaisaree, *International Criminal Law* (OUP 2001) 17–22, 67.
[43] 78 UNTS 277.

have ordered to be committed, such grave breaches, and shall bring such persons, regardless of their nationality, before its own courts'. However, it 'may also, if it prefers, and in accordance with the provisions of its own legislation, hand such persons over for trial to another High Contracting Party concerned, provided such High Contracting Party has made out a prima facie case'.[44] Article 147 of the fourth Geneva Convention defines 'grave breaches'—which are the most serious war crimes—as the following acts, if committed against persons or property protected by that Convention: wilful killing, torture or inhuman treatment, including biological experiments, wilfully causing great suffering or serious injury to body or health, unlawful deportation or transfer or unlawful confinement of a protected person, compelling a protected person to serve in the forces of a hostile Power, or wilfully depriving a protected person of the rights of fair and regular trial prescribed in the Convention, taking of hostages, and extensive destruction and appropriation of property, not justified by military necessity and carried out unlawfully and wantonly. The other three Geneva Conventions of 1949 also contain a similar definition of grave breaches, with necessary adjustmentfs to suit the purpose of the respective Conventions.

The 1948 Convention and the four Geneva Conventions of 1949 are often referred to as catalysts for the obligation to extradite or prosecute, as the following chapters will show.

[44] Geneva Convention for the amelioration of the condition of the wounded and the sick in armed forces in the field (75 UNTS 31), Art 49; Geneva Convention for the amelioration of the condition of wounded, sick and shipwrecked members of armed forces at sea (75 UNTS 85), Art 50; Geneva Convention relative to the treatment of prisoners of war (75 UNTS 135), Art 129; Geneva Convention relative to the protection of civilian persons in time of war (75 UNTS 287), Art 146.

2

The International Law Commission's Work on the Obligation to Extradite or Prosecute (*aut dedere aut judicare*)

I. Background

The International Law Commission (ILC) has established the criteria for the selection of new topics. They should reflect the needs of States in respect of progressive development and codification of international law; be sufficiently advanced in stage in terms of State practice to permit progressive development and codification; and be concrete and feasible for progressive development and codification. In this regard, the ILC should not restrict itself to traditional topics, but should also consider those that reflect new developments in international law and pressing concerns of the international community.[1] Topics can be suggested by States in the Sixth (Legal) Committee of the UN General Assembly, by the ILC Secretariat and, usually, by ILC members. To propose a topic, a syllabus needs to be developed for consideration of the ILC Working Group on Long-Term Programmes of Work. Once approved by that Working Group, with all necessary amendments and revisions, the topic will be submitted to the ILC Plenary for endorsement to be placed on the ILC's long-term programmes of work. The ILC normally has eight to ten active topics under its consideration each year. The person entrusted with direct responsibility for a topic submits his or her report for the consideration of the ILC. General statements on the report are made in the Plenary, normally held in the morning. After the end of the general statements, the ILC decides whether to refer the suggested draft articles, conclusions, or guidelines to a drafting committee. If the ILC decides to do so, the drafting committee will be set up for that topic comprising ILC members volunteering to be committee members plus the person responsible for the topic, the chair of the ILC Drafting Committee for that particular year, and the Rapporteur of the ILC report for that year. The committee meets in the afternoon to work on drafting, which is a time-consuming process and a main reason why the ILC cannot actively pursue more than eight to ten topics each year.

[1] (1997) ii YBILC (Part Two) 71–72 [238] and (2000) ii YBILC (Part Two) 131 [728].

The final outcome of a topic can be a set of draft articles to be submitted to the Sixth (Legal) Committee of the UN General Assembly (Sixth Committee) to take action upon. Draft articles by the ILC that have become international conventions include ones on diplomatic and consular relations,[2] the law of the sea,[3] the law of treaties,[4] and the 1998 Rome Statute of the International Criminal Court (ICC Statute).[5] The best-known draft articles that have not become an international convention but are authoritative and frequently cited by the International Court of Justice (ICJ) and international tribunals are the ILC's Articles on Responsibility of States for Internationally Wrongful Acts, adopted by the ILC in 2001. In 2006, one ILC Study Group produced its final report on 'Fragmentation of international law: difficulties arising from diversification and expansion of international law', which is more than 250 pages in length. Also in 2006, the ILC adopted the relatively concise 'Guiding Principles applicable to unilateral declarations of States capable of creating legal obligations'. The final outcome of the ILC's work on a particular topic is normally decided as the work on that topic progresses.

In 2004, the ILC put on its long-term programme of work the topic 'The obligation to extradite or prosecute (*aut dedere aut judicare*) in international law'. The syllabus was prepared by Zdislaw Galicki.[6] The Latin phrase *aut dedere aut judicare* was said to mean 'either extradite or prosecute', and a modern adaptation of the phrase *aut dedere aut punire* (either extradite or punish all offences by which another State is injured) used by Hugo Grotius in the early seventeenth century.[7]

According to the syllabus, in order to determine the effectiveness of the system based on the obligation to extradite or prosecute, three problems would need to be addressed: (1) the status and scope of application of the obligation under international law; (2) the hierarchy among the options under the obligation, provided that the requested State has a choice; and (3) practical difficulties in exercising *judicare*.[8]

A preliminary task in future codification work would be to complete a comparative list of relevant treaties and formulas used by them to reflect this obligation, which could be significantly strengthened by combining it with the principle of universality of suppression that denied 'safe haven' to criminals (which would not be the same thing as the principle of universality of jurisdiction or universality of competence of judicial organs).

[2] 1961 Vienna Convention on Diplomatic Relations (500 UNTS 95) and 1963 Vienna Convention on Consular Relations (596 UNTS 261).

[3] 1958 Geneva Convention on the High Seas (450 UNTS 82), 1958 Geneva Convention on the Continental Shelf (499 UNTS 311), 1958 Geneva Convention on the Territorial Sea and the Contiguous Zone (516 UNTS 205), and 1958 Geneva Convention on Fishing and Conservation of the Living Resources of the High Seas (559 UNTS 285).

[4] 1969 Vienna Convention on the Law of Treaties (1155 UNTS 331).

[5] 2187 UNTS 90.

[6] ILC, 'Report of the International Law Commission on the work of its 56th Session' (3 May–4 June and 5 July–6 Aug 2004) UN Doc A/59/10, Annex, 312.

[7] ibid 312 [2].

[8] Citing Michael Plachta, 'Aut dedere aut judicare: An Overview of Modes of Implementation and Approaches' (1999) 6 Maastricht J Euro & Comp L 332.

The syllabus mentioned the 1996 Draft Code's recognition of the existence of this obligation in Article 9, albeit exclusively in relation to a strictly limited and defined group of offences, described generally as crimes against the peace and security of mankind. The ILC was said to have introduced the concept of 'triple alternative', a possibility of parallel jurisdictional competence to be exercised not only by interested States, but also by international criminal courts.[9] Galicki alluded to the *Lockerbie* case before the ICJ, where Judge Weeramantry's dissenting opinion mentioned the existence of 'the rule of customary international law, *aut dedere aut judicare*',[10] while Judge Ajibola, also dissenting, opined that the requested State 'ha[d] a right recognized in international law and even considered by some jurists as *jus cogens*' to resort to the prosecution, in lieu of extradition, of the offender found in its territory.[11] A norm of *jus cogens* or a peremptory norm is a norm 'accepted and recognized by the international community of States as a whole from which no derogation is permitted and which can be modified only by a subsequent norm of general international law having the same character'.[12]

Galicki agreed with the view that, to be effective, the obligation had to be accepted as an indispensable element of the suppression of criminality and bringing offenders to justice in an international arena, and that the scope of this obligation should not be limited to international crimes as defined in international conventions.[13]

The topic 'The obligation to extradite or prosecute (*aut dedere aut judicare*)' was included in the ILC's current programme of work at its fifty-seventh session (2005), and Galicki appointed Special Rapporteur. The UN General Assembly endorsed this decision on 23 November 2005.

II. The ILC's Work 2006–2011

From 2006 to 2011, the ILC received and considered four reports by the Special Rapporteur. The Special Rapporteur presented his methodology in his preliminary report in 2006 that there were several main points to be considered from the beginning by the ILC.[14]

First, it was necessary to have a comprehensive comparative analysis of appropriate provisions concerning the obligation to extradite or prosecute contained

[9] In fact, the phrase 'third alternative' was used in the ILC's commentary to Article 9 of the Draft Code.

[10] *Questions of Interpretation and Application of the 1971 Montreal Convention arising from the Aerial Incident at Lockerbie*, Provisional Measures, Order of 14 Apr 1992 [1992] ICJ Rep 3, 52 (*Libyan Arab Jamahiriya v UK*) and 161 (*Libyan Arab Jamahiriya v USA*).

[11] ibid 82 and 187, respectively.

[12] Art 53, Vienna Convention on the Law of Treaties of 1969 (1155 UNTS 331). For an analysis of the content and case law on *jus cogens*, see Martti Koskenniemi, 'Fragmentation of International Law: Difficulties arising from the Diversification and Expansion of International Law', Report of the Study Group of the International Law Commission, UN Doc A/CN.4/L.682 (13 Apr 2006) §§374–79.

[13] Citing Plachta, 'Aut dedere aut judicare' 364.

[14] These points had already appeared as part of his preliminary plan of action accompanying the proposed syllabus for the topic submitted in 2004 (ILC, 'Report of . . . its 56th Session') §§21–28.

in the relevant conventions and other international instruments, together with a systematic identification of existing similarities and differences. Such analysis was to include the presentation of the evolution and development of the obligation to extradite or prosecute, from the 'Grotius formula' to the 'triple alternative', namely, extradite or punish; extradite or prosecute; extradite or prosecute or surrender to an international court.

Secondly, since the *aut dedere aut judicare* principle appears to be assimilated in many internal legislations, a systematic documentation of relevant legal provisions in domestic law and their actual implementation by States would be undertaken. The third step was to identify the sources of this obligation as deriving exclusively from international treaties, or as rooted also in customary norms. There was also the possibility of a mixed nature of the obligation in question when, for instance, *dedere* derived from conventional commitments, while *judicare* might be based on customary norms (or vice versa). The fourth initial task would be to establish as precisely as possible the existing mutual relationship and interdependence between the principle of universal jurisdiction and the obligation of *aut dedere aut judicare*. One of the most decisive factors to be established was the extent of the substantive application of the obligation to extradite or prosecute, either: (1) to all offences by which another State is particularly injured (*per* Grotius); or (2) to a limited category or categories of offences/crimes (eg to the 'crimes against the peace and security of mankind', or to 'international offences', or to 'crimes under international law', or to 'crimes under national law of international concern'). Identifying the possible criteria for such offences would be highly important. The content of the obligation to extradite or prosecute would be identified and analysed, taking into account its complex and alternative nature, including both the *dedere* and *judicare* limbs of this obligation. Such content was to encompass the conditions and exceptions to extradition, as well as grounds for establishing the necessary jurisdiction. The rights of States in case of the application and non-application of the *aut dedere aut judicare* obligation would also be discussed.

Galicki also proposed to consider the relations between the obligation to extradite or prosecute and other rules concerning jurisdictional competences of States in criminal matters, including the principle of 'universality of jurisdictional competences' as exercised by States or international judicial organs. The legal nature of particular obligations deriving under international law from the application of the obligation to extradite or prosecute should be defined, while paying special attention to: (1) the equality of alternative obligations (extradite or prosecute), or a prevailing position of one of them (hierarchy of obligations); (2) possible limitations or exclusions in fulfilling alternative obligations (eg non-extradition of own nationals, the political offences exception, limitations deriving from human rights protection); (3) any possible impact of such limitations or exclusions on another kind of obligation (eg the impact of extradition exceptions on alternatively exercised prosecution); (4) whether the obligation in question was a rule of substantive or procedural character, or of a mixed one; and (5) the position of the obligation in question in the hierarchy of norms of international law, be they a secondary rule, a primary rule, or a norm of *jus cogens*.

Finally, Galicki would analyse the relation between the obligation to extradite or prosecute and other principles of international law, such as State sovereignty, human rights protection, and universal suppression of certain crimes, as well as the impact of these principles on the extent of application of the obligation.[15]

Members of the ILC, reacting to the preliminary report by the Special Rapporteur, held varying views. All agreed that the objective of the obligation was to end impunity of persons suspected of having committed international crimes, especially those particularly grave crimes of international concern. Some members suggested that distinction be made between treaty-based crimes and crimes recognized under customary international law, such as war crimes, genocide, and crimes against humanity, while excluding from the scope of the topic crimes that were solely prosecuted under national laws. It was also suggested that the ILC focus on gaps in existing treaties, such as the execution of punishment and the lack of a monitoring system with regard to compliance with the obligation to prosecute. Some ILC members proposed that the ILC consider practical difficulties in the process of extradition, such as insufficiency of evidence, limitations on the extradition of nationals, and the failure to recognize the human rights of the person extradited. Others, however, cautioned against considering technical aspects of extradition law. The ILC generally agreed to focus on the obligation to extradite or prosecute, and not on the distinct but related concept of universal jurisdiction. Opinions were divided as to whether the ILC should analyse the third alternative, with those opposing it opining that the existing international criminal tribunals had their own *lex specialis* rules while those in favour of such analysis found it necessary for the ILC to pursue this task. On the whole, the ILC reached a general consensus that the scope of the topic should be limited as far as possible so as to concentrate on the issues directly connected with the obligation to extradite or prosecute, as well as on the analysis of the principal elements of the obligation, ie *dedere* and *judicare*.[16]

At the end of its annual session in 2006, the ILC requested information from governments on the following issues:

i. International treaties by which a State is bound, containing the obligation to extradite or prosecute, and reservations made by that State to limit the application of this obligation;
ii. Domestic legal regulations adopted and applied by a State, including constitutional provisions and penal codes of criminal procedures, concerning the obligation to extradite or prosecute (*aut dedere aut judicare)*;
iii. Judicial practice of a State reflecting the application of the obligation to extradite or prosecute (*aut dedere aut judicare)*;
iv. Crimes or offences to which the principle of the obligation *aut dedere aut judicare* is applied in the legislation or practice of a State.[17]

[15] Preliminary report, UN Doc A/CN.4/571 §61, footnotes omitted.
[16] ILC, 'Report of the International Law Commission on the work of its 58th Session' (1 May–9 June and 3 July–11 Aug 2006) UN Doc A/61/10 ch XI.
[17] ibid §30.

Only seven States responded to this request for information by the time the Special Rapporteur had finalized his second report in 2007.

The Special Rapporteur's second report took into account the views expressed in the Sixth Committee regarding his preliminary report. He stated the need to recapitulate the gist of his preliminary report in the light of the fact that the ILC election in late 2006 had replaced around half of the ILC members. The second report was a revised version of his preliminary report, adding comments received from governments to date. Taking into account the considerations made in his preliminary and second reports, the Special Rapporteur suggested the following formulation of the first draft article:

Article 1. Scope of application

The present draft articles shall apply to the establishment, content, operation and effects of the alternative obligation of States to extradite or prosecute persons under their jurisdiction.[18]

In their general comments, ILC members expressed opinions, in particular, on the source of the obligation to extradite or prosecute, its relationship with universal jurisdiction, the scope of the obligation and its two constitutive elements, and the 'triple' alternative. While some members found Draft Article 1 as proposed to be acceptable in principle, others found it difficult for the ILC to take a position on the scope of the draft articles on the topic without knowing the Special Rapporteur's view on subsequent issues, including that of the source of the obligation to extradite or prosecute. It was suggested that the Special Rapporteur present a systematic survey of the relevant international treaties in the field. Although some States had replied to the ILC's request for information, the ILC found the debates in the Sixth Committee and the comments received from governments insufficient, but that, nevertheless, the Special Rapporteur and the ILC were to approach the topic on an independent basis, taking into account comments made by States, including, if appropriate, making proposals for the progressive development of international law in the field.[19]

At the end of its annual session in 2007, the ILC sought further information from governments on the following questions, which were slightly modified from the ones asked in 2006:

i. International treaties by which a State is bound, containing the principle of universal jurisdiction in criminal matters; is it connected with the obligation *aut dedere aut judicare*?
ii. Domestic legal regulations adopted and applied by a State, including constitutional provisions and penal codes or codes of criminal procedure, concerning the principle of universal jurisdiction in criminal matters; is it connected with the obligation *aut dedere aut judicare*?

18 UN Doc A/CN.4/585 §76.

19 ILC, 'Report of the International Law Commission on the work of its 59th Session' (7 May–5 June and 9 July–10 Aug 2007) UN Doc A/62/10 ch IX.

iii. Judicial practice of a State reflecting the application of the principle of universal jurisdiction in criminal matters; is it connected with the obligations *aut dedere aut judicare*?

iv. Crimes or offences to which the principle of universal jurisdiction in criminal matters is applied in the legislation and practice of a State; is it connected with the obligation *aut dedere aut judicare*?

At the same session the ILC also indicated its desire for information on the following questions:

i. Whether the State has authority under its domestic law to extradite persons in cases not covered by a treaty or to extradite persons of its own nationality?

ii. Whether the State has authority to assert jurisdiction over crimes occurring in other States that do not involve one of its nationals?

iii. Whether the State considers the obligation to extradite or prosecute as an obligation under customary international law and if so to what extent?[20]

In June 2008, the Special Rapporteur submitted his third report, taking account of the debates in the ILC and the Sixth Committee as well as information given by twenty States in reply to the ILC's questions. He presented the following draft articles.

Article 1 Scope of application

The present draft articles shall apply to the establishment, content, operation and effects of the legal obligation of States to extradite or prosecute persons [under their jurisdiction] [present in the territory of the custodial State] [under the control of custodial State].

Article 2 Use of terms

1. For the purposes of the present draft articles:
   (a) 'extradition' means ....;
   (b) 'prosecution' means ....;
   (c) 'jurisdiction' means ....;
   (d) 'persons under jurisdiction' means.......;
   ...

2. The provisions of paragraph 1 regarding the use of terms in the present draft articles are without prejudice to the use of those terms or to the meanings which may be given to them [in other international instruments or] in the internal law of any State.

Article 3 Treaty as a source of the obligation to extradite or prosecute

Each State is obliged either to extradite or to prosecute an alleged offender if such an obligation is provided for by a treaty to which such State is a party.[21]

[20] ILC, 'Report of International Law Commission on the work of its 66th Session' UN Doc A/61/10 ch XI §§31–32.

[21] UN Doc A/CN.4/603 §§116, 121, 123.

The Special Rapporteur emphasized a need for a wider response from States on the issues identified by the ILC.[22]

Importantly, the Special Rapporteur allegedly found a shift in the ILC's approach to the topic. In his view, while the majority of the ILC members in 2006 adopted a cautious approach to the relationship between the obligation to extradite or prosecute and universal jurisdiction as well as the role of customary international law vis-à-vis the aforesaid obligation, the majority of the ILC members from 2007 onwards were more 'permissive' in their approach. He therefore had to reconsider the topic anew in the light of this more 'permissive' approach.[23]

In their comments on the third report, some members of the ILC questioned the methodology used and encouraged the Special Rapporteur to actively engage in an analysis of the main questions arising from the subject and make specific proposals for the ILC to move ahead with the topic, without awaiting comments and information from governments, relying instead on the rich State practice and the legal literature in the field. Others abstained from commenting on the substantive issues that had already been addressed in the previous reports, while some other members indicated their wish to comment on the report the following year. In reply, the Special Rapporteur reiterated that only a few States had provided their answers to the ILC's questions, but he agreed to utilize a more expeditious and independent approach to the topic. He stated that his next report would focus on the main substantive issues, such as the sources of the obligation to extradite or prosecute, and its content and scope, including the 1996 Draft Code, and relevant procedural issues, such as the conditions for the triggering of the obligation to extradite or prosecute.[24] Having witnessed little substantive progress so far, the ILC decided to set up an open-ended working group on the topic under the chairmanship of Alain Pellet, the mandate and membership of which were to be determined in 2009.

III. The 2009 General Framework

The Special Rapporteur did not submit his report in 2009. The ILC thus found it necessary to convene the working group under Pellet to assist the Special Rapporteur in discharging his task.

The Working Group agreed that its mandate would be to draw up a general framework for consideration of the topic in order to specify the issues to be addressed by the Special Rapporteur and their order of priority. With regard to the methodology for approaching the topic, the Working Group emphasized the importance of taking into account national legislation and decisions. It also raised the possibility of drawing on the work of certain academic institutions or non-governmental organizations.[25]

[22] ibid §6. [23] ibid §§42–45.

[24] ILC, 'Report of the International Law Commission on the work of its 60th Session' (5 May–6 June and 7 July–8 Aug 2008) UN Doc A/63/10 ch XI.

[25] ILC, 'Report of the International Law Commission on the work of its 61st Session' (4 May–5 June and 6 July–7 Aug 2009) UN Doc A/64/10 §201.

The aim of the general framework was to facilitate the work of the Special Rapporteur in the preparation of his future reports. It would be for the Special Rapporteur to determine the exact order of the questions to be considered, as well as the structure of, and linkage between, his planned draft articles on the various aspects of the topic.[26]

This general framework (General Framework) was subsequently referred to umpteen times in the ILC and the Sixth Committee. Therefore, it is necessary to reproduce it here in full. The General Framework reads thus:

List of questions/issues to be addressed

(a) **The legal bases of the obligation to extradite or prosecute**

(i) The obligation to extradite or prosecute and the duty to cooperate in the fight against impunity;

(ii) The obligation to extradite or prosecute in existing treaties:
Typology of treaty provisions; differences and similarities between those provisions, and their evolution (cf. conventions on terrorism);

(iii) Whether and to what extent the obligation to extradite or prosecute has a basis in customary international law;*

(iv) Whether the obligation to extradite or prosecute is inextricably linked with certain particular 'customary crimes' (e.g. piracy);*

(v) Whether regional principles relating to the obligation to extradite or prosecute may be identified.*

(b) **The material scope of the obligation to extradite or prosecute**
Identification of the categories of crimes (e.g. crimes under international law; crimes against the peace and security of mankind; crimes of international concern; other serious crimes) covered by the obligation to extradite or prosecute according to conventional and/or customary international law:

(i) Whether the recognition of an offence as an international crime is a sufficient basis for the existence of an obligation to extradite or prosecute under customary international law;*

(ii) If not, what is/are the distinctive criterion/criteria? Relevance of the *jus cogens* character of a rule criminalizing certain conduct?*

(iii) Whether and to what extent the obligation also exists in relation to crimes under domestic laws?

(c) **The content of the obligation to extradite or prosecute**

(i) Definition of the two elements; meaning of the obligation to prosecute; steps that need to be taken in order for prosecution to be considered 'sufficient'; question of timeliness of prosecution;

(ii) Whether the order of the two elements matters;

(iii) Whether one element has priority over the other—power of free appreciation (*pouvoir discrétionnaire*) of the requested State?

(d) **Relationship between the obligation to extradite or prosecute and other principles**

(i) The obligation to extradite or prosecute and the principle of universal jurisdiction (does one necessarily imply the other?);

[26] ibid §203.

(ii) The obligation to extradite or prosecute and the general question of 'titles' to exercise jurisdiction (territoriality, nationality);
(iii) The obligation to extradite or prosecute and the principles of *nullum crimen sine lege* and *nulla poena sine lege*;**
(iv) The obligation to extradite or prosecute and the principle *non bis in idem* (double jeopardy);**
(v) The obligation to extradite or prosecute and the principle of non-extradition of nationals;**
(vi) What happens in case of conflicting principles (e.g.: non extradition of nationals *v* no indictment in national law? obstacles to prosecute *v* risks for the accused to be tortured or lack of due process in the State to which extradition is envisaged?); constitutional limitations.**

(e) **Conditions for the triggering of the obligation to extradite or prosecute**
(i) Presence of the alleged offender in the territory of the State;
(ii) State's jurisdiction over the crime concerned;
(iii) Existence of a request for extradition (degree of formalism required); Relations with the right to expel foreigners;
(iv) Existence/consequences of a previous request for extradition that had been rejected;
(v) Standard of proof (to what extent must the request for extradition be substantiated?);
(vi) Existence of circumstances that might exclude the operation of the obligation (e.g. political offences or political nature of a request for extradition; emergency situations; immunities).

(f) **The implementation of the obligation to extradite or prosecute**
(i) Respective roles of the judiciary and the executive;
(ii) How to reconcile the obligation to extradite or prosecute with the discretion of the prosecuting authorities;
(iii) Whether the availability of evidence affects the operation of the obligation;
(iv) How to deal with multiple requests for extradition;
(v) Guarantees in case of extradition;
(vi) Whether the alleged offender should be kept in custody awaiting a decision on his or her extradition or prosecution; or possibilities of other restrictions to freedom?;
(vii) Control of the implementation of the obligation;
(viii) Consequences of non-compliance with the obligation to extradite or prosecute.

(g) **The relationship between the obligation to extradite or prosecute and the surrender of the alleged offender to a competent international criminal tribunal (the 'third alternative')**
To what extent the 'third' alternative has an impact on the other two.

[* It might be that a final determination on these questions will only be possible at a later stage, in particular after a careful analysis of the scope and content of the obligation to extradite or prosecute under existing treaty regimes. It might also be advisable to examine the customary nature of the obligation in relation to specific crimes.

** This issue might need to be addressed also in relation to the implementation of the obligation to extradite or prosecute (f).].[27]

Chairman Pellet reported to the ILC Plenary that it was obviously crucial to know whether the obligation was exclusively treaty-based or also had a source in customary law, an issue left open by the General Framework. In any case, the ILC's work on

[27] ibid §204.

the topic had to be continued, because the regime of treaty obligations to extradite or prosecute was far from clear, and nothing prevented the ILC from engaging in the progressive development of international law, to which the topic undoubtedly lent itself.[28] The questions raised in (e) to (g) concerning the conditions that triggered the obligation, the implementation of the obligation and its relationship to the 'third alternative' of surrender to a competent international criminal tribunal, though technical, were far from trivial, and the responses that might be given would surely be of great use to States.[29] The General Framework was merely intended to facilitate the Special Rapporteur's work on future reports; it would be his task to determine the order, structure, and interrelationship of the draft articles. Opposing views had emerged within the Working Group on a number of points, particularly the order in which the questions were to be addressed and whether the ILC should adopt a general approach emphasizing the sources of the obligation or a more specific approach centred on the relevant treaty provisions and the customary or treaty regimes applicable to specific offences. Some members considered it essential for the ILC to examine the customary basis of the obligation, while others thought that the ILC did not need to settle that question or could defer it until after a thorough examination of State practice. Differing views were also expressed on whether and to what extent the question of surrender to an international tribunal should be addressed. Some members thought the focus should be less on extradition and more on the obligation to prosecute when extradition did not take place. All members agreed, however, that the ILC's work on the topic should not include detailed consideration of extradition law or the principles of international criminal law. With regard to methodology, the importance of taking account of domestic legislation and decisions was stressed and the possibility raised of drawing on the work of certain academic institutions and non-governmental organizations.[30]

In 2010, the Special Rapporteur, yet again, did not present his report. The Working Group held two meetings in July 2010, chaired by Enrique Candioti, temporary chairman in the absence of Pellet. The Working Group continued its discussions with the aim of specifying the issues to be addressed to facilitate further the Special Rapporteur's work. Before it was a document prepared by the Secretariat entitled 'Survey of multilateral conventions which may be of relevance for the Commission's work on the topic "the obligation to extradite or prosecute (*aut dedere aut judicare*)"',[31] hereinafter referred to as the Secretariat's Survey. The Secretariat's Survey identified sixty-one multilateral instruments, at the universal and regional levels, that contain provisions combining extradition and prosecution as alternative courses of action for the punishment of offenders. It proposed a description and a typology of the relevant instruments in the light of these provisions, and examined the preparatory work of certain key conventions that have served as models in the field. For some provisions, it also reviewed reservations made. The Secretariat's Survey pointed out the differences and similarities between the reviewed provisions

[28] UN Doc A/CN.4/SR.3029 (13 Aug 2009) §57. [29] ibid §59.
[30] ibid §60. [31] UN Doc A/CN.4/630.

in different conventions and their evolution. Overall conclusions were offered in the Survey as to: (1) the relationship between extradition and prosecution in the relevant provisions; (2) the conditions applicable to extradition under the various conventions; and (3) the conditions applicable to prosecution under the various conventions. The Secretariat's Survey will be discussed in detail in Chapter 4.

The Working Group also had before it a 9-page working paper prepared by Special Rapporteur Galicki, entitled 'Bases for discussion in the Working Group on the topic "The obligation to extradite or prosecute (*aut dedere aut judicare*)" '.[32] The paper contained observations and suggestions based on the 2009 General Framework. It also drew upon the Secretariat's Survey.

In this working paper, the Special Rapporteur drew attention to questions concerning the legal bases, material scope, and content of the obligation to extradite or prosecute; the relationship between this obligation and other principles; the conditions for triggering the obligation; the implementation of the obligation; and the 'third' (previously called 'triple') alternative. The Special Rapporteur suggested that the Working Group determine, in the light of the Secretariat's Survey, whether it would be advisable for the ILC to adopt a general approach to the topic or whether it should focus its attention on certain specific categories of obligations (such as those found in conventions on terrorism that had become the mainstay of international conventions suppressing crimes of an international dimension). In this regard, he advised the Working Group to consider which typology of treaty provisions would better serve the objectives pursued by the ILC. The Working Group was also asked to determine, in the light of the conventional practice described in the Secretariat's Survey, whether it would be advisable to examine the material scope of the obligation to extradite or prosecute on the basis of a classification of the crimes concerned. In particular, a question was raised whether the focus would be on certain categories of crime—for instance, whether the obligation to extradite or prosecute applicable to grave breaches under the four Geneva Conventions of 1949, stipulating that each High Contracting Party thereto shall bring perpetrators of grave breaches before its own courts, extended to other crimes under international law, such as other war crimes, crimes against humanity, or genocide; or whether the obligation included in many conventions on terrorism extended to other offences of terrorism not covered in those conventions or to other crimes of international concern.

The paper invited the Working Group to consider the relationship between the two elements of the obligation to extradite or prosecute. The Working Group could determine, for example, whether, in the light of the case law of the Committee against Torture—set up to monitor the implementation of the 1984 Convention against Torture and Other Cruel, Inhuman or Degrading Treatment or Punishment[33]—the various provisions contained in contemporary conventions should be interpreted as imposing an obligation to prosecute as soon as the presence of the alleged offender in the territory of the State was ascertained, and whether a similar obligation existed in customary international law for one or more categories of crime. The Special

[32] UN Doc A/CN.4/L.774. [33] 1465 UNTS 85.

Rapporteur deemed it appropriate for the Working Group to examine the extent to which the obligation to extradite or prosecute was linked to the principle of universal jurisdiction, at least for certain categories of crime, and in particular whether the duty of the State to establish its jurisdiction over a certain crime when the alleged offender was present in its territory was a necessary element to ensure the proper implementation of the said obligation. A question could be raised whether the obligation was triggered by the presence of the alleged offender in the territory of the State or by the refusal of a previous request for extradition. The Working Group could also explore, in the light of the conventional practice in the field, to what extent other issues relating to the request for extradition (such as the standard of proof, political nature of the offence, immunities, and prosecutorial discretion enjoyed by national judicial authorities) would affect the operation of the obligation.

In response, the Working Group affirmed the continuing relevance of the 2009 General Framework, several aspects of which were elucidated by the Secretariat's Survey, including issues concerning the typology of treaty provisions and differences and similarities in the formulation of the obligation to extradite or prosecute in these provisions and their evolution. It was noted that, in seeking to find answers to the questions in the General Framework, the multilateral treaty practice on which the Secretariat's Survey had focused needed to be complemented by a detailed consideration of other aspects of State practice (including, but not limited to, national legislation, case law, and official statements of governmental representatives). In addition, as far as the duty to cooperate in the fight against impunity seemed to underpin the obligation to extradite or prosecute, a systematic assessment of State practice of that duty was necessary. This would clarify the extent to which that duty influenced, as a general rule or in relation to specific crimes, the work on the topic, including the material scope, the content of the obligation to extradite or prosecute, and the conditions for the triggering of that obligation. Taking into account the ILC's practice in progressive development and codification of international law, the Working Group reaffirmed that the general orientation of future reports of the Special Rapporteur should be towards presenting draft articles for consideration by the ILC, based on the General Framework.[34]

The Special Rapporteur submitted his fourth report in 2011,[35] which, building upon his three previous reports, sought to address the question of sources of the obligation to extradite or prosecute. The report focused on treaties and custom. The Special Rapporteur presented three draft articles thus:

Article 2 Duty to cooperate

1. In accordance with the present draft articles, States shall, as appropriate, cooperate among themselves, and with competent international court [*sic*] and tribunals, in the fight against impunity as it concerns crimes and offences of international concern.

[34] ILC, 'Report of the International Law Commission on the work of its 62nd Session' (3 May–4 June and 5 July–6 Aug 2010) UN Doc A/65/10 §340, and also Report to the Plenary by Candioti, Acting Chairman of Working Group, 3071st meeting 30 July 2010 (UN Doc A/CN.4/SR.3071 (11 July 2011) 5–6).

[35] UN Doc A/CN.4/648.

2. For this purpose, the States will apply, wherever and whenever appropriate, and in accordance with these draft articles, the principle to extradite or prosecute (*aut dedere aut judicare*).

Article 3 Treaty as a source of the obligation to extradite or prosecute

1. Each State is obliged either to extradite or to prosecute an alleged offender if such an obligation is provided for by a treaty to which such State is a party.
2. Particular conditions for exercising extradition or prosecution shall be formulated by the internal law of the State party, in accordance with the treaty establishing such obligation and with general principles of international criminal law.

Article 4 International custom as a source of the obligation *aut dedere aut judicare*

1. Each State is obliged either to extradite or to prosecute an alleged offender if such an obligation is deriving from the customary norm of international law.
2. Such an obligation may derive, in particular, from customary norms of international law concerning [serious violations of international humanitarian law, genocide, crimes against humanity and war crimes].
3. The obligation to extradite or prosecute shall derive from the peremptory norm of general international law accepted and recognized by the international community of States (*jus cogens*), either in the form of international treaty or international custom, criminalizing any one of acts listed in paragraph 2.

The debate in the ILC after receiving the fourth report focused mainly on the question of methodology and the general approach to be taken in addressing the issues raised by the topic, bearing in mind the work of the Working Group on the topic in 2009 and 2010 and the continuing relevance of the General Framework.

Maurice Kamto, Chairman of the ILC in 2011, apprised the Sixth Committee as follows. While the ILC considered the fourth report useful in focusing on treaties and custom as sources of the obligation to extradite or prosecute, the fourth report had not examined the issues sufficiently to allow the ILC to draw informed conclusions on the direction to be taken on the topic. In particular, concerns were expressed about the draft articles as proposed and the analysis on which they were based. The Special Rapporteur's methodology in dealing separately with the two main sources of international law—treaties and customary law—and therefore proposing two separate draft articles was conceptually problematic since there was no need for a draft article to demonstrate the existence of a rule in a treaty or under custom. On the contrary, the focus ought to be on the obligation to extradite or prosecute and on the way that treaties and custom evidenced the rule, rather than on treaties or custom as the source of the obligation. Part of the report also posed a number of questions concerning State practice, in particular legislation or case law involving crimes or categories of crime in respect of which the obligation to extradite or prosecute had come into play and it was unclear whether a court or tribunal had relied, in that respect, on customary international law.[36]

[36] UN Doc A/C.6/66/SR §79. For details of the Special Rapporteur's problematic methodology, see ILC, 'Report of the International Law Commission on the work of its 63rd Session' (26 April–3 June and 4 July–12 Aug 2011) UN Doc A/66/10 §§301–04 and accompanying notes.

It should be added that some ILC members considered this topic to be a complex one with 'implications for other aspects of the law, including questions of prosecutorial discretion, questions of asylum, the law on extradition, the immunity of State officials from foreign criminal jurisdiction, peremptory norms of international law, as well as universal jurisdiction, thereby posing problems in terms of the direction to be taken and what need[s] to be achieved'.[37] However, the complexity of a topic is not a decisive factor that deters the ILC from taking up and accomplishing its work on such a topic. Unlike topics that the ILC has abandoned for lack of support within the ILC and the Sixth Committee, such as 'Shared natural resources' which was abandoned in 2010, the present topic was of practical relevance to States and many States had requested the ILC to give a priority treatment to it. Special Rapporteur Galicki himself argued that there was 'rich State practice and legal literature in the field' of the obligation to extradite or prosecute.[38]

With respect to customary international law, as of 2012, only twenty-nine States[39] had submitted written information on their national legislation and judicial decisions. The lack of information from States posed a particular problem in the progress of this topic. The Special Rapporteur noted that 'extensive State practice could be an indication of the existence of a developing rule in customary law.'[40] In fact, the Special Rapporteur could have taken into account comparative legal studies in the field undertaken by, for example, the International Committee of the Red Cross (ICRC) and Amnesty International.

On the other hand, the Special Rapporteur's fourth report adopted a seemingly low standard of proof for the existence of customary international law as a source of the obligation to extradite or prosecute. He sought to rely on the general criminalization of the most serious crimes under international law, called 'core crimes', and the pleadings of the Counsel for Belgium in *Questions relating to the Obligation to Prosecute or Extradite (Belgium v Senegal)* then pending before the ICJ.[41] In his address to the Sixth Committee in 2011, he explained the difficulty of proving the existence of a customary international legal obligation to extradite or prosecute. He identified 'the particular categories of crimes that might give rise to such customary obligation, limited as to its scope and substance but recognized as binding by the international community of States.'[42] Several States (including Italy, Sri Lanka, Portugal, and Singapore) had serious difficulties with the legal methodology used by the Special Rapporteur. They disagreed with him that a customary international law obligation to extradite or prosecute automatically followed from the fact that

[37] UN Doc A/66/10 §306.
[38] ILC UN Doc A/63/10 §322.
[39] Twenty-nine States have replied to the Commission's request for information relating to this topic in 2006 (UN Doc A/61/10 §§30–32) and in 2007 (UN Doc A/62/10 §§31–33). They are Austria, Croatia, Japan, Monaco, Qatar, Thailand, UK, Chile, Ireland, Lebanon, Mexico, Slovenia, Sweden, Tunisia, USA, Latvia, Serbia, Sri Lanka, Kuwait, Poland, Guatemala, Mauritius, Netherlands, Russian Federation, Argentina, Belgium, Canada, South Africa, and Yemen. (UN Docs A/CN.4/579 and Add 1–Add 4; A/CN.4/599; and A/CN.4/612).
[40] ILC UN Doc A/63/10 ch XI §329.
[41] UN Doc A/CN.4/648 (31 May 2011) 5–24.
[42] UN Doc A/C.6/66/SR.28 (2 Dec 2011) §73.

customary international law prohibited a specific form of conduct or characterized such conduct as a crime.[43] States wanted the answer to the question whether the obligation was customary in nature according the established rule on the identification of customary international law. In their views, if the obligation was not customary, then the ILC might embark on progressive development of international law for this obligation, as suggested by the Nordic countries[44] and Malaysia[45] in the Sixth Committee in 2011.

At the Sixth Committee debate in 2011,[46] while France and Spain showed frustration with the lack of substantive progress in the ILC's work on the topic, Iran was the only one going as far as asking the ILC to either immediately terminate it 'since it seemed unlikely that the [ILC] would find sufficient evidence of the existence of a customary obligation to extradite or prosecute', or, if the ILC were to continue, for the Special Rapporteur to confine himself to his existing mandate. However, an overwhelming majority of States considered the topic important and meriting a priority treatment in the ILC's programme of work.[47] New Zealand and the Netherlands specifically reminded the ILC of the relevance of the 2009 General Framework for the ILC's future work.

IV. The ILC's Working Group 2012–2014

Neither Galicki nor Pellet was a member of the ILC for the quinquennium 2012–16. The ILC decided in May 2012 to appoint the present author as chairman of the Working Group in place of Pellet. No Special Rapporteur was to be appointed until after the Working Group decided on the future of this topic and found the need for such appointment. The re-establishment of this Working Group came at the time when the ICJ was being expected to deliver its judgment in *Questions relating to the Obligation to Prosecute or Extradite (Belgium v Senegal)* towards the end of the ILC's annual session in 2012.

In 2012 and 2013, the Working Group was open to all ILC members, with between seventeen and twenty-four members attending each of the meetings. In 2014, the Working Group was limited to the chairman plus only ten other ILC members to streamline the debate which had become circular and repetitious in 2012 and 2013.

The ILC in 2012 comprised twelve new members, including this present author. Several of the members who had served in the 2006–11 quinquennium seriously doubted the feasibility of the ILC pursuing this topic further, with no draft articles

[43] UN Doc A/C.6/66/SR.26 (7 Dec 2011) §42; UN Doc A/C.6/66/SR.27 (8 Dec 2011) §26, 75; UN Doc A/C.6/66/SR.28 (2 Dec 2011) §31. Cf also Israel (UN Doc A/C.6/66/SR.28 (2 Dec 2011) §25).

[44] UN Doc A/C.6/66/SR.26 (7 Dec 2011) §11.

[45] UN Doc A/C.6/66/SR.28 (2 Dec 2011) §7.

[46] UN Docs A/C.6/66/SR.18 (2 Dec 2011); A/C.6/66/SR.19 (22 Nov 2011); A/C.6/66/SR.20 (23 Nov 2011); A/C.6/66/SR.25 (9 Dec 2011); A/C.6/66/SR.26 (7 Dec 2011); A/C.6/66/SR.27 (8 Dec 2011); A/C.6/66/SR.28 (2 Dec 2011).

[47] France, El Salvador, Vietnam, and the Netherlands, for example.

having ever been referred to a drafting committee, and with the debates both in the ILC and the Sixth Committee going round in circles. Members, old and new, coming from States that could not extradite without treaty obligations insisted the obligation could not be a rule of customary international law, otherwise their respective States would have been bound to extradite outside treaty. Several other members were open to the possibility that the obligation was customary in nature, either extant or emerging, at least in relation to serious crimes of international concern.

The chairman of the Working Group presented four informal working papers each year in 2012 and 2013. The chairman presented one informal working paper at the start of the ILC session in 2014, with most of the Working Group meetings in 2014 devoted to drafting the final report of the ILC on the topic.

Substantive issues raised in these informal working papers will be analysed in Chapters 3–7. The following narrative account of what transpired in the Working Group meetings is intended to explain the context in which the Working Group discussed these substantive issues as well as related procedural issues. As already pointed out, the discussion in the Working Group was frequently circular and repetitive.

The first informal working paper, dated 22 May 2012, kept members abreast of the developments and debates to date, both in the ILC and the Sixth Committee. The chairman proposed that the right methodology for the ILC to pursue would be to focus on the obligation to extradite or prosecute as evidenced in treaties and customary international law, including the material scope and the content of this obligation, the relationship between the obligation and other principles, conditions for the triggering of the obligation, the implementation of the obligation, and, finally, the relationship between the obligation and the surrender of the alleged offender to a competent international criminal tribunal.[48] If some new rules should be suggested for adoption by States, the ILC ought to make this clear.

The chairman proposed, for an illustrative purpose only, that the draft articles could proceed in the following manner:

Preamble: *aut dedere aut judicare* as a vital tool to fight impunity

Art 1: Scope of application[49]
Art 2: Use of terms[50]
Art 3: Sources of the obligation to extradite
(1) Bilateral and multilateral treaties
(2) Reciprocity
(3) Comity
(4) Customary international law
(5) Others

[48] Special Rapporteur Galicki's much criticized methodology proceeded, to a large extent, on the basis that the obligation to surrender the alleged offender to a competent international criminal tribunal was evidence of a rule of customary international law that obligated States to extradite or prosecute perpetrators of crimes listed in the Statutes of the respective international criminal tribunals.

[49] See the Special Rapporteur's second report, UN Doc A/CN.4/603, 24.

[50] ibid 25.

Art 4: Sources of the obligation to prosecute
  (1) National law (and bases of jurisdiction, including universal jurisdiction)[51]
  (2) International law (bearing in mind the difference between monism and dualism)

Art 5: The material scope and extent of the obligation to extradite *or* prosecute
  (1) Obligation of means or obligation of results?
  (2) Conditions for the triggering of the obligations
  (3) The implementation of the obligation
  (4) Relationship between the obligation and other principles
  (5) The obligation to prosecute *or* extradite (*prosequi vel dedere*)?
  (6) Enforcement in cases of failure to fulfill the obligation (e.g. UN Security Council in the *Lockerbie* case)

Art 6: The relationship between the obligation and the surrender of the alleged offender to a competent international criminal tribunal

Art 7, Art 8 *etc.* . . .

In the chairman's view, the points raised in the 2009 General Framework could find their respective places within these articles. He also cautioned that care had to be taken to ensure that the draft articles focus on the *obligation* to extradite or prosecute, and not on detailed treatment of the law on extradition. Besides, it was pointed out, an extensive compilation of national law and regulations on extradition in all regions of the world and in the English, French, and Spanish languages could be found on the website of the International Money Laundering Information Network (IMoLIN).[52] There were some other databases with relevant information on extradition law, such as the website of the Asian Development Bank/OECD Anti-Corruption Initiative for Asia-Pacific.[53] Another source of information on extradition by States could be found on the website of the UN and Justice Information Network.[54] Any questions put by the ILC to States ought to avoid duplicating the information already available in the public domain.

The first meeting of the Working Group on 25 May 2012 was divided on whether the ILC should continue its work on the topic while the ICJ was deliberating its judgment in *Belgium v Senegal*. Some members considered it best for the ILC to wait for the judgment before going ahead, given the symbiotic relationship between the ICJ and the fact that the issues raised in that case addressed many of the issues before the ILC. Others argued that the ILC could proceed independently of the ICJ's judgment as time was of the essence for the ILC to make progress on the topic at hand, and the scope of the topic was much broader than the issues to be decided by the ICJ.

The majority in the Working Group seemed to favour the ILC addressing universal jurisdiction to the extent that it had an impact on the obligation to extradite or prosecute. However, it was unclear for them to what extent the ILC had to look into universal jurisdiction in this context. Some members did not believe that

[51] National laws of some States that are enacted to implement treaty obligations also apply equally to all offenders irrespective of whether such offenders are nationals of States Parties to the treaty.

[52] <https://www.imolin.org>, accessed 30 November 2017.

[53] <www.oecd.org/document/53/0,3343,en_34982156_34982441_39354805_1_1_1_1,00.html>, accessed October 2017.

[54] <http://www.uncjin.org/Laws/extradit/extindx.htm>, accessed October 2017.

customary law could be discussed independently of universal jurisdiction—only when there was some form of universal jurisdiction could the State comply with the obligation, although States at the Sixth Committee were divided on whether the ILC should address universal jurisdiction in this topic at all. Other members argued that the ILC should not dwell too much on universal jurisdiction—although the obligation to extradite or prosecute and universal jurisdiction were interrelated, they were also distinct and, as such, were to be analysed separately. According to another view, if the obligation were to be discussed without universal jurisdiction the topic would be reduced to two matters: (1) systematization with a view to codification of treaties, including analysing whether there was a customary rule of international law on the obligation to extradite or prosecute; and (2) how States would cooperate in the implementation of treaties and cross-border matters. It was also stated that the ILC should not undertake a separate comprehensive study of universal jurisdiction because universal jurisdiction was not the central tenet of this topic, but just one base of jurisdiction under international law on which the obligation to extradite or prosecute rested. In other words, it would be sufficient to explore universal jurisdiction only to the extent necessary to establish the obligation to extradite or prosecute. Arguably, this approach was adopted by Special Rapporteur Doudou Thiam in the 1996 Draft Code, Article 8 of which explored universal jurisdiction only to the extent that it was the practical foundation of the obligation to prosecute for the core crimes listed in that Code.[55]

One member expressed a view on the third alternative, contending that, given its complexity, it should be undertaken only once the sources and foundations of the obligation to extradite and prosecute were established by the ILC. In the opinion of this member, the third alternative was an exception to the obligation to extradite or prosecute in certain cases, and to begin research on the exception before ascertaining the scope of the rule might lead to complications in future research.

With respect to other matters concerning the topic, the 2009 General Framework was considered a good starting point. The obligation to extradite was considered by many members to be clearer in comparison to the obligation to prosecute. What was the obligation to prosecute and how would one know when the obligation was fulfilled? This also depended on criminal processes within the State, and a survey by the ILC would not be easy given the difference in national criminal practice—there were variations in prosecutorial discretion, sentencing policy, and so forth.

A question was raised as to whether there was sufficient general practice to justify codification of the obligation to extradite or prosecute. Some States, such as the USA, considered customary international law not providing a significant basis for an obligation beyond the wording of treaties—States only fulfilled this obligation to the extent of the treaties that they were party to. Although customary law was not the sole purpose of this topic, it was argued, would it be useful to codify the extradite-or-prosecute clauses in treaties in so far as the obligation was treaty specific?

[55] §(6), Commentary to Art 8 of the Draft Code.

A contrary argument was made, however, that it would be necessary to look at both practice and doctrine. An important issue was whether the repetitive use of provisions on universal jurisdiction in combination with the obligation to extradite or prosecute in multilateral conventions was one source of evidence of customary international law. For many years, multilateral conventions had begun to focus on crimes of international concern, such as genocide, crimes against humanity, and war crimes. There were also transnational crimes which affected the international community as a whole. As the targeted conduct affected the international rule of law, the obligation to extradite or prosecute was not just about the fight against impunity but also about strengthening the international rule of law. There were certain treaty-based crimes, such as the terrorism, that could be studied in the context of this obligation. In other words, according to this latter view, the ILC should concentrate more on sources of the obligation other than customary international law. The neat distinction between codification and progressive development of international law was very hard to apply in practice and it was not the ILC's policy to keep this neat distinction—usually it was mentioned only in the commentary and even then only when the draft article in question was a clear instance of progressive development. According to yet another view, the duty to cooperate in the fight against impunity needed to be addressed either as part of the discussion or separately, building on the draft article on international cooperation proposed by Special Rapporteur Galicki in his fourth report.

One member did not think the General Framework was good—it had too many elements to be a useful roadmap. Instead, according to this member, the ILC should identify exactly what the topic was dealing with, failing which it should produce a final report that summarized all the findings and difficulties to date. Yet another member clarified that Special Rapporteur Galicki's problems were related to a lack of information from States, and this was also the key reason for setting up the Working Group in 2009. That Working Group's analysis was useful but it did not have to be followed strictly, and the ILC in 2012 could choose between the many questions raised in the General Framework.

Another member opined that if the ILC were to continue with the topic it had to do substantial research on the customary international law aspect of the obligation, so that, based on that research, the ILC could determine what could be done. A view was expressed that the ILC needed a paper on the customary international law nature of the obligation in order to put the matter to rest. The role of reciprocity and comity in relation to the extradition of offenders would need to be analysed in assessing whether the obligation was a customary rule. Yet another view contended that if the obligation was a customary rule then the problem would be resolved as to the future work of the ILC and the issue would be one of determining what crimes it applied to. However, if the obligation was not a customary rule then the ILC could focus on international judicial cooperation and mutual legal assistance matters instead.

As correctly pointed out by some members, the Secretariat's Survey suggested that it would be impossible to harmonize the rules on extradition and prosecution in the various multilateral conventions as it would upset the delicate balance struck by States in the individual conventions.

The chairman of the Working Group submitted the second informal working paper on 30 May 2012 in the light of the discussion in the first meeting. At the second meeting, it was suggested that a further detailed analysis was needed before the ILC could reach a tentative conclusion on whether the obligation to extradite or prosecute was exclusively a treaty-based obligation. The ILC might refine questions posed to States, emphasizing what information the ILC needed, asking pertinent questions and showing the importance of what States thought and what State practice was. The ILC might determine whether regional principles for the obligation to extradite or prosecute could be identified.

It was pointed out by several members that the complexity of the topic should not be a factor in determining whether the ILC continued or discontinued this topic. It was also pointed out that the prevailing mood after the last meeting was not very optimistic. This topic involved entering either a field not warranted by State practice or fields already addressed by the ILC in the past; namely, the 1996 Draft Code. However, this topic had been considered an important topic by the Sixth Committee.

A view was expressed that the ILC could study in more detail the multilateral conventions dealing with special categories of crime, so that international cooperation to end impunity could be strengthened. For example, where one State did not request extradition thereby preventing the trigger of the obligation to extradite or prosecute in a treaty—how did the non-requesting State comply with the object and purpose of that treaty? The topic should also distinguish between core and non-core crimes. The 1996 Draft Code was originally intended to include more crimes than those presently contained in it, and the reduction in the number of crimes in the Draft Code was due to a lack of agreement in the ILC at that time on the inclusion of certain crimes. However, the inclusion of the finally selected crimes in the 1996 Draft Code did not affect the status of other crimes under international law, and the adoption of the Draft Code in 1996 did not prevent further development of that area of law.

According to several members, it was important that the ILC continue to use the General Framework for guidance.

Members coming from the States that could extradite only on the basis of existing treaty obligations reiterated their opposition to the suggestion that the obligation was one of customary international law.

The second meeting of the Working Group also discussed the question of the end result that this topic could seek to achieve, that is, a set of conclusions or draft articles? Some members indicated their conviction that the topic should be concluded with a final report in the form of conclusions because there was unlikely to be much progress in codification or progressive development of the obligation to extradite or prosecute. The conclusions would include a discussion of the progress of the ILC's work on this topic thus far, including a section on the difficulties faced and the reasons for removing the topic from the ILC's programme of work. The majority of the Working Group, however, would prefer the ILC to continue with the topic but without deciding on the final form of the final outcome as yet. In their opinion, if the ILC proceeded on this topic the final form could be draft articles or guidelines or best practices for States.

The Sixth Committee's response to the ILC's analysis of the substantive obligations on States would be a relevant factor in determining the final form. Admittedly, the final form would influence the content of the conclusions/articles and even the course of the research. Draft articles were likely to be more in the realm of codification, whereas best practices could better reflect progressive development of international law.

The chairman's third informal paper was submitted on 25 June 2012. This forty-page paper focused on the substance of the chairman's second informal working paper and responded to the problems raised by members. It referred to the lack of substantive progress on the debate on universal jurisdiction in the Sixth Committee that had been going on since 2011; issues related to customary international law and treaties; a possibility of analysing the obligation in the light of specific crimes; and a possible roadmap for moving forward. It also explained the rationale behind Articles 8 and 9 of the 1996 Draft Code, that is, the need for an effective system of criminalization and prosecution. The chairman confirmed that the main focus of the topic would be the obligation to extradite or prosecute, and not universal jurisdiction. With respect to customary international law, there were studies by other secondary sources that could be useful to the ILC in identifying State practice.

The third informal working paper also pointed out that States had been asked to comment on whether there was an obligation *aut dedere aut judicare* under customary international law without reference to a specific crime. Such a general approach did not address the fact that the obligation was not of a general, free-standing nature but was always with regard to a specific crime, for example, an obligation to extradite or prosecute for grave breaches of the 1949 Geneva Conventions. A 'free-standing obligation' approach was subject to criticism by some States, including the USA.[56] Other States, including Russia, similarly noted that while they disputed the existence of a general obligation to extradite or prosecute under customary international law, they believed such an obligation could exist with regard to specific crimes such as genocide.[57] Argentina also suggested progressing with a review of specific crimes as opposed to a more general approach to the obligation under customary international law.[58] A crime-specific approach also had the advantage of posing narrower questions to governments, thereby easing the burden on resources faced by governments in answering questions posed to them by the ILC. The success of a crime-specific approach could be seen in the questionnaire created by the UN Office on Drugs and Crime (UNODC) on the implementation of the 2000 UN Convention against Transnational Organized Crimes for the first reporting cycle.[59]

The paper alluded to the practice in South East Asia and Oceania, with the overwhelming trend of using reciprocity or comity outside treaty arrangements,

[56] *The obligation to extradite or prosecute (aut dedere aut judicare): Comments and information received from Governments (Addendum)*, 5 June 2007, UN Doc A/CN.4/579/Add 2 §§1–8.

[57] *The obligation to extradite or prosecute (aut dedere aut judicare): Comments and information received from Governments*, 30 May 2008, UN Doc A/CN.4/599 §§47–55.

[58] UN Doc A/C.6/62/SR.22 §58.

[59] *Information submitted by States in their responses to the checklist/questionnaire on the implementation of the United Nations Convention against Transnational Organized Crimes for the first reporting cycle: Note by Secretariat*, 6 Oct 2008, UN Doc CTOC/COP/2008/CRP 7.

noting also that Laos, Cambodia, and Timor Leste announced their policy of 'extradition of offenders to friendly States'. With regard to the Secretariat's Survey, States Parties to the relevant conventions might disagree on how to implement the obligation to extradite or prosecute—was it an obligation of means or result? Chairman Pellet himself was of the view that the regime of treaty obligation to extradite or prosecute was far from clear, and that nothing prevented the ILC from progressively developing the obligation. Instead of trying to harmonize treaty regimes horizontally, the ILC could try to codify articles vertically by using a model widely utilized in multilateral conventions. On the scope of crimes to be covered, a question was raised whether there should be other crimes than the crimes found in the 1996 Draft Code; for example, piracy, terrorism, and other crimes of comparable concern to the international community. The ILC, it was suggested, could also assess the rule of law at the national and international levels as a basis to rationalize the obligation to extradite or prosecute.

Members of the Working Group found it interesting that the 1996 Draft Code's Article 9 on the obligation to extradite or prosecute was progressive development even for core crimes and even though the wording of Article 9 might seemed more indicative of codification. States would have needed to join the Draft Code to be bound by the obligation to extradite or prosecute under Article 9. The ILC should consider whether something had changed since 1996, bearing in mind developments like the 1998 Rome Statute of the ICC, ad hoc international criminal tribunals, national legislation, and so forth, to ascertain if there was perhaps a customary international law norm for the core crimes. A view was expressed that even if a customary rule had emerged the question was whether the ILC should draft a new article when one had already existed in the 1996 Draft Code. This view alluded to the fact that in 1988 the Drafting Committee on the Draft Code, after considering at length whether to draft a detailed provision on the obligation to extradite or prosecute dealing with questions of jurisdiction and extradition or a short and general article stating only the basic principle, had concluded that it would be impossible to draft a detailed article that would satisfy all ILC members.[60] Similarly, it was, arguably, unlikely even today for the ILC to reach a more detailed provision than the one in the 1996 Draft Code.

In trying to research whether such a norm of customary international law for the obligation to extradite or prosecute existed today, it would be very important to look at national laws comprehensively and in a systematic survey. According to one view, while some States evidently accepted that the obligation was a customary international law norm, this acceptance probably did not extend worldwide. This view preferred not to rely heavily on Amnesty International's reports on the topic[61] since Amnesty International appears to have looked at national legislation in a very limited manner, and without substantiating whether the legislation was intended

[60] ILC, 'Report of the International Law Commission on the work of its 40th Session' (9 May–29 July 1988) UN Doc A/40/10 vol I, 272 [37].

[61] Amnesty International, *International Law Commission: The Obligation to Extradite or Prosecute (*Aut Dedere Aut Judicare) (2009).

to implement treaty obligations or was enacted because the State considered it was bound by the obligation to extradite or prosecute under customary international law (*opinio juris*). Besides, some States might be able to prosecute core crimes such as crimes against humanity even though they were not specifically labelled as such. State practice also had to be considered from both the prosecution and extradition sides. A State might have a law on prosecution and a law on extradition but not have a view that it was bound by an obligation to extradite or prosecute. In the USA, for example, it was established practice that in general an individual might not be extradited without an extradition treaty in place. There was one exception[62] which was a very limited exception expressed in terms of comity and was not an outright obligation. It perhaps even demonstrated a broader rule by having a narrow exception. This suggested that the ILC should look at the national law as a whole rather than focusing on specific aspects. Despite the extradition exception discussed earlier, it was hard to see the USA consider itself as under an obligation to prosecute persons in the absence of US statute. On the extradition side, the USA was similarly unlikely to see itself bound to extradite without a US statute. A question was also raised as to how any proof of *opinio juris* in extradition practices could be relevant to the singular obligation to extradite *or prosecute* as opposed to a mere obligation to extradite. The chairman responded to this question that extradition practices were relevant to the said obligation if they were accompanied by statements of *opinio juris* that the extraditions were undertaken pursuant to a belief in the existence of an obligation to extradite or prosecute the alleged offenders, and that they were not conducted out of a belief in an obligation to extradite without more.

According to certain members of the Working Group, acts done pursuant to comity and reciprocity could be a source of *opinio juris* and State practice when supported by relevant declarations. Other members countered that *opinio juris* referred to the mental state of the State in explaining its conduct, indicating that States were acting pursuant to a legal obligation, whereas reciprocity and comity pointed in exactly the opposite direction. There was nothing surprising about the number of States that extradited without a treaty. In South Africa, for instance, this was provided for in legislation but it was purely discretionary. Given its discretionary character, how could there be *opinio juris*? It was unclear how extradition practices absent a treaty necessarily moved the ILC much further in discussion of the obligation to extradite or prosecute, and not just about extradition practices of States. It was also noted that if States explicitly acted on the basis of reciprocity, there would seem to be no accompanying *opinio juris*. Could States be acting out of political pressure, moral pressure, or expediency, as in the case of terrorism, human trafficking, and other non-core crimes? On the other hand, it was pointed out, core crimes might not be of special relevance to the States concerned because the issues directly faced by the States were not core crimes but were, for example, terrorism and human or drug trafficking. In response, the chairman reminded members that States such as Timor Leste and Vietnam often engaged in extradition practices because,

[62] 18 USC 3181(b).

according to their public statements, they believed they were under a legal obligation to extradite in the fight against impunity. However, in the absence of formal extradition mechanisms, these States resorted to extraditions through the application of reciprocity and comity. Furthermore, the chairman did not advocate that the obligation *aut dedere aut judicare* could derive exclusively from comity and reciprocity; only when such acts were accompanied by relevant State declarations that the conduct was pursuant to a belief of *opinio juris* did the acts contribute to the formation of customary international law. The ILC would thus have to analyse the relevant extradition practices in the light of accompanying declarations to determine whether State practice and *opinio juris* existed in support of the obligation to extradite or prosecute under customary international law.

Regarding the question whether this obligation was a general principle of international law, a view was expressed that this led to the question of what this source of law meant. General principles operated within national legal systems which were then extrapolated as operating on the international legal level, and it was hard to see how this could be envisaged unless there was a consistent obligation *aut dedere aut judicare* practised between States. General principles were also found to exist in situations where the rule related to what it meant to be law, for example later in time superseded earlier in time, but the obligation to extradite or prosecute was unlikely to operate in that way, either. In addition, the ILC's main task was codification or progressive development of customary international law and not identification of general principles of law. General principles and customary international law were different sources of law. In the history of international law, the Permanent Court of International Justice (PCIJ) introduced the concept of general principles of law to prevent *non liquet*. The judgment of the ICJ and the PCIJ needed to be viewed with caution—sometimes they used 'principles of international law' when what they meant was customary international law.

In relation to progressive development of the law, some members noted that since Article 9 of the 1996 Draft Code did not attract widespread State adherence post-1996, it would not make sense in doing something comparable today. However, a view was expressed that although the ratification of a large number of treaties containing the obligation *aut dedere aut judicare* did not necessarily lead to the formation of a 'free-standing' obligation to extradite or prosecute (ie without reference to a specific crime) under customary international law, Australia had suggested in the Sixth Committee that 'if the Commission wished to proceed with the drafting of an obligation, it should draw upon elements in existing treaties, supplemented by such changes as it considered desirable'.[63] In the event of the ILC engaging in progressively developing a set of guidelines for States on the obligation, the general trends in such treaties could be adopted.

It was suggested that exploring the third alternative was viable. However, a question arose whether States not party to an international criminal tribunal in question would have an obligation to surrender offenders to the tribunal. On the other hand, it was claimed, today's proliferation in international tribunals suggested that there

[63] UN Doc A/C.6/66/SR.28 §2.

might be room to argue in favour of the existence of a customary international law norm to surrender offenders to the tribunals in lieu of prosecution by States. Amnesty International, for instance, posited that States Parties to the 1998 Rome Statute had enacted implementing legislation beyond their obligations under that Statute and under the Genocide Convention, that is, legislation containing the obligation to extradite or prosecute for genocide even though the State was not under a treaty obligation to do so; hence, a possible proof of *opinio juris*.

Some members of the Working Group considered the 'best practices' approach as a good alternative in the event that hard and fast rules were not crafted by the ILC, as it could be used to promote good practices by States. The UNODC had been trying very hard to promote the principle of combating impunity through cooperation through best practices. States had to extradite or prosecute and this could be done without a treaty as long as it was not prohibited by internal law. A problem was that certain States lacked the necessary criminalization in internal law for prosecution to proceed. States very often did not feel compelled by UNODC initiatives. The ILC, however, enjoyed the credibility to formulate best international legal practices to guide States. Best practices of States amounted to standard laws that would make it possible for States to determine the content of their obligations to extradite or prosecute vis-à-vis their internal law. A question was raised, though, as to whether the ILC could become engaged in producing standard laws.

Some members found in the Secretariat's Survey certain trends and common features that the ILC could extract to produce best practices. Although these might not be sufficient to establish customary international law, they would at least clarify some aspects of the obligation to extradite or prosecute. For example, in the conventions concluded after the 1970 Hague Convention for the Suppression of Unlawful Seizure of Aircraft,[64] there was a common trend that the custodial State had to submit the case of the alleged offender to a competent authority if it did not extradite and this was without exception. This obligation was supplemented by additional provisions that require State parties to: (1) criminalize the relevant offence under its domestic laws; (2) establish jurisdiction over the offence when there was a link to the crime or when the alleged offender was present on their territory and was not extradited; (3) make provisions to ensure the alleged offender be under custody and there be a preliminary enquiry; and (4) treat the offence as extraditable.[65] An analysis of the Secretariat's Survey revealed that of the 61 conventions surveyed, forty-seven conventions were drafted on or after 1970 with approximately three-quarters of these conventions emulating this 'Hague formula' as contained in the 1970 Hague Convention. In particular, under the prosecution limb of the obligation, the conventions only emphasized that the case be submitted to a competent authority for the purpose of prosecution. This was in contrast to the wording of the grave breaches regime under the four Geneva Conventions of 1949, stipulating: 'Each High Contracting Party . . . shall bring such persons . . . before its own

[64] (1971) 10 ILM 133.

[65] Secretariat's Survey §109.

courts.' Under the Hague formula, the custodial State had a wider margin of appreciation between the extradition and prosecution alternatives.[66]

There was some reluctance within the Working Group squarely to address universal jurisdiction in the context of the obligation to extradite or prosecute, as the Sixth Committee had on its agenda 'The Scope and Application of the Principle of Universal Jurisdiction'. Within the Sixth Committee, some States such as Cuba[67] preferred leaving the topic entirely outside the purview of the ILC whereas other States such as Switzerland[68] preferred to have the ILC address the obligation to extradite and prosecute and universal jurisdiction jointly. Given the lack of consensus, some members of the Working Group reiterated that it would be perhaps best for the ILC to work primarily on the obligation to extradite or prosecute, addressing universal jurisdiction only as it arose incidentally in conjunction with that obligation. Another view opined that the obligation to extradite or prosecute could be considered in the context of universal jurisdiction, and not vice versa.

Certain members of the Working Group interpreted the statements in the Sixth Committee saying that this topic was a 'matter of priority' as merely suggesting that if nothing more could be done the ILC needed to end the topic. According to these members, the ILC would lose no credibility if the topic were ended on sound grounds. For them, whether the ILC could do something substantively depended on whether there was customary international law on the obligation to extradite or prosecute and, if so, what its scope was. Customary international law had not been confronted directly so far, and this was the topic's biggest problem. Besides, the ILC should not keep asking States questions, since whether there was a rule in custom did not depend on whether the States said there was such a rule, but on State practice. An opinion was expressed that it was imperative for the ILC to conduct a research on the possible customary obligation to extradite or prosecute for core crimes.

In presenting his fourth informal working paper, dated 12 July 2012, the chairman of the Working Group explained the gist of the paper as follows.

The ILC should engage in a study on the customary nature of the obligation to extradite or prosecute for specific crimes of serious concerns in general, and not just the crimes listed in Article 9 of the 1996 Draft Code. Such a study (and any positive conclusions) would not be a repetition of the work engaged by the ILC under the 1996 Draft Code. If a norm did exist under customary international law today, this conclusion in and of itself progressed beyond the work done in 1996 because the obligation was drafted as progressive development at that time. Thus, even if Article 9 of the 1996 Draft Code were to be reproduced *in pari materia*, it would not diminish the normative value of the ILC finding a customary international law obligation to extradite or prosecute today.

Any study on customary international law by the ILC should involve an extensive analysis of domestic legislation, judicial decisions, and other State declarations. The study should also assess the impact of recent developments in international law such

[66] ibid §116. [67] UN Doc A/C.6/66/SR.27 §57.
[68] UN Doc A/C.6/66/SR.26 §18.

as the establishment of the ICC and ad hoc international criminal tribunals, the adoption by the UN General Assembly of resolutions on the fight against impunity for serious crimes, and statements by other regional and international bodies.

The study should also dedicate itself to analysing the impact of universal jurisdiction on the obligation to extradite or prosecute. In particular, what were the ramifications of such an obligation on the concept of mandatory universal jurisdiction? The ILC should avoid the criticism directed at it in 1996 when it adopted Article 8 on universal jurisdiction without undertaking a study on that topic.[69] In the event that the ILC found a customary obligation to extradite or prosecute for specific crimes, it could engage in drafting articles based on the 'Hague formula' and the 1996 Draft Code. The articles so formulated had to evaluate the precise relationship between the alternatives of extradition and prosecution vis-à-vis the gravity of the crime involved, the grounds (if any) on which extradition might be refused, the establishment of jurisdiction over the offence by the custodial State, the surrender to a competent international tribunal, the transfer to a third State, and so forth.

In the event that the aforesaid study indicated that there was no obligation to extradite or prosecute under extant customary international law, the ILC could engage in progressive development of the law. Given the precedent for progressive development found in Article 9 of the 1996 Draft Code, the ILC could seek to expand the list of crimes to which the obligation was applicable. While some States such as France[70] and Iran[71] preferred to have the topic concluded in the event that there was no obligation under customary international law, it was equally true that many States[72] believed the obligation played a crucial role in the fight against impunity. The currently emerging trend of accountability might make States more receptive to progressive development than they were in 1996. Arguably, the reason the progressive development postulated in 1996 did not translate successfully into State practice was because those developments were overshadowed by the advent of the ICC set up by the 1998 Rome Statute. However, the same fate needed not follow today.

A progressively developed obligation to extradite or prosecute for serious crimes could fill the lacuna in the law of individual criminal responsibility. While regimes such as those conceived under the 1998 Rome Statute relied on complementarity, the reality was a failure to engage individual accountability at a national level. The successful formulation and adoption of a regime on the obligation to extradite or prosecute for serious crimes could galvanize States into ensuring an effective system of individual criminal responsibility. In crafting a regime, the ILC could look to the framework of the 1996 Draft Code and the general trends noted in the Secretariat's Survey in drafting provisions that reflected progressive development. As stated with regard to codification, the postulated articles had to evaluate the precise relationship between the alternatives of extradition and prosecution vis-à-vis the gravity of the

[69] This was the target of criticism by the UK. *Comments and Observations received from Governments*, UN Doc A/CN.4/448 and Add 1, 99.

[70] UN Doc A/C.6/66/SR.20 §9.

[71] UN Doc A/C.6/66/SR.27 §47.

[72] eg Denmark, Finland, Iceland, Norway, and Sweden, UN Doc A/C.6/66/SR.26 §10; Switzerland (ibid §18); El Salvador (ibid §24); Italy (ibid §42); Peru (ibid §64); Belarus (UN Doc A/C.6/66/SR.27 §41); Russia (ibid §64); and India (ibid §81).

crime involved, the grounds (if any) on which extradition might be refused, the establishment of jurisdiction over the offence by the custodial State, the surrender to a competent international tribunal, the transfer to a third State, and so on.

Once the ILC concluded a set of draft articles on a regime for the obligation *aut dedere aut judicare* it could recommend that the UN General Assembly adopt the articles as a convention pursuant to Article 23 of the ILC's Statute.[73] In the alternative, it was also possible for the ILC to adopt the conclusions as a set of guidelines that States could rely on to enhance their practice on bilateral and multilateral levels.

Given that the ILC had not yet discussed the list of crimes that could fall within the scope of the topic, the ILC should commence with analysing the state of the law vis-à-vis the 'core crimes' of genocide, war crimes, and crimes against humanity. This would be in line with the emphasis on core crimes noted by some States[74] and ILC members. This approach also had the benefit of building on the 1996 Draft Code to assess if the progressive development in Article 9 of that Draft Code reflected established customary international law today. The suggestion of beginning with core crimes did not imply that the ILC should limit itself to a study of core crimes alone at this preliminary stage. It merely suggested a convenient starting point in the absence of consensus within the ILC on a list of crimes to be covered by the obligation. The chairman of the Working Group would be interested in receiving the following information from States:

i. Does the State have domestic legislation criminalizing crimes against humanity, war crimes or genocide?
ii. Is the reason for criminalization a treaty obligation?
iii. Domestic legislation, including constitutional and penal provisions, on the obligation to extradite or prosecute for crimes against humanity, war crimes or genocide.
iv Judicial decisions on the obligation to extradite or prosecute for crimes against humanity, war crimes or genocide.
v. Does the State extradite alleged offenders to States with which it does not have an extradition treaty?
vi. In the absence of an extradition request or upon the refusal of an extradition request, does a competent national authority review the case for prosecution?
vii. In the absence of positive State practice on the obligation to extradite or prosecute for crimes against humanity, war crimes, and genocide, are there

[73] Article 23, Statute of the International Law Commission:

1. The Commission may recommend to the General Assembly:
   (a) To take no action, the report having already been published;
   (b) To take note of or adopt the report by a resolution;
   (c) To recommend the draft to Members with a view to the conclusion of a convention;
   (d) To convoke a conference to conclude a convention.
2. Whenever it deems it desirable, the General Assembly may refer drafts back to the Commission for reconsideration or redrafting.

[74] Norway (UN Doc A/C.6/66/SR.26 §11); Russia (UN Doc A/CN.4/599 §55).

instances of State practice where the State has *refused* to both extradite and prosecute alleged offenders for these crimes? If yes, for what reasons?

viii. Has the State requested the extradition of an alleged offender for crimes against humanity, war crimes or genocide? Was there a jurisdictional link to the alleged offender on the basis of territoriality of the crime, nationality of the offender, or nationality of the victim? In the absence of the aforementioned jurisdictional bases, was the State exercising universal jurisdiction?

Alternatively

Does the State have the authority to seek extradition when the offence is not committed on its territory, the alleged offender is not its national, and the victims of the crime are not its nationals?

ix. Does the State have the authority to prosecute persons when the alleged offence is not committed on its territory, the alleged offender is not its national, and the victims of the crime are not its nationals?

The chairman of the Working Group also suggested that the ILC could formulate its work of progressive development in terms of guidelines for States to adopt in their practice should the ILC deem draft articles inappropriate. Throughout its history, the ILC had for varying reasons produced final outcomes in the forms of guidelines, guiding principles, model agreements, or suggestions for State practice. In one instance it even produced a final outcome in the form of articles while recommending that in substance they be used as guidelines for State conduct. This method was in contrast to the usual approach of producing draft articles intended for review and final adoption as a convention by States. Thus, contrary to the concerns voiced by certain members, these precedents suggest that the ILC was not precluded from, and should not fear, producing standard-setting instruments.

The earliest example of such guidelines is found in the 1954 Draft Articles produced on 'present statelessness'. The topic fell into the realm of progressive development and was compounded by complexities of varying domestic provisions and internal political sensitivities. The ILC formulated its proposals on that topic in the form of seven draft articles with commentaries as part of its final report on nationality, including statelessness. However, in doing so the ILC noted:

> In view of the great difficulties of a non-legal nature which beset the problem of present statelessness, the Commission considered that the proposals adopted, though worded in the form of articles, *should merely be regarded as suggestions which Governments may wish to take into account when attempting a solution of this urgent problem.*[75]

A more recent example is the topic on the 'unilateral acts of States' that was concluded in 2006 in the form of the 'Guiding Principles applicable to the unilateral declarations of States capable of creating legal obligations'.[76] In choosing to tread the path of

[75] (1954) ii YBILC §36, emphasis added.

[76] UN Doc A/61/10 §§176–77.

guidelines for progressive development, the ILC was motivated by, *inter alia*, non-uniformity of State practice and the diversity of legal cultures between States.[77]

Other examples of standard-setting guidelines, guiding principles, model agreements, or suggestions for future State practice are found in the final products for topics such as the 'Model Rules on Arbitral Procedure',[78] articles on the law of transboundary aquifers,[79] and the 'Guide to Practice on Reservations to Treaties'.[80]

The chairman of the Working Group stressed the need for the ILC to avoid duplication of efforts. The Council of Europe Committee of Experts on the Operation of European Conventions on Co-operation in Criminal Matters (PC-OC)[81] had produced in 2006 a publication on 'Extradition, European Standards'. Chapter 3 ('*Aut dedere, aut judicare* in transnational procedures') of that publication was devoted to the application/effect of the *aut dedere aut judicare* principle in the 1957 European Convention on Extradition[82] as well as in other Council of Europe conventions that give effect to this principle.[83] Since 2006, the PC-OC has been working on ways to simplify extradition (*dedere*), in particular by modernizing its procedures. The Extradition Convention has been supplemented by two additional protocols, the Third Additional Protocol,[84] which was opened for signature in November 2010 (and entered into force in May 2012) and the Fourth Additional Protocol,[85] opened for signature on 20 September 2012, on the occasion of the thirty-first Council of Europe Conference of Ministers of Justice in Vienna, Austria. As an alternative to extradition, the PC-OC has also worked on ways to improve and simplify the transfer of proceedings (the application of the *aut dedere aut judicare* principle under Article 6(2) of the European Convention on Extradition), among others. This was done in the framework of the development of practical guidelines on jurisdiction and transfer of proceedings, including a model request form.

The chairman reminded the Working Group of UN General Assembly Resolution A/RES/66/98 in 2011 on the 'Report of the International Law Commission on the work of the sixty-third session', paragraph 8 of which invited the ILC 'to continue to give priority to, and work towards the conclusion of, the topics "Immunity of State officials from foreign criminal jurisdiction" and "The obligation to extradite or prosecute (aut *dedere aut judicare)*" '.[86]

In response, some members of the Working Group opined that the UN General Assembly did not seem to insist that the ILC move forward substantively regarding the topic of *aut dedere aut judicare*, but rather that the ILC should decide what to do with it, and that it would be worse for the ILC to go forward only to realize it

77 ibid §§173–75. 78 (1953) ii YBILC §§15 and 22–43.

79 In resolution 66/104, the UN General Assembly recommended that the articles be considered by Member States when negotiating future agreements or arrangements for the management of their transboundary aquifers, as appropriate (UNGA Res 104 (2011) 9 Dec 2011).

80 *Official Records of the General Assembly, Sixty-sixth Session, Supp 10* (A/66/10) 61, 75, 76, and A/66/10/Add 1.

81 www.coe.int/tcj, accessed October 2017. 82 ETS 24.

83 http://www.coe.int/t/dghl/standardsetting/pc-oc/978-92-8716076-8.pdf>, accessed October 2017.

84 CETS 209. 85 ETS 46. 86 UNGA Res 98 (2011) 3.

was not a good idea a few years later. These members suggested that the Working Group submit a report to the ILC Plenary comprising four points. First, there was no value in pursuing a further study of treaty regimes since the Secretariat's Survey had already done just that. Secondly, the ILC had not identified a specific problem or difficulty faced by States in fulfilling their treaty obligations, in the sense that there was never a particular aspect of the treaty regimes that needed to be studied or clarified. While the application of facts to a treaty could be difficult, as was the dispute facing the ICJ in *Belgium v Senegal* then pending before the ICJ, the application of facts to law was not something that the ILC could resolve. Thirdly, most of the debate had focused on customary international law, and with respect to customary international law or progressive development in relation to core crimes the ILC had already addressed this in the 1996 Draft Code. Fourthly, with regard to an obligation under custom for non-core crimes, the Working Group might benefit from the ICJ judgment in *Belgium v Senegal*, expected to be rendered later that month.

However, an opposite view was expressed that it would be too premature to definitively conclude on what to do in 2012. The ILC needed to await the Sixth Committee's decision following the ICJ's judgment in *Belgium v Senegal*. If the ILC were to conclude the consideration of this topic soon, it needed to explain why the points raised in the 2009 General Framework no longer appeared to be analysed by the ILC. The ILC needed to be careful about the implications of abandoning this topic, lest the ILC hindered future development of the law in this area. The 1996 Draft Code also allowed the ILC to encourage progressive development for the obligation. The ILC had to wait to take a decision on the future of this topic in 2013.

According to some Working Group members, the ILC's report to the Sixth Committee and the UN General Assembly for the year 2012 should not include any specific question directed to States. If the proposed questions in the chairman's fourth informal working paper were raised in an abstract way without a prior analysis of the ICJ judgment in *Belgium v Senegal* and without a more detailed reflection on the future of this topic, those questions might not be appropriate and they might also give an impression that the ILC had made a decision on the future direction of this topic.

One ILC member, Donald McRae, had written in April 2012 on the ILC's work, stating that the topic of the obligation to extradite or prosecute was well advanced in terms of State practice, unlike some other topics of the ILC.[87] McRae explained to the Working Group that, as evidence of customary international law, State practice had to be accompanied by *opinio juris*; hence, widespread State practice did not necessarily contribute to the formation of customary international law.

The ICJ rendered its judgment in *Belgium v Senegal* on 20 July 2012.[88] Belgium instituted proceedings against Senegal in respect of a dispute concerning Senegal's compliance with its obligation to prosecute Hissène Habré, former President of Chad who had been living in exile in Senegal, for acts including crimes of torture

[87] Donald McRae, 'The Work of the International Law Commission: 2006–2011: Progress and Prospects' (2012) 106 AJIL 322.

[88] *Questions relating to the Obligation to Prosecute or Extradite (Belgium v Senegal)* [2012] ICJ Rep 422.

and crimes against humanity allegedly committed by him in Chad as perpetrator, co-perpetrator, or accomplice, or to extradite him to Belgium for the purposes of criminal proceedings. Belgium based its claims on the 1984 UN Convention against Torture and Other Cruel, Inhuman or Degrading Treatment or Punishment as well as on customary international law. The ICJ ruled that Senegal, by failing to make immediately a preliminary inquiry into the facts relating to the crimes allegedly committed by Habré, had breached its obligation under Article 6(2) of the Convention.[89] It also found Senegal, by failing to submit the case of Habré to its competent authorities for the purpose of prosecution, to be in breach of its obligation under Article 7(1) of the Convention.[90] Consequently, the ICJ held that Senegal was, without further delay, to submit the case of Habré to its competent authorities for the purpose of prosecution, if it did not extradite him.

The Working Group met briefly on 24 July 2012 to have a preliminary exchange of views on the impact of the judgment on the topic. Since the ILC's session in 2012 was nearing the end, the chairman of the Working Group was entrusted with presenting an informal working paper for consideration of the Working Group in May 2013, analysing all the issues raised thus far and taking into account the views expressed in the Sixth Committee in October 2012 on the ILC's Annual Report of 2012, including the impact of the aforesaid ICJ judgment on the future direction of this topic.

The comments made by States at the Sixth Committee in 2012 indicated that a majority[91] favoured a substantive study being continued on the topic, with only a minority[92] electing to remove the topic from the ILC's active agenda. Their reaction to Chapter IX (The obligation to extradite or prosecute (*aut dedere aut judicare*)) of the Report of the sixty-fourth session of the International Law Commission[93] can be summarized as follows.

[89] Art 6 of the Torture Convention provides:

1. Upon being satisfied, after an examination of information available to it, that the circumstances so warrant, any State Party in whose territory a person alleged to have committed any offence [under this Convention] is present shall take him into custody or take other legal measures to ensure his presence. The custody and other legal measures shall be as provided in the law of that State but may be continued only for such time as is necessary to enable any criminal or extradition proceedings to be instituted.
2. Such State shall immediately make a preliminary inquiry into the facts.

[90] '1. The State Party in the territory under whose jurisdiction a person alleged to have committed any offence referred to in article 4 is found shall in the cases contemplated in article 5, if it does not extradite him, submit the case to its competent authorities for the purpose of prosecution.'

[91] Slovenia (Doc A/C.6/66/SR.20 §9); Norway (Doc A/C.6/66/SR.26 §§10–11); Switzerland (ibid §18); El Salvador (ibid §26); Greece (ibid §37); Italy (ibid §42); Sri Lanka (Doc A/C.6/66/SR.27 §27); Cuba (ibid §58); Russian Federation (ibid §64); Portugal (ibid §75); New Zealand (ibid §84); Malaysia (Doc A/C.6/66/SR.28, §7); Ireland (ibid §19); Republic of Korea (ibid §27); Japan (ibid §36); Algeria (ibid §46); Netherlands (ibid §60); Romania (ibid §68).

[92] France (Doc A/C.6/66/SR.20, §46); Iran (Doc A/C.6/66/SR.27, §47); USA (ibid §92); UK (Doc A/C.6/66/SR.28, §12).

[93] UNGA 'Report of the International Law Commission, Sixty-fourth session' (7 May–1 June and 2 July–3 Aug 2012) GAOR 67th Session Supp No 10 (A/67/10) 116–20.

First, the five Nordic countries (Denmark, Finland, Iceland, Norway, and Sweden), El Salvador, Japan, Netherlands, Portugal, and Thailand explicitly asked the ILC to continue with this topic. There was general consensus among the delegations of these States that the fight against impunity for perpetrators of serious international crimes was a principal legal policy objective of the international community and the ILC's work in this field could potentially be a significant contribution to the development of an effective international criminal justice system. As pointed out by one delegation, pursuant to UN General Assembly Resolution 3074 of 1973 on the Principles of international cooperation in the detection, arrest, extradition, and punishment of persons guilty of war crimes and crimes against humanity, States unanimously agreed to cooperate and assist each other in combating such impunity.

Some of these delegations said the ICJ Judgment in *Belgium v Senegal* confirmed the key role played by the obligation *aut dedere aut judicare*, together with the principle of universal jurisdiction, in the enforcement of international criminal law and in preventing and countering impunity. According to one delegation, the ICJ's statement that the purpose of this kind of obligation was to prevent alleged perpetrators of acts of torture from going unpunished, by ensuring that they could not find refuge in any State Party to the Convention against Torture, brought new elements to the debate and showed the importance and relevance of this topic. While the ICJ Judgment did not address the question of whether the obligation to prosecute or extradite had attained a customary law status, the Judgment was considered to have shed some light on how the provisions containing such obligation were to be interpreted, applied, and implemented in a treaty. Important questions had been raised about the sources of such obligation and its relationship with the surrender of an alleged offender to a competent international court and tribunal. These and other questions had yet to be provided with clear answers.

These delegations generally concurred that codification and further clarification of applicable international law on this issue would help ensure maximum effect and compliance with existing rules. It was also suggested that the ILC ascertain the status of the obligation as it required further clarification as to the meaning and the nature of the obligation. Several of these delegations contended that, taking both progressive development of international law and its codification into account, any absence of a clear determination or agreement on the customary nature of the obligation could not be regarded as an insurmountable obstacle to further consideration of the topic. If necessary, steps towards progressive development of international law in relation to the obligation might be considered.

According to one of the delegations, the ILC's apparent uncertainty regarding its future work on the topic was attributable to a lack of systematization and a failure to establish specific objectives rather than to the nature of the obligation itself. This delegation referred to the fact the in 2004 the ILC had indicated that the topic had attained a sufficient level of maturity to warrant codification with the possible inclusion of some elements of progressive development based, *inter alia*, on the real needs of States. In the view of the delegation, the situation had not changed significantly since then. Besides, the feasibility of the topic was not dependent on identification of the obligation as a customary norm or a principle of international law since its existence was now incontrovertible by virtue of its recognition in various international treaties.

Another delegation concurred with the view of those ILC members who contended that the focus, taking both progressive development of international law and its codification into account, could be on the obligation to extradite or prosecute as evidenced especially in multilateral treaties, including the material scope and the content of the obligation, the relationship between the obligation and other principles, conditions for the triggering of the obligation, the implementation of the obligation, as well as the relationship between the obligation and the surrender of the alleged offender to a competent international criminal tribunal.

One other delegation considered this topic useful for providing a basis for the ongoing discussion of 'The Scope and Application of the Principle of Universal Jurisdiction' in the Sixth Committee.

In sum, these delegations supported the continuation of this topic in the ILC as a matter of priority, so as to produce a final outcome which elaborated rules of international law to guide States in this field.

Secondly, the following States made suggestions on how the ILC should proceed with this topic, in a more or less business-as-usual manner without mentioning the termination of this topic: Algeria, Belarus, Congo, Cuba, India, Italy, Malaysia, New Zealand, Poland, Romania, Russia, Singapore, Slovenia, and Vietnam.

Like those supporting the ILC's continuation with the topic, they considered the ILC's topic 'Immunity of State officials from foreign criminal jurisdiction' and that of 'The obligation to extradite or prosecute (*aut dedere aut judicare*)' in the context of combating impunity. One of the delegations even reiterated its consistent calls for expanding the scope of the obligation to extradite or prosecute to cover 'the gravest crimes with international repercussions' so as to 'help at least partially fill the gaps in the fight against impunity that individual States are hopelessly trying to address by unilateral extension of their universal jurisdiction'.

It was agreed that interpretation of this obligation concerned the international community at large, given the prevalence of such clauses in a whole segment of international treaties, including those on counter-terrorism. An in-depth analysis would be required of the ICJ Judgment in *Belgium v Senegal* to assess its implication for this topic. By analysing State practice, the ILC could ascertain whether the obligation was one of customary international law of general application.

Some of these delegations contended that the existence of the obligation to extradite or prosecute under international customary law had not been formally established by the ILC, except in certain cases relating to the most serious crimes, such as serious violations of international humanitarian law, genocide, war crimes, crimes against humanity, and, probably, acts of terrorism. It was suggested that the ILC analyse this obligation in the context of specific crimes as well as study the topic in the context, or independently, of universal jurisdiction and analyse how this would affect the obligation in the customary law sense. However, in the opinion of several of these delegations, absence of the customary nature of the obligation should not pose insurmountable difficulties in the further consideration of the topic.

It was also proposed that a thorough reflection on the existence of the principles dealing with jurisdictional gaps in general or in specific areas might be worth exploring and a study of these elements could be appropriate.

Even though several of the delegations recognized that an attempt to harmonize different multilateral treaty regimes on the obligation to extradite or prosecute was less than a meaningful exercise, they opined that further consideration of the topic would be useful for the interpretation and implementation of the existing treaties on the subject.

In the view of one delegation, the fight against impunity before domestic courts was addressed by several items on the ILC's agenda and the Sixth Committee: the obligation to extradite or prosecute, the immunity of State officials from foreign criminal jurisdiction, and the scope and application of the principle of universal jurisdiction. In this context, the ILC was asked to deliberate on a comprehensive approach to these matters and take into consideration the possibility of including in the ILC's agenda an item incorporating the above issues, namely 'State responsibility to end impunity for international crimes'.

The *third* group of States opposed or doubted the usefulness of the continuation of this topic. They were France, Hungary, Iran, Republic of Korea, South Africa, Spain, and the UK. They lamented the little substantive progress in the ILC's work on the topic, after so many years. Moreover, harmonization of the different multilateral treaty regimes would have been a less than meaningful exercise, especially since the excellent Secretariat's Study of 2010 had dealt with these matters rather fully. An assessment of the actual interpretation, application, and implementation of the obligation to extradite or prosecute clauses in a particular situation, such as in *Belgium v Senegal* before the ICJ, would not be useful to the development of the topic unless it could provide some general principles in international law. Besides, it was argued, this topic had become an area of law to which the ILC could not presently make any more contribution to the ILC's 1996 Draft Code, Article 9 of which already contained an obligation to extradite or prosecute for core crimes. According to Iran, the Draft Code had not been well received in State practice.

The *fourth* group of States expressed some reservation about the continuation of this topic, but would have no objection if the ILC decided to continue, provided that certain conditions were met. According to Austria, since the obligation was derived from specific treaty obligations and not customary international law, these individual treaty provisions could be of a different content so that a harmonization would hardly be feasible. However, if the ILC decided to pursue this topic, Austria recommended that it consider also the 2009 General Framework as it would be a valuable supplement to the previous work done by Special Rapporteur Galicki. Israel, for its part, shared the considerable doubts by some ILC members regarding the usefulness of continuing with this topic. However, if the ILC were to proceed, stressed Israel, the legal source for 'the principle to extradite or prosecute' was solely derived from treaty-based obligations, and there was not any sufficient basis under current international law or State practice to extend these obligations beyond binding international treaties that explicitly contained such obligations.[94]

The *fifth* group of States (El Salvador, Malaysia, New Zealand, and the USA) looked forward to the Working Group chairman's working paper to be submitted in 2013, reviewing the various perspectives in relation to the topic in the light of the ICJ's Judgment in *Belgium v Senegal* and any further developments. El Salvador particularly urged the ILC to reassess its objectives for the topic and to prepare a work plan that systematically identified the issues to be addressed. New Zealand encouraged further consideration of the relationship of this topic with universal jurisdiction.

Singapore looked forward to a speedy appointment of a new Special Rapporteur for the topic to build on Special Rapporteur Galacki's work, which would be given greater impetus by the ICJ Judgment in *Belgium v Senegal*.

On the customary international law status of the obligation, Israel joined Austria, UK, and the USA in asserting unequivocally that the obligation to extradite or prosecute was not one of customary international law but was treaty-based. In Cuba's view, the obligation arose from the presence of the alleged perpetrator in the territory of a State, but only if there was a treaty or a declaration of reciprocity between the States involved.

The Republic of Congo's position was somewhat nuanced. While considering the 'primary sources' of the obligation to be multilateral treaties and being 'aware of the difficulty in proving the existence of the obligation to extradite or prosecute under customary international law', Congo considered it vital for the ILC to establish 'general principles and clear rules that would constitute the legal regime governing the obligation to extradite or prosecute, as well as the serious crimes to which extradition could apply, without, however, undermining the right of each State to establish, in its domestic law, the crimes subject to extradition'. For Algeria, the existence of the obligation under international customary law had not been formally established by the ILC, except in certain cases relating to the most serious crimes, such as serious violations of international humanitarian law, genocide, war crimes, and crimes against humanity, and Algeria strongly appealed for adding terrorism to this category.

The 1996 Draft Code was alluded to in the interventions by Iran, Republic of Korea, New Zealand, and South Africa as containing the obligation to extradite or prosecute for the core crimes in international law. With the exception of New Zealand, these States considered the Draft Code to have said enough of what the ILC was trying to do regarding the obligation to extradite or prosecute.

The following States referred to universal jurisdiction in relation to this topic: Belarus, Cuba, France, Ghana, India, Iran, Israel, Japan, New Zealand, the five

[94] It should be noted that Art 16(a) of Israel's Penal Code provides: 'Israel penal law shall apply to foreign offences which Israel, by multilateral international conventions, has undertaken to punish even if they are committed by a person who is not an Israeli national or resident of Israel regardless of where they were committed.' By virtue of Article 9(b) of the Penal Code, '[t]here shall be no prosecution for a foreign offence save by the Attorney-General or with his written consent, upon his determination that such is in the public interest' (Law no 626/1996 (1996) 30 Israel L Rev 5, quoted in Luc Reydams, *Universal Jurisdiction: International and Municipal Legal Perspectives* (OUP 2003) 159).

Nordic countries, Peru, Portugal, Romania, Russia, and Slovenia. Of these States, those contending that the topic should be analysed separately from universal jurisdiction were France, India, Iran, Israel, Russia, and Slovenia. According to France, universal jurisdiction and '*aut dedere aut judicare*' were different issues. India considered the two issues not interrelated in the sense that one was dependent on the other. India thus agreed with those ILC members who had opted to delink the topic from that of universal jurisdiction. According to Russia, the obligation to extradite or prosecute was substantially different from universal jurisdiction in its 'pure' form—jurisdiction was exercised not only upon the consent but also upon the request of another State which could exercise its jurisdiction itself on the basis of traditional linkages. Therefore, added Russia, two fundamental negative effects of 'pure' universal jurisdiction were excluded when States fulfilled the obligation to extradite or prosecute: first, the risk of interstate conflicts was absent; and, second, it was highly probable that the State requesting extradition would provide maximum assistance to the requested State in establishing the circumstances of the crime. For Iran, there was a substantial difference between the two concepts, universal jurisdiction being of a procedural nature. Belarus was the only State insisting that the two topics should be analysed together. New Zealand, Peru, Portugal, and Romania merely referred to the close relationship between the obligation and universal jurisdiction.

In general, Austria, Netherlands, and Vietnam considered the 2009 General Framework a valuable supplement to the ILC's work. In the Netherlands' opinion, the ILC's work should eventually result in presenting draft articles based on that General Framework.

Ghana and Peru did not clearly indicate their position one way or another in their respective interventions on this topic.

In a related development, in October 2012, the chairman of the Working Group on the Scope and Application of the Principle of Universal Jurisdiction under the Sixth Committee circulated an informal note containing a list of essential elements of a working concept of universal jurisdiction. The subject-matter of that topic would be: '(1) focused on criminal matters; (2) exercised by national courts/tribunals; (3) exercised exceptionally; (4) based on the nature of certain crimes under international law, not on territoriality, personality or protective principles; and (5) distinct from (a) jurisdiction of international criminal courts/tribunals, (b) obligation to extradite or prosecute (*aut dedere aut judicare*), and (c) other forms of extra-territorial jurisdiction'.

On 14 December 2012, the UN General Assembly adopted by consensus Resolution 67/92 entitled 'Report of the International Law Commission on the work of its sixty-third and sixty fourth sessions', operative paragraph 8 of which invited the ILC 'to continue to give priority to the topics "Immunity of State officials from foreign criminal jurisdiction" and "The obligation to extradite or prosecute (*aut dedere aut judicare*)" '.[95] The drafting history of this operative paragraph should shed light on its true meaning.

[95] UNGA Res 67/92 (14 Jan 2013). Cf the identical draft resolution (UNGA Doc A/C.6/67/L.13 (7 Nov 2012)) adopted by consensus by the Sixth Committee on 16 Nov 2012.

During the informal consultation on the draft resolution on this agenda item held on 6 and 7 November 2012,[96] one delegation proposed deletion of the reference to the topic 'The obligation to extradite or prosecute (*aut dedere aut judicare*)', because her delegation was in favour of the ILC terminating this topic. This proposal was opposed by another delegation on the grounds that several delegations, including hers, were in favour of the ILC continuing to pursue its work on this topic. Yet another delegation proposed that this operative paragraph also include reference to the topic 'Protection of persons in the event of disasters' in view of the number and magnitude of disasters currently faced by States in all parts of the world. This latter proposal was opposed by another delegation that explained that this operative paragraph had been inserted to remind the ILC that the Sixth Committee had decided to include the item 'Scope and application of the principle of universal jurisdiction' in its agenda since 2009, and that the ILC was to expedite its work on the other two topics related to universal jurisdiction in order to allow the Sixth Committee to benefit from the ILC's work. Adding any reference to the topic 'Protection of persons in the event of disasters' in this operative paragraph, it was argued, would not be appropriate as protection of persons in the event of disasters had nothing to do with combating impunity of perpetrators of crimes of international concern.

The coordinator of the draft resolution reminded the delegations participating in the informal consultation that whereas operative paragraph 8 of the resolution on the same agenda item as adopted in 2011 had invited the ILC 'to continue to give priority to, and work towards the conclusion of, the topics "Immunity of State officials from foreign criminal jurisdiction" and "The obligation to extradite or prosecute (*aut dedere aut judicare*)" ',[97] the wording ', and work towards the conclusion of,' had been dropped from the current draft resolution. This, according to the coordinator, was to defer to the ILC's decision on how to proceed with these two topics, and the adoption of this draft resolution in 2012 would be without prejudice to the Sixth Committee's position on this operative paragraph in the following years. Eventually, after extensive consultations among interested delegations, operative paragraph 8 of the draft resolution remained unchanged and was adopted as such by the Sixth Committee and, subsequently, the UN General Assembly.

The chairman of the ILC Working Group on the Obligation to Extradite or Prosecute submitted his first informal working paper for the year 2013 on 5 April 2013, totalling 114 pages. On 14 May 2013, the Working Group met to consider the paper. In the light of the positive reaction in the Sixth Committee to the continuation of this topic, the chairman insisted that it would be best for the ILC to continue its work. In his view, should strong consensus on the discontinuation of the topic eventually emerge within the Sixth Committee and the ILC, the conclusion of the topic would no doubt be appropriate. This did not imply that the ILC should abdicate to the will of States its responsibility as a body of independent legal experts. On the contrary, if there was a clear consensus within the ILC that no substantive progress on a topic was viable there

[96] This author was present as a passive observer throughout the informal consultation process.
[97] UNGA Res 66/98 (13 Jan 2012).

was an onus on the ILC to communicate this decision to the Sixth Committee, notwithstanding the latter's expectations. On the other hand, when the Sixth Committee was clearly in favour of the substantive development of a topic, the ILC should work harder on it. The symbiotic relationship between States and the ILC is best captured in the following quote:

> The interaction between the Commission, a permanent body of legal experts serving in their personal capacity, and Governments, through a variety of means ... is at the core of the system created by the General Assembly for the promotion, with the assistance of the Commission, of the progressive development of international law and its codification ...
>
> ...
>
> ... [However, the] fact that the Commission is a subsidiary organ of the General Assembly has not prevented wide acceptance in the Sixth Committee of the view that the Commission should have a substantial degree of autonomy ...[98]

In the chairman's opinion, if the ILC found no customary law obligation to extradite or prosecute and there was not anything more that the ILC could contribute, it could choose to terminate consideration of this topic. Yet, such a decision would definitely disappoint the great number of States and the general public who had been looking forward to the ILC's final product on this obligation as an authoritative and essential tool in the fight against impunity. If the ILC found convincing evidence that the obligation had become a norm of customary international law or at least was emerging as such a norm, it might choose to present either draft articles or a set of guidelines. Those aspects of the topic that were not of customary nature might well be 'progressively developed'. The focus should be on substantive aspects, and not on procedural aspects (such as an extradition or prosecution mechanism) except in so far as such procedural aspects impact the substantive aspects.[99] However, one might find it difficult to imagine how draft articles on the obligation to extradite or prosecute[100] could be used, bearing in mind the existence of this obligation in a variety of forms in multilateral conventions.[101] One writer proposed that what was needed was not draft articles which applied in respect of the obligation regardless of its wording, but 'guidelines that [might] assist States in interpreting the particular version of the obligation that concerns them' in order to encourage a

[98] *The Work of the International Law Commission* (8th edn, United Nations 2012) vol I, 71, 77.

[99] Special Rapporteur Galicki wrote in his second report: 'Some Members [of the Commission] cautioned against considering the technical aspects of extradition law. What was specific to the topic and the precise meaning of the Latin maxim *aut dedere aut judicare* was that, failing an extradition, an obligation to prosecute arose. The focus, therefore, should be on the conditions for triggering the obligation to prosecute. The view was expressed that the Commission should not deal with all the collateral rules on the subject, which were linked to it but not necessarily part of it. It was also proposed that the focus should be limited to the elaboration of secondary rules' (Doc A/CN.4/585 §15). Cf also ibid §47, where Galicki also acknowledged that 'the application of some limitations traditionally imposed on extradition' might raise problems or even make it impossible to implement the '*dedere*' part of the obligation *aut dedere aut judicare.*

[100] Cf Special Rapporteur Galicki's proposed draft articles in his third report (Doc A/CN.4/603 10 June 2008, paras 110–29) and, three years later, in his fourth report (Doc A/CN.4/648 31 May 2011, §§40, 70–71, and 95). Cf also his second report (Doc A/CN.4/585 §§76–104).

[101] Claire Mitchell, *Aut Dedere Aut Judicare: The Extradite or Prosecute Clauses in International Law* (Graduate Institute of International and Development Studies 2009) 75.

more flexible approach, allowing particular features of each treaty to be taken into consideration,[102] and this would involve the ILC in, *inter alia*, drafting a model *aut dedere aut judicare* clause.[103]

Instead of either draft articles or guidelines, the chairman suggested that the ILC might choose to present a set of conclusions with commentaries regarding the obligation to extradite or prosecute in order to inform States where this obligation currently stood. A set of conclusions resulting from a systematic analysis would encourage further developments in the direction of subsequent establishment in customary international law, if the obligation had not yet attained a customary law status. If the obligation had already become a customary international norm, the set of conclusions would be a point of reference for States.

The chairman also alluded to the possibility of appointing a new Special Rapporteur to present his or her work on this topic, but, in any case, the ILC should finalize this topic by the end of the ILC's annual session in 2015 or, at the latest, in 2016.

Some members of the Working Group suggested that the ILC draft a model law or clause on the obligation to extradite or prosecute, focusing on international cooperation to end impunity for core crimes. Other members were in favour of the ILC filling the gaps in international criminal law, including the lack of the obligation to extradite or prosecute in relation to crimes against humanity, war crimes in international armed conflicts other than grave breaches, war crimes in non-international armed conflicts, as well as the very rudimentary international cooperation regime for the crime of genocide. In response, the chairman suggested that the ILC could draft the Guide to Practice on the Obligation to Extradite or Prosecute, or Guiding Principles Applicable to the Obligation to Extradite or Prosecute, or Model Rules or Model Law (or Draft Statute or Draft Code) on the Obligation to Extradite or Prosecute. The ILC might embark upon drafting rules, for example, as suggested by Special Rapporteur Galicki:

(a) The obligation to prosecute or extradite is imposed on the custodial State in whose territory an alleged offender is present;
(b) The custodial State has an obligation to take action to ensure that such an individual is prosecuted either by the national authorities of that State or by another State which indicates that it is willing to prosecute the case by requesting extradition;
(c) The custodial State has an obligation to take the necessary and reasonable steps to apprehend an alleged offender and to ensure the prosecution and trial of such an individual by a competent jurisdiction;
(d) The obligation to extradite or prosecute applies to a State which has custody of 'an individual alleged to have committed a crime'.[104]

Such rules would correspond closely to the reasoning of the ICJ in *Belgium v Senegal* in relation to the mechanism to combat impunity under the Convention against

[102] ibid. [103] ibid 77.

[104] UN Doc A/CN.4/585 §114, quoting §3 of the commentary to Art 9 of the Draft Code (1996) ii YBILC (Part Two) 31.

Torture of 1984, proceeding from the establishment of jurisdiction (Art 5), the obligation to engage a preliminary inquiry (Art 6), and the obligation to prosecute or extradite (Art 7).

Whatever the title of the final outcome of the ILC's work on the topic, the chairman suggested that it should have the following contents, most of which are referred to in the 2009 General Framework.

First, the preamble should make it clear that the obligation aimed at enhancing international cooperation in the fight against impunity for serious crimes of international concern.

Secondly, as agreed by the Working Group, the articles or principles which followed should focus on the substantive aspects rather than the procedural aspects of the obligation. The substantive aspects would include criminalization, prescriptive jurisdiction, and extradition or prosecution of alleged offenders. The procedural aspects, on the other hand, would focus on extradition procedures and other procedural matters of legal cooperation between States.[105]

Thirdly, regarding the material scope of the obligation, the list of offences enumerated in Articles 8 and 9 of the 1996 Draft Code encompasses aggression, genocide, crimes against humanity, crimes against UN and associated personnel, and war crimes. However, pursuant to Article 8 (Establishment of jurisdiction) of the Draft Code, jurisdiction over the crime of aggression shall rest with an international criminal court although the court of the State whose leaders participated in the act of aggression could try its own nationals for this crime. Aggression is, thus, not subject to Article 9 (Obligation to extradite or prosecute) of the Draft Code. The ILC's commentary reveal that, in 1996 when the Draft Code was adopted, Articles 8 and 9 were justified on the basis of the grave nature of the crimes involved and the desire to combat impunity for individuals who committed those crimes.[106]

In the Sixth Committee, Algeria has proposed the inclusion of international terrorism in any list of core crimes under international law to be subject to a customary law obligation to extradite or prosecute. Nonetheless, there is unlikely to be consensus among States whether international terrorism is a crime proscribed by *jus cogens*. For instance, the Argentine Supreme Court has held in *Lariz Iriondo* that terrorism is a 'regular crime', since it has not yet been classified as an international crime in the sense of being proscribed under customary international law and, as such, it is subject to regular statutes of limitations.[107]

[105] This classification is similar to Special Rapporteur Galicki's classification of relevant treaties into: (1) 'substantive treaties' which define particular offences and require their criminalization plus the prosecution or extradition of offenders; and (2) 'procedural conventions' which deal with extradition and other matters of inter-State legal cooperation. See UN Doc A/CN.4/571 §35 and UN Doc A/CN.4/648 §§42–46.

[106] *Draft Code of Crimes against the Peace and Security of Mankind with Commentaries*, UN Doc A/51/10 Art 8(3), (4), and (8), and Art 9(2).

[107] *Office of the Public Prosecutor v Lariz Iriondo*, L.845.XL, Vol 328; ILDC 125 (AR 2005) 10 May 2005. The Court therefore rejected Spain's extradition request for an alleged member of the Basque separatist organization ETA to stand trial in Spain for alleged acts of terrorism in Spain, owing to the statutes of limitations on the crimes of terrorism.

During the advent of widespread acts of piracy off the coast of Africa in recent years, joint international efforts have been undertaken to suppress piracy. One of the questions faced by the States whose naval vessels have apprehended suspected pirates is where their prosecution is to be held.[108] The idea of setting a special court outside the States of nationality of the accused and victims has also been broached.[109] The chairman of the Working Group therefore raised the possibility of including the crime of piracy within the context of the topic 'The obligation to extradite or prosecute'.[110]

Developments since 1996, including the 1998 ICC Statute, would have to be taken into account. Therefore, the chairman recommended that the ILC enumerate the following crimes to be covered by the obligation: genocide, crimes against humanity, war crimes in international armed conflicts (including grave breaches and non-grave breaches), war crimes in non-international armed conflict, torture beyond the context of a crime against humanity or war crime, and any other crime in relation to which the State adopting the final outcome of the ILC's work on this topic would be bound by conventional law to extradite or prosecute the offender, as in the case of acts of terrorism.

In relation to genocide, in the chairman's view, the international cooperation regime could be strengthened beyond the rudimentary regime under the Genocide Convention. As pointed out by Special Rapporteur Galicki, while that Convention

[108] See eg Kenneth Manusama, 'Prosecuting Pirates in the Netherlands: The Case of the *MS Samanyolu*' (2010) 49 Military L & L of War Rev 141, 143–44, 162–63.

[109] eg the proposal submitted by Jack Lang, Special Adviser on Legal Issues related to Piracy off the Coast of Somalia, to the UN Security Council on 25 Jan 2011.

[110] Article 105 of the 1982 UN Convention on the Law of the Sea (1833 UNTS 3) provides: 'On the high seas, or in any other place outside the jurisdiction of any State, every State may seize a pirate ship or aircraft, or a ship or aircraft taken by piracy and under the control of pirates, and arrest the persons and seize the property on board. The courts of the State which carried out the seizure may decide upon the penalties to be imposed, and may also determine the action to be taken with regard to the ships, aircraft or property, subject to the rights of third parties acting in good faith'. Nowhere in the 1982 Convention is there any provision on extradition. However, there is an extradite-or-prosecute provision in the 1988 Rome Convention for the Suppression of Unlawful Acts against the Safety of Maritime Navigation (1678 UNTS 201), Arts 3 and 4 of which are broad enough to cover acts of piracy as well.

Article 6(4) of the 1988 Rome Convention stipulates: 'Each State Party shall take such measures as may be necessary to establish its jurisdiction over the offences set forth in article 3 in cases where the alleged offender is present in its territory and it does not extradite him to any of the States Parties which have established their jurisdiction in accordance with paragraphs 1 and 2 of this article.'

Article 6(1) of the 1988 Rome Convention concerns: (1) the flag State of the ship against which the offence is committed; (2) the territorial State; and (3) the State of nationality of the victim. Article 6 para 2 authorizes a State Party to also establish its jurisdiction over any such offence when: (1) it is committed by a stateless person whose habitual residence is in that State; or (2) during its commission a national of that State is seized, threatened, injured, or killed; or (3) it is committed in an attempt to compel that State to do or abstain from doing any act.

There is difference of opinion on whether the wording 'where the alleged offender is present in its territory' under Art 6(4) applies to the situation where an alleged offender is in custody on board a warship that apprehends him or her. Some authors opine that it does so apply, while some others argue that it does not since the person is not within the 'territory', but within the 'jurisdiction', of the flag State of the warship. For the former view, see Robin Gesiss and Anna Petrig, *Piracy and Armed Robbery at Sea: The Legal Framework for Counter-piracy Operations in Somalia and the Gulf of Aden* (OUP 2011) 163–64.

does contain obligations for its Contracting Parties to prosecute (where the genocide was committed on its territory) and to extradite, these are not an *aut dedere aut judicare* obligation that requires States to elect either to extradite or prosecute. Therefore, in Galicki's opinion, if a person accused of committing genocide elsewhere is present on a State territory, the said State might be obliged to extradite the accused to a requesting State with which it has an extradition treaty or other extradition arrangements, but the former State is not obliged to prosecute the accused irrespective of whether an extradition request was made by the latter State.[111] This is affirmed by the ICJ in *Case Concerning Application of the Convention on the Prevention and Punishment of the Crime of Genocide (Bosnia and Herzegovina v Serbia and Montenegro)*.[112] The ILC might instead adopt the reasoning of the Federal Court of Australia in *Re Thompson; Ex parte Nulyarimma* that although conventional law does not impose an obligation to extradite or prosecute, 'the obligation imposed by customary law on each nation State is to extradite or prosecute any person, found in its territory, who appears to have committed any of the acts cited in the definition of genocide set out in the [Genocide] Convention'.[113]

With regard to the crime of aggression, the chairman suggested that ILC consider whether more could be done in term of international cooperation to extradite or prosecute the perpetrator of aggression in the light of the 2010 Kampala Amendment to the ICC Statute that incorporates the crime of aggression as a crime within the ICC's jurisdiction.[114]

Fourthly, regarding the content of the obligation to extradite or prosecute, the chairman suggested that the ILC provide answers to the General Framework's questions about the definition of the 'extradite' and the 'prosecute' elements, the meaning of the obligation to prosecute, steps to be taken in order for prosecution to be considered 'sufficient', the question of timeliness of prosecution, whether the order of the two elements matters, and whether one element has priority over the other. In passing, the chairman suggested that the ILC might find it unhelpful to retain the Latin formula '*aut dedere aut judicare*'. In the past, some ILC members including Special Rapporteur Galicki, doubted the use of this Latin formula, especially in relation to the term '*judicare*' which they considered as not reflecting precisely the scope of the term 'prosecute'.[115]

For the latter view, see Douglas Guilfoyle's review of the said book by Gesiss and Petrig in (2011) 11 Int'l Crim L Rev 910, 912.

[111] Fourth report (UN Doc A/CN.4/648) n 34. [112] [2007] ICJ Rep 43 §§442, 449.

[113] [1999] FCA 1192 (*per* Wilcox J).

[114] Resolution RC/Res. 6 (11 June 2010); UN Doc C.N.651.2010.TREATIES-8 (29 Nov 2010).

[115] In his preliminary report, the then Special Rapporteur Galicki discussed various Latin formulas relevant to this topic; namely, *aut dedere aut judicare; aut dedere aut punire; judicare aut dedere; aut dedere aut prosequi; aut dedere, aut judicare, aut tergiversari*; and *aut dedere aut poenam persequi* (Doc A/CN.4/571 §§5–8). Some ILC members doubted the use of the Latin formula *aut dedere aut judicare* tentatively chosen by the Special Rapporteur, especially in relation to the term '*judicare*' which they considered as not reflecting precisely the scope of the term 'prosecute'. Even the Secretariat's Survey thinks that the widely used Hague formula should, strictly speaking, be described as '*aut dedere aut prosequi*' (Secretariat's Survey §146). However, Galicki, while sharing this doubt, considered it rather premature at that time to focus on the precise definition of terms, leaving them to be defined in a future draft article on 'Use of terms' (Special Rapporteur's third report (UN Doc A/CN.4/603 §§36–37)).

The ILC might, therefore, be content simply with the terminology 'the obligation to extradite or prosecute', with the understanding that whether the mandatory nature of 'extradition' or that of 'prosecution' has priority over the other depends on the context and applicable legal regime in particular situations.

The power of free appreciation (*pouvoir discrétionnaire*) of the requested State also needed to be explored. Article 9 of the 1996 Draft Code simply provides: 'Without prejudice to the jurisdiction of an international criminal court, the State Party in the territory of which an individual alleged to have committed a crime [under the Draft Code] is found shall extradite or prosecute that individual.' Article 10 of the Draft Code then proceeds to reproduce a standard formula used in extradition treaties as well as multilateral treaties with a provision obligating States Parties to extradite offenders to other States Parties. At least two ILC members, James Crawford and PS Rao, opposed the formula in Article 9 of the 1996 Draft Code which would impose on the custodial State an automatic obligation of prosecution and obliterate its prosecutorial discretion. They proposed the formula used in Article 7 of the 1970 Hague Convention for the Suppression of Unlawful Seizure of Aircraft, pursuant to which the custodial State merely has an obligation to submit the case to its competent authorities for the purpose of prosecution.[116] The major concern of these two ILC members was the need to preserve the prosecutorial discretion not to prosecute in cases of lack of sufficient evidence.

While the said provision of Article 9 of the Draft Code was adopted as it is now, the ILC stated in its commentary to this provision:

> The obligation to extradite or prosecute is imposed on the custodial State in whose territory an alleged offender is present. The custodial State has an obligation to take action to ensure that such an individual is prosecuted whether by the national authorities of that State or by another State which indicates that it is willing to prosecute the case by requesting extradition.[117]

This commentary shows that the obligation to prosecute arises independently of any request for extradition.[118] However, the commentary does not shed light on whether prosecutorial discretion in other cases, such as the lack of public interest of the custodial State, was permissible under Article 9 of the Draft Code.[119] Since prosecuting or extraditing perpetrators of core crimes under international law would be in the common interest of the international community as a whole,[120] the chairman of the Working Group submitted that the custodial State would have no prosecutorial discretion over such crimes except in cases of lack of sufficient evidence.

As for the steps to be undertaken in order for prosecution to be considered sufficient as well as the timeliness of the prosecution, the choice of means to fulfil the

[116] UN Doc A/CN.4/SER.A/1996 at 50–51, cited in Raphäel van Steenberghe, 'The Obligation to Extradite or Prosecute: Clarifying its Nature' (2011) 9 J Int'l Crim Justice 1089, 1109.
[117] UN Doc A/51/10 ch II 31 [3] of the commentary to Art 9. See also Secretariat's Survey §147.
[118] Secretariat's Survey §129 and accompanying footnotes.
[119] van Steenberghe, 'The Obligation to Extradite or Prosecute' 1110.
[120] Cf *Belgium v Senegal* §§68-69, 91.

obligation to extradite or prosecute remains in the hands of the State in whose territory the alleged offender is present. As pointed out by the ICJ in *Belgium v Senegal*, 'the competent authorities involved remain responsible for deciding on whether to initiate a prosecution, in light of the evidence before them and the relevant rules of criminal procedure'.[121] However, the steps taken by the State must be scrutinized in the light of the object and purpose of international instruments or any other source of international obligation binding on that State, and such object and purpose are most likely to be making more effective the fight against impunity.[122] In cases of crimes proscribed by *jus cogens*, it is submitted, the obligations to end impunity are ones of result, and not simply obligations of conduct, and it is in the public interests of the State in whose territory the suspect is present to take steps to prosecute or extradite the person.[123] As explained by Judge Cançado Trindade,

> The conduct of the State ought to be one which is conducive to compliance with the obligations of result (in the *cas d'espèce*, the proscription of torture). The State cannot allege that, despite its good conduct, insufficiencies or difficulties of domestic law rendered impossible the full compliance with its obligation (to outlaw torture and to prosecute perpetrators of it); and the Court cannot consider a case terminated, given the allegedly 'good conduct' of the State concerned.[124]

The timeliness of the prosecution must be such that it would not lead to injustice; hence, necessary actions must be undertaken within a reasonable time limit.[125]

It could be argued, however, that, after acting in good faith, the forum State might decline to prosecute the alleged offender if such prosecution would encounter or has encountered so many legal and practical problems as to make the prosecution unlikely to succeed in the forum State.[126]

[121] ibid §90.

[122] See the reasoning of the ICJ, ibid §§85–86. NB: Judge Yusuf, in his Separate Opinion in that case, disagreed with the ICJ's interpretation of the facts regarding the steps taken by Senegal in relation to Mr Habré. He thought that the ICJ did not properly assess Senegal's legal system and practice (Sep Op of Judge Yusuf, §§13–17).

[123] Cf Section 153c (3) of the German Criminal Procedure Code (Federal Law Gazette, Part I, 3799) which provides that the prosecutor may, at any stage, dismiss a case concerning an offence committed outside German territory 'if the conduct of proceedings poses the risk of serious detriment to the Federal Republic of Germany or if other public interests of overriding importance present an obstacle to prosecution'. This present author submits that prosecuting crimes proscribed by *jus cogens* would not be seriously detrimental to any State or other significant public interests in that State, including Germany.

[124] Sep Op of Judge Cançado Trindade in *Belgium v Senegal* §50 and see also his full reasoning in §§43–51. However, Judge Xue rightly pointed out in the same case that one should not overlook practical difficulties, including financial and evidentiary burdens, encountered in trials of international crimes, as experienced by the various international criminal tribunals and special tribunals (Dissenting Op of Judge Xue, §§44–47).

[125] Cf Sep Op of Judge Çancado Trindade, ibid §§148, 151–53; Dissenting Op of Judge ad hoc Sur in the same case at §50; and Dissenting Op of Judge Xue, also in the same case, §28. Judge ad hoc Sur considered that there was no dispute between the Parties regarding the interpretation of the Convention against Torture, but that there was a dispute between them on the application of the Convention and Senegal's delay in this respect (Dissenting Op §§10–11, 52).

[126] Cf *Chili Komitee Nederland v Pinochet*, Ct App of Amsterdam, 4 Jan 1995 (1997) 28 Netherlands YBIL 363–65, in which the Court of Appeal held that the Dutch Public Prosecutor did not err in refusing to prosecute former Chilean President Pinochet while visiting Amsterdam because Pinochet might be entitled to immunity from prosecution and any necessary evidence to substantiate his prosecution

There is also a possibility, envisaged by Special Rapporteur Galicki, where a State might wish to fulfil both parts of the obligation, for instance by prosecuting, trying, and sentencing an offender and then extraditing or surrendering the offender to another State for the purpose of enforcing the judgment.[127]

There was widespread agreement in the Working Group that universal jurisdiction was a crucial component of the obligation to extradite or prosecute. Although universal jurisdiction and the obligation are two distinct legal concepts, States must establish necessary jurisdiction before they may prosecute perpetrators of crimes. Except where there is a regime change, perpetrators of core crimes are unlikely to be prosecuted in the territory where they have committed their crimes and the State intending to prosecute them may not have any jurisdictional *nexus* with the crimes or the perpetrators except through the establishment of universal jurisdiction.[128] The ICJ in *Belgium v Senegal* has clarified that the performance by the State of its obligation to establish the universal jurisdiction of its courts over the crime of torture is a necessary condition for enabling a preliminary inquiry (Art 6(2) of the Convention against Torture), and for submitting the case to its competent authorities for the purpose of prosecution (Art 7(1) of that Convention). The purpose of all these obligations, according to the ICJ, 'is to enable proceedings to be brought against the suspect, in the absence of his extradition, and to achieve the object and purpose of the Convention, which is to make more effective the struggle against torture by avoiding impunity for the perpetrators of such acts'.[129]

The standard of proof and the existence of circumstances that might exclude extradition or prosecution, such as immunities, the political offence exception to extradition, protection of human rights as a ground for denying extradition, and so forth, more appropriately belonged to public international law as well as extradition law in general, and guidance on these matters ought to be sought from these other areas of law[130] without the ILC having to provide an analysis thereon. However, formal extradition requests entailed important human rights protections which might be absent from informal forms of dispatching the accused to another State, such as extraordinary renditions. Under extradition law of most, if not all, States, the necessary requirements to be satisfied included double criminality, *ne bis in idem, nullem crimen sine lege*, specialty, and non-extradition of the accused to stand trial on the grounds of ethnic origin, religion, nationality, or political views. Indeed,

would be in Chile with which the Netherlands had no cooperative arrangements regarding criminal proceedings. See Kimberley N Trapp, *State Responsibility for International Terrorism* (OUP 2011) 88 n 132.

[127] Preliminary report, UN Doc A/CN.4/571 §§49–50.

[128] It should be recalled that the 'Obligation to extradite or prosecute' in Art 9 of the 1996 Draft Code is closely related to the 'Establishment of jurisdiction' under Art 8 of the Draft Code, which requires each State Party thereto to take such measures as may be necessary to establish its jurisdiction over genocide, crimes against humanity, crimes against United Nations and associated personnel, and war crimes, irrespective of where or by whom those crimes were committed. The ILC's commentary to Art 8 makes it clear that universal jurisdiction is envisaged (UN Doc A/51/10 §7).

[129] *Belgium v Senegal* §74.

[130] See eg Catherine Heard and Daniel Mansell, 'The European Arrest Warrant: The Role of Judges When Human Rights Are at Risk' (2011) 2 New J Euro Crim L 133, for the protection of human rights in the extradition system among EU Member States.

the European Court of Human Rights has held that a deportation carried out as a disguised extradition so as to circumvent the requirements of extradition is neither lawful nor compatible with the 'right to security of person' under Article 5 of the European Convention on Human Rights.[131] While States may find it easier to resort to deportation to rid themselves of suspected criminals, the chairman of the Working Group submitted that deportation might be insufficient to fulfil the obligation to extradite or prosecute unless there was a guarantee that the deported persons would be prosecuted in the States with the necessary jurisdiction.[132] Therefore, the rules/principles to be drafted by the ILC would have to ensure that the custodial State either prosecute or extradite the offender, and not deport or expel or pursue some other method of getting rid of the offender in lieu of extradition from or prosecution by the custodial State.

With respect to Australia's suggestion for the ILC to draw upon elements in existing treaties, to be supplemented by such changes as the ILC considered desirable,[133] this exercise by the ILC could establish best practices for States to emulate in relation to *aut dedere aut judicare*. An authoritative statement on this matter may be found in Judge Yusuf's Separate Opinion in *Belgium v Senegal*, where he divided international conventions containing the formula *aut dedere aut judicare* into two broad categories.

The first category comprises clauses that impose an obligation to extradite, and in which prosecution becomes an obligation only after the refusal of extradition. These conventions are structured in such a way as to give priority to extradition to the State in whose territory the crime is committed. The majority of these conventions do not impose any general obligation on States Parties to prosecute the alleged offender, and prosecution by the State on whose territory the alleged offender is present becomes an obligation only if a request for extradition has been refused, or some factors such as nationality of the alleged offender exist. Examples of this first category are Article 9(2) of the 1929 International Convention for the Suppression of Counterfeiting Currency,[134] Article 15 of the 2003 African Union Convention on Preventing and Combating Corruption,[135] and Article 5 of the Optional Protocol to the Convention on the Rights of the Child on the sale of children, child prostitution, and child pornography.[136] The second category of international conventions comprises clauses that impose an obligation to prosecute, with extradition being an available option, as well as clauses that impose an obligation to prosecute, with extradition becoming an obligation if the State fails to submit the case for prosecution. Such clauses in this second category can be found in, for example, the relevant provisions of the four Geneva Conventions of 1949, Article 7(1) of the 1970 Hague Convention for the Suppression of Unlawful Seizure of Aircraft, and Article 7(1) of the Convention

[131] *Bozano v France* (1986) 9 EHRR 297 §§53–54. Also cited in Mitchell, *Aut Dedere Aut Judicare*, 64.
[132] Cf Mitchell, ibid. [133] UNGA Doc A/C.6/66/SR.28 (2 Dec 2011) §2.
[134] 112 LNTS 371.
[135] Available at <http://www.refworld.org/docid/493fe36a2.html>, accessed 26 October 2017.
[136] UN Doc A/RES/54/263.

against Torture.[137] It could be said that the first category of treaties relate to 'transnational crimes such as corruption, drug trafficking or organized crime', whereas the second category deal with 'international crimes' which 'offend mankind'.[138]

In *Belgium v Senegal*, the ICJ has construed the Convention against Torture, in particular the obligations under Article 6(2) and Article 7(1), finding that the principal obligation under Article 7 is to submit the case for prosecution and that extradition is not strictly speaking an obligation but an alternative option available to the State which, if chosen, would relieve the State of its obligation to prosecute.[139] Since the relevant prosecute-or-extradite provisions of the Convention against Torture are modelled upon those of the 1970 Hague Convention, the ICJ's ruling also elucidates the meaning of the prosecute-or-extradite regime under the 1970 Hague Convention and other conventions that have followed the same formula. As the ICJ has also held that torture is a crime proscribed by *jus cogens*, the prosecute-or-extradite formula under the Convention against Torture could also serve as a model formula for the prosecute-or-extradite regime governing core crimes proscribed by *jus cogens*, such as genocide, crimes against humanity, and war crimes.

In relation to non-core crimes, the chairman thought that the Secretariat's Survey already answered the questions raised by the 2009 General Framework concerning the obligation to extradite or prosecute in existing treaties, that is, typology of treaty provisions, as well as differences and similarities between those provisions and their evolution.[140] The chairman suggested that States would have options as to which conventional formula on the obligation to extradite or prosecute/prosecute or extradite best suited their objectives in particular circumstances. There was nothing meaningful the ILC could add to the Secretariat's Survey.

It may be recalled that the General Framework lists *the legal bases of the obligation to extradite or prosecute* as the *first* item on the list of questions/issues. Special Rapporteur Galicki's fourth report dealt at length with the issue of the duty to cooperate in the fight against impunity as a legal basis of the obligation to extradite or prosecute.[141] In support of his contention that such duty to cooperate was well established as a principle of international law, Galicki cited Article 1(3) of the UN Charter, the 1970 Declaration on Principles of International Law concerning Friendly Relations and Cooperation among States in accordance with the Charter of the United Nations,[142] the preamble to the 1998 Rome Statute of the ICC,

[137] Sep Op of Judge Yusuf in *Belgium v Senegal* §§19–22. Cf also Belgium's commentary submitted to the ILC in 2009, where Belgium identified two types of treaty: (1) treaties that contain an *aut dedere aut judicare* clause with the obligation to prosecute conditional on refusal of a request for extradition of the alleged perpetrator of an offence; and (2) treaties that contain a *judicare vel dedere* clause with the obligation on States to exercise universal jurisdiction over perpetrators of the offences under the treaties, without making this obligation conditional on refusal to honour a prior extradition request (Doc A/CN.4/612 §15, quoted by Special Rapporteur Galicki in his fourth report, §85 and n 56).

[138] Cf Mitchell, *Aut Dedere Aut Judicare*, 66.

[139] *per* ICJ President Tomka, Provisional summary of record of the 3148th meeting of the International Law Commission, Doc A/CN.4/SR.3148 (17 Aug 2012) 21. See also §3, Declaration of Judge Donoghue in *Belgium v Senegal*.

[140] See UN Doc A/CN.4/630 §3.

[141] UN Doc A/CN.4/648 §§26–40.

[142] UN Doc A/RES/25/2625 (24 Oct 1970).

Guideline XII of the Guidelines of the Committee of Ministers of the Council of Ministers of the Council of Europe on eradicating impunity for serious human rights violations dated 30 March 2011, and Belgium's comments submitted to the ILC in 2009, among others. He concluded that the duty to cooperate with either international tribunals or national courts in the fight against impunity might be realized in the best and most effective way by the application of the principle *aut dedere aut judicare*[143] and proceeded to propose Draft Article 2: Duty to cooperate,[144] accordingly. Reaction in the Sixth Committee to this Draft Article was mixed. While some delegations were in favour of the general thrust of reflecting this duty to cooperate, others would prefer to distinguish the duty in relation to States on the one hand, and vis-à-vis international tribunals on the other hand. Yet, some other delegations considered the Draft Article ambiguous, vague, or abstract. It was also observed that combating impunity was essentially a political goal, which could not crystallize into an explicit legal obligation.[145]

However, such duty to cooperate as a legal basis of the obligation to extradite or prosecute could find support from the reasoning of the ICJ in *Belgium v Senegal* where the ICJ found a common interest of the international community to put an end to impunity for perpetrators' crimes, such as torture, proscribed by *jus cogens*.[146] It could also be supported by the conclusion of a Trial Chamber of the ICTY in *Furundžija* that 'one of the consequences of the *jus cogens* character bestowed by the international community upon the prohibition of torture is that every State is entitled to investigate, prosecute and punish or extradite individuals accused of torture, who are present in a territory under its jurisdiction', independently of any treaty obligation.[147]

The *sixth* set of questions/issues in the General Framework related to *the implementation of the obligation to extradite or prosecute.* Answers to the questions directly involving extradition law in general would need to be found in the body of that law.

The respective roles of the judiciary and the executive differ from one legal system to another. Non-compliance with the obligation to extradite or prosecute by any State organ, be it the judiciary or the executive, entails State responsibility. However, as the ICJ has held in *Application of the Convention on the Prevention and Punishment*

[143] UN Doc A/CN.4/648 §39.

[144] Art 2 Duty to cooperate

1. In accordance with the present draft articles, States shall, as appropriate, cooperate among themselves, and with competent international court [*sic*] and tribunals, in the fight against impunity as it concerns crimes and offences of international concern.
2. For this purpose, the States will apply, wherever and whenever appropriate, and in accordance with these draft articles, the principle to extradite or prosecute (*aut dedere aut judicare*).

[145] Topical summary of the discussion held in the Sixth Committee of the General Assembly during its sixty-sixth session, prepared by the Secretariat (Doc A/CN.4/650) §46.

[146] *Belgium v Senegal* §§68–69, 99.

[147] *Prosecutor v Anto Furundžija* (Judgment) ICTY-95-17/1 (10 Dec 1998) §156. But it is argued by Mitchell (*Aut Dedere Aut Judicare*, 33) that 'this decision indicates only an entitlement to exercise universal jurisdiction over and take other measures against those who are alleged to have violated a *jus cogens* norm; it does not indicate that there is an obligation to do so.'

of the Crime of Genocide (Bosnia and Herzegovina v Serbia and Montenegro), the ICJ's established jurisprudence is that claims against a State involving charges of exceptional gravity must be proven by fully conclusive evidence, at a high level of certainty appropriate to the seriousness of the allegation.[148]

Despite the Working Group chairman's efforts just mentioned at length, discussions in the subsequent meetings of the Working Group in 2013 focused on the need for the Working Group to submit a report to show to the Sixth Committee that there had been *some* progress on this topic at the ILC. The elements to be included in the report would be a summary of the work done by the ILC, including core findings of the Secretariat's Survey going through the various treaty regimes, which was helpful in identifying the different models of *aut dedere aut judicare* and the differences even within models; and a synthesis and recollection of the reports of former Special Rapporteur Galicki. In addition, the report ought to discuss the ICJ's Judgment in *Belgium v Senegal* and questions arising therefrom, for example the meaning of submitting a matter to prosecution in a broad sense when there was an obligation of the kind found in the Torture Convention, as well as elements that could be included in a national statute for States attempting to adhere to an obligation of *aut dedere aut judicare* that it had under one or more treaty regime.

The Working Group agreed that the said report would not be the final report but should be a progress report. Some members added that States might be asked as to what aspects of the obligation to extradite or prosecute the ILC should focus on, such as the content of the obligation, including its enforcement provision. Regarding the focus of the obligation on crimes, some members opined that focusing on specific crimes—genocide, crimes against humanity, and war crimes other than grave breaches—would leave out a rather large portion of international law where this particular obligation operated. In other words, they considered the topic to be more about looking at *aut dedere aut judicare* in a more systematic fashion, and not about any specific crime.

The Working Group asked the chairman to draft an outline of the Working Group's report to the ILC's plenary, which he did on 3 June 2013, as follows.

1. **Introduction**:
    1.1 Crime and punishment as a general principle of law recognized by civilized nations
    1.2 The importance of the obligation to extradite or prosecute, particularly the role this obligation plays in the fight against impunity, recognized since the time of *Grotius*
    1.3 The 1996 Draft Code of Crimes against the Peace and Security of Mankind focused only on core crimes. Arguments have been made that the obligation to extradite or prosecute core crimes proscribed by *jus cogens* has become, or is becoming, a rule of customary international law. However, since the obligation to extradite or prosecute is a broad concept covering all crimes, and not just the aforesaid core crimes, the Commission has found it unnecessary to examine the question of customary international law in order to write this Report.

148 [2007] ICJ Rep 43, 129–30, citing *Corfu Channel (United Kingdom v Albania)* [1949] ICJ Rep 4, 17.

1.4 Use of the Latin terminology *aut dedere aut judicare*

2. **Summary of the Commission's prior work since 2006**
   2.1 Four reports and one working paper by the Special Rapporteur, four draft articles, and questions put to States
   2.2 The 2009 General Framework
   2.3 The Secretariat's Survey (2010)
   2.4 Work of the Working Group during the present quinquennium (7 Informal Working Papers and this Report)
3. **Core findings of the Secretariat's Survey**, going through the various treaty regimes, which are helpful in identifying the different models of *aut dedere aut judicare* and the differences even within models, including the typology of provisions in such treaties as well as the relationship between extradition and prosecution in the relevant clauses of the treaties. (These conclusions could be useful for States to understand the nature and meaning of the obligation, its temporal scope and its implementation under the different treaty regimes.)

   Important gaps to be closed in the existing conventional regime governing the obligation to extradite or prosecute: (i) the lack of international conventions with this obligation in relation to crimes against humanity, war crimes other than grave breaches, and war crimes in non-international conflict; and (ii) the very rudimentary regime under the Genocide Convention
4. **Implementation of the obligation to extradite or prosecute:**
   4.1 Meaning of the implementation of the obligation to extradite or prosecute, e.g. as explained by the ICJ in *Belgium v Senegal* re: the Convention against Torture, and, arguably, with respect to the other conventions following the 1970 Hague Convention formula
   4.2 National measures necessary to adhere to the obligation under international law (whether pursuant to a treaty or outside treaty): criminalization, establishment of jurisdiction (especially **universal jurisdiction**), obligation to investigate/primary inquiry, apprehension of the accused, and submission of the case to the prosecuting authorities (which may or may not result in the institution of proceedings) OR extradition, if an extradition request is made by another State with the necessary jurisdiction and capability to prosecute the accused
   4.3 The relationship between the obligation to extradite or prosecute and the surrender of the alleged offender to a competent international criminal tribunal (the 'third alternative'), especially how treaty provisions which only contain the obligation to extradite or prosecute, but not the obligation to surrender a person to such tribunal, may be interpreted
   4.4 Enforcement of obligation to prosecute when extradition is refused (or *vice versa*) and consequences of non-compliance
5. **Guidance as to the elements that could be included in a national statute** [The international law dimension explained in Part 4.2 will be considered from a domestic criminal law dimension in Part 5. The Report could state that national law and procedure on extradition and prosecution, respectively, continue to apply *mutatis mutandis* to the national implementation of the obligation to extradite or prosecute, except insofar as stipulated in this Report to the contrary.]
   5.1 Crimes to be covered by the obligation to extradite or prosecute (arising from treaty obligations or outside treaty): criminalization *plus* the minimum penalty requirement of at least one year of imprisonment
   5.2 Priority of the obligation to prosecute over the obligation to extradite, or *vice versa*

5.3 Content of the obligation to prosecute:
 5.3.1 definition of the obligation to prosecute; establishment of the necessary jurisdiction (including **universal jurisdiction**);
 5.3.2 steps to be taken in order for prosecution to be considered sufficient and question of timeliness;
 5.3.3 question of the power of free appreciation or discretion of the prosecuting authorities (*pouvoir discrétionnaire*) after carrying out a preliminary investigation; and
 5.3.4 whether the availability of evidence affect the operation of the obligation.
5.4 Content of the obligation to extradite:
 5.4.1 definition of the obligation to extradite (esp. vis-à-vis deportation, extraordinary rendition and other informal forms of dispatching the accused to another State);
 5.4.2 double criminality: conduct-based test is to be preferred to elements-of-crime test;
 5.4.3 timing to determine double criminality—usually at the time the conduct occurred, but preferably at the time of the extradition request;
 5.4.4 reciprocity or treaty arrangements if constitutionally required;
 5.4.5 multiple requests for extradition; and
 5.4.6 measures to be taken where there is no extradition granted because of a certain limitation under the domestic law of the requested State (e.g. political offence exception to extradition, 'human rights/humanitarian' exception, or some constitutional limitations such as non-extradition of nationals).
5.5 Conditions triggering the obligation to extradite or prosecute: mere presence of the alleged offender in the territory of the State?
5.6 Immunities of the accused; amnesty; the statute of limitations; *non bis in idem*; *nullum crimen sine lege* and *nulla poena sine lege*
5.7 Option to fulfil both elements of the obligation: prosecuting the accused and then extraditing the convicted person to another State for the purpose of enforcing the judgment
5.8 Respective roles of the judiciary and the executive

Epilogue [Questions to the Sixth Committee]:
- This Report is only a **progress report** to the Sixth Committee, ***unless*** the Sixth Committee finds that there is nothing more for the Commission to contribute on this topic.
- If the Sixth Committee wishes the Commission to continue to work on this topic, in which other areas not covered by the Report does the Sixth Committee wish the Commission to work on?

The Working Group met on 5 June 2013 to consider the above outline suggested by the chairman. The chairman explained that to a large extent he followed proposals and some elements that members had indicated ought to be included. The chairman also suggested that the Latin term *aut dedere aut judicare* be dropped, on the understanding that whether extradition or prosecution has priority over the other depends on the context.

In summarizing the Secretariat's Survey, the chairman suggested that the report go through the various treaty regimes helpful in identifying the various models of *aut dedere aut judicare* provisions, including the typology of the treaties. Here, it would be useful to indicate that there were some gaps that ought to be closed, especially the lack of international conventions for war crimes and crimes against humanity and the very rudimentary regime under the Genocide Convention.

The chairman was open to the possibility that some States had enacted legislation even without treaty obligations to extradite or prosecute.

He pointed out that in the law of most States there was a minimum penalty requirement of five years, but the minimum norm under extradition treaties was a one-year sentence of imprisonment, so the ILC should make it as broad as possible. Certain treaties like the Torture Convention gave priority to the obligation to prosecute. Steps to be taken for prosecution to be considered sufficient and the question of timeliness were covered by the ICJ Judgment in *Belgium v Senegal*. The question of the availability of evidence was also captured by the Judgment in *Belgium v Senegal*.

In the chairman's opinion, the definition of the obligation to extradite was different from deportation, extraordinary rendition, or other forms of sending the accused to another state. There had been some debate over whether a State had to adhere to the double criminality rule. Crimes against humanity were not criminalized as such under many statutes. However, in so far as a conduct amounting to a crime against humanity was criminalized in some way, for example as murder, the double criminality requirement should be deemed to have been fulfilled.

The chairman referred to a perceptible trend towards adopting the time of the extradition request rather than the act as the relevant time. This would be important if one looked at the *Pinochet* case in the UK House of Lords.[149] Only one or two charges survived from the original extradition request because much of the conduct was not criminalized under the law of England and Wales at the time of the conduct in question.

Where there were multiple requests for extradition, there ought to be a consideration of good faith. The chairman emphasized that if the requested State extradited the person to a requesting State that had no intention of prosecuting the person, a serious breach of international legal obligation by the requested State would ensue.

The General Framework listed many limitations, but the chairman only selected those he considered to be relevant. Under the heading immunity of the accused, the chairman suggested a brief mention that this issue was under consideration by the ILC. For amnesty, the ILC needed to consider possibilities where amnesties were not accepted. Since the post-WWII Nuremberg trials, through the ICC Statute and the Special Tribunal for Sierra Leone Statute, prosecution went ahead although some amnesty had been granted. There also ought not to be any statute of limitations for core crimes. He agreed with Special Rapporteur Galicki's idea of a State prosecuting the person and then extraditing him to another State to carry out the sentence.

On the introduction, some members of the Working Group were concerned with the expression 'as a general principle of law recognized by civilized nations'. This reminded them of Article 38 of the ICJ Statute, and there was much controversy as to the nature and content of these general principles. One member emphasized that 'crime and punishment' was a general principle of law, and, from that, the Working

[149] *R, ex parte Pinochet v Bartle and Commissioner of Police for the Metropolis* [1999] UKHL 17.

Group could extrapolate the obligation, recognized since the time of Grotius. Others did not consider 'crime and punishment' was a general principle of law at all. Besides, some concern was expressed that what the ILC purported to do here was to describe the obligation to extradite or prosecute more than the fact that 'crime and punishment' was or was not a general principle of law. For them, the focus of this *aut dedere aut judicare* project was ending impunity and with due respect to the rule of law, and this should be made clear.

A view was expressed that the ILC should continue exploring the customary international law basis of the obligation, and that it would be too much to say that the ILC found it unnecessary to continue to discuss this point. The chairman proposed that the introduction should take note of the argument that the obligation to extradite or prosecute in relation to core crimes had become a norm of customary international law; however, since the obligation was meant to cover all crimes and not just core crimes, the ILC considered it unnecessary to consider this question at this stage. The chairman thought this would disappoint numerous States in the Sixth Committee, particularly those hoping for a norm of customary international law binding on States that were recalcitrant or apathetic. However, some members of the Working Group suggested the Working Group abandon any attempt to decide whether or not there was a rule of customary international law on *aut dedere aut judicare*. In their view, members could not arrive at a unanimous opinion on this issue, and it would not help the further promotion of any such rule, which many people would like to see. Thus, it was more or less agreed in the Working Group that it was not necessary, at this time, to go into the question of the customary international law status of *aut dedere aut judicare*. According to certain members, to the extent the 1996 Draft Code had already provided the obligation or prosecute for core crimes, the ILC did not consider it necessary to further discuss this in accordance with core crimes, and discussing the customary nature was only useful if the ILC wanted to produce draft articles.

Sir Michael Wood, the member of the Working Group who had served as counsel for Belgium in *Belgium v Senegal*, clarified that the principles he had deduced from that Judgment which the chairman was using as part of the Report were simply an attempt to deduce from *Belgium v Senegal* the principles of implementation in relation to the Torture Convention. On the other hand, a view was expressed that a very comprehensive distillation of the main conclusions of the ICJ in *Belgium v Senegal* did have application in all circumstances where the Torture Convention was at issue, and perhaps broader ramifications, certainly for all provisions in the relevant treaties using the Hague formula, and probably beyond.

The Working Group proceeded to analyse the ICJ's reasoning in *Belgium v Senegal* which treats the obligation 'to submit the case to the competent authorities for the purpose of prosecution' under Article 7(1) of the Torture Convention as synonymous with the obligation to prosecute,[150] which is normally implemented *after* the State has performed its other obligations in the preceding Articles of the

[150] *Belgium v Senegal* §90.

Convention against Torture, including the criminalization of torture through appropriate legislation, the establishment of universal jurisdiction, and a preliminary inquiry.[151] These might all be the necessary preconditions for the good faith fulfilment of the obligation to prosecute. Indeed, the ICJ describes these obligations collectively as 'elements of a single conventional mechanism aimed at preventing suspects from escaping the consequences of their criminal responsibility, if proven'. The ICJ emphasizes that Article 7(1) requires the State concerned to submit the case to its competent authorities for the purpose of prosecution, irrespective of the existence of a prior request for the extradition of the offender. Extradition is thus an alternative, which, if requested, allows the requested State to relieve itself of its obligations to prosecute. The two options are not of equal weight. Prosecution has the status of an 'international obligation under the convention, the violation of which is a wrongful act engaging the responsibility of the State', whereas extradition is merely an option that the Convention offers the State.[152]

By using 'the obligation to prosecute' synonymously with the obligation to submit the case to competent authorities for the purpose of prosecution, the ICJ limits the scope of the obligation, at least where it is contained in provisions following the 1970 Hague Convention formula. The ICJ emphasizes that this obligation does not necessarily result in the institution of proceedings, as such a decision rests with the authorities, depending on the evidence before them and the criminal procedure of the custodial State. Recalling the history of the Convention, the ICJ considers that the obligation under the Hague Convention was 'formulated in such a way as to leave it to those authorities to decide whether or not to initiate proceedings, thus respecting the independence of State parties' judicial systems'.[153] This strikes a balance between the competing interests of State sovereignty and the fight against impunity. It should be considered whether the obligation to prosecute might have more substantive content in contexts other than treaties following the 1970 Hague Convention formulation. The ICJ also notes that both the 1970 Hague Convention and the Convention against Torture emphasize 'that the authorities shall take their decision in the same manner as in the case of any ordinary offence of a serious nature under the law of the state concerned'.[154]

Although the ICJ has found the prohibition of torture to have become part of customary international law and a peremptory norm (*jus cogens*), it rules the Torture Convention to be applicable only to acts after its entry into force of that Convention for the State concerned, since there is nothing in the Convention evincing an intention to the contrary.[155]

Finally, the ICJ considers Senegal's argument that it took the necessary measures to institute proceedings against Habré, and referred the matter to the African Union, but that it was restricted financially and by the authority of the judgment of the ECOWAS Court of Justice that compelled Senegal to amend its Penal Code to avoid violating the principle of non-retroactivity, as Habré's acts had not been criminalized in Senegal at the time of their commission. The ICJ rejected these arguments by

[151] ibid §91. [152] ibid §95. [153] ibid §90. [154] ibid. [155] ibid §100.

Senegal as being insufficient to justify Senegal's tardiness in implementing its obligation to prosecute under the Convention. The ICJ holds that it is implicit in the Convention that this obligation 'must be implemented within a reasonable time, in a manner compatible with the object and purpose of the Convention',[156]and proceedings under the obligation to prosecute must be undertaken without delay. This serves the dual aim of fulfilling the Convention's object and purpose and guaranteeing the suspect fair treatment at all stages of the proceedings. The ICJ's ruling that Senegal should have taken all measures to implement its obligation to prosecute as quickly as possible, and in particular once the first complaint had been filed against Habré, may be extrapolated to all other Conventions following the Hague formula.

Certain members of the Working Group doubted whether the guidance of elements that could be included in national law should be included in the report. Some States might give direct effect to the treaty provision on *aut dedere aut judicare*. Some States, such as the UK, had very detailed extradition laws. If the Working Group was to have this section, some of these elements were perhaps too detailed. Instead, a very general provision stipulating that States needed criminalization, extraterritorial jurisdiction, and perhaps an extradition provision would be sufficient. The draft by the chairman was a little too detailed in going into extradition law, in particular the roles of the executive and the judiciary which were matters that should be reserved for States to decide.

A view was expressed that the ILC should explain also that since the 1996 Draft Code, a number of elements had strengthened the obligation to extradite or prosecute, in particular the obligation to cooperate against international crimes. This was enshrined in the 2004 ICJ advisory opinion on *Legal Consequences of the Construction of a Wall in the Occupied Palestinian Territory*.[157]

According to certain members of the Working Group, once the ILC explained the general measures to be taken to implement the obligation to extradite or prosecute, a number of other points needed not be raised any longer. Besides, the ILC might not be in a position to propose a model draft law or guidelines for national statutes, because the provisions in national statutes were very diverse. For example, under the French Criminal Code, there was an extremely complicated provision on the obligation to extradite or prosecute, and it would be unimaginable for the ILC to propose general rules for French law that would apply to other States as well. Matters raised in relation to extradition law were extremely sensitive and complex and would in all likelihood require several years of work by the ILC.

With regard to possible exceptions to extradition, some members believed that these involved numerous far-reaching issues and extensive case law. A problem in relation to human rights and refugee law alone could occupy the ILC for a whole annual session. Yet some other members saw the value in retaining guidelines for national authorities regarding the implementation, or elements of, the obligation. However, it was doubted whether the ILC could accomplish this within the context

[156] ibid §114. [157] [2004] ICJ Rep 136.

of the 2013 report—there was a big difference between doing this as a model law when the ILC had a Special Rapporteur who had worked for several years on this topic, on the one hand, and including what could be a model law in the report submitted to the Sixth Committee, on the other hand. Other members considered it necessary for the ILC to provide guidelines to national authorities on making more effective use of the national legislation in order to implement the obligation *aut dedere aut judicare*, especially when bearing in mind the importance of judicial co-operation in suppressing crimes of international concern.

On amnesty or a statute of limitations, a view was stated that these were particularly sensitive areas in States in transition from a dictatorship to a democratic system of government and where amnesties were part of the transition. In fact, the law of such States included provisions that were incompatible with the concepts of international law regarding certain crimes.

Some concern was expressed regarding the word 'enforcement' of the obligation, because it implied making effective the obligation of prosecuting the person even when extradition was denied for a lawful reason. The word 'implementation' might be more correct.

The Working Group then proceeded to make drafting changes to the draft report by its chairman which, on 31 July 2013, was taken note of by the Plenary of the ILC.[158] That report (hereinafter 'the 2013 report of the Working Group') subsequently appears as Annex A to the Report of the ILC on the work of its sixty-fifth session.[159] The sixteen-page 2013 report of the Working Group will not be reproduced here as it is substantially the same as the Final Report of the ILC on this topic in 2014 and appears in the Appendix to this book. The Final Report merely adds answers to the questions raised in the Sixth Committee in relation to the 2013 report of the Working Group.

At a meeting of the Sixth Committee of the UN General Assembly on 4 November 2013, the Chairman of the International Law Commission introduced the 2013 report of the Working Group as follows:

The report of the Working Group is intended to summarize and highlight particular aspects of the work of the Commission on this topic.

The report conceptualizes the topic by placing it within the broader framework of the efforts to combat impunity, while respecting the rule of law. It also recalls the importance of the obligation in the work of the Commission, summarizes the work done thus far, and offers suggestions that might be useful for States parties to conventions containing the obligation.

The report addresses issues relevant to the topic against the background of the Secretariat Survey (2010) and the Judgment of 20 July 2012 of the International Court of Justice in *Questions relating to the Obligation to Prosecute or Extradite (Belgium v Senegal)*. In doing so, the Working Group did not consider it necessary to delve further into the question of customary international law.

[158] ILC, 'Report of the International Law Commission on the work of its 65th Session' (6 May–7 June and 8 July–9 Aug 2013) UN Doc A/68/10 §149.

[159] ibid Annex A.

The 2013 report of the Working Group was generally well received. According to several delegations, the report was a particularly valuable resource in relation to its examination and interpretation of the obligation encapsulated in multilateral conventions as well as the Judgment of the ICJ in *Belgium v Senegal* while also answering several questions which had been raised during the ILC's work on this topic. The delegation of Israel was the only one that queried whether any broad implications could be derived from the specific circumstances presented in that Judgment. The Czech delegation was the only one that contended that the report contained certain problematic conclusions, in particular, it was argued, the report did not adequately reflect the contrary position of States on the prohibition of the resort to expulsion in order to circumvent an extradition procedure under Draft Article 13 of the Draft Articles on Expulsion of Aliens adopted by the ILC at first reading in 2012.

The positions taken by States regarding the future of this topic can be summarized as follows.

Portugal, Italy, Australia, Chile, Romania, New Zealand, Mexico, and Thailand explicitly supported the ILC's continued deliberation on this topic, reiterating the practical importance and continued relevance of this topic in the fight against impunity. For its part, Portugal hoped to see the ILC providing some answers to the already existing questions raised during the ILC's work on this topic, including the new elements which the *Belgium v Senegal* case brought into the discussion that would help the ILC develop a set of harmonized rules. Italy considered the obligation to extradite or prosecute as a normative mechanism aimed at filling the lacunae that might allow those responsible for the most serious crimes to escape prosecution and punishment. Italy, thus, looked forward to further progress in the ILC's analysis of the issues involved. New Zealand thought there was merit in examining whether an obligation to extradite or prosecute existed under customary international law in relation to specific crimes and encouraged further work to be done on this topic including its relationship with universal jurisdiction. Chile and Mexico both agreed that the ILC should examine whether the obligation had become a rule of customary international law, although Mexico clarified that the examination of the elements of the *aut dedere aut judicare* principle did not necessarily depend on the conclusion as to the customary status of such principle—work should therefore continue in parallel on both fronts. Mexico also proposed that the ILC analyse the priority between the obligation to prosecute and the obligation to extradite; the scope of the obligation to prosecute; and the relationship with *erga omnes* or *jus cogens* obligations. Mexico further clarified that the analysis of the last-mentioned relationship was closely related to the 'obligation to prosecute or extradite' as it involved determining in respect of whom the obligation existed; who could eventually request extradition; and who had a legal interest in invoking the international responsibility of a State for being in breach of its 'obligation to prosecute or extradite'.

Romania, Chile, and Thailand requested the ILC to address the existing gaps in the conventional regime governing the obligation to extradite or prosecute in relation to crimes against humanity, war crimes, and genocide. Chile and Thailand suggested that the ILC develop a model set of provisions or formulae to close such gaps or improve the conventional regime in this regard. Thailand added that this undertaking would assist the joint initiative of Argentina, Belgium, Netherlands, and Slovenia for the adoption of a new international instrument on mutual legal assistance and extradition concerning the effective investigation and prosecution of perpetrators of all the major international crimes, including crimes against humanity. Details of the aforesaid joint initiative appear in Chapter 8.

Chile and Thailand also encouraged the Commission to explore the relationship between the obligation to extradite or prosecute and the third alternative of surrendering a suspect to a competent international criminal tribunal.

Another group of States, comprising France, Poland, Austria, South Africa, Malaysia, Belarus, and Cuba made suggestions on how the ILC should proceed, in a business-as-usual manner without mentioning the termination of this topic.

Like Chile and Thailand, France considered that the link between the obligation to extradite or prosecute and the mechanisms put in place by international jurisdictions deserved particular attention. Poland suggested shifting the focus of this topic towards areas that were still not covered by this obligation: for example, some of the crimes against humanity, war crimes other than grave breaches, and war crimes in non-international armed conflict. In Austria's opinion, although the scope of the obligation to extradite or prosecute and the method and form of its implementation under specific treaty provisions varied so considerably that it would be difficult to establish a common regime, it might be possible to identify some common features. Austria suggested that the 2009 General Framework could be of assistance to the Working Group chaired by the present author. According to South Africa, the future of this topic should be dependent on the approach that the ILC decided to take with regard to the proposed inclusion of the topic 'Crimes against humanity' in the ILC's agenda. South Africa would not be convinced about the 'efficiency' of continuing with the topic 'The obligation to extradite or prosecute (*aut dedere aut judicare*)' if the ILC decided to include in its current agenda the topic 'Crimes against humanity' whose primary 'hard obligation' would be an *aut dedere aut judicare* obligation for crimes against humanity. However, six days earlier, on 29 October 2013, South Africa had asked the ILC to reconsider whether the topic 'Crimes against humanity' was to be placed on the ILC's current programme of work, since there might be other ways to address the issue of improving cooperation between States in relation to serious crimes, bearing in mind also that there were ongoing initiatives in this regard, such as the joint initiative of Argentina, Belgium, Netherlands, and Slovenia. Malaysia considered it premature for the ILC to draft any article on *aut dedere aut judicare* in so far as the ILC had not yet determined whether or not the obligation to extradite or prosecute had become a rule of customary international law. Malaysia, therefore, suggested that the ILC undertake an in-depth study to ascertain the aforesaid status of such obligation before the ILC proceeded to embark on progressive development in this area of international criminal law. Belarus raised the issue of the final product of the ILC's work on this topic. In its view, the lack of the clear understanding on the expectation of the ILC and the Sixth Committee as to the final product hindered the real progress. Belarus suggested that the final product of this topic could be guiding principles and commentaries on the implementation of the obligation. Lastly, Cuba considered it essential to review the general principles governing extradition and the grounds for refusing extradition, taking into account Article 3 ('Mandatory grounds for refusal') of the UN Model Treaty on Extradition.[160] Additionally, Cuba deemed it appropriate, in the context of the ILC's work on this topic, to establish a general framework of extraditable offences, without prejudice to the sovereign right of each State to determine under its national laws those offences for which extradition would be granted.

Four other States simply presumed that the ILC would continue its work on the topic. They were Peru, Japan, Indonesia, and Israel. Peru opined that the inclusion of the topic 'Crimes against humanity' in the long-term programme of work of the ILC would also complement the Commission's work on *aut dedere aut judicare*. Indonesia welcomed the reconstitution of the Working Group to evaluate the progress of work on the topic and to explore possible future options to be taken by the ILC. While Japan considered the 2013 report of the Working Group a positive development, it emphasized that a concrete outcome had to be addressed in the next few sessions. Israel, for its part, believed that recent legal developments had proved that the obligation to extradite or prosecute was 'not merely a theoretical subject, but a practical legal tool requiring States to implement their treaty obligation to extradite or prosecute as part of the international fight against impunity'. It then made several comments on the substance of the 2013 report of the Working Group. However, the delegations of Hungary, USA, UK, and Republic of Korea suggested that the ILC could not make a greater contribution to this topic than it had done already, and that, therefore, the topic be terminated. While agreeing with the recommendation in the 2013 report of the Working Group that any efforts in this area should focus on specific 'gaps in the present conventional regime' rather than a broad-based approach, the US delegation thought that the report in and of itself allowed the ILC 'to bring to closure its work on this topic'. Similarly, the Czech Republic and Russia expressed their dissatisfaction with the 'lack of substantial progress' and would like to see the termination of this topic or doubted whether this topic should be continued.

Spain doubted the usefulness of this topic because the obligation to extradite or prosecute operated in very different ways in different conventional regimes, and there was 'not even a decision' as to whether such an obligation was part of customary international law or a general principle of law. Spain added that 'the difficult systematization of this obligation' made it seriously doubt the viability of the topic.

While making statements on the topic, Singapore and Iran did not clearly indicate their respective positions as to whether the ILC should continue with the topic. Singapore said it was not clear how the ILC intended to proceed, particularly in the light of suggestions made by some members of the ILC of the possibility of suspending or terminating this topic. Singapore concluded by saying that it would study closely the suggestions of the Working Group. This present author met with Djamshid Momtaz of Iran after his rather vague statement in the Sixth Committee. Momtaz explained that

160 UNGA Res 88 (1997).

he was Chairman of the ILC in 2005, when the topic was put on the current agenda and Galicki appointed Special Rapporteur. According to him, the ILC at that time intended to examine whether the obligation had a customary international legal basis or was solely treaty-based. However, he felt the ILC lost its way as its work on this topic proceeded. He therefore suggested that the ILC take stock of its work on the topic thus far and decide on the best course for the future, irrespective of whether or not the Sixth Committee would eventually refer the topic 'Scope and Application of the Principle of Universal Jurisdiction' to the ILC, since universal jurisdiction—being 'procedural in nature'—was substantially different from the obligation to extradite or prosecute.

The States that asserted unequivocally that the obligation was not one of customary international law but was treaty-based were the UK, USA, Austria, South Africa, Israel, Malaysia, Iran, and Cuba.[161]

The relationship between universal jurisdiction and this topic was mentioned by France, UK, South Africa, New Zealand, Malaysia, Belarus, Cuba, Israel, Thailand, and Iran. Five of them were in favour of the ILC taking up the issue of universal jurisdiction within the context of this topic, whereas the other five were opposed to such an endeavour.

For South Africa, an effective *aut dedere aut judicare* obligation had to involve universal jurisdiction in some form or another. In other words, this topic was to include, as a major element, universal jurisdiction or, at the very least, aspects of universal jurisdiction. Belarus considered it meaningful for the ILC to conduct a research on the obligation to extradite or prosecute and the specific aspects of the concept of universal jurisdiction with a view to identifying customary international law. New Zealand and Thailand both encouraged the ILC to study the relationship between the obligation to extradite or prosecute and universal jurisdiction. According to Cuba, the Working Group should evaluate whether it was appropriate to specify the crimes to which the obligation to extradite or prosecute and universal jurisdiction would be applied, bearing in mind that abuse of the principle of universal jurisdiction had negative effects on State sovereignty.

On the other hand, France, UK, Malaysia, Israel, and Iran contended that either the topic should be analysed separately from universal jurisdiction or the ILC should avoid examining universal jurisdiction altogether.[162]

On 16 December 2013, the UN General Assembly adopted without a vote Resolution 68/112 entitled 'Report of the International Law Commission on the work of its sixty-third and sixty-fifth sessions', operative paragraph 7 of which '*Invites* the International Law Commission to continue to give priority to the topics "Immunity of State officials from foreign criminal jurisdiction" and "The obligation to extradite or prosecute (*aut dedere aut judicare*)" '.[163]

[161] At the Sixth Committee debate on this topic in 2012, Austria, Israel, UK, and USA had stated this same position.

[162] At the Sixth Committee debate on the topic 'The obligation to extradite or prosecute (*aut dedere aut judicare*)' in 2012, France, India, Iran, Israel, Russia, and Slovenia had taken this same position.

[163] UNGA Res 112 (2013), UN Doc A/RES/68/112. This operative paragraph is identical to operative paragraph 8 of UN General Assembly Resolution 67/92 entitled 'Report of the International Law Commission on the work of its sixty-third and sixty fourth sessions', UNGA Res 92 (2012).

The drafting history of this operative paragraph 7 is quite interesting. During the informal consultation on the draft resolution on this agenda item held on 5 November 2013,[164] the UK delegation proposed that the reference to the topic 'The obligation to extradite or prosecute (*aut dedere aut judicare*)' in the draft operative paragraph which subsequently became operative paragraph 7 of Resolution 68/112 be 'replaced with the topic by Sir Michael Wood on identification of customary international law' because her delegation was in favour of the ILC terminating the former topic. Another proposal was made by the Russian delegation, also suggesting the deletion of the reference to the former topic from the draft operative paragraph but without suggesting that it be replaced with another topic. However, the delegations of Portugal, Thailand, Iran, Venezuela, and Argentina, all of whom preferred to keep the topic 'The obligation to extradite or prosecute (*aut dedere aut judicare*)' as one of the ILC's two priority topics, opposed both proposals. On 15 November 2013, the Sixth Committee adopted the draft resolution without a vote, with the aforesaid draft operative paragraph remaining unchanged.[165]

The chairman of the Working Group, in the first informal working paper of 2014, proposed possible options for the ILC in relation to this topic, in the light of the debate at the Sixth Committee in October and November 2013, starting from the most modest option and moving to more ambitious ones.

The most modest option would be the final report of the Working Group, to be adopted by the ILC, addressing the remaining issues raised in the Sixth Committee in 2013; namely, the customary international law status of the obligation to extradite or prosecute, gaps in the existing conventional regime, universal jurisdiction, the third alternative, and other ancillary issues. It should also endorse the 2013 report of the Working Group, subject to any reservations by ILC members who disagreed with particular points in that report.

The second option was in relation to customary international law.

In 2013, the chairman of the Working Group had submitted an informal working paper analysing at length the customary international law status of the obligation to extradite or prosecute. The final report to be adopted by the ILC by the end of the 2014 session could list the national legislation dealing with the obligation to extradite or prosecute, judgments of national courts faced with the question, claims regarding the obligation to extradite or prosecute before foreign courts, pertinent statements made by States, and relevant resolutions of international organizations. The final report might conclude that only a relatively few States (ie twenty-nine States) had responded to the questions posed by the ILC in relation to this topic;[166]

[164] UN Doc A/C.6/68/L.24. This present author was a passive observer at the informal consultation.

[165] Report of the Sixth Committee to the UN General Assembly on the Report of the International Law Commission on the work of its sixty-third and sixty-fifth sessions, UN Doc A/68/464 (19 Nov 2013) §10. This draft resolution appears as draft resolution II attached to UN Doc A/68/464.

[166] No State has replied to the request by the ILC in 2011 for comments on the following: 'Are there, in the legislation of States or in the case law of domestic tribunals, certain crimes or categories of crimes in respect of which the obligation to extradite or prosecute has been implemented? If so, has a court or tribunal ever relied, in this respect, on customary international law?' (UN Doc A/66/10 §§45 and 46). The summary of the comments made by States in the Sixth Committee in 2011 in response to the

the information available to the ILC, including that from various sources in the public domain, was not sufficient for the ILC to determine definitively whether or not the obligation to extradite or prosecute had become a rule of customary international law or is acquiring such status. Therefore, a further study was needed. In this regard, the Nordic countries had stated that there were reasons to conclude that the obligation to extradite or prosecute was acquiring a customary status with regard to core crimes such as genocide, crimes against humanity, war crimes, torture, and acts of terrorism.[167] Outside the Nordic region, Belgium had postulated that there was a universal obligation of customary nature to suppress crimes of international humanitarian law. However, in Belgium's view, for serious offences other than crimes of international humanitarian law, there was only the obligation under treaties either to extradite or prosecute.[168]

In comparison, the Netherlands and Sri Lanka did not confine the customary international legal status of the obligation to extradite or prosecute to core crimes only. The former takes the position that 'the duty to extradite or prosecute [was] known to result from treaty law *or customary international law*, and that point need[ed] not [to] be reiterated'.[169] In a similar vein, Sri Lanka stated that extensive State practice in acceding to treaties containing the obligation to extradite or prosecute would point to the existence of a customary international law status of such obligation.[170]

However, other States had not stated unequivocally, either in their respective written responses to the ILC's request for comments/information or in the Sixth Committee, that the obligation to extradite or prosecute was one of customary international law or was acquiring such status. On the contrary, some of them had posited

last-mentioned request for comments reads thus: 'Commenting on State practice, some delegations observed that their domestic legislation, as well as bilateral extradition and multilateral treaties, contained provisions concerning the obligation to extradite or prosecute. In some instances, the legislation on extradition was residual in nature, applying in the absence of treaty relations with a State seeking extradition. Moreover, the legislation in question, as well as bilateral extradition treaties, did not specify any core crimes nor any particular category of crimes concerning which extradition would apply. Other delegations observed that although their domestic law did not explicitly refer to *aut dedere aut judicare* there were relevant provisions in that regard with respect to specific crimes. Indeed, the principle *aut dedere aut judicare* was applied regularly and consistently, both in domestic implementing legislation giving effect to relevant conventions and in related case law. Some delegations also noted that none of their national courts had relied on customary international law to implement the obligation to extradite or prosecute' (Doc A/CN.4/650 (20 Jan 2012) §45).

167 UN Doc A/C.6/62/SR.22 §33. At the Sixth Committee debate on this topic four years later in 2011, the delegation of Norway speaking on behalf of the Nordic countries stated that 'there was probably a basis in customary international law for an obligation to extradite or prosecute, but a more thorough analysis of specific crimes and identification of the core crimes that gave rise to the obligation was needed' (UN Doc A/C.6/66/SR. 26 §11).

168 UN Doc A/CN.4/612 §34. Belgium cited in support of this position the 1996 Draft Code of Crimes against the Peace and Security of Mankind, various UN General Assembly resolutions on the suppression of war crimes and crimes against humanity, positions frequently taken by the UN General Assembly and the UN Security Council on the need to combat impunity, and the fourth through sixth preambular paragraphs of the 1998 Rome Statute of the International Criminal Court (ibid §§32–33).

169 Statement by the Netherlands in the Sixth Committee (UN Doc A/C.6/66/SR.28 §60), emphasis added.

170 UN Doc A/C.6/66/SR.27 §27 (*per* Mr Hakeem, Minister of Justice of Sri Lanka).

unequivocally that this obligation was solely treaty-based. It could be argued that these last-mentioned States were 'persistent objectors'[171] and were, thus, not bound by any emerging customary international legal obligation to extradite or prosecute.

The chairman reminded the Working Group of the need to close existing gaps in treaties regarding the obligation to extradite or prosecute. He also brought to the attention of the Working Group a study by Chatham House, according to which the ILC's future work on the topic should concentrate on drafting a treaty containing the obligation to extradite or prosecute in respect of core international crimes as well as emulate the extradite-or-prosecute mechanism developed in the Hague formula and incorporated in the 1984 UN Convention against Torture and, most recently, in the 2006 International Convention for the Protection of All Persons from Enforced Disappearance.[172]

Instead of drafting a set of model provisions to close the gaps in the existing conventional regime regarding the obligation to extradite or prosecute, it should be recalled that Article 9 of the 1996 Draft Code already stipulates an obligation to extradite or prosecute for, *inter alia*, genocide, crimes against humanity, and war crimes. Nonetheless, as the 2013 report of the Working Group had pointed out, while there were various formulae in the different conventions containing this obligation and States might choose which formula would be most appropriate in a particular circumstance, the Hague formula served as a model for most of the contemporary conventions with this obligation. The Hague formula, as incorporated in the Convention against Torture, would be recommended for States undertaking to close the gaps in the existing conventional regime. The ICJ Judgment in *Belgium v Senegal*, as analysed in the 2013 report of the Working Group, would be helpful in construing the Hague formula to be adopted.

A model extradite-or-prosecute provision based on the Hague formula as adjusted in the light of Article 9 of the 1996 Draft Code, might read:

> Without prejudice to the jurisdiction of an international criminal court or any other court with competent jurisdiction, the State Party in the territory of which an individual alleged to have committed a crime set out in article … [genocide], … [crimes against humanity], or … [war crimes] is found shall, if it does not extradite him, be obliged, without exception whatsoever and whether or not the offence was committed in its territory, to submit the case to its competent authorities for the purpose of prosecution.

Alternatively, a variation of such a model might follow Article 11(1) of the 2006 International Convention for the Protection of All Persons from Enforced Disappearance,[173] which stipulates:

> The State party in the territory under whose jurisdiction a person alleged to have committed [an act of genocide/a crime against humanity/a war crime] is found shall, if it does not

[171] *Asylum case (Colombia v Peru)* [1950] ICJ Rep 266, 277–78; *Fisheries case (United Kingdom v Norway)* [1951] ICJ Rep 116, 131.

[172] Miša Zgonec-Rožej and Joanne Foakes, 'International Criminals: Extradite or Prosecute?', Chatham House Briefing Paper, Doc. IL BP 2013/01, July 2013.

[173] 2716 UNTS 3.

extradite that person or surrender him or her to another State in accordance with its international obligations or surrender him or her to a competent international criminal tribunal or any other competent court whose jurisdiction it has recognized, submit the case to its competent authorities for the purpose of prosecution.

With respect to the issue of universal jurisdiction, the chairman mentioned the joint proposal submitted by the Czech Republic, Guatemala, Liechtenstein, and Switzerland to the Sixth Committee's Working Group on the Scope and Application of the Principle of Universal Jurisdiction in 2013 for the ILC to undertake a study of certain aspects of universal jurisdiction that could assist the Sixth Committee's Working Group. Several delegations had been supportive of or open to that proposal, with some highlighting that the ILC's study should complement, not supersede, the role of the Sixth Committee. Some delegations had found it premature at the current stage of the discussions. Other delegations had stressed that discussion of the item should remain within the Sixth Committee exclusively for the time being.[174]

[174] UN Doc A/C.6/68/SR.23 §104.
The joint proposal by the Czech Republic, Guatemala, Liechtenstein, and Switzerland reads:

> *OP2bis Expresses* its willingness to consider, at its sixty-ninth session, the possibility of inviting the International Law Commission to undertake a legal study on the reliance of national courts on the principle of universal jurisdiction in criminal proceedings, and to inform the General Assembly about its findings by the end of its current quinquennium [2012–2016].

The joint proposal was introduced orally by Switzerland as follows:

> Firstly, this would be a limited mandate of the ILC. The idea is not to task the ILC to source out the entire agenda item that we are discussing in the Sixth Committee and this WG, the scope and application of the principle of universal jurisdiction. Rather, the ILC would be invited to write a study on the reliance of national courts on the principle of universal jurisdiction. The ILC could thus analyse the instances in which universal jurisdiction has been used in practice. How often did this happen so far? Under what circumstances? In which set of conditions? Did the practice of national courts evolve over time? What legal difficulties arose in the context of relying on universal jurisdiction? The ILC has done such analytical studies before. Famously, in 2006 it produced a widely recognized report on fragmentation of international law, which could serve as a model.
>
> Secondly, such a study of the ILC would be deeply relevant for our work. It would allow us to examine the application of the principle of universal jurisdiction, and by extension whether the principle has been relied on in a non-judicious manner, on a fair and objective basis. We all recognize the concern of delegations that believe the principle of universal jurisdiction has been relied upon in a non-judicious or abusive manner. An analytical study would help us in our discussion.
>
> Thirdly, the mandate of the ILC would be time-bound. It would not be a never-ending one. The Sixth Committee would remain in charge. Of course this could be discussed, but in our thinking, we would kindly ask the ILC to complete the study within the current quinquennium, that is, until 2016. That is in three years.
>
> Fourthly, the proposal to task the ILC with the writing of a study would be without prejudice to the separate question how the Sixth Committee paces its consideration of the principle of universal jurisdiction. It would be up to all of us to discuss whether it would be best to await the results of the ILC or whether we wished to continue deliberating the topic on an annual basis, as we have done so far.
>
> Mr. Chair, in a nutshell, I believe our proposal would be limited, relevant, time-bound and complementary. It seeks to be a constructive contribution to the work of the Sixth Committee.

The chairman of the ILC Working Group reminded its members that the topic 'Extraterritorial Jurisdiction', an initiative of the Secretariat of the ILC, had been put on the ILC's long-term programme of work since 2006.[175] That topic also covered the 'universality principle' and the proposed outline on an instrument on extraterritorial jurisdiction[176] included limitations on the extraterritorial assertion of jurisdiction[177] and dispute resolution. Therefore, the ILC might proceed to analyse universal jurisdiction within the context of the obligation to extradite or prosecute, taking into consideration also the proposed outline for the topic 'Extraterritorial Jurisdiction'. Above all, when the 12th Session of the Assembly of States Parties to the Rome Statute of the ICC discussed an item entitled 'Special Segment as requested by the African Union: "Indictment of sitting Heads of State and Government and its consequences on peace and reconciliation" ', it was 'generally highlighted' that thanks to the principle of complementarity under the Rome Statute, '[a]ccountability should be first and foremost pursued at the national level.'[178] Implementation of the obligation to extradite and prosecute, including through universal jurisdiction, would apparently fulfil this objective.

In the light of the foregoing, the chairman of the ILC Working Group suggested that the final report of the ILC might propound the following conclusions regarding universal jurisdiction in the context of the obligation to extradite or prosecute. First, while the obligation to extradite or prosecute was distinct from universal jurisdiction, the latter was a crucial component for prosecuting alleged perpetrators of crimes of international concern, particularly when the alleged perpetrator was not prosecuted in the territory where the crime had been committed. Secondly, when a State Party to an international instrument sought to extradite or prosecute a national of another State Party pursuant to that instrument by means of an exercise of universal jurisdiction, any dispute between the two States Parties concerning such exercise shall be settled as provided in that instrument itself. Thirdly, should a State seek to exercise universal jurisdiction outside a treaty binding on the States concerned, these States shall settle their dispute in accordance with Chapter VI (Pacific Settlements of Disputes) of the UN Charter.[179]

[175] ILC, 'Report of... its 58th Session' Doc A/61/10 Annex E.

[176] This comprises (1) a general duty to cooperate, (2) a duty to give notice, (3) a duty to review extraterritorial measures, (4) a general right to countermeasures, and (5) a dispute resolution mechanism.

[177] These limitations encompass (1) sovereignty, territorial integrity, and non-intervention, and (2) comity (ie the presumption against extraterritoriality, foreign State compulsion doctrine, and principle of reasonableness).

[178] Closing remarks of the President of the Assembly of States Parties to the Rome Statute of the ICC, 13th Mtg of the Assembly, 28 Nov 2013, 'Official Records of the Assembly of States Parties to the Rome Statute of the International Criminal Court', 12th session, The Hague, 20–28 Nov 2013 (ICC-ASP/12/20), vol I Annex IX 84.

[179] The principles of good faith and abuse of rights seem quite relevant to disputes over an exercise of universal jurisdiction. For some useful articles on these principles, see Anthony D'Amato, 'Good Faith' in Rudolf Berhardt (ed), *Encyclopedia of Public International Law*, vol 1 (North Holland 1992) 599–601; Michael Byers, 'Abuse of Rights: An Old Principle, A New Age' [2002] 47 McGill LJ 389; Alexander Kiss, 'Abuse of Rights' in *Max Planck Encyclopedia of Public International Law* (Dec 2006); and Steven Reinhold, 'Good Faith in International Law' (2013) 2 UCL Journal of Law & Jurisprudence 40.

With respect to the third alternative, the chairman referred to the positions expressed in the Sixth Committee in 2013. Chile, France, and Thailand suggested that the ILC analyse the relationship or link between the obligation to extradite or prosecute and the mechanisms put in place by international jurisdictions/competent international criminal tribunals. However, Canada and the United Kingdom were opposed to this. Canada considered surrender to an international criminal tribunal to be substantially different from an act of extradition, the latter involving bilateral State-to-State action.[180] For the UK, 'there [were] specific rules expressly covering transfers to an international criminal tribunal'.[181]

During the visit by the President of the ICJ to the Sixth Committee on 1 November 2013, this present author asked the ICJ President why the ICJ in *Belgium v Senegal* did not answer the question as to whether Senegal had an obligation to extradite Habré to Belgium if Senegal did not prosecute him. The ICJ President replied that a more careful reading of the Judgment would provide the answer to that question. In his opinion, while some scholars might prefer something more, the parties to the case were satisfied with the Judgment and had been following up on it. Paul Rietjens, Director-General of Legal Affairs of the Ministry of Foreign Affairs of Belgium and Belgium's Agent in *Belgium v Senegal*, who was also at the meeting, added that Belgium had always aimed at having Senegal extradite Habré to Belgium if Senegal did not prosecute him. However, he was pleased with Senegal's taking immediate steps to implement the Judgment with Belgium's assistance, thereby turning what had been a dispute before the ICJ into international cooperation between the Parties.

On 22 August 2012, just over a month after the ICJ Judgment in *Belgium v Senegal*, Senegal and the African Union signed an agreement to set up 'Extraordinary African Chambers' within the Senegalese court system to try Habré. On 19 December 2012, the Senegalese National Assembly passed the Extraordinary Chambers Statute setting up the Extraordinary African Chambers composed of the trial chamber and the appeals chamber to try 'the persons most responsible for international crimes committed in Chad between 7 June 1982 and 1 December 1990'. Each Chamber is composed of two Senegalese judges and one non-Senegalese judge who presides over the proceedings. On 8 February 2013, the Chambers officially opened pre-trial investigations.

This kind of 'internationalization' within a national court system was not unique—it followed the example of the Extraordinary Chambers in the Courts of Cambodia set up to try Khmer Rouge leaders. The establishment of the Extraordinary African Chambers by the agreement between Senegal and the African Union together with the participation of national and foreign judges in these Chambers made such arrangements similar to those concerning the Special Court for Sierra Leone, set up by an agreement between the UN and the Government of Sierra Leone, and the Special Tribunal for Lebanon, set up by the agreement between the UN and the Government

[180] UN Doc A/CN.4/612 §35.
[181] Statement of the UK delegation in the Sixth Committee on 4 Nov 2013.

of Lebanon to try those found responsible for the terrorist crime which killed the former Lebanese Prime Minister Rafiq Hariri and others.

Surrendering Habré to the Extraordinary African Chambers could be considered a 'third alternative' to the two alternatives of, first, Senegal extraditing Habré to Belgium or to any other requesting State entitled to seek his extradition from Senegal; and, second, Senegal submitting the case of Habré to competent Senegalese authorities for the purpose of his prosecution within Senegal's own national judicial system. The Extraordinary African Chambers could be categorized as a competent international criminal court whose jurisdiction Senegal had recognized. However, if the Chambers were not to be considered as an international criminal court, they could still be recognized as 'any other competent court whose jurisdiction Senegal has recognized'.

Therefore, the chairman of the Working Group proposed that the ILC include the third alternative for the implementation of the obligation to extradite or prosecute following the aforesaid example of the prosecution of Habré.[182]

With regard to other matters, Mexico had suggested that the ILC analyse, *inter alia*, (1) the priority between the obligation to extradite or prosecute; and (2) the scope of the obligation to prosecute. For Cuba, the ILC should establish 'a general framework of extraditable offences'. Belarus was even more specific, stating that the final product of this topic could be formulated as commentaries and guiding principles on the implementation of the obligation. All these positions could be considered together.

The chairman suggested that the ILC reply to these questions as follows. The 2013 report of the Working Group summarized the typology of provisions in multilateral instruments containing the obligation to extradite or prosecute as elucidated in the Secretariat's Survey, and the implementation of such obligation under the Torture Convention as construed by the ICJ in *Belgium v Senegal*. Although answers to the questions raised by Mexico could be found in the Secretariat's Survey and the relevant part of the 2013 report, the final report of the Commission could streamline such answers, which would form part of the general framework mentioned by Cuba and the guiding principles, alluded to by Belarus, on the implementation of the obligation to extradite or prosecute.

The ILC Working Group chairman recommended that since scope of the obligation to prosecute had already been elaborated in the 2013 report of the Working Group, it needed not be repeated in the final report of the ILC on this topic.

Mexico also raised the issue of 'the legal interest and the impact with regard to international responsibility of the *aut dedere aut judicare* principle when this involved *erga omnes* obligations or *jus cogens* norms, such as the prohibition of torture'. In

[182] The said conclusions would also be supported by eg Council of Europe, *Extradition, European Standards: Explanatory notes on the Council of Europe convention and protocol and minimum standards protecting persons subject to transnational criminal proceedings* (Council of Europe 2006), where it is stated: 'In the era of international criminal tribunals, the principle [of *aut dedere aut judicare*] may be interpreted *lato sensu* to include the duty of the state to transfer the person to the jurisdiction of an international organ, such as the International Criminal Court' (ibid 119, footnote omitted).

Mexico's opinion, such analysis was closely related to the 'obligation to prosecute or extradite' because it entailed determining: (1) in respect of whom the obligation existed; (2) who could eventually request extradition; and (3) who had a legal interest in invoking the international responsibility of a State for being in breach of its 'obligation to prosecute or extradite'.

The ILC Working Group chairman explained that obligations *erga omnes* designated the scope of application of the relevant law and the procedural consequences following from it. They were owed to the international community as a whole and all States had a legal interest or a general right of standing (*locus standi*) in their compliance and were, thus, entitled to invoke State responsibility in case of breach of such obligations irrespective of their particular interest in the matter. It had now become accepted that all *jus cogens* norms constitute *erga omnes* obligations; however, not all of the latter constituted the former.[183] For *erga omnes* obligations to be *jus cogens*, or 'peremptory norms', such obligations must have attained the status of non-derogable rules of international 'public policy' which rendered void other non-peremptory rules coming into conflict with them.[184]

The choice of terminology 'prosecute or extradite' employed by Mexico seemed to reveal that what Mexico had in mind was the scenario in *Belgium v Senegal*, where the ICJ interpreted the object and purpose of the Convention against Torture as giving rise to 'obligations *erga omnes partes*', or 'collective interests' of the treaty parties,[185] with each State Party having a 'common interest' in compliance with such obligations and, consequently, each State Party was entitled to make a claim concerning the cessation of an alleged breach by another State Party.[186] In dispositive paragraph 6 of the Judgment, the ICJ unanimously found that Senegal 'must, without further delay, submit the case of Hissène Habré to its competent authorities for the purpose of prosecution, if it does not extradite him'.[187] The ICJ saw no need to decide whether Belgium also had a special interest, as an injured State, with respect to Senegal's compliance with the relevant provisions of the Convention against Torture in Habré's case.[188] This fact, when read in conjunction with dispositive paragraph 6 of the Judgment, led to different interpretations among Members of the ICJ in that case.

[183] Koskenniemi 'Fragmentation of International Law', UN Doc A/CN.4/L 682 §§380–409.

[184] Michael Byers, 'Conceptualising the Relationship between *Jus Cogens* and *Erga Omnes* Rules' (1997) 66 Nordic JIL 211; and cf Christian J Tams, *Enforcing Obligations* Erga Omnes *in International Law* (CUP 2010) 138–56.

[185] This terminology is alluded to in Koskenniemi, 'Fragmentation of International Law', UN Doc A/CN.4/L 682 §§390, 393, referring to Art 48(1)(a) of the ILC's Draft Articles on State Responsibility (UN Doc A/56/10, 56): '1. Any State other than the injured State is entitled to invoke the responsibility of another ... if: (a) The obligation breached is owed to a group of States including that State, and is established for the protection of a collective interest of the group; ...'

[186] *Belgium v Senegal* §§67–70. See also Judge Cançado Trindade (Sep Op §§104–8), and Judge Donoghue (Declaration §§9–17). *Contra*: Dissenting Opinion of Judge Xue, §§2–23, and Dissenting Opinion of Judge ad hoc Sur, §§13, 19–20. Cf also the criticisms by Judge Skotnikov (Sep Op §§9–22).

[187] *Belgium v Senegal* §122(6). Cf also §58 of Judge ad hoc Sur's Dissenting Opinion.

[188] *Belgium v Senegal* §70.

For Judge Owada and Judge ad hoc Sur it meant Belgium was not in a legal position to claim Mr Habré's extradition to Belgium from Senegal.[189] In Judge Donoghue's opinion, the Court did not come to any conclusions regarding Belgium's extradition requests.[190] Likewise, Judge Skotnikov considered the issue of the validity of Belgium's request for Habré's extradition unsolved.[191] Judge Yusuf opined that Senegal was not under an obligation to extradite Habré to Belgium unless Senegal decided to do so simply because it wanted to relieve itself of the obligation to submit his case for prosecution by its own authorities and on its own territory.[192] Finally, Judge Xue stressed that Senegal was to decide on Belgium's extradition request as soon as possible so as to, as Senegal had declared, submit Habré's case to the competent authorities for prosecution.[193] Judge Xue added that if the African Union decided to set up a special tribunal to try Habré, Senegal's surrender of Habré to such a tribunal would not be a breach of Senegal's obligation under Article 7(1) of the Convention against Torture, 'because such a tribunal is created precisely to fulfil the object and purpose of the Convention; neither the terms of the Convention nor the State practice in this regard prohibits such an option'.[194]

Interestingly, an academic analysis of the Judgment concluded that the ICJ did not order Senegal to extradite Habré to Belgium because the Convention against Torture did not stipulate that any State Party thereto was automatically entitled to seek extradition of an alleged perpetrator of torture from another State Party that refused to prosecute such person.[195]

The issue raised by Mexico, therefore, deserved an answer. It comprised what Portugal described as the new elements that the *Belgium v Senegal* case brought into the discussion on the topic.

The chairman of the Working Group submitted that the ILC give the following answers to the questions raised by Mexico.

First, as pronounced by the ICJ in *Belgium v Senegal*, the obligation to punish a violation of *jus cogens* norms, such as the prohibition of torture, was owed by every State Party to a convention proscribing such violation to all the other States Parties to that convention.

Secondly, as a logical consequence of the first answer, all those other States Parties had a legal interest in invoking the international responsibility of a State Party for being in breach of its obligation to extradite or prosecute.

Thirdly, a State which could eventually request extradition would have to be a State Party to the relevant convention containing the obligation to extradite or prosecute,

[189] Declaration of Judge Owada, §§21–23, and Dissenting Opinion of Judge ad hoc Sur, §§45–46, 59–60.

[190] Declaration of Judge Donoghue, §5.

[191] Sep Op of Judge Skotnikov, §8. However, he concluded that the ICJ's ruling had settled the dispute between the Parties as to how the execution of an obligation arising from the Convention against Torture was to be understood (ibid §23). *Contra:* Judge ad hoc Sur disagreed that the Court had actually settled the dispute between the Parties (Dissenting Opinion of Judge ad hoc Sur, §§1–4, 13, 25).

[192] Sep Op of Judge Yusuf, §24.

[193] Dissenting Opinion of Judge Xue, §48.

[194] ibid §42.

[195] André Nollkaemper, 'Wither *Aut Dedere?* The Obligation to Extradite or Prosecute after the ICJ's Judgment in Belgium v Senegal', Amsterdam Law School Legal Studies Research Paper No 2013-47, 18.

provided that the requesting State had jurisdiction as well as was willing and able to prosecute the alleged offender. This third answer was not expressly given by the ICJ in *Belgium v Senegal* but was implicit in the Separate Opinion of Judge Skotnikov in that case. According to the learned Judge, by ruling that Belgium was entitled to invoke Senegal's responsibility without necessarily having a special interest in Senegal's compliance with the Convention against Torture, the Court was able to avoid dealing at the merits stage with two difficult questions. The first one related to whether Belgium had established its jurisdiction in respect of Habré in accordance with Article 5(1) of the Convention, despite the fact that none of the alleged victims was of Belgian nationality at the time of the alleged offences. The second question concerned the fact that, subsequent to its request for Habré's extradition, Belgium repealed a part of its legislation that had permitted it to exercise universal jurisdiction.[196] Of course, the chairman of the Working Group further submitted, in exercising its jurisdiction to prosecute a violator of a *jus cogens* norm, the prosecuting State would have to respect applicable international human rights of the accused.[197]

The chairman also suggested the option of appointing a new Special Rapporteur to finalize the ILC's work on this topic. Several States that still preferred the ILC to continue with this topic did not accept that the 2013 report of the Working Group had brought closure to the topic. A final report by the ILC as envisaged in the first option would necessarily be relatively concise and the Sixth Committee would not have before it a public record of more transparent and thorough exchanges of views in the ILC as would be the case if a Special Rapporteur were to be entrusted with the topic. As a solution, the ILC might appoint a new Special Rapporteur to present his or her report addressing the outstanding issues for consideration by the ILC during the second part of the session in 2014. The contents of the report of the new Special Rapporteur would be the same as those of the final report of the ILC as proposed in the first option. However, the report of the new Special Rapporteur would analyse the customary international law status of the obligation to extradite or prosecute in more detail. ILC Members would comment on the report by the new Special Rapporteur and the ILC's annual report would reflect the positions taken by the members. The Sixth Committee would reflect on these reports in October/November 2014. The ILC would adopt the final report, after taking into account the debate in the Sixth Committee, and conclude its work on the topic in 2015.

The chairman also alluded to the fact that the General Framework continued to be mentioned[198] as a possible roadmap for the ILC to pursue. However, ILC members

[196] Sep Op of Judge Skotnikov, §§3–4. See also Nollkaemper, 'Wither *Aut Dedere*?' 19.

[197] See eg Council of Europe, *Extradition, European Standards* ch 4, 'Material human rights guarantees as limitations to extradition'; Danai Azaria, *Code of Minimum Standards of Protection to Individuals Involved in Transnational Proceedings*, Report to the Committee of Experts on Transnational Criminal Justice, European Committee on Crime Problems, Council of Europe [PC-TJ/Docs 2005/PC-TJ (2005) 07 E Azaria], Strasbourg, 16 Sept 2005.

[198] At the Sixth Committee debate in 2012, Austria, the Netherlands, and Vietnam considered the 2009 General Framework a valuable supplement to the work of the Commission. In the Netherlands' opinion, the work of the Commission should eventually result in presenting draft articles based on that General Framework. At the Sixth Committee debate in 2013, Austria reiterated the usefulness of the 2009 General Framework to the work of the present Working Group.

would have to ask whether after the exhaustive deliberations in this Working Group in 2012–14 there were any elements or aspects in the General Framework that still deserved to be analysed by the ILC in the context of the topic.

The ones that probably still deserved to be so analysed by the ILC were, first of all, '(a) The legal bases of the obligation to extradite or prosecute' under sub-heading '(v)—Whether regional principles relating to the obligation to extradite or prosecute may be identified'. In the chairman's opinion, if 'regional principles' meant 'regional customary international law', then it could be confidently stated that at least among the Nordic countries the obligation to extradite or prosecute was acquiring a customary status with regard to core crimes such as genocide, crimes against humanity, war crimes, torture, and acts of terrorism. Beyond the context of regional custom, certain regional principles might exist, for example, the principle of prosecution of nationals in lieu of extradition followed by the fifteen Central and South American States abiding by Article 345 of the Bustamante Code of International Private Law, adopted at the Sixth International Conference of American States in Havana in 1928,[199] and Argentina.[200] The same regional principle was also enshrined in Article 6 of the 1957 European Convention on Extradition binding on the forty-seven European Member States of the Council of Europe. Other principles—such as non-extradition of a person to the requesting State where the person might face a death penalty, extradition on the basis of reciprocity, and so forth—applied to the law or practice governing extradition in general, and were not specifically related to the application of the obligation to extradite or prosecute.

With regard to '(b) The material scope of the obligation to extradite or prosecute', especially '(i) Whether the recognition of an offence as an international crime is a sufficient basis for the existence of an obligation to extradite or prosecute under customary international law'; and '(iii) Whether and to what extent the obligation also exists in relation to crimes under domestic laws?', the chairman thought that the answers had already been discussed in the Working Group in 2012 and 2013. Likewise, there seemed to be nothing that the ILC could add in relation to '(c) The content of the obligation to extradite or prosecute'.

The chairman then called attention to paragraph (d) (iii), (iv), and (vi) of the General Framework on the 'relationship between the obligation to extradite or prosecute and other principles', namely *nullum crimen sine lege* and *nulla poena sine lege; non bis in idem* (double jeopardy); the situations of conflicting principles (eg non-extradition of nationals *versus* no indictment in national law; obstacles to prosecute *versus* risks for the accused to be tortured or lack of due process in the State to which extradition is envisaged); and constitutional limitations. He also alluded to '(e) Conditions for the triggering of the obligation to extradite or prosecute',

199 OAS, Law & Treaty Ser No 34. It provides that States Parties to the Code are not obliged to extradite their nationals, but the nation that does not extradite one of its nationals is obliged to prosecute that national. The fifteen States Parties to the Code are Bolivia, Brazil, Chile, Costa Rica, Cuba, Dominican Republic, Ecuador, El Salvador, Guatemala, Haiti, Honduras, Nicaragua, Panama, Peru, and Venezuela.

200 UN Doc A/CN.4/579/Add 2 §§11–12. This is despite the fact that Argentina is not party to the Bustamante Code.

sub-paragraph '(v) Standard of proof (to what extent must the request for extradition be substantiated)', and '(vi) Existence of circumstances that might exclude the operation of the obligation (e.g. political offences or political nature of a request for extradition; emergency situations; immunities)'. He also took note of '(f) The implementation of the obligation to extradite or prosecute', sub-paragraph '(i) Respective roles of the judiciary and the executive'; '(ii) How to reconcile the obligation to extradite or prosecute with the discretion of the prosecuting authorities'; '(iii) Whether the availability of evidence affects the operation of the obligation'; '(iv) How to deal with multiple requests for extradition'; '(v) Guarantees in case of extradition'; '(vi) Whether the alleged offender should be kept in custody awaiting a decision on his or her extradition or prosecution; or possibilities of other restrictions to freedom?'; and '(viii) Control of the implementation of the obligation'. In his view, elements (d), (e), and (f) of the General Framework would neatly cover those suggested by the delegation of Cuba in the Sixth Committee. Part 4 (Implementation of the obligation to extradite or prosecute) of the 2013 report of the Working Group had already covered part of these elements.

The chairman of the Working Group pointed out that, according to the Secretariat's Survey, multilateral conventions on extradition usually stipulated the conditions applicable to the extradition process, including possible grounds of refusal. Nearly all the conventions with the obligation to extradite or prosecute specified that extradition was subject to the conditions provided by the law of the requested State. This implied that the requested State had the right to refuse extradition on the basis of the provisions of its domestic legislation. Such grounds of refusal might be connected to the offence (eg the statute of limitations had expired, the double criminality or the rule of specialty was not satisfied, the requirement of *nullum crimen sine lege* and *nulla poena sine lege* or *non bis in idem* was not met, or the crime was subject to the death penalty in the requesting State) or not so connected (eg the individual was granted political asylum or there exist humanitarian reasons to deny extradition).[201]

The Secretariat's Survey also explained that the degree of specificity of the rules concerning the conditions applicable to extradition varied depending on several factors. The inclusion of more detailed provisions had sometimes taken into account the specific concerns expressed during the course of negotiations (eg non-extradition of nationals, application or non-application of the political exception or fiscal exception clauses), the particular nature of the offence (for instance, the risk of refusal of extradition based on the political character of the offence appears to be more acute with respect to certain crimes) and a certain evolution in the drafting of the relevant provisions to take into account problems that might have been overlooked in the past (eg the possible triviality of the request for extradition or the protection of the rights of the alleged offender) or to take into account new developments or a changed environment.[202]

What the ILC might usefully assert in this matter, submitted the chairman of the Working Group, was that whatever the conditions under domestic law or a treaty

[201] Secretariat's Survey §139. [202] ibid §142.

pertaining to extradition, they had to be applied in good faith, without shielding an alleged offender from prosecution in or extradition to an appropriate criminal jurisdiction. Besides, in the case of crimes proscribed by *jus cogens* the object and purpose of the relevant domestic law and/or applicable treaty had to ensure that there be no impunity for perpetrators of such crimes. Hence, these crimes could never be considered political offences that constitute an exception to extradition.[203]

Even more ambitiously, the chairman of the Working Group suggested that the ILC might go beyond what was suggested in the General Framework and embark upon a *full-scale* (yet manageable) *progressive development of international law.* The ILC might, as suggested by Australia, draw upon elements in existing treaties containing the obligation to extradite or prosecute, to be supplemented by such changes as the ILC considers desirable.[204] Should the ILC wish to undertake this task, it might find it useful to proceed by updating the 1996 Draft Code in the light of developments since 1996, while also taking into consideration the General Framework. An outline of such undertaking, probably leading to a set of conclusions plus commentaries, might read thus:

(1) General introduction: to enhance international cooperation in the fight against impunity for serious crimes of international concern and close the existing gaps in the conventional regime
(2) Material scope (*ratione materiae*) of the obligation = all core crimes + X*

[*The core crimes would comprise war crimes beyond grave breaches, war crimes in internal armed conflicts, all crimes against humanity, and genocide. X would be piracy, acts of terrorism (which are not necessarily acts of 'international' terrorism already covered by the sectoral conventions on terrorism), aggression in the light of the 2010 Kampala Amendment to the ICC Statute, and other crimes that may become ones of serious concern to the international community in the future.]

(3) Criminalization plus establishment of jurisdiction, including universal jurisdiction
(4) A model clause of the obligation to extradite or prosecute
(5) International cooperation**

[203] A good example to be emulated would be Art 1 of the Additional Protocol, 15 Oct 1975, to the 1957 European Convention on Extradition (ETS 86), which reads:

> For the application of Article 3 [on political offences] of the Convention, political offences shall not be considered to include the following:
> a. the crimes against humanity specified in the Convention on the Prevention and Punishment of the Crime of Genocide adopted on 9 December 1948 by the General Assembly of the United Nations;
> b. the violations specified in Article 50 of the 1949 Geneva Convention for the Amelioration of the Condition of the Wounded and Sick in Armed Forces in the Field, Article 51 of the 1949 Geneva Convention for the Amelioration of the Condition of Wounded, Sick and Shipwrecked members of Armed Forces at Sea, Article 130 of the 1949 Geneva Convention relative to the Treatment of Prisoners of War and Article 147 of the 1949 Geneva Convention relative to the Protection of Civilian Persons in Time of War;
> c. any comparable violations of the laws of war having effect at the time when this Protocol enters into force and of customs of war existing at that time, which are not already provided for in the above-mentioned provisions of the Geneva Conventions' (*Council of Europe Treaty Series No 086).*

[204] UNGA Doc A/C.6/66/SR.28 (2 Dec 2011) §2.

[**The Commission could draw upon inspirational statements, such as that of operative paragraph 1 of UN General Assembly Resolution 3074 of 1973 on Principles of International Cooperation in the Detection, Arrest, Extradition and Punishment of Persons Guilty of War Crimes and Crimes against Humanity, that:

'[w]ar crimes and crimes against humanity, wherever they are committed, shall be subject to investigation and the persons against whom there is evidence that they have committed such crimes shall be subject to tracing, arrest, trial, and, if found guilty, to punishment.'

The duty to cooperate in the fight against impunity as a legal basis of the obligation to extradite or prosecute could also find support from the reasoning of the International Court of Justice in *Belgium v Senegal* where the Court found a common interest of the international community to put an end to impunity for perpetrators' crimes proscribed by *jus cogens* such as torture.[205] It could also be supported by the conclusion of a Trial Chamber of the International Criminal Tribunal for the former Yugoslavia (ICTY) in *Furundžija* that 'one of the consequences of the *jus cogens* character bestowed by the international community upon the prohibition of torture is that every State is entitled to investigate, prosecute and punish or extradite individuals accused of torture, who are present in a territory under its jurisdiction', independently of any treaty obligation.][206]

(6) Substantive rules of the obligation to extradite or prosecute—as elaborated in the 2013 report of the Working Group and in the relevant parts of this Informal Working Paper
(7) Procedural rules of the obligation to extradite or prosecute[207]
(8) Conclusions.

In the chairman's opinion, if the ILC decided to embark on the options elaborated above, a Special Rapporteur would have to be appointed and the topic would have to be concluded by the end of 2016. The chairman pointed out that the present topic had been included on the ILC's current programme of work since 2005, and it was the lack of substantive progress during the years 2005–12 that caused frustration and, consequently, some doubts about its feasibility. If the ILC were to finalize this topic in 2016, the time spent on this (ie 2005–16) would be a little longer than the one spent on some other topics (that had witnessed more consistent substantive progress), such as 'Expulsion of aliens' (2004–14). It would, however, be much shorter than that of the topic 'State responsibility', which spanned 45 years, from the appointment of the first Special Rapporteur (Francisco V García Amador) in 1956

[205] *Belgium v Senegal* §§68–69, 99.

[206] *Prosecutor v Anto Furundžija* (Judgment) ICTY-95-17/1.

[207] The ILC could embark on elaboration of secondary rules, but not all the collateral rules. As Special Rapporteur Galicki wrote in his second report:

> Some Members [of the Commission] cautioned against considering the technical aspects of extradition law. What was specific to the topic and the precise meaning of the Latin maxim *aut dedere aut judicare* was that, failing an extradition, an obligation to prosecute arose. The focus, therefore, should be on the conditions for triggering the obligation to prosecute. The view was expressed that the Commission should not deal with all the collateral rules on the subject, which were linked to it but not necessarily part of it. It was also proposed that the focus should be limited to the elaboration of secondary rules. (UN Doc A/CN.4/585 §15)

Cf also ibid §47, where Galicki also acknowledged that 'the application of some limitations traditionally imposed on extradition' might raise problems or even make it impossible to implement the '*dedere*' part of the obligation *aut dedere aut judicare*.

to the finalization of that topic in 2001, with James Crawford as the fifth, and last, Special Rapporteur.

V. The ILC's Final Report of 2014

The Working Group met on 6 May 2014 to consider the chairman's various suggestions elaborated above. Some members were adamant that it would not be necessary to appoint the Special Rapporteur at this stage, and that nothing useful could be added to the 2013 report of the Working Group. It was also suggested that dealing with the customary international law status of the obligation would entail the risk of moving backward from 1996 Draft Code which already contained an article on this obligation 'in customary international law'. Any gaps would have to be dealt with under the ILC's topic 'Crimes against humanity'. This view would prefer the issue of universal jurisdiction be considered by the ILC as another topic independently from the topic of the obligation to extradite or prosecute. Another member was of the opinion that universal jurisdiction was a question of whether international law permitted a State, if it wished, to exercise jurisdiction in a certain situation; it was not an obligation. A view was also expressed that the third alternative was a very complex matter, requiring a number of years to consider (eg to what extent extradition treaties were applicable when there was a referral to the ICC; what the treaty instrument at issue was; and what would happen when there was an extradition request parallel to a transfer). A view was stated that codification of regional principles regarding the obligation was not the ILC's task, and the ILC could not take the place of the parties to the treaties or the implementing bodies of the treaties. Several members deplored that the Sixth Committee had generally not been specific regarding what the ILC should do apart from expressing their appreciation of the 2013 report of the Working Group. In sum, those members supporting these arguments would simply have the 2013 Report updated and the topic terminated.

Members coming from States that could not extradite without treaty reiterated their position that it would be very difficult to identify an existing norm of customary international law on the obligation to extradite or prosecute. In their opinion, many States did not have national statutes that would allow them to fulfil that obligation, and the ones that did have such statutes typically allowed, but did not require, the prosecutor to act. In addition, many States did not extradite if they perceived in a requesting State problems relating to a fair trial or other aspects of the proceedings. The ICJ in *Belgium v Senegal* obviously was not squarely addressing customary international law. There were some views by ICJ judges in that case that one could read into them certain conclusions, but the ILC would need to be very cautious in construing the respective opinions of these judges. By pointing to the divide in the ICJ, it implied uncertainty about the customary status of the obligation to extradite or prosecute and this might not be desirable. Therefore, if the ICJ did not wish to make statements that could frustrate the development of customary international law, then the ILC ought not to make a statement that might make it more difficult for the law to evolve. The ILC could simply refer to the 1996 Draft Code and States would understand what the ILC meant. It would be very bad for the ILC to conclude that there was no customary international law, as that would stop it from developing, so the ILC should not take up a definitive position on this point. It was suggested that the ILC could simply point out that the ICJ opined that it did not need to give an opinion on this point, but that the ILC had already recommended a formulation in Article 9 of the 1996 Draft Code.

Some members of the Working Group reiterated that the ILC's discussion on the obligation to extradite or prosecute was quite circular and it was impossible to move forward with new angles. According to them, this present author (as chairman of the Working Group) was the driving force of this topic; otherwise, it would have been dropped in 2012. However, if the ILC were to continue with the topic, it would not necessarily be a success, and if the ILC were to drop it, it would not necessarily be a failure but simply a recognition of the fact that the ILC had arrived at the conclusion that, after analysing the different aspects of the topic, there was little more that the ILC could add.

Regarding the relationship with *erga omnes* and *jus cogens* norms, some members considered it a question of interpretation of conventional norms. It was pointed out that while all obligations established by *jus cogens* norms also had the character of *erga omnes* obligations, the reverse was not necessarily true, as *erga omnes* obligations (eg some obligations relating to the global commons) might not be established by peremptory norms of general international law.[208] In *Belgium v Senegal*, this issue was treated as it was in the context of multilateral conventions. The ICJ was saying: because both the parties to that dispute were parties to the Torture Convention they did have a common interest to ensure that acts of torture be prevented and if they occurred, the authors would not enjoy impunity. The ICJ did not touch upon *jus cogens* as such. All these treaties, even if not related to *jus cogens* norms, could create an *erga omnes* situation. In other words, in a treaty regime there was an *erga omnes* element to that, which was not tied to whether the underlying offence was a *jus cogens* offence or not.

Instead of a model clause, it was recommended that the ILC refer first to the 1996 Draft Code and posit that since then there had been subsequent developments to be taken into account (eg in the case of enforced disappearance), there existed a new formula comprising necessary elements that should be emulated. The ILC might add to this formula a linkage with the transfer of offenders to international criminal tribunals.

The Working Group found no need to answer the following questions posed in the General Framework: the legal basis of the obligation, including the issue of customary international law from regional perspectives; the scope of the obligation; and the relation between the obligation and other principles, mainly about extradition

[208] Cf Koskenniemi, 'Fragmentation of International Law', UN Doc A/CN.4/L 682 §38, citing as two examples of the obligations relating to the global commons; namely, Art 1 of the Treaty on Principles Governing the Activities of States in the Exploration and Use of Outer Space, including the Moon and Other Celestial Bodies (610 UNTS 205), and Art 136 of the 1982 UN Convention on the Law of the Sea.

law (although the chairman was asked to write briefly in the final report that this belonged to constitutional law and domestic law of the States concerned).

The Working Group approved the Final Report, as appears in the Appendix to this book, which is a slightly revised version of the 2013 report of the Working Group, merely adding answers to the questions raised in the Sixth Committee in relation to the 2013 report of the Working Group. The Final Report was subsequently endorsed by the Plenary of the ILC as the Final Report of the ILC on this topic.

The reaction in the Sixth Committee to the Final Report was as follows.

Delegations welcomed the adoption by the ILC of its Final Report on this topic, emphasizing further that the obligation to extradite or prosecute constituted a key tool in the fight against impunity. The fact that observations made by States during the previous debates in the Sixth Committee had been taken into account in the preparation of the Final Report was particularly welcomed.

Several delegations observed that the Final Report, together with the Secretariat's Survey, constituted useful and practical guidance for States in implementing the obligation. The Final Report was seen as an appropriate conclusion of the work on this topic. Some delegations, nevertheless, regretted that the work had not yielded more detailed results on the fulfilment or application of the obligation to extradite or prosecute. In that regard, it was suggested that the ILC consider preparing recommendations concerning its implementation. However, doubts concerning the topic and the issues that needed to be considered in relation to it were also reiterated; it was noted that enormous uncertainties remained with regard to key aspects of the matter.

Several delegations reiterated their view that the said obligation only resulted from specific treaty provisions, and not from customary international law. Noting also that the obligation varied considerably in its formulation, content, and scope in the conventional framework, they observed that it would be futile to attempt to harmonize these diverse treaty arrangements. Taking into account the different types of treaty provisions containing the obligation, it was pointed out that when drafting treaties, States were well placed to decide which formula of the obligation best suited their objective in a particular circumstance. However, the view was also expressed that the obligation might find its basis in customary international law if that was the source for the crimes in question.

It was noted that the ILC's work had elucidated two important considerations concerning the application of the obligation to extradite or prosecute; namely, the gap between the existence of the obligation and its implementation and the need to ensure its wider application. In that connection, the ILC's attempt to identify lacunae in the present conventional regime on the obligation with respect of crimes of international concern was welcomed by several delegations. The ILC was encouraged to consider a broader application of the obligation while considering related topics, in particular 'Crimes against humanity'. The view was also expressed that the obligation must be applied in accordance with the principles of the UN Charter, as well as considered in the light not only of State practice but of the relationship between international law and domestic law. It was also stressed that the existence of international criminal tribunals needed to be taken into account when considering the obligation to extradite or prosecute.

References were also made to the analysis in the Final Report of the ICJ Judgment in *Belgium v Senegal*, which helped to elucidate the topic further. However, some delegations doubted that any far-reaching conclusions could be drawn from the findings in that Judgment.

Concerning the question of the relationship of the obligation to extradite or prosecute with other principles, some delegations reiterated their view that the obligation and the principle of universal jurisdiction were distinct concepts. However, it was also pointed out that any meaningful consideration of the topic would have to be centred on the principle of universal jurisdiction.[209]

The UN General Assembly adopted its resolution on the report of the ILC for the year 2014, operative paragraph 3 of which: '*Takes note* of the final report on the topic "The obligation to extradite or prosecute (*aut dedere aut judicare*)" contained in paragraph 65 of the report of the International Law Commission, and encourages its widest possible dissemination'.[210] In conclusion, the termination of the ILC's work on this topic largely resulted from the circumstances prevailing at that time. The topic was considered appropriate for the ILC's work in 2005. However, there was no substantive progress during 2006–11. In addition, the ILC usually cannot take up more than eight to ten topics at the same time. In 2012 and 2013, the ILC was hard pressed to accommodate several new topics in its active agenda, including 'Formation and evidence of customary international law' (which was included in the active agenda on 2012 and the title of which has subsequently been changed to 'Identification of customary international law'), and 'Crimes against humanity' (which was included in the active agenda by the end of the ILC's annual session in 2014). A few members even suggested that the ILC combine the topic 'Obligation to extradite or prosecute (*aut dedere aut judicare*)' with that of 'Crimes against humanity', with the appointment of two 'Joint', or 'Co-', Special Rapporteurs. Besides, some members suggested to the chairman of the Working Group that the ILC might consider postponing consideration of the former topic to a subsequent date. Yet some other members who considered that there was sufficient evidence for the obligation to be a rule of customary international law, or at least an emerging one, deplored the ILC's 'premature' conclusion of this topic.

The ILC's Final Report of 2014, as appears in the Appendix of this book, has left unanswered several significant substantive questions on the obligation to extradite or prosecute. It is, nonetheless, a good starting point for in-depth analysis of important issues pertaining to the obligation to extradite or prosecute which are not already covered in the Final Report.

[209] ILC, 'Report of the International Law Commission on the work of its 66th Session': Topical summary of the discussion held in the Sixth Committee of the General Assembly during its 69th session, prepared by the Secretariat (UN Doc A/CN.4/678 (21 Jan 2015)) §§102–07.

[210] UNGA Res 118 (2014).

PART II

SUBSTANTIVE LAW

3

Customary International Law Analysis

I. Theory Behind and the Key Characteristics of 'Core Crimes', as Opposed to 'Non-Core Crimes', and the Importance of Their Prosecution

As pointed out in Chapter 2, several members of the International Law Commission's Working Group on the Obligation to Extradite or Prosecute (*aut dedere aut judicare*) recommended the ILC to focus on core crimes under international law, such as genocide, war crimes, and crimes against humanity, in analysing whether the obligation was of a customary international law nature. Special Rapporteur Galicki himself proposed Draft Article 4 on the basis that the commission of crimes in violation of *jus cogens* norms would entail the obligation to extradite or prosecute under customary international law.

Galicki could have found support for this position from the writing in 1996 by Bassiouni positing:

> International crimes that rise to the level of *jus cogens* constitute *obligatio erga omnes* which are inderogable. Legal obligations which arise from the higher status of such crimes include the duty to prosecute or extradite, the non-applicability of statutes of limitations for such crimes, the non-applicability of any immunities up to and including Heads of State, the non-applicability of the defense of 'obedience to superior orders' (save as mitigation of sentence), the universal application of these obligations whether in time of peace or war, their non-derogation under 'states of emergency', and universal jurisdiction over perpetrators of such crimes.[1]

In Bassiouni's view, according to the legal literature, *jus cogens* crimes comprised aggression, genocide, crimes against humanity, war crimes, piracy, slavery and slave-related practices, and torture. The legal basis in support of this conclusion consisted of: (1) international pronouncements, or *opinio juris*, reflecting the recognition that these crimes were deemed part of general customary law; (2) the language in preambles or other provisions of treaties applicable to these crimes that indicated these crimes' higher status in international law; (3) the large number of States that had ratified treaties related to these crimes; and (4) the ad hoc international

[1] M Cherif Bassiouni, 'International Crimes: *Jus Cogens* and *Obligatio Erga Omnes*' (1996) 59 L & Contemp Prob 63.

investigations and prosecutions of perpetrators of these crimes.[2] He conceded, however, that the then existing State practices were few and far between and were insufficient to establish a solid legal basis to argue that the obligations deriving from *jus cogens* crimes were actually carried out as established by law, or at least as perceived in the writings of progressive jurists. In other words, it was yet uncertain in international customary law as substantiated by State practice whether the inclusion of a crime in the category of *jus cogens* created legal rights or non-derogable duties *erga omnes*, including the duty to prosecute or extradite, as suggested in the legal literature.[3]

There are two crucial questions in this regard. First, what are the 'core crimes' proscribed by *jus cogens*? Second, does the proscription by *jus cogens* in and of itself give rise to the obligation to extradite or prosecute perpetrators of the crimes so proscribed?

In attempting to answer the first question, the 1996 Draft Code of Crimes against the Peace and Security of Mankind could be relevant. At its first reading in 1991, the list of crimes covered by the Draft Code comprised twelve crimes: aggression; threat of aggression; intervention; colonial domination and other forms of alien domination; genocide; apartheid; systematic or mass violations of human rights; exceptionally serious war crimes; recruitment, financing, and training of mercenaries; international terrorism; illicit traffic in narcotic drugs; and wilful and severe damage to the environment.[4] In 1995 and 1996, the ILC reduced the number of crimes in the final Draft Code to four: aggression, genocide, war crimes, and crimes against humanity. A fifth, crimes against United Nations personnel, was added at the last moment on the basis of its magnitude, the seriousness of the problem of attacks on such personnel, and 'its centrality to the maintenance of international peace and security'.[5]

The ILC had originally intended, in 1983, to include those crimes that it deemed 'the most serious international offences [. . .] determined by reference to a general criterion and also to the relevant conventions and declarations pertaining to the subject', thereby excluding the less grave ones.[6] However, by 1996, instead of the seriousness of the criminal conduct or of its effects, the ILC had opted for tradition and the Nuremberg legacy as the criteria of the definition of the crimes. The primary reason for this appears to have been the unfavourable comments by twenty-four States to the list of twelve crimes proposed in 1991.[7] The ILC was faced with the possibility that while the extended list of crimes proposed in 1991 was consistent with the requirement of 'most grave international crimes', it would not be accepted by the Sixth Committee and, as such, the Draft Code would be a mere academic exercise. As noted by one ILC member: 'Excessive zeal could only lead to yet another draft being consigned to the archives in New York.'[8] Thus,

[2] ibid 68. [3] ibid 74. [4] (1991) ii YBILC (Part Two) 95–97.
[5] Doc ILC (XLVIII)/CRD.2 of 3 June 1996, 3 (conclusion).
[6] (1983) ii YBILC (Part Two) §§46–48 and 69(a).
[7] UN Doc A/CN.4/448 (1 Mar 1993) and Add 1.
[8] *per* Christian Tomuschat at 2380th Meeting (UN Doc A/CN.4/SR.2380, 6).

in his thirteenth report submitted in 1995, the Draft Code's Special Rapporteur Doudou Thiam reduced the list of crimes to six: aggression; crimes against humanity; war crimes; genocide; international terrorism; and illicit traffic in narcotic drugs.[9] By 1996, this had been further reduced to exclude international terrorism and illicit traffic in narcotic drugs. The provisional summary records of the 2379th Meeting to the 2386th Meeting of the ILC in 1995 indicate that the reduction was received favourably by a majority of the ILC members but there was also a strong dissenting minority.[10]

Also in 1996, Bassiouni contended that 'the establishment of a permanent international criminal court having inherent jurisdiction over these [core] crimes would be a convincing argument for the proposition that crimes such as genocide, crimes against humanity, and war crimes are part of *jus cogens* and that obligations *erga omnes* to prosecute or extradite flow from them'.[11]

It is now established that the terminology 'core crimes' in international criminal law usually refers to the crimes of genocide, war crimes, crimes against humanity, and aggression.[12] It derives from the post-Second World War history and the legacy of the Nuremberg and Tokyo Military Tribunals.[13] As stipulated in the 1998 Rome Statute of the International Criminal Court,[14] the crimes just mentioned constitute 'the most serious crimes of concern to the international community as a whole'.[15] This concept of 'core crimes' was a focal point of discussion during the establishment of the International Criminal Court and drafting of the ICC Statute.[16] Although it is still debatable whether the list of core crimes should be expanded,[17] the concept of core crimes is firmly entrenched in legal parlance. It identifies those crimes that are universally condemned as unacceptable by the international community in contrast with other categories of crimes such as transnational crimes or other treaty-based

[9] Thirteenth report by Special Rapporteur Thiam, UN Doc A/CN.4/466 (24 Mar 1995) §3.

[10] Martin C Ortega, 'The ILC Adopts the Draft Code of Crimes against the Peace and Security of Mankind' (1997) 1 Max Planck Yearbook of UN Law 283, 298.

[11] Bassiouni, 'International Crimes', 73–74.

[12] Matthew Peter, 'The Proposed International Criminal Court: A Commentary on the Legal and Political Debates regarding Jurisdiction that Threaten the Establishment of an Effective Court' (1997) 24 Syracuse JIL & Commerce 177, 188; Douglas Guilfoyle, *International Criminal Law* (OUP 2016) chs 7–11.

[13] Bruce Broomhall, 'Towards the Development of an Effective System of Universal Jurisdiction for Crimes Under International Law' (2001) 35 New England L Rev 399, at 399; Steven R Ratner, Jason S Abrams, and James L Bischoff, *Accountability for Human Rights Atrocities in International Law: Beyond the Nuremberg Legacy* (3rd edn, OUP 2009) 14.

[14] 2187 UNTS 90.

[15] Rome Statute, 4th preambular paragraph and Art 5.

[16] See, generally, Benjamin Ferencz, 'International Criminal Courts: The Legacy of Nuremberg' (1998) 10 Pace Int'l L Rev 203; Jelena Pejic, 'Establishing an International Criminal Court: Major Unresolved Issues in the Draft Statute', A Position Paper of the Lawyers Committee for Human Rights (revised and updated May 1998), <http://www.iccnow.org/documents/LCHRUnresolvedIssues.pdf>, accessed 13 November 2017.

[17] See eg Astrid Reisinger Coracini, '"Amended Most Serious Crimes": A New Category of Core Crimes within the Jurisdiction but out of the Reach of the International Criminal Court?' (2008) 21 Leiden JIL 699; UN Press Release, *Terrorism Should be 'Core Crime' of Proposed International Court—India Tells Preparatory Committee*, 27 Mar 1996 (<http://www.un.org/News/Press/docs/1996/19960327.l2766.html>, accessed 13 November 2017).

crimes.[18] Beyond the ICC's regime, it has been contended that States have, in recent years, asserted universal jurisdiction, even in the absence of treaty obligations, to punish perpetrators of genocide, war crimes, crimes against humanity, and torture which they consider to be 'core crimes' or 'international crimes' proscribed by *jus cogens*.[19]

In 2017 the ILC's Drafting Committee on the topic 'Immunities of State officials from foreign criminal jurisdiction' provisionally adopted Draft Article 7 listing 'crimes under international law in respect of which immunity *ratione materiae* shall not apply'; namely, crime of genocide, crimes against humanity, war crimes, crime of apartheid, torture, and enforced disappearance, adding also that these crimes are to be understood according to their definition in the treaties enumerated in the annex to the Draft Articles. For the crime of genocide, it is as defined in Article 6 of the Rome Statute of the ICC and Article II of the 1948 Genocide Convention.[20] Crimes against humanity are those stipulated in Article 7 of the Rome Statute, whereas war crimes are as defined in Article 8(2) of the same Statute. The crime of apartheid is as defined in Article II of the 1973 International Convention on the Suppression and Punishment of the Crime of Apartheid.[21] Torture is as defined in Article 1(1) of the 1948 Convention against Torture and Other Cruel, Inhuman or Degrading Treatment or Punishment.[22] Enforced disappearance is as defined in Article 2 of the 2006 International Convention for the Protection of All Persons from Enforced Disappearance.[23]

The Drafting Committee used the phrase 'crimes under international law' to highlight that Draft Article 7 relates only to 'crimes that have their foundation in the international legal order' and 'are defined on the basis of international law, rather than domestic law'. The phrase reflects the language previously used by the ILC, for example in the Principles of International Law Recognized in the Charter of the Nürnberg Tribunal and in the Judgment of the Tribunal, 1950[24] (Principles I–III and V–VII), the Draft Code of Offences against the Peace and Security of Mankind, 1954 (Art 1) and the Draft Code of Crimes against the Peace and Security of Mankind, 1996 (Art 1 para 2). Some members of the Drafting Committee were in favour of a general reference to 'the most serious crimes recognized under international law', or a similar formulation, instead of listing specific crimes, leaving open the scope of the paragraph and allowing it to incorporate new developments in international law, in particular in international criminal law. Other members

[18] See also Neil Boister, 'The Exclusion of Treaty Crimes from the Jurisdiction of the Rome Statute of the International Criminal Court' (1998) 3 Journal of Armed Conflict Law 27.

[19] Cf Amnesty International, *Universal Jurisdiction: A Preliminary Survey of Legislation Around the World* (2011). See also Michael J Kelly, 'Cheating Justice by Cheating Death: The Doctrinal Collision for Prosecuting Foreign Terrorists—Passage of Aut Dedere Aut Judicare into Customary Law & Refusal to Extradite Based on the Death Penalty' (2003) 20 Arizona J International & Comparative L 491, *passim*, esp 521; and Jan Wouters, 'The Obligation to Prosecute International Law Crimes' in *The Need for Justice and Requirements for Peace and Security*, Proceedings of the Bruges Colloquium 'Impératifs de justice et exigences de paix et de sécurité', 9–10 Sept 2004 (College of Europe 2005) 17–32; Roger O'Keefe, *International Criminal Law* (OUP 2015) 47–84.

[20] 78 UNTS 277. [21] 1035 UNTS 167. [22] 1465 UNTS 85.

[23] 2716 UNTS 3. [24] (1950) ii YBILC §97.

opined that a reference to 'serious crimes' was too vague, and that the inclusion of a detailed list of crimes was to be preferred, noting that criminal law demanded specificity. The latter was the position the Drafting Committee eventually adopted. The preponderance of views in the Drafting Committee favoured the inclusion of genocide, war crimes, and crimes against humanity as these are 'the core crimes contained in the Rome Statute of the International Criminal Court and their prohibition is reflected in customary international law'. For some members, their prohibition is constitutive of *jus cogens*. The terminology 'crime of genocide' rather than genocide was adopted by the Drafting Committee in order to mirror the language used in the 1948 Genocide Convention and the Rome Statute. Beyond these 'core crimes', the prevailing view within the Drafting Committee was to include torture, enforced disappearance, and apartheid as separate crimes.

The Drafting Committee also debated whether to include the crime of aggression. Some members who supported the inclusion considered the crime of aggression to be the supreme international crime and pointed to its inclusion in earlier work of the ILC in the field of international criminal law, such as the 1950 Nürnberg Principles, the 1954 Draft Code of Offences, and the 1996 Draft Code of Crimes. However, some members referred to the pending activation of the Kampala amendment on aggression by the Assembly of States Parties to the ICC Statute, and suggested that any action on inclusion or non-inclusion should be kept pending until 2018. Other members with reservations regarding the inclusion of the crime of aggression observed that national courts were not necessarily well placed to prosecute all crimes falling under the jurisdiction of an international court, and there was no practice of national courts prosecuting the crime of aggression. The Drafting Committee eventually decided not to include the crime of aggression, but suggested that the Special Rapporteur reflect the various viewpoints on this issue in the commentaries, to afford an opportunity to States to comment on the matter. The Drafting Committee also declined to include the crime of corruption in the list despite its seriousness. In the opinion of some members, corruption was not an international crime, as it did not derive its criminal character from international law. Rather, corruption was a crime under domestic law that often required transnational cooperation for its effective prevention and punishment. It was pointed out that the 2003 UN Convention against Corruption[25] did not actually define corruption, but rather called for measures to prevent and combat it more efficiently. Indeed, there were many crimes dealt with in treaties that did not qualify as 'crimes under international law', such as the crimes of slavery, human trafficking, child prostitution and child pornography, piracy, and terrorism; hence, the Drafting Committee decided not to include them in Draft Article 7.[26]

The drafting history of Draft Article 7 is of direct relevance to the understanding why in 2017 the ILC Drafting Committee included or excluded crimes the

[25] (2004) 43 ILM 37.

[26] Statement of the Chairman of the Drafting Committee on 20 July 2017, <http://legal.un.org/docs/?path=./ilc/documentation/english/statements/2017_dc_chairman_statement_iso.pdf&lang=E>, accessed 13 November 2017.

perpetrators of which were not to be accorded immunity *ratione materiae* from foreign criminal jurisdiction. However, it also sheds light on why the Drafting Committee considered some crimes to be 'core crimes' and beyond 'core crimes' which crimes were 'crimes under international law' for the purposes of Draft Article 7. This present author begs to differ from the Drafting Commitee in one respect: in relation to the discussion on the obligation to extradite or prosecute under customary international law, core crimes are, it is hereby submitted, those crimes proscribed by *jus cogens*. Regarding the crime of aggression, the UK House of Lords has unanimously decided in *R v Jones (Margaret)*, in the context of the invasion of Iraq, that although there was a crime of aggression under customary international law, there was no such crime as the crime of aggression under the law of England and Wales since it had not been incorporated or assimilated into domestic criminal law by a statute.[27] That may be so. However, it is incorrect to state that no national court has ever prosecuted the crime of aggression. Thailand has done so. After the end of the Second World War, *Field Marshal Plaek Phibunsongkhram*, Thailand's Prime Minister between 1941 and 1944, was charged under Thai law with voluntarily joining Japan in waging a war of aggression that seriously endangered world peace. The Thai Supreme Court held in March 1946 that since the War Criminal Act[28] which criminalizes the crime of aggression for the first time entered into force on 11 October 1945, it could not be applied retroactively to the defendant's conduct prior to that date.[29] Although the defendant was acquitted because the provision of the Act of 1945 was held to be null and void due to its violation of the principle of legality (*nullum crimen sine lege*), the prosecution is a precedent that there has been national prosecution for the crime of aggression. Therefore, there can be national prosecution of the crime of aggression, should States undertake to do so.

Admittedly, domestic criminal laws of several States make no distinction between core crimes and non-core crimes. For example, Mexico's International Extradition Act, which applies when there is no treaty with the State seeking extradition, does not specify a particular category of crimes, or 'core crimes', to which extradition will apply, and most of Mexico's bilateral extradition treaties take the same approach.[30]

English courts do, at times, distinguish between core crimes and non-core crimes. In one case before the UK House of Lords, for example, it was noted that while the Torture Convention distinguishes between torture and 'other cruel, inhuman or degrading treatment', Article 2(2) of the Convention precludes derogations in any circumstances only in the case of torture, and the international obligation upon States Parties to assume universal criminal jurisdiction over torture does not apply to the lesser forms of ill-treatment. Therefore, the prohibition of ill-treatment falling short of torture is not considered to be *jus cogens*; nor does it engage the same fundamental considerations of English public policy that justify

[27] [2007] 1 AC 136, followed in *R (on the application of General Abdulwaheed Shannan Al Rabbat v West Minister Magistrate Court* [2017] EWHC 1969 (Admin).

[28] Royal Govt Gazette, vol 62/58 (11 Oct 1945) at 591.

[29] Case no 2/4/2489, Sup Ct Judgment no 1/2489 of 23 Mar 1946.

[30] Statement by Mexico before the Sixth Committee (UN Doc A/C.6/66/SR.18 (2 Dec 2011) §56). El Salvador's law does not make such a distinction, either (UN Doc A/C.6/66/SR.26 (7 Dec 2011) §24).

treating torture as an exception to the foreign act of State doctrine (ie English courts will not sit in judgment of another foreign State's acts done within the latter's own territory).[31]

In any event, the relevance of the 'fight against impunity' for core crimes and its relation to the obligation to extradite or prosecute was noted by several States in the Sixth Committee of the UN General Assembly in 2011.[32] The linkage between characterizing a crime as a 'core crime' and the arguably automatic triggering of the obligation to extradite or prosecute has been stressed by the Nordic countries, among others.[33] Even as early as 2007, the Nordic countries:

> felt that there were grounds to claim that the obligation [to extradite or prosecute] had or was acquiring customary status with regard to crimes such as genocide, crimes against humanity, war crimes, torture and terrorist crimes. The Commission had concluded in its 1996 Draft Code of Crimes against the Peace and Security of Mankind that genocide, crimes against humanity and war crimes would fall under the obligation *aut dedere aut judicare*. The importance of the practical commitment of States to ending impunity for those crimes was also reflected in the Rome Statute of the International Criminal Court, which built on the principle of complementarity. The anti-terrorist conventions and protocols adopted under United Nations auspices contained a consistently formulated *aut dedere aut judicare* obligation upon the State party in whose territory the alleged offender was present to either extradite that person or submit the case to its competent authorities for prosecution. Security Council resolution 1373 (2001) and subsequent resolutions on terrorism also helped to consolidate the obligation by urging all States to become parties to the relevant instruments and by expressly stating that terrorist offenders must be brought to justice. The obligation was a common feature in modern criminal law conventions but specific formulations differed and the clauses did not always set forth a clear obligation.[34]

In its comment submitted to the ILC in 2009, Belgium considered that:

> there is a universal obligation to suppress crimes of international humanitarian law [ie crimes against humanity, genocide, and war crimes]. This obligation is customary in light of the many consistent positions expressed by the international community on this issue. It takes the form of 'prosecute or extradite' [*judicare vel dedere*] rather than 'extradite or prosecute' [*aut dedere aut judicare*]. However, for serious offences other than crimes of international

[31] *Belhaj & Rahmatullah (no 1) v Straw & Ors* [2017] UKSC 3 at §§279–80 (*per* Lord Sumption).

[32] eg Denmark, Finland, Iceland, Norway, and Sweden, UN Doc A/C.6/66/SR.26 at §10; Switzerland (ibid §18); El Salvador (ibid §24); Italy (ibid §42); Peru (ibid §64); Belarus (UN Doc A/C.6/66/SR.27, §41); Russia (ibid §64); and India (ibid §81).

[33] Norway's statement in the Sixth Committee on behalf of the Nordic countries (UN Doc A/C.6/66/SR.26 (7 Dec 2011) §11). See also the statement of Algeria (UN Doc A/C.6/66/SR.28 (2 Dec 2011) §46). Belarus puts it somewhat differently—the nature of the primary obligation determines the corresponding secondary obligation to extradite or prosecute; however, it would be premature to deduce that the secondary obligation automatically acquired all the characteristics of the primary one (UN Doc A/C.6/66/SR.27 (8 Dec 2011) §41). Contra: Singapore does not agree that because customary international law prohibits a specific form of conduct or characterized such conduct as a crime it automatically follows that there is a customary international legal obligation on the part of States to extradite or prosecute (UN Doc A/C.6/66/SR.28 (2 Dec 2011) §31).

[34] UN Doc A/C.6/62/SR.22 (4 Dec 2007) §33.

humanitarian law, there is only the obligation either to extradite or prosecute, and this is solely a treaty obligation.[35]

In Belgium's view, crimes against humanity, genocide, and war crimes 'pose a threat, both qualitatively and quantitatively, to the most fundamental values of the international community' and, therefore, must be suppressed by direct prosecution of the alleged perpetrators or extradition of those responsible to any State that wishes to prosecute them. In 2011, Algeria stated in the Sixth Committee that the existence of the obligation to extradite or prosecute in the sense of international customary law had not been formally established by the ILC except in certain cases relating to the most serious crimes, such as serious violations of international humanitarian law, genocide, war crimes, and crimes against humanity. Algeria strongly appealed to the ILC for adding terrorism to this category.[36]

It may be recalled that the second related question is whether the proscription by *jus cogens* norm in and of itself gives rise to the obligation to extradite or prosecute the crimes so proscribed.

Let's start with the notion of *jus cogens* and its consequences. Article 53 of the 1969 Vienna Convention on the Law of Treaties[37] stipulates that treaties conflicting with a peremptory norm of general international law (*jus cogens*) at the time of its conclusion is void. Such a norm is that from which no derogation is permitted and that can be modified only by a subsequent norm of general international law having the same character.

In 2016, the ILC started its work on the topic '*Jus cogens*', renamed 'Peremptory norms of general international law (*jus cogens*)' in 2017. The first report of the Special Rapporteur on that topic provides an extensive background history of *jus cogens* norms, an essential element of which is to serve to protect fundamental values of the international community or international public order (*ordre public*).[38] The International Court of Justice (ICJ) has stated that the prohibition on the use of force,[39] the prohibition of genocide,[40] and the prohibition of torture[41] have become peremptory norms (*jus cogens*). The ICTR Appeals Chamber stated in *Nyiramasuhuko* that in setting up the ICTR the UN Security Council had the authority to limit jurisdiction of the ICTR in relation to crimes against humanity 'subject to respect for peremptory norms of international law (*jus cogens*)'.[42] According

[35] UN Doc A/CN.4/612 (26 Mar 2009) §21. Belgium cited in support of this position: the Draft Code of Crimes against the Peace and Security of Mankind, various UN General Assembly resolutions on the suppression of war crimes and crimes against humanity, the many positions taken by the UN General Assembly and the UN Security Council on the need to combat impunity, and the fourth through sixth preambular paragraphs of the ICC Statute (ibid §20).

[36] UNGA Doc A/C.6/66/SR.28 (2 Dec 2011) §46.

[37] 1155 UNTS 331.

[38] UN Doc A/CN.4/693 (8 Mar 2016) §63.

[39] *Military and Paramilitary Activities in and against Nicaragua (Nicaragua v United States)* [1986] ICJ Rep 14, 100–01 [190].

[40] *Case Concerning Armed Activities on the Territory of the Congo (New Application: 2002) (Democratic Republic of Congo v Rwanda)* [2006] ICJ Rep 6, 31–32 [64].

[41] *Questions relating to the Obligation to Prosecute or Extradite (Belgium v Senegal)* [2012] ICJ Rep 422, 457 [99].

[42] *Prosecutor v Nyiramasuhuko* (Judgment) ICTR-98-42, App Ch (14 Dec 2015) §2136.

to the Constitutional Court of South Africa, a State's duty to prevent impunity is particularly pronounced with respect to the norms, such as the prohibition on torture, that are widely considered 'peremptory and therefore non-derogable'.[43]

Jus cogens is often linked in the legal literature to the obligation *erga omnes*. The latter was referred to in the following dictum of the International Court of Justice in *Barcelona Traction*:

> 33. [A]n essential distinction should be drawn between the obligations of a State towards the international community as a whole, and those arising vis-à-vis another State in the field of diplomatic protection. By their very nature the former are the concern of all States. In view of the importance of the rights involved, all States can be held to have a legal interest in their protection; they are obligations *erga omnes*.
>
> 34. Such obligations derive, for example, in contemporary international law, from the outlawing of acts of aggression, and of genocide, as also from the principles and rules concerning the basic rights of the human person, including protection from slavery and racial discrimination. Some of the corresponding rights of protection have entered into the body of general international law (*Reservations to the Convention on the Prevention and Punishment of the Crime of Genocide*, Advisory Opinion, I.C.J. Reports 1951, p. 23); others are conferred by international instruments of a universal or quasi-universal character.[44]

After reviewing thirteen reports by Special Rapporteur Doudou Thiam, fifteen annual reports by the ILC, and eight documents containing comments from governments, this present author finds that the obligation to extradite or prosecute in Articles 8 (Establishment of jurisdiction) and 9 (Obligation to extradite or prosecute) of the 1996 Draft Code appears to reflect the progressive development of international law at that time. The obligation to extradite or prosecute for the core crimes of genocide, crimes against humanity, war crimes, and crimes against the United Nations and associated personnel was derived from 'a number of multilateral conventions'[45] in which it is contained. While treaties can be a source of customary international law, it is only the case when the treaty reflects State practice and *opinio juris*. The existence of a rule of customary international law must be demonstrated according to the standard established by the ICJ's jurisprudence. In *Questions relating to the Obligation to Prosecute or Extradite (Belgium v Senegal)*, Judge Greenwood's questions to the Counsel for Belgium and Senegal emphasized the need for proof of actual State practice in recognizing the obligation to prosecute or extradite in addition to the fact that the obligation is contained in multilateral conventions. Such strict positivist adherence to State practice and *opinio juris* in the formation of customary international law is also evidenced in *Jurisdictional Immunities Case (Germany v Italy)*. This process was not followed in the 1996 Draft Code. In

[43] *National Commissioner of the South African Police Service v the Southern African Human Rights Litigation Centre and Others*, 2014 (12) BCLR 1428 (CC) §4.

[44] *Barcelona Traction, Light and, Power Company, Limited (Belgium v Spain)*, Second Phase [1970] ICJ Rep 3.

[45] UN Doc A/51/10 §(3) of the commentary to Art 8.

fact, Special Rapporteur Thiam himself conceded that the obligation *aut dedere aut judicare* in Articles 8 and 9 was unsupported by State practice when he said:

As a general rule, States did not consider that they were bound to try an alleged offender in the case where an application for extradition was rejected. The same was true where no application for extradition was made. That obligation did, of course, exist in some conventions having a specific purpose, but not in all conventions. It was thus not provided for in the Conventions on genocide and on apartheid and had no general effect. *If [Articles 8 and 9] were adopted, it would be the first provision of universal effect in the matter.*[46]

From the ILC's commentaries to Articles 8 and 9 of the 1996 Draft Code, it appears that the obligation *aut dedere aut judicare* was based on principle of logic rather than evidence of actual State practice (notwithstanding the repetitive use of such obligation in treaties). These Articles were justified on the basis of the grave nature of the crimes involved and the desire to combat impunity for individuals who commit those crimes through an effective system of criminalization and prosecution rather than actual State practice and *opinio juris*.[47] The relevant part of that discussion in the ILC is:

[I]t was open to question whether [Arts 8 and 9] must be applied only to States Parties to the Code or to all States.... [I]f the draft Code became a convention, the theoretical reply to the question would need to be assessed in the light of the ... Vienna Convention on the Law of Treaties ... It would thus be necessary to establish to what extent the principle *aut dedere aut judicare* had gained acceptance as a customary rule binding on States not parties to the Code. From a practical standpoint, not to concede that the scope of that principle was *erga omnes* would amount to a weakening of the system of the Code.[48]

The refusal to extend the obligation in Articles 8 and 9 to all States as opposed to the formulation of 'States Parties' also suggests that the provisions were not a codification of international law as it stood in 1996. This point was specifically raised by the UK.[49]

To conclude, at the time of their adoption in 1996, Articles 8 and 9 of the 1996 Draft Code of Crimes Against the Peace and Security of Mankind represented progressive development and were based on the need to combat impunity vis-à-vis the core crimes numerated therein. Since the completion of the 1996 Draft Code, there may have been significant developments in international law that can evince State practice and *opinio juris*. It is trite that due to the seriousness, magnitude, and often widespread scope of commission of the core crimes of genocide, crimes against humanity, torture, and serious violations of international humanitarian law in a State territory, State officials are usually involved either directly or indirectly in their perpetration. Unless there is a regime change in the territorial State, the absence of

[46] ILC, 'Report of the International Law Commission on the work of its 39th Session' (4 May–17 July 1987) UN Doc A/42/10 §36 (emphasis added).

[47] UN Doc A/51/10 §§(3), (4), and (8) of the commentary to Art 8, and §(2) of the commentary to Art 9.

[48] ILC, 'Report of the International Law Commission on the work of its 46th Session' (2 May–22 July 1994) UN Doc A/49/10 at 80 [142].

[49] *Comments and Observations received from Governments*, UN Doc A/CN.4/448 and Add 1, 99 [12].

international cooperation to extradite or prosecute perpetrators of core crimes will give them impunity from the punishment they duly deserve.

The rest of this Chapter will faithfully adhere to the established methodology for the identification of customary international law in order to prove whether the Netherlands is correct in declaring that '[T]he duty to extradite or prosecute is known to result from treaty law *or customary international law*, and that point need not be reiterated.'[50]

II. Customary International Law Analysis

In 2016 the ILC adopted on first reading the draft conclusions on identification of customary international law; namely, 'the way in which the existence and content of rules of customary international law are to be determined'. The process involves ascertaining whether there is a general practice, on the one hand, and whether that practice is accepted as law (*opinio juris*), on the other hand, having regard to the overall context, the nature of the rule, and the particular circumstances in which the evidence in question is to be found.

A general practice is primarily the practice of States that contributes to the formation, or expression, of rules of customary international law, although in certain cases, the practice of international organizations also contributes to the aforesaid. Conduct of other actors is not practice that contributes to the formation, or expression, of rules of customary international law, but may be relevant when assessing the said general practice. The relevant practice must be general in the sense that it must be sufficiently widespread and representative, as well as consistent. Provided that the practice is general, no particular duration is required.

The requirement of acceptance as law (*opinio juris*) means that the practice in question must be undertaken with a sense of legal right or obligation, and not mere usage or habit. Evidence of such acceptance may take a wide range of forms, including public statements made on behalf of States; official publications; government legal opinions; diplomatic correspondence; decisions of national courts; treaty provisions; and conduct in connection with resolutions adopted by an international organization or at an intergovernmental conference. Failure to react over time to a practice may serve as evidence of acceptance as law (*opinio juris*), provided that States were in a position to react and the circumstances called for some reaction.

A rule set forth in a treaty may reflect a rule of customary international law if it is established that the treaty rule: (1) codified a rule of customary international law existing at the time when the treaty was concluded; (2) has led to the crystallization of a rule of customary international law that had started to emerge prior to the conclusion of the treaty; or (3) has given rise to a general practice that is accepted as law (*opinio juris*), thus generating a new rule of customary international law. The fact

[50] Statement by the Netherlands in the Sixth Committee (UN Doc A/C.6/66/SR.28 (2 Dec 2011) §60, emphasis added).

that a rule is set forth in a number of treaties may, but does not necessarily, indicate that the treaty rule reflects a rule of customary international law.

A resolution adopted by an international organization or at an intergovernmental conference cannot, of itself, create a rule of customary international law although it may provide evidence for establishing the existence and content of a rule of customary international law, or contribute to its development. Indeed, a provision in a resolution so adopted may reflect a rule of customary international law if it is established that the provision corresponds to a general practice that is accepted as law (*opinio juris*).

Decisions of international courts and tribunals, in particular of the ICJ, concerning the existence and content of rules of customary international law are a subsidiary means for the determination of such rules. Regard may be had, as appropriate, to decisions of national courts concerning the existence and content of rules of customary international law, as a subsidiary means for the determination of such rules.

Teachings of the most highly qualified publicists of the various nations may serve as a subsidiary means for the determination of rules of customary international law.

Where a State has objected to a rule of customary international law while that rule was in the process of formation, the rule is not opposable to the State concerned for so long as it maintains its objection, which must be clearly expressed, made known to other States, and maintained persistently.

A rule of particular customary international law, whether regional, local, or other, is a rule of customary international law that applies only among a limited number of States. To determine the existence and content of such a rule, it is necessary to ascertain whether there is a general practice among the States concerned that is accepted by them as law (*opinio juris*).[51]

The ILC's draft conclusions on the identification of customary international law are intended 'to produce authoritative guidance for those called upon to identify customary international law, including national and international judges'.[52] When the issue of the customary status of the obligation to extradite or prosecute arose in the Working Group on the Obligation to Extradite or Prosecute (*aut dedere aut judicare*), the chairman of the Working Group found useful as a guidance the International Law Association's *Statement of Principles Applicable to the Formation of General Customary International Law* (ILA's Statement of Principles).[53] The ILA's work is more detailed and complex in its explanation than the ILC's draft conclusions, which mainly aim at non-international lawyers. Thus, the ILA's Statement of Principles of 2000 remains pertinent to the analysis of whether the obligation *aut dedere aut judicare* is one of customary international law.

[51] ILC, 'Report of the International Law Commission on the work of its 68th Session' (2 May–10 June and 4 July–12 August 2016) UN Doc A/71/10 §62.

[52] ILC, 'Report of the International Law Commission on the work of its 63rd Session' (26 April–3 June and 4 July–12 August 2011) UN Doc A/66/10 Annex A §4.

[53] International Law Association, 'Final Report of the Committee on Formation of Customary (General) International Law' (2000).

When the ICJ or an international tribunal of similar standing has an occasion to directly address the question whether the obligation to extradite or prosecute is a rule of general or regional customary international law, the parties concerned will have to present evidence of State practice and *opinio juris* in support of their respective arguments.

The International Court of Justice has repeatedly laid down the criteria for identifying a rule of customary international law.[54] A relatively recent authoritative pronouncement by the ICJ on the determination of the existence of customary international law appears in its Judgment in *Jurisdictional Immunities of the State (Germany v Italy: Greece Intervening)*. The ICJ enunciates that in order to determine, in accordance with Article 38(1)(*b*) of its Statute,[55] the existence of 'international custom, as evidence of a general practice accepted as law',

> it must apply the criteria which it has repeatedly laid down for identifying a rule of customary international law. In particular, as the Court made clear in the *North Sea Continental Shelf* cases, the existence of a rule of customary international law requires that there be a 'settled practice' together with *opinio juris* (*North Sea Continental Shelf (Federal Republic of Germany/Denmark; Federal Republic of Germany/Netherlands), Judgment, I.C.J. Reports, 1969*, p. 44, §77). Moreover, as the Court has also observed,
>
>> It is of course axiomatic that the material of customary international law is to be looked for primarily in the actual practice and *opinio juris* of States, even though multilateral conventions may have an important role to play in recording and defining rules deriving from custom, or indeed in developing them. (*Continental Shelf (Libyan Arab Jamahiriya/Malta), Judgment, I.C.J. Reports 1985*, pp. 29–30, §27.)
>
> In the present context, State practice of particular significance is to be found in the judgments of national courts faced with the question whether a foreign State is immune, the legislation of those States which have enacted statutes dealing with immunity, the claims to immunity advanced by States before foreign courts and the statements made by States, first in the course of the extensive study of the subject by the International Law Commission and then in the context of the adoption of the United Nations Convention [on Jurisdictional Immunities of States and Their Property of 2004]. *Opinio juris* in this context is reflected in particular in the assertion by States claiming immunity that international law accords them a right to such immunity from the jurisdiction of other States; in the acknowledgment, by States granting immunity, that international law imposes upon them an obligation to do so; and, conversely, in the assertion by States in other cases of a right to exercise jurisdiction over foreign States. While it may be true that States sometimes decide to accord an immunity more extensive than that required by international law, for present purposes, the point is that the grant of immunity in such a case is not accompanied by the requisite *opinio juris* and therefore sheds no light upon the issue currently under consideration by the Court.[56]

In *Germany v Italy*, the ICJ scrutinized State practice in the form of national legislation of the ten States referred to by the Parties in that case which had legislated specifically for the subject of State immunity.[57] In arriving at the conclusion that customary international law as evidenced by State practice in the form of judicial decisions

[54] In accordance with Art 38(1)(*b*) of the ICJ's Statute, ie the existence of 'international custom, as evidence of a general practice accepted as law'.

[55] (1945) 39 AJIL Supp 215.

[56] [2012] ICJ Rep 99, 122–23 [55].

[57] ibid 130–01 [70–71].

supports the proposition that State immunity for *acta jure imperii* continues to extend to civil proceedings for acts occasioning death, personal injury, or damage to property committed by the armed forces and other organs of a State in the conduct of armed conflict, even if the relevant acts take place on the territory of the forum State,[58] the ICJ analysed the judgments of national courts of eleven European States (Belgium, Germany, Netherlands, France, Italy, UK, Ireland, Slovenia, Poland, Serbia, and Greece), two non-European States (Brazil and Egypt), as well as a few decisions of the European Court of Human Rights.[59]

In a similar vein, before arriving at the conclusion that, under customary international law as it presently stands, a State is not deprived of immunity by reason of the fact that it is accused of serious violations of international human rights law or the international law of armed conflict,[60] the ICJ in *Germany v Italy* analysed 'a substantial body of State practice ... particularly evident in the judgments of national courts'[61] of six European States (Italy, Greece, France, Slovenia, Poland, and the UK), two non-European States (Canada and New Zealand), as well as two judgments of the European Court of Human Rights.[62]

It could be argued that the ICJ in *Germany v Italy* did not spend time combing through State practice of all or a majority of States in the process of identifying the said rule of customary international law because the practice of the relatively few States analysed by it showed the absence of consistent State practice to support the existence of a rule of customary international law in question. It could be equally argued, however, that the ICJ usually does not analyse practice of all or a majority of States in order to identify rules of customary international law.

An authoritative explanation of the ICJ's practice in identifying rules of customary international law is that of Judge Peter Tomka, who was Vice President of the ICJ at the time of *Germany v Italy* and immediately became President of the ICJ right after that case until February 2015. Judge Tomka explains the methodology used by the ICJ in *Germany v Italy* in his speech at the Conference on 'The Judge and International Custom' held in Paris in September 2012.[63]

In *Germany v Italy*, the ICJ found there was little need to prove the existence of a customary rule of State immunity, referring primarily to the International Law Commission's extensive survey of State practice as confirmed by the record of national legislation, judicial decisions, assertions of a right to immunity, and the comments of States on what became the 2004 UN Convention on Jurisdictional Immunities and Their Property.[64] The important question in *Germany v Italy* was whether a tort exception to State immunity was a rule of customary international law and applicable in the circumstances of the case. In answering this question, the

[58] ibid 134–45 [77–78]. [59] ibid 131–34 [72–76]. [60] ibid 139 [91].

[61] ibid 137 [84–85]. [62] ibid 136–38 [83–87] and 139 [90].

[63] Speech of Judge Peter Tomka. President of the ICJ, *The Judge and International Custom* (Council of Europe 2012) 27. This speech also appears as a chapter entitled 'Customary International Law in the Jurisprudence of the World Court: The Increasing Relevance of Codification' in Liesbeth Lijnzaad and the Council of Europe (eds), *The Judge and International Custom* (Brill/Nijhoff 2016). The citation in this book refers to the former publication, not the latter one.

[64] UN Doc A/59/508.

ICJ did not turn directly to individual stances of State practice and *opinio juris*, but instead scrutinized evidence relating to the 1972 European Convention on State Immunity[65] and the UN Convention on Jurisdictional Immunities and Their Property, which were not binding on either Germany or Italy, the latter Convention being not yet even in force. The ICJ found that neither convention could be used as evidence of customary international law regarding whether a tort exception applied to situations of armed conflict. The European Convention explicitly did not applied to armed conflict, whereas the UN Convention's broadly drafted tort exception could not be taken as representing customary international law in so far as it applied to armed conflict in the light of the ILC's commentary on the Draft Articles on which the Convention was based and various reservations by States Parties to that UN Convention.[66] Judge Tomka clarifies further:

> Only after having determined that the relevant codifications could not be used as evidence of a customary rule did the Court continue to consider the question by reference to an extensive survey of 'State practice in the form of judicial decisions', accompanied by '*opinio juris*, as demonstrated by the positions taken by States and the jurisprudence of a number of national courts which have made clear that they considered that customary international law required immunity' (§77 of the Judgment). Without determining the status of the tort exception in general, the Court concluded that no customary exception existed for torts during armed conflict.[67]

In determining whether State immunity foreclosed civil proceedings in that case, the ICJ 'looked into individual circumstances and practice and expressions of *opinio juris*' as well as relevant provisions of the codification instruments concerning State immunity. Since the existence of the rule of State immunity under customary international law was beyond dispute, the ICJ found no need to examine the extensive State practice and *opinio juris*. However, the ICJ had to look for the existence of exceptions to the said rule through 'a survey of the primary sources of the custom itself'.[68] According to Judge Tomka, the ICJ has always taken 'a pragmatic approach to determining the existence and content of international custom, considering whether a rule has been convincingly identified before moving on to consider the primary evidence of State practice and *opinio juris*.'[69]

The four particular methods that have played an important role in the ICJ's assessment of evidence of customary international law, depending on the circumstances before the ICJ, are: '1) referring to multilateral treaties and their *travaux préparatoires*, 2) referring to United Nations resolutions and other non-binding documents which are drafted in normative language, 3) considering whether an established rule applies to current circumstances as a matter of deduction and 4) resorting to an analogy'.[70] Judge Tomka has clarified further that each of these methods depends on the existence of a certain situation. For example, 'for the [ICJ] to refer to a treaty or resolution, one must have been adopted on the topic, and for [the ICJ] to rely on

[65] ETS 074.

[66] Tomka, *The Judge and International Custom*, 44–45, citing §56 of the ICJ Judgment in *Germany v Italy*.

[67] ibid 45. [68] ibid 46. [69] ibid 47. [70] ibid.

existing rules by deduction or analogy, the logical step must suggest itself as reasonable'.[71] On *opinio juris*, Judge Tomka explains that:

in practice, the Court has never found it necessary to undertake [an inquiry into a 'settled practice' together with *opinio juris*] for every rule claimed to be customary in a particular case and instead has made use of the best and most expedient evidence available to determine whether a customary rule of this sort exists. Sometimes this entails a direct review of the material elements of custom on their own, while more often it will be sufficient to look to the considered views expressed by States and bodies like the International Law Commission as to whether a rule of customary law exists and what its content is, or at least to use rules that are clearly formulated in a written expression as a focal point to frame and guide an inquiry into the material elements of custom.[72]

With respect to the obligation to extradite or prosecute, Chapter 2 of this book informs readers that the ILC did not embark on the process of identifying the existence or non-existence of a rule of customary international law on that obligation. No drafting committee was ever set up to consider the ILC's work on this topic; hence, no commentary exists to elucidate the ILC's finding on State practice and *opinio juris* or, in the event that the obligation was not a customary rule, to suggest progressive development of international law regarding the obligation. Therefore, there is no 'ready-made' source of reference from the ILC for anyone interested in finding the existence or non-existence of the obligation to extradite or prosecute under customary international law.

The ICJ in *Questions relating to the Obligation to Prosecute or Extradite (Belgium v Senegal)* ruled it had no jurisdiction to entertain Belgium's claims relating to Senegal's alleged breaches of obligations under customary international law because at the date of Belgium's filing of the Application the dispute between Belgium and Senegal did not relate to breaches of obligations under customary international law.[73] The ICJ predominantly confined itself to an analysis of the mechanism to combat impunity under the Convention against Torture of 1984, especially the relationship between the different articles on the establishment of jurisdiction (Art 5), the obligation to engage a preliminary inquiry (Art 6), and the obligation to prosecute or extradite (Art 7). Moreover, *Belgium v Senegal* was confined to the obligations regarding crimes against humanity and war crimes in internal armed conflicts.

Judge Abraham and Judge ad hoc Sur were the only two judges who dissented on this point.[74] They further concluded the ICJ should not have upheld Belgium's claim of the existence of the customary international law obligation to prosecute or extradite.

In his Separate Opinion, Judge Abraham considered there was insufficient evidence, based on State practice and *opinio juris*, of a customary obligation for States to prosecute before their domestic courts those individuals suspected of war crimes or crimes against humanity on the basis of universal jurisdiction, even when limited to the case where the suspect was present in the territory of the forum State. In his

[71] ibid. [72] ibid 29. [73] [2012] ICJ Rep 422, 444–45 [53–55], 462 [122(2)].
[74] Sep Op of Judge Abraham, ibid 471–76 [3–20]; Dis Op of Judge ad hoc Sur, ibid 610 [17].

view, first, the practice of fifty-one States presented by Belgium represented 'only a minority within the international community, which is in any event insufficient to establish the existence of a universal customary rule'. Secondly, some of these States might have enacted their national legislation 'on the basis of a particular interpretation of their conventional obligations' and, apart from the fact that such interpretation was 'not universally shared', this fact did not demonstrate the existence of an *opinio juris* regarding the existence of an obligation to establish 'universal jurisdiction' outside any conventional obligations. Finally, 'certain States among the 51—and probably many of them', such as France, might have extended the jurisdiction of their courts over the crimes in question 'on the basis of a purely unilateral choice of sovereign decision, without in any sense believing that they were required to do so by some international obligation, whether conventional or customary—but solely in the belief that international law entitled them to do so'.[75]

In the dissenting opinion of Judge ad hoc Sur, the ICJ's ruling on its lack of jurisdiction to decide on Belgium's claim related to breaches of obligations under customary international law seemed to have resulted from a twofold concern by the ICJ. First, the ICJ avoided 'being drawn into a lengthy discussion which might delay the deliberation in the case'. Second, the ICJ avoided 'having to find that the customary rule invoked by Belgium did not exist, so as not to hinder its possible subsequent establishment in customary law, and thus to maintain the uncertainty surrounding this point, pending further developments'. In his view, despite the ICJ's silence, or perhaps because of such silence, 'it seems clear that the existence of a customary obligation to prosecute or extradite, or even simply to prosecute, cannot be established in positive law'.[76]

A few members of the ILC's Working Group on the Obligation to Extradite or Prosecute (*aut dedere aut judicare*) surmised that the then ICJ President Peter Tomka's answer to this author's question on 24 July 2012, during his official visit to the ILC, hinted that Judges Abraham and Sur had implicitly disclosed the deliberations in the ICJ which had found the obligation to extradite or prosecute to be non-existent under customary international law.[77] However, these members of the Working Group ought to bear in mind the Separate Opinion of Judge Cançado Trindade,

[75] Sep Op of Judge Abraham, ibid 476 [21], 477 [24–25], and 478–80 [31–39].

[76] Dis Op of Judge ad hoc Sur, ibid 610 [18]. Judge ad hoc Sur seems to be one of the proponents of the so-called 'voluntarist' theory of customary international law, positing that the key to customary international law is not belief (*opinio juris*) but the will of States. See Sur, 'La Coutume international. Sa vie, son œuvre' (1986) 3 Droits, Revue français de théorie juridique 111, 122–23 and the criticism of this theory in the ILA's Statement of Principles 38–40.

[77] Judge Tomka replied to this author's criticism of Judge Abraham's 'unrealistically high threshold for evidence of *opinio juris*' thus: 'It was not appropriate for him to comment on the views of his colleagues: some were prolific writers, while others expressed their views only when necessary. He would therefore prefer to refrain from commenting on the separate opinion of Judge Abraham. Opinions and judgments should speak for themselves. His role as President of the Court was simply to remind colleagues that in their opinions they should not disclose the confidential nature of deliberations, and that the purpose of a separate opinion was not to criticize the judgment, but to explain why the judge concerned could not endorse the interpretation of the conclusions of the Court. It was for the reader to draw his or her own conclusions as to whether the separate opinion provided a more convincing analysis of the situation and the rules in question' (Provisional summary of record of the 3148th meeting of the ILC, UN Doc A/CN.4/SR.3148 (17 Aug 2012) 21).

one of the most prolific writers on the ICJ's bench, who wrote that the ICJ 'did not express itself well' on this point.[78] Since the ICJ's determination of whether there was a dispute on the question of customary international law rested on purely factual considerations of the case at issue, what the ICJ 'really wished to say' was that:

> '*there was no material object for the exercise of its jurisdiction* in respect of obligations under customary law, rather than a lack of its own jurisdiction per se. The finding that, in the circumstances of the present case, a dispute did not exist between the contending parties as to the matter at issue, *does not necessarily mean that, as a matter of law, the Court would automatically lack jurisdiction*, to be exercised in relation to the determination of the existence of a dispute concerning breaches of alleged obligations under customary international law.'[79]

In the same vein, Judge Sebutinde, who must have been present during the ICJ's deliberations of the case, stated categorically that the record before the ICJ showed that in the diplomatic exchanges between the Parties in the period prior to the date of Belgium's filing the Application, no claim had ever been made by Belgium relating to Senegal's alleged breach of any international obligations other than those under the Convention against Torture. Hence, the ICJ did not have jurisdiction to examine Belgium's claims concerning Senegal's alleged breach of its obligation *aut dedere aut judicare* on the basis of rules of international law other than the Convention against Torture.[80]

In any case, any reference to the existence or non-existence of the customary law obligation in *Belgium v Senegal* was to the obligation in the cases of crimes against humanity and war crimes in internal armed conflicts. It did not touch upon such obligation in the context of genocide, war crimes in international armed conflicts, or other crimes of international concern.

Let's now apply in the context of the obligation to extradite or prosecute the criteria which, according to the ICJ in *Germany v Italy*, the ICJ has repeatedly laid down for the purpose of identifying a rule of customary international law. In order to have an international customary law status, the obligation to extradite or prosecute must be substantiated by the following:

(i) 'settled practice' of States as evidenced by judgments of national courts faced with the question, the legislation of those States which have enacted statutes dealing with the obligation, the claims regarding the obligation before foreign courts, and the statements made by States in the course of the extensive study of the subject by the International Law Commission as well as in other contexts related to this topic;

(ii) *opinio juris* as reflected in particular by the assertion by States claiming the existence of the obligation, in the acknowledgement that international law

[78] *Belgium v Senegal* [2012] ICJ Rep 422, 544 [143] (Sep Op of Judge Cançado Trindade).

[79] ibid 544 [144] (emphasis original, footnote omitted), and cf also ibid 543–44 [141–43]. NB Judge Cançado Trindade is well-known for his opposition to a 'voluntarist reasoning, focused on the will of States within the confines of the strict and static inter-State dimension' (ibid 553 [166]).

[80] ibid 604 [41–42] (Sep Op of Judge Sebutinde).

imposes upon them the obligation to extradite or prosecute offenders of certain crimes; and

(iii) multilateral conventions recording and defining rules deriving from custom, or indeed developing them.

In *Belgium v Senegal*, Judge Sir Christopher Greenwood specifically asked Belgium the following questions:

> With regard to the argument that Senegal is in breach of a customary international law obligation to prosecute or extradite, please indicate:
> (1) which States have provided for their courts to possess jurisdiction over
> (i) war crimes committed in an armed conflict not of an international character; and
> (ii) crimes against humanity; in cases where the alleged offence occurred outside their territory and neither the alleged offender nor the victims were their nationals;
> (2) what instances there are of States exercising jurisdiction or granting extradition in such cases; and
> (3) what evidence exists that States consider that international law requires them to prosecute or extradite in such cases.
> The question relates solely to customary international law and not to action taken pursuant to treaty obligations such as those arising under the Convention against Torture.[81]

Judge Greenwood's questions, it should be stressed once again, focused specifically on two of the so-called 'core crimes'—crimes against humanity and war crimes (and he specifically focused only on war crimes in non-international armed conflicts). Judge Greenwood's first two questions are related to State practice, or the *objective element* of customary international law.[82] His third question addresses the *subjective element*, or *opinio juris*, in customary international law.

A. State practice (objective element)

State practice encompasses verbal acts as well as physical acts in public, formally manifesting States' will in their international legal relations.[83] Abstentions or omissions may, in appropriate circumstances, manifest such will, as in, for example, an abstention from pursuing a particular course of action following a protest from another State.[84] For a new rule of customary international law to materialize, an indispensable requirement would be that within the period in question, short though it might be, State practice, including the practice of States whose interests are specially affected, should have been both extensive and virtually uniform in support of such

[81] ICJ Doc CR 2012/5, Verbatim Record of the Public Sitting on 16 Mar 2012 at 34.

[82] According to the International Law Association, State practice, which is the most characteristic and the most important component of customary international law, is to be described as the 'objective' element, and not the 'material' element, so as to avoid confusion with the jurisdictionally distinct concept of 'material source of law' (ILA's Statement of Principles 13).

[83] ILA's Statement of Principles 14–15; and *Fisheries* case (*United Kingdom v Norway*) [1951] ICJ Rep 116, 124–25.

[84] ILA's Statement of Principles 15–16.

a rule.[85] *The State practice in question need not be universal.*[86] As the International Law Association has explained, as long as a State practice is sufficiently representative and widespread, it is not normally necessary for even a majority of States to have engaged in the practice, provided there is no significant dissent.[87] Besides, if all 'specially affected States' are represented, it is not necessary for a majority of States in the world to have participated in such State practice; but if 'specially affected States' do not accept the practice, it cannot crystallize into a rule of general customary law.[88]

In this light, Judge Abraham's Separate Opinion in *Belgium v Senegal* that the practice of 51 out of 193 States was insufficient to establish customary international law is, with due respect, highly questionable. The learned Judge's aforesaid conclusion is not supported by, among others, the ICJ's analysis of State practice in *Germany v Italy*.

As mentioned in Chapter 2, the ILC sought from States information of relevance to the customary international law analysis of the obligation to extradite or prosecute. In 2006 the Commission requested governments to submit information concerning their legislation and practice with regard to the said obligation. In the following year the Commission further requested information from Governments concerning their legislation and practice with regard to the obligation to extradite or prosecute and its possible connection with universal jurisdiction. Twenty-three States responded in writing and the second and third reports of Special Rapporteur Galicki analysed the responses received by the time of these reports,[89] but not in the context of the criteria on the determination of the existence of customary international law as reaffirmed by the ICJ in *Germany v Italy*.

In 2011, the ILC requested comments from States whether there were, in the legislation of States or in the case law of domestic tribunals, certain crimes or categories of crimes in respect of which the obligation to extradite or prosecute had been implemented, and, if so, whether a court or tribunal had ever relied, in this respect, on customary international law.[90] The summary of the comments made by States in the Sixth Committee in response to the last-mentioned request for comments is not quite enlightening. Some delegations observed that their domestic legislation, as well as bilateral extradition and multilateral treaties, contained provisions concerning the obligation to extradite or prosecute, although in some instances, the legislation on extradition was residual in nature, applying in the absence of treaty relations with a State seeking extradition. The legislation in question, as well as bilateral extradition treaties, also did not specify any core crimes nor any particular category of crimes concerning which extradition would apply. While the domestic law of other delegations did not explicitly refer to *aut dedere aut judicare*, there were relevant provisions in that regard with respect to specific crimes. Indeed, the principle *aut dedere aut judicare* was applied regularly and consistently, both

[85] *North Sea Continental Shelf* cases [1969] ICJ Rep 3, 43 [74]. See further, ILA's Statement of Principles 20–26.

[86] ILA's Statement of Principles 23–24. [87] ibid 25. [88] ibid 26.

[89] UN Doc A/CN.4/585 §§ 61–72 and UN Doc A/CN.4/603 §§69–93.

[90] UN Doc A/66/10 §§45–46.

in domestic implementing legislation giving effect to relevant conventions and in related case law. Some delegations noted, however, that none of their national courts had relied on customary international law to implement the obligation to extradite or prosecute.[91]

In trying to establish the existence in the present day of a customary norm on the obligation to extradite or prosecute, it is crucial to have a systematic survey that analyses national laws comprehensively rather than focusing superficially on specific aspects of these laws. In particular, State practice needs to be analysed from both the prosecution and the extradition sides. A State may have a law on prosecution and a law on extradition and not have a view that it is bound by an obligation to extradite or prosecute.

An in-depth analysis of all the available relevant information, including information from other reliable sources, is therefore needed to ascertain whether the obligation to extradite or prosecute has become part and parcel of customary international law.

(1) *National legislation dealing with the obligation* aut dedere aut judicare

Judge Greenwood's first question concerns assertion of jurisdiction on the basis of universality, or universal jurisdiction. In order to be able to prosecute an alleged offender found in its territory, a State has first to criminalize the crime in question and establish jurisdiction over it, even if the act constituting the crime occurs outside its territory and neither the offender nor the victim is of its nationality.[92] One commentator rightly defines universal jurisdiction as 'prescriptive jurisdiction over offences committed abroad by persons who, at the time of commission, are non-resident aliens, where such offences are not deemed to constitute threats to the fundamental interests of the prescribing State or, in appropriate cases, to give rise to effects within its territory'—it is a base of jurisdiction that does not require any link or *nexus* with the forum State.[93]

Universal jurisdiction and the obligation *aut dedere aut judicare* are not automatically linked. While universal jurisdiction enables a State to establish jurisdiction where the forum State has no jurisdictional nexus with the crime or the offender except for the presence of the offender in its territory, universal jurisdiction per se does

[91] 'Report of the International Law Commission on the work of its sixty-third Session' (2011): topical summary of the discussion held in the Sixth Committee of the General Assembly during its sixty-sixth session, prepared by the Secretariat (UN Doc A/CN.4/650 (20 Jan 2012) §45). Amnesty International has criticized the reports/information/comments submitted by States in response to the ILC's requests/questions as 'often partial, contradictory or simply mistaken' (Amnesty International, *International Law Commission: The Obligation to Extradite or Prosecute* (Aut Dedere Aut Judicare) (2009) 21).

[92] Cf *Belgium v Senegal* [2012] ICJ Rep 422, 584 [2] (Declaration of Judge Donoghue).

[93] Roger O'Keefe, 'Universal Jurisdiction: Clarifying the Basic Concept' (2004) 2 J Int'l Crim Justice 735, 745. This definition is more comprehensive than that propounded in the Joint Sep Op of Judges Higgins, Kooijmans, and Buergenthal in *Arrest Warrant of 11 April 2000 (Dem Rep Congo v Belgium)* [2002] ICJ Rep 3, 75 [42], that universal jurisdiction is 'more accurately' defined as 'the jurisdiction to establish a territorial jurisdiction over persons for extraterritorial events'.

not create an obligation to extradite or prosecute.[94] However, several international instruments, such as the universally ratified four Geneva Conventions of 1949, provide for universal jurisdiction over the offences covered by these instruments plus the alternative option to extradite alleged offenders to another State for the purpose of prosecution.[95]

Belgium's written reply to Judge Greenwood's first question seemed to have derived from the most recent and exhaustive research up to the first quarter of 2012.[96]

Belgium listed the following twenty-four States that explicitly conferred jurisdiction on their courts to prosecute crimes against humanity and war crimes committed in an armed conflict not of an international character: Armenia, Australia, Azerbaijan, Belarus, Belgium, Bosnia and Herzegovina, Bulgaria, Burundi, Canada, Croatia, Czech Republic, Estonia, Finland, France, Germany, Kenya, Luxembourg, Malta, Moldova, Montenegro, Netherlands, Norway, Philippines, and Poland.[97]

Belgium also listed the following twenty-seven States that conferred jurisdiction on their courts to prosecute by reference to the crimes against humanity and war crimes committed in an armed conflict not of an international character cited in the 1998 Rome Statute of the International Criminal Court: Argentina, Bolivia, Burkina Faso, Cameroon, Costa Rica, Cuba, Cyprus, Denmark, Ethiopia, Georgia, Latvia, Lithuania, Mexico, New Zealand, Nicaragua, Panama, Portugal, Samoa, Senegal, Slovenia, South Africa, Spain, Switzerland, Timor-Leste, Trinidad and Tobago, Uganda, and Uruguay.[98] Although the ICC Statute has no provision on the obligation to extradite or prosecute,[99] national legislation of several States that

[94] Report of the AU-EU ad hoc Technical Expert Group on the Principle of Universal Jurisdiction (Annex to Council of the European Union Doc 8672/1/09/ Rev 1 (16 Apr 2009) §11; Belgium's position in UN Doc A/CN.4/612, §§18, 20, 24–25, and South Africa's position in ibid §59; Amnesty International, *ILC: The Obligation to Extradite or Prosecute* 7–9.

[95] See Chapter 1 n 44. According to Claus Kreβ ('Reflection on the *Iudicare* Limb of the Grave Breaches Regime' (2009) 7 J Int'l Crim Justice 789), what the *iudicare* limb of the grave breaches regime actually entails is a duty to investigate and, where so warranted, to prosecute and convict.

[96] The main source used by Belgium was Amnesty International, *Universal Jurisdiction—a Preliminary Survey*). See Oral Proceedings in *Belgium v Senegal* (19 Mar 2012) 26 [23]. For Special Rapporteur Galicki's summary of information provided by States on domestic regulations adopted and applied concerning the obligation to extradite or prosecute, see his third report (UN Doc A/CN.4/603) §§69–83, 90–93.

[97] Supplementary replies from Belgium to the questions put to it by Judge Greenwood at the close of the public hearing held on 16 Mar 2012, <http://www.icj-cij.org/files/case-related/144/17640.pdf>, accessed 13 November 2017. Interestingly, Belgium did not include Senegal in this list despite the fact that Senegal had enacted a number of legislative reforms in 2007 which brought its domestic law into conformity with the Convention against Torture as well as formally proscribed the crime of genocide, crimes against humanity, war crimes, and other violations of international humanitarian law. The amendments also enable prosecution, on the basis of universal jurisdiction, offenders who are present in Senegal's jurisdiction. These legislative reforms were cited in the ICJ Judgment in *Belgium v Senegal* [2012] ICJ Rep 422, 435 [28].

[98] Supplementary replies from Belgium, <http://www.icj-cij.org/files/case-related/144/17640.pdf>.

[99] The ICC Statute stipulates, in its preamble, that States Parties to the Statute are determined to end impunity for the perpetrators of the most serious crimes of concern to the international community as a whole, and that it is the duty of every State to exercise its criminal jurisdiction over those responsible for international crimes. Art 89 of the Statute obligates States Parties to cooperate with the ICC, including surrendering such persons to the ICC. Special Rapporteur Galicki opines: '[A] concept of the principle of universal jurisdiction and competence, especially in later years, is often connected with

has been enacted to implement their obligations under the ICC Statute expressly includes the obligation to extradite or prosecute perpetrators of genocide, crimes against humanity, and war crimes.[100] Peru[101] and Paraguay[102] should be added to this list, too.

Have the States listed by Belgium also provided for their courts to possess universal jurisdiction beyond the context of crimes against humanity and war crimes in internal armed conflicts, and especially beyond the context of implementing treaty obligations?

According to Amnesty International, as early as September 2001, domestic laws or national jurisprudence of at least forty-five States provided for universal jurisdiction over 'ordinary crimes', including 'ordinary crimes of international concern' such as piracy and hostage taking as well as certain crimes under international law which could be prosecuted only to the extent the conduct was defined as an ordinary crime under national law.[103] The list of States falling into this category include: Algeria, Burundi, Cameroon, Colombia, Croatia, Democratic Republic of the Congo, Ecuador, Georgia, Hungary, Jordan, Kazakhstan, Kyrgyzstan, Lao PDR, Latvia, Lithuania, Macedonia [The former Yugoslav Republic of], Moldova, Monaco, Mongolia, Paraguay, Romania, Russia, Slovakia, Syria, Tajikistan, Turkey, Turkmenistan, Ukraine, Uzbekistan, Vietnam, and Yemen.[104]

Those States listed by Amnesty International as having either national laws or jurisprudence providing for universal jurisdiction over certain war crimes, as of September 2001, include: Antigua and Barbuda, Bahamas, Barbados, Belize, Bosnia and Herzegovina, Botswana, Brazil, Canada, Côte d'Ivoire, Croatia, Democratic Republic of the Congo, Dominica, Ecuador, Fiji, Gambia, Ghana, Greece, Guyana, Guatemala, Honduras, Hungary, India, Iran, Ireland, Jamaica, Kiribati, Lao PDR, Latvia, Lesotho, Liberia, Liechtenstein, Lithuania, Luxembourg, Macedonia [The former Yugoslav Republic of], Moldova, Monaco, Mongolia, Nicaragua, Nigeria, Panama, Papua New Guinea, Paraguay, Philippines, Poland, Romania, Russia, St Kitts and Nevis, St Lucia, St Vincent and the Grenadines, Samoa, San Marino, Seychelles, Sierra Leone, Singapore, Slovakia, Solomon Islands, Swaziland, Tajikistan, Tanzania, Timor-Leste, Trinidad and Tobago,

the establishment of international criminal courts and their activities. In practice, however, the extent of such quasi-universal "jurisdiction and competence" depends on the number of States accepting the establishment of such courts and is not directly connected with the obligation to extradite or prosecute.' (Preliminary report, UN Doc A/CN.4/571 §21).

[100] Raphäel van Steenberghe, 'The Obligation to Extradite or Prosecute: Clarifying its Nature' (2011) 9 J Int'l Crim Justice 1089, 1097.

[101] Act no 18.026, Cooperation with the ICC in combating genocide, war crimes, and crimes against humanity, 25 Sept 2006 (Official Gazette, 4 Oct 2006), and Art 9, second paragraph, draft bill no 1615/2012-CR (18 Oct 2012) entitled 'Law on the Crimes against International Human Rights Law and International Humanitarian Law'.

[102] Paraguay's Law on the Implementation of the Rome Statute of the International Criminal Court, approved by the Senate on 4 Aug 2016.

[103] Amnesty International, *Universal Jurisdiction: UN General Assembly Should Support This Essential International Justice Tool* (2010) 15–16 and n 23.

[104] ibid 19.

Turkmenistan, Tuvalu, Uganda, UK, Ukraine, Uruguay, Uzbekistan, Vanuatu, Vietnam, and Zimbabwe.[105]

States identified by Amnesty International as having either national laws or jurisprudence providing for universal jurisdiction over all, some, or several crimes against humanity, as of September 2001, include: Algeria [apartheid], Bosnia and Herzegovina, Croatia [apartheid], Ecuador, Georgia, Ghana [slave trade, trafficking in women, and apartheid], Hungary, Iraq [slavery, trafficking in human persons], Kyrgyzstan [apartheid], Lao PDR [apartheid], Latvia [apartheid], Liberia [apartheid], Lithuania, Macedonia [The former Yugoslav Republic of], Monaco [sexual slavery and other forms of sexual violence], Mongolia [apartheid], Nicaragua [slave trade and trafficking in women and children], Panama [apartheid and enforced disappearance], Paraguay [enforced disappearance], Philippines, Poland, Romania [apartheid], Russia [apartheid], Tajikistan, Timor-Leste, Ukraine, Uruguay [enforced disappearance], Uzbekistan [apartheid], Vanuatu [slave trading and trafficking in persons], and Vietnam [apartheid].[106]

States identified by Amnesty International as having either national laws or jurisprudence providing for universal jurisdiction over genocide, as of September 2001, include: Bosnia and Herzegovina, Brazil, Canada, Colombia, Croatia, Ecuador, Georgia, Honduras, Hungary, Ghana, Kyrgyzstan, Latvia, Lithuania, Luxembourg, Macedonia [The former Yugoslav Republic of], Mexico, Nicaragua, Panama, Poland, Romania, Russia, Slovakia, Tajikistan, and Timor-Leste.[107]

States listed by Amnesty International as having either national laws or jurisprudence providing for universal jurisdiction over torture, as of September 2001, include: Algeria, Brazil, Canada, Colombia, Croatia, Ecuador, Georgia, Greece, Guatemala, Honduras, Hungary, Iceland, Ireland, Kazakhstan, Kyrgyzstan, Latvia, Liechtenstein, Lithuania, Luxembourg, Macedonia [The former Yugoslav Republic of], Mexico, Monaco, Mongolia, Panama, Paraguay, Poland, Romania, Russian Federation, Slovakia, Sri Lanka, Tajikistan, Timor-Leste, Turkey, Turkmenistan, UK, Ukraine, Uruguay, and Uzbekistan.[108]

Reporting the results of an updated preliminary survey of legislation around the world in September 2012, Amnesty International concludes that 166 (ie approximately 86%) of the 193 UN Member States have defined one or more core crimes under international law (ie genocide, crimes against humanity, war crimes, and torture) as crimes in their national law, although many of them have failed to define all of these crimes as crimes under national law and in many instances the definitions of such crimes under national law are not consistent with those under international law. Among the 193 UN Member States, 147 States (ie around 76.2% of the total) have provided for universal jurisdiction over one or more of these crimes. Another sixteen States (or 8.29%) can exercise universal jurisdiction over conduct constituting a crime under international law, but only as an ordinary crime under national law. A total of ninety-one States (or approximately 47.1%) have provided for

[105] ibid 19–20. [106] ibid 20. [107] ibid. [108] ibid.

universal jurisdiction over ordinary crimes, even when the conduct does not amount to a crime under international law.[109]

In Amnesty International's assessment, the fact that approximately three-quarters of the UN Member States have authorized their courts to exercise universal jurisdiction over one or more crimes under international law and almost half of the UN Member States have authorized their courts to exercise universal jurisdiction over ordinary crimes constitutes 'evidence of *opinio juris* since such legislation indicates that two branches of each State—the legislature and the executive—believe that such legislation is fully compatible with the State's obligations under international law [and] there are almost no examples of other States making formal objections to the enactment of such criminal legislation'.[110]

In the context of analysing the obligation to extradite or prosecute under customary international law, what matters is national legislation that provides for jurisdiction over an offence *plus* the obligation to extradite or prosecute outside treaty obligations. This is not the case with regard to, for example, El Salvador's Penal Code, Article 10 of which expressly recognizes universal jurisdiction without establishing an exhaustive list of crimes—it applies to all crimes that impair legal rights that are internationally protected by specific agreements or rules of international law, or entail a serious breach of universally recognized human rights.[111] As another example, Ghana's Courts Act of 1993 (Act 459) stipulates in section 56(4), on the criminal jurisdiction of the Courts, that the Courts shall have jurisdiction over any person (whether a citizen or not) for the following offences under Ghana's law: '(a) slave trade or traffic in slaves; (b) piracy; (c) traffic in women or children; ... (e) genocide; ... (h) hijacking; (i) unlawful traffic in narcotics; (j) attacks on any international communications system, canal or submarine cable; ... (m) traffic in obscene publications; ...' Article 1 of the Geneva Conventions Act of Ghana, 2009 (Act 708) stipulates that for the exercise of jurisdiction, indictments may be issued against any person of whatever nationality who commits an offence whether within or outside Ghana.[112] In yet another example, South Africa has 'utilized the principle of universal jurisdiction as set out in the *Princeton Principles on Universal Jurisdiction*'. The serious crimes under international law subject to South Africa's universal jurisdiction include piracy, slavery, war crimes, crimes against peace, crimes against humanity, genocide, and torture.[113] Since there seems to be no extradite-or-prosecute provision in the domestic law of El Salvador, Ghana, or South Africa,

[109] Amnesty International, *Universal Jurisdiction—a Preliminary Survey of Legislation Around the World—2012 Update* (2012) 2, 12, and Annexes I and II.

[110] ibid 2.

[111] Legislative Decree no 1030 (26 Apr 1997), in force 20 Apr 1997. UNGA, 'Report of the Secretary-General on the scope and application of the principle of universal jurisdiction' (2012) UN Doc A/67/116 (28 June 2012) 2–4. The Penal Code was recently amended to harmonize the definition of torture under the Penal Code with that of the Convention against Torture, which El Salvador has ratified (ibid 3–4).

[112] ibid 4–5.

[113] UN Doc A/CN.4/612 § 57. The Princeton Principles on Universal Jurisdiction will be discussed in Chapter 5.

national legislation of these States does *not* count as State practice on the obligation to extradite or prosecute under customary international law.

In contrast, the Penal Code (Law no 11.179) of Argentina, one of the States cited by Belgium in *Belgium v Senegal*, provides for universal jurisdiction over most crimes. Besides, Argentina's extradition law of 1885 stipulates that where Argentina is not bound to hand over the offenders sought for extradition, they shall be tried by Argentine courts and sentenced to the penalties specified by law for crimes or offences committed within Argentina's territory.[114]

The 2003 Criminal Code of Bosnia and Herzegovina, another State cited by Belgium, does impose a mandatory duty to prosecute non-nationals who have committed abroad a crime against a foreign State or other non-nationals, provided that the crime is punishable by no less than five years' imprisonment under the law of the territorial State and extradition to another State has not been granted by Bosnia and Herzegovina.[115] More specifically, Article 12(1)(*c*) of the Criminal Code stipulates that the criminal legislation of Bosnia and Herzegovina shall apply to anyone who, outside its territory, perpetrates '[a] criminal offence Bosnia and Herzegovina is bound to punish according to *the provisions of international law*, international treaties or intergovernmental agreements'.[116]

In Canada, the obligation to extradite or submit the matter for prosecution applies to crimes of universal jurisdiction recognized as such by treaties binding on Canada or by customary international law.[117]

Article 14(4) and (5) of Croatia's Criminal Code of 2003 provides for universal jurisdiction over any offence against values protected by international law, provided that the alleged offender has been arrested in Croatia and has not been extradited.[118] Croatia itself has informed the ILC that its Law on International Legal Assistance in Criminal Matters, in force since 1 July 2005, stipulates that when an extradition from Croatia is not permissible, its national judicial body may, at the request of a foreign judicial body, take over criminal prosecution for an offence committed abroad, even without an extradition agreement with the requesting State provided that an assurance of reciprocity is given by the requesting State.[119]

Even before the adoption of the 1998 Rome Statute of the International Criminal Court, Article 5(3) of Cuba's Penal Code of 1987 provides for universal jurisdiction over, *inter alia*, 'crimes against humanity, human dignity or collective health', provided that the accused is present in Cuban territory and is not extradited to another State.[120]

[114] Amnesty International, *Universal Jurisdiction: The Duty of States to Enact and Implement Legislation* (2001) ch 4 at 10.

[115] Art 12 (1)(c), (4), and (5) of the 2003 Criminal Code of Bosnia and Herzegovina (Amnesty International, *ILC: The Obligation to Extradite or Prosecute* 11–12).

[116] Amnesty International, *ILC: The Obligation to Extradite or Prosecute* 11, emphasis added.

[117] UN Doc A/CN.4/612 §48.

[118] Amnesty International, *Universal Jurisdiction—a Preliminary Survey . . . 2012 Update* 44.

[119] UN Doc A/CN.4/579 §22.

[120] Law no 62 of 29 Dec 1987, quoted in Amnesty International, *ILC . . . International Justice Tool* 16 n 24. See also Amnesty International, *Universal Jurisdiction: A Preliminary Survey of Legislation Around the World* (2011) 44; and Cuba's statement before the Sixth Committee on 6 Nov 2012 (UN Doc A/C.6/67/SR. 22 §§87–90).

By virtue of Article 3 of the 2004 Penal Code of the Democratic Republic of the Congo, any person who, outside the territory of the Democratic Republic of the Congo, is guilty of an offence punishable by at least two months' imprisonment, may be prosecuted in the Democratic Republic of the Congo if not extradited to another State.[121]

Section 8(1) subparagraph 6 of Denmark's Penal Code of 1992 stipulates that acts committed outside Danish territory shall also come within Danish criminal jurisdiction, irrespective of the nationality of the perpetrator where transfer of the accused for legal proceedings in another State is rejected, and provided that according to Danish law the act is punishable with a sentence more severe than one year of imprisonment.[122]

Section 8 of Finland's Penal Code, 39/1889, as amended, provides for the duty to extradite an alleged offender to stand trial for a crime committed outside Finland and punishable by at least six months' imprisonment, provided that the territorial State has requested Finland to prosecute the person in a Finnish court or to extradite the alleged offender to stand trial for the offence, but Finland has denied the extradition request.[123]

Sections 1 and 6–12 of Germany's Code of Crimes Against International Law (or VStGB), in force since 30 June 2002, provide for universal jurisdiction of German courts over genocide, crimes against humanity, and war crimes, even in the absence of a nexus with Germany after the commission of the crimes.[124] Section 7(2) subparagraph 2 of Germany's Penal Code stipulates that German criminal law also applies to any criminal act committed abroad by the offender who was a foreigner at the time of commission of the offence and punishable by the law of the territorial State, provided that he or she is present in Germany and is not extradited, although the offence is an extraditable offence under the German Extradition Act, because a request for extradition is not made or is rejected, or because extradition is not feasible.[125]

By virtue of Article 328M of Malta's Criminal Code of 2006, Maltese courts shall have jurisdiction over acts of terrorism, financing of terrorism, and any ancillary offences where the extradition of the alleged offender to another State for such an offence is refused by Malta.[126]

Article 137(2) of the 2003 Montenegro Criminal Code provides that Montenegro's criminal legislation shall apply to a foreigner who commits abroad, against a foreign

[121] Amnesty International, *Universal Jurisdiction: A Preliminary Survey* 46–7.

[122] Quoted in Luc Reydams, *Universal Jurisdiction: International and Municipal Legal Perspectives* (OUP 2003) 127–28. Only the Minister of Justice of Denmark has the authority to bring a prosecution (ibid 128).

[123] Amnesty International, *ILC: The Obligation to Extradite or Prosecute* 14, and see also *Universal Jurisdiction: A Preliminary Survey* 55.

[124] Máximo Langer, 'The Diplomacy of Universal Jurisdiction: The Political Branches and the Transnational Prosecution of International Crimes' (2011) 105 AJIL 1, 11.

[125] Reydams, *Universal Jurisdiction* 143–44. See also Amnesty International, *Universal Jurisdiction: A Preliminary Survey* 57–58.

[126] Amnesty International, *ILC: The Obligation to Extradite or Prosecute* 15.

State or another foreigner, a criminal offence punishable under the law of the territorial State by at least five years' imprisonment, provided that the alleged offender is present in Montenegro but is not extradited to another State.[127]

Article 20 of Panama's Penal Code of 2007 stipulates that all crimes committed by a foreigner abroad, if such foreigner is not extradited, shall be subject to investigation and prosecution under Panama's criminal legislation.[128]

Article 5 of Portugal's Penal Code of 2006 imposes on Portugal the duty to prosecute if a foreigner is present within Portugal and the extradition or apprehension under an European arrest order is not granted by Portugal. The Code applies to all crimes, except those provided in the Act implementing the 1998 Rome Statute of the ICC in which case the alleged offender shall be surrendered to the ICC.[129]

The Swiss Penal Code, as amended on 18 June 2010 and in force as of 1 January 2011, stipulates in Article 264*m* that a person who commits an act of genocide, crime against humanity, or war crime while abroad is guilty of an offence if he is in Switzerland and is not extradited to another State or delivered to an international criminal court whose jurisdiction is recognized by Switzerland. Where neither the victim nor the perpetrator of the offence committed abroad is a Swiss national, the prosecution, with the exception of measures to secure evidence, may be abandoned or may be dispensed with if: (1) a foreign authority or an international criminal court whose jurisdiction is recognized by Switzerland is prosecuting the offence and the suspect is extradited or surrendered to the court; or (2) the suspect is no longer present in Switzerland and is not expected to return there. Moreover, where the person has been acquitted of the same offence abroad in a legally binding judgment or where the sentence imposed abroad has been served, pardoned, or prescribed (*prescrite*), such person shall not be liable to further prosecution in Switzerland for the offence unless the acquittal, or pardon, or application of the time limits to execution of the sentence abroad has the objective of unjustifiably shielding the offender from punishment. Separately, the 2009 Swiss Military Penal Code, Article 10 (1*bis*), provides for universal jurisdiction over certain war crimes committed abroad if the alleged offender is found in Switzerland and is not extradited or surrendered to an international criminal court whose jurisdiction is recognized by Switzerland.[130]

Belgium itself exercises universal jurisdiction over foreign nationals who have committed any of the following offences outside Belgium: sexual offences against minors, exploitation of prostitution or trafficking in persons; female genital mutilation; failure to comply with some of the rules governing activities of marriage brokers; acts of corruption; acts of marine pollution; counterfeiting; serious violations of international humanitarian law; acts of terrorism; and any offence that, under international treaty law or international customary law, must be prosecuted irrespective of the State in which it was committed and of the nationality of its

[127] Reydams, *Universal Jurisdiction* 15. See also Amnesty International *Universal Jurisdiction: A Preliminary Survey* 82–83.

[128] Amnesty International, *ILC: The Obligation to Extradite or Prosecute* 15.

[129] ibid 16, and see also *Universal Jurisdiction: A Preliminary Survey* 93.

[130] Amnesty International, *Universal Jurisdiction: A Preliminary Survey* 109.

perpetrator(s) and even where Belgium has not refused an extradition request.[131] However, on 5 August 2003, Belgium enacted the Law relating to Serious Violations of International Humanitarian Law, Article 27 of which amends the Criminal Code, the Code of Criminal Procedure, and the Judiciary Act, to the effect that only persons who have become Belgium nationals or residents after their commission of the offence can be prosecuted on the basis of universal jurisdiction for genocide, crimes against humanity, and war crimes.

Latvia and Slovenia each declares, without providing details, that it has concluded a number of bilateral treaties with different States that include the obligation to extradite or prosecute.[132]

Many States not listed by Belgium in its reply to Judge Greenwood's first question also have legislation authorizing the exercise of universal jurisdiction where extradition is denied.

By virtue of Article 65(1) subparagraph 2 of Austria's Penal Code of 1975, Austrian courts may exercise universal jurisdiction, beyond treaty obligations, over offences committed abroad, provided that (1) the acts are also punishable where they are committed, (2) the suspect, if not an Austrian national, is present in Austrian territory, and (3) the suspect cannot be extradited to the territorial State for reasons other than the nature and characteristics of the offence (that is, either because of the absence of an extradition request from the territorial State even though Austria has offered extradition, or because of the absence of cooperation in criminal matters between Austria and the territorial State).[133] The offences need not be crimes under international law such as genocide, crimes against humanity or war crimes.[134] However, under Article 9(3) of Austria's Statute on Extradition and Mutual Assistance in Criminal Matters of 1979, the public prosecutor may refrain from prosecuting an offence if Austria's criminal jurisdiction is based only on Article 65(1) subparagraph 2 and it is not against public interest to refrain from prosecution, in particular when punishment would not deter the commission of offences by others, or when a thorough investigation is not possible due to the lack of cooperation from the territorial State.[135]

Pursuant to Article 4 of Cabo Verde's Penal Code of 2003, Cabo Verde's national law shall apply to crimes under international law committed abroad when the alleged offender is present in any territory under Cabo Verde's jurisdiction and Cabo Verde does not grant extradition.[136]

Article 16 of Colombia's Penal Code (Law 599/2000 of 24 July 2000) stipulates that the Code shall apply to foreigners present in Colombia who have committed a

[131] UN Doc A/CN.4/612, §§21–23. See also Amnesty International, ibid 30–31.

[132] UN Doc A/CN.4/579/Add 1 §15 (Slovenia) and UN Doc A/CN.4/579/Add 2 §10 (Latvia).

[133] Amnesty International, *Universal Jurisdiction: The Duty of States* ch 6 at 5–6. See also UN Doc A/CN.4/579 §37, and Reydams, *Universal Jurisdiction* 96–97.

[134] eg in *Public Prosecutor v Milan T* (1963) 28 ILR 341, the Austrian Supreme Court upheld the prosecution of the defendant, a Yugoslav national, for the offence of fraud committed in Yugoslavia after Austria had denied his extradition to Yugoslavia on human rights grounds (Judgment of 29 May 1958).

[135] Reydams, *Universal Jurisdiction* 96–97 and n 10.

[136] Amnesty International, *ILC: The Obligation to Extradite or Prosecute* 12.

crime abroad against another foreigner, provided that the crime in question is not political, that it is punishable by at least three years' imprisonment, and that an extradition from Colombia is not granted.[137]

Article 10 of Italy's Penal Code of 1930, as amended, provides for universal jurisdiction over crimes committed abroad by a foreigner against another foreigner, if the Minister of Justice demands the prosecution of the offender, the offender is present in Italy, the crime is punishable by at least three years' imprisonment, and the offender is not extradited by Italy.[138]

Lebanon has declared unequivocally that 'the Lebanese State is bound by the principle "extradite or prosecute" (*aut dedere aut judicare*) with respect to both Lebanese nationals and any alien or stateless person in Lebanon who has committed criminal acts abroad'.[139] A foreigner, a request for whose extradition is refused on the grounds of the absence of the legal requirements provided for in relevant international agreements, or, in the absence of any such agreement, in Lebanese domestic law, must be arraigned before the Lebanese courts for trial in accordance with Article 23 of the Lebanese Penal Code of 1943, as amended.[140]

Article 119(2) of the former Yugoslav Republic of Macedonia's Criminal Code of 1996 stipulates an 'extradite or prosecute' obligation for all crimes committed abroad by a foreigner against another foreigner found in the former Yugoslav Republic of Macedonia and punishable by at least five years' imprisonment.[141]

Pursuant to Article 3 of Peru's Penal Code of 1991, Peru's national criminal legislation may apply to foreigners when a request for extradition is denied by Peru.[142] Article 78 of Peru's Code of Military and Police Justice of 1 September 2010 provides for universal jurisdiction over war crimes in international as well as non-international armed conflict.[143]

By virtue of Article 9 of Serbia's Criminal Code 2005, courts may exercise jurisdiction over any foreigner who commits a crime abroad against another foreigner which is punishable by at least five years' imprisonment under the law of the territorial State, if the foreign offender is found in Serbia and is not extradited.[144] The *aut dedere aut judicare* principle is 'fully reflected' in cases of non-Serbian nationals who commit an offence abroad and Serbia denies requests for their extradition.[145] In such cases, 'there is the obligation to prosecute [on the basis of universal principle] the alleged offender in Serbia for the same offence under the terms of either the national legislation or an international treaty which has precedence over the national legislation'.[146] Serbia has concluded bilateral treaties containing this obligation with several States.[147]

Article 8 of Somalia's Penal Code of 1964 provides for universal jurisdiction over an offence committed by a foreigner against another foreigner abroad, provided that

[137] ibid and also Amnesty International, *Universal Jurisdiction: A Preliminary Survey* 41.
[138] Amnesty International, *Universal Jurisdiction: A Preliminary Survey* 66.
[139] UN Doc A/CN.4/579/Add 1 §35.
[140] ibid §§33–34.
[141] Amnesty International, *ILC: The Obligation to Extradite or Prosecute* 14–15.
[142] ibid 15–16.
[143] Legislative Decree 1094, cited ibid 17.
[144] Amnesty International, *Universal Jurisdiction: A Preliminary Survey* 101.
[145] UN Doc A/CN.4/579/Add 2 §§45–46.
[146] ibid §§15 and 45, and see also §39.
[147] ibid §§13–14. See also Amnesty International, *ILC: The Obligation to Extradite or Prosecute* 16.

it is a crime in the territorial State, that the offender is found in Somalia when the complaint is made, and that the offender is not extradited to the territorial State or the State of nationality of the offender.[148]

Sweden can exercise universal jurisdiction over 'international crimes' which are not part of Swedish national law, such as crimes against humanity, provided that the offence in question falls within the scope of the national criminal law of Sweden and the least severe punishment for the crime in Swedish law is imprisonment for four years or more. In addition, prosecution over 'crimes against international law' committed outside Sweden is permissible if authorized by the Swedish Government. A 'crime against international law' is defined as 'a serious violation of a treaty or agreement with a foreign power or an infraction of a generally recognized principle or tenet relating to international humanitarian law concerning armed conflicts'.[149]

National law of several States, mainly with a civil law tradition, prohibits extradition of nationals.[150]

An authoritative commentary to the grave breaches regime under the 1949 Geneva Conventions explains that as most national laws and international conventions on extradition prohibit the extradition of nationals of the State detaining them, the State must bring the said nationals before its own courts for prosecution.[151] As the four Geneva Conventions of 1949 are universally ratified or acceded to by all States of the international community, it can be concluded that as least in relation to the grave breaches regime, all States are bound to prosecute its nationals suspected of committing a grave breach or hand them over to another State which has made out a prima facie case.

Beyond the grave breaches regime under the four Geneva Conventions, the practice of States which do not extradite their nationals is quite extensive and virtually uniform in the one direction of prosecuting such nationals before the courts of the State of the nationality of the offenders in lieu of extradition. This conclusion is substantiated by the following examples of State practice which is both representative and widespread.

A number of these States have concluded bilateral treaties with other States containing an obligation to prosecute the alleged offender when his or her extradition is refused by the requested State solely on the basis of the nationality of the said person. This is in line with a long-established practice, as authorized for example by Article 345 of the Bustamante Code of International Private Law, adopted at the Sixth International Conference of American States in Havana in 1928,[152] Article 8 of the International Convention for the Suppression of Counterfeiting

[148] Amnesty International, *Universal Jurisdiction: A Preliminary Survey* 104.

[149] Swedish Criminal Code, ch 2 section 3.6 and ch 22 section 6. See also UN Doc A/CN.4/579/Add 1 §§51–63.

[150] See further Zsuzsanna Deen-Racsmány, 'A New Passport to Impunity? Non-Extradition of Naturalized Citizens versus Criminal Justice' (2004) 2 J Int'l Crim Justice 761.

[151] Jean S Pictet (ed), *The Geneva Conventions of 12 August 1949: Commentary*, vol 3 (ICRC 1960) 623.

[152] OAS, Law & Treaty Ser No 34. It provides that States Parties to the Code are not obliged to extradite their nationals, but the nation that does not extradite one of its nationals is obliged to prosecute that national.

Currency of 1929,[153] and Article 6 paragraph 2 of the 1957 European Convention on Extradition.[154] Such is the case of Austria, in its bilateral extradition treaties with Canada and with the USA.[155] So is the case of Argentina, in its bilateral extradition treaties with Australia, Belgium, Bolivia, Brazil, Colombia, Italy, Netherlands, Paraguay, Republic of Korea, Spain, and Switzerland.[156]

Article 27 of the Political Constitution of Guatemala stipulates that extradition is governed by the provisions of international treaties binding on Guatemala. A number of such treaties contain the *aut dedere aut judicare* clause. The aforesaid Article 27 also prohibits extradition of Guatemalan nationals in the case of political offences, but makes an exception for crimes against humanity or crimes against international law, in accordance with treaties binding on Guatemala.[157]

By virtue of Article 7 of Monaco's Law 1222 (28 December 1999) on extradition, the principle *aut dedere aut judicare* is implemented when extradition is refused solely on the basis of the nationality of the alleged offender.[158] Monaco has concluded bilateral extradition treaties that provide for the possibility of prosecuting a person if extradition is refused on the ground of nationality with Italy, Australia, France, and Belgium, among others.[159] When extradition is refused on other grounds, the principle *aut dedere aut judicare* will be applied only if the Courts of Monaco have jurisdiction on foreigners for offences committed abroad.[160] Most of these offences are not based on universal jurisdiction, except for the offence of torture and a crime or offence against another alien if the alien offender is found in Monaco in the possession of items acquired through the commission of the crime/offence.[161]

Ireland's Extradition Act 1965, as amended, governs extradition with States other than Member States of the European Union. The obligation to extradite is paramount, and recourse to prosecution in Ireland is considered only where extradition of an Irish citizen is not permitted because of the absence of reciprocal arrangements.

[153] 112 LNTS 371. Art 8 of the 1929 Convention stipulates: '[I]n countries where the principle of the extradition of nationals is not recognized, nationals who have returned to the territory of their own country after the commission abroad of an offence in Article 3 should be punishable in the same manner as if the offence had been committed in their own country, even in a case where the offender has acquired his nationality after the commission of the offence.'

[154] 'If the requested Party does not extradite its national, it shall at the request of the requesting Party submit the case to its competent authorities in order that proceedings may be taken if they are considered appropriate' (ETS 24). Art 4 of the United Nations Model Extradition Treaty, adopted by UN General Assembly resolution 45/116 of 14 Dec 1990 (UN Doc A/RES/45/116), stipulates eight optional grounds for refusal to extradite. The first ground is: '(a) If the person whose extradition is requested is a national of the requested State. Where extradition is refused on this ground, the requested State shall, if the other State so requests, submit the case to its competent authorities with a view to taking appropriate action against the person in respect of the offence for which extradition had been requested.'

[155] UN Doc A/CN.4/579 §§5–6. It is interesting to note, however, that Canada, one of the States cited by Austria, denies categorically that any of the fifty-one bilateral treaties to which Canada is party contains an obligation to extradite or submit the matter for prosecution (UN Doc A/CN.4/612 §43). But see Canada's earlier statement in Doc A/CN.4/612 §§ 39–40, which recognizes the importance to the international community of the obligation to prosecute under multilateral as well as bilateral treaties where the requested State refuses to extradite its own nationals.

[156] UN Doc A/CN.4/612 §7.

[157] UN Doc A/CN.4/599 §§13–18.

[158] UN Doc A/CN.4/579 §25.

[159] ibid §12.

[160] ibid §27.

[161] Arts 8 and 9, Code of Penal Procedure of Monaco.

Nonetheless, in practice Ireland has not refused extradition requests on the grounds of Irish nationality.[162]

Article 5(1)(h) of Malta's Criminal Code imposes on Malta a duty to prosecute an alleged offender where the extradition request has been denied by Malta because of the suspect's Maltese nationality or because the offence incurs the death penalty in the requesting State.[163]

As previously mentioned, both Lebanese law and Serbian law authorize the exercise of universal jurisdiction as well as contain an extradite-or-prosecute provision. As Lebanon does not extradite its own nationals, it tries Lebanese nationals before Lebanese courts for their crimes committed abroad against foreigners in accordance with the jurisdiction *ratione personae* provided in Article 20 of its Penal Code.[164] As for nationals of Serbia who cannot be extradited to another State, they may be prosecuted in Serbia for offences committed abroad under the terms of the national legislation or relevant treaties.[165]

By virtue of the relevant provisions of the Russian Criminal Code of 1996 as amended, Russia exercises universal jurisdiction over those crimes in respect of which it is bound by an international treaty to exercise criminal jurisdiction. Such crimes include 'crimes against the peace and security of mankind'; a crime of aggression; offences related to weapons of mass destruction; the use of prohibited means of waging war; genocide, ecocide; mercenary activities; attacks on internationally protected persons or institutions; hostage taking; hijacking of an aircraft, sea vessel, or railway train; and piracy.[166] However, under other relevant laws, if Russia refuses to extradite a person to a foreign State and has jurisdiction over the said person (including on the basis of universal jurisdiction), Russia's competent authorities seek the case file from the requesting State with a view to his prosecution in Russia. This applies also to cases where the persons sought for extradition are Russian nationals, whose extradition to another State is prohibited by Russian law.[167]

Beyond the context of States prosecuting their respective nationals in lieu of extradition, is national law of States virtually uniform in imposing the obligation to extradite or prosecute on the relevant national authorities? The information on national law of States all over the world shows that there are at least fifteen European States, five South American States (including Cuba), three African States, one Asian State, and one North American State that have provided for their courts to possess universal jurisdiction over, as well as for the relevant authorities to prosecute, offenders who are not extradited to another State, irrespective of the nationality of these offenders. The total number of twenty-five States from five continents is much more representative and widespread for the purpose of proving State practice than the total number States cited by the ICJ in *Germany v Italy* as evidence of State practice in that particular ICJ Judgment.

[162] UN Doc A/CN.4/579/Add 1 §26.
[163] Amnesty International, *ILC: The Obligation to Extradite or Prosecute* 15.
[164] UN Doc A/CN.4/579/Add 1 §§29–30.
[165] UN Doc A/CN.4/579/Add 2 §16.
[166] UN Doc A/CN.4/599 §41.
[167] ibid §§42–44.

In terms of the types of offence or crime covered by the obligation to extradite or prosecute under national law, there is divergence in practice. For instance, Austria explains that its legislation does not distinguish between certain categories of crime or offence, since all crimes and offences punishable under the Austrian Penal Code are subject to this obligation stipulated in sections 64 and 65 of the Austrian Penal Code.[168] Chile says there are no limitations in its legislation and practice that would prevent the application of the principle of the obligation *aut dedere aut judicare* to certain crimes or offences.[169] Slovenia applies the principle *aut dedere aut judicare* to all crimes proscribed in Slovenia's Penal Code of 2005, including crimes under international humanitarian law and relevant treaties binding on Slovenia; namely, genocide, crimes against the civilian population, crimes against the wounded and the sick, war crimes against prisoners of war, war crimes of using unlawful weapons, unlawful killing and wounding of the enemy, maltreatment of the sick and wounded and of prisoners of war, abuse of international symbols, trafficking in persons, international terrorism, endangering persons under international protection, taking of hostages, unlawful manufacturing and trade with narcotic drugs, and enabling opportunity for consumption of narcotic drugs, among others.[170] Article 55 of Tunisia's Act no 75 of 2003 (10 December 2003) gives Tunisian courts universal jurisdiction over terrorist crimes committed abroad by a stateless person or a foreigner present on Tunisian territory whose extradition has not been requested by the competent foreign authorities prior to the rendering of a final judgment against him by the competent Tunisian court.[171] Under Serbia's law, the obligation to extradite or prosecute on the basis of universal jurisdiction applies to all crimes considered as offences under the law of the requesting State and punishable by at least five years' imprisonment as well as offences criminalized 'under the principles of law recognized by the international community'.[172] In Canada, the obligation to extradite or prosecute applies to crimes of universal jurisdiction where provided by treaties binding on Canada. Canada also has 'the capacity to extradite or prosecute for non-treaty based crimes of universal jurisdiction'.[173]

Most States have national legislation that implements treaty obligations. For example, in Poland, the obligation *aut dedere aut judicare* applies to any crimes or offences covered by international treaties binding on Poland.[174] As another example, Mauritius's Convention for the Suppression of the Financing of Terrorism Act 2003, enacted to implement Mauritius's obligations under the said Convention, provides for the application of the principle *aut dedere aut judicare* to offences of financing terrorism.[175]

The above information reveals that, beyond the context of prosecution of nationals in lieu of their extradition and the context of implementing treaty obligations, national legislation of eleven States provides for the obligation to extradite or prosecute all crimes without any distinction. National legislation of eight States provides for

[168] UN Doc A/CN.4/579 §45.
[169] UN Doc A/CN.4/579/Add 1 §77.
[170] ibid §80.
[171] ibid §66.
[172] UN Doc A/CN.4/579/Add 2 §44.
[173] UN Doc A/CN.4/612 §36.
[174] UN Doc A/CN.4/579/Add 4 §8.
[175] Doc A/CN.4/599 §24.

the obligation to extradite or prosecute crimes punishable by a minimum term of imprisonment ranging from two months to five years. National legislation of one State provides for the obligation to extradite or prosecute offences of terrorism. National legislation of five States provides for the obligation to extradite or prosecute crimes against international law, such as crimes against humanity. Finally, national legislation of three States applies the obligation to extradite or prosecute to crimes of universal jurisdiction.

(2) *Judgments of national courts faced with the question*

Belgium replied to Judge Greenwood's second question that, to its knowledge, there were 'some half-dozen cases' in which the courts of certain States have tried non-nationals for crimes against humanity or war crimes committed in an armed conflict not of an international character committed outside the forum State and neither the victims nor the alleged perpetrators were nationals of the forum State. Belgium cited the following cases: decision 53/1993 of the Constitutional Court of Hungary dated 13 October 1993, judgment of 18 April 1997 of Switzerland's Division 1 Military Tribunal (Lausanne) in *Grabez*, judgment of 27 April 2001 of the Swiss Military Court of Cassation in *Niyonteze*, judgment of the Netherlands' Supreme Court in *Knesevic* dated 11 November 1997, judgment of the Netherlands' Court of Appeal at The Hague on 29 January 2007 and judgment of the Netherlands' Supreme Court on 8 July 2008 in *Habibullah Jalalzoy and Heshamuddin Hesam*, judgment of Canada's Superior Court (Criminal Division) in *Munyaneza* dated 22 May 2009, judgment of Belgium's *Cour d'assises* in *Ntezimana* et al of 8–9 June 2001 and in *Nzabonimana* et al of 29 June 2005, judgment of the French Court of Cessation in *Munyeshiaka* dated 6 January 1998, judgment of the South African Constitutional Court in *Basson* dated 10 March 2004, and judgment of the Central African Republic's Court of Cessation in *Patassé* et al dated 11 April 2006.[176]

There are many more cases of exercise of universal jurisdiction by national courts which were not included by Belgium in the above list.

In late 2009, a court in Brussels, Belgium, sentenced a Rwandan national named *Ephrem Nkezabera*, widely known as the 'genocide banker', to thirty years' imprisonment for war crimes including murders and rapes during Rwanda's national upheavals in 1994.[177]

Finland's court of appeal in Helsinki upheld, on 30 March 2012, the district court's decision convicting *François Bazaramba*, a Rwandan refugee, of genocide in

[176] Supplementary replies from Belgium, <http://www.icj-cij.org/files/case-related/144/17640.pdf>; Oral Proceedings in *Belgium v Senegal* (19 Mar 2012), ICJ Doc 2012/6, 26–27 [24] and accompanying footnotes. See also UN Doc A/CN.4/599 §32 (judicial practice in the Netherlands). For Special Rapporteur Galicki's summary of the information provided by States on judicial practice reflecting the application of the obligation to extradite or prosecute, see his third report (UN Doc A/CN.4/603) §§84–89.

[177] <http://www.abc.net.au/news/2009-12-02/court-jails-rwandas-genocide-banker/1165298>, accessed 14 November 2017.

Rwanda, his country of origin, and sentencing him to life imprisonment.[178] On 10 December 2012, Finland's Supreme Court, without giving any reason, declined to hear Bazaramba's appeal.

In Germany, the court in *Prosecutor v Dost* convicted a Dutch national for selling narcotic drugs in the Netherlands.[179] In 1997 the Higher Regional Court at Düsseldorf convicted *Nikola Jorgíc*, a Bosnian Serb, of acting with intent to commit 11 counts of genocide, murder of twenty-two people and dangerous assault and deprivation of liberty in Bosnia in 1992. The Court found jurisdiction over the case pursuant to Article 6 no 1 of the German Criminal Code. In the Court's reasoning, there was a legitimate link for criminal prosecution in Germany, as this was in accordance with Germany's military and humanitarian missions in Bosnia and Herzegovina and Jorgíc had resided in Germany for more than twenty years and had been arrested there. In addition, international law did not prohibit German courts from trying the case. In particular, neither Article VI of the Genocide Convention nor Article 9 of the ICTY Statute excluded the jurisdiction of German courts over acts of genocide committed outside Germany by a foreigner against foreigners. His conviction and life sentence were affirmed on appeal by the Federal Court of Justice.[180] In 2000, the Federal Constitutional Court dismissed Jorgíc's constitutional challenge, *inter alia*, that customary international law and Article VI of the Genocide Convention prohibited the exercise of universal jurisdiction over genocide.[181]

In May 2011, the Munich District Court, after seven months of trial of 90-year-old *Ivan (John) Demjanjuk*, convicted and sentenced him to five years' imprisonment for being an accomplice in mass murder of 27,900 persons in the Sobibor extermination camp in Poland in 1943. It was one of the first times in German legal history that a non-German national stood trial for the murder during the Third Reich of non-German nationals outside Germany. The Munich District Court's jurisdiction was based on the premises that the accused had been a German civil servant.[182] He died in March 2012 while awaiting his appeal to be heard by the German Appellate Court.

In January 2011, a trial commenced in Frankfurt, Germany, against *Onesphore Rwabukombe*, a former mayor in Rwanda, on charges of genocide, murder, incitement to genocide, and incitement to murder committed in Rwanda in 1994. In December 2015, he was convicted by the Higher Regional Court of Frankfurt of committing genocide and sentenced to life imprisonment.[183]

[178] UNGA, 'Report of the Secretary-General on the scope and application of the principle of universal jurisdiction' (2012) UN Doc A/67/116 (28 June 2012) 7 [28].

[179] Judgment of 20 Oct 1976 (74 ILR 166). Cited in Amnesty International, *ILC . . . International Justice Tool* 34.

[180] Judgment of 26 Sept 1997 and Appeal Judgment of 30 Apr 1999 (case no 3 StR 215/98), respectively. Cited in Amnesty International, *ILC . . . International Justice Tool* 34. The reasoning of the Düsseldorf Court was affirmed by the European Court of Human Rights in *Jorgíc v Germany* (no 74613/01, ECHR 2007-III).

[181] Judgment of 12 Dec 2000 (case no 2 BvR 1290/99). Cited in Amnesty International, *ILC . . . International Justice Tool* 34.

[182] Karin Matussek, 'Demjanjuk Convicted of Helping Nazis to Murder Jews During the Holocaust', *Bloomberg* (New York 12 May 2011).

[183] 'Onesphore Rwabukombe gets life sentence in Germany over Genocide', *New Times* (Kigali 29 Dec 2015).

In May 2011, a court in Stuttgart, Germany, started the trial of *Ignace Murwanashyaka* and *Straton Musoni*, accused of thirty-nine counts of war crimes and twenty-six counts of crimes against humanity committed in eastern Congo between 2008 and 2009. In September 2015 the Higher Regional Court of Stuttgart convicted the former of four counts of aiding and abetting war crimes and of leading a foreign terrorist organization. He was sentenced to thirteen years' imprisonment. The Court acquitted Musoni of war crimes and crimes against humanity for lack of sufficient evidence, but convicted him of leading a foreign terrorist organization and sentenced him to eight years' imprisonment. This was the first judgment in Germany under a law that allows Germany to exercise universal jurisdiction over war crimes, crimes against humanity, and genocide.[184]

In the Netherlands, *Sebastien Nzapali*, a national of the Democratic Republic of the Congo, was convicted in April 2004 for torture committed in the then Zaire.[185] In July 2011 the Netherlands' Appeals Court sentenced *Joseph Mpambara*, a Rwandan national, to life imprisonment for the crime of genocide, war crimes, and torture committed in Rwanda in 1994. He had been arrested in Amsterdam in 2006, after first arriving in the Netherlands in 1998 with a fake passport and seeking asylum.

In April 2005, a Spanish court convicted *Adolfo Francisco Scilingo*, a former Argentine naval officer, of crimes against humanity, including extrajudicial execution, committed against Argentines in Argentina. In July 2007, the Spanish Supreme Court increased his sentence but changed his conviction to the crimes of murder and unlawful detention, which constituted crimes against humanity according to international law.[186]

As early as 1948, a Swiss military court exercised universal jurisdiction to convict *Ernst Haldiman*, a German national, for his participation as a member of an SS commando unit in a massacre in Belgium during the Second World War.[187]

Jacques Mungwarere, a Rwandan refugee living in Canada since 1998, was arrested in Canada in November 2009 in cooperation with Rwanda's Genocide Fugitive Tracking Unit. He was charged with one count of genocide and one count of crime against humanity in Rwanda in 1994. He was acquitted of all charges in July 2013 as the Prosecution had failed to prove his guilt beyond any reasonable doubt.[188] The prosecution, however, shows the willingness of Canada to exercise universal jurisdiction over these crimes.

Despite such impressively widespread practice of national courts exercising universal jurisdiction over different categories of crime, what really matters in the analysis of the obligation to extradite or prosecute is national court decisions specifically

[184] 'Rwandan rebel leaders jailed in Germany for war crimes', *Guardian* (London 28 Sept 2015).

[185] Judgment of the Rotterdam District Court, 7 Apr 2004. Cited in Amnesty International, *ILC . . . International Justice Tool* 38.

[186] Cited ibid 41. [187] ibid 45.

[188] 'Canadian court acquits refugee Jacques Mungwarere of genocide in Rwanda' *Canadian Press* (Toronto 5 July 2015).

addressing the obligation to extradite or prosecute. The judgments must not be based on implementation of treaty obligations, such as in the following decisions.

In *The Prosecution v Refik Saric*, Denmark's Eastern Division of High Court (Third Chamber), on 25 November 1994, convicted Refik Saric, a Croat refugee living in Denmark, for war crimes committed in a Croat-administered prison camp in Bosnia from 1 July to 20 August 1993. His offences of committing bodily harm of an especially grievous, brutal, or dangerous nature and ill-treatment were proscribed under Sections 245–46 of the Danish Penal Code. Saric was sentenced to eight years' imprisonment and permanently barred from entering Danish territory thereafter. This conviction and sentence were affirmed by the Danish Supreme Court on 15 August 1995.[189] The Danish Court asserted jurisdiction on the basis of the extradite-or-prosecute provision of Section 8(1) subparagraph 5 of the Danish Penal Code which implements the grave breaches regime under Articles 129 and 130 and Articles 146 and 147, respectively, of the Third and Fourth Geneva Conventions of 12 August 1949 relating to the protection of victims of war.[190] However, in *Lee Urzua* et al *v Pinochet*, the Danish Director of Public Prosecution declined to prosecute former Chilean President Pinochet for alleged persecution and torture in Chile upon complaints by Chilean exiles living in Denmark. In his reasoning, Danish jurisdiction on the basis of the extradite-or-prosecute provision of Section 8(1) subparagraph 5 of the Danish Penal Code which, in this case, implemented the Convention against Torture, only existed if the suspect was present in Denmark. He also added that if the crimes for which Pinochet was accused of amounted to genocide, Article VI of the Genocide Convention only provided for the jurisdiction of the territorial State or an international tribunal.[191]

In 1997, the Bavarian Higher Regional Court convicted *Novislav Dijacić* of aiding murder and attempted murder, amounting to grave breaches of the Fourth Geneva Convention of 1949.[192]

On 21 February 2001, the German Federal Court of Justice upheld the judgment of the Düsseldorf Higher Regional Court of 29 November 1999 in *Maksim Sokolović*, which sentenced Sokolović, a Bosnian Serb, to nine years' imprisonment for having taken part in 1992 in genocide and other crimes on the territory of the former Yugoslavia. The Federal Court of Justice affirmed that the application of the principle of universal jurisdiction was justified in cases of genocide and grave breaches of the Fourth Geneva Convention of 1949. The Federal Court of Justice left open as to whether it was necessary to establish a nexus with Germany for prosecution to be undertaken in Germany, although it preferred to consider it unnecessary to demonstrate such a nexus where the jurisdiction of German courts was founded on an international treaty binding on Germany and which obliged it to take steps to prosecute.[193] This precedent was followed in

[189] <http://www.internationalcrimesdatabase.org/Case/743>, accessed 17 November 2017.
[190] Reydams, *Universal Jurisdiction* 128–29.
[191] Opinion of 3 Dec 1998, case no 555/98, cited in Reydams, ibid 129.
[192] Judgment of 23 May 1997, cited in Amnesty International, *ILC… International Justice Tool* 35.
[193] *Bundesgerichtshof*, Decision of the Third Criminal Senate of 21 Feb 2001, 3 StR 372/00.

Kjuradj Kusljić.[194] It may be recalled that the 1948 Genocide Convention does not impose the obligation to extradite or prosecute. The fact that some national courts err in interpreting the Genocide Convention as imposing a treaty obligation *aut dedere aut judicare* somehow negates any presumption that these courts apply *aut dedere aut judicare* as a rule of customary international law, and not treaty law.

France's *Cour de Cassation* (Criminal Law Chamber) held in the *Disparu de Beach* case that the relevant Articles of the French Criminal Code authorize French courts to prosecute and try any person, if in France, who, outside France's territory, commits torture as defined in Article 1 of the Convention against Torture of 1984 to which France is party.[195]

The High Court of Colombo, Sri Lanka, in *Ekanayake v Attorney General* convicted a Sri Lankan national under the Offences against Aircraft Act no 24 of 1982 for having hijacked an Alitalia aircraft from New Delhi, India, to Bangkok, Thailand, demanding a ransom from the Italian Government. The Supreme Court of Sri Lanka, in dismissing the defendant's appeal challenging the High Court's jurisdiction, took into consideration the following international instruments containing the obligation to extradite or prosecute to which Sri Lanka had become party and which were specifically mentioned in the preamble to the Act of 1982: the 1963 Tokyo Convention on Offences and Certain Other Acts Committed on Board Aircraft; the 1970 Hague Convention for the Suppression of Unlawful Seizure of Aircraft; and the 1971 Montreal Convention for the Suppression of Unlawful Acts against the Safety of Civil Aviation.[196]

In the United Kingdom, the nature of the obligation to extradite or prosecute was discussed in the litigation surrounding the extradition of General *Pinochet* of Chile. The UK applies the obligation to extradite or prosecute in accordance with its national legislation enacted to implement multilateral conventions containing such an obligation to which the UK is a State Party. The UK thus extradites individuals, including British nationals, to other States to stand trial for, for example, terrorism offences, provided that the extradition is not barred for other reasons. The UK has also prosecuted those allegedly responsible for torture and hostage taking elsewhere.[197]

[194] Judgment, Federal Supreme Court, 21 Feb 2001 [BGH 3 StR 244/00—*Bechluss v 21. February 01*]. See Amnesty International, *GERMANY: End Impunity through Universal Jurisdiction*, No Safe Haven Series 3 (2008) 98. The reasoning that the Genocide Convention imposed an obligation to extradite or prosecute departed from the one used by German courts in the earlier case of *Nikola Jorgíc* (no 74613/01, ECHR 2007-III) .

[195] 04-87.245, Arrêt numéro 7513 du 10 janvier 2007. Cited in Amnesty International, *ILC: The Obligation to Extradite or Prosecute* 25.

[196] [1988] 1 Sri Lanka Law Rep 46.

[197] UN Doc A/CN.4/579 §§42–44. However, in *T v Secretary of State for the Home Department* [1996] AC 742, a case concerning asylum (and not extradition) of an alleged Algerian terrorist, Lord Mustill states, obiter: 'Another weapon in the fight against terrorism has been the revival of the doctrine, propounded by Hugo Grotius (De Jure Belli ac Pacis lib 2, c 21, ss 3 and 4), "*aut dedere aut punire*", that states are under an international obligation either to return criminals (or at least certain types of criminal) to the place where their crimes were committed, or to prosecute and if appropriate punish them locally. This idea was to a limited extent a feature of the 1937 League of Nations Convention (arts 9 and

For example, in *Faryadi Sarwar Zardad*, a former Afghan armed group leader, was convicted on 18 July 2005 of torture and hostage taking in Afghanistan.[198]

There is no known judicial decisions in the United States which apply the obligation to extradite or prosecute except as provided in conventions to which the United States is a party, as in *United States v Yousef*,[199] where the US Court of Appeals for the Second Circuit held that the 1971 Montreal Convention creates 'a jurisdictional agreement among contracting States to extradite or prosecute offenders who commit the acts proscribed by the treaty'.[200] In US law,[201] the 1996 amendments to the existing US extradition law permit an exception, allowing the USA to extradite, in the exercise of comity and in the absence of a treaty, persons other than US citizens, nationals, or permanent residents who have committed crimes of violence against US nationals abroad.[202] The Fifth Circuit Court of Appeals has upheld the constitutionality of these amendments on the grounds that 'although some authorization by law is necessary for the Executive to extradite, neither the Constitution's text nor . . . [relevant jurisprudence] require that the authorization comes in the form of a treaty'.[203] The US Government is not precluded from trying to apply *aut dedere aut judicare* to other States having custody of offenders the USA wishes to prosecute where the domestic legal system of that custodial State permits extradition absent a treaty.[204] The fact that the exception to extradition absent a treaty under US law is based on comity, and not international customary law, dilutes the force of any argument in favour of citing the US practice in support of the existence of *aut dedere aut judicare* as a rule of customary international law.

In contrast to the above national court decisions applying *aut dedere aut judicare* as a treaty obligation, there are national court decisions specifically addressing the obligation to extradite or prosecute even absent a treaty.

10), and has now been given a more general effect by international and national legislation. Thus, by s 4(1) of the 1978 Act the United Kingdom has assumed extra-territorial jurisdiction over the long list of crimes contained in Sch 1: a list which, as already observed, is amply wide enough to cover the crimes of which the appellant is said to be guilty. The assumption of extra-territorial jurisdiction goes further. In relation to a much smaller group of activities, directed at particularly vulnerable targets, the United Kingdom has by statute assumed jurisdiction over criminal acts irrespective both of the offender's nationality and of the place where the acts are done.'

198 *R v Zardad*, cited in Amnesty International, *ILC: The Obligation to Extradite or Prosecute* 47.

199 327 F 3d 56, 96 (2d Cir 2003).

200 Doc A/CN.4/579/Add 2 §56.

201 18 USC §§3184–95 (2001).

202 18 USC §§3181(*b*): 'The provisions of this chapter shall be construed to permit, in the exercise of comity, the surrender of persons, other than citizens, nationals, or permanent residents of the United States, who have committed crimes of violence against nationals of the United States in foreign countries without regard to the existence of any treaty of extradition with such foreign countries if the Attorney General certifies, in writing, that—(1) evidence has been presented by the foreign government that indicates that had the offences been committed in the United States, they would constitute crimes of violence as defined in section 16 of this title; and (2) the offenses charged are not of a political nature.'

203 *Ntakirutimana v Reno*, 184 F 3d 419, 426 (5th Cir 1999). *Certiorari denied*: 528 US 1135 (2000). See Michael John Garcia and Charles Doyle, *Extradition to and from the United States: Overview of the Law and Recent Treaties* (Congressional Service Report for Congress, 17 Mar 2010) 3–4.

204 As in the case of eg Art 10 of the Italian Constitution, and Art 15 section 4 of the Russian Constitution. See Kelly, 'Cheating Justice by Cheating Death' 517.

In *Aguilar Diaz* et al *v Pinochet*, the Court of First Instance of Brussels ruled it was competent to try General Pinochet, former President of Chile, in a case brought by Chilean exiles living in Belgium, referring to 'the general principle of international law *aut dedere aut judicare* (the obligation to extradite or prosecute) [that] imports the necessity of combating impunity of crimes under international law and the responsibility of State authorities to ensure punishment of such crimes irrespective of the place of commission'.[205]

The Federal Court of Australia in *Re Thompson; Ex parte Nulyarimma* has held that 'the obligation imposed by customary law on each nation State is to extradite or prosecute any person, found in its territory, who appears to have committed any of the acts cited in the definition of genocide set out in the [Genocide] Convention'.[206] However, the Court held in that particular case that it was one thing to say Australia had such an international customary legal obligation to prosecute or extradite a person suspected of having committed a crime of genocide found in its territory; it was another thing to say that, without legislation to that effect, such a person might be put on trial for genocide before an Australian court. As Australia had not by that time enacted legislation to criminalize genocide, the accused could not be tried for genocide in an Australian court.[207]

Austria's judicial practice in this matter is quite interesting. In Austria's response to the International Law Commission's request for information, Austria considers the principle *aut dedere aut judicare* as having 'a crucial role in the Austrian practice', but Austrian court decisions instituting proceedings in Austria following the refusal of extradition do not explicitly refer to Section 65(1) second paragraph of the Austrian Penal Code which incorporates the said principle. Be that as it may, Austria reaffirms that '[t]he lack of Austrian court decisions . . . does not reflect the great importance of the principle *aut dedere aut judicare* in Austrian judicial practice.'[208] In actual practice and despite the absence of any explicit reference by Austrian courts to the extradite-or-prosecute provision under Austrian law, Austrian courts have exercised universal jurisdiction to prosecute, after Austria's non-extradition of the accused to the territorial State, those foreigners accused of committing 'ordinary crimes' (such as fraud)[209] as well as 'core crimes under international law'. In *Public Prosecutor v Cvjetkovic*, the Austrian Supreme Court ruled that, after Austria had notified Bosnia of the arrest in Austria of a Serbian national suspected of having committed genocide, complicity in genocide, murder and complicity in murder,

[205] Order of 6 Nov 1998 [1999] 118 J des Tribunaux 308. See also Reydams, *Universal Jurisdiction* 114–15.

[206] [1999] FCA 1192 (*per* Wilcox J).

[207] After this judgment, Australian Parliament started working on drafting legislation to criminalize genocide. Eventually, genocide is criminalized under the International Criminal Court Act of 2002, enacted to implement Australia's obligations under the 1998 Rome Statute of the ICC which Australia ratified on 1 July 2002.

[208] UN Doc A/CN.4/579 §37. This has led Galicki to express his concern that since there was no Austrian court decision instituting proceedings following the refusal of extradition that explicitly referred to such provision, this 'seemed to weaken the importance of the principle *aut dedere aut judicare* in Austrian judicial practice' (Special Rapporteur Galicki's second report, UN Doc A/CN.4/585 §70).

[209] See *Public Prosecutor v Milan T* (1963) 28 ILR 341.

and complicity in arson as part of the ethnic cleansing in the former Yugoslavia and Bosnia did not react to the Austrian notification owing to the then ongoing armed conflict in the former Yugoslavia, Austria was competent under domestic law and international law to prosecute the said accused.[210]

Nevertheless, since Austria has repeatedly stated in the Sixth Committee[211] that it does not consider the obligation to extradite or prosecute to be a rule of customary international law, any invocation of Austria's State practice in support of the existence of such a rule of customary international law will have to be taken with a grain of salt.

The Chilean Supreme Court stated in *Villa Grimaldi* that although prosecuting crimes against humanity should preferably be the responsibility of the territorial State, all States are also authorized to investigate and prosecute when the investigation in the territorial State was neither efficient nor effective.[212] In *Benjamín Cevallos Jones and Ramón Cáceres*, the Chilean Supreme Court reiterated that every State member of the international community is obliged to prosecute and punish persons alleged to have committed crimes against humanity.[213]

Peru's Constitutional Court stated in *Huaura, José Enrique Crousillat Lopéz Torres* that torture and enforced disappearances are subject to universal jurisdiction based on the obligation to extradite or prosecute since they are 'acts contrary to the interests of mankind as a whole'.[214] The National Court of Spain in the *Martinez de Perón* case, while denying Argentina's extradition request for an alleged perpetrator of imprisonment, enforced disappearances, and torture during 1 July 1974 and 24 March 1976, stated that if an extradition was not granted, Spain was obligated to submit the case to its own competent authorities for prosecution. However, the Court held that the facts of the case under consideration did not qualify as crimes against humanity and, therefore, prosecution was barred by statutory limitations.[215]

Switzerland's practice in this matter is illuminating. In the case of former Rwandan Minister of Environment *Gaspard Ruhumuliza*, Rwanda filed the request on 5 August 2008 to have him extradited from Switzerland to stand trial in Rwanda for genocide, conspiracy to commit genocide in a joint criminal enterprise with the then interim

[210] Judgment of 13 July 1994, discussed in Reydams, *Universal Jurisdiction* 99–101.

[211] See Chapter 2.

[212] Case no 2707-2006 of 3 Oct 2006, quoted in Amnesty International, *ILC... International Justice Tool* 32 n 72.

[213] Case no 8113-08 of 29 Sept 2009, quoted in Amnesty International, ibid 33 n 73.

[214] Judgment of 8 Aug 2008, File 01271-2008-PHC/TC (cited in Note 7-1-SG/35 of 18 May 2010 from the Permanent Mission of Peru to the United Nations, New York, to the Office of Legal Affairs of the United Nations Secretariat, on the scope and application of the principle of universal jurisdiction at section (c), and Amnesty International, *ILC: The Obligation to Extradite or Prosecute* 26).

[215] Judgment of 28 Apr 2008. Cited in Amnesty International, ibid 26–27. See also the *obiter dictum* of the Spanish Supreme Court of 27 June 2007, overruling a judgment by a first instance court and declaring that Spain had jurisdiction to try non-nationals allegedly responsible for smuggling of migrants found on the high seas, where the Supreme Court stated that States were under the duty to enact legislation with respect to crimes under international law, including the *aut dedere aut judicare* principle. Quoted in Amnesty International, *ILC... International Justice Tool* 42 n 114.

government, complicity in genocide, and crimes against humanity in Rwanda in 1994 or, failing his extradition, to have him prosecuted in Switzerland. On 29 June 2009, the Swiss Government sent a diplomatic note to inform Rwanda of its refusal to extradite the accused 'because of the situation in Rwanda regarding human rights and because the suspicions put forward to support the request for extradition [were] not sufficiently backed up. … [since] the facts in the extradition request were not sufficiently detailed to allow Switzerland to determine if the conditions for extradition were fulfilled'. However, the Swiss Government also informed its Rwandan counterpart that Rwanda was entitled to request the Swiss authorities to take steps to prosecute the accused in Switzerland, provided that Rwanda also furnish the Swiss authorities with a detailed and comprehensive description about the offences allegedly committed by the accused as well as evidence to substantiate the charges against him. The Rwandan Government consequently sent such information and evidence to the Swiss authorities concerned.[216]

On 25 July 2012, the Swiss Federal Criminal Court issued a decision in criminal complaints against *General Khaled Nezzar*, former Algerian Minister of Defence, accused of war crimes and tortures committed during the Algerian civil war in 1992–2000, who was arrested while in transit in Switzerland.[217] Pursuant to the Swiss Penal Code, as amended and in force since 1 January 2011, Titles 12*bis*, 12*ter*, and 12*quater* codify the proscription of genocide, crimes against humanity, and war crimes, respectively. Article 264*m* provides for the extradite-or-prosecute regime. The Federal Criminal Court held Article 264*m* applicable to the cases against General Nezzar as prohibition of non-retroactivity was not applicable to procedural rules, especially provisions governing the competence of domestic authorities.[218] It rejected the contention by Nezzar's counsel that Swiss authorities could exercise jurisdiction only if extradition of the accused to Algeria was impossible. The Court held that prosecution in the State where the crimes had been committed or in the State of nationality of the accused was preferred, and, therefore, Swiss authorities had jurisdiction only if the other State expressly or implicitly declined to pursue criminal investigation, as was the case at hand. The Court cited judicial precedents that the proviso 'if he or she is not extradited' covered the situation where the accused was not transferred for whatever reason. In the present complaints, Algeria did not seek Nezzar's extradition and no criminal investigation had been or could be instituted against him in Algeria where he had been granted an amnesty under Order no 06-01 of 27 February 2006.[219] Moreover, Algeria was not party to the Rome Statute of the ICC, which would have subjected the accused to the jurisdiction of the ICC.[220] Nonetheless, the Swiss prosecutor allowed Nezzar to leave Switzerland for Algeria on the latter's promise that he would take part in subsequent proceedings

[216] Office fédéral de la justice, Communiqués, OFJ, 30.06.2009, 'La Suisse refuse d'extrader un Rwandais: Le Rwanda peut présenter à la Suisse une demande de délégation de la poursuite pénale'; *Sunday Times* (Kigali 5 July 2009); and Edwin Musoni, 'Rwanda: Genocide Suspect on Swiss Government Welfare Scheme', *New Times* (Rwanda 13 June 2012).

[217] Case no BB.2011.140. [218] ibid §2.3. [219] ibid §3.4. [220] ibid §3.6.

in Switzerland. The Federal Criminal Court held that in relation to the requirement that the accused is present on Swiss territory, it sufficed for the presence of the accused to be in Switzerland at the moment of the court hearing of the charge against him and interrogation by the prosecutor.[221]

The South African Constitutional Court has held in the *Zimbabwe Torture Docket Case* that the international crimes of piracy, slave-trading, war crimes, crimes against humanity, genocide, torture, and apartheid require States, 'even in the absence of binding international treaty law', to suppress such conduct because all States have an interest as they violate values that constitute the foundation of the world public order.[222] Although the alleged acts of torture in that case were perpetrated in Zimbabwe, by and against Zimbabwean nationals, and none of the perpetrators was present in South Africa, the duty to combat torture was held to travel beyond the borders of Zimbabwe since torture formed part of the category of crimes in which all States had an interest under customary international law to repress them. Therefore, South Africa could, 'through universal jurisdiction, assert prescriptive and, to some degree, adjudicative jurisdiction by investigating the allegations of torture as a precursor to taking a possible next step against the alleged perpetrators such as a prosecution or an extradition request'.[223]

Slovenia has confirmed it does apply the principle *aut dedere aut judicare* in practice. However, there are no special centralized records or gathering of information on individual cases where its prosecutors initiated criminal proceedings or took over prosecution of Slovenian nationals or foreign nationals from the requesting State in lieu of extradition as a result of the application of *aut dedere aut judicare*. Thus, Slovenia cannot provide the International Law Commission with the numerical data with regard to its judicial practice applying *aut dedere aut judicare*.[224]

In Serbia, neither the extradition of accused or sentenced persons nor their possible prosecution in Serbia is made conditional on the existence of an international treaty. The principle of universal jurisdiction is enshrined in Serbian domestic law, whereby Serbian courts may exercise universal jurisdiction over foreigners where requests for their extradition have been denied. Although it is 'very uncommon' for Serbian courts to exercise universal jurisdiction, this is because all requirements for extradition have been met and the foreigners extradited from Serbia, and not

[221] ibid §3.1. The Court rejected Nezzar's contention that he had immunity for acts committed during his term of office as Minister of Defence. However, in Jan 2017 the Office of the Attorney General of Switzerland dropped his prosecution on the ground that the acts allegedly committed by him could not be war crimes since there was no armed conflict in Algeria at that time. Later in Jan 2017, the civil parties in the case announced they would appeal the decision before the Federal Criminal Court.

[222] *National Commissioner of the South African Police Service v Southern African Human Rights Litigation Centre and Another* (CCT02/14) [2014] ZACC 30 §§35–37.

[223] ibid §49 (footnotes omitted).

[224] UN Doc A/CN.4/579/Add 1 §76.

because of the absence of evidence of Serbia's State practice in support of the obligation to extradite or prosecute.[225]

Non-extradition of nationals may be a basis for the obligation to prosecute.

Argentine courts have dealt with the obligation to extradite or prosecute 'in a limited number of cases' where extradition has been refused because of the nationality of the person sought. As Argentina cannot extradite its own nationals, their prosecution becomes the alternative to extradition. However, none of these cases have reached judgment due to the requesting foreign courts' failure to provide the relevant background information to their Argentine counterparts.[226]

Canada has informed the International Law Commission that there is no particular practice regarding the obligation to extradite or prosecute, whether from a judicial, prosecutorial, or law enforcement perspective, nor are there any particular crimes or offences to which the obligation is applied or not applied, as Canada permits and regularly authorizes the extradition of its own nationals; hence, the application of this obligation 'rarely, if ever, surfaces in Canada'.[227]

Chile mentions two cases in 2006 where the Chilean Supreme Court affirmed judgments of lower courts which rejected extradition of Chilean nationals to another State and which stated that the persons in question be tried in Chile for the offence of which they were accused.[228] One case concerned Argentina's request for the extradition of Chilean national *Rafael Washington Jara Macias*. The other concerned Argentina's request for the extradition of Chilean national *Juan León Lira Tobar*.

In September 2012 a court in Geneva, Switzerland, ordered *Erwin Sperisen*, Guatemala's former National Director of Police who had been arrested in Switzerland on 31 August 2012, to remain for at least three months in administrative detention while awaiting trial for alleged extrajudicial executions in Guatemala by members of the Guatemalan police under his command in 2005 and 2006. Sperisen is a Guatemalan-Swiss national and Switzerland cannot extradite its nationals. In June 2014, he was convicted and sentenced by a Swiss court to life imprisonment, which sentence was upheld on appeal on 12 May 2015.[229]

From 1997 to 2007, Serbia denied extradition requests 'in very few instances', primarily because these involved Serbian nationals. Serbia did not proceed to prosecute these individuals in Serbia because their offences did not fulfil the conditions required to consider them as offences under international instruments providing for the obligation to extradite or prosecute and no other State requested Serbia to prosecute them or gave Serbia evidentiary material necessary for such prosecution. Serbia asserted that there were 'many more instances in practice' where foreign States declined extradition requests from Serbia, did not proceed to prosecute the individuals sought by Serbia in lieu of extradition, and even released them, although,

[225] UN Doc A/CN.4/579/Add 2 §47. [226] ibid §§11–12.

[227] UN Doc A/CN.4/612 §53. [228] UN Doc A/CN.4/579/Add 1 at 105.

[229] http://www.swissinfo.ch/eng/swiss-guatemalan_former-guatemala-police-chief-sperisen-has-life-sentence-upheld/41426910, accessed 15 November 2017.

sometimes, these individuals were subsequently extradited to Serbia by other States where they happened to be found and arrested on an international warrant.[230]

According to the information provided to the International Law Commission by Monaco, Thailand, South Africa, Ireland, and Mexico, there is no domestic court case in these States specifically referring to the obligation *aut dedere aut judicare*.[231] In Latvia, there is 'not much judicial practice of Latvia reflecting the obligation *aut dedere aut judicare*', and the three instances cited by Latvia concern extradition only.[232]

A general conclusion regarding the analysis of judgments and *obiter dicta* of national courts faced with the question related to the obligation to extradite or prosecute, disregarding cases of prosecution of nationals in lieu of their extradition, is that courts of at least eight States (four from Europe, one from Oceania, one from Africa, and two from South America) in at least nine cases have asserted the existence of this obligation outside treaty. The crimes that were subject to these decisions varied from ordinary crimes to war crimes, genocide, crimes against humanity, torture, and enforced disappearance. The number of national court decisions in this respect is roughly equal to the respective total numbers of national court decisions cited by the ICJ in *Germany v Italy* as conclusive evidence of customary international law in that Judgment.

(3) *Claims regarding the obligation* aut dedere aut judicare *before foreign courts*

There are reports that the Netherlands' judiciary asked their German counterpart to extradite alleged Nazi criminal *Herbertus Bikker*, a Dutch-German national, to the Netherlands or, if such extradition were to be denied, prosecute them in German courts.[233] Eventually, the district court of Hagen, Germany, ruled in February 2004 that he was unfit to stand trial in Germany.

Amnesty International mentions investigating Judge Santiago Pedraz of Madrid who asserted, in response to the denial by Guatemalan courts to grant five extradition requests by Spain, that the obligation to extradite or prosecute was based not only on conventional law, but also on customary international law owing to the *jus cogens* character of the prohibition of genocide and crimes against humanity.[234]

230 UN Doc A/CN.4/579/Add 2 §§53–54.

231 UN Doc A/CN.4/579 §40 (Monaco), ibid §41 (Thailand), UN Doc A/CN.4/612 §63 (South Africa), UN Doc A/CN.4/579/Add 1 §73 (Ireland), and ibid §75 (Mexico).

232 UN Doc A/CN.4/579/Add 2 §52.

233 Deen-Racsmány, 'A New Passport to Impunity?' 761–62.

234 Amnesty International, *ILC: The Obligation to Extradite or Prosecute* 26. The investigating judge considered that Guatemala was in breach of its international legal duty by refusing to either investigate former Guatemalan President Rios Montt in Guatemala or extradite him to Spain. However, Rios Montt was wanted in Spain not only for the alleged genocide of the Mayan population in Guatemala during an armed conflict but also for crimes against internationally protected persons in the Spanish Embassy in Guatemala City in 1981 allegedly committed by Guatemalan officials (ibid 25–26). In other words, Spain was asserting jurisdiction over Rios Montt for crimes against Spanish nationals as well. See further details on this case in Langer, 'The Diplomacy of Universal Jurisdiction' 36–37.

(4) *Statements made by States*

Chapter 2 has already listed States that made statements in the Sixth Committee of the UN General Assembly to the effect that the obligation to extradite or prosecute was not one of customary international law but was treaty-based.[235] In addition, Australia opines that it is doubtful that customary international law currently imposes any obligation to extradite or prosecute.[236]

However, Argentina has contended that the customary law status of the said obligation must be analysed on a case-by-case basis according to the type of the crime in question. It cautions, though, that the fact that the crime is a core crime (ie genocide, crime against humanity, or war crime) does not in and of itself warrant any conclusion regarding the application of the obligation to extradite or prosecute to that crime.[237]

For Russia, the existence of an obligation under customary international law may not be necessarily inferred from the existence of a number of treaties containing such an obligation.[238] Similarly, the existence of a customary rule obligating States to exercise their criminal jurisdiction or to accede to extradition requests in respect of a specific type of crime may not be readily inferred from the existence of a customary rule proscribing this type of crime.[239] Russia believes that important evidence of *opinio juris* could derive from national courts' judgments or States' official declarations that pronounce explicitly that the refusal to extradite gives rise to an obligation of the requested State to refer the case to its competent authorities for the purpose of prosecution.[240] Russia does not yet see such 'convincing evidence of the existence of a customary rule *aut dedere aut judicare*'.[241] Nonetheless, it hastens to add, '[t]he question of the establishment of an obligation *aut dedere aut judicare* in customary international law with respect to a small number of criminal acts that arouse the concern of the entire international community [ie primarily genocide, war crimes, and crimes against humanity] merits separate analysis.'[242]

China considers the obligation to extradite or prosecute to be treaty-based although it might also become an international customary law obligation with regard to the crimes under customary international law as acknowledged by the international community. Such crimes should be primarily international crimes, transnational crimes endangering the common interest of the international community under international law, and serious crimes endangering the national and public interest under domestic law.[243]

[235] Several of these States, eg the USA and South Africa, have consistently made this position known. See eg US written response in UN Doc A/CN.4/579/Add 2 §§1–8; and South Africa's written response in UN Doc A/CN.4/612 §68. For a succinct description of policy considerations in implementing US extradition laws, see Adam B Abelson, 'The Prosecute/Extradite Dilemma: Concurrent Criminal Jurisdiction and Global Governance' (2010) 16 UC Davis JIL & Policy 101, 112–13.

[236] UN Doc A/C.6/SR.28 (2 Dec 2011) §2.

[237] Doc A/C.6/62/SR.22 §58. [238] UN Doc A/CN.4/599 §§48–50.

[239] ibid §51. [240] ibid §54. [241] ibid. [242] ibid §55.

[243] UN Doc A/C.6/62/SR.22 §62.

According to Canada, 'for the vast majority of crimes, the obligation to extradite or prosecute does not and should not apply and, where applicable, the scope of the obligation should be defined by treaty ... as part of the international community's collective efforts to deny a safe haven to terrorists and other criminals'.[244] This rationale harks back to the distinction, made in the debate leading to the conclusion of the Rome Statute of the ICC in 1998, between 'treaty-based crimes' (such as terrorism) and core crimes of concern to the international community as a whole (ie genocide, crimes against humanity, war crimes, and aggression).[245] Canada seems to imply that the obligation to extradite or prosecute outside treaty ought to apply to these core crimes.

Thailand informed the Sixth Committee on 6 November 2012 that States in the South East Asian region have been actively cooperating in extraditing or prosecuting perpetrators of crimes of common concern, such as international terrorism, drug trafficking, and human trafficking, among others. Thailand is a member of the steering group for the Bali Process on People Smuggling, Trafficking in Persons, and Related Transnational Crimes, comprising forty-six members and twenty-nine observers.[246] Besides, there has been the International Legal Cooperation against Terrorism stream under the framework of the Bali Regional Meeting on Counter-International Terrorism, with more than twenty States from Asia, Oceania, Western Europe, and North America participating.[247] It was stressed that 'the States participating in these two processes feel legally bound to extradite or prosecute perpetrators of serious crimes of international concern under their respective domestic law, and the majority of them can extradite such offenders without a treaty', and that '[t]his kind of practice can crystallize into regional customary law.'[248]

Tunisia reports on the numerous bilateral agreements concluded by Tunisia relating to judicial cooperation, most of which provide explicitly for the obligation to 'extradite or prosecute' as in, for example, its agreements with Libya, Algeria, Lebanon, Morocco, Jordan, Mauritania, UAE, Egypt, Kuwait, Syria, Qatar, Yemen, Italy, France, Bulgaria,

[244] UN Doc A/CN.4/612 §41.

[245] See eg Preparatory Committee on the Establishment of the International Criminal Court, Press Release L/2766, 6th Meeting (PM) 27 Mar 1996.

[246] The forty-six members comprise forty-one States and three territories (Australia, Indonesia, New Zealand, and Thailand (as the four members of the Steering Group of the Bali Process) and Afghanistan, Bangladesh, Bhutan, Brunei Darussalam, Cambodia, China, DPR Korea, Fiji, France (on behalf of New Caledonia), Hong Kong SAR, Macau SAR, India, Iran, Iraq, Japan, Jordan, Kiribati, Lao PDR, Malaysia, Maldives, Mongolia, Myanmar, Nauru, Nepal, Pakistan, Palau, Papua New Guinea, Philippines, Rep of Korea, Samoa, Singapore, Solomon Islands, Sri Lanka, Syria, Timor Leste, Tonga, Turkey, USA, Vanuatu, and Vietnam, plus the International Organization for Migration (IOM) and the UN High Commission for Refugees (UNHCR).

[247] The participating States include Australia, Brunei Darussalam, Canada, Cambodia, China, Fiji, France, India, Indonesia, Japan, Republic of Korea, Laos, Malaysia, Myanmar, New Zealand, Papua New Guinea, the Philippines, the Russian Federation, Singapore, Thailand, Timor Leste, USA, and Vietnam.

[248] A copy of the statement is on file with the present author, who chaired the International Legal Cooperation against Terrorism stream of the Bali Process.

Czechoslovakia, Turkey, Hungary, Poland, Greece, Portugal, Senegal, Mali, Côte d'Ivoire, and China, respectively.[249]

In sum, according to the statements made by several States there could be a rule of customary obligation to extradite or prosecute (or, according to Belgium, to prosecute or extradite) in relation to the core crimes of genocide, crimes against humanity, and war crimes. They differ as to whether other serious crimes such as terrorism should also fall under the purview of this customary obligation. This divergence of opinions is due to the fact that States face different threats of criminal nature, and this difference is reflected accordingly in the different national priorities in suppressing such threats.

(5) Resolutions of international organizations

Resolutions of the UN General Assembly may, in so far as they claim to enunciate binding international rules and not merely political statements, constitute evidence of the existence of customary international law, help to crystallize emerging customary international law, or contribute to the formation of new international customary law.[250] Statements in a resolution indicating what the law should be like (*lex ferenda*) can contribute to the crystallization or formation of new customary law. On the other hand, statements in a resolution signifying what the law currently is (*lex lata*) constitute rebuttable evidence that such law is already in existence.[251] The language of the resolution, the number of supporting States—in particular specially affected States—and the circumstances of its adoption including statements during the process of adoption are relevant factors in determining whether the resolution (one or more provisions of which may or may not be repeated in other resolutions) expressly or impliedly declares the law.[252] While there is no requirement that a specific expression of *opinio juris* be followed by simultaneous State practice, a customary rule will not be created if the subsequent State practice contradicts the resolution.[253]

Resolutions that show a clear intent by their supporting States to make new law or declare existing law can, in a very exceptional case, lay down general customary law if these resolutions are adopted unanimously or almost unanimously. The near-unanimity must at least include all representative groups of States that are specially affected by the rule in question as well as important State actors or groups of State actors in the field in question.[254] The International Law Association cites the Declaration on Friendly Relations as an example of this kind of resolution.[255]

[249] UN Doc A/CN.4/579/Add 1 §21.

[250] ILA's Statement of Principles 55–56. See also the ICJ's Advisory Opinion in *Legality of the Threat or Use of Nuclear Weapons* [1996] ICJ Rep 226, 254 [70].

[251] ILA's Statement of Principles 56–59. [252] ibid 58–61. [253] ibid 61 and n 168.

[254] ibid 61–65.

[255] ibid 62, citing in support of this conclusion the ICJ's analysis in *Military and Paramilitary Activities in and against Nicaragua (Nicaragua v United States of America)* (Merits) [1986] ICJ Rep 14, 100 regarding the Declaration on Principles of International Law concerning Friendly Relations and Cooperation among States in Accordance with the Charter of the United Nations (UNGA Res 2625 (XXV) of 24 Oct 1974). Cf also Anthea Elizabeth Roberts, 'Traditional and Modern Approaches to Customary International Law: A Reconciliation' (2001) 95 AJIL 757, 758–59, 763, 765.

Logically, the above analysis as to whether UN General Assembly resolutions can contribute to the formal creation of a new rule of customary international law or declare the existence of one such rule applies *mutatis mutandis* to resolutions of international conferences of a universal character.[256]

Two of the oft-cited UN General Assembly resolutions that are relevant to the obligation to extradite or prosecute are UN General Assembly Resolution 2840 (XXVI) of 18 December 1971 entitled 'Question of the punishment of war criminals and of persons who have committed crimes against humanity'[257] and UN General Assembly Resolution 3074 (XXVIII) of 3 December 1973 entitled 'Principles of international co-operation in the detection, arrest, extradition and punishment of persons guilty of war crimes and crimes against humanity'.[258] Paragraph 1 of the former Resolution 'urges all States . . . to put an end to and to prevent war crimes and crimes against humanity and to ensure the punishment of all persons guilty of such crimes, including their extradition to those countries where they have committed such crimes'. Paragraph 5 of the latter Resolution stipulates, '[p]ersons against whom there is evidence that they have committed war crimes and crimes against humanity shall be subject to trial and, if found guilty, to punishment, as a general rule in the country in which they committed those crimes [and, i]n that connection, States shall cooperate on questions of extraditing such persons.' No States voted against these Resolutions, and those who abstained did so mainly because of the alleged imprecise definition of the crimes addressed in the Resolutions at that time.[259]

In addition, the Economic and Social Council (ECOSOC) adopted without a vote ECOSOC Resolution 1989/65 of 24 May 1989 entitled 'Effective prevention and investigation of extra-legal, arbitrary and summary executions'.[260] Principle 18 of the Principles annexed to the Resolution provides:

> Governments shall ensure that persons identified by the investigation as having participated in extra-legal, arbitrary or summary executions in any territory under their jurisdiction are brought to justice. Governments shall either bring such persons to justice or co-operate to extradite any such persons to other countries wishing to exercise jurisdiction. This principle shall apply irrespective of who and where the perpetrators or the victims are, their nationalities or where the offence was committed.

UN General Assembly Resolution 44/159 on summary and arbitrary executions of 15 December 1989,[261] adopted without a vote, stated in its preamble that the UN General Assembly welcomed this ECOSOC Resolution.

In *Belgium v Senegal*, Judge Cançado Trindade mentioned, in support of his analysis on 'The Struggle against Impunity in the Law of the United Nations', the UN Commission on Human Rights' resolution 2003/72 of 24 April 2003,[262] paragraph 10 of which recognizes that crimes such as genocide, crimes against humanity, war

[256] ILA's Statement of Principles 65–66.

[257] UNGA Res 2840 (1971).

[258] UNGA Res 3074 (1973).

[259] van Steenberghe, 'The Obligation to Extradite or Prosecute' 1100-1; Amnesty International, *ILC . . . International Justice Tool* 55.

[260] E/CN.4/RES/1989/65.

[261] UNGA Res 44/159.

[262] E/CN.4/RES/2003/72.

crimes, and torture are violations of international law, and perpetrators of such crimes should be prosecuted or extradited by States, and which further urged all States to take effective measures to implement their obligations to prosecute or extradite perpetrators of such crimes.[263]

On 8 April 2005, the Assembly of the Inter-Parliamentary Union, which is an international organization of parliaments, unanimously adopted the resolution entitled 'The Role of Parliaments in the Establishment and Functioning of Mechanisms to Provide for the Judgment and Sentencing of War Crimes, Crimes against Humanity, Genocide and Terrorism with a view to Avoiding Impunity'. The preamble of this resolution stated, *inter alia*, 'each State has the obligation and the duty to prosecute or extradite the perpetrators of war crimes, crimes against humanity, crimes of genocide and terrorist crimes, irrespective of the location of the crime or the nationality of the perpetrator'.[264]

Belgium, in its written response to Judge Greenwood's third question, cited the relevant resolutions of the UN General Assembly, treaty texts, UN Security Council resolutions calling on States to combat impunity of perpetrators of war crimes and crimes against humanity, UN Security Council resolutions adopted under Chapter VII of the UN Charter to put an end to serious crimes that constitute a threat to international peace and security (as in the cases of the former Yugoslavia and Rwanda), Sixth Committee debates on the scope and application of the principle of universal jurisdiction, and academic writings.[265] Decisions in resolutions adopted by the UN Security Council acting under the UN Charter's Chapter VII (which authorizes the Council to take coercive measures with respect to 'threats to the peace, breaches of the peace, and acts of aggression') are binding on UN Member States pursuant to Article 25 of the Charter.[266]

The UN Security Council resolutions cited by Belgium did not include those concerning international terrorism.[267] In relation to international terrorism, operative paragraph 2 of UN Security Council Resolution 1566 (2004),[268] adopted under Chapter VII of the UN Charter, '[*c*]*alls upon* States to cooperate fully in the fight against terrorism, especially with those States where or against whose citizens terrorist acts are committed, in accordance with their obligations under international law, in order to find, deny safe haven and bring to justice, on the basis of the

[263] *Belgium v Senegal* [2012] ICJ Rep 422, 539–40 [131] (Sep Op of Judge Cançado Trindade).

[264] IPU Doc no 13 (112th IPU Assembly).

[265] Supplementary replies from Belgium, <http://www.icj-cij.org/files/case-related/144/17640.pdf>.

[266] Art 25 reads: 'The Members of the United Nations agree to accept and carry out the decisions of the Security Council in accordance with the present Charter.'

[267] Cf the argument that the obligation *aut dedere aut judicare* has been further developed by the UN General Assembly and the UN Security Council, especially in relation to terrorist acts in Guido Acquaviva, '*Aut Dedere Aut Judicare*' in Antonio Cassese (ed), *The Oxford Companion to International Criminal Justice* (OUP 2009) 253–54 (citing UNGA Res 49/60 of 9 Dec 1994; UNSC Res 731 (1992); UNSC Res 748 (1992); UNSC Res 883 (1993); and *Questions of Interpretation and Application of the 1971 Montreal Convention arising from the Aerial Incident at Lockerbie (Libyan Arab Jamahiriya v United Kingdom)* (Preliminary Objections) [1998] ICJ Rep 3).

[268] UNSC Res 1566 (8 Oct 2004) UN Doc S/RES/1566.

principle to extradite or prosecute, any person who supports, facilitates, participates or attempts to participate in the financing, planning, preparation or commission of terrorist acts or provides safe havens'. Operative paragraph 4 of this Resolution calls upon States to become party to the relevant international conventions and protocols. This latter paragraph somehow diminishes the sanctity of the 'obligations under international law ... on the basis of the principle to extradite or prosecute' under operative paragraph 2, as such obligations are largely treaty-based, unless it could be proved that at the time of the adoption of the Resolution the principle to extradite or prosecute had already existed under customary international law. The same could be said of UN Security Council Resolution 1456 (2003),[269] not adopted pursuant to Chapter VII of the UN Charter. While calling upon States to become party to all relevant international conventions and protocols relating to terrorism, operative paragraph 3 of this latter Resolution provides: 'States must bring to justice those who finance, plan, support or commit terrorist acts or provide safe havens, in accordance with international law, in particular on the basis of the principle to extradite or prosecute.'[270]

In analysing the customary international law aspect of the obligation *aut dedere aut judicare* in his fourth report,[271] Special Rapporteur Galicki stated that those invoking a customary international law obligation to prosecute or extradite usually quoted the UN General Assembly's Declaration on Territorial Asylum of 1967[272] as the earliest international recognition of a customary law obligation to prosecute perpetrators of crimes against humanity.[273] He then referred to the drafting history of this Declaration to show that it was not intended to propound legal norms or to change existing rules of international law, but to lay down 'broad humanitarian and moral principles' to be relied on by States in their asylum practices.[274] Proceeding on the basis of the drafting history of this one General Assembly resolution alone, Special Rapporteur Galicki surprisingly concluded in a sweeping manner, 'This language suggests that, from the outset, the General Assembly resolutions and other binding international instruments concerning the prosecution of crimes against humanity were meant to be aspirational only, and not intended to create any legal duties.'[275]

Senegal, in its written comments on Belgium's written replies to Judge Greenwood's questions in *Belgium v Senegal*, relied on the drafting history of the resolution on the said Declaration to reach the same conclusion as Galicki's, but

[269] UNSC Res 1456 (20 Jan 2003) UN Doc S/RES/1456.

[270] See also Claire Mitchell, *Aut Dedere Aut Judicare: The Extradite or Prosecute Clauses in International Law* (Graduate Institute of International and Development Studies 2009) 10–11.

[271] UN Doc A/CN.4/648 (31 May 2011) §§74–96. [272] UNGA Res 2312 (1967).

[273] UN Doc A/CN.4/648 (31 May 2011) §75. Art 1(2) of the Declaration stipulates: 'The right to seek and to enjoy asylum may not be invoked by any person with respect to whom there are serious reasons for considering that he has committed a crime against peace, a war crime or a crime against humanity, as defined in the international instruments drawn up to make provision in respect of such crimes.'

[274] (1967) Yearbook of the United Nations 758–59, quoted in Galicki's fourth report, UN Doc A/CN.4/648 (31 May 2011) §§74–96, §76.

[275] Galicki's fourth report, ibid §77.

without specifically referring to his analysis.[276] However, Senegal merely touched upon UN General Assembly resolutions as evidence of the customary law nature of the obligation *aut dedere aut judicare*. Senegal did not rebut Belgium's contention that the other sources cited by Belgium could be evidence of such customary law status of the obligation. Senegal appeared to make a distinction between primary and secondary obligations when it argued:

> Senegal regards the fight against impunity for serious crimes under international law as a fundamental principle which is beyond dispute. …
>
> While the prohibition of torture has certainly acquired the status of a (primary) peremptory norm (and has done so irrespective of its origins, conventional or customary), it is not clear that the secondary *aut dedere aut judicare* obligation deriving from that norm has also assumed the status of a peremptory norm of a customary origin. Such a status is far from accepted by the international community as a whole, as shown by the positions taken by States during the work of the International Law Commission [citing Special Rapporteur Galicki's fourth report].[277]

In this present author's opinion, statements in the various resolutions of international organizations mentioned earlier in this section evince that States strongly feel they are obliged to take effective measures to extradite or prosecute perpetrators of core crimes under international law. This conviction is echoed in the Sixth Committee during the debate on the obligation to extradite or prosecute, as shown in Chapter 2. The fact that a number of States are of the position that the obligation is treaty-based must be considered in its proper context. First, most, if not all, of these States cannot extradite absent a treaty. Second, there are widespread concerns about the potential abuse of universal jurisdiction, a matter closely related to the obligation *aut dedere aut judicare*, and the States sharing this concern appear to prefer the obligation to exist only in treaties binding on the States in question so that there would be no dispute regarding the exercise of any head of jurisdiction, including universal jurisdiction. Therefore, statements in the pertinent resolutions must be considered in the light of all other relevant factors in order to determine whether the obligation to extradite or prosecute for core crimes has become a norm of customary law.[278] In the case of terrorism, the resolutions urge States to take measures to suppress acts of terrorism by becoming States Parties to the relevant multilateral treaties on international terrorism, and, consequently, any obligation *aut dedere aut judicare* for these crimes will be treaty-based.

[276] Further written comments of the Government of Senegal on the supplementary replies of the Belgian Government to the question put to Belgium by Judge Greenwood at the close of the hearing held on 16 Mar 2012, <http://www.icj-cij.org/files/case-related/144/17646.pdf>, accessed 20 August 2017.

[277] ibid 1.

[278] Roberts, 'Traditional and Modern Approaches to Customary International Law' 763, argues that the ICJ has relied on resolutions couched in both mandatory and hortatory languages, and that even mandatory language is still ambiguous as it can represent either a moral, treaty, or customary obligation. Roberts also cites in support of her argument the example of the ICJ's treatment of the Declaration on Principles of International Law concerning Friendly Relations in *Nicaragua v United States of America* (Merits) [1986] ICJ Rep 14, 107 [203–04].

B. *Opinio juris* (subjective element)

Judge Greenwood's third question in *Belgium v Senegal* appears to echo the pronouncement of the ICJ in *North Sea Continental Shelf* that:

> Not only must the acts concerned amount to a settled practice, but they must also be such, or be carried out in such a way, as to be evidence of a belief that this practice is rendered obligatory by the existence of a rule requiring it. The need for such a belief, i.e. the existence of a subjective element, is implicit in the very notion of the *opinio juris sive necessitates*. The States concerned must therefore feel that they are conforming to what amounts to a legal obligation. The frequency, or even habitual character of the acts is not itself enough. There are many international acts, e.g. in the field of ceremonial and protocol, which are performed almost invariably, but which are motivated only by considerations of courtesy, convenience or tradition, and not by any sense of legal duty.[279]

As Belgium has rightly pointed out, it is not always possible to draw a clear distinction between the material (objective) element and the mental (subjective) element of custom, and that the ICJ itself has established the existence of *opinio juris* through the existence of a certain State practice in this matter.[280] For example, the ICJ in the *Gulf of Maine* case has held that the presence of customary rules in the *opinio juris* of States can be tested by 'induction based on the analysis of a sufficiently extensive and convincing practice'.[281]

The International Law Association makes a distinction between, *inter alia*, the different stages in the life of a customary rule, and especially the time when it begins to be formed, on the one hand, and the time when it is already established, on the other.[282] The ILA concludes that it is only sometimes necessary to establish the existence of a subjective element separately from the existence of the objective element (State practice) of customary international law.[283]

According to the ILA, '[o]nce a customary rule has become established, States will naturally have a belief in its existence; but this does not *necessarily* prove that the subjective element needs to be present during the *formation* of the rule.'[284] In addition, it is in fact often difficult or even impossible to disentangle the objective and the subjective elements of customary international law.[285] In the opinion of the ILA, if it can be shown that States generally *believe* that a pattern of conduct fulfilling the conditions of being State practice is permitted as a legal right or, as the case may be,

[279] [1969] ICJ Rep 3, 44 [77].

[280] Supplementary replies from Belgium <http://www.icj-cij.org/files/case-related/144/17646.pdf>, 2 [6], citing *Delimitation of the Maritime Boundary in the Gulf of Maine Area (Canada/United States of America)* [1984] ICJ Rep 246, 299 [111]; *Nicaragua v United States of America* (Merits) [1986] ICJ Rep 14, 98 [184]; and *Germany v Italy* [2012] ICJ Rep 99, 122 [55]. See also T Meron, 'Revival of Customary Humanitarian Law' (2005) 99 AJIL 817, 819.

[281] *Delimitation of the Maritime Boundary in the Gulf of Maine Area* 299 [111], cited Supplementary replies from Belgium <http://www.icj-cij.org/files/case-related/144/17646.pdf>, 13 [20]. This is also the position of the International Committee of the Red Cross (ICRC), see Jean-Marie Henckaerts and Louise Doswald-Beck, *Study on Customary International Humanitarian Law* vol 1 (CUP 2005), Rules, xl–xli.

[282] ILA's Statement of Principles 30.

[283] ibid 7 [(a)].

[284] ibid 7 [(b)], emphasis original.

[285] ibid 7 [(c)].

required by law in the sense of a legal obligation, 'this is *sufficient* for it to be law; but it is not *necessary* to prove the existence of such a belief' although such a belief may be inferred.[286] The ILA clarifies further:

> [I]t is not always, and probably not even usually, *necessary* to prove the existence of any sort of subjective element in addition to the objective element, but (a) where it is *present*, that may be *sufficient* to establish the existence of a customary rule binding on the State(s) in question; and (b) proof of its *absence* may mean that such a rule has not come into existence, either because the practice is not a sort which 'counts' towards the formation of a customary rule [as in the case of mere comity or purely conventional obligations], or because persistent objection has prevented a general rule from emerging, or at any rate has prevented its binding the particular objector(s).[287]

The ILA alludes to the 'numerous examples where the ICJ has simply referred to the constant and uniform practice of States, without any reference to the subjective element'.[288]

Since what a State actually believes is 'undiscoverable', such belief in the context of *opinio juris* may be 'discovered' from either what a State says it believes or what can reasonably be implied from the said State's conduct.[289] Thus, the Appeals Chamber of the Special Tribunal for Lebanon, when elaborating the customary nature of the crime of terrorism, assumes as a starting point 'the presumption of the existence of *opinio juris* whenever a finding is made of a consistent practice', and to deny the existence of a customary rule in such circumstances would require finding 'the reasons of expediency or those based on comity or political convenience that support the denial of the customary rule'.[290]

Also, as the ILA points out, 'a substantial manifestation of acceptance (consent or belief) by States that a customary rule exists may compensate for a relative lack of practice, and vice versa'.[291]

When reviewing State practice it must be borne in mind that the requirement of actual material conduct does not translate into conduct by a specific number or percentage of States.[292] Where there is strong proof of *opinio juris*, a lack of State practice has not impeded the formation of a rule of customary international law. Notwithstanding the lack of actual State practice, in *Nicaragua v USA* the ICJ

[286] ibid 30–31 and Section 16 at 32, emphasis original.

[287] ibid 31–32 and Section 17 at 34–38, emphasis original.

[288] ibid 40–41 and n 99, citing *Fisheries case* [1951] ICJ Rep 116, 128 (low, as opposed to high, water mark as the starting point for measurement of the territorial sea); *Nottebohm (Second Phase)* [1955] ICJ Rep 4, 23 (definition of nationality); *Barcelona Traction* [1970] ICJ Rep 3, 42 [70] (attribution of nationality to corporations); *Continental Shelf (Libya/Malta)* [1985] ICJ Rep 13, 33 [34] (exclusive economic zone now a part of customary international law).

[289] Cf ILA's Statement of Principles 33.

[290] *Interlocutory Decision on the Applicable Law: Terrorism, Conspiracy, Homicide, Perpetration, Cumulative Charging* (Special Tribunal for Lebanon App Ch) 16 Feb 2011 §101.

[291] ILA's Statement of Principles Section 19 at 40–42. The ILA cites the example of the ICJ's ruling in *Nicaragua v United States of America*, 107. While the ICJ in that case re-emphasized the need for both the objective and subjective elements, it demanded very little evidence of actual State practice in the light of clear-cut proof of the *opinio juris* of the international community in such international instruments as the Declaration on Principles of International Law concerning Friendly Relations.

[292] ILA's Statement of Principles 25.

derived the customary rules against the non-use of force and non-intervention from, *inter alia,* the Declaration on Principles of International Law Concerning Friendly Relations.[293] This may be particularly relevant in establishing the customary nature of the obligation *aut dedere aut judicare* where a majority of States in the world do not have an occasion to extradite or prosecute perpetrators of core crimes. Strong *opinio juris* may exist in the form of State declarations, and statements by governments at the Sixth Committee qualify as unilateral State declarations and proof of *opinio juris.* General Assembly resolutions, even if they are not binding, can, in certain circumstances, provide evidence important for establishing the existence of a rule or the emergence of *opinio juris.*[294] Resolution 2840 of 1971 and Resolution 3074 of 1973 have been cited to prove the existence of an obligation *aut dedere aut judicare* vis-à-vis the core international crimes of genocide, war crimes, and crimes against humanity.[295]

The European Committee on Crime Problems of the Council of Europe reminds Member States that the *aut dedere aut judicare* principle is already enshrined in Article 6 paragraph 2 of the 1957 European Convention on Extradition[296] whereby the requested State Party which refuses to extradite a national shall, at the request of the requesting State Party, submit the case to its competent authorities so that proceedings may be taken.[297] The Committee advises the Council of Europe to reinforce the application of the *aut dedere aut judicare* principle as a means of prosecuting war crimes effectively in cases where universal jurisdiction cannot be exercised because of the lack of political will on an international level and the methodological difficulties regarding the scope of the principle of universal jurisdiction.[298]

The analysis just mentioned shows 'sufficiently convincing and extensive' State practice in different geographical regions in prosecuting perpetrators of a variety of crimes when the alleged offenders are not extradited for some reason. Positions taken by States indicate strongly that the extradite-or-prosecute/prosecute-or-extradite regime applies in particular to core crimes under international law. This practice is far from universal and the statements are far from unanimous, though. Yet, the practice is at least relatively as 'sufficiently convincing and extensive' as that cited by the ICJ in *Germany v Italy* in support of the ICJ's proof of existence of a norm of customary international law in that Judgment.[299]

[293] Roberts, 'Traditional and Modern Approaches to Customary International Law' 758.

[294] *Legality of the Threat or Use of Nuclear Weapons* 255 [70].

[295] van Steenberghe, 'The Obligation to Extradite or Prosecute' 1100.

[296] Art 4 of the United Nations Model Extradition Treaty (UN Doc A/RES/45/116).

[297] Secretariat memorandum prepared by the Directorate General of Human Rights Affairs (DGHL), *Draft Opinion of the European Committee on Crime Problems (CDPC) on Parliamentary Assembly Recommendation 1953 (2011) on The Obligation of Member States and Observer States of the Council of Europe to Co-operate in the Prosecution of War Crimes*, Doc CDPC (2011) 5 [7].

[298] ibid 5 [11].

[299] The present author would not go so far as Roberts, 'Traditional and Modern Approaches to Customary International Law' (758, 764–65) who argues that 'modern custom' that emphasizes *opinio juris* rather than State practice 'is derived by a *deductive* process that begins with general statements of rules rather than particular instances of practice'. In Roberts's opinion, since 1945, international law has expanded to include many *moral* issues, eg human rights, and this development moves from State values to human values, and from a liberal State system to a welfare system in which 'State practice is

C. Multilateral conventions recording and defining rules deriving from custom, or indeed developing them

The plethora of multilateral conventions that refer to the obligation *aut dedere aut judicare* raises the complex issue of customary international law obligations arising from treaties. The International Court of Justice has recognized the ability of treaties to give rise to customary rules under exceptional circumstances, that is, the relevant treaty provisions need to be of a 'fundamentally norm-creating' character.[300] To prove the existence of the obligation *aut dedere aut judicare* as a rule of customary international law, one has to consider also the practice of non-States Parties to the relevant multilateral treaties with provisions on the said obligation. This is to ascertain that the obligation is not merely implemented by States because these States are bound by treaty obligations. However, this does not *ipso facto* prevent the conduct of State Parties from contributing to the formation of the obligation under customary international law. Where practice of State Parties reveals *opinio juris sive necessitates* as opposed to mere *opinio juris conventionalis,* that conduct becomes proof of customary international law.[301]

Multilateral conventions can assist in the 'crystallization' of emerging rules of customary international law when State practice is developing in parallel with the drafting of such conventions, as in the case of the exclusive economic zone under the 1982 UN Convention on the Law of the Sea,[302] which took thirteen years to conclude.[303] In exceptional and extremely rare cases, a multilateral treaty may give rise to new customary rules (or assist in their creation) 'of its own impact' if it is widely adopted by States with the clear intention to create new customary law, and not a merely conventional norm.[304] The provision in question must be of a 'fundamentally norm-creating character'—that is, with the necessary degree of generality and compulsoriness in its observance among States.[305] Arguably, this was the case of common Article 3 to the four Geneva Conventions of 12 August 1949[306] which creates obligations extending beyond the States Parties to the Conventions,[307] and the Martens Clause in paragraph 8

less important in forming modern customs because these customs prescribe ideal standards of conduct rather than describing existing practice', as in the example of the customary prohibition of torture which expresses a 'moral abhorrence of torture rather than an accurate description of State practice'. Hence, according to Roberts, '[t]he moral content of modern custom explains the strong tendency to discount the importance of contrary State practice in the modern approach', and such contrary State practice is usually treated as 'breaches of the relevant rule'.

[300] *North Sea Continental Shelf* 44 [77].

[301] van Steenberghe, 'The Obligation to Extradite or Prosecute' 1100.

[302] 1833 UNTS 3.

[303] ILA's Statement of Principles 49–50.

[304] ibid 50–54.

[305] ibid 52–54, citing the ICJ in *North Sea Continental Shelf* 41–43 [70–74].

[306] Geneva Convention for the amelioration of the condition of the wounded and the sick in armed forced in the field (75 UNTS 31), Geneva Convention for the amelioration of the condition of wounded, sick and shipwrecked members of armed forces at sea (75 UNTS 85), Geneva Convention relative to the treatment of prisoners of war (75 UNTS 135), Geneva Convention relative to the protection of civilian persons in time of war (75 UNTS 287).

[307] ILA's Statement of Principles 52.

of the Preamble to the 1907 Hague Convention IV Respecting the Laws and Customs of War on Land.[308]

There is a contention that the obligation *aut dedere aut judicare* has become part of customary international law in relation to the grave breach regime under the Geneva Conventions of 1949 and Additional Protocols, whereby each High Contracting Party undertakes to prosecute alleged perpetrators of grave breaches before its court or to hand them over to another High Contracting Party which has made out a prima facie case.[309] However, even in the case of the four Geneva Conventions of 1949 that have been universally ratified, not all States Parties thereto have domestic law to enable prosecution of violators of the grave breach regime under these Conventions.[310] Furthermore, not until 1995 was anyone prosecuted for alleged commission of a grave breach, and the prosecution was undertaken in the International Criminal Tribunal for the former Yugoslavia,[311] not a domestic court of States Parties to the Geneva Conventions. There is a dilemma here. An analysis of customary international law involves examining evidence of State practice as evidence of customary international law. Yet, even though States become party to multilateral treaties, they may not faithfully enact domestic legislation or take steps to implement their treaty obligations despite the obligation *pacta sunt servanda* as well as another cardinal rule in the law of treaties, that is, a party may not invoke the provisions, or shortcomings, in its internal law as a justification for its failure to perform a treaty.[312] Inconsistent State practice is not fatal to the formation of customary international law as long as the non-conforming conduct is accepted as a violation of the law and is not justified.[313] Given the lack of domestic provisions explicitly dealing with the obligation to extradite or prosecute, the position of States on their domestic laws is key. For example, in *Belgium v Senegal* Senegal acknowledged the violation of its international law obligations when it failed to enact legislation for the prosecution of the core crimes.[314] Thus, the inconsistent practice of Senegal does not detract from the formation of a rule of international customary law.

The ILC sought information from States regarding treaties containing a provision on the obligation to extradite or prosecute to which they were parties, and twenty-three States responded to this request.[315] In addition, Amnesty International has

[308] 36 Stat 2277, cited in the ICJ's *Nuclear Weapons* Advisory Opinion [1996] ICJ Rep257 [78] and 259 [84].

[309] Acquaviva, '*Aut Dedere Aut Judicare*' 254.

[310] See eg the judgments of French courts to the effect that as the Geneva Conventions had no direct effect in the national legal systems and France had not enacted legislation to implement the Geneva Conventions, France could not exercise extraterritorial jurisdiction over grave breaches under these Conventions (Brigitte Stern, 'International Decision: *In re Javor* and *In re Munyeshyaka*' (1999) 93 AJIL 525, 527).

[311] *Prosecutor v Duško Tadić* (IT-94-1).

[312] As codified in Arts 26 and 27, Vienna Convention on the Law of Treaties 1969 (1155 UNTS 331).

[313] *Nicaragua v United States of America*, 98 [186].

[314] See generally, Counter-memorial of the Republic of Senegal, *Questions relating to the Obligation to Extradite or Prosecute (Belgium v Senegal)*, vol 1 <http://www.icj-cij.org/files/case-related/144/16931.pdf>, accessed 17 November 2017, esp at 37 [218].

[315] UN Doc A/CN.4/579, UN Doc A/CN.4/579/Add 1–Add 4, UN Doc A/CN.4/599, and UN Doc A/CN.4/612. Cf the Special Rapporteur Galicki's third report (UN Doc A/CN.4/603) §§63–68.

published two memoranda on international treaties with universal jurisdiction and the obligation *aut dedere aut judicare*. The first one, published in 2001, included twenty-one such conventions concluded between the years 1929 and 2000.[316] The second one, published in 2009, was devoted to the presentation of the obligation *aut dedere aut judicare* in the context of the ILC's work, providing information on reservations, declarations, signatures, and ratifications as well as quoting provisions of the treaties dealing directly with universal jurisdiction and the obligation *aut dedere aut judicare*.[317] According to Amnesty International, there are at least thirty-seven international or regional instruments containing the obligation *aut dedere aut judicare*.[318]

The ILC Secretariat's Survey of June 2010[319] identifies sixty-one multilateral instruments at both the universal and regional levels that contain provisions combining extradition and prosecution as alternatives for the punishment of offenders. There is a great diversity in the formulation, content, and scope of the obligation to extradite and prosecute in conventional practice which might vary from one category of crimes to another and, in some cases, from one convention to another dealing with the same category of crimes. The Secretariat's Survey is discussed in Chapters 2 and 4 of this book. Special Rapporteur Galicki analysed the Secretariat's Survey in his fourth report[320] and the outcome of his analysis was a draft article entitled 'Treaty as a source of the obligation to extradite or prosecute', and not a conclusion as to whether such treaties recorded and defined rules deriving from custom, or indeed developed them.[321] This was despite the fact that some delegations in the Sixth Committee asked the ILC to analyse whether the accumulation of treaties containing the obligation *aut dedere aut judicare* and their wider acceptance by States signify the existence of an emerging rule of custom.[322]

There are legal scholars who argue that if a State has become party to a large number of treaties containing a variation of the *aut dedere aut judicare* principle, there is strong evidence that it intends to be bound by this generalizable provision, and that such practice should lead to the entrenchment of this principle in customary law because the said State articulates the belief that *aut dedere aut judicare* is an accepted norm, thereby satisfying the requirement of *opinio juris* when establishing customary norms.[323] In *Questions of Interpretation and Application of the 1971 Montreal Convention arising from the Aerial Incident at Lockerbie (Libyan Arab Jamahiriya v United Kingdom) and (Libyan Jamahiriya v United States of America)*,

[316] Amnesty International, *Universal Jurisdiction: The Duty of States*.
[317] Amnesty International, *ILC: The Obligation to Extradite or Prosecute*.
[318] ibid 21 and Annexes I and III.
[319] UN Doc A/CN.4/630 (18 June 2010).
[320] UN Doc A/CN.4/648 §§59–69.
[321] ibid §§70–72.
[322] Topical summary of the discussion held in the Sixth Committee of the General Assembly during its sixty-sixth session, prepared by the Secretariat (UN Doc A/CN.4/650 §44).
[323] Colleen Enache-Brown and Ari Fried, 'Universal Crime, Jurisdiction and Duty: The Obligation of Aut Dedere Aut Judicare in International Law' (1998) 43 McGill LJ 613, 629.

Judge Weeramantry, dissenting from the main Judgment on other points, seemed to subscribe to this argument when he referred to 'the principle of customary international law *aut dedere aut judicare*' which was 'well-established'.[324] However, in the same Orders, Judges Evensen, Tarassov, Guillaume, and Aguilar Mawdsley jointly stated that, as of 1992, 'in general international law there [was] no obligation to prosecute in default of extradition'.[325]

In 2010, Amnesty International published a paper focusing mainly on universal jurisdiction but, in one of the chapters, also reviewing widespread ratification of international legal instruments with the obligation to extradite or prosecute 'foreigners suspected of committing certain crimes abroad against other foreigners'.[326] For instance, as of the publication of the 2010 paper there were 167 States Parties to the 1979 International Convention on the Taking of Hostages,[327] 147 States Parties to the Convention against Torture,[328] 164 States Parties to the 1997 Convention for the Suppression of Terrorist Bombing,[329] and 146 States Parties to the 2003 UN Convention against Corruption.[330]

There is a dilemma here. The ICJ in *North Sea Continental Shelf* has held that ratification of a treaty by a large number of States may transform the treaty's provisions into customary law by influencing practice of non-States Parties.[331] Nevertheless, the more widespread ratification of a treaty, the fewer there are non-States Parties whose practice is vital to the transformation from treaty obligations to customary law.[332] Moreover, as the ICJ has clarified, where a State takes action to implement a treaty obligation, 'no inference could legitimately be drawn as to

[324] Provisional Measures, Orders of 14 Apr 1992 [1992] ICJ Rep at 69 (UK order) and 179 (USA order). Judge Weeramantry wrote: 'Another aspect of the 1971 Montreal Convention is that it does not interfere with the principle of customary international law *aut dedere aut judicare* [which is] an important facet of a State's sovereignty over its nationals and the well-established nature of this principle is evident from the following description: "The widespread use of the formula 'extradite or prosecute' either specifically stated, explicitly stated in a duty to extradite, or implicit in a duty to prosecute or criminalize, and the number of signatories to these numerous conventions, attests to the existing general *jus cogens* principle." (M Cherif Bassiouni, *International Extradition: United States Law and Practice*, 1987, p. 22.)' Special Rapporteur Galicki also added that Judge Ajibola, another dissenting judge in the Orders just mentioned, confirmed the existence of 'a right recognized in international law and even considered by some jurists as *jus cogens*' (Special Rapporteur's preliminary report (UN Doc A/CN.4/571 §55). However, on close scrutiny, what Judge Ajibola actually referred to was the right of a State not to extradite its own nationals. (See: Provisional Measures, Orders of 14 Apr 1992 [1992] ICJ Rep at 81–82 (UK order).)

[325] Provisional Measures, Orders of 14 Apr 1992 [1992] ICJ Rep at 24 (UK order) and 135 (USA order). The full statement on this point reads: 'In so far as general international law is concerned, extradition is a sovereign decision of the requested State, which is never under an obligation to carry it out. Moreover, in general international law there is no obligation to prosecute in default of extradition. Although since the days of Corvarruvias and Grotius such a formula has been advocated by some legal scholars, it has never been part of positive law. This being so, every State is at liberty to request extradition and every State is free to refuse it. Should it refuse, a State is not obliged to prosecute.'

[326] Amnesty International, *ILC ... International Justice Tool* ch III.

[327] 1316 UNTS 205. [328] 1465 UNTS 85. [329] 2149 UNTS 256.

[330] (2004) 43 ILM 37. [331] [1969] ICJ Rep 3, 43–44.

[332] RR Baxter, 'Treaties and Custom' (1970) 129 Recueil des Cours de l'Académie de Droit International 27, 73.

the existence of a rule of customary international law'.[333] However, States can be bound by the same rule both on the level of treaty law and on that of customary international law.[334]

Since there is still some debate as to whether the *aut dedere aut judicare* obligation has now become a customary international law obligation, there can be no presumption that treaties with a provision containing such obligation codify existing customary international law.[335] At most, such treaties can provide the 'impulse or model for the formation of a new customary rule' through a sufficiently extensive, representative, and uniform State practice outside the treaty framework among non-States Parties to such treaties themselves and/or between the non-States Parties and the States Parties to the treaties.[336]

In some cases, frequent repetition in widely accepted multilateral conventions may provide evidence of the recognition by the international community that a rule is of general law,[337] as in the case of various humanitarian conventions discussed by the ICJ in *Legality of the Threat or Use of Nuclear Weapons*.[338]

Because the multilateral treaties containing the obligation to extradite or prosecute have diverging formulae, it is difficult to find one standard 'model' on the obligation to extradite or prosecute that fits the definition of being of a 'fundamentally norm-creating character' in the sense of having the necessary degree of generality and compulsoriness in its observance among States.[339] Given the internal balance to each provision that were deliberately negotiated by States, any attempt to harmonize a customary international law obligation is unlikely to reflect a codification of international law or be acknowledged by States as acceptable progressive development. Even in the case of the Hague formula which provides the precursor for most contemporary treaties containing the obligation to extradite or prosecute, the ambiguity of this obligation in the 1970 Hague Convention was noted by the Secretariat's Survey.[340] Lastly, it could be argued that there is insufficient data on State practice and *opinio juris* in the absence of treaty obligations to indicate the existence of the obligation as a rule of customary international law. It is primarily for this last reason that Russia[341] and the USA[342] objected to the existence of a 'free-standing' obligation *aut dedere aut judicare.*

In *North Sea Continental Shelf*, the ICJ reasons that where a treaty permits reservations to all or certain of its provisions, those provisions are not declaratory of existing customary law.[343] The International Law Association has declined to adopt

333 [1969] ICJ Rep 3, 43 [76].

334 *Nicaragua v United States of America* 95 [178].

335 Cf ILA's Statement of Principles 43–44.

336 ibid 46–47, citing *North Sea Continental Shelf* 41, 43–44 [71, 75–76].

337 ILA's Statement of Principles 48. The ILA here stresses that the test as to whether this recognition is there remains 'qualitative rather than quantitative'.

338 Advisory Opinion, *Use of Nuclear Weapons* [1996] ICJ Rep 226, 256–59 [74–84].

339 [1969] ICJ Rep 3, 41–43 [70–74].

340 Secretariat's Survey §130.

341 *The obligation to extradite or prosecute (aut dedere aut judicare): Comments and information received from Governments*, 30 May 2008, UN Doc A/CN.4/599 §52.

342 ibid *(Addendum)*, 5 June 2007, UN Doc A/CN.4/579/Add 2 §§1–8.

343 [1969] ICJ Rep 3, 38–39 [63]: '[S]peaking generally, it is a characteristic of purely conventional rules and obligations that, in regard to them, some faculty of making unilateral reservations may, within

the ICJ's reasoning. According to the ILA, reservations might be permitted for some diplomatic reason and this does not in itself prove that those provisions to which the reservations are permitted are not rules of customary international law—and if they were customary international law, the mere fact that the treaty obligations could be removed or reduced would not affect their customary status.[344]

Most reservations to the multilateral treaties with the provision on the obligation to extradite or prosecute are related to non-extradition of nationals (Belgium, Brazil, Ecuador, Mongolia, and Panama); non-extradition of anyone for crimes carrying the death penalty or life imprisonment under the law of the requesting State (Portugal); non-extradition to stand trial on the grounds of ethnic origin, religion, nationality, or political views (Belgium); the condition that a State is obligated to prosecute only after receiving and rejecting an extradition request (Netherlands); the right not to submit any particular case for prosecution if the alleged offender is dealt with under national security and preventive detention laws (Malaysia); extradition only under specific treaty arrangements with the requesting State (St Kitts and Nevis and the USA); non-extradition for political offences (Belgium, Croatia, Cyprus, Estonia, Hungary, Iceland, Italy, Malta, Montenegro, Netherlands, San Marino, Sweden, and the former Yugoslav Republic of Macedonia), and the establishment of national jurisdiction only where the prosecution by another State having jurisdiction is not to be expected (Austria). In sum, these reservations do not dilute the essence of the obligation to extradite or prosecute, as they only condition the exercise of such obligation to fit the particular requirements under the respective domestic laws.

Logically, in so far as a particular crime is not a 'core crime' proscribed by *jus cogens* a State will have difficulty in finding legal justifications to extradite or prosecute a national of another State which is not party to the applicable multilateral convention binding on them both.

In conclusion, what may be said of the role of multilateral conventions with an extradite-or-prosecute provision in recording, defining, or developing rules deriving from custom in this matter is as follows. At most, the widespread adherence to multilateral conventions containing the obligation to extradite or prosecute in one format or another signifies States' conviction that they are obliged by international law to extradite or prosecute perpetrators of serious crimes of international concern and the conventions merely provide the necessary mechanism to realize this obligation. States are provided with the 'impulse' to commit themselves to prosecute perpetrators of crimes under international law or to extradite such persons to a State able and willing to prosecute them or to surrender them to a competent international criminal court.[345] In other words, it could be argued that States are

certain limits, be admitted—whereas this cannot be so in the case of general or customary international law rules and obligations which, by their very nature, must have equal force for all members of the international community, and cannot therefore be the subject of any right of unilateral exclusion exercisable at will by any one of them in its own favour.'

344 ILA's Statement of Principles, 44–45.

345 Cf Amnesty International, *ILC… International Justice Tool* 65. See also Robert Zimmermann, *La Coopération judiciare internationale en matière pénale* (3rd edn, Brylant 2009) 701–11.

bound by the same rule both on the level of treaty law and on that of customary international law.[346]

A number of States can only extradite according to binding treaty obligations. The fact that these States have become parties to virtually all of the treaties containing a provision on the obligation to extradite or prosecute could be considered as evidence of their conviction that there exists a customary international law obligation to extradite or prosecute serious crimes of common concern that they need to implement under their domestic legal system. The domestic law of the following States could probably be considered in this context: Armenia,[347] Burundi,[348] Cyprus,[349] Estonia,[350] Timor-Leste,[351] and Turkmenistan,[352] among others. Interestingly, Kuwait and Sweden have referred to the Rome Statute of the ICC as containing *aut dedere aut judicare* provisions.[353]

D. Conclusions of the analysis on customary international law

Special Rapporteur Galicki took note that the Sixth Committee looked up to the ILC for the answer to the question whether the obligation *aut dedere aut judicare* had a customary nature.[354] He then quoted in full the statement of Belgium's Counsel in *Belgium v Senegal* before the ICJ on 6 April 2009 on the customary international law obligation on States to prosecute or extradite perpetrators of crimes against humanity, genocide, and war crimes.[355] The sources cited by the Counsel for Belgium were operative paragraph 1 of UN General Assembly Resolution 3074 of 1973 entitled 'Principles of international co-operation in the detection, arrest, extradition and punishment of persons guilty of war crimes and crimes against humanity', Article 9 of the Draft Code of Crimes against the Peace and Security of Mankind, the preamble of the ICC Statute, the 1948 Genocide Convention, the four Geneva Conventions of 1949, and the 1984 Convention against Torture.[356] The identification of certain categories of crime as crimes of international concern, opined Galicki, might be recognized as 'a good directory of customary rules appropriate to

[346] Cf *Nicaragua v United States of America* 95 [178].

[347] Criminal Code of 2003, Art 15(3) stipulates: '[F]oreign citizens and stateless persons not permanently residing in Armenia who committed a crimes outside Armenian territory are subject to criminal liability under the Criminal Code of the Republic of Armenia, if they committed such crimes which are provided in an international treaty binding on Armenia' (Amnesty International, *Universal Jurisdiction: A Preliminary Survey* 26).

[348] Penal code of 2009, Art 10 (universal jurisdiction subject to extradition treaties), see Amnesty International, *Universal Jurisdiction: A Preliminary Survey* 38.

[349] Criminal Code, section 5(1)(e)(v)—universal jurisdiction over offences under any treaty binding on Cyprus, see Amnesty International, ibid 45.

[350] Penal Code of 2007—universal jurisdiction over all acts if the punishability of the acts arises from an international agreement binding on Estonia, see Amnesty International, ibid 53.

[351] Penal Code of 2009, Art 8(b)—universal jurisdiction pursuant to any international convention or treaty, Amnesty International, ibid 113.

[352] Criminal Code of 1998, Art 8(2)—universal jurisdiction where provided for in international treaties, see Amnesty International, ibid 115.

[353] UN Doc A/CN.4/599, 11 (Table 2).

[354] Special Rapporteur's fourth report, UN Doc A/CN.4/648 (31 May 2011) §§78–81.

[355] ibid §§82–83. [356] ibid n 55.

serve as bases for the obligation to extradite or prosecute'.[357] While conceding that there were some doubts whether the obligation *aut dedere aut judicare* possessed characteristics of *jus cogens*,[358] Galicki proceeded to take what was considered by 'some commentators' as 'the next logical step'[359] by proposing the following draft article:

Article 4

International custom as a source of the obligation *aut dedere aut judicare*

1. Each State is obliged either to extradite or to prosecute an alleged offender if such an obligation is deriving from the customary norm of international law.
2. Such an obligation may derive, in particular, from customary norms of international law concerning [serious violations of international humanitarian law, genocide, crimes against humanity and war crimes].[360]
3. The obligation to extradite or prosecute shall derive from the peremptory norm of general international law accepted and recognized by the international community of States (*jus cogens*), either in the form of international treaty or international custom, criminalizing any one of acts listed in paragraph 2.[361]

As already pointed out in Chapter 2, several States have expressed their disagreement with the conclusion that the customary nature of the obligation *aut dedere aut judicare* could necessarily be inferred from the existence of customary rules proscribing specific international crimes.[362] It is also argued by one scholar that the *erga omnes* and the *jus cogens* concepts do not as such lead to the formation of any source of international law, including custom, as the *erga omnes* concept plays a role in the law of State responsibility while the *jus cogens* concept relates to the law of State responsibility and the law of treaty, but these laws are 'technically alien to individual criminal responsibility'.[363]

Besides, Galicki's referring to the Genocide Convention in support of his conclusion is puzzling in so far as he also admitted that while the Genocide Convention did contain obligations for States to prosecute (where the genocide was committed on its territory) and to extradite, these were not an *aut dedere aut judicare* obligation which required States to elect either to extradite or prosecute. Therefore, in his opinion, if a person accused of committing genocide elsewhere was present on a State territory, the said State might be obliged to extradite the accused to a requesting State with

[357] ibid §91. Galicki (ibid §88) quoted William Schabas's contention that the recognition of an offence as an international crime gives rise to duties on the States with respect to investigation, prosecution, and extradition; ie the obligation *aut dedere aut judicare* (William Schabas, *The UN Criminal Tribunals: The Former Yugoslavia, Rwanda and Sierra Leone* (CUP 2008) 158).

[358] Special Rapporteur's fourth report, UN Doc A/CN.4/648 (31 May 2011) §94.

[359] Cf ibid §92.

[360] The list of crimes and offences in the square brackets 'seems to be still open and subject to further consideration and discussion', ibid §96.

[361] ibid §95.

[362] Topical summary of the discussion held in the Sixth Committee of the General Assembly during its sixty-sixth session, prepared by the Secretariat (UN Doc A/CN.4/650) §48.

[363] van Steenberghe, 'The Obligation to Extradite or Prosecute' 1092 and accompanying footnotes. Also, Mitchell, *Aut Dedere Aut Judicare* 33.

which it had an extradition treaty or other extradition arrangements but the former State was not obliged to prosecute the accused irrespective of whether an extradition request was made by the latter State.[364] His view seems to echo the ICJ's in the *Bosnian Genocide* case.[365] However, the Federal Court of Australia in *Re Thompson; Ex parte Nulyarimma* has enunciated differently, that 'the obligation imposed by customary law on each nation State is to extradite or prosecute any person, found in its territory, who appears to have committed any of the acts cited in the definition of genocide set out in the [Genocide] Convention'.[366] The Federal Court of Australia appears to proceed on the basis that although conventional law does not impose an obligation to extradite or prosecute, the *jus cogens* prohibition of genocide whose definition is codified in the Genocide Convention gives rise to a customary international law obligation to extradite or prosecute genocidaires.

It has been suggested that the customary international law duty to prosecute international crimes is emerging concerning prosecutions based on territoriality, and perhaps nationality, jurisdiction, and that international crimes are subject to permissive, as opposed to mandatory, universal jurisdiction by States.[367] Permissive universal jurisdiction means what a State may do on its own territory in order to investigate and prosecute crimes committed abroad and where neither the victim nor the offender is a national of the forum State.[368] This permissive universal jurisdiction only applies to prescriptive jurisdiction, which is about what a State may do *on its own territory* when investigating and prosecuting crimes committed abroad, not about *enforcement jurisdiction*, which is what a State may do *on the territory of other States* when prosecuting such crimes.[369] A State may not exercise *enforcement jurisdiction* outside its territory, failing permission of the other State concerned.[370] This

[364] Fourth report (UN Doc A/CN.4/648) n 34, quoting with approval Mitchell, *Aut Dedere Aut Judicare* 9.

[365] The ICJ's interpretation of the obligation under Art 6 of the Genocide Convention ('Persons charged with genocide or any of the other acts enumerated in Article 3 shall be tried by a competent tribunal of the State in the territory of which the act was committed, or by such international penal tribunal as may have jurisdiction with respect to those Contracting Parties which shall have accepted its jurisdiction.') is to the effect that this Article merely obligates Contracting Parties to institute and exercise territorial criminal jurisdiction as well as to cooperate with the international penal tribunal, including by accepting the jurisdiction of that tribunal (*Case Concerning Application of the Convention on the Prevention and Punishment of the Crime of Genocide (Bosnia and Herzegovina v Serbia and Montenegro)* [2007] ICJ Rep 43, 226–27 [442], 229 [449]).

[366] [1999] FCA 1192 (*per* Wilcox J).

[367] Robert Cryer, Håkan Friman, Darryl Robinson, and Elizabeth Wilmshurst, *An Introduction to International Criminal Law and Procedure* (2nd edn, CUP 2010) 72–73. Gerhard Werle et al, *Principles of International Criminal Law* (2nd edn, TMC Asser Press 2009) 198 and 954, asserts that the so-called mandatory universal jurisdiction has so far been universally recognized only for war crimes in international armed conflicts, as enshrined in the grave breach regime of the 1949 Geneva Conventions.

[368] Cf *Arrest Warrant of 11 April 2000 (Dem Rep Congo v Belgium)* [2002] ICJ Rep 3, 167–68 [49], 172–73 [56] (Dis Op of Judge ad hoc Van den Wyngaert).

[369] ibid 167–68 [49].

[370] ibid. See also Roger O'Keefe, 'Universal Jurisdiction: Clarifying the Basic Concept' (2004) 2 J Int'l Crim Justice 735, 740, 745, 750, 754, and 759; Karinne Coombes, 'Universal Jurisdiction: A Means to End Impunity or a Threat to Friendly International Relations?' (2011) 43 George Wash Int'l Law Rev 419, 436–39, 459–66.

is why an obligation to extradite or prosecute requires the presence of the accused within the forum State.[371]

Writing in 2009, Amnesty International asserted: 'The existence of an obligation [to extradite or prosecute] or its beginning could reasonably be presumed . . . at least regarding crimes under international law, such as genocide, crimes against humanity, war crimes, torture, enforced disappearances, and extralegal, arbitrary or summary executions.'[372]

Another empirical study on the subject, also published in 2009, concluded that, in view of the universal participation in the Geneva Conventions of 1949 and the recent increases in frequency of prosecutions of alleged perpetrators of grave breaches, there was 'at least an emerging customary obligation operating outside the [Geneva] Conventions themselves to extradite or prosecute'.[373] Indeed, the ICTY Appeals Chamber has held that national courts of any State are under 'a customary-law obligation to try or extradite persons who have allegedly committed grave breaches of international humanitarian law'.[374] This is also the case of the offence of torture, where there is 'a growing willingness' by States to recognize an obligation to either extradite or prosecute persons accused of torture, and this obligation exists independently of the Convention against Torture itself.[375]

However, this latter study reached a different conclusion in relation to genocide. It was pointed out that as of 2009 only fifty-seven States had enacted legislation to allow them to prosecute genocidaires present in their territory whom they did not extradite, and there was no universal prosecution of perpetrators of genocide. The study concluded there was 'not yet enough State practice' to find the existence of a customary international law obligation to extradite or prosecute for the crime of genocide.[376] With due respect, this contention ignores the fact that customary international law may crystallize from widespread practice of 'specially affected States'. In the context of the obligation to extradite or prosecute genocide, 'specially affected States' are those in whose territory genocide is committed or genocidaires are present. Genocide has been actively prosecuted in the past few decades in the ICTY and the ICTR, set up by the UN Security Council acting under Chapter VII of the UN Charter. The ICC itself has also taken up cases of alleged genocide. All States are bound by their obligations under Chapter VII of the UN Charter to surrender genocidaires to the ICTY or the ICTR where either tribunal has jurisdiction. States Parties to the ICC Statute are bound to surrender genocidaires to the ICC. National prosecution of perpetrators who committed genocide prior to or during the Second World War has also been pursued in domestic courts, as documented earlier in this chapter. It should be borne in mind, too, that acts constituting genocide under international law are serious criminal offences under national law of all States despite the

371 Cf *Arrest Warrant* [2002] ICJ Rep 3, 80 [57] (Joint Sep Op of Judges Higgins, Kooijmans, and Buergenthal).

372 Amnesty International *ILC: The Obligation to Extradite or Prosecute* 27–28.

373 Mitchell, *Aut Dedere Aut Judicare* 30.

374 *Prosecutor v Tihomir Blaskic* (Judgment on the Request of the Rep of Croatia for Review of the Decision of Trial Chamber II of 18 July 1997) IT-95-14, App Ch (29 Oct 1997) §29.

375 Mitchell, *Aut Dedere Aut Judicare* 30.

376 ibid 31 and Annex 3.

absence of the opprobrious label 'genocide' attached to such offences in national law, and their sentence is severe in proportion to the gravity of the acts. Therefore, the obligation to extradite or prosecute such serious criminal offences should be considered in the present context as well.

In addition, according to available information as of 2009, only 129 States had enacted national legislation to implement the grave breach regime under the universally ratified 1949 Geneva Conventions.[377] This means States do not always enact national legislation to implement their treaty obligations. A fortiori, when States enact national legislation, outside treaty obligations, to provide for prosecution on the basis of universal jurisdiction if they deny extradition of the person sought by another State, as discussed earlier in this chapter, such act should be considered as strong evidence of *opinion juris* of these States regarding the obligation to extradite or prosecute under customary international law.

To recapitulate, the process of identification of customary international law is a complex one and there is no scientific or mathematical formula to prove that a rule is or is not one of customary international law. Be that as it may, this present author submits, according to the available information and the preceding analysis and based on the standard of assessment of State practice by the ICJ, it may be concluded that the obligation *aut dedere aut judicare* has crystallized or at least is in the process of crystallizing into a rule of customary international law for the core crimes proscribed by *jus cogens*. For treaty-based crimes such as international terrorism, the obligation to extradite or prosecute appears in different treaty formulae.[378]

To conclude otherwise would mean applying the rules on identification of customary international law *too* stringently, or *too* 'formalistically', bearing in mind also that today's world is a world of nearly 200 States (as well as other international actors) whose practice is not usually well documented.

In addition, the application of the two-element approach of identification of customary international law in different fields (or for different types of rules) may differ. Fortunately, armed conflicts are not widespread all over the world and serious human rights violations are confined to some, not all, States. The practice of these States is, more often than not, to shield perpetrators of crimes from prosecution; hence, their practice, even as specially affected States, cannot be determinative of the customary international law status of a rule against impunity. In the former Yugoslavia, Rwanda in 1994, and in the mass execution situation during the Khmer Rouge regime in Cambodia, it is the 'imperatives of humanity' or 'the dictate of public conscience' of the rest of the members of the international community of

377 ibid Annex 3.

378 Cf Stoyan Minkov Panov, 'The Obligation *Aut Dedere Aut Judicare* ("Extradite or Prosecute") in International Law: Scope, Content, Sources and Applicability of the Obligation "Extradite or Prosecute" ', PhD thesis (Birmingham 2016), ch 4: 'Customary Law and the *Aut Dedere Aut Judicare* Obligation'. Panov concludes that the obligation to extradite or prosecute has formed or crystallized as a rule of customary international law for core crimes or some *jus cogens* prohibition such as torture, genocide, grave breaches of international humanitarian law, including war crimes, and crimes against humanity. The obligation is emerging as a rule of customary international law for offences against the safety of civil aviation and hijacking, terrorism-related activities, international drug trafficking, and crimes against UN and associated personnel.

States that constitutes both State practice and *opinio juris*. In other words, identification of a particular customary rule of customary international law under any field of international law, be it international human rights law, international humanitarian law and international criminal law, among others, must be considered in its proper context including the surrounding circumstances.

In *Kupreškić* et al, the Trial Chamber of the ICTY was discussing whether reprisals against civilians could be justified in modern days. Reprisals against civilians in combat zones are prohibited by Article 51(6) of the Additional Protocol I of 1977, and reprisals against civilian objects are outlawed by Article 52(1) of the said Additional Protocol. The ICTY asked a question whether these provisions, assuming that they were not declaratory of customary international law, had subsequently been transformed into general rules of international law. The Trial Chamber proceeded to state that:

> Admittedly, there does not seem to have emerged recently a body of State practice consistently supporting the proposition that one of the elements of custom, namely *usus* or *diuturnitas* has taken shape. This is however an area where *opinio iuris sive necessitatis* may play a much larger role than *usus*, as a result of the aforementioned Martens Clause. In the light of the way States and courts have implemented it, this Clause clearly shows that principles of international humanitarian law may emerge through a customary process under the pressure of the demands of humanity or the dictates of public conscience, even where State practice is scant or inconsistent. The other element, in the form of *opinio necessitatis*, crystallizing as a result of the imperative of humanity or public conscience, may turn out to be the decisive element heralding the emergence of a general rule or principle of humanitarian law.[379]

The ICTY Trial Chamber in that case was finding that the Marten Clause had long been recognized as a rule of customary international law, and the fact that recently there had not been a body of State practice that used this Clause, presumably because there had not been armed conflicts of the scale comparable to those in the former Yugoslavia in the early 1990s, did not negate the existence of such customary rule. This is subsequently made clear when the Trial Chamber stated that after the First World War 'it became clear to States that norms of international humanitarian law were not intended to protect State interests; they were primarily designed to benefit individuals *qua* human beings'. It added that '[t]his trend marks the translation into legal norms of the "categorical imperative" formulated by [the German philosopher Immanuel] Kant in the field of morals: one ought to fulfil an obligation regardless of whether others comply with it or disregard it.'[380] The same, it is hereby submitted, could be said of the obligation to extradite or prosecute in the present days.

A dilemma that needs to be tackled is the so-called 'Baxter paradox'. According to Harvard Law School Professor, and subsequently ICJ Judge Richard Baxter, it will become more difficult to assess what is the state of customary law outside treaty law when the number of parties to a treaty increases.[381] In the case of widely ratified treaties only a few States, which are not party, would be creating customary

[379] *Prosecutor v Zoran Kupreškić* et al (Judgment) IT-95-16-T, T Ch (14 Jan 2000) §527.
[380] ibid §518. [381] Baxter, 'Treaties and Custom' 64, 73.

law. In some fields of law it will moreover become impossible to ascertain the status of customary law outside treaty law. For example, in the case of the four Geneva Conventions of 1949, it would be impossible to assess the status of customary law outside the Conventions, as there are virtually no States outside this treaty regime. This is why, in 2005, the study by the International Committee of the Red Cross on customary international humanitarian law emphasized that the practice of States must not be excluded in determining the customary law status of a treaty provision.

On the other hand, the then ICJ President Tomka informed the Paris Conference in September 2012 that: 'In any event, widespread participation in a codification convention has never, in the jurisprudence of the Court, been sufficient on its own for the confirmation of a customary rule.'[382] Judge Tomka cited *Nicaragua v United States of America*, in which the ICJ had to decide whether, when States abstained from threatening or using force or from intervening, they had been motivated by a sense that customary international law, and not the UN Charter alone, proscribed such actions. Tomka stressed that the crux of the ICJ's inquiry in that case was on *opinio juris*, not State practice.[383]

In order to clarify the relationship between customary law and treaty law, the authoritative opinion in 1978 of the then ICJ President Jiménez de Aréchaga classified the way a treaty can interact with customary international law. According to him, a treaty can, first, have a declaratory effect of codifying existing law. Secondly, a treaty can have a crystallizing effect in the sense of codifying an emerging rule. Thirdly, a treaty may have a generating effect and represent constitutive evidence of acceptance as law, which will contribute to the formation of customary law.[384]

The Joint Separate Opinion of Judges Higgins, Kooijmans, and Buergenthal in *Arrest Warrant* is illuminating in relation to the identification of international law. On the question whether States are entitled to exercise such jurisdiction over persons accused of serious international crimes who have no connection with the forum State and are not present in the State's territory, while, after considering the practice of a handful States, the Judges found no established practice indicating the exercise of such jurisdiction, they did not find evidence of an *opinio juris* that deemed it unlawful, either. In addition, the growing number of multilateral treaties for the punishment of serious international crimes which contained the *aut dedere aut prosequi* provisions tended to be carefully drafted so as not to preclude the exercise of universal jurisdiction by national courts in these types of case. They concluded that while there might be no general rule specifically authorizing the right to exercise universal jurisdiction, the absence of a prohibitive rule and the growing international consensus on the need to punish crimes regarded as most heinous by the international community indicated that the exercise of such universal jurisdiction would not be unlawful.[385] It is hereby submitted that there is no prohibitive rule against

[382] *The Judge and International Custom* 39.
[383] ibid 39–40.
[384] Jiménez de Aréchaga, 'International Law in the Past Third of a Century' (1978) 159 Recueil des Cours de l'Académie de Droit International 1, 12–23.
[385] [2002] ICJ Rep 3, 68–79 [19–52]. This is in line with the reasoning of the ICJ in the *Nuclear Weapons* Advisory Opinion, where the ICJ opined that there was no prohibitive rule against the threat

the assumption by States of the obligation to extradite or prosecute perpetrators of core crimes under international law, either. As will be seen in Chapters 5–7, States are wary about possible 'abuse' of criminal prosecution for political purposes. If the exercise of the obligation to extradite or prosecute is in good faith, with due regard to the applicable rules of universal jurisdiction as well as immunities of State officials, it cannot be unlawful and is, thus, permissible as a rule of customary international law. The obligation to extradite or prosecute can, thus, be a reasonable and functional rule of customary international law for the international community.[386]

Treaty-based crimes, such as international terrorism, have been rather comprehensively covered by multilateral treaties, as will be shown in Chapter 4. States have undertaken to cooperate in suppressing serious crimes of common concern and what needs to be done is to ensure that they faithfully implement their treaty obligations.

Since certain States have strongly opposed giving a customary nature to the obligation to extradite or prosecute because of some concern over incompatibility with their domestic law on extradition and State jurisdiction, the ascription of a customary status to the obligation as a 'rule' (that is,'the obligation as conceived independently of the implementation system to which it is generally associated and which provides obligations concerning both extradition and State jurisdiction')[387] does *not* bind those States which were 'persistent objectors' while this customary obligation was in the process of emerging.[388] These persistent objectors are States that can extradite only on a basis of binding treaty obligations and have persistently and openly objected to and openly dissented from the position that there exists the obligation to extradite or prosecute beyond binding international legal instruments that contain such obligation. These persistent objectors include the USA[389] and the other States mentioned in Chapter 2.

or use of nuclear weapons as such, and that it could not be concluded definitively whether there was a prohibitive rule proscribing the unlawfulness of the threat or use of nuclear weapons in the extreme circumstance of self-defence, in which the very survival of a State would be at stake (Advisory Opinion in *Legality of the Threat or Use of Nuclear Weapons* 238 [21], and *dispositif* §2(E) of the Advisory Opinion). See also Dapo Akande, 'Nuclear Weapons, Unclear Law?: Deciphering the *Nuclear Weapons* Advisory Opinion of the International Court' (1997) 68 British YBIL 165, 213–15; Ole Spiermann, '*Lotus* and the Double Structure of International Legal Argument' in Laurence Boisson de Chazournes and Philippe Sands (eds), *International Law, the International Court of Justice and Nuclear Weapons* (CUP 1999) ch 9 esp 131–48.

[386] Cf David J Bederman, *The Spirit of International Law* (University of Georgia Press 2002) 37, on the argument that *opinio juris* can be proven when States 'follow a custom out of a sense that it is reasonable and functional for the international community'.

[387] van Steenberghe, 'The Obligation to Extradite or Prosecute' 1091, 1105, and 1116.

[388] *Asylum (Colombia v Peru)* [1950] ICJ Rep 266, 277–78; *Fisheries (United Kingdom v Norway)* [1951] ICJ Rep 116, 131. See also ILA's Statement of Principles 27–29 and 61; Curtis A Bradley and Mitu Gulati, 'Withdrawing from International Custom' (2010) 120 Yale LJ 202; Joel P Trachtman, 'Persistent Objectors, Cooperation, and the Utility of Customary International Law' (2011) 21 Duke J Int'l & Comp L 221.

[389] See eg general comments of the USA in UN Doc A/CN.4/579/Add 2 §§1–2.

4

The Obligation to Extradite or Prosecute for Non-Core Crimes as Treaty Obligations

The obligation to extradite or prosecute perpetrators of non-core crimes can be found in various conventions outside customary international law.

This chapter will first set out to explain the operation of the various provisions on the obligation to extradite or prosecute under the conventions covered by the ILC Secretariat's Survey of Multilateral Conventions dated 18 June 2010 (Secretariat's Survey). It will then address pertinent issues of international law pertaining to the implementation of these provisions; namely, double criminality *ratione materiae* and *ratione temporis*; the political offence exception; and the existence of humanitarian reasons to deny extradition. As the issue of immunity relates to the scope of the obligation to extradite or prosecute in both customary international law and treaties, it will be addressed in Chapter 6. However, this book will not address the principles of *nullum crimen sine lege* and *nulla poena sine lege* and that of *non bis in idem* (double jeopardy) which are common in domestic legal systems of the world and which are not peculiar to the obligation to extradite or prosecute.

I. Conventional Provisions on the Obligation to Extradite or Prosecute

The Secretariat's Survey involves an extensive survey of sixty-one universal and regional multilateral conventions that contain the obligation to extradite or prosecute as alternative courses of action for the punishment of alleged offenders.[1] The Survey describes the typology of the provisions in the various conventions and the preparatory work leading to their adoption.[2] The Survey also contains conclusions on the relationship between extradition and prosecution in the relevant provisions, the conditions applicable to extradition under the various conventions, and the conditions applicable to prosecution under the various conventions.[3] States may

[1] *Survey of multilateral conventions which may be of relevance for the work of the International Law Commission on the topic 'The obligation to extradite or prosecute (*aut dedere aut judicare*)'*, 18 June 2010, UN Doc A/CN.4/630 §4.

[2] ibid. [3] ibid §5.

choose the provision pertaining to the obligation to extradite or prosecute in any of these conventions which best suits their interest.

The essence of the Secretariat's Survey is as follows.[4]

A. Typology of provisions in multilateral instruments

The provisions on the obligation to extradite or prosecute contained in multilateral instruments can be classified as falling into four categories, based on chronological and substantive criteria: (1) the 1929 International Convention for the Suppression of Counterfeiting Currency and other instruments following the same model; (2) regional conventions on extradition; (3) the four Geneva Conventions of 1949 and the 1977 Additional Protocol I; and (4) the 1970 Hague Convention for the Suppression of Unlawful Seizure of Aircraft and other conventions following the same model.

The classification reflects an evolution in the drafting of provisions combining extradition and prosecution provisions and is useful in understanding the influence of certain conventions (such as the 1929 Counterfeiting Convention or the 1970 Convention for the Suppression of Unlawful Seizure of Aircraft) on conventional practice. It also highlights some fundamental similarities in the scope and content of provisions pertaining to the same category and reveals some general tendencies in the field. However, the classification is not intended to reflect a rigid separation, as some instruments concerning the same category are often very different in their content, and, in some instances, drafting techniques adopted in certain conventions have been followed in instruments belonging to a different category.

With respect to the mechanism under the 1929 International Convention for the Suppression of Counterfeiting Currency,[5] a distinction is made between nationals and non-nationals of the State concerned. It further recognizes that States employ different practices with regard to the exercise of extraterritorial jurisdiction and therefore does not oblige States to assert jurisdiction in every case in which extradition is refused.[6] The 1929 Convention serves as a prototype for other subsequent instruments.[7] Typically, this model: (1) criminalizes the relevant offence that States Parties undertake to make punishable under their domestic laws; (2) makes provision for prosecution and extradition that takes into account the divergent views of States with regard to the extradition of nationals and the exercise of extraterritorial jurisdiction,

[4] The author is grateful to Trevor Pascal Chimimba, Senior Legal Officer, Codification Division, Office of the UN Legal Counsel, for the faithful and detailed summary of the Secretariat's Survey that appears here.

[5] 112 LNTS 371.

[6] *Proceedings of the International Conference for the Adoption of a Convention for the Suppression of Counterfeiting Currency, Geneva, 9th April to 20th April 1929* (C.328.M.114.1929.II) annex III 234.

[7] The instruments include: (1) the 1936 Convention for the Suppression of the Illicit Traffic in Dangerous Drugs (198 LNTS 301); (2) the 1937 Convention for the Prevention and Punishment of Terrorism (League of Nations Doc C.546M.383 (1937)); (3) the 1950 Convention for the Suppression of the Traffic in Persons and of the Exploitation of the Prostitution of Others (96 UNTS 271); (4) the 1961 Single Convention on Narcotic Drugs (520 UNTS 204); and (5) the 1971 Convention on Psychotropic Substances (1019 UNTS 175).

the latter being permissive rather than mandatory; (3) contains provisions that impose an obligation to extradite, with prosecution coming into play once there is refusal of extradition; (4) establishes an extradition regime under which States undertake, under certain conditions, to consider the offence as extraditable; (5) limits the infringement of the convention upon the States' approach to the question of criminal jurisdiction as a question of international law; and (6) contains a non-prejudice clause with regard to each State's criminal legislation and administration.

While the provisions of the 1929 Convention are followed very closely in the subsequent instruments within the same category, some instruments contain terminological differences, some of which appear to be of editorial nature, while others modify the substance of the obligations undertaken by States Parties.

As for the regional conventions and arrangements on extradition, they also contain provisions that combine options of extradition and prosecution.[8] These instruments, while bearing in mind the regional peculiarities and traditions, have essentially been aimed at regulating cooperation in extradition matters. Even though they contain provisions combining the options of extradition and prosecution, they have emphasized the obligation to extradite (which is regulated in detail) and have only contemplated prosecution as an alternative to avoid impunity in the context of that cooperation. It is possibly assumed also that the territorial State will in any event take the necessary steps to prosecute in respect of offences committed on its territory. As extradition is conceived as a means to ensure the effectiveness of criminal jurisdiction, States Parties have a general duty to grant extradition. However, the framework has detailed provisions containing conditions and exceptions, including mandatory and discretionary grounds for refusal. For instance, extradition of nationals is prohibited or subject to specific safeguards. There is also need to satisfy the requirement of double criminality. Moreover, extradition will be refused with regard to political offences: if the person will be subjected to torture or other inhuman or degrading treatment or punishment; when extradition will be incompatible with humanitarian considerations in view of the age or health of the person sought; when an amnesty has been granted; if *ne bis in idem* applies; or when the offence is punishable by the death penalty in the requesting State which is not provided for by the law of the requested State.

Provisions in the foregoing two groups of agreements and arrangements have been subject to modification and adjustment over time, particularly in respect of conditions and exceptions. It may also be recalled that UN General Assembly has adopted the Model Treaty on Extradition[9] which provides an alternative to the provisions on the extradition aspect of the said agreements and arrangements.

[8] These instruments include: (1) the 1928 Convention on Private International Law (OAS, Law & Treaty Ser No 34), also known as the Bustamante Code, under Book IV (International Law of Procedure), Title III (Extradition); (2) the 1933 Inter-American Convention on Extradition (165 LNTS 20); (3) the 1981 Inter-American Convention on Extradition (OAS, Treaty Ser No 60); (4) the 1957 European Convention on Extradition (359 UNTS 273); (5) the 1994 Economic Community of West African States (ECOWAS) Convention on Extradition (Doc A/P1/8/94); and (6) the Scheme for the Extradition of Fugitive Criminals between Commonwealth Countries (or the London Scheme for Extradition within the Commonwealth) (M Cherif Bassiouni (ed), *International Criminal Law*, vol 2 (3rd edn, Martinus Nijhoff 2008) Appendix 1).

[9] UNGA Res 116 (XLV) (14 Dec 990) as amended by UNGA Res 88 (LII) (12 Dec 1997).

The third group of instruments comprise the four Geneva Conventions of 1949 which contain an identical mechanism for the prosecution of persons accused of having committed grave breaches.[10] Its underlying principle is the establishment of universal jurisdiction over grave breaches of the Conventions. Pursuant to the first paragraph of the common Article, the parties 'undertake to enact any legislation necessary to provide effective penal sanctions for persons committing, or ordering to be committed, any of the grave breaches' of the Conventions. In its second paragraph, the common Article specifies that:

> Each High Contracting Party shall be under the obligation to search for persons alleged to have committed, or to have ordered to be committed, such grave breaches, and shall bring such persons, regardless of their nationality, before its own courts. It may also, if it prefers, and in accordance with the provisions of its own legislation, hand such persons over for trial to another High Contracting Party concerned, provided such High Contracting Party has made out a prima facie case.

Under the third paragraph, the High Contracting Parties shall take measures to suppress all acts contrary to the Conventions other than the grave breaches. Pursuant to the fourth paragraph, the accused 'shall benefit by safeguards of proper trial and defence' in all circumstances, and that those safeguards shall not be less favourable than those provided by Article 105 and the following Articles of the third Geneva Convention relative to the Treatment of Prisoners of War.

Under this mechanism, there is an obligation to prosecute. Extradition is an option available to the State, provided the other Contracting Party establishes a prima facie case. The obligation to undertake measures against an alleged offender is not conditional upon any jurisdictional considerations of States. The obligation to search for and prosecute an alleged offender seems to exist irrespective of any request for extradition by another party.[11]

The Protocol Additional to the Geneva Conventions of 12 August 1949, and relating to the Protection of Victims of International Armed Conflicts (Protocol I) 1977[12] makes the common Article applicable to Protocol I by *renvoi*. Under its Article 85(1), '[t]he provisions of the Conventions relating to the repression of breaches and grave breaches, supplemented by this Section, shall apply to the repression of breaches and grave breaches of this Protocol.' Article 85(3) explicitly provides that the grave breaches enumerated in the Geneva Conventions and Protocol I shall be considered war crimes. Moreover, Article 88(2), on mutual assistance in criminal matters in connection with proceedings brought in respect of grave breaches, specifies that the parties to Protocol I shall, when the circumstances allow, cooperate in

[10] Geneva Convention for the amelioration of the condition of the wounded and the sick in armed forces in the field (75 UNTS 31) Art 49; Geneva Convention for the amelioration of the condition of wounded, sick and shipwrecked members of armed forces at sea (75 UNTS 85) Art 50; Geneva Convention relative to the treatment of prisoners of war (75 UNTS 135) Art 129; Geneva Convention relative to the protection of civilian persons in time of war (75 UNTS 287) Art 146.

[11] See Jean Pictet (ed), *The Geneva Conventions of 12 August 1949: Commentary*, vol 4 (ICRC 1958) 593.

[12] 1125 UNTS 3.

extradition matters. In this regard, due consideration shall be offered to the request of the State in whose territory the offence has occurred. Nevertheless, this duty is subject to the rights and obligations established in the Geneva Conventions and in Article 85(1) of the Additional Protocol. Article 88(3) provides that the law of the requested party shall apply in all cases, and that the provisions of paragraphs (1) and (2) of Article 88 shall not 'affect the obligations arising from the provisions of any other treaty of a bilateral or multilateral nature which governs or will govern the whole or part of the subject of mutual assistance in criminal matters'.

With regard to the fourth group of instruments, the 1970 Hague Convention for the Suppression of Unlawful Seizure of Aircraft,[13] containing 'The Hague formula', is a contemporary manifestation of a conventional mechanism that combines the options of extradition and prosecution. It is a variation of the Geneva Conventions formula. The Hague formula is contained in many other instruments adopted subsequently.[14]

In its original form, the Hague formula was aimed at making it obligatory to prosecute acts of unlawful seizure of aircraft, based on a system of multiple jurisdictions.

[13] (1971) 10 ILM 133.

[14] These include: the 1971 Organization of American States (OAS) Convention to Prevent and Punish the Acts of Terrorism Taking the Form of Crimes against Persons and Related Extortion that are of International Significance; the 1971 Convention for the Suppression of Unlawful Acts against the Safety of Civil Aviation; the 1973 Convention on the Prevention and Punishment of Crimes against Internationally Protected Persons, including Diplomatic Agents; the 1977 European Convention on the Suppression of Terrorism; the 1977 Organization of African Unity Convention for the Elimination of Mercenarism in Africa; the 1979 International Convention against the Taking of Hostages; the 1979 Convention on the Physical Protection of Nuclear Material; the 1984 Convention against Torture and Other Cruel, Inhuman or Degrading Treatment or Punishment; the 1985 Inter-American Convention to Prevent and Punish Torture; the 1987 South Asian Association for Regional Cooperation (SAARC) Regional Convention on Suppression of Terrorism and the 2004 Additional Protocol thereto; the 1988 Protocol for the Suppression of Unlawful Acts of Violence at Airports Serving International Civil Aviation, Supplementary to the Convention for the Suppression of Unlawful Acts against the Safety of Civil Aviation; the 1988 Convention for the Suppression of Unlawful Acts against the Safety of Maritime Navigation; the 1988 UN Convention against Illicit Traffic in Narcotic Drugs and Psychotropic Substances; the 1989 International Convention against the Recruitment, Use, Financing and Training of Mercenaries; the 1994 Inter-American Convention on the Forced Disappearance of Persons; the 1994 Convention on the Safety of United Nations and Associated Personnel and its the 2005 Optional Protocol; the 1996 Inter-American Convention against Corruption; the 1997 Inter-American Convention against the Illicit Manufacturing of and Trafficking in Firearms, Ammunition, Explosives, and Other Related Materials; the 1997 Organization for Economic Cooperation and Development (OECD) Convention on Combating Bribery of Foreign Public Officials in International Business Transactions; the 1997 International Convention for the Suppression of Terrorist Bombings; the 1998 Convention on the Protection of the Environment through Criminal Law; the 1999 Criminal Law Convention on Corruption; the 1999 Second Protocol to the Convention for the Protection of Cultural Property in the Event of Armed Conflict; the 1999 International Convention for the Suppression of the Financing of Terrorism; the 2000 Optional Protocol to the Convention on the Rights of the Child on the sale of children, child prostitution and child pornography; the 2000 UN Convention against Transnational Organized Crime and its Protocols; the 2001 Council of Europe Convention on Cybercrime; the 2003 African Union Convention on Preventing and Combating Corruption; the 2003 UN Convention against Corruption; the 2005 International Convention for the Suppression of Acts of Nuclear Terrorism; the 2005 Council of Europe Convention on the Prevention of Terrorism; the 2006 International Convention for the Protection of All Persons from Enforced Disappearance; the 2007 Association of Southeast Asian Nations (ASEAN) Convention on Counter-Terrorism; the 2010 Protocol Supplementary to the Convention for the Suppression of Unlawful Seizure of Aircraft; and the 2010 Convention on the Suppression of Unlawful Acts Relating to International Civil Aviation.

The obligation to prosecute was placed on the State of registration of the aircraft and the State of landing if the alleged offender left the aircraft in the latter State.[15] The system contains 'the obligation of apprehension of the alleged offender, a possibility of extradition, the obligation of reference to the competent authority and the possibility of prosecution'.[16] The overall logic of this system was maintained, with minor amendments by the Hague Conference.[17] The draft submitted by the Legal Committee contained the main elements of the mechanism that was later to be enshrined in the 1970 Hague Convention, including a provision imposing on States Parties, if they do not extradite, an obligation to submit the case to their competent authorities for prosecution.[18] At the consideration of the final draft in plenary, a compromise text was submitted that replaced the phrase 'whatever the motive for the offence' with 'without exception whatsoever',[19] and this amendment was adopted by the Conference.[20] In the course of the debate on Article 8, which obliged Contracting States to include the offence as an extraditable one in extradition treaties, it was clarified that this provision did not make extradition itself mandatory or automatic.[21] Paragraph 2 was added following a proposal whereby, *inter*

[15] The Chairman of the subcommittee (Gilbert Guillaume, the delegate from France, who later became a judge and President of the ICJ), during the proceedings of the Legal Committee, indicated that the subcommittee had started its work with a US proposal to establish priority jurisdiction for the State of registration of the aircraft in the case of unlawful seizure and to provide for extradition of the alleged offender to the State of registration of the aircraft even in exceptional cases, but that the majority of the States considered that, while this proposal presented the advantage of efficiency, it would probably not be accepted universally because of the then existing traditional extradition practice (ICAO, Legal Committee, Thirtieth meeting (3 March 1970) §12, in *Seventeenth Session (Montreal, 9 February–11 March 1970, Minutes and Documents relating to the Subject of Unlawful Seizure of Aircraft* (Doc 8877-LC/161)). A similar proposal was later put forward by the USA at the Conference. See generally, *International Civil Aviation Organization, International Conference of Air Law, The Hague, December 1970, Volume I: Minutes* and *International Civil Aviation Organization, International Conference of Air Law, The Hague, December 1970, Volume II: Documents.*

[16] ICAO, Legal Committee, Thirtieth meeting (3 Mar 1970) §15, in *Seventeenth Session.* As for draft Art 6 (on procedures for arrest, detention, and preliminary enquiry), the Chairman also noted that it was, as draft Art 9, borrowed from the Tokyo Convention (ibid §16).

[17] ICAO, Legal Committee, Thirty-fourth meeting (5 Mar 1970) §16, in *Seventeenth Session* (following a vote of the Committee).

[18] See 'Draft Convention' (SA Doc No 4), reproduced in *International Conference*, vol 2, 15–23. Draft Art 7 reads as follows: 'The Contracting State which has taken measures pursuant to Article 6, paragraph 1 [to take the alleged offender into custody or ensure his presence] shall, if it does not extradite the alleged offender, be obliged to submit the case to its competent authorities for their decision whether to prosecute him. These authorities shall take their decision in the same manner as in the case of other offences.'

[19] In the original proposal by Kenya, the phrase was 'without exception', but this was modified to add the word 'whatsoever', as proposed by the USSR, to reflect the wording of UN General Assembly resolution 2645 (XXV) (25 Nov 1970) on aerial hijacking or interference with civilian air travel, condemning, 'without exception whatsoever, all acts of aerial hijacking or other interference with civil air travel, whether originally national or international, through the threat of use of force, and all acts of violence which may be directed against passengers'. See *International Conference*, vol 1, Tenth plenary meeting, §§8 and 21.

[20] For the debate, see *International Conference*, vol 1, §7–64.

[21] ibid, Twelfth meeting of the Commission of the Whole, International Air Transport Association Observer (§26); see also the USA (§16) and India (§20). This point was also made in response to two amendments (SA Doc No 6 by Senegal and SA Doc No 64 by Tanzania) aimed at modifying the text of the provision to ensure that the Convention did not replace national laws governing extradition, notably

alia, 'the Contracting States which make extradition conditional on the existence of a treaty *shall* recognize the present Convention as the legal basis for extradition'. While this proposal was justified as filling a loophole in the Legal Committee's draft with respect to States that make extradition conditional on the existence of a treaty, and thus received some support, it was opposed by several delegations who did not want the Convention to constitute the basis for extradition. Such concerns were repeated in plenary in the final debate on the draft convention and, following a heated discussion, the proposal was amended to provide that the State concerned '*may at its option* consider this Convention as the legal basis for extradition in respect of the offence'.

The constituent elements of the mechanism contained in the various subsequent instruments that have adopted variations of the Hague formula include: (1) the criminalization of the relevant offence, which the States Parties undertake to make punishable under their domestic law, with penalties commensurate with the gravity of the offence; (2) an obligation to take such measures as may be necessary to establish jurisdiction over the offence when a State Party has a particular link with it—these obligatory and discretionary bases of jurisdiction vary from instrument to instrument; (3) provisions regarding measures to take the offender into custody and to proceed to a preliminary inquiry into the facts; (4) provision under which the State Party in whose territory the alleged offender is found shall, if it does not extradite him, submit the case to its competent authorities for the purpose of prosecution; and (5) provisions under which the State Party undertakes, under certain conditions, to consider the offence as an extraditable one.

While the Hague formula has served as a model for the drafting of the relevant provisions, many of these instruments have modified the original terminology, sometimes affecting the substance of the obligations undertaken. In particular, there are differences in the characterization of the offence to denote its seriousness, in some instances explicitly providing that the relevant offence should not be justifiable by considerations of a political, philosophical, ideological, racial, ethnic, religious, or other similar nature. There are also variations of the obligation by which the States Parties take such measures to establish their jurisdiction over the offence in the case where the alleged offender is in their territory and they do not extradite him. Moreover, there are variants in the formulation of the provision relating to submission of a case to competent authorities for the purpose of prosecution if the alleged offender is not extradited. There are also differences in relation to conditions and exceptions concerning extradition. In particular, for the purpose of extradition, the political exception (a political offence or as an offence connected with a political offence or as an offence inspired by political motives) or the fiscal exception clause is

on the granting of asylum in cases of political hijackings (see Tanzania (§11)). While the amendments were supported by delegations who insisted on the need to respect the sovereignty of States (United Arab Republic (§10); Tunisia (§§17–18); Rwanda (§19); Venezuela (§22); Ceylon (§§23–24); and Kuwait (§25)), they were rejected by the Commission of the Whole (§§30–31). Another proposal by Tanzania to avoid the implication that extradition should be resorted to automatically and to safeguard the validity of existing treaties was also rejected (see Thirteenth meeting of the Commission of the Whole §§39–42).

applicable in some instruments, while not applicable in others, especially the more recent conventions. Certain conventions specify that their provisions shall not be interpreted so as to impair the right of asylum. At the same time, some conventions provide that a request for extradition shall not be granted or mutual assistance denied in certain circumstances. These would include (1) where the requested State Party has substantial grounds for believing that the request is made for the purpose of prosecuting or punishing a person on discriminatory grounds and/or that the person's position may be prejudiced for that reason; (2) where there are substantial grounds for believing that the person would be in danger of being subjected to torture or other inhuman or degrading treatment or punishment; (3) if the requested Party has substantial grounds for believing that the person's position may be prejudiced because communication with the appropriate authorities of the State entitled to exercise rights of protection cannot be effected; or (4) if it appears to the requested State that it is unjust or inexpedient to surrender or return the fugitive offender by reason of the trivial nature of the case, by reason of the request for the surrender or return of a fugitive offender not being made in good faith or in the interests of justice, or for any other reason.

B. Relationship between extradition and prosecution in the relevant clauses

Provisions containing the obligation to extradite or prosecute share two fundamental characteristics: their objective to ensure the punishment of certain offences at the international level, and their use, for that purpose, of a mechanism combining the possibility of prosecution by the custodial State and the possibility of extradition to another State. Beyond these basic common features, provisions in multilateral conventions greatly vary, including in terms of the relationship they establish between these two possible courses of action. Although the relationship between the obligation to extradite or prosecute is not identical, the relevant provisions seem to fall into two main categories: (1) those clauses for which the obligation to prosecute is only triggered by the refusal to surrender the alleged offender following a request for extradition; and (2) those imposing an obligation to prosecute *ipso facto* when the alleged offender is present in the territory of the State, which the latter may be liberated from by granting extradition.

As the first category concerns instruments containing clauses imposing an obligation to prosecute only when extradition has been requested and not granted, States Parties (at least those that do not have a special link with the offence) do not have a general obligation *ipso facto* to prosecute the alleged offender present in their territory. When a State receives a request for extradition, these instruments recognize the possibility for the State to refuse to surrender the individual, either for reasons explicitly contemplated in the conventions themselves or on grounds based on its own national legislation. If it decides not to grant extradition, however, the State has the obligation to prosecute the individual. In other words, these conventions appear to give some priority to the option of extradition and provide the alternative of prosecution as a safeguard against impunity. In effect, these conventions appear to follow what was originally foreseen by Hugo Grotius when he referred to the principle *aut dedere aut punire*: when appealed to, a State should either punish the guilty person as he deserves, or it should entrust him to the discretion of the party making the appeal.[22]

It ought to be underlined that instruments under this category adopt very different mechanisms for the punishment of offenders, which may affect the interaction between extradition and prosecution. In some instances, there are detailed provisions concerning the prosecution of offences subject of the instrument, while in other cases the process of extradition is regulated in greater detail. The 1929 Counterfeiting Convention and subsequent conventions inspired by it belong to this category. The overall structure of the mechanism for the punishment of offenders in these conventions is based on the idea that the State in whose territory the crime was committed will request the extradition of the offender who has fled to another country, and that extradition should, in principle, be granted. These conventions, however, recognize that States may be unable to extradite in some cases (most notably, when the individual is their national or when they have granted asylum to him) and provide for the obligation to prosecute as an alternative.[23]

The multilateral conventions on extradition also fall into this category. By their very nature, the application of the rules of judicial cooperation and mutual assistance provided in them is triggered by the submission of a request for extradition. These conventions are based on the general undertaking by States Parties to surrender to one another all persons against whom the competent authorities of the requesting Party are proceeding for an offence or who are wanted for the carrying out of a sentence or detention order. This obligation to extradite, however, is subject to a number of conditions and exceptions. They provide for an alternative obligation to prosecute the offender whenever his extradition is refused, particularly on the grounds that he is a national of the requested State, as a mechanism to avoid impunity.

Some of the conventions that follow the Hague Formula could also be included in this category, whenever the relevant clause is to be interpreted as subjecting the obligation to prosecute to the refusal of a request for extradition.[24]

Clauses imposing an obligation to prosecute *ipso facto*, with the possible alternative of extradition, include all those clauses that impose an obligation upon States Parties to prosecute any person present in their territory who is alleged to have committed a certain crime. This obligation to prosecute exists *ipso facto* in that it arises as soon as the presence of the alleged offender in the territory of the State concerned is

[22] Hugo Grotius, *De Jure Belli ac Pacis*, Book II, chapter XXI, section IV (Francis W Kelsey tr, Clarendon/Humphrey Milford 1925) 527–29 at 527.

[23] See Marc Henzelin, *Le Principe de l'universalité en droit penal international: Droit et obligation pour les États de poursuivre et de juger selon le principe de l'universalité* (Helbing & Lichtenhahn/Faculté de droit de Genève/Bruylant 2000) 286 (who qualifies the system as *primo dedere secundo prosequi*).

[24] Christian Maierhöfer, '*Aut dedere—aut iudicare*': *Herkunft, Rechtsgrundlagen und Inhalt des völkerrechtlichen Gebotes zur Strafverfolgung oder Auslieferung* (Duncker & Humblot 2006) 349–50; Claire Mitchell, *Aut Dedere Aut Judicare: The Extradite or Prosecute Clauses in International Law* (Graduate Institute of International and Development Studies 2009).

ascertained,[25] regardless of any request for extradition. It is only when such a request is made that an alternative course of action becomes available to the State, namely the surrender of the alleged offender to another State for prosecution. In the absence of a request for extradition, the obligation to prosecute is absolute, but, once such a request is made, the State concerned has the discretion to choose between extradition and prosecution.

The clearest example would be the relevant common Article of the 1949 Geneva Conventions which provides that each State party 'shall bring' persons alleged to have committed, or to have ordered to be committed, grave breaches to those Conventions, regardless of their nationality, before its own courts, but 'may also, if it prefers', hand such persons over for trial to another State Party concerned. While this provision appears to give a certain priority to prosecution by the custodial State, it also recognizes that this State has the discretion to opt for extradition,[26] provided that the requesting State has made out a prima facie case.[27] When Austria was unable to extradite a stateless Palestinian who had grown up in a refugee camp in Syria and was seeking asylum in Austria to stand trial in war-torn Syria for the killing of twenty unarmed or wounded soldiers during an armed conflict in Syria, an Austrian court in Innsbruck tried the accused, convicted, and sentenced him to life imprisonment. This is a good example of the implementation of the said common Article of the Geneva Conventions.[28]

Article 7 of the 1970 Hague Convention for the Suppression of Unlawful Seizure of Aircraft provides that '[t]he Contracting State in the territory of which the alleged offender is found shall, if it does not extradite him, be obliged [. . .] to submit the case to its competent authorities for the purpose of prosecution.' Even though the text does not seem to resolve unequivocally the question of whether the obligation to prosecute arises *ipso facto* or only once a request for extradition is submitted and not

[25] On the need for the accused to be present in the territory of the State concerned as a precondition of the assertion of universal jurisdiction, see the Joint Separate Opinion of Judges Higgins, Kooijmans, and Buergenthal appended to the judgment of the International Court of Justice in *Arrest Warrant of 11 April 2000 (Democratic Republic of the Congo* v *Belgium)* [2002] ICJ Rep 3, 80 [57]; see also President Guillaume's Separate Opinion, ibid 39–40 [9]. See also Gilbert Guillaume, 'Terrorisme et droit international' (1989) 215 Recueil des cours de l'Académie de droit international 287, 368–9. For a view according to which the presence of the alleged offender in the territory of the State is not required for prosecution under the relevant provision of the 1949 Geneva Conventions, see Henzelin, *Le Principe de l'universalité en droit penal international*, 354.

[26] See eg Declan Costello, 'International Terrorism and the Development of the Principle *Aut Dedere Aut Judicare*' (1975) 10 J Int'l L & Economics 486; M Cherif Bassiouni and Edward M Wise, *Aut Dedere Aut Judicare: The Duty to Extradite or Prosecute in International Law* (Martinus Nijhoff 1995) 15; Maierhöfer, '*Aut dedere—aut iudicare*' 349–50. For authors who emphasize the priority attributed to prosecution in the Geneva Conventions, see Luigi Condorelli, 'Il sistema della repressione dei crimini di Guerra nelle Convenzioni di Ginevra del 1949 e nel primo protocollo addizionale del 1977' in P Lamberti Zanardi and G Venturini (eds), *Crimini di guerra e competenza delle giurisdizioni nazionali: Atti del Convegno, Milano, 15–17 maggio 1997* (Giuffrè 1998) 35–6; Henzelin, *Le Principe de l'universalité en droit penal international*, 353 (who qualifies the model of the Geneva Conventions as *primo prosequi secundo dedere*).

[27] Art 88(2) of Additional Protocol I to the Geneva Conventions calls on States Parties to 'give due consideration to the request of the State in whose territory the alleged offence has occurred', thus hinting at the idea that prosecution by the latter State would be preferable.

[28] 'Austria convicts asylum seeker of Syria war crimes' (*BBC News*, 11 May 2017) <http://www.bbc.com/news/world-europe-39879305>, accessed 9 November 2017.

granted, in a finding relating to a similar provision contained in Article 7 of the 1984 Convention against Torture and Other Cruel, Inhuman or Degrading Treatment or Punishment,[29] the Committee against Torture has found that:

> the obligation to prosecute the alleged perpetrator of acts of torture does not depend on the prior existence of a request for his extradition. The alternative available to the State party under article 7 of the Convention exists only when a request for extradition has been made and puts the State party in the position of having to choose between (a) proceeding with extradition or (b) submitting the case to its own judicial authorities for the institution of criminal proceedings, the objective of the provision being to prevent any act of torture from going unpunished.[30]

In *Belgium v Senegal*, the International Court of Justice (ICJ) has considered Article 7(1) as requiring:

> [T]he State concerned to submit the case to its competent authorities for the purpose of prosecution, irrespective of the existence of a prior request for the extradition of the suspect. ... The obligation to submit the case to the competent authorities, under Article 7, paragraph 1, may or may not result in the institution of proceedings, in the light of the evidence before them, relating to the charges against the suspect.
>
> However, if the State in whose territory the suspect is present has received a request for extradition in any of the cases envisaged in the provisions of the Convention, it can relieve itself of its obligation to prosecute by acceding to that request.[31]

Therefore, it follows that, pursuant to the Torture Convention, the choice between extradition and submission for prosecution does not mean that the two alternatives are to be given the same weight. Extradition is an option offered to the State Party by the Convention, whereas prosecution is international obligation under the Convention, violation of which is a wrongful act that would engage the responsibility of the State.[32]

This obligation does not necessarily imply that proceedings will be taken, let alone that the alleged offender will be punished. The formula used in the Hague Convention should, strictly speaking, be described as '*aut dedere aut prosequi*'.[33]

Although the Article in question does not establish a temporal limit for performance of the obligation, the ICJ has found that the text necessarily implies that it must be implemented within a reasonable time, in a manner compatible with the object and purpose of the Convention.[34]

[29] 1465 UNTS 85. Under this provision, '[t]he State Party in the territory under whose jurisdiction a person alleged to have committed any offence referred to in article 4 is found shall in the cases contemplated in article 5, if it does not extradite him, submit the case to its competent authorities for the purpose of prosecution.'

[30] *Guengueng* et al *v Senegal*, Merits, UN Doc CAT/C/36/D/181/2001 §9.7.

[31] [2012] ICJ Rep 422, 456 [94–95].

[32] ibid §95.

[33] See also Guillaume, 'Terrorisme et droit international' 354 and 368; Henzelin, *Le Principe de l'universalité en droit penal international*, 302 and 304–06.

[34] [2012] ICJ Rep 422, 460 [114]. In relation to the Geneva Conventions, although the text of the common Article is not unequivocal in this regard, the commentary explains that the obligation to search for the alleged offender (which constitutes a preamble to prosecution) arises '[a]s soon as a Contracting Party realizes that there is on its territory a person who has committed such a breach' (Pictet, *The Geneva Conventions*, 593).

In Article 9 of the ILC's 1996 Draft Code of Crimes against the Peace and Security of Mankind, the State Party in whose territory an individual alleged to have committed these crimes is found 'shall extradite or prosecute that individual'. It was stated that the obligation to prosecute arose independently from any request for extradition. The custodial State had an obligation 'to take action to ensure that such an individual is prosecuted either by the national authorities of that State or by another State which indicated that it was willing to prosecute the case by requesting extradition'.[35]

With respect to the option of extradition, the conventions also differ in the mechanisms they establish to provide a legal basis for extradition in respect of the relevant offences. Multilateral conventions on extradition, as well as a few conventions following the Hague formula,[36] directly impose upon States Parties a general obligation to extradite, subject to certain conditions. The 1949 Geneva Conventions do not address the issue of the legal basis for extradition, and Article 88 of its Additional Protocol I only calls on States Parties to cooperate in the matter of extradition,without prejudice to their obligations arising from other treaties on the subject of mutual assistance in criminal matters. The majority of the conventions, however, establish a system by which the relevant offence shall be deemed to be included as an extraditable offence in any existing extradition treaty between States Parties and such States undertake to include the offence as an extraditable offence in every future extradition treaty to be concluded among them, which is usually combined with provisions whereby States Parties which make extradition conditional on the existence of a treaty may consider the relevant convention as the legal basis of extradition and States Parties which do not make extradition conditional on the existence of a treaty shall recognize the offence as an extraditable offence between themselves.

Besides the multilateral conventions on extradition (which usually stipulate the conditions applicable to the extradition process, including possible grounds of refusal), nearly all the conventions specify that extradition is subject to the conditions provided by the law of the requested State. This implies that the requested State has the right to refuse extradition on the basis of the provisions of its domestic legislation. Such grounds of refusal may be connected to the offence (eg the statute of limitations has expired, the double criminality or the rule of speciality is not satisfied, or the crime is subject to the death penalty in the requesting State) or not so connected (eg the individual was granted political asylum or there exist humanitarian reasons to deny extradition).

Some conventions have included more elaborate provisions relating to the extradition process, which affect the operation of the clauses on prosecution and extradition. The degree of specificity of the rules concerning the conditions applicable to extradition have varied depending on several factors. Among them, the inclusion of more

[35] §(3) of the commentary to Art 9 (1996) ii YBILC (Part Two) 31. Reference should also be made to the commentary to Art 8 (whereby each State party 'shall take such measures as may be necessary to establish its jurisdiction' over the crimes set out in the draft code 'irrespective of where or by whom those crimes were committed').

[36] eg the 1999 Organization of African States' Convention on the Prevention and Combating of Terrorism (Omer Elagab and Jeehan Elagab (eds), *International Law Documents Relating To Terrorism* (3rd edn, Routledge-Cavendish 2007) 491).

detailed provisions has sometimes taken into account the specific concerns expressed during the course of negotiations (eg non-extradition of nationals, application or non-application of the political exception or fiscal exception clauses), the particular nature of the offence (for instance, the risk of refusal of extradition based on the political character of the offence appears to be more acute with respect to certain crimes), and a certain evolution in the drafting of the relevant provisions to take into account problems that may have been overlooked in the past (for instance, the possible triviality of the request for extradition or the protection of the rights of the alleged offender) or to take into account new developments or a changed environment. The reasons for the adoption of a certain type of regulation appear to depend on the particularities of each convention and its negotiating history, and should be assessed on the basis of a detailed examination of the relevant preparatory works. In order to make an accurate assessment of the scope of the obligations incumbent upon States under the clauses that combine the options of extradition and prosecution, the relevant provisions should not be read in isolation. These provisions are but one element of an overall mechanism for the punishment of offenders provided for under the relevant international instruments, which usually also includes rules relating to the criminalization of certain offences, the establishment of jurisdiction, the search for and arrest of alleged offenders, rules on cooperation in criminal matters, and the regime of extradition.

The Secretariat's Survey represents a holistic analysis of the relevant treaty obligations. It is unlikely that a more in-depth analysis of the provision would shed any more light on the treaty obligations. In addition, as already pointed out several times, it is not possible to harmonize the various provisions on the obligation to extradite or prosecute for all crimes. Each convention reflects its own internal balance that was achieved by States during the preparatory conferences. The variations in the provisions relating to prosecution and extradition appear to be determined by several factors, including the geographical, institutional, and thematic framework in which each convention is negotiated, and the specific concerns voiced by delegations.

Nevertheless, as the ILC's Final Report on the Obligation to Extradite or Prosecute (*aut dedere aut judicare*) has pointed out, one of the most relevant trends appears to be the 'Hague formula' that serves 'as a model for most of the contemporary conventions for the suppression of specific offences'.[37] Of the sixty-one conventions surveyed by the ILC Secretariat in 2010, forty-seven conventions were drafted on or after 1970 with approximately three-quarters of those conventions adopting the Hague formula. In these post-1970 Hague Conventions there is a common trend that the custodial State shall, without exception, submit the case of the alleged offender to a competent authority if it does not extradite. This obligation is supplemented by additional provisions that require State parties: (1) to criminalize the relevant offence under its domestic laws; (2) to establish jurisdiction over the offence when there is a link to the crime or when the alleged offender is present on their territory and is not extradited; (3) to make provisions to ensure the alleged offender is under custody and there is a preliminary enquiry; and (4) to treat the offence as extraditable.[38] In particular, under

[37] Secretariat's Survey §91. [38] ibid §109.

the prosecution limb of the obligation, the conventions only emphasize that the case be submitted to a competent authority for the purpose of prosecution. To a lesser extent, there is also a trend of stipulating that, absent prosecution by the custodial State, the alleged offender must be extradited *without exception whatsoever*. In addition to these elements, most of the conventions also adopt the additional provisions on criminalization, establishment of jurisdiction, and so forth, already mentioned.

The ILC's Final Report on the topic 'Obligation to extradite or prosecute (*aut dedere aut judicare*)', as appears in the Appendix to this book, explains the implementation of the Hague formula as clarified by the ICJ in the context of the Torture Convention.

As a matter of following best practices, States should emulate Article 11(1) of the 2006 International Convention for the Protection of All Persons from Enforced Disappearance,[39] stipulating:

> The State party in the territory under whose jurisdiction a person alleged to have committed [a crime under the Convention] is found shall, if it does not extradite that person or surrender him or her to another State in accordance with its international obligations or surrender him or her to a competent international criminal tribunal or any other competent court whose jurisdiction it has recognized, submit the case to its competent authorities for the purpose of prosecution.

Such a provision allows the possibility for the obligation to extradite or prosecute to be satisfied by a 'third alternative' of surrendering the alleged offender to a competent international criminal tribunal or a competent court whose jurisdiction the State concerned has recognized, thereby ensuring that there be no impunity for perpetrators of crimes covered by the convention in question.

Apart from the treaty regime, States may cooperate on an ad hoc basis to extradite offenders wanted for serious crimes, such as acts of terrorism and human trafficking. For example, the Joint Statement by the 23 States from Asia, Oceania, Western Europe, and North America participating in the First Workshop on International Legal Cooperation against Terrorism under the framework of the Bali Regional Meeting on Counter-Terrorism, in January 2005, under the chairmanship of the present author, declares:

> Increasingly, countries see it in their interests to cooperate as fully as possible, and to avoid being seen as providing a safe haven for terrorists. Bilateral and multilateral treaties provide the foundation for international cooperation. The overwhelming trend is for countries to use reciprocity undertakings on an ad hoc basis, outside their treaty obligations, when providing legal assistance. Some States do not require a reciprocity undertaking in order to provide assistance.[40]

[39] 2716 UNTS 3.

[40] Joint Statement on the Outcomes of the 1st Workshop, on file with the author. The said twenty-three participating States were: Australia, Brunei Darussalam, Canada, Cambodia, China, Fiji, France, India, Indonesia, Japan, Republic of Korea, Laos, Malaysia, Myanmar, New Zealand, Papua New Guinea, Philippines, Russia, Singapore, Thailand, Timor Leste, USA, and Vietnam. On file with the present author. The Process was set up after the bombings carried out by the terrorist group Jemaah Islamiyah in Bali, Indonesia, in October 2002 killing 202 victims (including 88 Australians, 38 Indonesians, and nationals of 20 other States) as well as injuring 209 other victims.

In addition, Annex 2 to the Chairman's Report of the Second Workshop on that matter, held on 27–29 June 2005, also under the chairmanship of the present author, summarizes responses from the seventy officials and experts from twenty-six participating States that:

> Normally countries use an extradition law/treaty as the basis for the preparation and application for extradition. For countries that do not have an extradition treaty, many of them use reciprocity as a basis for extradition, insofar as not prohibited by their domestic laws. . . .[41]

This practice of extradition absent a treaty has also been promoted among the forty States and three territories participating in the Bali process (Regional Ministerial Conference) on People Smuggling, Trafficking in Persons and Related Transnational Crime.[42]

II. International Legal Issues Pertaining to the Implementation of the Provisions on the Obligation to Extradite or Prosecute: Double Criminality, Political Offence Exception, and Human Rights Exceptions

The ILC's Final Report on the obligation to extradite or prosecute recognizes that under extradition law of most if not all States the necessary requirements to be satisfied include double criminality, *ne bis in idem, nullem crimen sine lege*, speciality, and non-extradition of the suspect to stand trial on the grounds of ethnic origin, religion, nationality, or political views.[43] The Report stresses that any condition under domestic law or a treaty pertaining to extradition must not be applied in bad faith, with the effect of shielding an alleged offender from prosecution in or extradition to an appropriate criminal jurisdiction, and that in the case of core crimes, the object and purpose of the relevant domestic law and/or applicable treaty is to ensure that perpetrators of such crimes do not enjoy impunity, implying that such crimes can never be considered political offences and be exempted from extradition.[44]

The application of the rule against double jeopardy (*ne bis in idem*) is well-established in the practice of States,[45] and will not be analysed here, in the context

[41] The 26 participating States were: Australia, Brunei Darussalam, Cambodia, Canada, China, Fiji, Germany, India, Indonesia, Italy, Japan, Republic of Korea, Laos, Malaysia, Myanmar, Netherlands, New Zealand, Papua New Guinea, Philippines, Russia, Singapore, Thailand, Timor Leste, United Kingdom, USA, and Vietnam. On file with the author.

[42] The 41 States and 2 territories are: Australia, Indonesia, New Zealand, and Thailand (as the four members of the Steering Group of the Bali Process) and Afghanistan, Bangladesh, Bhutan, Brunei Darussalam, Cambodia, China, North Korea, Fiji, France (on behalf of New Caledonia), Hong Kong, Macau, India, Iran, Iraq, Japan, Jordan, Kiribati, Lao PDR, Malaysia, Maldives, Mongolia, Myanmar, Nauru, Nepal, Pakistan, Palau, Papua New Guinea, Philippines, Rep. of Korea, Samoa, Singapore, Solomon Islands, Sri Lanka, Syria, Timor Leste, Tonga, Turkey, Vanuatu, and Vietnam. On file with the author.

[43] Final Report §22. [44] ibid §59.

[45] See eg Gerard Conway, '*Ne bis in idem* in International Law' (2003) 3 Int'l Crim L Rev 217; John AE Vervaele, '*Ne bis in idem*: Towards a Transnational Constitutional Principle in the EU?' (2013) 9 Utrecht L Rev 211.

of the obligation to extradite or prosecute. As for the statute of limitations for core crimes, there is widespread acceptance in both State practice and the legal literature that core crimes proscribed by *jus cogens* are not subject to the statute of limitations.[46] For non-core crimes, the requested State may refuse to grant extradition of the offender if the statute of limitations for the crime for which the person is sought has expired.

There are three aspects of the extradition law of States that may impede the implementation of the obligation to extradite or prosecute even though this obligation is incorporated in the relevant treaties binding on the States; namely, the requirement of double criminality in extradition; the political offence exception to extradition; and the human rights exceptions to the obligation to extradite the requested person.

A. Double criminality

In order to extradite a person to another State, it is an established customary practice that the offence in question must be an offence in both the requesting and the requested States. This rule is called 'double criminality' or 'dual criminality', designed to ensure reciprocal respect for the principle *nullum crimen sine lege* (no person shall be subject to a criminal punishment for a conduct that is not criminalized by law).[47] This is a main reason why treaties with the obligation to extradite or prosecute require States Parties to criminalize the offences proscribed by the treaties in their domestic criminal law.

Double criminality has three dimensions: substantive, temporal, and jurisdictional.

In terms of substance, the UN Office on Drugs and Crime's Model Law on Extradition (2004) recommends that:

> In determining whether an offence is an offence punishable under the laws of [country adopting the law] and the requesting State, it shall not matter whether:
> a) The laws of both [country adopting the law] and the requesting State place the acts or omissions constituting the offence within the same category of offences or denominate the offence by the same terminology or define or characterize it in the same way;
> b) The constituent elements of the offence may be different under the laws of both [country adopting the law] and the requesting State, it being understood that the totality of the acts or omissions as presented by the requesting State shall be taken into account.[48]

In other words, the 'conduct-based' test, focusing on the substantive underlying conduct as an offence, as opposed to the 'elements of crimes-based' test, focusing on technical terms or definitions of the offence, is to be preferred. The former test

[46] eg Art 29, Rome Statute of the ICC; 1968 Convention on the Non-Applicability of Statutory Limitations to War Crimes and Crimes against Humanity (754 UNTS 73); ICRC, *Customary International Law*, Rule 160. Statute of Limitations<https://ihl-databases.icrc.org/customary-ihl/eng/docs/v1_rul_rule160>, accessed 9 November 2017.

[47] Neil Boister, *An Introduction to Transnational Criminal Law* (OUP 2012) 218.

[48] <https://www.unodc.org/pdf/model_law_extradition.pdf>, accessed 9 November 2017, Sect 3(3), footnote omitted.

made it possible for Chile to extradite former Peruvian President Alberto Fujimori to stand trial in Peru. On 11 July 2007, a lower court in Chile, applying the elements of crimes test denied his extradition to Peru on charges of corruption and crimes against humanity because the majority of crimes Fujimori was charged with did not exist under Chilean law. This ruling was overturned by the Chilean Supreme Court on 21 September 2007, ruling that Fujimori was to be extradited to stand trial for the killings of twenty-five people in two separate massacres in 1991 and 1992 and for corruption although the killings were not criminalized as crimes against humanity under Chilean law at the time of the alleged killings.[49] This test for double criminality is incorporated in several extradition treaties and instruments[50] and is to be recognized as a best practice. Indeed, as early as in 1922 the US Supreme Court held that US law did not require the name by which the crime is described in the two States shall be the same, nor that the scope of the liability shall be coextensive, or, in other respects, the same in the two States; it is enough if the particular act charged is criminal in both jurisdictions.[51]

As for the temporal dimension, a clear illustration is the ruling by the UK House of Lords in *Pinochet (No 3)*, where it was held that all offences except torture for which Pinochet was being sought for extradition from the UK to Spain were not crimes under English law at the time of their commission. Hence, Pinochet was to be extradited to stand trial for torture only.[52]

Most of the participating States in the Workshop on International Legal Cooperation against Terrorism under the framework of the Bali Regional Meeting on Counter-Terrorism in 2005, mentioned at the end of section I above, explained that they determined double criminality at the time the conduct occurred, rather than when the request for assistance was received. However, they also witnessed 'a perceptible trend' towards determining double criminality at the time of the request. A part of such a trend is the judgment in August 2015 of a High Court of South Africa in *Patel Usman Ismail v State*, where the Court begs to differ from the ruling of the UK House of Lords in *Pinochet (No 3)*. Criticizing the approach adopted by the House of Lords in *Pinochet (No 3)* as too restrictive, the South African High Court reasons that even if the reasoning of the House of Lords in that case could be accepted as correct, it was an interpretation of the English Extradition Act, and, more particularly, of the definition of the term 'extradition crime' within the context of that statute, against the unique background and history of that law and in terms of the principles of UK law, not universally. The case at bar involves the interpretation

[49] Megan Hass, 'Fujimori Extraditable!: Chilean Supreme Court Sets International Precedent for Human Rights Violations' (2008) 39 Univ Miami Inter-Amer L Rev 373.

[50] Kimberly Prost, 'No Hiding Place: How Justice Need Not be Blinded by Borders' in Steven David Brown (ed), *Combating International Crime: the Longer Arm of the Law* (Routledge-Cavendish 2008) 123, 135–36, citing the example of Canada Extradition Act, SC 1999, c18 s 3(2); cf Gavan Griffith and Claire Harris, 'Recent Developments in the Law of Extradition' (2005) 6 Melbourne JIL 33, 37–42.

[51] *Collins v Loisel* 259 US 309, 312 (1922). See also *Heilbronn v Kendall* 775 F Supp 1020 (WD Mich 1991).

[52] *R v Bow Street Metropolitan Stipendiary Magistrate and Others, ex parte Pinochet Ugarte* (No 3) [2000] 1 AC 147, 194 (*per* Lord Browne-Wilkinson).

of Article 1 of the 2000 Extradition Agreement between South Africa and the USA[53] which provides that the States Parties 'agree to extradite to each other, pursuant to the provisions' of the Treaty 'persons whom the authorities in the Requesting State have charged with or convicted of an extraditable offence'. Article 2.1 of the Treaty provides that an offence shall be an extraditable offence if it is punishable under the laws of both States by deprivation of liberty for a period of at least one year or by a more severe penalty. Properly construed, Article 2.1 of the Treaty, which has to be interpreted consistently with the definition of 'extraditable offence' in South Africa's Extradition Act no 67 of 1962, is held not to refer to conduct that would have constituted an offence in South Africa at the time of its commission in the foreign State, but to refer to conduct which will constitute an offence in South Africa at least at the time of the extradition request, if not at the time when the enquiry is being conducted by the magistrate. This 'reasonable interpretation' of the definition in the Act and of the said Article is said to be in line with the preferred interpretation of many of the States who are signatories to the European Convention on Extradition, sub-article 2.1 of which is very similar in wording to the definition of 'extraditable offence' in the South African Act and to sub-article 2.1 of the 2000 Treaty. The wording of the definition of 'extraditable offence' in section 1of the Act is clearly non-retrospective, referring to conduct that must be an offence at the time of the extradition request in South Africa and not at a time of its commission in the foreign State.[54]

In October 2013, the Committee of Experts on the Operation of European Conventions on Co-operation in Criminal Matters conducted a survey of the practice of twenty European States on the reference moment to be applied when considering double criminality as regards extradition requests. According to the participating experts, the States that consider as determinative for the purpose of double criminality the moment when the offence was committed are France, Poland, and the UK. The following States consider as determinative for the purpose of double criminality the moment when the offence was committed, *provided* that it is also a crime at the time of the extradition request: the Czech Republic, Denmark, Georgia, Hungary, Italy, and Latvia. The States that consider as determinative for the purpose of double criminality the moment when the extradition request is received are Croatia, Finland, and Iceland. The States that consider as determinative for the purpose of double criminality the moment when the decision on the extradition request is made are Germany, Sweden, and Switzerland. For Greece, Portugal, Slovenia, and Ukraine, the double criminality must exist at the time of the commission of the offence, the receipt of the extradition request, and the decision on the request.[55]

With regard to the jurisdictional dimension of double criminality, it is closely related to the substantive and temporal dimensions discussed earlier in this section—if there is no jurisdiction, there is no criminality even when the conduct-based

[53] GNR 7100 of 29 June 2009.

[54] [2015] 4 All SA 382 (GJ), High Court of South Africa, Gauteng Local Division, Johannesburg (18 Aug 2015), upheld by the Supreme Court of Appeal on 1 December 2016.

[55] Compilation of replies to the questionnaire on the reference moment to be applied when considering double criminality as regards extradition requests, Council of Europe Doc PC-OC/Docs 2013/

test of double criminality is applied flexibly. For example, the Prosecutor of the International Criminal Tribunal for Rwanda (ICTR) requested that the trial of *Michel Bagaragaza* for conspiracy to commit genocide, genocide, complicity in genocide, and violations of the Geneva Conventions of 1949 and Additional Protocol II of 1977[56] committed in Rwanda in 2004 be transferred to Norway. Both the ICTR Trial and Appeals Chambers rejected this request in 2006. Norwegian law, as it stood in 2006, had a general provision providing jurisdiction over certain crimes, including homicide and serious bodily injury, when committed abroad by a foreigner, provided that the prosecution was authorized by the King. Norway submitted that the said provisions would cover the underlying acts alleged in the indictment against Bagaragaza, and that Bagaragaza's alleged genocidal intent, as well as the number of his victims, could be taken into account under provisions allowing for the most severe penalties in aggravating circumstances, thus fully reflecting the gravity of the crimes charged. The ICTR found against the transfer of the trial to Norway because Norway lacked the necessary jurisdiction as it could not charge the crime of genocide as defined in the ICTR Statute,[57] noting that the crime of homicide did not require proof of genocidal intent, an essential element of the crime of genocide under the Statute. It was held that the basis of the ICTR's authority to refer its cases to national jurisdictions flows from the ICTR Statute, Article 8 of which specified that the ICTR had concurrent jurisdiction with national authorities to prosecute 'serious violations of international humanitarian law', thereby allowing the ICTR only to refer cases where the State would charge and convict for those international crimes listed in the ICTR Statute.[58] The ICTR Prosecutor's subsequent effort, in 2007, to have the case transferred to be tried in the Netherlands also failed after the Dutch court had ruled, in similar case involving a Rwandan national, that it did not have jurisdiction to try the accused for genocide. Therefore, in implementing the obligation to extradite or prosecute under treaties, States Parties thereto must ensure that they have jurisdiction under their national law to exercise the widest jurisdiction permissible under international law in order to prosecute persons accused of committing any offence under the respective treaties.

For EU Member States, the requirement of double criminality is subject to the European Arrest Warrant (EAW) Framework Decision of 13 June 2002 on the European arrest warrant and the surrender procedures between Member States.[59] Article 2(2) of the Framework Decision provides the list of categories of offence which 'shall, under the terms of this Framework Decision and without verification of the double criminality of the act, give rise to surrender pursuant to a European arrest warrant'. This is provided that they are punishable in the Member State issuing

PC-OC(2013)12 (14 Nov 2013). The answer from the expert from Belgium is too vague for the present author to arrive at any definite conclusion.

56 1225 UNTS 609. 57 (1994) 33 ILM 1598.

58 *Prosecutor v Michel Bagaragaza* (Decision on Rule 11*bis*) ICTR-05-86-AR11*bis* (30 Aug 2006) §§13–16.

59 2002/584/JHA.

the arrest warrant by a custodial sentence or a detention order for a maximum period of at least three years and as they are defined as such by the law of the issuing Member State (ie not necessarily by the law of the requested State as well). The list includes arson, crimes within the jurisdiction of the International Criminal Court, hostage taking, rape, murder, causing grievous bodily injury, acts of terrorism, organized or armed robbery, participating in a criminal organization, trafficking in human beings, illicit drug trafficking, and unlawful seizure of aircraft or ships.

B. Political offence exception

The political offence exception features prominently in extradition practice.[60] Its two-fold rationale is to maintain a neutral position in internal political conflicts in another State, and to prevent the surrender of an offender to a jurisdiction where there is a risk that his trial or punishment might be unfairly influenced by political considerations.[61] What is a 'political' offence is usually subject to the determination of States requested to extradite persons, and there is no objective test that enjoys universal acceptance.[62]

After the First World War, the Netherlands refused to extradite German Emperor Kaiser Wilhelm II to stand trial for his roles in initiating and waging the First World War, on the grounds that the crime of the supreme offence against international morality and the sanctity of treaties he was charged with was political in nature and not punishable under Dutch law.[63] Things started to change after the Second World War, when the London Agreement setting up the International Military Tribunal at Nuremberg to try major war criminals[64] did away with any excuse not to surrender the persons sought to the Tribunal. Article 3 of the Agreement simply obligated States Parties thereto to, *inter alia*, take the necessary steps to make available for the investigation of the charges and trial of the major war criminals detained by them who were to be tried by the Tribunal at Nuremberg. The International Military Tribunal for the Far East set up by the Proclamation of the Supreme Commander for the Allied Powers to try and punish the major war criminals in the Far East was to mete out 'stern justice' to these criminals, without any exception.[65] Ad hoc international criminal tribunals established by the UN Security Council acting under

[60] See ICRC, *Customary International Law* database, ch 44 Practice relating to Rule 161. International Cooperation in Criminal Proceedings, Section D. Political offence exception to extradition, available at <https://ihl-databases.icrc.org/customary-ihl/eng/docs/v2_cha_chapter44_rule161_sectiond>, accessed 9 November 2017.

[61] *per* Lord Diplock in *Cheng v Governor of Pentonville Prison* [1973] AC 931, 945.

[62] See the detailed analysis of Reinhardt J in the US case of *Quinn v Robinson* 783 F 2d 776 (9th Cir 1986); C van den Wijngaert, *The Political Offence Exceptions to Extradition: The Delicate Problem of Balancing the Rights of the Individual and the International Public Order* (Kluwer 1980).

[63] Tim McCormack, 'From Sun Tzu to the Sixth Committee' in THL McCormack and GI Simpson (eds), *The Law of War Crimes: National and International Approaches* (Kluwer 1997) 44–48.

[64] Agreement by the Government of the United States of America, the Provisional Government of the French Republic, the Government of the United Kingdom of Great Britain and Northern Ireland, and the Government of the Union of Soviet Socialist Republic for the Prosecution and Punishment of the Major War Criminals of the European Axis of 8 August 1945, 82 UNTS 279.

[65] Second preambular paragraph, Special proclamation by the Supreme Commander for the Allied Powers at Tokyo, 19 January 1946, Treaties and Other International Acts Series 1589 at 20.

Chapter VII of the UN Charter also did away with the political offence exception, requiring States to comply without undue delay with any order by a Trial Chamber to surrender or transfer the accused to the Tribunal.[66]

The Genocide Convention is the first convention on core crimes of international law to explicitly stipulate, in Article VII, that genocide and the other acts related to genocide 'shall not be considered as political crimes for the purpose of extradition'. The prohibition and punishment of war crimes since the days of the Nuremberg Tribunal make it unimaginable that there could be a political offence exception to the extradition of war criminals, although some of them might commit such heinous acts out of patriotism and although the Geneva Conventions and their Additional Protocols may not explicitly exclude the political offence exception to extradition as does the Genocide Convention. There is no international treaty specifically focusing on crimes against humanity, unlike the crime of genocide or war crimes. Yet, crimes against humanity are no ordinary crimes—they must be committed as part of a widespread or systematic attack against the civilian population. To categorize such crimes as political offences would ignore the underlying facts that they are usually committed pursuant to a political objective or ideology.[67] So is the crime of aggression.[68] The ICRC has compiled an impressive list of examples of State practice to support the conclusion that genocide, war crimes, and crimes against humanity are not political offences.[69]

Torture, even when not committed as part of a widespread or systematic attack against the civilian population to qualify as a crime against humanity, has gained recognition as a crime proscribed by *jus cogens*, as the ICJ has held in *Belgium v Senegal*. Although the Convention against Torture does not have a provision excluding an act of torture from being considered a political offence, as does the Genocide Convention, the relevant provisions of the Torture Convention entail the same effect. Article 2(2) of the Torture Convention provides that '[n]o exceptional circumstances whatsoever, whether a state of war or a threat of war, internal political instability or any other public emergency, may be invoked as a justification for torture.' States Parties to the Torture Convention are required by Article 4 thereof to ensure that all acts of torture, attempted torture, and complicity or participation in torture are offences under their criminal law punishable by appropriate penalties that take into account their grave nature.

Beyond the prosecution of core crimes, the implementation of the political offence exception is in a state of flux. There have been extensive discussions of the gist

[66] eg Art 29, ICTY Statute ((1993) 32 ILM 1159) and Art 28, ICTR Statute.

[67] The Third report of the Special Rapporteur of the ILC on the topic 'Crimes against humanity' posits that the political exception is intended to cover conducts in the nature of activism seeking political change, and that 'there is support for the proposition that crimes such as genocide, crimes against humanity and war crimes should not be regarded as "political offences"' (Doc A/CN.4/704, §§43–44).

[68] As Carl von Clausewitz puts it, 'The political object is the goal, war is the means of reaching it, and the means can never be considered in isolation from their purposes' (*On War* (Michael Howard and Peter Pret trs, Princeton University Press 1976) 87).

[69] ICRC, *Customary International Law* database, ch 44 'Practice relating to Rule 161'.

of this subjective application of the political exception.[70] There can be 'pure political offences' in the sense of being directed solely at the State without affecting civilians and without being accompanied by the commission of a common crime. Examples of pure political offences include treason, espionage, sedition, and conspiracy to overthrow the government. 'Relative' political offences are those with *either* a combination of a common crime with a pure political offence *or* a common crime that is perpetrated pursuant to a political agenda. There are no fewer than three approaches in practice to relative political offences. First, the Anglo-American 'political incidence' approach requires that for an offence to be a political one, it must be 'incidental to and [form] part of political disturbances', as in the case of *In re Castioni* where a Swiss citizen killed a member of the local government in the course of the fighting during a violent anti-government demonstration, with no evidence of a private grudge against the deceased.[71] However, since there had to be two or more parties in the State, each seeking to impose the government of their own choice on the other, acts by anarchists do not qualify as political offences.[72] This approach has been followed in the US, as in *Artukovic v Boyle* where the extradition of a former pro-Nazi Croatian government official was denied despite evidence of his complicity in the execution of 200,000 Serb prisoners.[73] In another case, a US court denied the extradition to the UK of a member of the provisional Irish Republican Army (Provisional IRA) fighting for an independent republic for the whole of Ireland who killed a British soldier in an ambush in Northern Ireland, holding the conduct to be a political offence.[74] To circumvent this political offence exception for Provisional IRA members, the USA and the UK concluded the Supplementary Treaty Concerning the Extradition Treaty in 1985 to explicitly exclude acts of terrorism from the political offence exception.[75]

A more rigorous test for the political offence exception is the test of 'predominant motive' or 'proportionality' as practised in Switzerland, whereby the political character of the crime must outweigh its characteristics as a common crime. In the Swiss case of *Ktir v Ministère Public Fédéral* decided in 1961, for example, it was held that, in order to be a political offence, the conduct must have a predominantly political

[70] eg Ivan A Shearer, *Extradition in International Law* (Manchester University Press 1971) 166–93; Geoff Gilbert, *Transnational Fugitive Offenders in International Law: Extradition and Other Mechanisms* (Martinus Nijhoff 1998) 203–315, and *Responding to International Crimes* (2nd edn, Martinus Nijhoff 2006) 193–287. One succinct and illustrative analysis on the issue is by R Stuart Phillips, 'The Political Offence Exception and Terrorism: Its Place in the Current Extradition Scheme and Proposals for Its Future' (1997) 15 Dickinson JIL 337, 341–49.

[71] *In re Castioni* (1891) 1 QB 149, 150–52.

[72] *In re Meunier* (1894) 2 QB 415, 419.

[73] *Artukovic v Boyle* 140 F Supp 245 (SD Cal 1956), 170 F Supp 383 (SD Cal 1959).

[74] *In re Doherty* (1984) 599 F Supp 270, 272–76 (SDNY 1984). Cf *Quinn v Robinson*, another IRA-related case, where a US Court of Appeal held that Quinn was to be extradited because his killing of a London policeman in 1975 as part of the struggle for the IRA's cause had occurred in England, not Northern Ireland, and the political 'uprising' did not extend to England (783 F 2d 776 (9th Cir 1986)). See also M Cherif Bassiouni, *International Extradition: United States Law and Practice* (6th edn, OUP 2014) 679–712.

[75] (1985) 24 ILM 1105. See also Kathleen A Basso, 'The 1985 U.S.-U.K. Supplementary Extradition Treaty: A Superfluous Effort?' (1989) 12 Boston College Int'l & Comp L Rev 301. This Treaty has been subsequently amended.

character in the sense of being 'the sole means' of safeguarding and attaining a political aim.[76] Three years later, the Swiss court in *Watkin v Ministère Public Fédéral* explains that for a conduct to qualify as a political offence it must acquire a predominantly political character by the circumstances under which it is committed, especially by its motive and purpose. The act must be committed in the course of 'a struggle for or against those in power' or aims at 'saving persons from a power which tolerates no opposition', provided that 'the harm inflicted is proportionate to the object pursued and the interests involved are sufficiently important, if not to justify, then at least to provide a legal excuse for, the damage done by an offender to certain legally recognizable values'.[77] It is not settled whether this is an objective or subjective test, and Swiss courts are not consistent in their treatment of terrorists in the context of political offence claims.[78] Besides, there is a fallacy in the *Watkin* reasoning if taken to its extreme. As the Federal Court of Appeal of Canada states, *obiter*, in *Gil v Canada (Minister of Employment and Immigration)*:

> A very serious crime, such as murder, may be accepted as political if the regime against which it is committed is repressive and offers no scope for freedom of expression and the peaceful change of government or government policy. Under such a regime the claimant might be found to have had no other option to bring about political change. On the other hand, if the regime is a liberal democracy with constitutional guarantees of free speech and expression ... it is very difficult to think of any crime, let alone a serious one, which we would consider to be an acceptable method of political action. To put the matter in concrete terms, the plotters against Hitler might have been able to claim refugee status [in Canada]; the assassin of John F. Kennedy could never do so.[79]

A crucial question is who is to judge whether a regime is or is not repressive? This naturally rests with the court of the State requested to extradite an offender to another State, does it not?

Another approach, called the 'mixed' Continental approach, weighs the offender's motive against the seriousness of the crime—the more serious the crime, the more likely that extradition will be granted.[80] Yet, there is inconsistent application of this test.

Due to the elusiveness of the aforesaid approaches to determine the political offence exception,[81] some authors propose a rule of thumb that when violence is directed against a government or its institution it is revolution, when it is directed

[76] (1961) 34 ILR 143, 145–47. For the early history of this test as applied by a Swiss court in 1908, see Richard Bach Jensen, *The Battle against Anarchist Terrorism: An International History, 1878–1934* (CUP 2014) 332.

[77] (1964) 72 ILR 614, 616–17.

[78] Phillipps, 'The Political Offence Exception and Terrorism' 346–48.

[79] *Gil v Canada (Minister of Employment and Immigration)* (1997) 107 ILR 147, 167. The case was about the application of refugee law in Canada. The Court applied the 'incidence' test of political offence in the light of case law in the UK, USA, and elsewhere. It concluded on the facts of the case that the bombings of commercial stores owned by those allegedly supporting the government in that case lacked the nexus with any realistic political objective, and that the bombings were 'unacceptable as a form of political protest against any regime, however repressive, totalitarian or dictatorial' (ibid 168).

[80] Phillipps, 'The Political Offence Exception and Terrorism' 348–49.

[81] See further LC Green, 'Terrorism and Armed Conflict: The Plea and the Verdict' (1989) 19 Israel YB Hum Rights 131, 138–43.

against civilians and civilian property it is terrorism.[82] Nevertheless, there is no universal support in State practice for this proposed rule, as appeared from the case law mentioned earlier in this section.

With respect to international efforts to harmonize the practice on the political offence exception, Section 4, under the heading 'Offences of political nature', of the UN Office on Drugs and Crime's Model Extradition Treaty (2004),[83] recognizes that extradition '[shall not be granted] [may be refused], if the offence for which it is requested is an offence of a political nature', in which case the competent authorities of the States concerned shall, as appropriate, consult with a view to facilitating the resolution of the matter. This is without prejudice to offences in respect of which the requested State has assumed an obligation, pursuant to any multilateral convention or bilateral treaty or arrangement, either not to consider them as offences of a political nature for the purpose of extradition or to take prosecutorial action in lieu of extradition. An accompanying footnote suggests that States may also qualify that the following conducts do not constitute an offence of political nature for the purpose of extradition: murder or manslaughter; inflicting serious bodily harm; kidnapping, abduction, hostage-taking or extortion; using explosives, incendiaries, devices, or substances in circumstances in which human life is likely to be endangered or serious bodily harm or substantial property damage is likely to be caused; and an attempt or conspiracy to engage in counselling, aiding, or abetting another person to engage in, or being an accessory after the fact in relation to any of the conducts just referred to.

The ASEAN Treaty on Mutual Legal Assistance in Criminal Matters of 29 November 2004[84] allows States Parties not to provide legal assistance if the offence in question is of a political nature. It specifically clarifies that the following offences shall not be offences of a political nature: killing or injuring a Head of State or his/her immediate family member; killing or injuring a Head of Government or a Cabinet Minister; offences proscribed by international conventions binding on the parties to extradite or prosecute; or any attempt, abetment, or conspiracy to commit any of the above offences. Although the Treaty governs taking of evidence or statements of persons, effecting services of judicial documents, and executing searches and seizures, its provision on the scope of political offence exception is illuminating for the application of the political offence exception in the context of extradition, too.

The States participating in the Bali Process against international terrorism mentioned in section I are more ambitious. Their Joint Statement issued in 2005 asserts that offences under the UN terrorist-related conventions are not regarded as political offences, irrespective of whether the State requesting assistance is party to the conventions. Some States rely on case law rather than legislation to determine whether an offence is of a political character. In any event, the 'emerging norm of customary international law' does not recognize terrorist offences as political offences.

[82] Phillipps, 'The Political Offence Exception and Terrorism' 357, agreeing with Richard Allan, 'Terrorism, Extradition & International Sanctions' (1993) 3 Alb LJ Sci & Tech 327, 329.

[83] <https://www.unodc.org/pdf/model_law_extradition.pdf>, accessed 11 August 2017.

[84] ASEAN Legal Instruments No 9, available at <http://agreement.asean.org/home/index/2.html>, accessed 11 August 2017.

However, international conventions against terrorism are not uniform in excluding the offences covered by these respective conventions from being political offences. The 1963 Tokyo Convention on Offences and Certain Other Acts Committed on Board Aircraft [85] allows its States Parties not to take 'any action in respect of offences against penal law of a political nature'.[86] The other conventions and protocols adopted between 1963 and 1997 Terrorist Bombing Convention are silent on the political exception to extradition and prosecution. Article 5 of the 1997 Convention requires each State Party to adopt necessary measures to ensure that the criminal acts within the scope of this Convention, 'in particular where they are intended or calculated to provoke a state of terror in the general public or in a group of persons or particular persons, are under no circumstances justifiable by considerations of a political, philosophical, ideological, racial, ethnic, religious or other similar nature and are punished by penalties consistent with their grave nature'. The provision in Article 5 of the 1997 Convention has been followed by several subsequent conventions, such as Article 6 of the 2005 International Convention for the Suppression of Acts of Nuclear Terrorism.[87] When the 2010 Beijing Protocol Supplementary to the 1979 Hague Convention for the Suppression of Unlawful Seizure of Aircraft [88] was adopted in September 2010, its draftsmen deemed it necessary to stipulate in Article XII of the Protocol, which amends the 1970 Hague Convention, that the offences are not to be considered as political offences that are exempt from extradition and mutual legal assistance.

Treaties with the provision on the obligation to extradite or prosecute can thus be categorized into four broad categories in relation to the political offence exception. First, some treaties expressly recognize the political offence exception to extradition. Secondly, others expressly exclude the political offence exception to extradition. Thirdly, some other treaties are silent on the political offence exception. Finally, the rest of the treaties specify that the political offence exception shall be interpreted by them in a certain manner.

Article 30 of the 1969 Vienna Convention on the Law of Treaties[89] provides that where States are parties to successive treaties relating to the same subject matter, if a treaty specifies that it is subject to, or that it is not to be considered as incompatible with, an earlier or later treaty, the provisions of that other treaty prevail. When all the parties to the earlier treaty are parties also to the later treaty but the earlier treaty is not terminated or suspended, the earlier treaty applies only to the extent that its provisions are compatible with those of the later treaty. When the parties to the later treaty do not include all the parties to the earlier one, as between States Parties to both treaties the earlier treaty applies only to the extent that its provisions are compatible with those of the later treaty; but as between a State party to both treaties and a State party to only one of the treaties, the treaty to which both States are parties governs their mutual rights and obligations. However, although many treaties with the provision on the obligation to extradite or prosecute may address international

[85] 704 UNTS 219. [86] Art 2 of the 1963 Convention.
[87] UN Doc A/RES/59/290 (2005). [88] ICAO Doc 9959. [89] 1155 UNTS 331.

terrorism, each of them focuses on a different subject matter of international terrorism, be it the *modus operandi* or target of an act of terrorism. The rule on successive treaties just mentioned is, therefore, not applicable.

The fourth category of treaties, which specify that the political offence exception shall be interpreted by States Parties in a particular manner, may affect the interpretation of the political exception in other treaties, pursuant to the customary international law of treaty interpretation as codified in Article 31 of the 1969 Vienna Convention on the Law of Treaties.[90] According to this Article, in the interpretation of treaties:

3 There shall be taken into account, together with the context:
 (*a*) any subsequent agreement between the parties regarding the interpretation of the treaty or the application of its provisions;
 (*b*) any subsequent practice in the application of the treaty which establishes the agreement of the parties regarding its interpretation;
 (*c*) any relevant rules of international law applicable in the relations between the parties.
4. A special meaning shall be given to a term if it is established that the parties so intended.

Article 32 of the 1969 Vienna Convention under the heading 'Supplementary Means of Interpretation' provides that supplementary means of interpretation, including the preparatory work of the treaty and the circumstances of its conclusion, may be resorted to in order to confirm the meaning resulting from the application of Article 31, or to determine the meaning when the interpretation according to Article 31 *either* leaves the meaning ambiguous or obscure *or* leads to a result that is manifestly absurd or unreasonable.

In 2016, the International Law Commission (ILC) adopted a set of draft conclusions on the topic 'Subsequent Agreements and Subsequent Practice in relation to the interpretation of treaties'.[91] Draft conclusion 2 affirms that Articles 31 and 32 of the 1969 Vienna Convention set forth, respectively, the general rule of interpretation and the rule on supplementary means of interpretation; these rules also apply as customary international law. Draft conclusion 7 on possible effects of subsequent agreements and subsequent practice in interpretation posits:

1. Subsequent agreements and subsequent practice under Article 31, paragraph 3, contribute, in their interaction with other means of interpretation, to the clarification of the meaning of a treaty. This may result in narrowing, widening, or otherwise determining the range of possible interpretations, including any scope for the exercise of discretion which the treaty accords to the parties.
2. Subsequent practice under Article 32 can also contribute to the clarification of the meaning of a treaty.

[90] The ICJ has held that the rule in Art 31 of the Vienna Convention is a rule of customary international law (*Case concerning Kasikili/Sedudu Island (Botswana/Namibia)* [1999] ICJ Rep 1405, 1059 §18 and the cases cited therein).

[91] Report of the International Law Commission on the Work of the Sixty-eighth Session (2 May–10 June and 4 July–12 August 2016), Doc A/71/10, ch VI. See also an in-depth analysis of this provision in Georg Nolte (ed), *Treaties and Subsequent Practice* (OUP 2013) Parts 1 (Doctrinal Aspects), 2 (Practical Significance), 3 (Interpretation and Change), and 5 (Reports of the ILC Study Group on Treaties Over Time).

3. It is presumed that the parties to a treaty, by an agreement subsequently arrived at or a practice in the application of the treaty, intend to interpret the treaty, not to amend or to modify it. The possibility of amending or modifying a treaty by subsequent practice of the parties has not been generally recognized. The present draft conclusion is without prejudice to the rules on the amendment or modification of treaties under the Vienna Convention on the Law of Treaties and under customary international law.

Draft conclusion 10 clarifies that an agreement of the parties under Article 31(3)(a) and (b) of the Vienna Convention requires a common understanding regarding the interpretation of a treaty that the parties are aware of and accept. Though it may be taken into account, such an agreement need not be a legally binding one.

What is worrisome is the exclusion of the exercise of the right of self-determination from several treaties on international terrorism.

For example, although Article 15 of the 2005 International Convention for the Suppression of Acts of Nuclear Terrorism explicitly excludes the application of the political offence exception from the extradition of persons sought for the offences under that Convention, Article 4 of the same Convention provides:

1. Nothing in this Convention shall affect other rights, obligations and responsibilities of States and individuals under international law, in particular the purposes and principles of the Charter of the United Nations and international humanitarian law.

The provision in Article 4(1) of the 2005 Convention also appears in Article 19 of the 1997 International Convention for the Suppression of Terrorist Bombings[92] and Article VI of the 2010 Beijing Protocol, among others. The genesis of this kind of provision is the exclusion clause in the Draft Comprehensive Convention on International Terrorism under consideration at the UN General Assembly since the 1990s. The formula aims at excluding the exercise of the right of self-determination recognized under Article 1(2) of the UN Charter from the scope of these conventions.[93] In effect, while States must reject the political offence exception when considering requests for extradition of perpetrators of offences under the respective conventions, they may refuse to extradite the persons if the offences (which would have otherwise been acts of international terrorism) are in the pursuit of the right to self-determination by 'freedom fighters' to liberate their territory from foreign colonialism or occupation. This is the understanding of members of the Organization of the Islamic Cooperation (OIC), enunciated during the drafting of the Comprehensive Convention and echoing the approach in the OIC Convention on Combating International Terrorism of 1999,[94] Article 2 of which recognizes

[92] 2149 UNTS 256.

[93] Draft Art 3 [18] of the Draft Comprehensive Convention on International Terrorism reads: '1. Nothing in this Convention shall affect other rights, obligations and responsibilities of States and individuals under international law, in particular the purposes and principles of the Charter of the United Nations and international humanitarian law' (A/C.6/65/L. 10, annex II). Art 1(2) of the UN Charter specifically recognizes 'the principle of equal rights and self-determination of peoples'.

[94] Convention of the Organization of the Islamic Conference on Combating International Terrorism, 1 July 1999, Annex to Resolution No 59/26-P, available at <http://www.refworld.org/docid/3de5e6646.html>, accessed 10 November 2017.

that '[p]eoples' struggle including armed struggle against foreign occupation, aggression, colonialism, and hegemony, aimed at liberation and self-determination in accordance with the principles of international law shall not be considered a terrorist crime.'[95]

On 31 October 2016, Rohan Parera, chairman of the Working Group of the UN General Assembly's Sixth Committee on Measures to Eliminate International Terrorism, informed an informal meeting of permanent representatives to the United Nations in New York of the latest developments on the Draft Comprehensive Convention as follows. There was consensus among States that it was necessary to clearly define an act of terrorism as well as the need to distinguish between an act of terrorism and the right to self-determination. Besides, the Convention would be without prejudice to international humanitarian law and it would aim at ensuring that there be no impunity for perpetrators of acts of terrorism. The latest draft that the chairman of that Working Group considered to be well-balanced is still not acceptable to all groups of States, unfortunately.[96]

The deadlock is cause by the difference of opinion between the OIC and the rest of UN Member States relating to Draft Article 3 [18] of the Draft Comprehensive Convention on International Terrorism. Both sides agree with paragraph 1 of that Draft Article, which has already been incorporated in several conventions against international terrorism as mentioned above, stipulating: '1. Nothing in this Convention shall affect other rights, obligations and responsibilities of States and individuals under international law, in particular the purposes and principles of the Charter of the United Nations and international humanitarian law.' Although there is broad support for a paragraph providing that '[t]he activities of armed forces during an armed conflict, as those terms are understood under international humanitarian law, which are governed by that law, are not governed by the present Convention,' the OIC considers the wording of draft paragraph 2 to be failing to cover the situation of national liberation movements which are not 'armed forces' but are 'parties' to an armed conflict in situations of 'foreign occupation'. The OIC has, therefore, submitted the following counterdraft: 'The activities of the parties during an armed conflict, including in situations of foreign occupation, as those terms are understood under international humanitarian law, which are governed by that law, are not governed by this Convention.'

The Arab Convention for the Suppression of Terrorism,[97] adopted by the Council of Arab Ministers of the Interior and the Council of Arab Ministers of Justice in April 1998, follows the approach of giving recognition to freedom fighters. All Arab States are members of the OIC. Article 1(3) of the Arab Convention stipulates that

[95] See further Katja LH Samuel, *The OIC, the UN and Counter-Terrorism Law-Making: Conflicting or Cooperative Legal Orders?* (Hart 2013) 338ff.

[96] The latest draft appears in the Report of the Ad Hoc Committee established by General Assembly Resolution 51/ 210 of 17 December 1996, Sixteenth session (8–12 April 2013) UNGA Doc A/68/37 Annex II.

[97] League of Arab States, Arab Convention on the Suppression of Terrorism, 22 April 1998, available at <http://www.refworld.org/docid/3de5e4984.html>, accessed 10 November 2017.

the offences under five international conventions against terrorism, including the 1963 Tokyo Convention and the 1970 Hague Convention, shall also be regarded as terrorist offences under the Arab Convention, except when the conventions are not ratified by States Parties to the Arab Convention or where offences have been excluded by their legislation. Article 2 of the Arab Convention then provides:

(a) All cases of struggle by whatever means, including armed struggle, against foreign occupation and aggression for liberation and self-determination, in accordance with the principles of international law, shall not be regarded as an offence. This provision shall not apply to any act prejudicing the territorial integrity of any Arab State.
(b) None of the terrorist offences indicated in [Article 1] shall be regarded as a political offence. . . .

Subparagraph (b) proceeds to exclude the following offences from being regarded as a political offence, 'even if committed for political motives': (i) attacks on the kings, Heads of State or rulers of the contracting States or on their spouses and families; (ii) attacks on crown princes, vice-presidents, prime ministers or ministers in any of the Contracting States; (iii) attacks on persons enjoying diplomatic immunity, including ambassadors and diplomats serving in or accredited to the Contracting States; (iv) premeditated murder or theft accompanied by the use of force directed against individuals, the authorities or means of transport and communications; (v) acts of sabotage and destruction of public property; or (vi) the manufacture, illicit trade in or possession of weapons, munitions or explosives, or other items that may be used to commit terrorist offences.

Subparagraph (a), by specifically excluding liberation and self-determination that prejudices the territorial integrity of any Arab State, was traditionally understood as allowing freedom fighters to liberate the Palestinian territory from Israel, without the States Parties to the Arab Convention assuming an obligation to extradite them to be prosecuted for what would normally qualify as acts of terrorism. Hence, common enemies such as Al-Qaeda and the terrorist group called the Islamic State of Iraq and the Levant (ISIL), whose acts prejudice the territorial integrity of Arab States are terrorists who can be extradited to a State Party to the Arab Convention.[98] Things have changed, though. The diplomatic dispute among Arab States starting on 5 June 2017 has put the implementation of the Arab Convention to the test. Bahrain, Saudi Arabia, UAE, and Egypt cut diplomatic ties with Qatar which they accused of supporting 'terrorist organizations', including Hamas and the Muslim Brotherhood, thereby undermining the Palestinian Authority and Egypt, respectively. Yemen, Maldives, Mauritania, Senegal, and Libya soon joined in cutting diplomatic ties with Qatar, while Jordan and Djibouti downgraded their diplomatic relations with that State. Although Hamas, which has exercised de facto governing authority over the Gaza Strip since 2007, is considered a terrorist organization by Israel, USA, and several allies of the United States, Qatar treats it as a legitimate

[98] See eg Mohammad El-Sayed Selim, 'Arab Perceptions of Soft Security Issues' in Hans Günther Brauch et al (eds), *Coping with Global Environmental Change, Disasters and Security: Threats, Challenges, Vulnerabilities and Risks* (Springer 2011) 327, 329–31.

resistance movement. Less than three weeks later, Bahrain, Saudi Arabia, UAE, and Egypt issued a thirteen-point demand to Qatar, including that Qatar hand over all individuals wanted by the four States for terrorism; sever links with ISIL, al-Qaeda, the Muslim Brotherhood, and the Lebanese Shia militant group Hezbollah; and expel any members of Iran's Revolutionary Guard from Qatar. With regard to the link to al-Qaeda, Qatar was alleged to be backing Haya Tahrir al-Sham, previously known as al-Nusra Front, which is one of the most active jihadist groups fighting Syrian government forces to overthrow President Bashar al-Assad.

In order to end the conundrum, the recognition of 'legitimate freedom fighters' in the exercise of self-determination in the present era must be put in its proper perspective. The oft-cited justification for such recognition derives from Article 1(2) of the UN Charter—the purposes of the UN encompass developing friendly relations among nations 'based on respect for the principle of equal rights and self-determination of peoples'.

Of relevance is UN General Assembly Declaration on Principles of International Law concerning Friendly Relations and Co-operation among States in accordance with the Charter of the United Nations,[99] the pertinent part of which declares:

> Nothing [in the principle of equal rights and self-determination of peoples] shall be construed as authorizing or encouraging any action which would dismember or impair, totally or in part, the territorial integrity or political unity of sovereign and independent States conducting themselves in compliance with the principle of equal rights and self-determination of peoples as described above and thus possessed of a government representing the whole people belonging to the territory without distinction as to race, creed or colour.
>
> Every State shall refrain from any action aimed at the partial or total disruption of the national unity and territorial integrity of any other State or country.

In addition, the 1993 Vienna Declaration and Programme of Action,[100] adopted by the Second World Conference on Human Rights, states in paragraph I:

> 2. All peoples have the right of self-determination. By virtue of that right they freely determine their political status, and freely pursue their economic, social and cultural development.
>
> Taking into account the particular situation of peoples under colonial or other forms of alien domination or foreign occupation, the World Conference on Human Rights recognizes the right of peoples to take any legitimate action, in accordance with the Charter of the United Nations, to realize their inalienable right of self-determination. The World Conference on Human Rights considers the denial of the right of self-determination as a violation of human rights and underlines the importance of the effective realization of this right.
>
> In accordance with the Declaration on Principles of International Law concerning Friendly Relations and Cooperation Among States in accordance with the Charter of the United Nations, this shall not be construed as authorizing or encouraging any action which would dismember or impair, totally or in part, the territorial integrity or political unity of sovereign and independent States conducting themselves in compliance with the principle of equal

[99] UN Res 2625 (XXV) (1970). [100] UNGA Doc A/CONF.157/23.

rights and self-determination of peoples and thus possessed of a Government representing the whole people belonging to the territory without distinction of any kind.

These instruments and their relevance to the right to self-determination have been analysed by Judge Yusuf and Judge Cançado Trindade in the *Kosovo* Advisory Opinion by the ICJ. The ICJ in that case found it unnecessary to resolve the radically different views of whether, outside the context of non-self-governing territories and peoples subject to alien subjugation, domination, and exploitation, the international law of self-determination confers upon part of the population of an existing State a right to separate from that State, and whether international law provides for a right of 'remedial secession' and, if so, in what circumstances.[101] According to Judge Yusuf and Judge Cançado Trindade, post-colonial self-determination has two dimensions, internal and external. Internal self-determination is in the context of the relationship between peoples and their own State, especially (1) a right of the entire population of the State to determine its own political, economic, and social destiny and to choose a representative government; and (2) a right of a defined part of the population, which has distinctive characteristics on the basis of race or ethnicity, to participate in the political life of the State, to be represented in its government, and not to be discriminated against. External self-determination serves as 'remedial secession' and an exception to the cardinal rule of territorial integrity of States. External self-determination is permissible if (1) the State denies such groups the exercise of their right of internal self-determination; and (2) subjects them to systematic discrimination, persecution due to racial or ethnic characteristics, and egregious violations of human rights (eg torture, mass killing, ethnic cleansing, mass forced displacement of the population, and inhuman treatment) or international humanitarian law. Denial of autonomous political structures or a decision by the UN Security Council to intervene could be an additional criterion to be considered. All possible remedies for the realization of internal self-determination must be exhausted before external self-determination can be invoked.[102]

If the opinions of the two learned judges of the ICJ in the *Kosovo* Advisory Opinion are to be accepted as correct, the political offence exception to the treaty obligation to extradite or prosecute is to be applied in the following ways.

First, where the political offence exception is expressly allowed by treaties or required to be applied by domestic law of the requested State, the exception must be narrowly construed to cover 'pure' political offences not involving violence and/or physical damage caused to their victims.

Secondly, 'relative' political offences normally fall under the purview of one or more treaties proscribing acts of terrorism. Perpetrators of these offences are to be presumed to be extraditable. The presumption for the exception in such offences to be narrowly construed is justified by UN Security Council resolutions adopted

[101] *Accordance with international law of the unilateral declaration of independence in respect of Kosovo* [2010] ICJ Rep 403, 438 [82–83].

[102] Sep Op of Judge Yusuf, ibid 618, 621 [9ff]; Sep Op of Judge Cançado Trindade, ibid 523, 593 [174ff].

under Chapter VII of the UN Charter in order to combat international terrorism, which bind all UN Member States. The resolutions unequivocally reject any political or other excuses for acts of terrorism. For example, UN Security Council Resolution 1566 (2004) on threats and international security caused by terrorist acts provides in its operative paragraph 3:

> *Recalls* that criminal acts, including against civilians, committed with the intent to cause death or serious bodily injury, or taking of hostages, *with the purpose to provoke a state of terror* in the general public or in a group of persons or particular persons, *intimidate a population or compel a government or an international organization* to do or abstain from doing any act, *which constitute offences within the scope of and as defined in the international conventions and protocols relating to terrorism, are under no circumstances justifiable by considerations of a political*, philosophical, ideological, racial, ethnic, religious or other similar *nature*, and *calls upon* all States to [prevent/punish such acts].[103] (Emphasis added.)

Where treaties specify that the political offence exception shall be interpreted by them in a certain manner, as in the case of self-determination, the perpetrators must fulfil the conditions set by the Swiss test of predominant motive or proportionality, and the cause in question must fulfil the conditions for (internal) self-determination elaborated by Judges Yusuf and Cançado Trindade in the *Kosovo* Advisory Opinion.

It may be wise to have a treaty provision that excludes in a sweeping manner any political consideration in relation to extradition. A good example is Article 13(1) of the 2006 International Convention for the Protection of All Persons from Enforced Disappearance, which reads:

> For the purposes of extradition between States Parties, the offence of enforced disappearance shall not be regarded as a political offence or as an offence connected with a political offence or as an offence inspired by political motives. Accordingly, a request for extradition based on such an offence may not be refused on these grounds alone.

C. Human rights exceptions

Article 2 of the 1966 International Covenant on Civil and Political Rights (ICCPR)[104] obligates each State Party to the ICCPR to undertake to respect and to ensure to all individuals within its territory and subject to its jurisdiction the rights recognized in the ICCPR, including the right to life under Article 6 and the right not to be subjected to torture or to cruel, inhuman, or degrading treatment or punishment under Article 7 thereof. The Human Rights Committee of eighteen independent experts set up under the ICCPR to monitor the implementation of the ICCPR by its States Parties has issued General Comment no 31 that the Article 2 obligation entails an obligation not to extradite, deport, expel, or otherwise remove a person from their territory, where there are substantial grounds for believing that there is a real risk of irreparable harm, such as that contemplated by Articles 6 and 7

[103] UNSC Res 1566 (8 Oct 2004) UN Doc S/RES/1566.

[104] 999 UNTS 171.

of the ICCPR, either in the country to which removal is to be effected or in any State to which the person may subsequently be removed.[105]

The ICCPR has 169 States Parties as of this writing and many of its States Parties still retain the death penalty. However, other States, mostly Western European States, Australia, Canada, New Zealand, and States that have abolished the death penalty, cannot extradite a person to the requesting State which may impose a death penalty on the person if convicted. Serious crimes such as terrorist offences often carry the death penalty. It is the prerogative of the judiciary rather than the executive whether the death penalty is imposed. Yet, in some jurisdictions, the executive can commute the sentence to life imprisonment or bring a lesser charge. Where the requested State is prohibited by its own law or treaty obligation to extradite a person accused of committing an offence that carries the death penalty in the requesting State, a solution could be for the requesting State to give an undertaking to the requested State that the death penalty will not be sought or carried out.

For European States party to the 1950 European Convention on Human Rights,[106] Article 2 of the Convention protects the right to life, whereas Article 3 thereof proscribes torture as well as inhuman or degrading treatment or punishment. The European Court of Human Rights has held, in *Al-Saadoon and Mufdhi v the United Kingdom*, that although the death penalty had not violated international norms at the time when the Convention was drafted, there had been a subsequent development towards its absolute abolition, in law and in practice, within all the forty-seven Council of Europe Member States/States Parties to the Convention. Protocol no 6 to the Convention abolishes the death penalty in time of peace, whereas Protocol no 13 does so in all circumstances. All but three States Parties to the Convention had signed and ratified Protocol no 13. Consequently, Article 2 of the Convention had been amended so as to prohibit the death penalty in all circumstances, and the death penalty, which involved the deliberate and premeditated destruction of a human being by the State authorities, causing physical pain and intense psychological suffering as a result of the foreknowledge of death, could be considered inhuman and degrading and, as such, contrary to Article 3 of the Convention.[107] However, the European Court of Human Rights allows extradition to proceed where it considers, on a case-by-case basis in the light of the prevailing circumstances, that a diplomatic undertaking or assurance by the requesting State not to seek or carry out the death penalty against the person sought is adequate, convincing, and will be implemented by that State in good faith.[108]

[105] CCPR/C/21/Rev1/Add13 (26 May 2004) §12.

[106] ETS 5.

[107] No 61498/08, ECHR 2010. For an earlier case deciding that extradition of an offender to the US where there was a serious likelihood that he would be sentenced to death was a violation of Art 3 of the European Convention on Human Rights, see *Soering v the United Kingdom* (1989) 11 EHRR 439.

[108] The assurances were found to be adequate in eg *Einhorn v France*, no 71555/01, decision on admissibility ECHR 2001-XI; *Salem v Portugal*, no 26844/04 (9 May 2006); *Boumedienne and Others v Bosnia and Herzegovina*, nos 38703/06, 40123/06, 43301/06, 43302/06, 2131/07, and 2141/07, decision on admissibility (18 Nov 2008); *Babar Ahmad and Others v the United Kingdom*, nos 24027/07, 11949/08, and 36742/08, decision on admissibility (8 July 2010); *Harkins and Edwards v the United*

Regarding the obligation not to extradite or surrender a person to face torture or inhuman and degrading treatment or punishment, the ICTY Trial Chamber has authoritatively held in *Prosecutor v Furundžija* that since the prohibition of torture laid down in human rights treaties 'enshrines an absolute right, which can never be derogated from, not even in time of emergency', and that the prohibition on torture is a peremptory norm or *jus cogens*, States are 'barred by international law from expelling, returning or extraditing a person to another State where there are substantial grounds for believing that the person would be in danger of being subjected to torture'.[109] Although the prohibition of inhuman and degrading treatment or punishment has yet to be recognized as *jus cogens*, it is submitted that States Parties to the ICCPR and other human rights instruments prohibiting inhuman and degrading treatment or punishment do have treaty obligations not to extradite a person from their territory to another State where there are substantial grounds for believing that there is a real risk of that person being subject to inhuman and degrading treatment or punishment in that other State.[110] The assurance by the receiving/requesting State is evaluated in the same way as in the case of the person facing or risking the death penalty.[111] In addition to limitations regarding the death penalty and torture, as well as inhuman and degrading treatments or punishment, there is a broader human rights limitation to extradition.

While a crime cannot be regarded as some form of political activism and is not a 'political offence' as such, extradition may be denied where a requesting State is pursuing the extradition on account of the individual's political opinions or where the State is making its request for extradition as a means of persecuting an individual for his or her political views or for other reasons extraneous to his or her guilt of the charged offence.[112] A standard provision in multilateral conventions as well as bilateral extradition treaties allows the requested State to deny an extradition request where it has substantial grounds for believing that the request has been made for the purpose of prosecuting or punishing a person on account of that person's sex, race, religion, nationality, ethnic origin, or political opinions or that compliance with the request would cause prejudice to that person's position for any

Kingdom, nos 9146/07 and 32650/07 (17 Jan 2012); and *Rrapo v Albania*, no 58555/10 (25 Sept 2012). The assurances were found to be either inadequate or non-existent in eg *Bader and Kanbor v Sweden*, no 13284/04 (8 Nov 2005); *Al Nashir v Poland*, no 28761/11 (24 July 2014); and *AL (XW) v Russia*, no 44095/14 (29 Oct 2015).

[109] *Prosecutor v Furundzija* (Judgment) IT-95-17/I-T (10 Dec 1998) §144.

[110] See eg *Saadi v Italy* (2009) 49 EHRR 30 §§128–30, in which the European Court of Human Rights held that there can be no deportation or extradition of a person to another State where substantial grounds have been shown for believing that there is a real risk of treatment incompatible with the right not to be subjected to torture or to inhuman or degrading treatment or punishment under Art 3 of the European Convention on Human Rights, after examining the foreseeable consequences of sending the applicant to the receiving State, bearing in mind the general situation there and his or her personal circumstances. Cf also *Babar Ahmad and Others v the United Kingdom* (2012) 56 EHRR 1.

[111] See *Othman (Abu Qatada) v the United Kingdom* (2012) 55 EHRR 1 §189.

[112] The third report of the Special Rapporteur of the ILC on the topic 'Crimes against humanity', A/CN.4/704 §§49, 74.

one of these reasons.[113] States are also concerned that the extradited person must receive a fair trial in the requesting State, as required, for example, by Article 14 of the ICCPR and Article 6 of the European Convention on Human Rights. Where the person challenges his or her extradition on the ground that the right to a free trial in the requesting State will be violated, the competent authorities must scrutinize the challenge and ensure that the person is not extradited if the right is not guaranteed in the requesting State.[114] For example, in April 2017 a French court of appeal rejected Serbia's request for the extradition of former Kosovo Prime Minister Ramush Haradinaj to stand trial in Serbia for war crime charges, after concluding he would not have a fair and balanced trial in Serbia.

In conclusion, if the State where the accused is found cannot extradite him to stand trial in the requesting State for fear that his human rights will be jeopardized, the former State must either prosecute the person or, in the event that it does not have adequate resources to do so, extradite him to another State which has concurrent jurisdiction and can fulfil the human rights obligations in question, taking into account the competing interests of the territorial State, the State of nationality of the victim, the State of nationality of the offender, and the availability of evidence that would secure the effective prosecution of the offender. An example of concurrent jurisdiction may be found in the case of Ricardo Miguel Cavallo, a former Argentine navy commander of a detention centre in Buenos Aires where at least 614 victims were allegedly tortured and killed. He had been extradited from Mexico to Spain in 2003 to face charges of genocide and other crimes under Spanish law that allowed offences committed abroad to be tried in Spain if the accused was not facing prosecution in his own country. Spain stopped his prosecution after Argentina, the territorial State where the offences had allegedly been committed, requested his extradition. He was re-extradited from Spain to Argentina on 31 March 2008, after Mexico approved his re-extradition, to stand trial for killing and torturing left-wing activists during the 'dirty war' of 1976–83. In October 2011 he was sentenced to life imprisonment after being found guilty of thirteen counts of premeditated murder, twelve counts of torture aggravated by the political persecution of the victims, and twelve counts of aggravated unlawful deprivation of liberty and aggravated robbery.[115]

[113] See eg Art 14(15) of the UN Convention against Corruption; Art 9 of the International Convention against the Taking of Hostages; Art 6(6) of the 1988 United Nations Convention against Illicit Traffic in Narcotic Drugs and Psychotropic Substances; Art 12 of the International Convention for the Suppression of Terrorist Bombings; Art 15 of the International Convention for the Suppression of the Financing of Terrorism; and Art 13(7) of the International Convention for the Protection of All Persons from Enforced Disappearance.

[114] As in the European Court of Human Rights' decision in *Ahorugeze v Sweden*, no 37075/09 (4 June 2012).

[115] *Prosecutor v Ricardo Cavallo,* Trial Oral Federal No 5, Argentina, Case no 1298 (26 Oct 2011) <http://www.asser.nl/upload/documents/20121101T041309-Cavallo%20Tribunal%20Buenos%20Aires%20Fallo%2028-12-2011.pdf>, accessed 14 July 2017.

5

Universal Jurisdiction and the Obligation to Extradite or Prosecute

I. Rationale for Universal Jurisdiction

The generally accepted definition of universal jurisdiction (UJ) is that it is 'the jurisdiction to establish a territorial jurisdiction over persons for extraterritorial events'[1] where neither the victims nor offenders are nationals of the forum State.

An oft-cited rationale for UJ is that because of the atrocious nature of the crime in question, each State has a vested interest in its suppression and punishment despite the absence of a *nexus* with the forum State, otherwise its perpetrator may escape punishment.[2] As the Appeals Chamber of the ICTY in *Prosecutor v Tadić* puts it, 'Universal jurisdiction [is] nowadays acknowledged in the case of international crimes.'[3] This is also the view of the ICTY Trial Chamber in *Prosecutor v Furundžija* that as international crimes are universally condemned wherever they occur, every State is entitled to prosecute and punish the perpetrators of such crimes.[4]

In the *Arrest Warrant* case between the Democratic Republic of the Congo and Belgium before the International Court of Justice, the dispute involved the arrest

[1] *Arrest Warrant of 11 April 2000 (DR Congo v Belgium)* [2002] ICJ Rep 3, 75 [42] (Joint Sep Op of Judges Higgins, Kooijmans, and Buergenthal). For an authoritative account of the history of universal jurisdiction, see M Cherif Bassiouni, 'The History of Universal Jurisdiction and Its Place in International Law' in Stephen Macedo (ed), *Universal Jurisdiction: National Courts and the Prosecution of Serious Crimes under International Law* (University of Pennsylvania Press 2006) 39.

[2] Stephen Macedo (ed), *Princeton Project on Universal Jurisdiction* (Princeton University Press 2001), Principle 1(1): '[U]niversal jurisdiction is criminal jurisdiction based solely on the nature of the crime, without regard to where the crime was committed, the nationality of the alleged or convicted perpetrator, the nationality of the victim, or any other connection to the State exercising such jurisdiction.' Also, Sienho Yee, 'Universal Jurisdiction: Concept, Logic, and Reality' (2011) 10 Chinese JIL 503, 504–05.

[3] Decision on the defence motion of interlocutory appeal on jurisdiction, IT-94-1, ICTY App Ch (2 Oct 1995) §62.

[4] Judgment, IT-95-17/1-T, T Ch (10 Dec 1998) §156, quoting the Supreme Court of Israel in *Eichmann* which is also endorsed by a US court in *Demjanjuk*, 'it is the universal character of the crimes in question ... which vests in every State the authority to try and punish those who participated in their commission' (*Attorney-General of the Government of Israel v Adolf Eichmann* (1968) 36 ILR 277, 298; *In the Matter of the Extradition of John Demjanjuk* 612 F Supp 544, 558 (ND Ohio 1985). See also *Demjanjuk v Petrovsky* 776 F 2d 571 (6th Cir 1985) cert denied, 475 US 1016, 106 S Ct 1198, 89 L Ed 2d 312 (1986), for a discussion of the universality principle as applied to the commission of war crimes.

warrant issued by a Belgian investigating judge in exercise of his purported universal jurisdiction for the arrest of the incumbent Minister of Foreign Affairs of DR Congo. DR Congo originally challenged the legality of the arrest warrant before the ICJ on two separate grounds: Belgium's claim to exercise a universal jurisdiction and the alleged violation of the immunities of the Minister for Foreign Affairs of DR Congo then in office. However, in the submissions in its Memorial, and in its final submissions at the close of the oral proceedings, DR Congo invoked only the second ground. The ICJ considered that, logically, the second ground was to be addressed only once there had been a determination in respect of the first ground, since it is only where a State has jurisdiction under international law in relation to a particular matter that there could be any question of immunities in regard to the exercise of that jurisdiction. However, in the case at bar, and in view of the final form of DR Congo's submissions, the ICJ addressed first the question whether, assuming that Belgium had jurisdiction under international law to issue and circulate the arrest warrant, Belgium in so doing violated the immunities of the then Minister for Foreign Affairs of DR Congo.[5] Having found Belgium in violation of the personal immunity (or immunity *ratione personae*) of the Minister of Foreign Affairs of DR Congo, the ICJ abstained from deciding on the issue of UJ originally raised by DR Congo.

Nevertheless, ICJ President Guillaume in his Separate Opinion believes it useful to explain his position on whether the Belgian judge had jurisdiction to issue the international arrest warrant. In his view, traditionally customary international law did recognize UJ over piracy; whereas in modern days UJ is conferred by treaties over offences covered in the respective treaties. Whenever the perpetrator of any of the offences covered by these treaties is found in the territory of a State, that State is under an obligation to arrest and then extradite or prosecute him. The State must have first conferred jurisdiction on its courts to try him if he is not extradited, thereby assuring universal punishment of the offences in question, as the perpetrators are denied refuge in all States. By contrast, none of these treaties has contemplated establishing jurisdiction over offences committed abroad by foreigners against foreigners when the perpetrator is not present in the territory of the State in question. Universal jurisdiction *in absentia* is, in Judge Guillaume's opinion, unknown to international conventional law.[6]

The Joint Separate Opinion of Judges Higgins, Kooijmans, and Buergenthal approaches UJ from a different angle. They consider the inaccurately termed 'universal jurisdiction principle' in treaties to be, in fact, a 'principle of obligation' for each State Party to establish the necessary jurisdiction over the crimes under the respective treaties. The question in *Arrest Warrant* was different: whether Belgium had the right to issue and circulate the arrest warrant if it so chose. While the Joint Separate Opinion finds there is no established practice in which States exercise UJ, properly so-called, there is no evidence of *opinio juris* that renders it illegal

[5] [2002] ICJ Rep 3, 18–19.

[6] ibid 37–40 [5–9] (Sep Op of President Guillaume).

either. Thus, while there is no general international law specifically authorizing the right to exercise UJ, the absence of a prohibitive rule and the growing international consensus on the need to punish the most serious crimes indicate that the arrest warrant issued by Belgium did not as such violate international law.[7] On UJ *in absentia*, it must be borne in mind that while some jurisdictions provide for trial *in absentia*, others do not. If a person must be within the jurisdiction at the time of the trial itself, that may be a prudent guarantee for the right of fair trial but has little to do with bases of jurisdiction recognized under international law. For the obligation to extradite or prosecute, there cannot be an obligation to extradite someone a State chooses not to try unless that person is present within that State's reach. Although 'these sensible realities' are critical for the obligatory exercise of the obligation to extradite or prosecute, they cannot be interpreted *a contrario* so as to exclude a voluntary exercise of a universal jurisdiction. There is no rule of international law (and certainly not the *aut dedere* principle) which makes illegal cooperative overt acts designed to secure the presence of perpetrators of international crimes within a State wishing to exercise jurisdiction. If a State chooses to exercise a universal criminal jurisdiction *in absentia*, it must also ensure that certain safeguards are put in place. These safeguards are 'absolutely essential to prevent abuse and to ensure that the rejection of impunity does not jeopardize stable relations between States'. First, a State contemplating bringing criminal charges based on universal jurisdiction must offer to the national State of the prospective accused person the opportunity itself to act upon the charges concerned. Secondly, such charges may only be laid by a prosecutor or *juge d'instruction* who acts in full independence, without links to or control by the government of that State. Thirdly, there should be some special circumstances that do require the exercise of an international criminal jurisdiction and if these have been brought to the attention of the prosecutor or *juge d'instruction*; for example, persons related to the victims of the case will have requested the commencement of legal proceedings. Finally, universal criminal jurisdiction must be exercised only over those crimes regarded as the most heinous by the international community, such as piracy and crimes against humanity.[8]

Judge ad hoc Van den Wyngaert appointed by Belgium, in her Dissenting Opinion, contends that international law does not prohibit States from enacting legislation allowing themselves to exercise prescriptive extraterritorial jurisdiction to investigate and prosecute war crimes and crimes against humanity committed abroad. In her view, international law permits and even encourages UJ to end impunity for such crimes—even *in absentia* (although there may be good political/practical reasons not to assert jurisdiction *in absentia*, for example international relations costs and the difficulty in obtaining the evidence in trials of extraterritorial crimes).[9] At the opposite end, Judge ad hoc Bula-Bula, appointed by DR Congo,

[7] ibid 75–79 [44–52] (Joint Sep Op of Judges Higgins, Kooijmans, and Buergenthal).
[8] ibid 79–83 [56–65].
[9] ibid 165–77 [44–67] (Dis Op of Judge ad hoc Van den Wyngaert).

states in his Separate Opinion that UJ is 'variable geometry' jurisdiction, selectively exercised against some States to the exclusion of others.[10]

Which one or more of the opinions of the ICJ judges in *Arrest Warrant* is/are correct? Could the Joint Separate Opinion of Judges Higgins, Kooijmans, and Buergenthal plus the Dissenting Opinion of Judge ad hoc Van den Wyngaert be correct, but the ongoing debate is merely about preventing the abuse of UJ?

II. International Developments Regarding Universal Jurisdiction

Where serious crimes of international concern are committed by State agents pursuant to an official or unofficial policy of the incumbent government leadership, the State of nationality of the offenders can usually shield them from the long arm of the law, except in two situations. First, there has been a regime change in that State and the new regime is opposed to its predecessor's heinous acts. Second, an offender visits another State and that other State is able and willing to exercise universal jurisdiction (UJ) over the person and the crime in question, and that person does not enjoy any immunity from the criminal jurisdiction of the State where he or she is present. Apart from that, UJ normally works vis-à-vis nationals of States with low leverage against the foreign State exercising UJ over the persons.

According to one study, from the trial of Adolf Eichmann in Israel in 1961 up to August 2010, out of the possible 1,051 defendants (including 259 in Spain, 235 in Germany, 261 in Canada, 85 in the UK, 70 in Australia, 63 in Belgium, 37 in France, 17 in Turkey, 16 in Switzerland, 12 in Norway, 11 in Sweden, 3 in Israel, and one in the USA), only 32 were tried on the basis of UJ, 24 of whom were Nazis, former Yugoslavs, and Rwandans. For five out of the eight remaining defendants (four Afghans and one Congolese), their State of nationality did not protest the UJ prosecution. The other two (one Mauritanian and one Tunisian) were nationals of 'low-leverage' States (but they were tried *in absentia* and did not serve any sentence). The other defendant was an Argentine tried in Spain over Argentina's protests. In the UK, there were only two defendants prosecuted under UJ—Anthony Sawoniuk (an ex-Nazi) prosecuted under the War Crimes Act of 1991 and convicted and sentenced in 1999 to life for murder of two Jews in Belarus in 1942; and Faryadi Sarwar Zardad (an ex-Afghan Mujahideen leader) prosecuted under section 134(1) of the Criminal Justice Act of 1988 and convicted in July 2005 of torture and hostage taking and sentenced to twenty years' imprisonment.[11]

After the mass influx of refugees and asylum seekers from Syria arriving in Europe in recent years, Germany, Sweden, Finland, Switzerland, Norway, Netherlands, and France, among others, have exercised UJ to prosecute Syrians suspected of

[10] ibid 133 [104] (Sep Op of Judge ad hoc Bula-Bula).

[11] Máximo Langer, 'The Diplomacy of Universal Jurisdiction: The Political Branches and the Transnational Prosecution of International Crimes' (2011) 105 AJIL 1, *passim*.

committing war crimes and/or crimes against humanity in Syria before their arrival in Europe.[12] This welcome trend is likely to continue for the foreseeable future.

Chapter 3 of this book endeavours to document State practice on UJ, which will not be repeated here. It should be noted that some States with UJ law have yielded to the pressure from several States whose nationals have been subject to the exercise of UJ.[13] In 2003, Belgium amended its UJ law passed in 1993. The 2003 Code of Criminal Procedure[14] recognizes the immunity defence based on a person's official capacity. Moreover, for Belgian courts to exercise jurisdiction over a serious crime committed outside Belgium, the accused must be a Belgian national or have his primary residence in Belgium; or the victim is a Belgian national or has had his or her actual place of normal and legal residence in Belgium for at least three years at the time of its commission; or where Belgium is bound by treaty to exercise jurisdiction over the case. Above all, unless the accused is a Belgian national or has his or her primary residence in Belgium, only the federal prosecutor may pursue such case, and his or her decision is not subject to appeal.[15]

Spain has amended its law in 2009 and 2014 to limit the scope of the exercise of UJ. Organic Act no 1/2009 of 3 November 2009[16] provides, *inter alia*, that, without prejudice to treaty provisions binding on Spain, for Spanish courts to have UJ over the offences enumerated under the Act,[17] the accused must be present in Spain, there are victims of Spanish nationality or that there is some special link with Spain and, in any event, there is no other State or competent international court that has initiated proceedings, including an effective investigation and, where appropriate, prosecution of such crimes. Proceedings already initiated in Spain shall be temporarily stayed if proceedings connected with the same offence and against the same accused are initiated by a court in another State or an international court. Organic Act no 1/2014 of 13 March 2014[18] expands the list offences subject to UJ to encompass, among others, torture, enforced disappearance, and corruption of public officials. It also requires that only the victim and the Public Prosecution Service have the legal standing to initiate proceedings in such cases.

[12] Useful links to news about these cases can be found in Human Rights Watch, 'Q&A: First Cracks to Impunity in Syria, Iraq: Refugee Crisis and Universal Jurisdiction in Europe' (20 Oct 2016) <https://www.hrw.org/news/2016/10/20/qa-first-cracks-impunity-syria-iraq>, accessed 10 November 2017.

[13] In the case of Belgium, see Malvina Halberstam, 'Belgium's Universal Jurisdiction Law: Vindication of International Justice or Pursuit of Politics?' (2003) 25 Cardozo L Rev 247; Jana Panáková, 'Law and Politics of Universal Jurisdiction' (2011) 3 Amsterdam Law Forum 49.

[14] 'Loi du 23 avril 2003 modifiant la loi du 16 juin 1993 relative a la répression des violations graves de droit international humanitaire et l'article 144ter du Code judicaire' and 'Loi du 5 août 2003 modifiant la loi du 16 juin 1993 relative a la répression des violations graves de droit international'.

[15] For a writing in support of this new Belgian law, see Roozbeh (Rudy) B Baker, 'Universal Jurisdiction and the Case of Belgium: A Critical Assessment' (2009) 16 ILSA Journal Int'l & Comp L 141.

[16] Official Gazette no 266 of 4 Nov 2009.

[17] Genocide and crimes against humanity; terrorism; piracy or unlawful seizure of aircraft; crimes related to the prostitution or corruption of minors or legally incompetent persons; trafficking in psychotropic, toxic, or narcotic drugs; illegal trafficking or smuggling of persons, whether or not they are workers; crimes relating to female genital mutilation if the perpetrators are present in Spain; and any other crime that should be prosecuted in Spain under an international treaty or agreement, especially treaties on international humanitarian law and human rights protection.

[18] Official Gazette no 63 of 14 Mar 2014.

With regard to the obligation to extradite or prosecute in UJ cases, Article 23(4)(a) of the original Organic Act no 6/1985, as amended in 2014, stipulates that Spanish courts shall have UJ over genocide, crimes against humanity, or war crimes against protected persons or property where proceedings are brought against a Spanish national, a foreign national who is a habitual resident in Spain, or a foreign national present in Spain whose extradition has been denied by Spanish authorities. Paragraph 4 of the Article, as amended, gives Spanish courts UJ over all the offences listed therein provided that the accused is a foreign national present in Spain whose extradition has been denied by Spanish authorities, if this is required under a treaty in force in Spain. Paragraph 5 excludes the UJ of Spanish courts over the offences listed in paragraph 4 in two situations, based on the principle of complementarity and that of subsidiarity, respectively. First, an international court set up by a treaty or agreement to which Spain is party has initiated proceedings. Second, the State where the offence is committed or the State of nationality of the accused has initiated proceedings and either the accused is not present in Spanish territory or proceedings have been initiated to extradite the accused to either of the aforesaid States or to surrender the accused to a competent international court, unless the extradition is not granted. The second exception is inapplicable where the State having jurisdiction over the case is unwilling or unable genuinely to undertake the investigation.

The Second Division of the Spanish Supreme Court shall determine unwillingness in a particular case by having regard to the principles of due process recognized by international law whether any one or more of the following exist: the proceedings or the national decision in the State concerned aims to shield the person from criminal responsibility; there is an unjustified delay in the proceedings in the circumstances inconsistent with the intention to bring the person to justice; and/or the proceedings are not conducted independently or impartially, but in a manner inconsistent with the intention to bring the person to justice. The Second Division of the Spanish Supreme Court shall determine inability in a particular case by considering whether, due to a total or substantial collapse or unavailability of its national judicial system, the State concerned is unable to apprehend the accused or the necessary evidence and testimony or is otherwise unable to carry out the proceedings.

As of 22 February 2016, the case of Argentine military officer Adolfo Scilingo was the first and only case of UJ to result in convictions from both the National High Court and the Supreme Court of Spain. Criminal proceedings in many UJ cases in Spain did not progress much due to a combination of three main factors. Some of the accused enjoyed immunity from the jurisdiction of Spanish courts by virtue of their status as incumbent or former Heads of State, Heads of Government, or Ministers of Foreign Affairs. In other cases, Spain extradited the accused to another State to face ongoing prosecution. In the rest of the cases, a third State denied extradition of the accused to Spain, as when the UK declined Spain's request to have former Chilean President Pinochet extradited from the UK to Spain.[19]

[19] Communication dated 22 Feb 2016 from the Spanish Ministry of Foreign Affairs and Cooperation in response to the request of the UN General Assembly for information and observations on the scope

The atrocities in Syria have brought a new lease of life to Spanish prosecution of those accused of such heinous acts in Syria. On 27 March 2017, Judge Eloy Velasco of Spain's national court in Madrid ruled that the Spanish court had jurisdiction to hear the criminal complaint of a Syrian-Spanish dual national over the torture and death of her brother in Syria allegedly at the hands of six accused; namely, Syria's Vice President Farouk al-Sharaa, a former foreign minister; Ali Mamlouk, head of Syria's National Security Bureau; General Jamil Hassan, head of Syria's air force intelligence; and senior officers running the prison where her brother had been detained and murdered.[20]

In June 2008, the African Union (AU) received the report of the Commission on the Use of the Principle of Universal Jurisdiction by Some Non-African States as Recommended by the Conference of Ministers of Justice/Attorneys General of the AU.[21] The report accepts UJ as a concept of international law in the cases of piracy, crimes against humanity, war crimes, torture under the Torture Convention, and, *potentially*, genocide, depending on the extent to which States are bound by the various sources of international law (be it customary or treaty law) providing for UJ. However, the expansive approach adopted by UJ proponents is discretionary, policy-oriented, and not legally oriented, with potentially disruptive effects creating judicial chaos due to a proliferation of litigation and the erosion of the principle of the sovereign equality of States. The report posits that UJ is subject to jurisdictional immunities. To avoid abuse of UJ, summons to a Head of State to appear in proceedings before the courts of another State must be subject to the consent of the Head of State concerned and diplomatic confidentiality. It substantiates this position by quoting the statement of the ICJ in *Djibouti v France* that where the consent of the Head of State is expressly sought in a request for testimony in court, this request which is transmitted in confidentiality through the intermediary of the competent authorities and in the form prescribed by the law cannot have infringed the immunities from jurisdiction enjoyed by the Head of State, or be an attack on the honour or dignity of the Head of State merely because this invitation is sent to him when he is in the forum State on an official function.[22] The report concludes, however, that the likelihood of abuse of a principle in international law does not nullify the existence of the concept or its applicability in the right circumstances.[23]

As a means to bridge differences in the understanding of the scope and application of UJ, the African Union and the European Union set up the AU-EU Technical ad hoc Expert Group on the Principle of Universal Jurisdiction in November 2008[24] in

and application of universal jurisdiction, Doc 16-05499 (E), available at: <http://www.un.org/en/ga/sixth/71/universal_jurisdiction/spain_e.pdf>, accessed 10 November 2017.

20 Nick Cumming-Bruce, 'High-Ranking Syrians Could Face Reckoning in Landmark Spain Case' (NY Times, 27 Mar 2017) <https://www.nytimes.com/2017/03/27/world/middleeast/syria-crime-torture-assad-war.html>, accessed 10 November 2017.

21 AU Doc EX.CL/411 (XIII), available at <http://archive.au.int/collect/oaucounc/import/English/EX%20CL%20411%20(XIII)%20_E.PDF>, accessed 10 November 2017.

22 *Certain Questions of Mutual Assistance in Criminal Matters (Djibouti v France)* [2008] ICJ Rep 117, 240 [179–80].

23 AU Doc EX.CL/411 (XIII) §86.

24 The independent experts appointed by the EU were Antonio Cassese (Italy), Pierre Klein (Belgium), and Roger O'Keefe (Australia). The independent experts appointed by the AU were: former

response to the AU's concerns over 'abusive applications of the principle of universal jurisdiction'. The ad hoc Expert Group was to clarify the respective understanding of the African and the European Union States on the principle of universal jurisdiction.[25] The Group, having met in January and March 2009, issued its report on 15 April 2009 with the following recommendations. The Group states categorically:

> International law, both customary and conventional, regulates States' assertion of universal criminal jurisdiction. States by and large accept that customary international law permits the exercise of universal jurisdiction over the international crimes of genocide, crimes against humanity, war crimes and torture, as well as over piracy. In addition, numerous treaties oblige States Parties to empower their criminal justice systems to exercise universal jurisdiction over the crimes defined in those treaties, although this obligation extends only to the exercise of such jurisdiction when a suspect is subsequently present in the territory of the forum State.[26]

In exercising UJ, a priority is to be given to a State having a significant link with the crime in question, especially the territorial State where the crime is committed. When exercising UJ, States have to bear in mind the need to avoid impairing friendly international relations. National criminal justice authorities considering exercising UJ 'should consider refraining from taking steps that might publicly and unduly expose the suspects, thereby discrediting and stigmatizing them, curtailing their right to be presumed innocent until found guilty by a court of law and hampering the discharge of their official functions'. National criminal justice authorities considering exercising UJ 'are legally bound to take into account all the immunities to which foreign State officials may be entitled under international law'. Where either the territorial State or the national State of the victim/accused seems 'manifestly unwilling or unable to prosecute the suspect, and the suspect is a foreign State official exercising a representative function on behalf of his or her State', the national criminal justice authorities considering exercising UJ should seek and issue a summons to appear or an equivalent measure, rather than an arrest warrant, for the suspect to appear before the court and to produce, with the assistance of counsel, any exculpatory evidence. States should specify an appropriate level of court for prosecuting such serious crimes.

In the same month of April 2009, the Non-Aligned Movement (NAM) Ministerial Meeting, held in Havana, Cuba, from 27 to 30 April 2009, adopted a resolution that, realizing 'the negative effects on international relations of the abuse of the Principle of Universal Jurisdiction', called upon States 'to refrain from such abuse' and urged them to discuss this matter in the UN General Assembly 'aiming at identifying the scope and limits of this Principle and establish a mechanism to monitor such implementation and to prevent its abuse in the future'.[27]

President of the International Court of Justice Mohammed Bedjaoui (Algeria), Chaloka Beyani (Zambia), and Chris Maina Peter (Tanzania).

[25] Report of the AU-EU Technical ad hoc Expert Group on the Principle of Universal Jurisdiction dated 15 April 2009, Annexed to the Council of the European Union Doc 8672/1/09 dated 16 April 2009 §2.

[26] ibid §9 (footnotes omitted).

[27] Final Document of the Ministerial Meeting of the Non-Aligned Movement Coordinating Bureau, Havana, Cuba, 27–30 Apr 2009 (Doc NAM 2009/MM/Doc1/Rev1 of 30 Apr 2009) §17.3.

Consequently, from 2009, the UN General Assembly has included on its agenda the topic 'The scope and application of the principle of universal jurisdiction' at the request of the Group of African States. The memorandum explaining the request for this inclusion states that while UJ is well established in international law, it applies to a very limited category of offences, such as piracy, slavery, torture, genocide, war crimes, and crimes against humanity occurring outside the territory of the State concerned irrespective of the nationality of the perpetrators. Universal justice is enshrined in Article 4(h) of the Constitutive Act of the African Union,[28] and many African States have expressed approval of UJ on a treaty basis, and existing practice shows that many States establish a jurisdictional link with the commission and punishment of such crimes as genocide, crimes against humanity, and war crimes. However, the scope and applicability of the UJ principle outside the context of applicable treaties and outside such jurisdictional links is unclear and remains to be settled or determined.

The memorandum notes that the AU itself undertook a study on the application and scope of UJ, elucidating the origin, nature, scope, applicability, and effects of the concept in the light of the jurisprudence of the ICJ on this issue, resolutions of the UN General Assembly, and declarations and decisions of the AU relevant to UJ, and the legal competence of States applying UJ. The study indicated that there was no dispute or controversy with UJ itself; the only issue was the extent of its application. Furthermore, while the ICJ had not directly addressed and made a determination on the extent and applicability of the principle, judges of the ICJ, particularly in the *Arrest Warrant* case, had made clear and unequivocal statements to the effect that the application of the principle was limited under international law. The study also indicated that the extent of the application of UJ had never been discussed at the UN level, and that there was no widespread State practice. The AU is concerned about UJ's ad hoc and arbitrary application, particularly towards African leaders. The application of UJ has to be consistent with international law and the conduct of international relations. Therefore, the Assembly of Heads of State and Government of the AU has referred the issue of the principle of UJ for discussion in the UN General Assembly with a view to establishing regulatory provisions for its application.[29]

The UN General Assembly requests the UN Secretary General to invite Member States to submit information and observations on the scope and application of the principle of UJ, including information on the relevant applicable international treaties, their domestic legal rules and judicial practice, and to prepare and submit to the General Assembly a report based on such information and observations. The UN General Assembly's Sixth Committee is also authorized to continue its consideration of the scope and application of the principle of UJ, without prejudice to the consideration of related issues in other forums of the United Nations.[30]

[28] OAU Doc CAB/LEG/23.15 (2001).

[29] Doc A/63/237/Rev1 (23 July 2009) annex.

[30] A/RES/64/117 (15 Jan 2010).

In October 2010, the African Group of States informed the Sixth Committee that as yet there was no generally accepted definition of UJ and no agreement on which crimes other than piracy and slavery it should cover or on the conditions for its application, and that UJ principle hardly existed in most domestic jurisdictions.

In October 2011, the Working Group on the Scope and Application of the Principle of Universal Jurisdiction was set up under the Sixth Committee of the UN General Assembly 'to undertake a thorough discussion of the scope and application of universal jurisdiction', open to all UN Member States and members of the specialized agencies and of the International Atomic Energy Agency.[31]

The Working Group first met in October 2011. Several delegations focused on the 'abuse or misuse' of UJ, as well as its potential application in an arbitrary, politically motivated, or selective manner, in disregard of international law. A view was expressed that the application of UJ had to have due regard to the UN Charter, human rights law and international humanitarian law, and the principles of judiciousness and good faith, as well as due process guarantees. There was a divergence of views with respect to the relevance of the immunity of foreign officials in the topic before the Working Group. Some delegations raised the need for future discussions on the interrelationships and distinctions of UJ from other concepts of international law, including the concept of *aut dedere aut judicare*; the complementary but distinct role of the jurisdiction of international criminal tribunals to provide accountability and fight impunity for international crimes; the potential role that the international settlement of disputes may play in the practical exercise of UJ; and the international legal responsibility that States may accrue for the abuse or misuse of UJ.

In a related development, on 15 September 2011 the UK amended its law on universal jurisdiction[32] by requiring the consent of the Director of Public Prosecutions before an arrest warrant could be issued in cases brought by private individuals against alleged perpetrators of crimes committed outside and with no connection to the UK (the so-called 'universal jurisdiction cases'). This puts an end to private individuals' right to initiate criminal prosecutions in such cases by applying to a magistrate for an arrest warrant. In the past, arrest warrants sought by private individuals were often seen by their opponents as being 'politically motivated', and the threats of arrest deterred high-profile foreign politicians such as former US Secretary of State Henry Kissinger, senior Chinese Communist Party official Bo Xilai, and former Israeli foreign minister Tzipi Livni from visiting the UK.

[31] A/RES/65/33 of 6 Dec 2010. *Disclosure*: In the autumn of 2011, the present author was nominated by the Asian Group in the Sixth Committee of the UN General Assembly to chair the Sixth Committee's Working Group on the Scope and Application of the Principles of UJ. However, the African Group wanted the chair to come from an African State since UJ had been used the most against Africans and, to a lesser extent, nationals of Latin American States. The African Group could not find a candidate of an ambassadorial rank to chair the Working Group, so the chair was given to the then permanent representative of Costa Rica to the United Nations, New York. The present author was, in return, given the chair of the Sixth Committee's Working Group on the Administration of Justice at the United Nations.

[32] Police Reform and Social Responsibility Act 2011 (C 13).

The Working Group chair issued a roadmap at the end of the debate in 2011.[33] A tentative list of crimes subject to UJ include: apartheid; corruption; crimes against humanity; crimes against peace/crime of aggression; enforced disappearances; genocide; piracy; slavery; terrorism; torture; transnational organized crime; and war crimes. The roadmap provides details of the application of UJ as appeared in Table 5.1.

Table 5.1 Application of UJ as in the 2011 Roadmap of the Working Group on UJ

Issues raised	
(a) Conditions for application	– International law, including the UN Charter – Good faith – Judiciousness – *Nulla poena sine lege/nullum crimen sine lege* – International human rights/international humanitarian law (IHL) obligations – Immunity
(b) Criteria for exercising jurisdiction	– Fight impunity – Avoidance of abuse/misuse – Not politically motivated, arbitrary, or discriminatory/selective – Last resort/complementary/exceptional – Jurisdictional links (with territoriality, nationality, etc)/conflict of competing jurisdiction – Consultations among concerned States – Inability and/or unwillingness to prosecute
(c) Procedural aspects	– Presence/absence of alleged offender – *Ne bis in idem*/double jeopardy – Statute of limitations – International due process guarantees – Prima-facie case – Judicial independence – Prosecutorial independence – Prosecutorial discretion
(d) Role of national judicial systems	– Exercisable by national judicial systems – Need for national legislation – Implementation of treaty obligations – Relationship between international law and domestic law
(e) Interaction with other concepts of international law	– Interaction with *aut dedere aut judicare* – Complementary to jurisiction of international criminal tribunals – Role of settlement of disputes – State responsibility for abuse
(f) International assistance and cooperation	– Mutual assistance and cooperation in criminal matters (investigations, evidence, judicial cooperation) – Extradition

[33] <https://papersmart.unmeetings.org/media2/1156492/oral_report_chair_51113-1-.pdf>, accessed 10 November 2017.

In October 2012, the chairperson circulated an informal note containing the following list of essential elements of a working concept of UJ: '(1) focused on criminal matters; (2) exercised by national courts/tribunals; (3) exercised exceptionally; (4) based on the nature of certain crimes under international law, not on territoriality, personality or protective principles; and (5) distinct from (a) jurisdiction of international criminal courts/tribunals, (b) obligation to extradite or prosecute (*aut dedere aut judicare*), and (c) other forms of extra-territorial jurisdiction'. No substantive progress has been achieved so far.

The Working Group continues to meet each year. On 4 November 2016, the chair of the Working Group presented her oral report on the meetings of the Working Group in 2016,[34] with an annex elaborating suggestions in the Working Group since 2011 as follows:

1. ***Definition of the concept of universal jurisdiction:***
   - To combat impunity
   - To protect the rights of victims
   - Achieving international justice/promoting justice
   - To address the most serious crimes of concern to the international community as a whole.

   (b) [*sic*] Relevant components Essential elements of a working concept of Universal Jurisdiction
   - Focused on criminal matters
   - Exercised by national courts/tribunals
   - Exercised exceptionally/exceptional character
   - Based on the nature of certain crimes under international law, and not on any other jurisdictional connection to the State exercising universal jurisdiction (including territoriality, nationality, passive personality or protective principles, as recognized under international law).

   (c) Distinction from other related concepts
   Distinct from:
   - Jurisdiction of international criminal courts/tribunals
   - Obligation to extradite or prosecute (*aut dedere aut judicare*)
   - Other forms of jurisdiction (including, territoriality, nationality, passive personality or protective principles, as recognized under international law).
2. ***Scope of UJ:***
   Crimes under UJ (the same as the ones enumerated in 2011)
   On the application of UJ, the Working Group summarized the progress made up to 2016 as appeared in Table 5.2 below.

[34] On file with the author. The Working Group held three meetings: on 13, 14, and 21 Oct 2016.

Table 5.2 The Pending Issues Pertaining to the Application of UJ as of November 2016

(a) Conditions for application	– International law, including the UN Charter – *Nulla poena sine lege/nullum crimen sine lege* – International human rights/IHL obligations – Immunity (it is recognized that there are multiple dimensions to this tier, including that application of the principle must be consistent with other principles of international law) – Discretionary/obligatory nature of the Principle
(b) Criteria for exercising jurisdiction	– Fight impunity – Avoidance of abuse/misuse – Not politically motivated, arbitrary, or discriminatory/selective – Last resort/complementary/exceptional – Jurisdictional links (with territoriality, nationality, etc)/conflict of competing jurisdiction – Consultations among concerned States – Inability and/or unwillingness to prosecute – National amnesties – Prosecutorial fiat and discretion – Good faith – Judiciousness
(c) Procedural aspects	– Presence/absence of alleged offender – *Ne bis in idem*/double jeopardy – Statute of limitations – International due process guarantees (including, *inter alia*, the presumption of innocence, the right to a fair trial, the right to minimum trial guarantees in full equality, the right to an adequate and effective appeals process) – Establishment of a prima-facie case before proceeding – Judicial independence – Prosecutorial independence – Prosecutorial discretion – International comity – Challenges of evidence gathering/ preservation in the exercise of UJ
(d) Role of national judicial systems	– Exercisable by national judicial systems – Primacy of national justice systems/complementary/role of complementarity – Implementation of obligations under international law – Necessity of national legislation – Relationship between international law and domestic law
(e) Interaction with other concepts of international law	– Interaction with immunity – Abuse – Distinction from *aut dedere aut judicare* – Complementary to jurisdiction of international criminal tribunals – Role of settlement of disputes – Questions of State responsibility for wrongful acts in the exercise of UJ, including, as appropriate, its abuse
(f) International assistance and cooperation	– Mutual assistance and cooperation in criminal matters (investigations, evidence, judicial cooperation) – Technical assistance and cooperation in the conduct of criminal matters (investigations, prosecution, evidence, judicial cooperation) – Extradition

Regarding the list of crimes, the chair explained that the most serious crimes of concern to the international community as a whole, and in respect of which UJ is exercisable, may include: crimes against humanity, genocide, piracy, slavery, torture, and war crimes, but this is without prejudice to the potential application of UJ with respect to 'other crimes under international law'. This is because the list just mentioned should not be interpreted as limiting or prejudicing in any way existing or developing rules of international law with respect to crimes under international law.

With respect to the application of UJ, the chair clarified that States should undertake to ensure that any action taken in their application of UJ be in conformity with the principles and purposes of the UN Charter and guided by the Declaration on Principles of International Law concerning Friendly Relations and Cooperation among States in accordance with the Charter of the United Nations.[35] In addition, States should abide by applicable international legal obligations concerning the immunity of State officials from foreign criminal jurisdiction, particularly with respect to Heads of State, Heads of Government, and Ministers of Foreign Affairs. Unless a specific treaty obligation stipulates to the contrary, primary jurisdiction for prosecuting crimes that could be subject to UJ is accorded to the territorial State where the crime is committed or the State of nationality of the alleged perpetrator. UJ is to be exercised exceptionally, when a State with primary jurisdiction is unable or unwilling to bring criminal proceedings against an alleged perpetrator. In such situation, the State seeking to exercise UJ is encouraged to inform and consult such other States with primary jurisdictional ties, in the process of initiation of any proceedings against any alleged perpetrator. National judicial systems exercising UJ should pay due regard to international law. Where national authorities have prosecutorial discretion over a crime in the exercise of UJ, they may take into account considerations and factors such as the international legal obligations of the State, including any action taken or being taken in any other jurisdictional forums; an examination of the practical difficulties of proceeding, including witness access and availability and evidence gathering; the public interests at stake; international comity; and the interests of justice. A State may, under its national law, condition its exercise of UJ on the presence of an alleged perpetrator in its territory, and the consent of a competent high authority such as the Attorney-General or the Public Prosecutor or his or her equivalent. Lastly, States should undertake the necessary steps to render mutual judicial assistance and cooperation to each other in the investigation and prosecution of crimes in the exercise of UJ, consistent with their obligations under international law.

Sudan and Algeria questioned who would decide whether a State was unable or unwilling to exercise primary jurisdiction. China insisted that crimes subject to UJ must be those crimes so prescribed by the relevant treaties or customary international law. China and Singapore opined that the list of crimes subject to UJ was still disputed. For China and India, piracy was the only crime subject to UJ under customary international law. The chair replied that the crimes in the latest list were those with the least opposition to their inclusion in the list, compared to transnational crimes and corruption. The African Group of States, Russia, Cuba, and Israel reiterated their

[35] UN GA Res 2625 (XXV) of 24 Oct 1970.

concern that UJ had been abused, being used as a political tool against certain States. The Czech Republic and Morocco considered the International Law Commission (ILC) to be the most appropriate forum to undertake the study on UJ, whereas the USA, UK, and Australia contended that the ILC had already had many topics on its agenda, and that the Sixth Committee was the most appropriate forum for States to bridge their differences on the scope and application of UJ.

It should be noted that in 2011 the African Union proposed that the UN establish an international commission on UJ as a subsidiary body of the UN General Assembly to serve as a regulatory body on the exercise of UJ by checking the validity, legality, and factual basis of indictments issued by judges in individual States and warrants before they can be approved for execution outside their own territories.[36] This proposal has met with opposition and is no longer pursued. For example, the Czech delegation opposed it in the Sixth Committee on 12 October 2011 on the ground that it would undermine the independence of the judiciary and be contrary to the obligations under human rights instruments, such as the right to equality before the courts and tribunals under Article 14(1) of the 1966 International Covenant on Civil and Political Rights[37] and the right to a fair trial under Article 6 of the European Convention for the Protection of Human Rights and Fundamental Freedoms.[38]

It can be seen that UJ has now been accepted by the Working Group as a principle distinct from that of the obligation to extradite or prosecute, although their interaction in the fight against impunity is well recognized.

III. The Future Direction for Universal Jurisdiction in the Context of the Obligation to Extradite or Prosecute

As the April 2009 report of the AU-EU ad hoc Expert Group on the Principle of Universal Jurisdiction explains, while the obligation *aut dedere aut judicare* is conceptually distinct from universal jurisdiction, where a State has this obligation,

> the establishment of jurisdiction, universal or otherwise, is a logically prior step: a State must first vest its courts with competence to try given criminal conduct. It is only once such competence has been established that the question whether to prosecute the relevant conduct, or to extradite persons suspected of it, arises. Moreover, the obligation to submit a case to the prosecuting authorities or to extradite applies as much in respect of an underlying jurisdiction based on territoriality, nationality, passive personality, *etc* as it does to universal jurisdiction. The obligation *aut dedere aut judicare* is nevertheless relevant to the question of universal jurisdiction, since [it] compels a [State] to exercise the underlying universal jurisdiction ... In short, a [State] is not only bound to empower its criminal justice system to exercise universal

[36] Report of the Secretary General, 'The scope and application of the principle of universal jurisdiction', UN Doc A/66/93 (20 June 2010) §168.

[37] 999 UNTS 171.

[38] ETS 5. The present author was in the meeting room of the Sixth Committee when this statement was made.

jurisdiction but is further bound actually to exercise that jurisdiction by means of either considering prosecution or extraditing.[39]

In other words, universal jurisdiction is a facet of extraterritorial jurisdiction that a custodial State may rely on to fulfil its obligation *aut dedere aut judicare*.[40] The International Law Commission rightly points out that some crimes may be subject to universal jurisdiction but not necessarily to the obligation to extradite or prosecute.[41]

This understanding of the place of universal jurisdiction vis-à-vis the obligation *aut dedere aut judicare* is consistent with the understanding of States in other regions outside the European Union and Africa, as evidenced from the statements of Cuba and Russia, among others, before the Sixth Committee of the UN General Assembly in 2011.[42] It is also supported by the ruling of the International Court of Justice in *Belgium v Senegal*, where the ICJ observed that 'the performance by the State of its obligation to establish the universal jurisdiction of its courts over the crime of torture [under the Convention against Torture in that case] is a necessary condition for enabling a preliminary inquiry ... and for submitting the case to its competent authorities for the purpose of prosecution'.[43]

The *aut dedere aut judicare* obligation is concerned with preventing impunity for certain crimes by obligating States either to prosecute or extradite the alleged offender to a requesting State that can ensure prosecution. This obligation does not prescribe or indicate a preference for the type of jurisdiction that a custodial State should exercise should it elect to prosecute rather than extradite the alleged offender.[44] Thus, if a State can exercise any other form of jurisdiction, universal jurisdiction is irrelevant to the fulfilment of the *aut dedere aut judicare* obligation. To this end, universal jurisdiction has been called a 'correlative obligation' to the obligation to extradite or prosecute.[45] A more accurate description, however, would classify universal jurisdiction as a facet of extraterritorial jurisdiction that a custodial State may rely on to fulfil its *aut dedere aut judicare* obligation.[46] Phrased differently, UJ complements the operation of the obligation to extradite or prosecute when the State in which a person suspected of having committed a crime does not have any other jurisdictional link with the crime in question. In such a situation, UJ enables the State to fulfil its obligation to prosecute the person.

[39] Report of the AU-EU Technical ad hoc Expert Group on the Principle of UJ, 15 April 2009 §11. See also Amnesty International, *Ending Impunity: Developing and Implementing a Global Action Plan Using Universal Jurisdiction* (2009) 13–14.

[40] See also Raphaël van Steenberghe, 'The Obligation to Extradite or Prosecute: Clarifying its Nature' (2011) 9 J Int'l Crim Justice 1089, 1104.

[41] ILC, 'Report of the International Law Commission on the work of its 58th Session' (26 Apr–3 June and 4 July–12 Aug 2011) UN Doc A/66/10 §324.

[42] UNGA Doc A/C.6/66/SR.27 (8 Dec 2011) §57 and §65 respectively.

[43] [2012] ICJ Rep 422, 451[74].

[44] Mitsue Inazumi, *Universal Jurisdiction in Modern International Law: Expansion of National Jurisdiction for Prosecuting Serious Crimes under International Law* (Intersentia 2005) 122.

[45] van Steenberghe, 'The Obligation to Extradite or Prosecute' 1104.

[46] ibid.

The conceptual distinction between the two rules is also relevant because it clarifies that universal jurisdiction does not affect the formation or the existence of a rule under customary law that obligates States to extradite or prosecute alleged offenders. The converse is equally accurate. The existence or non-existence of an *aut dedere aut judicare* obligation for a specific crime under customary international law does not imply the existence or non-existence of universal jurisdiction vis-à-vis that crime. Thus, Article 8 of the 1996 Draft Code of Crimes against the Peace and Security of Mankind incorporates universal jurisdiction as a necessary 'corollary' to the *aut dedere aut judicare* obligation under Article 9.[47] The ILC did not establish the customary international law nature of universal jurisdiction before incorporating it in the 1996 Draft Code.[48]

According to one view, jurisdiction is termed 'quasi-universal' when it has the same purpose as universal jurisdiction, but is authorized only by treaty.[49] In the case of a 'subsidiary', 'default', or 'fall-back' exercise of universal jurisdiction, the State whose sole connection to the crime is the presence of the alleged offender on its territory exercises 'subsidiary universal jurisdiction' to prosecute only if and when the State having primary jurisdiction over the alleged offender and the crime in question refuses to seek his extradition to that State.[50] In contrast, 'primary',[51] 'absolute', or 'mandatory' universal jurisdiction[52] is based on 'the *civitas maxima* perspective on universal jurisdiction: any member of the international community is entitled to prosecute in order to protect universally recognized important values and therefore no link with the trial forum is required ... [and] there is thus no requirement of *forum deprehensionis*'.[53] That is to say, a State seeks to prosecute the alleged offender irrespective of his presence in the territory of the said State or the absence of jurisdictional links with that particular State.[54] An example of 'mandatory' UJ in the

[47] UN Doc A/51/10, Art 8(6).

[48] This was the target of criticism by the UK that called the ILC's work on this point 'sketchy'. *Comments and Observations received from Governments*, UN Doc A/CN.4/448 and Add 1, 99.

[49] Commonwealth Secretariat, *Implementation Kits for the International Counter-Terrorism Conventions* (2002) 6 [16]. This type of universal jurisdiction is also called 'the co-operative general universality principle' or 'a form of bilateral cooperation in penal criminal matters' (Luc Reydams, *Universal Jurisdiction: International and Municipal Legal Perspectives* (OUP 2003) 28–29).

[50] The said subsidiary jurisdiction was proposed by Iran for inclusion in the Convention on the Prevention and Punishment of the Crime of Genocide, but was rejected by several other States. See Reydams, *Universal Jurisdiction* 50–51. See also Karinne Coombs, 'Universal Jurisdiction: A Means to End Impunity or a Threat to Friendly International Relations?' (2011) 43 George Wash Int'l Law Rev 419, 462–64.

[51] Reydams, *Universal Jurisdiction* 50.

[52] Robert Cryer, Håkan Friman, Darryl Robinson, and Elizabeth Wilmshurst, *An Introduction to International Criminal Law and Procedure* (2nd edn, CUP 2010) 73; Gerhard Werle et al, *Principles of International Criminal Law* (2nd edn, TMC Asser 2009) 70.

[53] Alexander Zahar and Göran Sluiter, *International Criminal Law: A Critical Introduction* (OUP 2008) 500.

[54] Cf The Brussels Principles Against Impunity and for International Justice, Principle 14(2): '2. International law does not require a state to exercise universal jurisdiction, should the presumed author of a serious crime not be present on its territory (jurisdiction in absentia). In the absence of jurisdiction of an international court, it would, however, be desirable that a state be able to exercise universal jurisdiction in absentia to make the fight against impunity more effective, even more so when the victims are present on the territory of the forum state. The exercise of such a jurisdiction should, however, not

context of the obligation to extradite or prosecute is the repression of grave breaches under the four Geneva Conventions of 1949 and Additional Protocol I of 1977, where the High Contracting Parties must search for and prosecute perpetrators of grave breaches under these instruments themselves, regardless of where, by whom, or against whom they are committed, or 'hand such persons over for trial to another High Contracting Party concerned'.[55] Many States and scholars continue to object to mandatory universal jurisdiction outside treaty.[56]

UJ may also be 'permissive', as in the case of piracy where any State may, if it chooses, exercise UJ to capture and try pirates it finds on the high seas or other areas beyond national jurisdiction of any State.[57]

On the other hand, the European Committee on Crime Problems (CDPC) of the Council of Europe contends that there is no international consensus on the definition and scope of universal jurisdiction since the exercise of universal jurisdiction is in practice often subject to legal limitations defined in national laws of the States concerned. Therefore, the CDCP advises the Council of Europe to be neutral in relation to the principle of universal jurisdiction and to 're-inforce the application of the principle *aut dedere aut judicare* as a means of prosecuting war crimes effectively in cases where universal jurisdiction cannot be exercised'.[58] In other words, *aut dedere aut judicare* underpins the international legal cooperation to suppress the crimes separately from the application of universal jurisdiction.[59]

The Sixth Committee's open-ended Working Group on the scope and application of the principle of universal jurisdiction has decided not to refer the topic under its mandate to the ILC as yet, while also keeping open a possibility for such referral

impede the exercise of the jurisdiction of the International Criminal Court.' (The Brussels Principles were adopted by the 'Brussels Group for International Justice' after the colloquium 'The Fight against Impunity: Stakes and Perspectives' (Brussels, 11–13 Mar 2002), available at <http://archive.iccnow.org/documents/BrusselsPrinciples6Nov02.pdf>, accessed 10 November 2017.

[55] Werle et al, *Principles of International Criminal Law* 70.

[56] eg Inazumi, *Universal Jurisdiction in Modern International Law* 143; M Cherif Bassiouni and Edward Wise, *Aut Dedere Aut Judicare: The Duty to Extradite or Prosecute in International Law* (Martinus Nijhoff 1995) 54; Lyal S Sunga, *The Emerging System of International Criminal Law: Developments in Codification and Implementation* (Kluwer Law International 1997) 254.

[57] Art 100 of the 1982 UN Convention on the Law of the Sea (1833 UNTS 3) codifies a rule of customary international law, stipulating all States shall cooperate to the fullest possible extent in the repression of piracy on the high seas or in any other place outside the jurisdiction of any State. See also Eugene Kontorovich, 'The Piracy Analogy: Modern Universal Jurisdiction's Hollow Foundation' (2004) 45 Harvard ILJ 183, and 'A Guantánamo on the Sea: The Difficulty of Prosecuting Pirates and Terrorists' (2010) 98 California L Rev 243, 251ff; Eugene Kontorovich and Steven Art, 'An Empirical Examination of Universal Jurisdiction over Piracy' (2010) North Western University School of Law, *Faculty Working Papers*, Paper 38, available at <http://scholarlycommons.law.northwestern.edu/facultyworkingpapers/38>, accessed 10 November 2017.

[58] Secretariat memorandum prepared by the Directorate General of Human Rights and Legal Affairs, *Draft Opinion of the European Committee on Crime Problems (CDPC) on Parliamentary Assembly Recommendation 1953 (2011) on the Obligation of Member States and Observer States of the Council of Europe to Co-operate in the Prosecution of War Crimes*, Doc CDPC (2011) 5 (14 Mar 2011) 3 [10–11]. Cf also Inazumi, *Universal Jurisdiction in Modern International Law* 25–30, 101–05, where the author finds that the definition of universal jurisdiction is itself disputed.

[59] Cf Doc CDPC (2011) 5 (14 Mar 2011) 3 [12].

'when appropriate'.[60] In fact, UJ in the context of the obligation to extradite or prosecute is different from the UJ under the Sixth Committee's agenda which has 'International assistance and cooperation' as one of the issues in the application of the UJ principle.[61] What the Sixth Committee has been analysing since 2011 is what may be called the doctrine of 'primary', 'absolute', or 'mandatory' universal jurisdiction based on the *civitas maxima* perspective. The genesis of Belgium seeking the extradition of former Chadian President Habré from Senegal to stand trial in Belgium was the complaint filed with a Belgian investigating judge on 30 November 2000 by a *Belgian national* of Chadian origin, which was subsequently joined by similar complaints of approximately twenty other persons before the same judge. The Agent of Belgium in *Belgium v Senegal* was at pains to point out to the ICJ in that case that:

> [The implementation of the obligation to prosecute or extradite in that case] is not about combating impunity by prosecuting 'on behalf of the international community' or 'on behalf of an entire continent' an individual suspected of crimes of torture, war crimes, crimes against humanity and crimes of genocide.... [I]t is about submitting to the competent national authorities, for the purpose of prosecution ... either in Senegal, the African country where the individual suspected of those crimes is present or, failing that, in Belgium, a country which has been seeking his extradition since 2005.[62]

Where a State has to resort to UJ for the purpose of *aut dedere aut judicare*, an initial step is to ascertain whether customary international law or a treaty establishes UJ for the crime in question. For example, the ICTY Appeals Chamber has held in *Blaskic* that the national jurisdictions of all States 'are required by customary law to judge or to extradite those persons presumed responsible for grave violations of international humanitarian law'.[63] It is possible that for certain 'treaty crimes' there is only an obligation to exercise 'universal jurisdiction' between the State parties *inter se* without a corresponding universal jurisdiction under customary international law.[64] Nonetheless, States may have the obligation to prosecute or extradite core

[60] Report to the plenary of the Sixth Committee by the chair of the Working Group on the scope and application of the principle of universal jurisdiction on 21 Oct 2011. See also the statement by Cuba in the Sixth Committee: 'Although the two were related, there were significant differences between the obligation to extradite or prosecute and the principle of universal jurisdiction. The [ILC] should focus on regulating the obligation to extradite or prosecute and leave the other matter to the [Sixth] Committee's Working Group on the scope and application of the principle of universal jurisdiction, which would decide whether to refer it to the [ILC]', UN Doc A/C.6/66/SR.27 (8 Dec 2011) §57. The UN General Assembly itself has recognized 'the diversity of views by States and the need for further consideration towards a better understanding of the scope and application of universal jurisdiction' (UNGA Doc A/RES/66/103 (13 Jan 2012) fourth preambular paragraph).

[61] Informal Working Paper of the Working Group on the Scope and Application of the Principle of Universal Jurisdiction, Doc A/C.6/66/WG.3/1 (21 Oct 2011) §II (3)(f).

[62] *per* Paul Rietjens, Agent of the Kingdom of Belgium, Hearings on 19 March 2012, ICJ Doc CR 2012/6, 50.

[63] *Prosecutor v Tihomir Blaskic* (Judgment on the Request of the Republic of Croatia for Review of the Decision of Trial Chamber II of 18 July 1997) IT-95-14-AR (29 Oct 1997) §29, citing in support of this customary obligation the United States military manual, *The Law of Land Warfare* (1956) §506(b).

[64] Bruce Broomhall, 'Towards the Development of an Effective System of Universal Jurisdiction for Crimes Under International Law' (2001) 35 New England L Rev 399, 401.

crimes under international law although the relevant treaties on those crimes do not specifically impose such obligation on their States Parties. This is the case of the crime of genocide.

The inclusion of genocide as a crime over which States may exercise UJ to prosecute in lieu of extradition is interesting. The European Court of Human Rights in *Jorgic v Germany* upheld the jurisdiction of German courts under German Criminal Code to try persons charged with genocide committed abroad, regardless of the defendant's and the victims' nationalities, and despite the wording of Article VI of the Genocide Convention,[65] to which Germany is party, that persons charged with genocide or any of the other acts enumerated in the Convention 'shall be tried by a competent tribunal of the State in the territory of which the act was committed, or by such international penal tribunal as may have jurisdiction with respect to those Contracting Parties which shall have accepted its jurisdiction'. In the Court's reasoning,

> the Contracting Parties to the Genocide Convention, despite proposals in earlier drafts to that effect, had not agreed to codify the principle of universal jurisdiction over genocide for the domestic courts of all Contracting States in [Article VI] . . . However, pursuant to Article I of the Genocide Convention, the Contracting Parties were under an *erga omnes* obligation to prevent and punish genocide, the prohibition of which forms part of the *jus cogens*. In view of this, the [German] national courts' reasoning that the purpose of the Genocide Convention, as expressed notably in that Article, did not exclude jurisdiction for the punishment of genocide by States whose laws establish extraterritoriality in this respect must be considered as reasonable (and indeed convincing). Having thus reached a reasonable and unequivocal interpretation of Article VI of the Genocide Convention in accordance with the aim of that Convention, there was no need, in interpreting the said Convention, to have recourse to the preparatory documents, which play only a subsidiary role in the interpretation of public international law (see Articles 31 §1 and 32 of the Vienna Convention on the Law of Treaties of 23 May 1969).[66]

The European Court of Human Rights also noted that this interpretation of Article VI of the Genocide Convention in the light of Article I of that Convention and the establishment of universal jurisdiction to try the applicant on charges of genocide was 'widely confirmed by the statutory provisions and case-law of numerous other Contracting States to the [European] Convention (for the Protection of Human Rights and Fundamental Freedoms) and by the Statute and case-law of the ICTY'. Furthermore, Article 9(1) of the ICTY Statute[67] was held to have confirmed the German courts' view, providing for concurrent jurisdiction for genocide of the ICTY and national courts, without any restriction to domestic courts of particular States.[68]

[65] 78 UNTS 277. [66] *Jorgić v Germany*, §68, ECHR 2007-III. [67] (1993) 32 ILM 1159.

[68] *Jorgić v Germany*, no 74613/01 §69. The European Court of Human Rights cited the relevant law of the following States authorizing the exercise of universal jurisdiction over the crime of genocide: Spain, France, Belgium (at least until 2003), Finland, Italy, Latvia, Luxembourg, the Netherlands

A question may be asked: in view of the latest development in the Sixth Committee with regard to UJ, how can the obligation to extradite or prosecute operate alongside UJ to end the impunity?

Potential abuse of UJ features prominently in the work of the Sixth Committee's Working Group on UJ. It may be recalled that AU-EU Technical ad hoc Expert Group on the Principle of Universal Jurisdiction was set up in November 2008 in response to the AU's concerns over 'abusive applications of the principle of universal jurisdiction'. As already pointed out above, the ad hoc Expert Group, in endeavouring to clarify the respective understanding of the African and the European Union States on the UJ principle, admits that States by and large accept that both customary international law and treaties permit the exercise of UJ and it then suggests how UJ is to be exercised, such as a priority is to be given to a State having a significant link with the crime in question, especially the territorial State where the crime is committed; the need to avoid impairing friendly international relations; and the need to respect the relevant immunities.

In the present author's opinion, most, if not all, of the concerns about potential abuse of UJ can be met by upholding the Princeton Principles on Universal Jurisdiction, adopted in January 2001 by a group of eminent scholars and jurists.[69] The commentary to the Principles acknowledges that all legal powers can be abused by wilfully malicious individuals, but the Princeton Principles 'do all that principles can do to guard against such abuses: they specify the considerations that conscientious international actors can and should act upon'.[70]

The 14 Principles[71] can be summarized as follows.

UJ is criminal jurisdiction based solely on the seriousness of the crime under international law, irrespective of where the crime was committed, the nationality of the alleged or convicted perpetrator, the nationality of the victim, or any other connection to the State exercising such jurisdiction. A State shall exercise UJ in good faith and in accordance with its rights and obligations under international law and national judicial organs shall construe national law in a manner that is consistent with these Principles. Serious crimes under international law to be subjected to UJ include piracy, slavery, war crimes, crimes against peace, crimes against humanity, genocide, and torture as well as 'other crimes under international law'. Amnesties for these crimes are generally inconsistent with the obligation of States to provide accountability thereto and the exercise of UJ with respect to these crimes shall not

(since 2003), Russia, Slovakia, Czech Republic, Hungary, Austria, Denmark, Estonia, Poland, Portugal, Romania, Sweden, and Switzerland (since 2000) (ibid §§53–54).

69 Adrian Arena, Lloyd Axworthy, Gary J Bass, M Cherif Bassiouni, William J Butler, Hans Corell, Param Cumaraswamy, EVO Dankwa, Richard A Falk, Tom Farer, Cees Flinterman, Mingxuan Gao, Menno T Kamminga, Michael Kirby, Bert B Lockwood, Stephen Macedo, Stephen P Marks, Michael O'Boyle, Diane F Orentlicher, Stephen A Oxman, Vesselin Popovski, Michael Posner, Yves Sandoz, Jerome J Shestack, former President of the International Court of Justice Stephen M Schwebel, Kuniji Shibahara, Anne-Marie Slaughter, Turgut Tarhanli, and Wang Xiumei. Although Law Lord Nicholas Browne-Wilkinson of the UK House of Lords participated in the project, he did not join in the adoption of the Principles.

70 <https://lapa.princeton.edu/hosteddocs/unive_jur.pdf>, 45, accessed 10 November 2017.

71 Reproduced in Macedo, *Princeton Project on Universal Jurisdiction* 18–25.

be excluded by amnesties that are incompatible with international legal obligations of the amnesty-granting State.

A State shall, where necessary, enact national legislation to enable the exercise of UJ; however, national judicial organs may rely on UJ even if their national legislation does not specifically provide for such jurisdiction. A State shall comply with all international obligations applicable to, *inter alia, prosecuting* and *extraditing* persons accused or convicted of crimes under international law. A State or its judicial organs shall refuse to entertain a request for extradition based on UJ if the person sought is likely to face a death penalty sentence or to be subjected to torture or any other cruel, degrading, or inhuman punishment or treatment, or if it is likely that the person sought will be subjected to sham proceedings in which international due process norms will be violated and no satisfactory assurances to the contrary are provided. A State that refuses to extradite on the aforesaid ground shall, when permitted by international law, *prosecute* the individual accused *or extradite* such person to another State where this can be done without exposing him or her to the aforementioned risks. A State exercising UJ may, for the purposes of prosecution, seek judicial assistance to obtain evidence from another State, provided that the requesting State has a good faith basis and that the evidence sought will be used in accordance with international due process norms. Prior criminal or accountability proceedings conducted in good faith in accordance with international norms and standards shall be recognized by other States, so that there can be no multiple prosecutions or punishment for the same conduct. Besides, statutes of limitations or other forms of prescription shall not apply to these serious crimes.

Where more than one State has or may assert jurisdiction over a person and where the State that has custody of the person has no basis for jurisdiction other than the principle of universality, that State or its judicial organs shall, in deciding whether to *prosecute* or *extradite*, base their decision on an aggregate balance of the following criteria: (1) multilateral or bilateral treaty obligations; (2) the place of commission of the crime; (3) the nationality connection of the alleged perpetrator to the requesting State; (4) the nationality connection of the victim to the requesting State; (5) any other connection between the requesting State and the alleged perpetrator, the crime, or the victim; (6) the likelihood, good faith, and effectiveness of the prosecution in the requesting State; (7) the fairness and impartiality of the proceedings in the requesting State; (8) convenience to the parties and witnesses, as well as the availability of evidence in the requesting State; and (9) the interests of justice. Where disputes arise from the exercise of UJ, States should settle their disputes by all available means of peaceful settlement of disputes and in particular by submitting the dispute to the International Court of Justice. Pending the determination of the issue in dispute, a State seeking to exercise UJ shall not detain the accused person nor seek to have that person detained by another State unless there is a reasonable risk of flight and no other reasonable means can be found to ensure that person's eventual appearance before the judicial organs of the State seeking to exercise its jurisdiction.

As regards immunities of the persons sought, Principle 5 of the Princeton Principles merely provides that the official position of any accused person, whether as Head of State or Government or as a responsible government official, shall not relieve such person of criminal responsibility nor mitigate punishment with respect to these serious crimes under international law.[72]

The commentary to the Princeton Principles clarifies that the Principles do not prevent a State from initiating the criminal process, conducting an investigation, issuing an indictment, or requesting extradition, when the accused is not present in that State.

On the illustrative list of serious crimes subjected to UJ, 'slavery' was included partly because of its historical ties to piracy, although only a few conventional provisions authorize the exercise of UJ for slavery. Although 'war crimes' were initially restricted to 'serious war crimes', namely, 'grave breaches' of the 1949 Geneva Conventions and Additional Protocol (AP) I thereto, the participants agreed to remove the word 'serious' to avoid the impression that some war crimes are not serious, although they also concurred that UJ should not be invoked to prosecute minor transgressions of the 1949 Conventions and AP I. Apartheid, terrorism, and drug trafficking offences were raised as candidates for inclusion. The Principles leave open the possibility that, in the future, other crimes not listed therein may be deemed of such a heinous nature as to warrant the application of UJ.[73]

'Especially difficult moral, political, and legal issues' surrounded immunities for former or incumbent heads of State, diplomats, and other officials. There are two distinct immunities from prosecution: substantive immunity and procedural immunity. The former would exonerate a person from criminal responsibility when he or she commits a crime in an official capacity—Principle 5 rejects this substantive immunity. However, under existing customary international law, 'in proceedings before national tribunals, procedural immunity remains in effect during a head of State's or other official's [*sic*] tenure in office, or during the period in which a diplomat is accredited to a host State'.[74] The commentary adds, though, that in the future, this procedural immunity may be called increasingly into question; hence, the participants in the Princeton Project 'opted not to try and settle on principles governing procedural immunity in order to leave space for future developments'.[75] The issue of immunity of State officials is analysed by this present author in Chapter 6.

The present author wishes to add that, as a rule, in so far as the State concerned exercises UJ in good faith, without ulterior political agenda and avoiding the criticisms against its potential 'abuse' and arbitrariness as much as possible, that State can prosecute the alleged offender in lieu of extradition without the State incurring State responsibility for international wrongful acts. The list of crimes subject to UJ under customary international law should be 'core crimes' proscribed by *jus cogens*, otherwise a State may exercise jurisdiction in the absence of any jurisdictional

[72] Cf Yee, 'Universal Jurisdiction' 527, where the author who opposes the principle of UJ suggests, *arguendo*, the exercise of UJ be subject to several conditions, eg '(1) limiting that exercise to the most heinous crimes such as, in addition to piracy, slavery, genocide, crimes against humanity and serious war crimes; (2) giving priority to the territorial State; (3) applying the clean-hands doctrine; (4) requiring a decision of the highest State authority to trigger the exercise; (5) respecting applicable immunities of officials and States; (6) possible approval of an international screening mechanism; and (7) the presence of the suspect.'

[73] Macedo, *Universal Jurisdiction* 29–30. [74] ibid 31. [75] ibid 32.

link between the State and the crime in question only where that State is obligated to do so under a treaty.

Where a crime violates a norm of *jus cogens*, a proper exercise of UJ over the perpetrator is most likely to meet the least opposition or resistance from the international community of nations. A case in point is the *Zimbabwe Torture Docket Case* decided by the Constitutional Court of South Africa, holding that the South African Police Service (SAPS) has a duty to investigate crimes against humanity committed in Zimbabwe by Zimbabweans against Zimbabweans.[76] While South Africa is a State Party to both the Convention against Torture and the ICC Statute, Zimbabwe is party to neither. It was alleged that six Cabinet Ministers and Directors General and the ruling party in Zimbabwe itself were implicated as suspects in the commission of these crimes. The Constitutional Court of South Africa explains:

> We have found that our applicable legislative scheme, understood in the light of international customary law and other international obligations, places an obligation on our country through the SAPS to investigate crimes against humanity, including torture, committed outside our territory. However, the universal jurisdiction to investigate international crimes is not absolute. It is subject to at least two limitations. The first limitation arises from the principle of subsidiarity. It requires that ordinarily there must be a substantial and true connection between the subject-matter and the source of the jurisdiction. And once jurisdiction is properly founded, the principle of non-intervention in the affairs of another country must be observed; investigating international crimes committed abroad is permissible only if the country with jurisdiction is unwilling or unable to prosecute and only if the investigation is confined to the territory of the investigating state. Simply put, we may not investigate or prosecute international crimes in breach of considerations of complementarity and subsidiarity.[77]

The second limitation is that of practicality, whereby 'it must be considered whether embarking on an investigation into an international crime committed elsewhere is reasonable and practicable in the circumstances of each particular case ... in light of all the relevant circumstances', particularly 'whether the investigation is likely to lead to a prosecution and accordingly whether the alleged perpetrators are likely to be present in South Africa on their own or through an extradition request ...'[78]

On the facts of that case, the Constitutional Court of South Africa concluded that, due to 'the international and heinous nature of the crime', South Africa had 'a substantial connection to it'. The Court considered as 'the cornerstone of the universality principle, in general, and the Rome Statute, in particular', the obligation 'to hold torturers, genocidaires, pirates and their ilk, the so-called *hostis humani generis*, the enemy of all humankind, accountable for their crimes, wherever they may have committed them or wherever they may be domiciled'. The alleged acts of torture were perpetrated in Zimbabwe, by and against Zimbabwean nationals, and none of the perpetrators was present in South Africa. However, 'the duty to combat torture travel[led] beyond the borders of Zimbabwe'. Torture formed part

[76] *National Commissioner of the South African Police Service v Southern African Human Rights Litigation Centre and Another* (CCT02/14) [2014] ZACC 30.
[77] ibid §61. [78] ibid §63–64.

of the category of crimes in which all States had an interest under customary international law. Therefore, South Africa could, through universal jurisdiction, assert prescriptive and, to some degree, adjudicative jurisdiction by investigating the allegations of torture as a precursor to taking a possible next step against the alleged perpetrators such as a prosecution or an extradition request. There was no evidence that Zimbabwe had launched any investigation or had indicated its willingness to do so, given the period of time since the alleged commission of the crimes. While conceding that political inter-State tensions were, in most instances, virtually unavoidable in implementing UJ, the exercise of UJ for purposes of the investigation of an international crime committed outside the territory of South Africa might occur in the absence of a suspect without offending international law. As South Africa was not exercising enforcement jurisdiction against the Zimbabwean suspects within the South African territory, this would not offend against the principle of non-intervention. Furthermore, there was a reasonable possibility that the SAPS would gather evidence that might satisfy the elements of the crime of torture allegedly committed in neighbouring Zimbabwe, and the possible presence of the suspects in South Africa in the future could not be discounted.[79] Of interest is the Court's opinion that in its investigation in the case at hand the SAPS could not readily discount the assistance offered by the Southern African Human Rights Litigation Centre (SALC), a non-governmental organisation based in Johannesburg providing support to human rights and public interest litigation within Southern Africa, either.

The limitation on the basis of practicality in the exercise of UJ may be demonstrated by the prosecution in the UK of *Kumar Lama*, a former colonel in the Nepalese Army. He was charged in the UK with two counts under section 134(1) of the UK Criminal Justice Act 1988 based on allegations that in May 2005 at an army barracks under his command he participated in the torture of two detainees who were members of Maoist forces fighting the Nepalese Government in an internal armed conflict in Nepal during 1996–2006. Section 134(1) allows the UK, as a State Party to the Torture Convention, to prosecute the offence of torture committed by 'a public official or person in an official capacity, whatever his nationality', provided that 'in the United Kingdom or elsewhere he intentionally inflicts severe pain or suffering on another in the performance or purported performance of his official duties'. He was arrested in January 2013 while on leave in the UK from his posting as a UN peacekeeper in South Sudan. The Nepalese Embassy in London lodged a protest with the British Government and demanded his immediate release on the ground that he was serving as a UN peacekeeper at the time of his arrest. However, the UN Secretary General waived his immunity because the alleged offences did not relate to Lama's functions of an expert on UN mission and had allegedly been committed prior to his function in the UN.

[79] ibid §§47, 49, 74–79. See also Mia Swart, 'Towards a Multi-Layered System of International Criminal Justice' in Evelyn A Ankumah (ed), *The International Criminal Court and Africa: One Decade On* (Intersentia 2016) 139, 150–52; Angela Mudukuti, 'Complementarity and Africa: Tackling International Crimes at the Domestic Level', ibid 489, 499.

His trial in the UK started in February 2015 but was adjourned on 18 March 2015 until August that year owing to the lack of a qualified interpreter. In August 2016, a jury exonerated him of one charge of torture but could not reach a verdict on the second charge. A month later he was formally acquitted of the other charge after the Crown had informed the court that there was no realistic prospect of conviction on the second charge due to inconsistencies in evidence. The prosecution was estimated to have cost approximately £1 million.[80] The exercise of UJ in this case has been criticized as inappropriate. According to one legal scholar, while UJ is supposed to be a tool to try extraordinary crimes through ordinary means, a domestic criminal court exercising UJ may not be appropriate as an organ of international criminal justice as the domestic court is mainly involved in finding guilt or innocence of the accused without considering the significant context in which the crimes were committed and their impact on the society, including the State authorities and/or institutions there. Trial in a foreign domestic criminal court thus risks distortion or undue disregard of the context of the commission of crimes, coupled with other inherent problems such as the language barrier as well as difficulties in presenting witnesses and evidence.[81]

The *Lama* episode informs us that in order to prosecute crimes on the basis of the exercise of universal jurisdiction there must be solid documentation of the evidence substantiating criminal charges against the accused. This may be lacking at prosecution by a State acting on its own without the support of relevant international organizations and other States. Nonetheless, the shortcomings of the exercise of universal jurisdiction in the *Lama* case are not necessarily the norm. Exercise of UJ by domestic courts is also useful when competent international criminal tribunals cannot get hold of the persons sought by such tribunals. On 16 February 2017, the District Court of Stockholm was able to convict and sentence *Haisam Omar Sakhanh*, a former member of a Syrian armed group fighting the Syrian Government, to life imprisonment for his participation in the summary execution 'under particularly cruel circumstances' of seven injured Syrian soldiers in Syria in 2012, one year before he was granted a refugee status in Sweden. He confessed to having personally shot one soldier dead, but argued that the death sentences against his victim had been carried out by a 'regularly constituted court' set up by a party to a non-international armed conflict in Syria. While the Swedish Court held that a non-State actor could establish a court during such conflict, the Syrian soldiers, including the one shot dead by Sakhanh, were executed less than two days after their capture: hence, without a fair trial.[82] Sakhanh was, therefore, convicted of war crimes under section 6 of

[80] 'Nepal torture charge colonel Kumar Lama cleared', *BBC* (6 Sept 2016) available at <http://www.bbc.com/news/uk-england-sussex-37290487>, accessed 10 November 2017.

[81] Devika Hovell, 'The "Mistrial" of Kumar Lama: Problematizating Universal Jurisdiction' (6 Apr 2017) EJIL Talk! <https://www.ejiltalk.org/the-mistrial-of-kumar-lama-problematizing-universal-jurisdiction/>, accessed November 2017.

[82] *Haisam Omar Sakhanh*, District Court of Stockholm, Case no B 3787-16, Judgment of 16 Feb 2017.

Chapter 22 of the then Swedish Penal Code[83] and on the basis of universal jurisdiction as the crimes had no nexus with Sweden whatsoever. The footage of the summary execution was published in the media in 2013 and the Italian authorities assisted their Swedish counterparts in identifying Sakhanh who used to stay in Italy. These played a crucial role in the success of the Swedish Court's exercise of universal jurisdiction in this case.[84]

As the authors of the Princeton Principles have correctly concluded, the establishment of international networks of cooperation will be especially important to the effective development of universal jurisdiction. Therefore, UJ 'can only work if different States provide each other with active judicial and prosecutorial assistance, and all participating States will need to insure that due process norms are being complied with'.[85]

In the final analysis, as a procedural safeguard against abuse/vexatious criminal prosecution, the Minister of Justice or equivalent of the forum State must authorize the prosecution in such cases. A screening process could emulate the pre-trial chamber mechanism in the ICC and other international criminal tribunals, plus stringent regulations/guidelines/rules against prosecutorial discretion which may entail arbitrary or over-aggressive exercise of prosecution.

[83] This provision penalizes, *inter alia*, crimes against international law or serious violations of a generally recognized principle of international humanitarian law concerning armed conflicts. The new Code as amended entered into force in July 2014.

[84] Christina Anderson, 'Syrian Rebel Gets Life Sentence for Mass Killing Caught on Video', *New York Times* (16 Feb 2017) available at <https://www.nytimes.com/2017/02/16/world/europe/syrian-rebel-haisam-omar-sakhanh-sentenced.html>, accessed 10 November 2017.

[85] Macedo, *Universal Jurisdiction* 44–45.

6

Scope of the Obligation to Extradite or Prosecute

I. A Single Obligation in the Alternative or Two Separate Obligations?

One crucial issue is whether the obligation to extradite or prosecute constitutes a single obligation in the alternative or two separate obligations.

The International Law Commission's commentary to Article 9 of the 1996 Draft Code of Crimes against the Peace and Security of Mankind appears to indicate that the ILC treated this obligation as a single obligation in the alternative.[1] The obligation to extradite or prosecute is a single obligation with two elements of extradition and prosecution. It is not two separate obligations, that is, an obligation to extradite and an obligation to prosecute. The singular nature of the obligation becomes clear when contrasted with instruments such as the 1948 Convention for the Prevention and Punishment of the Crime of Genocide.[2] That Convention contains obligations for States to prosecute (where the genocide occurred on its territory) and to extradite, but these are not an *aut dedere aut judicare* obligation, where a State is required to extradite *or* prosecute.[3] Thus, if a person accused of committing genocide elsewhere is present on a State's territory, that State may be obliged to extradite him or her to a requesting State with whom it has an existing extradition treaty or other extradition arrangements but that State is not obliged to prosecute the person, whether or not an extradition request is made. On the other hand, instruments such as the four Geneva Conventions of 1949[4] require, under a single provision, States to either extradite or prosecute alleged offenders present on their territory.[5]

[1] See Chapter 1 Section II. [2] 78 UNTS 277.

[3] Claire Mitchell, *Aut Dedere, aut Judicare: The Extradite or Prosecute Clause in International Law* (Graduate Institute of International and Development Studies 2009) ch 1 n 10.

[4] Geneva Convention for the amelioration of the condition of the wounded and the sick in armed forced in the field (75 UNTS 31); Geneva Convention for the amelioration of the condition of wounded, sick and shipwrecked members of armed forces at sea (75 UNTS 85); Geneva Convention relative to the treatment of prisoners of war (75 UNTS 135); Geneva Convention relative to the protection of civilian persons in time of war (75 UNTS 287).

[5] Geneva Convention for the amelioration of the condition of the wounded and sick in armed forces in the field (Art 49); Geneva Convention for the amelioration of the shipwrecked members of armed forces at sea (Art 50); Geneva Convention relative to the treatment of prisoners of war (Art 129); Geneva Convention relative to the protection of civilian persons in time of war (Art 146).

This obligation arises regardless of the place of the commission of the crime. The dispute surrounding the obligation *aut dedere aut judicare* is the extent of discretion custodial States have in choosing between the two options and whether the relationship between the elements of extradition and prosecution is alternative/equal or conditional/hierarchical.

The alternative structure of the obligation to extradite or prosecute derives from the Latin expression *aut dedere aut judicare.*[6] Edward M Wise, an eminent scholar in this field, also refers to the obligation as a single obligation in the alternative.[7] Special Rapporteur Galicki likewise adopted the terminology 'alternative' obligations.[8]

It is hereby submitted that *aut dedere aut judicare* is part and parcel of a single process in which international law recognizes individual criminal responsibility and the allocation of the role for States to ensure that individuals be held criminally responsible for the crimes committed by them. As eloquently put by Ratner, Abrams, and Bischoff, this process requires examining three subsidiary issues that essentially correspond to different strategies for providing international criminal responsibility. First, to what extent does international law *directly provide for individual (or other) culpability?* Secondly, to what extent does international law *obligate* some or all States or the global community at large to try and punish, or otherwise sanction, offenders? Thirdly, to what extent does international law *authorize* these same actors to try and punish, or otherwise sanction, offenders?[9] The obligation *aut dedere aut judicare* involves a State establishing jurisdiction under its domestic law in order to be able to detain, extradite, or put on trial an alleged offender found in its territory.[10] As such, it falls squarely within Ratner et al's second subsidiary issue. However, the obligation also overlaps to a certain extent with Ratner et al's third subsidiary issue which concerns exercising jurisdiction over the individual criminals under an internationally recognized basis of criminal jurisdiction, including universal jurisdiction where applicable. This is consistent with the contention by another commentator that the international obligation to extradite or prosecute has two components: the obligation to adapt internal law to ensure the inclusion of the obligation to extradite or prosecute, unless the obligation is directly applicable internally; and the establishment of competence to exercise jurisdiction over the offence when the alleged offender is present in any territory under the jurisdiction of the State concerned.[11] This is one single international legal obligation which has a 'two-tiered strategy'.[12]

[6] Zdzislaw Galicki (Special Rapporteur), Second report on the obligation to extradite or prosecute (*aut dedere aut judicare*), UN Doc A/CN.4/585 (11 June 2007) §89.

[7] Edward M Wise, 'The Obligation to Extradite or Prosecute' (1993) 27 Israel L Rev 268, 268.

[8] Zdzislaw Galicki (Special Rapporteur), Third report on the obligation to extradite or prosecute (*aut dedere aut judicare*), UN Doc A/CN.4/603 (10 June 2008) §76.

[9] Steven R Ratner, Jason S Abrams, and James L Bischoff, *Accountability for Human Rights Atrocities in International Law: Beyond the Nuremberg Legacy* (3rd edn, OUP 2009) 11 (emphasis original).

[10] See Commonwealth Secretariat, *Implementation Kits for the International Counter-Terrorism Conventions* (2002) 6 [15].

[11] Gérard Dive, Head of the International Humanitarian Law Unit of the Belgian Ministry of Justice, in *Extraditing Genocide Suspects From Europe to Rwanda*, Report of a Conference organized by REDRESS and African Rights at the Belgian Parliament, 1 July 2008, 42.

[12] ibid 44.

As explained in Chapter 4, where the obligation is contained in a treaty, the discretion custodial States have in choosing between the two elements depends on the specific wording and content of the obligation under that treaty. One author argues that the main reasons for the difference in the various conventions appear to be the seriousness and nature of the crime in question and the appropriateness of the forum used to punish the alleged offender. In his view, generally where the crime affects the international community as a whole, the custodial State appears to have free discretion in choosing between the extradition and prosecution. In contrast, where extradition is given a preference to prosecution it is over those crimes in which all States cannot conceptually be viewed as having an equal interest, since the interests safeguarded do not transcend State concerns'.[13] This conclusion is reinforced by a decision of the Committee against Torture, set up to monitor the implementation of the 1984 Convention against Torture and Other Cruel, Inhuman or Degrading Treatment or Punishment.[14] It is undisputed that nowadays torture is a universally condemned crime.[15] In *Suleymane Guengueng* et al *v Senegal*, the Committee:

> recalls that, under article 7 of the Convention, 'the State Party in the territory under whose jurisdiction a person alleged to have committed any offence referred to in article 4 is found shall in the cases contemplated in article 5, if it does not extradite him, submit the case to its competent authorities for the purpose of prosecution'. It notes that the obligation to prosecute the alleged perpetrator of acts of torture does not depend on the prior existence of a request for his extradition. The alternative available to the State party under article 7 of the Convention exists only when a request for extradition has been made and puts the State party in the position of having to choose between (a) proceeding with extradition or (b) submitting the case to its own judicial authorities for the institution of criminal proceedings, the objective of the provision being to prevent any act of torture from going unpunished.[16]

In *Belgium v Senegal*, the ICJ rules that States Parties to the Convention against Torture has obligations to criminalize torture, establish their jurisdiction, including universal jurisdiction, over torture so as to equip themselves with the necessary legal tool to prosecute this offence, and make an inquiry into the facts. The ICJ declares that '[t]hese obligations, taken as a whole, might be regarded as elements of a *single conventional mechanism* aimed at preventing suspects from escaping the consequences of their criminal responsibility, if proven.'[17]

In dispositive paragraph 6 of the Judgment, the ICJ unanimously found that Senegal 'must, without further delay, submit the case of Habré to its competent authorities for the purpose of prosecution, if it does not extradite him'.[18] Therefore, Senegal was required to cease its continuing wrongful act, in accordance with general

[13] Raphaël van Steenberghe, 'The Obligation to Extradite or Prosecute: Clarifying its Nature' (2011) 9 J Int'l Crim Justice 1089, 1113–14.

[14] 1465 UNTS 85.

[15] As affirmed by the ICJ in *Belgium v Senegal* [2012] ICJ Rep 422 §99.

[16] Decision of the Committee Against Torture under Article 22 of the Convention against Torture and Other Cruel, Inhuman or Degrading Treatment or Punishment, 36th Session, CAT/C/36/D/181/2001, 19 May 2006 §9.7.

[17] *Belgium v Senegal* [2012] ICJ Rep 422 §91 (emphasis added), and see also §§74–75.

[18] ibid §122(6). Cf also §58 of Judge ad hoc Sur's Dissenting Opinion.

international law on the responsibility for internationally wrongful acts, by taking action for the purpose of prosecution of Habré, should it not extradite him.[19]

On 24 July 2012, four days after the ICJ Judgment in *Belgium v Senegal*, ICJ President Tomka responded to the present author's question, during his visit to the ILC, that the ICJ had construed 'the principal obligation' under Article 7 of the Torture Convention as the obligation 'to submit the case for prosecution and that extradition [was] not strictly speaking an obligation but an alternative option available to the State which, if chosen, would relieve the State of its obligation to prosecute'.[20] In her Declaration appended to the Judgment, Judge Donoghue likewise contends that the obligation under Article 7(1) 'is to submit a case for prosecution', not an obligation to extradite or prosecute. With due respect, these views must be considered in their proper context. Paragraph 1 of Article 7 of the Torture Convention requires that the State Party in the territory under whose jurisdiction the offender is found shall, in the cases where it has established jurisdiction pursuant to Article 5, 'if it does not extradite him, submit the case to competent authorities for the purpose of prosecution'. This provision thus focuses on the obligation to prosecute, but this is normally implemented *after* the State has performed its other obligations in the preceding Articles, including the criminalization of torture through appropriate legislation, the establishment of universal jurisdiction, and a preliminary inquiry, as well as after taking a decision not to extradite the offender, collectively described by the ICJ as 'elements of a single conventional mechanism aimed at preventing suspects from escaping the consequences of their criminal responsibility, if proven'.

The way in which the ICJ in *Belgium v Senegal* answers the question on the scope of the obligation under Article 7(1) of the Torture Convention has led one author to comment that a question raised but not fully addressed in that case is: does a State that has custody over a person suspected of committing torture, but that is unwilling or unable to prosecute the person itself, also have an obligation to extradite the person to a State seeking extradition which is able and willing to prosecute the person?[21] It is hereby submitted that the answer must be in the affirmative. For example, on 21 April 2017, the Dutch Court of Appeal in 's-Hertogenbosch held *Guus Kouwenhoven*, a Dutch national, responsible as an accessory to war crimes committed in Liberia and parts of Guinea between August 2000 and December 2002, on the grounds, *inter alia*, that international law, in particular Articles 2 and 3 of the European Convention of Human Rights[22] contains a positive obligation on States to investigate and prosecute allegations of war crimes or crimes against humanity, and that UN Security Council Resolution 1674 (2006) on the protection

[19] *Belgium v Senegal* [2012] ICJ Rep 422 §121.

[20] *per* ICJ President Tomka, Provisional summary of record of the 3148th meeting of the ILC, UN Doc A/CN.4/SR.3148 (17 Aug 2012) 21. See also §3 of the Declaration of Judge Donoghue in *Belgium v Senegal*.

[21] André Nollkaemper, 'Wither Aut Dedere? The Obligation to Extradite or Prosecute after the ICJ's Judgment in Belgium v Senegal' (2013) 4 J Int'l Dispute Settlement 501.

[22] 1950 European Convention for the Protection of Human Rights and Fundamental Freedoms, ETS 5.

of civilians in armed conflict calls for an end to impunity for war crimes and crimes against humanity.[23] Although the Special Court for Sierra Leone has jurisdiction over 'serious violations of international humanitarian law and Sierra Leonean law committed in the territory of Sierra Leone since 30 November 1996',[24] it does not have jurisdiction over crimes committed in Guinea. Thus, surrendering the accused to the Special Court would not suffice. The Dutch Government could have surrendered him to the Special Court and, after he had served out his punishment by the Special Court, extradited/transferred him to face prosecution in Guinea. This would have been a cumbersome process, and Guinea might not be able or willing to prosecute *Kouwenhoven*. The two provisions of the European Convention cited by the Dutch Court do not unequivocally require prosecution of the offender. Article 3 broadly requires the High Contracting Parties ensure that no one shall be subjected to torture or to inhuman or degrading treatment or punishment. Article 2 stipulates the protection of the right to life to be accorded by the High Contracting Parties. It is more justifiable to rely on the Security Council Resolution, operative paragraph 8 of which '*Emphasizes* in this context the responsibility of States to comply with their relevant obligations to end impunity and to prosecute those responsible for war crimes, genocide, crimes against humanity and serious violations of international humanitarian law.'[25] In sum, by assuming the obligation to prosecute, the Dutch Government did not also assume the obligation to extradite/surrender due to the difficulties inherent in the extradition/surrender in the circumstances of the case.

II. General Principle of International Law

It may be recalled from Chapter 1 that the French Supreme Court (Criminal Chamber) in the *Barbie* case considered as a general principle of law recognized by all nations the obligation to return the perpetrator of a crime against humanity to the State where the crime was committed, to be tried there, and which the 1966 International Covenant on Civil and Political Rights (ICCPR)[26] and the European Convention on Human Rights refer to, and are regularly incorporated into the domestic legal order of higher authority than ordinary laws.[27] The very brief judgment of the French Supreme Court did not elaborate which provisions of the ICCPR and the Convention it was alluding to. It could be the right to an effective remedy under Article 2(3) of the ICCPR, and Article 13 of the Convention. The former stipulates:

[23] Dieneke De Vos, 'Corporate Accountability: Dutch Court convicts former "Timber baron" of war crimes in Liberia' <https://me.eui.eu/dieneke-de-vos/blog/corporate-accountability-dutch-court-convicts-former-timber-baron-of-war-crimes-in-liberia/#.WP2fKaR7cTE.twitter>, accessed 16 November 2017.

[24] Art 1(1), Statute of the Special Court of Sierra Leone (2178 UNTS 138).

[25] UNSC Res 1674 (28 Apr 2006) UN Doc S/RES/1674.

[26] 999 UNTS 171.

[27] Cour de Cassation [Cass] [supreme court for judicial matters] crim, 6 Oct 1983, Bull crim, No 83-93194 (Fr).

3. Each State Party to the present Covenant undertakes:
   (a) To ensure that any person whose rights or freedoms as herein recognized are violated shall have an effective remedy, notwithstanding that the violation has been committed by persons acting in an official capacity;
   (b) To ensure that any person claiming such a remedy shall have his right thereto determined by competent judicial, administrative or legislative authorities, or by any other competent authority provided for by the legal system of the State, and to develop the possibilities of judicial remedy;
   (c) To ensure that the competent authorities shall enforce such remedies when granted.

The latter provision reads: 'Everyone whose rights and freedoms as set forth in this Convention are violated shall have an effective remedy before a national authority notwithstanding that the violation has been committed by persons acting in an official capacity.'

Article 38(1)(c) of the Statute of the International Court of Justice[28] lists 'the general principles of law recognized by civilized nations' as one of the four sources of international law. The drafting history of Article 38 of the Statute of the Permanent Court of International Justice (PCIJ),[29] the precursor of the International Court of Justice (ICJ), shows that 'general principles of law recognized by civilized nations' are an autonomous source of international law to fill legal gaps so that the PCIJ would not have to make declarations of *non liquet*. The PCIJ might apply 'general principles of law recognized by civilized nations' simultaneously with 'international conventions, whether general or particular, establishing rules expressly recognized by the contesting States' and 'international custom, as evidence of a general practice accepted as law'.[30]

The notion of 'general principles' was introduced as a response to the perceived incompleteness in international law that could benefit greatly from drawing on its more established municipal counterparts.[31] The intention of the Commission of Jurists in 1920 in drafting the Statute was to avoid a *non liquet*. However, they were equally clear that this provision did not authorize the PCIJ to legislate.[32] Where the PCIJ would enter the realm of judicial legislation, the situation would not be one of *non liquet*. As usefully illustrated by one author:

Assume ... that the ICJ were to conclude that the massive environmental destruction caused by Iraq at the end of the Persian Gulf War was not prohibited by international law. This would certainly represent a gap in what the law ought to provide; indeed it might spur efforts to negotiate a treaty to address the problem of the effects of war on the environment. But it would

[28] (1945) 39 AJIL Supp 215. [29] 6 LNTS 379, 390.

[30] Permanent Court of International Justice/Advisory Committee of Jurists, *Procès-Verbaux of the Proceedings of the Committee*, 16 June–24 July 1920, 293ff. Also summarized in Fabián O Raimondo, *General Principles of Law in the Decisions of International Criminal Courts and Tribunals* (Martinus Nijhoff 2008) 17–21. See also ILC, 'Report of the International Law Commission on the work of its 69th Session' (1 May–2 June and 4 July–5 Aug 2017) UN Doc A/72/10, annex A (General principles of law).

[31] Alain Pellet, 'Article 38' in Zimmerman et al (eds), *The Statute of the International Court of Justice: A Commentary* (OUP 2006) 764–65.

[32] *Procès-Verbaux of the Proceedings of the Committee* 296 (La Pradelle), 309 (Root), 314 (Ricci-Busatti), 316 (Phillimore), and 319 (Hagerup).

not represent a finding of *non liquet*, since a legal rule would exist, albeit an unsatisfactory one. In contrast, a finding of *non liquet* would mean that the Court could not determine whether the environmental destruction caused by Iraq was prohibited or permitted by international law. There would be a gap, not in the law as it ought to be, but in the law as it is.[33]

The succinct definition provided by Lord Phillimore, the author of the proposal finally adopted in the PCIJ Statute, stipulates, '[T]he general principles … were these which were accepted by all nations *in foro domestico,* such as certain principles of procedure, the principle of good faith, and the principles of *res judicata*, etc.'[34]

More recently, the commentary to Article 38 by Alain Pellet lists three criteria in the identification of general principles: (1) they must be unwritten legal norms of a wide-ranging character; (2) they must be recognized in the municipal law of States; and (3) they must be transposable at the international level.[35] In practice, (1) and (2) are combined to mean that the principles must be widely accepted under municipal laws of States. It has been suggested that the reasoning of the ICJ in the *Barcelona Traction Case*[36] resembles the concept of the limited liability company that exists in systems of municipal law.[37] A detailed (but slightly outdated) exposition of the general principles that exist under international law was carried out by Bin Cheng in his seminal work *General Principles of Law as applied by International Courts and Tribunals*, published in 1953.[38] The principles identified include, *inter alia,* self-defence, necessity, and good faith. A more recent work by Giorgio Gaja[39] identifies the following examples of general principles as applied by the ICJ and other international courts or tribunals include the principles of good faith;[40] *res judicata*;[41] the full compensation of prejudice, by awarding to the injured party the *damnum emergens* and the *lucrum cessans*;[42] *uti possidetis*;[43] elementary considerations of humanity;[44] every State's obligation not knowingly to allow its territory to be used for acts contrary to the rights of other States;[45] and the general principle of procedural law that the plea of error cannot be allowed as an element vitiating consent if the party advancing it contributed by its conduct to the error, or could have avoided it,

[33] Daniel Bodansky, 'Non Liquet and the Incompleteness of International Law' in *International Law, the International Court of Justice and Nuclear Weapons* (CUP 1999) 156.

[34] *Procès-Verbaux of the Proceedings of the Committee* 335.

[35] Pellet, 'Article 38' 766.

[36] *Barcelona Traction, Light and Power Company, Limited (Belgium v Spain)* [1970] ICJ Rep 3.

[37] Ian Brownlie, *Principles of Public International Law* (7th edn, OUP 2008) 18.

[38] See, generally, Bin Cheng, *General Principles of Law as Applied by International Courts and Tribunals* (reprinted; Burlington 1987).

[39] Giorgio Gaja, 'General Principles of Law' in *Max Planck Encyclopedia of Public International Law* (OUP 2013).

[40] See Robert Kolb, *Good Faith in International Law* (Hart 2017)

[41] It means a final judgment on the merits of the case which is subject to no appeal and is binding upon the parties to the dispute; thus, each of the parties is precluded from pursuing litigation on a case on same issues between same parties. See *Boundary Dispute between Argentina and Chile concerning the Frontier Line between Boundary Post 62 and Mount Fitzroy* (22 RIAA 3-149) §68.

[42] The Latin terminologies mean direct loss and the interests or damages for the loss of reasonably expected profits or for loss of use of property, respectively. See *Amco Asia Co v Rep of Indonesia* [Award of 20 Nov 1984], ICSID Case no ARB/81/1 FA §267.

[43] The boundaries between colonies should be preserved after they become independent sovereign States. See *Frontier Dispute Case (Burkina Faso/Republic of Mali)* [1986] ICJ Rep 554 §§20, 24.

[44] *Corfu Channel (UK v Albania)* [1949] ICJ Rep 4, 22.

[45] ibid.

or if the circumstances were such as to put that party on notice of a possible error.[46] Another example is the principle that 'proof may be administered by means of circumstantial evidence'.[47]

According to Cassese, general principles of international law 'consist of principles inherent in the international legal system', whose identification 'does not require an in-depth comparative survey of all the major legal systems of the world, but can be carried out by way of generalization and induction from the main features of the international legal order'.[48] For example, general principles of law governing criminal trials include the principles of independent and impartial judiciary, presumption of innocence, fair and expeditious trial, and trial in the presence of the accused.[49]

The International Law Commission (ILC) agrees that although customary international law is the most common basis for peremptory norms of general international law (*jus cogens*), treaty provisions and general principles of law may also serve as bases for such peremptory norms if the necessary criteria for their elevation to that status are met.[50]

Could *aut dedere aut judicare* be a general principle of law recognized by civilized nations in their international judicial cooperation and domestic prosecution? For instance, could the obligation to extradite or prosecute be a general principle of 'the duty to cooperate in the fight against impunity' often referred to by, among others, the Nordic countries and Greece.[51] This duty has underpinned, *inter alia*, UN Security Council resolutions against international terrorism adopted under Chapter VII of the UN Charter. For example, UN Security Council Resolution 1566 (2004) calls upon States to cooperate fully in the fight against terrorism, in accordance with their obligation under international law, in order to find, deny safe haven to, and bring to justice, 'on the basis of the principle to extradite or prosecute', any person who commits an act of terrorism.[52]

[46] *Case concerning the Temple of Preah Vihear (Cambodia v Thailand)* [1962] ICJ Rep 6 §26.

[47] *Corfu Channel* 18.

[48] Antonio Cassese, *International Criminal Law* (2nd edn, OUP 2008) 21.

[49] ibid 378–94.

[50] Draft conclusion 5 (Bases for peremptory norms of general international law (*jus cogens*)) adopted by the ILC Drafting Committee on the topic 'Peremptory norms of general international law (*jus cogens*)' in 2017. See also the Special Rapporteur's second report on *jus cogens*, UN Doc A/CN.4/706 §§48–51.

[51] Statement of Norway before the Sixth Committee on behalf of the Nordic countries (UN Doc A/C.6/66/SR.26 (7 Dec 2011) §10. According to Greece, the duty to cooperate in this matter 'was indeed an overarching idea that might be considered to encompass the obligation to extradite or prosecute' (ibid §38). Cf Cuba's suggestion for the ILC to 'focus on establishing the general principles that governed extradition and on the grounds for refusing extradition, taking into account article 3 (Mandatory grounds for refusal) of the Model Treaty on Extradition, contained in annex to General Assembly resolution 45/116' (UN Doc A/C.6/66/SR.27 (8 Dec 2011) §55). What Cuba seems to suggest is the establishment of 'conditions' for extradition (eg double criminality) and 'grounds' for refusing extradition (eg the political offence exception), and not treating the obligation to extradite or prosecute as a general principle of law.

[52] Operative §2 of UNSC Res 1566 (2004). See also Andrea Bianchi, 'Security Council's Anti-terror Resolutions and their Implementation by Member States: An Overview' (2006) 4 J Int'l Crim Justice 1044, esp 1054–55.

The ILC's Working Group on the Obligation to Extradite or Prosecute (*aut dedere aut judicare*) was unanimous in not pursuing the possibility of the obligation to extradite or prosecute as a general principle of law, having concluded that the avenue of exploring such a possibility would be more difficult than that of analysing the existence of the said obligation in customary international law. First, general principles are premised on the notion that they operate within national legal systems and are then extrapolated to operate on the international legal level. In order to be a general principle of law, the obligation *aut dedere aut judicare* would have to be widely incorporated as such into municipal laws of a large number of States and as of 2012–14 when the Working Group was working on the topic there was no extensive comparative study to note the existence or non-existence of such a rule under the various municipal legal systems. Second, according to some members of the Working Group, while general principles are also found to exist in situations where a rule relates to what it means to be law, such as the general principle of later in time supersedes earlier in time, the obligation to extradite or prosecute is unlikely to operate that way.

This present author submits that the obligation to extradite or prosecute 'forms part' of a general principle of law known in national legal systems as 'subsidiarity'. For instance, Spanish courts, in applying 'the principle of subsidiarity', 'may exercise [universal] jurisdiction only if the offences are not being investigated and prosecuted effectively by another country or by an international court. Moreover, proceedings already initiated in Spain must be temporarily stayed if proceedings connected with the same offences are initiated by a court in another country or an international court.'[53]

Subsidiarity is best known as a general principle of European Union law, according to which the EU may only act where action of individual Members is insufficient.[54] However, in the context of criminal law, subsidiarity has the meaning as applied by Spanish courts, which are not alone in this regard. In *Zimbabwe Torture Docket Case*, the Constitutional Court of South Africa states that universal jurisdiction to investigate international crimes is subject to, *inter alia*, 'the principle of subsidiarity' requiring that 'ordinarily there must be a substantial and true connection between the subject-matter and the source of the jurisdiction', and that:

> once jurisdiction is properly founded, the principle of non-intervention in the affairs of another country must be observed; investigating international crimes committed abroad is permissible only if the country with jurisdiction is unwilling or unable to prosecute and only

[53] Communication dated 22 Feb 2016 from the Spanish Ministry of Foreign Affairs and Cooperation in response to the request of the UN General Assembly for information and observations on the scope and application of universal jurisdiction, Doc 16-05499 (E) at 4, <http://www.un.org/en/ga/sixth/71/universal_jurisdiction/spain_e.pdf>, accessed 16 November 2017.

[54] Art 5(3) of the Treaty on European Union (2008/C 115/ 01) provides: 'Under the principle of subsidiarity, in areas which do not fall within its exclusive competence, the Union shall act only if and in so far as the objectives of the proposed action cannot be sufficiently achieved by the Member States, either at central level or at regional and local level, but can rather, by reason of the scale or effects of the proposed action, be better achieved at Union level.'

if the investigation is confined to the territory of the investigating State. Simply put, we may not investigate or prosecute international crimes in breach of considerations of complementarity and subsidiarity.[55]

Subsidiarity is to be distinguished from 'complementarity'. The former connotes 'concurrent competence', whereas the latter accords the primacy to another court or tribunal or jurisdiction,[56] as in the case of the 1998 Rome Statute of the ICC,[57] preambular paragraph 10 and Article 1 of which provide that the ICC 'shall be complementary to national criminal jurisdictions',[58] deferring to the sovereign rights of States to prosecute perpetrators of crimes under the Rome Statute. However, the two principles share one thing in common: the inability or unwillingness of the State in whose territory the offender is present to prosecute that offender bestows upon another State or a competent international criminal tribunal the right to step in and prosecute the offender instead. Complementarity applies in a 'vertical' relation between States and an international organ such as the ICC. Subsidiarity refers to the sharing of competences at a 'horizontal' level among different States: a State other than the State with the *nexus* to the offence (such as the territorial State) may exercise jurisdiction only if the latter State is unwilling or unable to investigate and prosecute the offence in question. As provided in Article 153(f)(2)(4) of the German Code of Criminal Procedure,[59] the German public prosecution office may dispense with prosecuting a criminal offence under the German Code of Crimes against International Law 'if the offence is being prosecuted by an international court of justice or by a country on whose territory the offence was committed, a citizen of which is either suspected of the offence, or suffered injury as a result of the offence'. In Switzerland, Article 264m(1) of the Swiss Criminal Code[60] allows Swiss authorities to exercise criminal jurisdiction over genocide and war crimes committed abroad if the alleged perpetrator is in Switzerland and is not extradited to another State or surrendered to an international tribunal. By virtue of Article 246m(2), the Swiss authorities may decline to exercise jurisdiction over the said offence if a foreign authority or an international tribunal of which Switzerland recognizes jurisdiction is pursuing the offence and if the offender is extradited to that other State or surrendered to such international tribunal.

[55] *National Commissioner of the South African Police Service v Southern African Human Rights Litigation Centre and Another* (CCT02/14) [2014] ZACC 30 §61.

[56] Kristina Miskowiak, *The International Criminal Court: Consent, Complementarity and Cooperation* (DJØF 2000) 45–46.

[57] 2187 UNTS 90.

[58] Art 17 of the ICC Statute governs the situation of inability and unwillingness of States Parties which allow the ICC to step in. See further Markus Benzing, 'The Complementarity Regime of the International Criminal Court: International Criminal Justice between State Sovereignty and the Fight against Impunity' (2003) 7 Max Planck Yearbook of UN Law 591; Mohamed M El Zeidy, *The Principle of Complementarity in International Criminal Law: Origin, Development and Practice* (Martinus Nijhoff 2008); Jann K Kleffner, *Complementarity in the Rome Statute and National Criminal Jurisdictions* (OUP 2008).

[59] Federal Law Gazette [*Bundesgesetzblatt*] Part I pp 1074, 1319, as amended by Art 3 of the Act of 23 Apr 2014 (Federal Law Gazette Part I p 410).

[60] Criminal Code of 21 Dec 1937, SR 311.0.

The obligation to extradite or prosecute is, thus, part of the principle of subsidiarity—when the State with *nexus* to the offence does not seek extradition or is unable or unwilling to prosecute the offender, the State in whose territory the offender is present shall, either pursuant to a treaty or a customary international legal obligation, prosecute the offender in lieu of his or her extradition. Where the custodial State surrenders the offender to the ICC or another competent international tribunal in lieu of his or her prosecution in that State, it in effect resorts to the principle of complementarity in utilizing the third alternative to the obligation to extradite or prosecute. In either case, justice is to be done and seen to be done to victims of crimes in accordance with the right of victims to an effective remedy as referred to by the French Supreme Court (Criminal Chamber) in the *Barbie* case. Because Barbie's victims were French nationals and his crimes were committed in France, the French Court was exercising territorial as well as passive personality jurisdiction over Barbie, a foreign national, while citing the principle of subsidiarity in support. In the case of an offence committed by a non-French national abroad, Article 689-11 of the current French Code of Criminal Procedure[61] provides that criminal jurisdiction may be exercised only if no other international or national jurisdiction has requested the surrender or extradition of the alleged perpetrator, provided that the alleged perpetrator is a French permanent resident.

Although the German, Swiss, and French laws just mentioned do not use the word 'subsidiarity' or 'complementarity', they, in effect, apply these principles.

Subsidiarity is also mentioned in the literature. International criminal law is said to be 'ultimately based on the idea of the existence of a *jus puniendi* of the international community as a whole' the purpose of which is to protect genuine community values. This is evidenced by, *inter alia*, (1) the rule of *jus cogens* in Article 53 of the 1969 Vienna Convention on the Law of Treaties,[62] (2) the fourth preambular paragraph of the ICC Statute that the most serious crimes of concern to the international community as a whole must not go unpunished and that their effective prosecution must be ensured by taking measures at the national level and by enhancing international cooperation, and (3) the international obligations *erga omnes* referred to in the ICJ's *obiter dictum* in *Barcelona Traction* and Article 48(1)(b) of the ILC's Articles on State Responsibility. While the enforcement of such values is primarily entrusted to international criminal tribunals set up by treaties or the UN Security Council representing the 'collective will' and offering the best guarantee against hegemonic abuses, this does not rule out 'the existence of *subsidiary* or delegated powers of (groups of) States acting as fiduciaries of the common good'. [63]

[61] Code of Criminal Procedure (in force as of 2 Mar 1959), Art 689-11 enacted by LOI No 2010-930, 9 Aug 2010, Art 8.

[62] 1155 UNTS 331.

[63] Claus Kreβ and Kimberly Post in Otto Triffterer (ed), *Commentary on the Rome Statute of the International Criminal Court—Observers' Notes Article by Article* (2nd edn, CH Becks-Hart-Nomos 2008) 1611–12, citing *Prosecutor v Tadic* (Decision on the Defence Motion for Interlocutory Appeal on Jurisdiction) IT-94-1-AR72 (2 Oct 1995) §99 (emphasis added).

Subsidiarity does not apply vis-à-vis international criminal tribunals set up on an ad hoc basis by the UN Security Council acting under Chapter VII of the UN Charter. Thus, the ICTY and the ICTR has primacy over any national jurisdiction. However, the UN Security Council, although acting under Chapter VII of the Charter, specifically accords primacy of the Special Tribunal for Lebanon only over national courts of Lebanon.[64]

III. Immunity of State Officials from Foreign Criminal Jurisdiction

What happens where the persons sought pursuant to the 'extradite or prosecute' obligation are State officials, such as Heads of State, entitled to immunity from foreign criminal jurisdiction? Even treaties addressing crimes typically do not address the issue of immunity, leaving the matter to other treaties addressing immunities of classes of officials or to customary international law. Where treaties address the issue of immunity, there may be some exception, as in the case of Article IX of the 1994 Inter-American Convention on Forced Disappearance of Persons[65] stipulating that '[p]rivileges, immunities, or special dispensations shall not be admitted in such trials', but this is 'without prejudice to the provisions set forth in the Vienna Convention on Diplomatic Relations'.[66]

In the English case of *Pinochet (No 3)*, the House of Lords held that General Pinochet, a former President of Chile, had no immunity for acts of torture committed after the Torture Convention entered into force for the UK and the date of the entry into force of section 134 of the Criminal Justice Act of 1988 that implemented that Convention. To otherwise grant him immunity would negate the object and purpose of the Torture Convention that obligate its States Parties to end the impunity of those having perpetrated torture.[67] In contrast, the Belgian Supreme Court held in 2003 that Ariel Sharon, then incumbent Prime Minister of Israel, was entitled to immunity before Belgian courts since none of the international conventions relevant to the case at bar provided for an exception to that rule. Although Article IV of the 1948 Genocide Convention does exclude immunity, Article VI of the same convention provides only for prosecution before national courts of the State on whose territory the crimes under the Convention were committed, and before an international criminal court, but not for prosecution before national courts exercising universal jurisdiction. Regarding war crimes, neither the Rome Statute of the ICC, nor the four Geneva Conventions of 1949, nor the two additional protocols thereto of 1977 contains a provision that would prevent the defendant from evoking immunity from the jurisdiction of Belgian courts.[68]

[64] See further Cassese, *International Criminal Law* 336–46.
[65] (1994) 33 ILM 1429. [66] 500 UNTS 95.
[67] *R v Bow Street Metropolitan Stipendiary Magistrate and Others, ex parte Pinochet Ugarte (No 3)* [1999] UKHL 17.
[68] *Abbas Hijazi and others v Sharon and others (Decision related to the Indictment of Ariel Sharon, Amos Yaron and Others)* (2003) 42 ILM 596.

Immunity of State officials from foreign criminal jurisdiction has become a sensitive issue in modern-day international relations, when State officials sometimes face prosecution in a foreign State they visit or intend to visit or which seeks their extradition. The International Criminal Court has been facing the problem concerning the immunity of the incumbent President of Sudan against whom it has issued an arrest warrant for his surrender to the ICC.

There are two main types of immunity: personal immunity based on the official status of a person (immunity *ratione personae*) and functional immunity for acts performed by a person in an official capacity (immunity *ratione materiae*). The topic of immunity has been analysed extensively elsewhere.[69]

With respect to immunity *ratione personae*, the ICJ has held in *Arrest Warrant* that '[i]n international law it is firmly established that, as also diplomatic and consular agents, certain holders of high-ranking office in a State, such as the Head of State, Head of Government and Minister of Foreign Affairs, enjoy immunities from jurisdiction in other States, both civil and criminal.'[70] That case concerns the warrant issued by Belgium for the arrest of the incumbent Minister for Foreign Affairs of the Democratic Republic of the Congo. The ICJ reasons that in customary international law, the immunities accorded to Ministers for Foreign Affairs are not granted for their personal benefit, but to ensure the effective performance of their functions on behalf of their respective States. The nature of the functions exercised by a Minister for Foreign Affairs are such that, throughout the duration of his or her office, a Minister for Foreign Affairs when abroad enjoys full immunity from criminal jurisdiction and inviolability which protects the individual concerned against any act of authority of another State that would hinder him or her in the performance of his or her duties. In this respect, no distinction can be drawn between acts performed by a Minister for Foreign Affairs in an 'official' capacity and those claimed to have been performed in a 'private capacity', or, for that matter, between acts performed before the person concerned assumed office as Minister for Foreign Affairs and acts committed during the period of office. Even the mere risk that, by travelling to or transiting another State, a Minister for Foreign Affairs might be exposing himself or herself to legal proceedings could deter the Minister from travelling internationally when required to do so for the purposes of the performance of his or her official

[69] See the reports of the ILC Special Rapporteurs on the topic 'Immunity of State officials from foreign criminal jurisdiction'. Special Rapporteur Kolodkin's reports can be found at (2008) ii YBILC (Part One) 157, Docs A/CN.4/601 (preliminary report); A/CN.4/631 (second report); and A/CN.4/646 (third report). Special Rapporteur Escobar Hernández's reports can be found at Docs A/CN.4/654, A/CN.4/661, A/CN.4/673, A/CN.4/686, and A/CN.4/701.

See also eg Cassese, *International Criminal Law* 302–14; Dapo Akande and Sangeeta Shah, 'Immunities of State Officials, International Crimes, and Foreign Domestic Courts' (2010) 21 EJIL 815; Alexander Orakhelashvili, 'Immunities of State Officials, International Crimes, and Foreign Domestic Courts: A Reply to Dapo Akande and Sangeeta Shah' (2011) 22 EJIL 849; Dapo Akande and Sangeeta Shah, 'Immunities of State Officials, International Crimes, and Foreign Domestic Courts: A Rejoinder to Alexander Orakhelashvili' (2011) 22 EJIL 857; Ingrid Wuerth, 'Reassessing *Pinochet's* Legacy' (2012) 106 AJIL 731 and 'Foreign Official Immunity: Invocation, Purpose, and Exceptions' (2013) 23 Swiss Rev Int'l & Euro L 207; Roger O'Keefe, *International Criminal Law* (OUP 2015) 405–60.

[70] *Arrest Warrant of 11 April 2000 (Democratic Republic of the Congo v Belgium)* [2002] ICJ Rep 3, 20–21 [51].

functions. The ICJ has been unable to deduct from State practice any exception under customary international law to the rule according immunity from criminal jurisdiction and inviolability to incumbent Ministers for Foreign Affairs, where they are suspected of having committed war crimes or crimes against humanity.

After also examining the rules concerning the immunity or criminal responsibility of persons having an official capacity contained in the legal instruments creating international criminal tribunals, including Article 27 of the ICC Statute, the ICJ finds that these rules likewise do not enable it to conclude that any such exception exists in customarily international law in regard to national courts. Moreover, the rules governing the jurisdiction of national courts must be carefully distinguished from those governing jurisdictional immunities: jurisdiction does not imply absence of immunity, while absence of immunity does not imply jurisdiction. Thus, although various international conventions on the prevention and punishment of certain serious crimes impose on States *obligations of prosecution or extradition*, thereby requiring them to extend their criminal jurisdiction, such extension of jurisdiction in no way affects immunities under customary international law, including those of Ministers for Foreign Affairs. However, the *immunity* from jurisdiction enjoyed by incumbent Ministers for Foreign Affairs does not mean that they enjoy *impunity* in respect of any crimes they might have committed, irrespective of their gravity: jurisdictional immunity may bar prosecution for a certain period or for certain offences; it cannot exonerate the person to whom it applies from all criminal responsibility. Accordingly, there are circumstances where there can be criminal prosecution of the persons enjoying immunity *ratione personae*. These circumstances are where such persons are tried in their own countries, where the State that they represent or have represented decides to waive that immunity, where such persons no longer enjoy all the immunities accorded by international law in other States after ceasing to hold the office, and where such persons are subject to criminal proceedings before certain international criminal courts, where they have jurisdiction.[71]

It is now settled that under customary international law the 'troika' (the Head of State, Head of Government, and Minister of Foreign Affairs) as well as diplomatic agents and consular agents enjoy immunity *ratione personae* while they are in office and, after they leave office, for official acts performed while they were in office. This is affirmed by the ICJ in *Djibouti v France*.[72] In any case, constitutional Heads of State with merely nominal or ceremonial functions are not criminally responsible for acts performed by other State officials.[73]

By ruling that those entitled to personal immunity include 'certain holders of high-ranking office in a State, such as . . .' the ICJ in *Arrest Warrant* seems to indicate

[71] ibid 21–30 [53–71].

[72] *Certain Questions of Mutual Assistance in Criminal Matters (Djibouti v France)* [2008] ICJ Rep 177, 236–37.

[73] Statement of Thailand (UN Doc A/C.6/66/SR.26 (7 Dec 2011) §47), referring to the definition of the crime of aggression adopted by the Review Conference of the Rome Statute in 2010, which limits the category of persons who could commit such a crime to those 'in a position effectively to exercise control over or direct the political or military action of a State'.

that the list is not closed to the 'troika' of Head of State, Head of Government, and Minister for Foreign Affairs. However, the ICJ in *Djibouti v France* has denied immunity *ratione personae* to Djibouti's *procureur de la République* and Head of National Security.[74] This shows that being a high-ranking official within a State does not automatically entitle the official to immunity *ratione personae* before foreign criminal jurisdiction. Therefore, any extension of immunity *ratione persone* beyond the troika must be justified,[75] with criteria for such extension clearly identified.[76]

State practice on immunity *ratione personae* varies. China's position is that immunity *ratione personae* should not be limited to the troika, but should be accorded to high-level State officials engaged in international political, economic, trade, and cultural exchanges, bearing in mind each State's specific situation and political system.[77] The Swiss Federal Criminal Court in *Khaled Nezzar* recognized that the accused who was minister of defence of Algeria at the time of his alleged acts of war crimes enjoyed immunity *ratione personae* during his official term of office.[78] On the other hand, the Netherlands considers immunity *ratione personae*, which it considers to be 'absolute', limited to the troika only 'because of the changing balance between immunity and the growing desire to prevent impunity for international crimes'.[79] Belgium and Austria are of the view that State officials beyond the troika enjoy immunity under relevant treaties, such as the Vienna Convention on Diplomatic Relations of 1961, which is *lex specialis* and not customary international law.[80]

A compromise solution might be by postulating that any State official on an official visit overseas shall have immunity *ratione personae* in the State he or she visits provided that an appropriate visa and/or permission to stay is issued by the host State for the duration of his or her visit.[81] This was the case of Major Tomas Ricardo Anderson Hohatsu, a former official of Peru's Army Intelligence Service, sent by the Peruvian Government to appear before a hearing of the Inter-American Commission on Human Rights in Washington, DC in March 2000. Despite his being accused by the US authorities of having committed horrendous crimes in Peru in 1997, he was entitled to diplomatic immunity by virtue of his G-2 visa issued to accredited members of the Peruvian Mission to the Organization of American States. The G-2

[74] [2008] ICJ Rep 177, 243–44.

[75] Statement of New Zealand (UN Doc A/C.6/66/SR.27 (8 Dec 2011) §87). See, however, the statement of Algeria that restrictive interpretation to immunity *ratione personae* by confining it to the troika is not in conformity with current international norms or State practice (UN Doc A/C.6/66/SR.28 (2 Dec 2011) §44).

[76] Statements of India (UN Doc A/C.6/66/SR.27 (8 Dec 2011) §79) and Kenya (UN Doc A/C.6/66/SR.28 (2 Dec 2011) §52). Japan, however, considers it impracticable for the ILC to analyse the scope of immunity in all cases because of lack of State practice. Japan prefers the ILC to focus on the troika and perhaps other high-ranking State officials such as Cabinet ministers (ibid §35).

[77] UN Doc A/C.6/66/SR.27 (8 Dec 2011) §9.

[78] *A v Ministère Public de la Confédération, B and C*, Case no BB.2011.140, Decision of 25 July 2012.

[79] UN Doc A/C.6/66/SR.26 (7 Dec 2011) §§58–59.

[80] Statements of Belgium (ibid §66) and Austria (ibid §78).

[81] Cassese, *International Criminal Law* 311. See also the statement of Hungary (UN Doc A/C.6/66/SR.19 (22 Nov 2011) §56).

diplomatic visa is a non-immigrant visa which allows accredited representatives of any rank of foreign governments recognized by the USA to enter into the USA to work for an international organization and not for personal business or pleasure. This compromise will be in line with the 1969 Convention on Special Missions.[82] Waiver of such immunity is stipulated in Article 41 of the 1969 Convention.[83] The UK, which is not party to the 1969 Convention, accords immunity *ratione personae* to visiting ministers for whom international travel is intrinsic to their functions, such as incumbent ministers of defence and incumbent ministers of international trade.[84] Several States which are not party to the 1969 Convention accept the rationale of allowing foreign State officials to travel to a foreign State on an official visit without fear of being prosecuted in the host State.[85] Germany, which is not party to the Convention, cited personal immunity of *Rose Kabuye*, Chief of Protocol to the Rwandan President, in its decision not to arrest her during her official visit to Germany in April 2008.

Those enjoying immunity *ratione personae* will continue to enjoy immunity *ratione materiae* after they leave office, for *official acts* performed while in office.

Functional immunity (*ratione materiae*) derives from functional necessity (*ne impediatur legation* or *ne impediatur officium*) required by all State agents in performing their official duties. As the ICTY Appeals Chamber explains in *Blaskić*, State officials acting in their official capacity are 'mere instruments of a State and their official action can only be attributed to the State'. As such, they are immune from sanctions or penalties for conduct that is not private but undertaken on behalf of a State and 'not attributable to them personally but to the State on whose behalf they act'. Functional immunity is said to be 'a well-established rule of customary international law going back to the eighteenth and nineteenth centuries, restated many times since'.[86] The Supreme Court of Israel in *Eichmann* gives an alternative explanation based on the theory of 'act of State'. According to this theory, the act performed by a person as an organ of the State must be regarded as an act of that State alone and only that State bears responsibility therefor. Another State has no

[82] 1400 UNTS 231. See, in particular, Arts 1, 31(1), and 43 of the 1969 Convention. The Convention, which entered into force on 21 June 1985, was a direct product of the ILC's work.

[83] This would apparently also satisfy the suggestion for a case-by-case approach suggested by Peru (UN Doc A/C.6/66/SR.26 (7 Dec 2011) §61). Cf also the statements of Belgium, UN Doc A/C.6/66/SR.26 (7 Dec 2011) §70, Austria (ibid §80), and the Netherlands, UN Doc A/C.6/66/SR.26 (7 Dec 2011) §58.

[84] Statement of the UK (UN Doc A/C.6/66/SR.28 (2 Dec 2011) §10); General Shaul Mofaz—*Application for Arrest Warrant against General Shaul Mofaz*, Bow Street Magistrates' Court, London, 12 Feb 2004; and *Bo Xilai—Re Bo Xilai*, Bow Street Magistrates' Court, London, 8 Nov 2005, 128 ILR 713. Cf *Khurts Bat v The Investigating Judge of the German Federal Court and Others* [2011] EWHC 2029 (Admin).

[85] eg US Secretary of Defence Donald Rumsfeld—Decision of the German Prosecutor, 10 Feb 2005. Other States that are in support of this practice include Singapore (UN Doc A/C.6/66/SR.28 (2 Dec 2011) §29), China (UN Doc A/C.6/66/SR.27 (8 Dec 2011) §9) and Russia (UN Doc A/C.6/66/SR.27 (8 Dec 2011) §66). See also Ramona Pedretti, *Immunity of Heads of State and State Officials for International Crimes* (Brill Nijhoff 2015) 42.

[86] *Prosecutor v Blaskić* (Judgment on the Request of the Republic of Croatia for Review of a Decision of Trial Chamber II of 18 July 1997) IT-95-14-AR108*bis* (29 Oct 1997) §38.

right to punish the person who committed the act, save with the consent of the State whose mission he performed; otherwise, it would be interfering in the internal affairs of another State contrary to the cardinal international legal principle of equality of States based on their sovereignty.[87] In *Pinochet (No 3)*, the House of Lords has no difficulty in holding that there was immunity for the charge of murder and that of conspiracy to murder.[88] State practice in the UK, Canada, New Zealand, Australia, and the USA shows that immunity is accorded even in cases of alleged violation of *jus cogens*.[89]

However, where the act proscribed by a treaty can only be committed on behalf of the State, there can be no immunity *ratione materiae*. This is the case of torture as defined by Article 1(1) of the Convention against Torture to be an act 'inflicted by or at the instigation of or with the consent or acquiescence of a public official or other person acting in an official capacity.' This is why the UK House of Lords in *Pinochet (No 3)* rules that Pinochet enjoys no immunity for torture committed after the UK has become party to the Torture Convention and torture is a crime under UK law. The same reasoning is applicable to offences under the 2006 Enforced Disappearance Convention,[90] Article 2 of which defines 'enforced disappearance' as 'the arrest, detention, abduction or any other form of deprivation of liberty by agents of the State or by persons or groups of persons acting with the authorization, support or acquiescence of the State'.

What are the criteria for determining whether a State official has acted in an official capacity and the act performed is an official one for the purpose of enjoying immunity *ratione materiae*? France asks to what extent an 'act of an official as such' differs from an 'act falling within official functions'.[91] Spain prefers restrictive interpretation of 'official acts'.[92] The ILC considered this question in 2015. Of importance is the view of some ILC members that an 'act of State doctrine' was an entirely different legal concept from immunity *ratione materiae*. In general, there was support in the ILC for the assertion that an 'act performed in an official capacity' was defined in contradistinction to 'acts performed in a private capacity'. However, an act performed in a private capacity was not necessarily *acta jure gestionis*, nor was an act performed in an official capacity coterminous with *acta jure imperii*. Moreover, the distinction between an 'act performed in an official capacity' and an 'act performed in a private capacity had no relation whatsoever to the distinction between lawful

[87] Cited ibid. The Israeli Court then expresses reservations about this act of State doctrine which it considers inapplicable to war crimes and crimes against humanity. See also Akande and Shah, 'Immunities of State Officials' 826, where the authors posit that this is a substantive defence for the official not to be held legally responsibility for an act which is an act of the State. According to Ingrid Wuerth ('Foreign Official Immunity' 209), functional immunity ultimately protects States because it prevents them from being sued directly through the officials who work on their behalf.

[88] According to Lord Browne-Wilkinson, as to the charges of murder and conspiracy to murder, there was no reason why the ordinary rules of immunity should not apply and Pinochet should not be entitled to such immunity. Lord Hope of Craighead and Lord Hutton concur.

[89] See the authorities cited in Wuerth, 'Foreign Official Immunity' 220 nn 82–83.

[90] 2716 UNTS 3.

[91] Statement by France (UN Doc A/C.6/66/SR.20 (23 Nov 2011) §44).

[92] Statement of Spain (UN Doc A/C.6/66/SR27 (8 Dec 2011) §33).

and unlawful acts. Some ILC members were not convinced of a need to define an official act or an act performed in an official capacity for the purposes of the topic of 'Immunity of State officials from foreign criminal jurisdiction' since legal concepts tend to be indeterminate and did not always lend themselves to legal definition.[93] In the end, the ILC Drafting Committee on that topic provisionally adopted a definition of an 'act performed in an official capacity' for the purpose of immunity as 'any act performed by a State official in the exercise of State authority'.[94]

It is hereby submitted that whether a State official exercises State authority depends on whether an act performed by a State official apparently in an official capacity or as part of an official function is pursuant to the instruction of the State or under the authority of his or her functions; otherwise, the act is a 'private' one.[95]

An unsettled issue is whether *ultra vires* acts by State officials can give rise to the immunity *ratione materiae* of the officials performing such acts. Article 7 of the ILC's Articles on State Responsibility for Internationally Wrongful Acts[96] treat *ultra vires* acts as 'acts of the State under international law' for the purposes of State responsibility. However, there is no exact parallel between the law of State responsibility and the regime of immunity of State officials from foreign criminal jurisdiction, as recent developments in international criminal law have shown that an individual State agent and a State could both be held liable for the same act, the latter being State responsibility and the former being individual criminal responsibility. Although the ILC's Articles on State Responsibility have rejected the idea that a State might commit an international crime, Article 58 of the Articles stipulates that the rules of State responsibility provided therein 'are without prejudice to any question of the individual responsibility under international law of any person acting on behalf of a State'. Regarding Article 7 of the Articles on State Responsibility, the rationale there is that the State cannot take refuge behind the notion of *ultra vires* under domestic law of its organ or person or entity empowered to exercise elements of the governmental authority. This is different from the issue of immunity *ratione materiae* under international law. As pointed out in the ILC's commentary to Article 7: 'As a rule of attribution, Article 7 is not concerned with the question whether the conduct amounted to a breach of an international obligation. … [and equally], Article 7 is not concerned with the admissibility of claims arising from international wrongful acts committed by organs or agents acting *ultra vires* or contrary to instructions.'[97]

It is hereby submitted that when a government official performs an *ultra vires* act not attributable to the State, the official shall not enjoy immunity *ratione materiae.* Lord Steyn in the UK House of Lords' judgment in *Pinochet (No 1)* gives the

[93] ILC, 'Report of the International Law Commission on the work of its 67th Session' (4 May–5 June and 6 July–7 Aug 2015) UN Doc A/67/10 ch X §§204–05.

[94] Draft article 2(f) as provisionally adopted by the Drafting Committee in 2015.

[95] This author, thus, concurs with the ILC members who expressed this position in 2011 (ILC, 'Report of the International Law Commission on the work of its 66th Session' (26 April–3 June and 4 July–12 Aug 2011) UN Doc A/67/10 §135).

[96] 53 UN GAOR 56th Session Supp 10, 43.

[97] (2001) ii YBILC (Part Two) 47 §10 of the commentary to Art 7.

following illuminating examples of *ultra vires* acts from which their perpetrators shall not enjoy immunity.

> [T]he concept of an individual acting in his capacity as Head of State involves a rule of law which must be applied to the facts of a particular case. It invites classification of the circumstances of a case as falling on a particular side of the line. It contemplates at the very least that some acts of a Head of State may fall beyond even the most enlarged meaning of official acts performed in the exercise of the functions of a Head of State. If a Head of State kills his gardener in a fit of rage that could by no stretch of the imagination be described as an act performed in the exercise of his functions as Head of State. If a Head of State orders victims to be tortured in his presence for the sole purpose of enjoying the spectacle of the pitiful twitchings of victims dying in agony (what Montaigne described as the farthest point that cruelty can reach) that could not be described as acts undertaken by him in the exercise of his functions as a Head of State. Counsel for General Pinochet expressly, and rightly, conceded that such crimes could not be classified as official acts undertaken in the exercise of the functions of a Head of State. These examples demonstrate that there is indeed a meaningful line to be drawn.[98]

What distinguishes the acts mentioned in the quotation above and the murder and conspiracy to murder for which the House of Lords in *Pinochet (No 3)* rules that Pinochet has immunity is that the former had no connection to his function on behalf of the State whereas the latter were undertaken as part of his government policy to eliminate left-wing opponents for the sake of national security. However heinous such policy might be, it is not for a court of a foreign State to arrogate to itself the right to sit in judgment of the legitimacy of official acts in another State.

There are also US cases holding that an individual official of a foreign State is not entitled to immunity under the US Foreign Sovereign Immunity Act in an action against him for acts beyond the scope of his authority.[99]

Are there exceptions to immunity *ratione personae* and immunity *ratione materiae*?

Some States, such as the USA,[100] deny immunity to permanent residents/naturalized citizens living there.

According to several States, immunity of States as well as State officials from foreign criminal jurisdiction is inseparable from sovereignty of the State concerned; hence, no exceptions to immunity are allowed[101] even in cases of commission of

[98] *R v Bow Street Metropolitan Stipendiary Magistrate, ex p. Pinochet Ugarte* [1998] 4 All ER 897 (*per* Lord Steyn). Poland also opposes immunity *ratione materiae* for *ultra vires* acts (Note from the Permanent Mission of Poland to the United Nations, New York, 10 June 2015, transmitting an opinion of the Legal Advisory Committee to the Minister of Foreign Affairs of the Republic of Poland, on immunities of State officials from foreign criminal jurisdiction, at point 3: The *ultra vires* acts).

[99] *Xuncax v Gramajo* (1995) 886 F Supp 162, 175 (Dist Ct Massachusetts) and *Cabiri v Assasie-Gyimah* (1996) 921 F Supp 1189 (Dist Ct SD NY), both of which are cited by Lord Hoffmann in *Jones v Kingdom of Saudi Arabia* [2006] UKHL 26 §97.

[100] US Dept of State's Statement of Interest of the USA in *Yousuf v Samantar* 699 F3d 763 (4th Cir 2012).

[101] eg the statements of Niger (UN Doc A/C.6/66/SR.19 (22 Nov 2011) §43), China (UN Doc A/C.6/66/SR.27 (8 Dec 2011) §§10–11), Iran (ibid §45), and Israel (UN Doc A/C.6/66/SR.28 (2 Dec 2011) §22).

serious crimes under international law 'in an official capacity'.[102] Another view asserts that there is no exception to functional immunity.[103] An opposing view contends, however, that exercise of foreign jurisdiction is not a threat to sovereign independence or equality, as the 2004 UN Convention on Jurisdictional Immunities of States and Their Property[104] has shown.[105] Furthermore, it is argued, under customary international law there is no immunity *ratione materiae* for international crimes, and exceptions to immunity *ratione personae* are to be considered in the light of agreements between States, so as to ascertain whether there are treaty obligations precluding immunity.[106]

Many States consider developments since the Nuremberg Charter up to the advent of the ICC Statute as part and parcel of customary international law that denies immunity for serious crimes under international law. According to the Nordic countries, for example, the developments just mentioned are normative production and clarification of customary international law rules governing the scope for the invocation of immunities and, as such, have bearing on the general state of the law on immunity of State officials from foreign criminal jurisdiction.[107] A number of States are in favour of denying immunity to perpetrators of genocide, war crimes, and crimes against humanity (including other serious crimes such as ethnic cleansing and torture), relying particularly on the Joint Separate Opinion of Judges Higgins, Kooijmans, and Buergenthal in *Arrest Warrant* as correctly stating the current state of customary international law on immunity of State officials from foreign criminal jurisdiction.[108]

The Joint Separate Opinion reasons:

> 74. The increasing recognition of the importance of ensuring that the perpetrators of serious international crimes do not go unpunished has had its impact on the immunities which high State dignitaries enjoyed under traditional customary law. Now it is generally recognized that in the case of such crimes, which are often committed by high officials who make use of the power invested in the State, immunity is never substantive and thus cannot exculpate the offender from personal criminal responsibility. It has also given rise to a tendency, in the case of international crimes, to grant procedural immunity from jurisdiction only for as long as the suspected State official is in office.

[102] Statement of Indonesia, UN Doc A/C.6/66/SR.24 (1 Dec 2011) §72.

[103] Russia's statement, UN Doc A/C.6/66/SR.27 (8 Dec 2011) §66.

[104] UN Doc A/RES/59/38 (2005), not yet in force.

[105] Statement of Norway on behalf of the Nordic countries, UN Doc A/C.6/66/SR.26 (7 Dec 2011) §4.

[106] Statement of Belgium (ibid §§68–70), Austria (ibid §79), New Zealand (UN Doc A/C.6/66/SR.27 (8 Dec 2011) §86), and Portugal (ibid §§73–74) contend that there is 'a trend' against immunity in cases concerning international crimes that violate *jus cogens* norms.

[107] Statement of Norway on behalf of the Nordic countries, UN Doc A/C.6/66/SR.26 (7 Dec 2011) §§4–7. See also the statement of Greece, ibid §§31–36.

[108] Statement of Norway on behalf of the Nordic countries, ibid §7. Cf also the statements of Belgium, ibid §§68–70; Mexico (UN Doc A/C.6/66/SR.18 (2 Dec 2011) §54. Malaysia suggests that a distinction be made between immunity in cases of ordinary crimes and that in cases of grave crimes, with immunity for the latter to be avoided (UN Doc A/C.6/66/SR.28 (2 Dec 2011) §6). See also Cassese, *International Criminal Law* 304–10.

75. These trends reflect a balancing of interests. On the one scale, we find the interest of the community of mankind to prevent and stop impunity for perpetrators of grave crimes against its members; on the other, there is the interest of the community of States to allow them to act freely on the inter-State level without unwarranted interference. A balance therefore must be struck between two sets of functions which are both valued by the international community. Reflecting these concerns, what is regarded as a permissible jurisdiction and what is regarded as the law on immunity are in constant evolution. The weights on the two scales are not set for all perpetuity. Moreover, a trend is discernible that in a world which increasingly rejects impunity for the most repugnant offences, the attribution of responsibility and accountability is becoming firmer, the possibility for the assertion of jurisdiction wider and the availability of immunity as a shield more limited. The law of privileges and immunities, however, retains its importance since immunities are granted to high State officials to guarantee the proper functioning of the network of mutual inter-State relations, which is of paramount importance for a well-ordered and harmonious international system. . . .
79. . . . A State may exercise the criminal jurisdiction which it has under international law, but in doing so it is subject to other legal obligations, whether they pertain to the non-exercise of power in the territory of another State or to the required respect for the law of diplomatic relations or, as in the present case, to the procedural immunities of State officials. In view of the worldwide aversion to these crimes, such immunities have to be recognized with restraint, in particular when there is reason to believe that crimes have been committed which have been universally condemned in international conventions. It is, therefore, necessary to analyse carefully the immunities which under customary international law are due to high State officials and, in particular, to Ministers for Foreign Affairs.[109]

The Joint Separate Opinion finds no basis for the argument that Ministers for Foreign Affairs are entitled to the same immunities as Heads of State who, under traditional customary law, were seen as personifying the sovereign State. However, under customary international law, the incumbent Ministers for Foreign Affairs enjoy full immunity, for the purpose of ensuring the free performance of their official functions on behalf of their respective States, so that they can travel freely abroad on *official* trips whenever the need to do so arises.[110]

Nonetheless, the majority of the ICJ in *Arrest Warrant* has held that immunity *ratione personae* subsists even in case of serious crimes. Violation of a *jus cogens* norm, which is part of substantive law, does not necessarily remove immunity, which falls under the realm of procedural law, that is, procedural justice embodied in immunity cannot be sacrificed for the sake of substantive justice against impunity. This is affirmed by the ICJ in *Germany v Italy (Greece intervening)*, albeit in the context of State immunity, when it says:

Assuming for this purpose that the rules of the law of armed conflict which prohibit the murder of civilians in occupied territory, the deportation of civilian inhabitants to slave labour and the deportation of prisoners of war to slave labour are rules of *jus cogens*, there is no conflict between those rules and the rules on State immunity. The two sets of rules address different matters. The rules of State immunity are procedural in character and are confined

[109] *Arrest Warrant* [2002] ICJ Rep 3, 85–87.

[110] ibid 87–89 [81–85] (Joint Sep Op).

to determining whether or not the courts of one State may exercise jurisdiction in respect of another State. They do not bear upon the question whether or not the conduct in respect of which the proceedings are brought was lawful or unlawful.[111]

Therefore, the UK asserts categorically that the troika has absolute immunity *ratione personae* even in cases of international crimes. In its opinion, immunity *ratione materiae* can be waived by the State whose official is accused of a serious international crime, and the waiver can be implied by way of a treaty, as in the case of the Convention against Torture. The UK contends that there is little State practice to support an argument that there is no immunity *ratione materiae* in respect of certain other crimes under international conventions.[112] That may be true to a certain extent. Domestic courts in many States dismiss complaints against former officials of foreign States on the ground of immunity *ratione materiae*.[113] But this practice is not universal. On 25 July 2012, the Swiss Federal Criminal Court, while recognizing the immunity *rationae personae* of *Khaled Nezzar* as minister of defence of Algeria at the time of his alleged commission of war crimes in Algeria, ruled that this immunity did not subsist after his tenure in that position came to an end. Recognizing a clear trend in international law to restrict the immunity of persons as regards crimes proscribed by *jus cogens*,[114] the Court held that former State officials are not entitled to functional immunity (*ratione materiae*) for their conducts contrary to fundamental values of the international legal order.[115]

Statements in the Sixth Committee of the UN General Assembly continue to reveal diverging views and practices among States.

Mexico's practice in relation to Heads of State and Government and ministers of foreign affairs is to safeguard immunity *ratione personae*, which extends to acts performed by an official in the discharge of his official functions; this is considered a rule of customary international law. Mexico has no legislation providing specifically for the protection of Heads of State, or for a waiver of immunity, in connection with criminal offences. In practice, there have been instances of claims brought against former Heads of State for acts performed while in office in which the Governments concerned assumed the defence in order to protect the institution those persons had represented, usually the presidency. However, no official defence has been undertaken for such individuals where the acts were performed in a personal capacity. On the other hand, the Government of Mexico has safeguarded the immunity of former presidents from foreign judicial proceedings. Notwithstanding this current practice, Mexico is in favour of restricting immunity 'as a result of evolving international law' in cases of serious violations of human rights which are tantamount to grave crimes under international law.[116]

[111] *Jurisdictional Immunities of the State (Germany v Italy: Greece Intervening)* [2012] ICJ Rep 99 §93.

[112] UN Doc A/C.6/66/SR.28 (2 Dec 2011) §11.

[113] Wuerth, 'Reassessing *Pinochet's* Legacy', 731, citing, *inter alia*, the dismissal of criminal complaints against ex-US Secretary of Defence Rumsfeld in France (for alleged torture), ex-Chinese President Jiang in Germany, ex-US President Bush in Switzerland, and *Matar v Dichter* (Israeli official accused of torture and war crimes) in the US Ct App 2nd Cir 2009, thanks to their 'functional immunity'.

[114] *A v Ministère Public de la Confédération, B and C* §5.3.5.

[115] ibid §5.4.3.

[116] UN Doc A/C.6/66/SR.18 (2 Dec 2011) §§53–54.

In Belgium, immunity from criminal jurisdiction is governed by the 2003 Code of Criminal Procedure, which refers to the rules of customary and treaty-based international law. Immunity is therefore recognized only within the limits established by international law.[117] Belgium considers that under international law immunity *ratione materiae* is excluded for crimes under international law.[118] Regarding immunity *ratione personae*, it should be examined in light of agreements between States; States that are parties to the same treaty on international criminal law could be deemed to have declined *ipso facto* to invoke personal immunity for their officials if the treaty precludes the invocation of any form of immunity or provides that the official capacity of the alleged perpetrator is an element of the crime. Even in such a scenario, a State can choose to admit, in the context of an official visit, a person suspected of committing an international crime. However, the State remains bound to comply with any pre-existing obligation to cooperate with an international court, including the obligation to execute an arrest warrant issued by such a court.[119]

Under Germany's legal system, immunity of foreign State officials is addressed under Section 20 of the Judiciary Act, which refers explicitly to general rules of international law, including customary law, and required the courts to determine whether immunity exists in a given case.[120] Unlike Belgium, Germany takes the following position. Exceptions to the principle of immunity must be grounded in customary international law, and a violation of a *jus cogens* norm does not necessarily remove immunity because to conclude that such norms were superior to rules governing immunity would be to confuse rules of substantive law with rules of procedure. Immunity is not synonymous with impunity. State officials who committed unlawful acts bear full responsibility under the laws of their own States, and these States are required by their laws to exercise jurisdiction over such State officials. Waiver of immunity is always possible. The exercise of jurisdiction by the official's State and waivers of immunity are important tools in the common effort to combat impunity and States should be encouraged to make use of them. In cases involving grave crimes under international law, where these two mechanisms just mentioned have somehow proved ineffective, a balance has to be found between the need to ensure stability in international relations and the need to avoid impunity for grave crimes under international law, and the best way to proceed would be through international institutions such as the International Criminal Court.[121]

However, the German Federal Supreme Court (*Bundesgerichtshof*) has ruled that although espionage is an official act, public international law does not prohibit States from punishing foreign officials for acts of espionage[122] unless they are persons enjoying immunity under the 1961 Vienna Convention on Diplomatic Relations or the 1963 Vienna Convention on Consular Relations[123] or other specific

[117] UN Doc A/C.6/66/SR.26 (7 Dec 2011) §71. [118] ibid §69.
[119] ibid §70. [120] UN Doc A/C.6/66/SR.26 (7 Dec 2011) §85.
[121] ibid §§86–88.
[122] StR 347/92 of 30 July 1993, *juris*, §8; StB 11/91 of 29 May 1991, *juris*, §7.
[123] 596 UNTS 261.

treaties.[124] It should be noted that espionage is not listed as a grave/core crime under international law.

By virtue of Section 16 of the Netherlands' International Crimes Act of 2003, 'foreign heads of State, heads of government, and ministers of foreign affairs, as long as they are in office' enjoy personal or full immunity from the exercise of criminal jurisdiction by the Netherlands. They enjoy functional immunity after their term of office for acts performed during their term of office but this functional immunity does not extend to international crimes, including genocide, crimes against humanity, grave breaches of the four Geneva Conventions of 1949, breaches of the laws and customs of war in international and non international armed conflict, and the crime of torture.[125] This reflects 'a marked trend towards giving prosecution for international crimes precedence over functional immunity'; this 'strong' trend against impunity is 'not yet fully settled', though.[126]

There is consensus in the Sixth Committee as well as in the ILC that international law needs to balance between stability in international relations through the recognition of immunity of State officials from foreign criminal jurisdiction, on the one hand, and accountability—or denial of impunity—of perpetrators of crimes proscribed by peremptory norms, on the other hand.[127] While it is trite to state that immunity is not impunity, a question arises whether prosecution of perpetrators of international crimes is to be left solely to international criminal tribunals having jurisdiction over such crimes,[128] or whether States do have a crucial role to prosecute these perpetrators by denying any immunity they may assert. According to one research, between 1990 and 2009, sixty-five former Heads of State or Government were prosecuted for serious human rights or financial crimes, including Augusto Pinochet (Chile), Alberto Fujimori (Peru), Slobodan Milosevic (former Yugoslavia), Charles Taylor (Liberia and Sierra Leone), and Saddam Hussein (Iraq).[129] Only two out of five 'big names' just mentioned (Pinochet and Fujimori) were prosecuted in ordinary domestic criminal courts, and in their own States, however.

The ILC has put the topic 'Immunity of State officials from foreign criminal jurisdiction' on its active agenda since 2007, with Roman Kolodkin appointed Special Rapporteur. Kolodkin submitted three reports—one in 2008, and two in 2011. In

[124] 2 BvL 19/91, 2 BvR 1206/91, 2 BvR 1584/91 and 2 BvR 1601/93 of 15 May 1995, *juris*, §174.

[125] 'Immunity of Foreign State Officials: Advisory Report by the Netherlands Government Advisory Committee on Issues of Public International Law' (2011) 58 Netherlands IL Rev 461–62.

[126] Cited from the Netherlands' written reply to the questions posed by the ILC in 2014 relating to the topic 'Immunity of State officials from foreign criminal jurisdiction'. Poland also supports this 'trend' (Note from the Permanent Mission of Poland to the United Nations, New York, 10 June 2015, transmitting an opinion of the Legal Advisory Committee to the Minister of Foreign Affairs of the Republic of Poland, on immunities of State officials from foreign criminal jurisdiction, 12–15).

[127] ILC, 'Report … on the work of its 66th Session' §119; statements of Thailand (UN Doc A/C.6/66/SR.26 (7 Dec 2011) §45), Mexico (UN Doc A/C.6/66/SR.18 (2 Dec 2011) §§52–54), Romania (UN Doc A/C.6/66/SR.28 (2 Dec 2011) §65), Greece (UN Doc A/C.6/66/SR.26 (7 Dec 2011) §§29–36), Iran (UN Doc A/C.6/66/SR.27 (8 Dec 2011) §45), Russia (ibid §67), and Australia (UN Doc A/C.6/66/SR.28 (2 Dec 2011) §1).

[128] As contended by Germany, UN Doc A/C.6/66/SR.26 (7 Dec 2011) §87.

[129] Ellen L Lutz and Caitlin Reiger (eds), *Prosecuting Heads of State* (CUP 2009).

2012, the ILC appointed Concepción Escobar Hernández as Special Rapporteur to replace Kolodkin, who did not run for re-election to the ILC. Escobar Hernández submitted five reports, one each in 2012, 2013, 2014, 2015, and 2016.

Special Rapporteur Kolodkin observed that in the case of immunity *ratione personae*, 'the predominant view seemed to suggest that such immunity was absolute', with no exceptions.[130] Similarly, he was not convinced by the various rationales for exceptions to immunity *ratione materiae* 'in the context of crimes under international law', as these were not substantiated by evidence against immunity in State practice.[131] Some ILC members criticized Kolodkin for having set a very high standard that the exceptions must be grounded in customary law, without taking into account relevant trends that had an impact on immunity, in particular developments in human rights law and international criminal law which require the rule on immunity to be appropriately placed 'in the overall legal context'.[132] This latter view posited that everyone should be treated equally irrespective of his or her position, and State officials would not be presumed to be immune unless there are special reasons for such immunity, and this would not be the case in respect of grave crimes under international law.[133] As the principle of non-impunity for grave crimes under international law was a core value of the international community and, from the perspective of hierarchy of norms or conflicting norms, it was argued, the ILC should weigh in for accountability while, admittedly, State practice in this area was still far from uniform.[134]

Escobar Hernández is seen as more sympathetic to the view of the Joint Separate Opinion in *Arrest Warrant* and its adherents. The reports of these two Special Rapporteurs have elicited divergent views among ILC members as well as States in the Sixth Committee.

Up to 2016, the ILC provisionally adopted the following draft articles.

Part one

Introduction

Draft article 1
Scope of the present draft articles

1. The present draft articles apply to the immunity of State officials from the criminal jurisdiction of another State.
2. The present draft articles are without prejudice to the immunity from criminal jurisdiction enjoyed under special rules of international law, in particular by persons connected with diplomatic missions, consular posts, special missions, international organizations and military forces of a State.

[130] ILC, Report ... on the work of its 66th Session §113. Kolodkin later conceded that his use of the word 'absolute' was not entirely felicitous because even in case of immunity *ratione personae*, such immunity was limited in time and substance (ibid §193).

[131] ibid §§113–14 and 193–97.

[132] ibid §121. [133] ibid §§123 and 130–31. [134] ibid §124.

Draft article 2

Definitions

For the purposes of the present draft articles:

[...]

(e) 'State official' means any individual who represents the State or who exercises State functions.

(f) An 'act performed in an official capacity' means any act performed by a State official in the exercise of State authority.

Part two

Immunity *ratione personae*

Draft article 3

Persons enjoying immunity ratione personae

Heads of State, Heads of Government and Ministers for Foreign Affairs enjoy immunity *ratione personae* from the exercise of foreign criminal jurisdiction.

Draft article 4

Scope of immunity ratione personae

1. Heads of State, Heads of Government and Ministers for Foreign Affairs enjoy immunity *ratione personae* only during their term of office.
2. Such immunity *ratione personae* covers all acts performed, whether in a private or official capacity, by Heads of State, Heads of Government and Ministers for Foreign Affairs during or prior to their term of office.
3. The cessation of immunity *ratione personae* is without prejudice to the application of the rules of international law concerning immunity *ratione materiae*.

Part three

Immunity *ratione materiae*

Draft article 5

Persons enjoying immunity ratione materiae

State officials acting as such enjoy immunity *ratione materiae* from the exercise of foreign criminal jurisdiction.

Draft article 6

Scope of immunity ratione materiae

1. State officials enjoy immunity *ratione materiae* only with respect to acts performed in an official capacity.
2. Immunity *ratione materiae* with respect to acts performed in an official capacity continues to subsist after the individuals concerned have ceased to be State officials.
3. Individuals who enjoyed immunity *ratione personae* in accordance with draft article 4, whose term of office has come to an end, continue to enjoy immunity with respect to acts performed in an official capacity during such term of office.

In 2016 and 2017, the ILC considered Special Rapporteur Escobar Hernández's fifth report.[135] In her introduction of the fifth report on 26 July 2016, the Special Rapporteur stressed that this report formed a whole with her four previous reports and should thus be read in conjunction with them. The fifth report aimed to try to discover whether there were situations in which the immunity of State officials from foreign criminal jurisdiction was without effect, even where such immunity was potentially applicable because all normative elements were present and, if the answer was in the affirmative, to identify those situations. State practice would have to be analysed. In her opinion, although practice in relation to crimes under international law was varied, there was a clear trend towards considering the commission of such crimes as a bar to the application of the immunity, either because these crimes were not considered official acts or because they were considered an exception to the immunity owing to their gravity or to the fact that they undermined legal values and principles recognized by the international community as a whole. National courts' decisions recognizing the immunity for international crimes largely concerned immunity *ratione personae* and only very exceptionally immunity *ratione materiae*. She concluded that the commission of international crimes could currently be considered to constitute an exception to the immunity of State officials from foreign criminal jurisdiction based on a rule of international customary law, or at least a clear trend that reflected an emerging custom. The Special Rapporteur said her fifth report duly analysed the immunity in relation to the rest of the rules and institutions that made up the normative system of international law, in particular the principle of sovereign equality of States and that of sovereignty, especially the right to exercise jurisdiction, as well as international human rights law and international criminal law. An analysis was conducted on the relationship between the immunity and the main categories of rules of contemporary international law, such as *jus cogens*, the values and principles of international law, the concepts of combating impunity and ensuring accountability, plus the right of victims to redress, and the State's obligation to prosecute certain international crimes.

Some members of the ILC supported Special Rapporteur Escobar Hernández's conclusion that there was no immunity under customary international law for perpetrators of international crimes. They considered it imperative for the ILC to balance the sovereign equality of States and the stability of international relations, on the one hand, with the prevention and punishment of serious crimes of concern to the international community as a whole, on the other hand. It was also noted that atrocious crimes occurring in one State could cause instability and other negative impacts on not only the State where the crimes were committed but also neighbouring States and the international community at large. A request for the extradition of a State official suspected of committing such a crime would fulfil the obligation of States to prevent and punish that serious crime, while an invocation of immunity *ratione materiae* would open the door to impunity—immunity as a

[135] UN Doc A/CN.4/701 (14 June 2016).

procedural bar would become a substantive bar entailing impunity. This view was said to have the support of several States in the Sixth Committee.

Other ILC members disagreed, arguing that there was no consistent practice, or even a 'trend', against the non-applicability of the immunity, especially in the light of the ICJ Judgment in *Arrest Warrant*. These ILC members endorsed the conclusion reached in the second report of the previous Special Rapporteur Kolodkin[136] and the statements of a number of States in the Sixth Committee that there was no customary norm or trend towards the establishment of such a norm for exceptions to the immunity as substantiated by general practice or adequate evidence of their acceptance as law. They pointed out that a number of cases cited by Special Rapporteur Escobar Hernández in support of her conclusion concerned civil, not criminal, proceedings and many examples cited by her were related to State immunities, not the immunity of officials from foreign criminal jurisdiction at all. National laws implementing the ICC Statute were considered to be of dubious relevance, since they had been enacted solely for the purpose of implementing the treaty obligations of States Parties to that Statute, without also affecting immunities under customary international law. Immunity as a rule of customary international law was essentially procedural in nature and was completely different from the substantive law that determined whether a conduct of a State official was lawful or unlawful.

There was consensus in the ILC that the ILC could 'codify' the existing rule of customary international law (*lex lata*) of immunity *ratione personae*, which permitted no exception. There was no consensus on the answers to two questions. First, could the ILC do the same regarding immunity *ratione materiae*, or whether the ILC could, at most, only propose 'progressive development' of a rule (*lex ferenda*) governing this latter immunity as it had not yet attained the status of a rule of customary law? Secondly, would the ILC have to await Special Rapporteur Escobar Hernández's next report on procedural aspects related to the immunity which could prevent prosecutors or judges from initiating vindictive legal proceedings against foreign State officials?

In 2017, the ILC provisionally adopted Draft Article 7, according to which immunity *ratione materiae* from the exercise of foreign criminal jurisdiction shall not apply 'in respect of the following crimes under international law: crime of genocide; crimes against humanity; war crimes; crime of apartheid; torture; and enforced disappearance', as respectively defined in the treaties enumerated in the annex to the draft articles on the topic. The reason why these crimes have been singled out is already explained in Chapter 3 Section I and will not be repeated here.

The drafting history of Draft Article 7 is crucial to the understanding the ILC's position regarding the exception to immunity of State officials from foreign criminal jurisdiction.

First of all, the Plenary of the ILC had to decide by a show of hands whether to close the debate on the proposal to refer Draft Article 7 as proposed by the Special Rapporteur to the Drafting Committee at all. The vote by the ILC members present

[136] UN Doc A/CN.4/631.

and voting was twenty in favour, three against, and one abstention. At least two of the ILC members who had made statements in the Plenary against referring the Draft Article to the Drafting Committee were among the ILC members who were absent when the vote was called. Taking a decision by voting is rare and exceptional in the ILC where most decisions are by consensus.

After the provisional adoption of Draft Article 7 by the Drafting Committee it was necessary for the chair of the Drafting Committee to inform the ILC Plenary that 'the Drafting Committee proceeded in its work on the general understanding that the outcome of its work was without prejudice to, or taking a position on, the question whether the text of draft Article 7, or any part thereof, codified existing law—reflecting *lex lata*—or whether the result constituted an exercise in progressive development, reflecting *lex ferenda*'. Some members of the Drafting Committee participated without prejudice to 'the fundamental problems that they had with the text as proposed, as well as the text as finally adopted' because, in their view, the Drafting Committee was 'essentially embarking on a policy-making exercise as opposed to seeking the codification or progressive development of the law'.[137]

After receiving the oral report of the chair of the Drafting Committee, the ILC Plenary provisionally adopted, by a recorded vote (twenty-one in favour, eight against, and one abstention), the footnotes attached to the heading of Part Two (Immunity *ratione personae*) and to that of Part Three (Immunity *ratione materiae*), Draft Article 7, and the annex enumerating the list of crimes under international law for the purpose of Draft Article 7. The aforesaid identical footnotes read: 'The Commission will consider the procedural provisions and safeguards applicable to the present draft articles at its seventieth session [in 2018]'. The reference to 'provisions and safeguards' indicates that the procedural aspects of immunity are not restricted to the question of limitations and exceptions to immunity, but affect the Draft Articles on this topic as a whole.

The Annual Report of the ILC for the year 2017 explains the reasons behind the recorded vote, which is exceptionally rare in the ILC's practice, in the provisional adoption of Draft Article 7.

Those in favour considered that there has been a discernible trend towards limiting the applicability of immunity *ratione materiae* in respect of certain types of conduct which constitute crimes under international law. This trend is reflected in national judicial decisions taken by national courts. In rare cases, this trend has also been reflected in the adoption of national legislation that provides for exceptions to immunity *ratione materiae* in relation to the commission of international crimes. This trend has also been highlighted in the literature, and has been reflected to some extent in proceedings before international tribunals. In addition, fulfilling the purpose for which immunity was established (ie protecting the sovereign equality and legitimate interests of States) must be balanced with other existing standards or clash with the legal principles enshrined in such important sectors of contemporary

[137] Statement of the Chair of the Drafting Committee on the topic 'Immunity of State officials from foreign criminal jurisdiction', 20 July 2017, <http://legal.un.org/docs/?path=./ilc/documentation/english/statements/2017_dc_chairman_statement_iso.pdf&lang=E>, accessed 17 November 2017.

international law as international humanitarian law, international human rights law, and international criminal law, so that immunity is not turned into a procedural mechanism to block all attempts to establish the criminal responsibility of certain State officials arising from the commission of the most serious crimes under international law.

In contrast, the ILC members disagreeing with the provisional adoption of Draft Article 7 argued that national case law, national statutes, and treaty law do not support the exceptions asserted in Draft Article 7, and that the relevant practice showed no 'trend', temporal or otherwise, in favour of exceptions to immunity *ratione materiae* from foreign criminal jurisdiction. In the opinion of these latter ILC members, immunity is a procedural matter and, consequently, it is not possible to assume that the existence of criminal responsibility for any crimes under international law committed by a State official automatically precludes immunity from foreign criminal jurisdiction. They added that immunity does not depend on the gravity of the act in question or on the fact that such act is prohibited by the peremptory norm of international law; that the issue of immunity must be considered at an early stage of the exercise of jurisdiction, before the case is considered on the merits; that the lack of immunity before an international criminal court is not relevant to the issue of immunity from the jurisdiction of national courts; and that the establishment of a new system of exceptions to immunity, if not agreed upon by treaty, will probably harm inter-State relations and risks undermining the international community's objective of ending impunity for the most serious international crimes. Furthermore, these members thought the ILC, by proposing Draft Article 7, was conducting a 'normative policy' exercise of creating 'new law', with no relation to either the codification or the progressive development of international law. For them, there was a difference between procedural immunity from foreign jurisdiction and substantive criminal responsibility. They maintained that the recognition of exceptions to immunity was neither required nor necessarily appropriate for achieving the required balance as asserting exceptions to immunity that States have not accepted by treaty or through their widespread practice risks creating severe tensions, if not outright conflict, among States. These members also asserted that no decision can be taken on the issue of limitations and exceptions to immunity until the ILC has taken a position on the issue of procedural safeguards. This opinion was not, however, accepted by the majority of ILC members, who considered that the issue of the crimes to which immunity from jurisdiction *ratione materiae* does not apply can be dealt with separately at the present stage of the ILC's work. Nevertheless, in order to reflect the great importance attached by the ILC to procedural issues in the context of the topic of immunity, it was agreed that the current text of the Draft Articles should include the aforesaid footnotes.[138]

Secondly, the Special Rapporteur's proposed Draft Article 7 included a provision to the effect that the exception to immunity 'shall not apply to persons who enjoy immunity *ratione personae* during their term of office' and is 'without prejudice

[138] ILC, 'Report . . . on the work of its 69th Session' §§239–44.

to: (i) Any provision of a treaty that is binding on both the forum State and the State of the official, under which immunity would not be applicable; (ii) The obligation to cooperate with an international court or tribunal which, in each case, requires compliance by the forum State'.[139] This has been deleted by the Drafting Committee, thereby affirming that there is no exception whatsoever to immunity *ratione personae*. The chair of the Drafting Committee explains that, by explicitly limiting the scope of Draft Article 7 to immunity *ratione materiae*, the reference to immunity *ratione personae* in a following paragraph as proposed by the Special Rapporteur had become superfluous and could be deleted. He adds that '[t]he commentaries will further emphasize that the limitations and exceptions listed in draft Article 7 do not apply with respect to immunity *ratione personae*,' and that '[t]he commentary will also clarify that these limitations and exceptions are applicable to those officials that enjoyed immunity *ratione personae* whose term of office has come to an end.'[140]

In conclusion, the prevailing view and State practice support the conclusion that there is no exception to immunity *ratione personae*. On the contrary, there are exceptions to immunity *ratione materiae* under treaty and emerging State practice. It is conceivable that States exercising universal jurisdiction for the purpose of prosecuting instead of extraditing alleged perpetrators of 'core crimes'/'crimes under international law' are likely to deny immunity *ratione materiae* to such persons. This conclusion would not change, irrespective of the ILC's consideration of the procedural aspect of immunity in 2018.

There are eighteen points of summary on procedural issues regarding immunity in the third report of the first Special Rapporteur on the topic, Roman Kolodkin, which read:

(a) The question of the immunity of a State's official from foreign criminal jurisdiction must in principle be considered either at the early stage of court proceedings or even earlier at the pretrial stage, when the State that is exercising jurisdiction decides the question of taking, in respect of the official, criminal procedure measures which are precluded by immunity.

(b) Failure to consider the issue of immunity *in limine litis* may be viewed as a violation of the obligations of the forum State under the norms governing immunity. This also relates to the consideration of the question of immunity at the pretrial stage of the exercise of criminal jurisdiction at the time when the question of the adoption of measures precluded by immunity is decided. This, however, does not pertain to a situation in which the State of the official who enjoys immunity *ratione materiae* does not invoke his immunity or invokes it at a later stage in the proceedings.

(c) Only the invoking of immunity or a declaration of immunity by the official's State, and not by the official himself, constitutes a legally relevant invocation of immunity or declaration of immunity, i.e. they have legal consequences.

(d) In order to be able to invoke the immunity of that official, the official's State must know that corresponding criminal procedure measures are being taken or planned in respect of that person. Accordingly, the State that is implementing or planning such measures must inform the official's State in this regard.

139 UN Doc A/CN.4/701, 95.

140 ibid.

(e) When a foreign Head of State, Head of Government or minister for foreign affairs is concerned, the State exercising criminal jurisdiction itself must consider the question of the immunity of the person concerned and determine its position regarding its further action within the framework of international law. In this case, it is appropriate perhaps to ask the official's State only about a waiver of immunity. Accordingly, the official's State in this case does not bear the burden of raising the issue of immunity with the authorities of the State exercising criminal jurisdiction.

(f) When an official who enjoys functional immunity is concerned, the burden of invoking immunity lies with the official's State. If the State of such an official wishes to protect him from foreign criminal prosecution by invoking immunity, it must inform the State exercising jurisdiction that the person in question is its official and enjoys immunity since he performed the acts with which he is charged in an official capacity. If it does not do so, the State exercising jurisdiction is not obliged to consider the question of immunity *proprio motu* and, therefore, may continue criminal prosecution.

(g) When an official who enjoys personal immunity but is not one of the 'threesome' is concerned, the burden of invoking immunity lies with the official's State. If the State of such an official wishes to protect him from foreign criminal prosecution by invoking immunity, it must inform the State exercising jurisdiction that the person in question is its official and enjoys personal immunity since he occupies a high-level post which, in addition to participation in international relations, requires the performance of functions that are important for ensuring that State's sovereignty.

(h) The State of the official, regardless of his level, is not obliged to inform a foreign court of his immunity in order for that court to consider the question of immunity. The official's State may invoke the immunity of the official through the diplomatic channels and thereby inform the State exercising jurisdiction. This suffices in order for a court of that State to be obliged to consider the issue of immunity. The absence of an obligation on the part of a State to deal directly with a foreign court is based on the principle of sovereignty, the sovereign equality of States.

(i) The State invoking the immunity of its official is not obliged to provide grounds for immunity apart from those referred to in paragraphs (f) and (g) above.

The State (including its court) that is exercising jurisdiction, it would seem, is not obliged to 'blindly accept any' claim by the official's State concerning immunity.

However, a foreign State may not disregard such a claim if the circumstances of the case clearly do not indicate otherwise. It is the prerogative of the official's State, not the State exercising jurisdiction, to characterize the conduct of an official as being official in nature or to determine the importance of functions carried out by a high-ranking official for the purpose of ensuring State sovereignty.

(j) The right to waive the immunity of an official is vested in the State, not in the official himself.

(k) When a Head of State or Government or a minister for foreign affairs waives immunity with respect to himself, the State exercising criminal jurisdiction against such an official has the right to assume that that is the wish of the official's State, at least until it is otherwise notified by that State.

(l) The waiver of immunity of a serving Head of State, Head of Government or minister for foreign affairs must be express. The hypothetical situation in which the State of such an official requests a foreign State to carry out some type of criminal procedure measures in respect of the official possibly constitutes an exception. Such a request unequivocally involves a waiver of immunity with respect to these measures and in such a case the waiver is implied.

(m) A waiver of immunity of officials other than the 'threesome' but who have personal immunity, of officials who have functional immunity as well as of former officials who also have functional immunity may be either express or implied. Implied immunity in this case may be expressed, inter alia, in the non-invocation of immunity by the official's State.
(n) It would seem that, following an express waiver of immunity, it is legally impossible to invoke immunity. At the same time, an express waiver of immunity may in some cases pertain only to immunity with regard to specific measures.
(o) In the case of an initial implied waiver of immunity expressed in the non-invocation of the functional immunity of an official or the personal immunity of an official other than the 'threesome', immunity may, it would seem, be invoked at a later stage in the criminal process (inter alia, when the case is referred to a court).

At the same time, there is doubt as to whether a State which has not invoked such immunity in the court of first instance may invoke it at the stage of appeal proceedings. In any case, the procedural steps which have already been taken in such a situation by the State exercising jurisdiction in respect of the official at the time of the invocation of immunity may not be considered unlawful.
(p) A waiver by the State of the official of the latter's immunity makes it possible to exercise to the full extent foreign criminal jurisdiction in respect of that official. This pertains, inter alia, to jurisdiction in respect of acts performed by the official in an official capacity.
(q) Irrespective of the waiver of immunity with regard to its official, the official's State is not exempt from international legal responsibility for acts performed by that person in an official capacity.
(r) A State which invokes the immunity of its official on the basis that the act with which the official has been charged was of an official nature recognizes that the act constitutes an act by that State itself. This establishes the prerequisites for the international legal responsibility of that State and for the institution of international legal proceedings against it by actors that are entitled to do so.[141]

The procedural aspects of the topic have not been considered as contentious as their substantive counterparts.

The following are some of the views expressed at the Sixth Committee in 2011 about the procedural aspects of immunity.

The procedural aspects of immunity must strike a balance between the interests of the State and a fight against impunity on the one side, and the strengthening of inter-State cooperation on the other.[142] Immunity is to be addressed at the initial stage of judicial proceedings or even after the pre-trial stage.[143] According to one view, only the official's State can invoke the immunity of its officials.[144] However, a view has been expressed that the official concerned could play a part in invoking immunity by notifying the authorities of the State exercising jurisdiction.[145] While one view insists that waiver of immunity must be by the State and must always be

[141] UN Doc A/CN.4/646 §61.
[142] Statement of France, UN Doc A/C.6/66/SR.20 (23 Nov 2011) §45.
[143] Statements by Peru (UN Doc A/C.6/66/SR.26 (7 Dec 2011) §60) and India (UN Doc A/C.6/66/SR.27 (8 Dec 2011) §79).
[144] Statement by Indonesia, UN Doc A/C.6/66/SR.24 (1 Dec 2011) §72.
[145] Statement by Romania, UN Doc A/C.6/66/SR.28 (2 Dec 2011) §66.

explicit unless treaty obligations stipulate to the contrary, it also considers that the troika and other State officials should be treated differently in terms of the invocation and waiver of immunity.[146] A preference is also stated for the procedural aspects of immunity to be dealt with after definitive conclusions on the substantive aspects of immunity has been reached.[147] One delegation agrees with Kolodkin's views on procedural issues in his third report in so far as they relate to crimes other than those of international concern.[148]

146 Statement of Kenya, ibid §52.
147 Statement by Thailand, UN Doc A/C.6/66/SR.26 (7 Dec 2011) §48.
148 Statement by Greece, ibid §36.

7

The Third Alternative of Surrender to a Competent International Criminal Tribunal or a Hybrid Tribunal and its Impediments

Before the entry into force of the 1998 Rome Statute of the International Criminal Court[1] on 1 July 2002, the UN Security Council had to establish the International Criminal Tribunal for the former Yugoslavia (ICTY) and the International Criminal Tribunal for Rwanda (ICTR) in 1993 and 1994, respectively, to prosecute the worst mass atrocities since the Second World War. Other ad hoc or hybrid tribunals set up to prosecute crimes committed prior to 1 July 2002 and those crimes over which the ICC does not have temporal jurisdiction included the Extraordinary Chambers in the Courts of Cambodia (ECCC or the Khmer Rouge Tribunal), the Special Panels and the Serious Crimes Unit of the Dili District Court (or the East Timor Tribunal), the Special Court for Sierra Leone, and the Extraordinary African Chambers in Senegal to try former President of Chad Hissène Habré. The Iraqi Special Tribunal for Crimes against Humanity was set up by the Coalition Provisional Authority after the overthrow of President Saddam Hussein of Iraq and the military occupation of Iraq in 2003. The Iraqi Tribunal's jurisdiction *ratione temporis* was from 17 July 1968, the date of the Ba'athists coming into power in Iraq by a *coup d'état*, until 1 May 2004, the date of the US President's declaration of the end of the major hostilities against Iraq. In any case, Iraq was not party to the ICC Statute between July 2002 and 1 May 2004. The Special Tribunal for Lebanon was established to try all those responsible for the terrorist bombing on 14 February 2005 which killed the former Prime Minister of Lebanon Rafik Hariri and other persons. Although the incident occurred after the entry into force of the Rome Statute, neither Lebanon nor the State suspected of being behind the attack was party to the Rome Statute and, in any event, the International Criminal Court has no jurisdiction *ratione materiae* over the crimes within the jurisdiction of the Special Tribunal for Lebanon, which are terrorism, crimes and offences against life and personal integrity, illicit associations, and failure to report crimes and offences.[2]

[1] 2187 UNTS 90.

[2] See Michael P Scharf and Margaux Day, 'The *Ad Hoc* International Criminal Tribunals: Launching a New Era of Accountability' in William A Schabas and Nadia Bernaz (eds), *Routledge Handbook of International Criminal Law* (Routledge 2010) ch 5; Fidelma Donlon, 'Hybrid Tribunals', ibid ch 7;

The third alternative to the obligation to extradite or prosecute was used in the *Lockerbie* case, albeit in a unique circumstance. Two Libyan nationals were suspected of planting plastic explosives in a suitcase on Pan Am flight 103 leading to its explosion on 22 December 1988 above the Scottish village of Lockerbie, killing all the passengers and crew on board. Eleven villagers were also killed by the falling debris. The USA, the State of registration of the aircraft, and the UK demanded that Libya extradite the two Libyans to stand trial either in the USA or the UK. Libya refused, stating that it was fulfilling its obligation under Article 7 of the 1971 Montreal Convention for the Suppression of Unlawful Acts against the Safety of Civil Aviation[3] by prosecuting the suspects in Libya in lieu of extradition to either the USA or the UK. Libya explained that it was constitutionally prohibited from extraditing its nationals, and that the two accused Libyans would not receive a fair trial in the USA or the UK due to public sentiments surrounding the incident. The USA and the UK would not accept this, being suspicious that the suspected Libyans might be agents of the Libyan Government entrusted with carrying out the terrorist bombing against the US aircraft and its passengers; hence, their prosecution in Libya would be a mere sham. The USA and the UK resorted to UN Security Council resolutions adopted under Chapter VII of the UN Charter to compel Libya to extradite the accused. Libya responded by taking the USA and the UK to the International Court of Justice (ICJ). The proceedings in the ICJ, entitled *Questions of Interpretation and Application of the 1971 Montreal Convention arising from the Aerial Incident at Lockerbie (Libyan Arab Jamahiriya v United Kingdom)* and *(Libyan Arab Jamahiriya v United States of America)*, lasted from 1992 to 2003, when the three parties agreed to 'discontinue with prejudice the proceedings' as a result of their agreement in force in January 1999 for Libya to surrender the accused to stand trial by the Scottish High Court of Justiciary applying the law of Scotland in relation to the accused and the offences, but in the Netherlands, a neutral State, the law of which applied generally in every other aspect.[4]

The most recently set up ad hoc tribunal, and probably a most successful one, is former Chadian President Habré's trial before the Extraordinary African Chambers sitting in Senegal, as a third alternative to Senegal either prosecuting him or extraditing him to Belgium. The trial in the Trial Chamber started on 20 July 2015 and concluded on 11 February 2016, after testimony from ninety-three witnesses. On 30 May 2016, Habré was convicted by the Trial Chamber of torture, war crimes, and crimes against humanity, including having raped a woman himself, and was sentenced to life in prison. His crimes included sexual slavery and ordering the killing of 40,000 people. On 29 July 2016 Habré was ordered by the Trial Chamber to pay compensation to his victims of rape and sexual violence in the amount of

Masayoshi Mukai, 'Ad-hoc Tribunals: The Failure to Contribute to Precedence-setting for a Universal Model of International Justice' (2009) 3 Berkeley J Int'l Publicist 48; Ilias Bantekas and Susan Nash, *International Criminal Law* (3rd edn, Routledge 2007) 557–80; Roger O'Keefe, *International Criminal Law* (OUP 2015) 483–528.

[3] 974 UNTS 177.

[4] For a succinct account, see Bantekas and Nash, *International Criminal Law*, 577–80.

US$33,880 each, victims of arbitrary detention, torture, prisoners of war, and their survivors US$25,410 each, and his indirect victims US$16,935 each. The number of those entitled to the compensation was yet to be determined.

On 27 April 2017, the Extraordinary African Appeals Chamber, while acquitting Habré of the charge of rape introduced at the trial stage, upheld his other convictions for war crimes, crimes against humanity, and torture, and his life sentence. It also ruled that the millions of US dollars of compensation awarded to more than 4,000 victims was to be managed by a trust fund. This example shows that the third alternative to the obligation to extradite or prosecute can function satisfactorily. Article 10(3) of the Statute of the Extraordinary African Chambers[5] provides that the official position of an accused, whether as Head of State or Government, or as a responsible government official, shall not relieve him or her of criminal responsibility under this Statute, nor shall it, in and of itself, constitute a ground for reduction of sentence. This is reinforced by Article 20 of the same, stipulating that an amnesty granted to any person falling within the jurisdiction of the Extraordinary African Chambers with respect to the crimes under that Statute shall not be a bar to prosecution. Thus, like the ICTY, the ICTR, and other tribunals set up by the UN Security Council under Chapter VII of the UN Charter, the Extraordinary African Chambers, established under an agreement between the African Union and Senegal, does not face the problem of immunity of State officials that hinders the prosecution and/or extradition of these officials.

The advent of the aforesaid tribunals and 'irregular' courts reveals the following. One was set up to prosecute Europeans for crimes against Europeans. Two were established to punish crimes in the Middle East by Middle Eastern nationals against other Middle Eastern nationals. Two were set up in Asia to prosecute crimes by Asians against Asians. Three were set up to prosecute crimes by Africans against Africans. The other one was set up to prosecute crimes committed by African Arabs against Westerners. The States whose nationals were the targets of prosecution were mostly 'low-leverage' States, without any powerful friend among the permanent members of the UN Security Council endowed with the veto power to shield them from accountability from ad hoc or hybrid tribunals that needed the UN Security Council's blessings.[6]

The coming into existence of the permanent International Criminal Court should have ended the need to set up ad hoc international criminal tribunals or hybrid ones. As of this writing, there are 123 States Parties to the ICC Statute. The ICC has jurisdiction over genocide, war crimes, and crimes against humanity. The crime of aggression has been included by the amendments adopted in May 2010 which have entered into force after receiving the necessary thirty ratifications on 27 June 2016. States Parties to the Statute would be able to activate the ICC's jurisdiction over this crime after 1 January 2017. Therefore, pursuant to Article 15*bis* under the heading 'Exercise of jurisdiction over the crime of aggression (State referral, *proprio motu*)', the

[5] (2013) 52 ILM 1020.

[6] Cf Gary Jonathan Bass, *Stay the Hand of Vengeance: The Politics of War Crime Tribunals* (Princeton University Press 2000).

ICC may exercise jurisdiction only with respect to crimes of aggression committed one year after 27 June 2016, 'subject to a decision to be taken after 1 January 2017 by the same majority of States Parties as is required for the adoption of an amendment to the Statute'. However, a State Party may opt out by lodging a declaration with the ICC Registrar that it does not accept the ICC's jurisdiction over aggression. The withdrawal of such a declaration may be effected at any time and shall be considered by the State Party within three years. In respect of a State that is not a party to this Statute, the ICC shall not exercise its jurisdiction over the crime of aggression when committed by that State's nationals or on its territory. Where the Prosecutor concludes that there is a reasonable basis to proceed with an investigation in respect of a crime of aggression, he or she shall first ascertain whether the UN Security Council has made a determination of an act of aggression committed by the State concerned. The Prosecutor shall notify the UN Secretary-General of the situation before the ICC, including any relevant information and documents. Where the Security Council has made such a determination, the Prosecutor may proceed with the investigation in respect of a crime of aggression. Where no such determination is made within six months after the date of notification, the Prosecutor may proceed with the investigation in respect of a crime of aggression, provided that the Pre-Trial Division has authorized the commencement of the investigation in respect of a crime of aggression in accordance with the procedure applicable to the other crimes under the ICC's jurisdiction, and the Security Council has not adopted a resolution under Chapter VII of the UN Charter to request the ICC to defer the commencement or proceeding of the investigation or prosecution, respectively, for a period of twelve months; that request may be renewed by the Council under the same conditions. A determination of an act of aggression by an organ outside the ICC, be it the UN Security Council or the IC J or other bodies, shall be without prejudice to the ICC's own findings under the ICC Statute. Article 15*ter* of the ICC Statute on the ICC's exercise of jurisdiction over the crime of aggression by means of the UN Security Council's referral follows the same conditions as Article 15*bis*.

Due to a joint proposal by France and the UK submitted to the Assembly of States Parties to the ICC Statute held in November 2016, a facilitator was appointed to develop a common understanding of how the ICC jurisdiction would be exercised, to be approved by the Assembly in December 2017, so that the ICC's jurisdiction over the crime of aggression could be activated.

As of this writing, the ICC Prosecutor has been carrying out preliminary examination regarding the situations in Afghanistan (for alleged crimes against humanity and war crimes committed in Afghanistan since 1 May 2003), Gabon (for alleged crimes committed in Gabon since May 2016), Nigeria (for alleged crimes against humanity or war crimes committed in the Niger Delta, the Middle-Belt States, and in the context of armed conflict between Boko Haram and Nigerian security forces in Nigeria), Guinea (for alleged crimes against humanity committed in the context of the 28 September 2009 events in Conakry, Guinea), Colombia (for alleged war crimes committed since 1 November 2009 and alleged crimes against humanity committed since 1 November 2002), Iraq (for alleged war crimes committed by UK nationals in the context of the Iraq conflict and occupation from 2003 to 2008),

Palestine (for alleged crimes committed in the occupied Palestinian territory, including East Jerusalem, since 13 June 2014), registered vessels of Comoros, Greece, and Cambodia (with respect to the 31 May 2010 Israeli raid on the Humanitarian Aid Flotilla bound for Gaza Strip), and Ukraine (for alleged crimes committed in the context of the 'Maidan' protests since 21 November 2013 and other events in Ukraine since 20 February 2014).

Also as of this writing, the ICC Prosecutor has been undertaking the investigation of the situations in: Uganda (since 2004 after the referral by Uganda, currently focusing on alleged war crimes and crimes against humanity committed in the context of a conflict between the Lord's Resistance Army (LRA) and the national authorities in Uganda since 1 July 2002), DR Congo (since April 2004 after the referral by DR Congo, focusing on alleged war crimes and crimes against humanity committed in the context of armed conflict there since 1 July 2002), Darfur/Sudan (after the UN Security Council's referral in March 2005, focusing on alleged genocide, war crimes, and crimes against humanity committed in Darfur, Sudan, since 1 July 2002), Central African Republic (after the two self-referrals by that State, on (1) alleged war crimes and crimes against humanity committed in the context of a conflict in that State since 1 July 2002, with the peak of violence in 2002 and 2003; and (2) alleged war crimes and crimes against humanity committed in the context of renewed violence starting in 2012), Kenya (with the ICC Prosecutor opening *proprio motu* investigation in March 2010 on alleged crimes against humanity committed in the context of post-election violence in Kenya in 2007/08), Libya (after the Security Council's referral in February 2011, focusing on alleged crimes against humanity committed in the context of the situation in Libya since 15 February 2011), Côte d'Ivoire (with the ICC Prosecutor opening *proprio motu* investigation in October 2011 on alleged crimes within the jurisdiction of the ICC committed in the context of post-election violence in Côte d'Ivoire in 2010/11, and also since 19 September 2002 to the present), Mali (since January 2013 after Mali's self-referral, focusing on alleged war crimes committed in Mali since January 2012), and Georgia (with the ICC Prosecutor opening *proprio motu* investigation in January 2016 on alleged crimes against humanity and war crimes committed in the context of an international armed conflict between 1 July and 10 October 2008). On 8 May 2017 the ICC Prosecutor informed the UN Security Council that her Office was considering launching an investigation into alleged migrant-related crimes in Libya, including human trafficking. On 25 October 2017 the ICC Prosecutor was authorized to open *proprio motu* investigation into alleged crimes against humanity committed in Burundi or by nationals of Burundi outside Burundi since 26 April 2015 until 26 October 2017.

As of this writing, the ICC has had twenty-five cases, *all* of which are situations in Africa, with forty-two defendants, *all* of whom are Africans. Arrest warrants have been issued against fifteen accused who are still at large, *all* of whom are Africans, including the incumbent President of Sudan, the Minister of Interior of Sudan at the time of the issuance of the warrant, the Minister of National Defence of Sudan at the time of the warrant, Joseph Kony (Commander-in-Chief of the Lord's Resistance Army), and the alleged Supreme Commander of a Hutu militia group in Rwanda.

At the stage of preliminary examination of complaints ('communications') sent to the ICC Prosecutor, the ICC Prosecutor has decided not to investigate the situations in Honduras and Venezuela. It was alleged that after the *coup d'état* of 28 June 2009 in Honduras, crimes against humanity of murder, deportation and forcible transfer of population, imprisonment or other severe deprivation of physical liberty, persecution, rape and other forms of sexual violence, and other inhumane acts were committed. The ICC Prosecutor concluded after thorough legal and factual analysis that the information available was insufficient to provide a reasonable basis to believe that the alleged crimes amounted to crimes against humanity. The communications the ICC Prosecutor received regarding Venezuela related to events since 1 July 2002 including allegations of crimes against humanity against political opponents of the Government of Venezuela. The ICC Prosecutor determined that the ICC Statute threshold for seeking authorization to initiate an invitation into the situation in Venezuela was not met by the facts and evidence at her disposal. She has also concluded that, based on the information available, there was no reasonable basis to believe that the two incidents against South Korea caused by North Korea constituted a crime within the ICC's jurisdiction. These incidents were the shelling of Yeonpyeong Island on 23 November 2010 which resulted in the killing of South Korean marines and civilians and the injury of many others; and the sinking of a South Korean warship, the *Cheonan*, hit by a torpedo allegedly fired from a North Korean submarine on 26 March 2010, which resulted in the death of forty-six persons.

Although not all States are party to the ICC Statute, Article 13(b) of the Statute authorizes the UN Security Council, acting under Chapter VII of the UN Charter, to refer to the ICC Prosecutor a situation in which one or more of crimes within the ICC's jurisdiction appears to have been committed. Article 15*ter* does the same regarding the crime of aggression, subject to Article 15*bis*. These provisions on referral as well as the provision of Article 16 on the Security Council's request for the ICC to defer the investigation or prosecution of a crime under the ICC's jurisdiction ensure that all the permanent members of the Council, with their veto power, must unanimously agree to adopt the necessary Security Council resolution under Chapter VII of the UN Charter. However, allowing any permanent member of the Security Council to block any referral of a situation that may implicate its nationals or nationals of its ally/client State to the ICC Prosecutor has been criticized as creating a 'double standard' of international criminal justice. It is also not inconceivable that the Security Council, under the pressure of one or more of the permanent members, may adopt the resolution to defer investigation or prosecution before the ICC.

The so-called double standard has been subject to criticisms for being used to target only Africans despite the widespread mass atrocities committed or being committed in other continents.[7]

Why have all the cases actively pursued by the ICC involved Africans? It is true that there have been several self-referrals by African States Parties to the ICC Statute.

[7] See eg Hans Köchler, 'Justice and Realpolitik: The Predicament of the International Criminal Court' (2017) 16 Chinese JIL 1.

Of the 123 States Parties to the ICC Statute, 33 of them are African States, compared to 19 from Asia-Pacific, 18 from Eastern Europe, 28 from Latin America and the Caribbean, and 25 from Western European and other States. Yet, the ICC Prosecutor's *proprio motu* investigation and prosecution have been criticized for having focused mainly on Africans. Above all, why has not the UN Security Council referred the situation in Syria, a non-State Party to the ICC Statute, to the ICC? After the start of the March 2011 popular uprising against the Assad Government, fighting in Syria has spiralled out of control, with several parties to the armed conflict committing war crimes and crimes against humanity. The exact, or even estimated, number of dead and displaced persons will only be known once a comprehensive documentation is properly undertaken after the dawn of peace. In any case, the situation in Syria is at least of the same scale of seriousness as the conflicts in the former Yugoslavia and Rwanda leading to the creation by the UN Security Council of the ICTY and the ICTR, respectively. President Assad had as his allies certain permanent members of the UN Security Council with the veto power to prevent the referral of the situation in Syria to the ICC. In Iraq, another non-State Party to the ICC Statute, a terrorist group called the Islamic State of Iraq and the Levant (ISIL) have committed heinous war crimes and crimes against humanity, if not also genocide, since June 2014, although there were allegations that some of the parties fighting ISIL also committed core crimes of international concern. The UN Security Council has not referred the Iraqi situation to the ICC, either.

In contrast, the Security Council has referred the situation in Darfur, Sudan, to the ICC, and the ICC has issued an international arrest warrant against Sudan's incumbent President Al Bashir, among others.

I. Practical Difficulties and Principled Opposition to the Third Alternative

International criminal tribunals have no law enforcement agency of their own, relying on States to arrest and surrender/transfer offenders to them. Article 29 of the Statute of the ICTY[8] and Article 28 of that of the ICTR,[9] both set up by the UN Security Council, compel States to cooperate with them. Other tribunals, including hybrid tribunals, may have offenders extradited to stand trial there on the basis of inter-State extradition or by special arrangements or agreements with the States concerned. For example, the standard Agreement on Legal Assistance between the Special Tribunal for Lebanon and interested States stipulates that the State party thereto agrees to surrender to the Tribunal persons, including citizens, found in its territory whom the Tribunal has sought to arrest or has found guilty of a crime within the jurisdiction of the Tribunal.

Article 89(1) of the ICC Statute authorizes the ICC to transmit a request for the arrest and surrender of a person to 'any State on the territory of which the person

[8] (1993) 32 ILM 1159. [9] (1994) 33 ILM 1598.

may be found and shall request the cooperation of that State in the arrest and surrender of such a person'. The provision goes on to require 'States Parties' to comply with requests for arrest and surrender. Article 87 of the Statute, entitled 'Requests for cooperation: general provisions', sets out in paragraph 7 the consequences of the failure of a State Party to comply with a request to cooperate by the ICC—the ICC may make a finding to that effect and refer the matter to the Assembly of States Parties or, where the UN Security Council referred the matter to the ICC, to the Security Council. Article 87(5) stipulates that the ICC may invite any non-State Party to the ICC Statute to provide assistance on an ad hoc basis, and when a non-State Party which has entered into an ad hoc arrangement or an agreement with the ICC fails to cooperate thereunder, the ICC may so inform the Assembly of States Parties or, where the Security Council referred the matter to the ICC, the Security Council. Nevertheless, Article 112(2)(f) of the Statute merely provides that the Assembly shall consider any question relating to non-cooperation pursuant to Article 87(5) and (7) without clarifying what the Assembly is to do in this regard.[10] In the case of the UN Security Council, non-compliance with its resolutions passed under Chapter VII of the UN Charter entails sanctions imposed by the Council on non-complying States. However, it has been pointed out that on more than a dozen occasions when the Presidents of the ICTY and the ICTR requested the Security Council to enforce the Tribunals' requests to States to surrender the persons sought by the Tribunals the Council chose not to act, leaving States to use diplomatic and economic means at their disposal to force compliance with the requests for surrender.[11]

Prosecuting perpetrators of serious crimes of international concern by domestic courts has not been undertaken for various reasons, especially the lack of means and resources. The third alternative to the obligation to extradite or prosecute by means of surrendering offenders to the ICC seems attractive. However, this has run into difficulties due to the resistance of several States, party and non-party to the ICC Statute, not to cooperate with the ICC by arresting and surrendering the offenders sought by the ICC. Neither the Assembly of States Parties nor even the UN Security Council has been successful in forcing these States to do otherwise. The ICC itself recognizes this. In its Decision of 6 July 2017 on the non-compliance by South Africa with the ICC's request for the arrest and surrender of Sudanese President Al Bashir, Pre-Trial Chamber II of the ICC notes that States Parties have been referred to both the Assembly of States Parties and the UN Security Council in six instances in relation to failures to arrest and surrender Al Bashir. However, the past twenty-four meetings of the Security Council following the adoption of Resolution 1593 (2005)[12] which refers the situation in Darfur, Sudan, to the ICC leading to the arrest warrant against Al Bashir, have not resulted in measures against

[10] Otto Triffterer (ed), *Commentary on the Rome Statute of the International Criminal Court—Observers' Notes, Articles by Articles* (2nd edn, CH Becks-Hart-Nomos 2008) 1517–31, 1537–40, 1692.

[11] Daphna Shraga, 'Politics and Justice: The Role of the Security Council' in Antonio Cassese (ed), *The Oxford Companion to International Criminal Justice* (OUP 2009) 168, 173–74. Cf Göran Sluiter, 'Cooperation of States with International Criminal Tribunals', ibid 187.

[12] UNSC Res 1593 (31 Mar 2005) UN Doc S/RES/1593 [on Violations of International Humanitarian Law and Human Rights Law in Darfur, Sudan].

non-complying States Parties, despite proposals from different States to develop a follow-up mechanism concerning the referral of States to the Security Council by the ICC. The Chamber considers that these considerations further strengthen its belief that a referral of South Africa to the UN Security Council is not warranted as a way to obtain cooperation from South Africa.[13]

The gist of the principled opposition to the ICC can be found in the African Union's withdrawal strategy document dated 12 January 2017.[14] It commences by explaining that the (then) thirty-four African States which have ratified the ICC Statute 'initially embraced the rule of law movement as an extension of their commitments to Africa's emancipatory future', 'a solution for Africa's injustices'. Their moral conscience was significantly compelled by the violence in Africa in the 1980s and 1990s. It 'instigated feelings of indignity and anger' connected with the international community's inaction during the Rwandan genocide, the injustice of the South African apartheid, and 'the results of the long anti-colonial struggles against European imperialism'. However, 'the predominance of African subjects of international criminal justice [targeted by the ICC] has created suspicion about prosecutorial justice', with 'the patterns of only pursuing African cases being reflective of electivity and inequality'. A perception of double standard against African States is caused by 'the systemic imbalance in international decision-making processes' of the UN Security Council whose decisions are made on the basis of the interests of the permanent members rather than the legal and justice requirements, thereby raising questions about perceived fairness of the international justice system as a whole.[15] The UN Security Council's decision to refer the situation in Sudan, a non-State Party to the ICC Statute, especially with the consequential indictment of the incumbent Sudanese President Omar Al Bashir, 'has illustrated this seeming inequality' and 'selectivity'. The African Union, therefore, calls for solidarity among its Member States to oppose the prosecution against the Sudanese President, and to call on the UN Security Council to defer, pursuant to Article 16 of the ICC Statute, the ICC's prosecution against him, as well as against President Kenyatta and Deputy President Ruto of Kenya, a State Party to the ICC Statute.[16]

The withdrawal strategy sets out the following objectives:

a) Ensure that international justice is conducted in a fair and transparent manner devoid of any perception of double standards.
b) Institution of legal and administrative reforms of the ICC.
c) Enhance the regionalization of international criminal law.
d) Encourage the adoption of African Solutions for African problems.
e) Preserve the dignity, sovereignty and integrity of Member States.[17]

[13] *Decision under Art 87(7) of the Rome Statute on the non-compliance by South Africa with the request by the Court for the arrest and surrender of Omar Al Bashir* ICC-02/05-01/09, Pre-Trial Ch II, 6 July 2017, §138.

[14] <https://www.hrw.org/sites/default/files/supporting_resources/icc_withdrawal_strategy_jan._2017.pdf>, accessed 17 November 2017.

[15] ibid §§1–3. [16] ibid §4. [17] ibid §8.

The strategy alludes to the formal one-year notice of Burundi dated 27 October 2016 to withdraw from the ICC Statute following the April 2016 opening of an ICC preliminary investigation of violence in Burundi.[18] This followed South Africa's notice of 19 October 2016 to withdraw from the ICC Statute on the ground that the ICC Statute's treaty obligations are inconsistent with customary international law on 'diplomatic immunity' of sitting Heads of State, while also avowing that 'in complex and multi-faceted peace negotiations and sensitive post-conflict situations, peace and justice must be viewed as complementary and not mutually exclusive'.[19] The Gambia became the third African State to express the intention to withdraw from the ICC Statute, on 10 November 2016, giving its reason as being centred on the ICC's selectivity practices against Africans and especially their leaders. According to The Gambia, the said selectivity against Africans ignores 'crimes committed by the West ... [;] there are many Western countries, at least 30, that have committed heinous war crimes against independent sovereign States and their citizens since the creation of the ICC and not a single Western war criminal has been indicted'.[20] The Strategy notes, however, that Sierra Leone, Côte d'Ivoire, Zambia, Nigeria, Malawi, Senegal, and Botswana are among the African States opposing South Africa's withdrawal notification.[21]

The strategy lists the following proposed amendments to the ICC Statute.[22] South Africa proposes that Article 16 of the Statute be amended to allow a State with jurisdiction over a situation being investigated or prosecuted by the ICC to request the UN Security Council in turn to request the ICC to defer the aforesaid investigation or prosecution. Where the Security Council fails to decide on the State's request within six months of receipt, that State may request the UN General Assembly, pursuant to UN General Assembly's Uniting for Peace Resolution,[23] to assume the Security Council's deferral responsibility. Kenya proposes four amendments. First, the complementary principle in the preamble of the ICC Statute should recognize not only national but also 'regional' criminal jurisdictions. Secondly, trials in the absence of the accused in exceptional circumstances under Article 63(2) of the

[18] ibid §23. The notice became effective on 27 Oct 2017, with Burundi officially ceasing to be a State Party to the ICC Statute as of that date.

[19] ibid §24. [20] ibid §25. [21] ibid §26. [22] ibid §30.

[23] UNGA Res A/RES/377 (3 November 1950), the pertinent part of which reads:

1. Resolves that if the Security Council, because of lack of unanimity of the permanent members, fails to exercise its primary responsibility for the maintenance of international peace and security in any case where there appears to be a threat to the peace, breach of the peace, or act of aggression, the General Assembly shall consider the matter immediately with a view to making appropriate recommendations to Members for collective measures, including in the case of a breach of the peace or act of aggression the use of armed force when necessary, to maintain or restore international peace and security. If not in session at the time, the General Assembly may meet in emergency special session within twenty-four hours of the request therefor. Such emergency special session shall be called if requested by the Security Council on the vote of any seven members, or by a majority of the Members of the United Nations;
2. Adopts for this purpose the amendments to its rules of procedure set forth in the annex to the present resolution. ...

Cf Michael Ramsden, '"Uniting for Peace" in the Age of International Justice' (2016) 42 Yale JIL 1.

Statute should be made clearer; that is, the Trial Chamber must satisfy itself, on a case-by-case basis and as strictly necessary, that exceptional circumstances exist and alternative measures have been put in place, including changes to the trial schedule or temporary adjournment or attendance through the use of communications technology or through representation of Counsel. This is provided also that the rights of the accused are fully ensured in his or her absence, and that the accused has explicitly waived his or her right to be present at the trial. Thirdly, Article 27 of the Statute on the irrelevance of official capacity should be amended to ensure that Heads of State, their deputies, and any person acting or entitled to act as such be 'exempt from prosecution during their current term of office'; such exemption 'may be renewed by the ICC under the same conditions'. Thirdly, Article 70 of the Statute regarding offences against the administration of justice should be amended to encompass acts by ICC officials that are against the administration of justice by the ICC. Finally, Article 112(4) of the Statute, dealing with subsidiary bodies of the ICC, should be amended to 'operationalize' the Independent Oversight Mechanism (IOM) to carry out inspection, evaluation, and investigation of all the organs of the ICC, including the Office of the Prosecutor.

The withdrawal strategy calls on AU Member States to become party to the Malabo Protocol of 27 June 2014[24] so that the jurisdiction of the African Court of Human and Peoples' Rights could be expanded and the crimes listed under the ICC Statute prosecuted in Africa instead, with the Court being a regional judicial mechanism to exercise its mandate complementarily to the ICC.[25]

On 26 October 2016 the Dutch Ministry of Foreign Affairs and the Africa Legal Aid (AFLA) hosted a seminar on 'The International Criminal Court and Africa: One Decade On', with the ICC Prosecutor, a Gambian national, as the Keynote Speaker. She defended the ICC's record by pointing out the following. First, one had to look at the ICC's achievement from the perspective of victims of crimes under the ICC's jurisdiction. Granting impunity to perpetrators of these crimes would be tantamount to allowing serious atrocities to occur. All accused persons were accorded the right to defend themselves against the charges against them under the due process of law and according to international human rights law. Secondly, situations amounting to crimes against humanity under the ICC Statute occurred in Africa more frequently than elsewhere, as manifested by the fact that approximately 80 per cent of the UN peace-keeping operations were in Africa. Thirdly, although all the cases before the ICC had been the ones relating to Africa, most of them had been referred to the ICC by African States or by the UN Security Council. Fourthly, Senegal was the first State Party to the ICC Statute, and the

[24] Reproduced in Amnesty International, *Malabo Protocol: Legal and Institutional Implications of the Merged and Expanded African Court* (2016) 40–64. As of July 2017, the Protocol was signed by ten AU Member States; namely, Benin, Chad, Rep of Congo, Ghana, Guinea-Bissau, Kenya, Mauritania, Sierra Leone, São Tome & Principe, and Uganda. None has ratified it. The Protocol requires the ratifications/accessions of fifteen AU Member States for it to enter into force. See also Gerhard Werle and Morris Vormbaum (eds), *The African Criminal Court: A Commentary on the Malabo Protocol* (Springer 2017).

[25] Withdrawal strategy document <https://www.hrw.org/sites/default/files/supporting_resources/icc_withdrawal_strategy_jan._2017.pdf>, §36.

developments in Africa in the field of human rights, such as the work of the African Commission on Human and Peoples' Rights and the African Court on Human and Peoples' Rights, supplemented the ICC's mandate. Fifthly, the ICC's task was to punish perpetrators of crimes under its jurisdiction, which was a condition for peace and justice and an important factor in the promotion of stability and prosperity of the African Continent. In reply to a question whether the ICC was insensitive to the accusation by some African States that the ICC had been biased against Africa, the ICC Prosecutor responded that the ICC had to discharge its functions according to its Statute and Rules of Procedure and Evidence without any exception, otherwise its credibility and objective would be undermined.[26] The ambassador of Burundi to the Netherlands clarified that Burundi had to withdraw from the ICC Statute allegedly because of distortion in some quarters in Europe of the events in Burundi leading to the preliminary investigation by the ICC which tarnished the image of the Government of Burundi. The ambassador of Libya, while stating that the ICC had to prove that it was not politically biased, claimed that justice did not necessarily lead to peace. In his view, certain African States including Libya knew best how to attain peace, and sometimes forgiveness, not justice, might be crucial to peace. The ambassador of Sierra Leone, on the other hand, reiterated his State's support for the ICC as Sierra Leone had benefited from international criminal justice before.[27]

The ICC Prosecutor's reasoned responses have not laid to rest the concerns that the ICC has not prosecuted equally serious crimes committed outside Africa, and that the UN Security Council has not referred any situation outside Africa, however serious, to the ICC Prosecutor.[28]

The following analysis centres upon the notion of discriminatory justice cited by several States, especially those in Africa, as a major reason or excuse for resisting the request to surrender persons to the ICC. The other issues related to the third alternative to the obligation to extradite or prosecute will be dealt with in Section II as well as in Chapter 8. However, this book will not join the debate on the broader issue of UN Security Council reform which has been going on for decades without a chance of seeing the light of day in the foreseeable future.

Equality of persons under the law is well recognized in international instruments, starting from the 1948 Universal Declaration of Human Rights (UDHR).[29] Article

[26] The Office of the ICC Prosecutor issued a statement on 4 July 2016 refuting the allegation in an article in the British newspaper, the *Daily Telegraph*, two days earlier that the Office had 'already ruled out putting [former British Prime Minister] Tony Blair on trial for *war crimes*'. The Prosecutor explained that her Office was conducting a preliminary examination with respect to the situation in Iraq in order to determine whether there were reasonable grounds to open an investigation on the basis of reliable information independently assessed in accordance with the criteria under the ICC Statute as well as the existing jurisdiction of the ICC which did not then include the crime of aggression. (<https://www.icc-cpi.int/Pages/item.aspx?name=160704-otp-stat>, accessed 17 November 2017.)

[27] Verbatim note taken by a colleague of the present author's who attended the seminar.

[28] See eg Akbar Khan, 'Ten Years of International Court Practice—Trials, Achievements and Tribulations: Is the ICC Today What Africa Expects or Wants?' in Evelyn A Ankumah (ed), *The International Criminal Court and Africa: One Decade On* (Intersentia 2016) 433; Max du Plessis, 'Exploring Efforts to Resolve the Tension Between the AU and the ICC over the Bashir Saga', ibid 245.

[29] UNGA Res 217A (III) GAOR 3rd Session (Resolutions pt 1) 71, UN Doc A/810 (1948), reprinted in (1949) 43 AJIL (Supp) 127.

7 of the UDHR stipulates: 'All are equal before the law and are entitled without any discrimination to equal protection of the law. All are entitled to equal protection against any discrimination in violation of this Declaration and against any incitement to such discrimination.' Article 10 adds that everyone is entitled in full equality to a fair and public hearing by an independent and impartial tribunal, in the determination of his rights and obligations and of any criminal charge against him. Article 30 provides, though, that nothing in the UDHR may be interpreted as implying for any State, group, or person any right to engage in any activity or to perform any act aimed at the destruction of any of the rights and freedoms set forth herein. In other words, the fact that some violators of human rights set forth in the UDHR have not been brought to justice does not imply that other violators may also violate the said rights with impunity.

Article 2(1) of the widely ratified 1966 International Covenant on Civil and Political Rights (ICCPR)[30] obligates each State Party to respect and ensure to all persons within its territory and subject to its jurisdiction the rights recognized in the ICCPR without distinction of any kind, such as race, colour, sex, language, religion, political or other opinion, national or social origin, property, birth, or other status. Article 26 not only entitles all persons to equality before the law as well as equal protection of the law, but also prohibits any discrimination under the law and guarantees to all persons equal and effective protection against discrimination on any ground mentioned in Article 2(1). This must be read in conjunction with Article 5(1), which is similar to Article 30 of the UDHR.[31] The Human Rights Committee, set up to monitor the implementation of the ICCPR, has issued an observation in its General Comment no 18 (Non-Discrimination) that 'not every differentiation of treatment will constitute discrimination, if the criteria for such differentiation are reasonable and objective and if the aim is to achieve a purpose which is legitimate under the Covenant'.[32]

Article 14 of the 1950 European Convention of Human Rights[33] stipulates that the enjoyment of the rights and freedoms in this Convention 'shall be secured without discrimination on any ground such as sex, race, colour, language, religion, political or other opinion, national or social origin, association with a national minority, property, birth or other status'. The European Court of Human Rights has held in *Thlimmenos v Greece* that Article 14 is violated when persons of analogous situations are treated differently and when persons whose situations are significantly different are not treated differently.[34] The Court has consistently held that Article 14 ensures the equal treatment of those in relevantly similar situations.[35]

[30] (1967) 6 ILM 368.

[31] 'Nothing in the present Covenant may be interpreted as implying for any State, group or person any right to engage in any activity or perform any act aimed at the destruction of any of the rights and freedoms recognized herein or at their limitation to a greater extent than is provided for in the present Covenant.'

[32] HRI/GEN/1/Rev9 (vol i) §13.

[33] European Convention for the Protection of Human Rights and Fundamental Freedoms, ETS 5.

[34] [GC] no 34369/97 §44, ECHR 2000-IV.

[35] *Fredin v Sweden (no 1)*[1991] 13 EHRR 784 §60 and subsequent cases cited in Oddný Mjöll Arnardóttir, *Equality and Non-Discrimination under the European Convention on Human Rights* (Martinus Nijhoff 2003) 11[n 38].

In Africa, the 1981 African Charter of Human and Peoples' Rights[36] recognizes in Article 3 that every individual shall be equal before the law and entitled to equal protection of the law. Pursuant to Article 60, the African Commission on Human and Peoples' Rights shall draw inspiration from international law on human and peoples' rights, particularly from the provisions of various African instruments on human and peoples' rights, the UN Charter, the Charter of the Organization of African Unity, the UDHR, other instruments adopted by the UN and by African States in the field of human and peoples' rights as well as from the provisions of various instruments adopted within the UN Specialized Agencies of which the parties to the present Charter are members. Article 61 of the Charter requires the Commission also to take into consideration, as subsidiary measures to determine the principles of law, other general or special international conventions, laying down rules expressly recognized by Member States of the Organization of African Unity, African practices consistent with international norms on human and peoples' rights, customs generally accepted as law, general principles of law recognized by African States as well as legal precedents and doctrine.

Judge Conçado Trindade of the IC J is, therefore, right when he says:

> In that transcendental Advisory Opinion of 2003, the [Inter-American Court of Human Rights], in line with the humanist teachings of the 'founding fathers' of the *droit des gens (jus gentium)*, pointed out that, under that fundamental principle, the element of equality can hardly be separated from non-discrimination, and equality is to be guaranteed without discrimination of any kind. This is closely linked to the essential dignity of the human person, ensuing from the unity of human kind. The basic principle of equality before the law and non-discrimination permeates the whole operation of the State power, having nowadays entered the domain of *jus cogens*. In [my] concurring opinion, it was stressed that the fundamental principle of equality and non-discrimination permeates the whole *corpus juris* of the international law of human rights, has an impact in public international law, and projects itself onto general or customary international law itself, and integrates nowadays the expanding material content of *jus cogens*.[37]

In domestic law, US courts probably has the richest jurisprudence against discriminatory justice.

Both the US Constitution and federal law prohibit intentional discrimination on the basis of race, colour, or national origin. Under the Constitution's Fourteenth Amendment, '[n]o state shall ... deny to any person within its jurisdiction the equal protection of the laws.'[38] The Equal Protection Clause within that Amendment further prohibits certain law enforcement practices that discriminate based on race,

[36] (1982) 21 ILM 58.

[37] Dis Op of Judge Cançado Trindade in *Jurisdictional Immunities of the State (Germany v Italy)*, Counter-Claim, Order of 6 July 2010 [2010] ICJ Rep 310, 381[135] (footnotes omitted), citing the Inter-American Court of Human Rights' Advisory Opinion no 18 (17 Sept 2003), on the *Juridical Condition and Rights of Undocumented Migrants*, Series A No 18 (17 Sept 2003) §§83, 97–99, and 100–01.

[38] US Const amendment XIV §1. The Fifth Amendment guarantees due process of law to individuals in their dealings with the federal government, and this due process requirement has been interpreted to incorporate the Fourteenth Amendment's equal protection guarantee.

ethnicity, or national origin. This constitutional protection plays a role in racial discrimination claims regarding law enforcement. As the US Supreme Court has ruled in *Whren v United States*, the Equal Protection Clause under the Constitution 'prohibits selective enforcement of the law based on considerations such as race'.[39] After that decision, claimants may argue that the conduct of an individual officer was racially motivated.

In *United States v Armstrong*, the respondents were indicted on charges of conspiring to possess with intent to distribute more than fifty grams of cocaine base (crack) and conspiring to distribute the same as well as federal firearms offences. They filed a discovery motion asking for information from the government in order to prove that they were being selectively prosecuted because they were black and, consequently, for dismissal of the indictment. The US Supreme Court had to consider the showing necessary for a defendant to be entitled to discovery on a claim that the prosecution singled him out for prosecution on the basis of his race. In order to dispel the presumption that a prosecutor has not violated equal protection, a criminal defendant must present 'clear evidence to the contrary'. The requirements for a selective prosecution claim draw on 'ordinary equal protection standards'. The claimant must demonstrate that the federal prosecutorial policy 'had a discriminatory effect and that it was motivated by a discriminatory purpose'. To establish a discriminatory effect in a race case, the claimant must show that similarly situated individuals of a different race were not prosecuted. If discovery is ordered, the government must assemble from its own files documents that might corroborate or refute the defendant's claim. Discovery thus imposes many of the costs present when the government must respond to a prima facie case of selective prosecution; it will divert prosecutors' resources and may disclose the government's prosecutorial strategy. The justifications for a rigorous standard for the elements of a selective prosecution claim thus require a correspondingly rigorous standard for discovery in aid of such a claim. The required threshold of 'a credible showing of different treatment of similarly situated persons' adequately balances the government's interest in vigorous prosecution and the defendant's interest in avoiding selective prosecution. The Court concluded that the respondents in that case failed to show that the government declined to prosecute similarly situated suspects of other races.[40]

A law enforcement activity may violate the Equal Protection Clause even where discriminatory intent is not the decision maker's sole motive,[41] and the accused may argue that they were the victims of selective enforcement.

[39] *Whren v United States* 517 US 806, 813 (1996).

[40] *United States v Armstrong* 517 US 456, 465 (1996). See also *Washington v Davis* 426 US 229, 239–40 (1976). In one case, a US court has explained that '[i]f law enforcement adopts a policy, employs a practice, or in a given situation takes steps to initiate an investigation of a citizen based solely upon that citizen's race, without more, then a violation of the Equal Protection Clause has occurred' (*United States v Avery* 137 F 3d 343, 355 (6th Cir 1997)). Cf *Monroe v City of Charlottesville* where law enforcement officers were held to have violated the Equal Protection Clause when they administered or enforced a racially neutral policy in a manner that disproportionately affected a protected group and they acted with discriminatory intent (579 F 3d 380, 388 (4th Cir 2009).

[41] *Smith v Town of Clarkton* 682 F 2d 1055, 1066 (4th Cir 1982); *Orgain v City of Salisbury* 305 F App'x 90, 98 (4th Cir 2008) ('Notably, the Equal Protection Clause does not require Plaintiffs to prove that the challenged action rested solely on racially discriminatory purposes.').

Proof of discriminatory intent is, however, an essential element of such selective enforcement equal protection claims. An equal protection violation occurs when evidence shows that 'racial animus was one of several factors that, taken together', motivated the discriminatory acts.[42] To assess whether intentional discrimination animates a law enforcement activity, courts examine the totality of the circumstances with particular attention to factors the US Supreme Court has identified as most probative of discriminatory intent.[43] Those factors include evidence of discriminatory effects; evidence of departures from normal procedures; the specific sequence of events that led to the discriminatory practices at issue; and contemporaneous statements from a decision maker that reveal a discriminatory intent.[44]

However, if race or ethnicity is 'but one factor' and not the sole basis for a certain practice, it may be difficult to prove a violation of the Fourteenth Amendment.[45] For example, a US court in *Brown v City of Oneonta* concluded that there was no violation of the Equal Protection Clause where plaintiffs alleged that they were questioned solely on the basis of their race, where the physical description of the suspect provided by the victim of the crime included race among other factors.[46] Thus, it was decided in that case that only when race-based law enforcement decisions were a product of racial stereotyping by police officials, as opposed to the government's response to evidence developed from other sources, might constitutional issues arise.

A claimant can satisfy the requirement set by the US Supreme Court in *United States v Armstrong* that '[t]o establish discriminatory effect in a race case, the claimant must show that similarly situated individuals of a different race were not prosecuted'[47] by naming an individual who was not investigated in similar circumstances or through the use of statistical or other evidence 'address[ing] the crucial question of whether one class is being treated differently from another class that is otherwise similarly situated'.[48] However, US courts have explained that if racially motivated decision-making is shown, or an agency policy employs explicit racial criteria, the claimant need not demonstrate statistically that members of his or her racial or ethnic group were disproportionately targeted for enforcement.[49]

[42] *Orgain v City of Salisbury; Personnel Adm'r of Mass v Feeney* 442 US 256, 279 (1979).

[43] *Village of Arlington Heights v Metro Housing Dev Corp* 429 US 252, 266 (1977) (explaining that '[d]etermining whether invidious discriminatory purpose was a motivating factor [behind a law enforcement officer's actions] demands a sensitive inquiry into such circumstantial and direct evidence of intent as may be available').

[44] ibid 266–68 (1977); *Sylvia Dev Corp. v Calvert County* 48 F 3d 810, 819 (4th Cir 1995).

[45] *United States v Valenzuela* 2001 US Dist LEXIS 7679 (D Colo 31 May 2001) (denying motions to suppress, there being 'no persuasive evidence that the Trooper targeted any of these suspects solely because of their race').

[46] *Brown v City of Oneonta* 195 F 3d 111, 119 (2d Cir 1999) (distinguishing equal protection claims based on racially neutral policies applied discriminatorily from claims based on policies containing express racial classifications).

[47] *United States v Armstrong* 465.

[48] *Chavez v Illinois State Police*, 251 F 3d 612, 638 (7th Cir 2001). See also *Flowers v Fiore* 359 F 3d 24 (1st Cir 2004).

[49] *Brown v City of Oneonta* 221 F 3d 329, 337 (2d Cir 2000) ('[I]t is not necessary to plead the existence of a similarly situated non-minority group when challenging a law or policy that contains an express racial classification.').

Moreover, the equal protection doctrine requires that where race or ethnicity is the sole or 'predominant' factor behind the decision to stop or arrest, 'strict scrutiny' requires that the government demonstrate a 'compelling' justification served by 'narrowly tailored' means. 'Strict scrutiny' connotes an analytical framework requiring the government to demonstrate a 'close fit' between any distinction in treatment of its citizens on the basis of race and a 'compelling' law enforcement or national security interest. This may depend on the 'totality' of circumstances, not the least of which may be the magnitude of any public safety or national security interests at stake.[50] As one author summarized it, '[i]n the end ... even when formally strict, judicial scrutiny under the Equal Protection Clause must be ever sensitive to the circumstances in which government seeks to act and to the methods by which it seeks to achieve even its legitimate ends.'[51]

Nonetheless, the 'equitable standing doctrine' has been applied by US courts to deny an individual plaintiff, as opposed to a class action, the legal standing to seek injunctive relief against unconstitutional police practices unless he can show a 'substantial certainty' that he will suffer similar injury in the future.[52]

In addition to the Equal Protection Clause of the US Constitution, another constitutional Amendment and several federal statutes may provide a basis for racial profiling lawsuits.

The Fourth Amendment provides that '[t]he right of the people to be secure in their persons, houses, papers, and effects, against unreasonable searches and seizures, shall not be violated.'[53] Since even the temporary detention of an individual by police during a traffic stop for a limited purpose constitutes a seizure for Fourth Amendment purposes,[54] a traffic stop must be 'reasonable' under the circumstances,[55] and may not be solely based on race or other such factors.[56]

In *Terry v Ohio*, the US Supreme Court applies a 'totality of circumstances' test to determine the reasonableness of police investigatory traffic stops.[57] In *United States v Brignoni-Ponce*, the Court addresses the issue of race as a factor giving rise to reasonable suspicion of criminal activity, proposing a multi-factored analysis: 'Officers may consider the characteristics of the area ... usual patterns of traffic on the particular road, and previous experience with alien traffic.'[58] Moreover, in

[50] Cf *Hirabayashi v United States* 320 US 81 (1943); *Korematsu v United States* 323 US 214 (1944).

[51] Peter J Rubin, 'Reconnecting Doctrine and Purpose: A Comprehensive Approach to Strict Scrutiny after Adarand and Shaw' (2000) 149 U Pa L Rev 1, 5.

[52] *City of Los Angeles v Lyons* 461 US 95, 105–06 (1983) ('[Plaintiff] would have had not only to allege that he would have another encounter with the police but also to make the credible assertion ... that all police officers in Los Angeles always choke any citizen with whom they happen to have an encounter.').

[53] US Const amendment IV.

[54] *Whren v United States* 809–10; *United States v Branch* 537 F 3d 328, 334 (4th Cir 2008).

[55] The US Supreme Court found that reasonable, articulable suspicion was a sufficient ground for a police officer to stop and question a citizen briefly. Such suspicion must not be based on the officer's 'inchoate or unparticularized suspicion or "hunch," but [on] the specific reasonable inferences which he is entitled to draw from the facts in light of his experience'. *Terry v Ohio* 392 US 1, 27 (1968).

[56] The US Supreme Court has held in *Bivens v Six Unknown Narcotics Agents* 403 US 388 (1971) that plaintiffs can sue federal defendants in federal court for Fourth Amendment violations.

[57] *Terry v Ohio* 22–27.

[58] *United States v Brignoni-Ponce* 422 US 873, 884–85 (1975). *See also United States v Anderson* 923 F 2d 450, 455 (6th Cir 1991) ('Suspicions based solely on the race of the person stopped cannot give

United States v Weaver, a US court rules that federal drug enforcement agents can rely on racial characteristics if objective crime trend analysis validates the use of these characteristics as 'risk factors' in predicting criminal behaviour.[59] The Guidance regarding the Use of Race by Federal Law Enforcement Agencies[60] issued by the US Department of Justice prohibits the use of 'generalized stereotypes' based on race or ethnicity, and allows officers to consider racial factors in 'traditional law enforcement' activities only as part of a specific description or tip from an informant. However, the Guidance 'do[es] not affect current Federal policy with respect to law enforcement activities and other efforts to defend and safeguard against threats to national security or the integrity of the Nation's borders'. When federal law enforcement officers are 'investigating or preventing threats to national security or other catastrophic events (including the performance of duties related to air transportation security), or enforcing laws protecting the integrity of the Nation's borders', they may consider both race and ethnicity 'to the extent permitted by the Constitution and laws of the United States'.

The Violent Crime Control and Law Enforcement Act of 1994[61] prohibits law enforcement agencies from engaging in a pattern or practice of violating the US Constitution or laws. The statute grants the US authority to sue a state or local government for equitable and declaratory relief when a 'government authority . . . engage[s] in a pattern or practice of conduct by law enforcement officers . . . that deprives persons of rights, privileges, or immunities secured or protected by the Constitution or laws of the United States'. It thereby empowers the US Department of Justice, but not private victims, to bring civil actions against any police agency engaged in unconstitutional 'patterns or practices' and to 'obtain appropriate equitable and declaratory relief to eliminate the pattern or practices' of racial discrimination by such law enforcement agencies.

With respect to the practice of international criminal tribunals, the fact that the persons meting out criminal justice have also committed the same or similar crime (*tu quoque*) has been consistently rejected as a defence, for instance, by the US Military Tribunal sitting at Nuremberg under Control Council Law No 10,[62] and by the ICTY.[63]

In *Kanyabashi*, the Defence Counsel contended before the ICTR that there were numerous other areas of conflicts and incidents, such as Congo, Liberia, and

rise to a reasonable suspicion justifying a *Terry* stop.') Additionally, erratic behaviour and evasive acts by those under the observation of the police officer, as well as aspects of the motor vehicle, may support the reasonable suspicion necessary for an investigatory stop.

[59] *United States v Weaver*, 966 F 2d 391, 392 (8th Cir 1992).

[60] Guidance Regarding the Use of Race by Federal Law Enforcement Agencies, US Dept of Justice, Civil Rights Division (June 2003) <http://www.justice.gov/crt/about/spl/documents/guidance_on_race.pdf>, accessed 21 November 2017.

[61] 42 USC §14141.

[62] *In re Weizsaecker and Others*, US Military Tribunal, Nuremberg, 14 Apr 1949 (1955) 16 Ann Dig 344, 348.

[63] *Prosecutor v Zoran Kupreskic and Others* (Judgment) IT-95-16-T, T Ch II (14 Jan 2000) §§23, 125, 162, 511, 513, 515–24, 527–35, 765. See Kriangsak Kittichaisaree, *International Criminal Law* (OUP 2001) 272–73.

Somalia, where the UN Security Council took no action to create an international criminal tribunal, and that, consequently, individual criminal responsibility should not be pursued in the case of Rwanda. Trial Chamber I of the ICTR rejected this argument, reasoning that:

> The fact that the Security Council, for previously prevailing *geo-strategic and international political reasons*, was unable in the past to take adequate measures to bring to justice the perpetrators of crimes against international humanitarian law is not an acceptable argument against introducing measures to punish serious violations of international humanitarian law when this becomes an option under international law.[64]

In the *Celebici* case decided by the ICTY Appeals Chamber in 2001,[65] one of the accused persons relied on a test drawn from US case law, and in particular *United States of America v Armstrong*, on the required threshold for selective prosecution claims. It may be recalled that, pursuant to this test, the complainant must prove first that he or she was singled out for prosecution for an improper motive, and secondly, that the Prosecutor elected not to prosecute other similarly situated defendants. The ICTY Appeals Chamber agreed with the ICTY Prosecutor that in order to satisfy this test there must be clear evidence of the intent of the Prosecutor to discriminate on improper motives, and that other similarly situated persons were not prosecuted. The Appeals Chamber went on to observe that other jurisdictions that recognize an ability for judicial review of a prosecutorial discretion also indicate that the threshold is a very high one.[66] The Appeals Chamber found it unnecessary to select between such domestic standards, as it was not appropriate for it simply to rely on the jurisprudence of any one jurisdiction in determining the applicable legal principles. In its view, the provisions of the ICTY Statute and the relevant principles of international law sufficed. The breadth of the discretion of the Prosecutor, and the fact of her statutory independence, imply a presumption that the prosecutorial functions under the Statute are exercised regularly, which presumption may be rebutted by evidence establishing that the discretion has in fact not been exercised in accordance with the Statute; for example, in contravention of the principle of equality before the law in Article 21of the Statute.[67] This would require evidence from which a clear inference can be drawn that the Prosecutor was motivated in that case by a factor inconsistent with that principle. Because the principle is one of equality of persons before the law, it involves a comparison with the legal treatment of other persons

[64] *Prosecutor v Kanyabashi* (Decision on the Defence Motion on Jurisdiction) ICTR-96-15-T, T Ch II (18 June 1997) §36 (emphasis added).

[65] *Prosecutor v Zejnil Delalic, Zdravko Mucic, Hazim Delic, and Esad Landzo* (*Celebici Case*) (Judgment) IT-96-21-A, App Ch (20 Feb 2001).

[66] Citing *Chief Constable of Kent and Crown Prosecution Service, ex parte GL* (1991) Crim App R 416; *R v Inland Revenue Commissioners, ex parte Mead and Cook* [1993] 1 All ER 772; *R v Power* [1994] 1 SCR 601. The ICTY Appeals Chamber also recognized that in Australia there may be a principle pursuant to which proof of a selective prosecution may give rise to some relief, including, for example, the exclusion of evidence: *Hutton v Kneipp* [1995] QCA 203.

[67] Paragraph 1 of Art 21 provides: 'All persons shall be equal before the [ICTY].' Art 21 is under the heading 'Rights of the accused', and the other paragraphs of that Article relate to the right to a fair and public hearing, the presumption of innocence, and the minimum guarantees, in full equality, during the entire process of prosecution.

who must be similarly situated for such a comparison to be a meaningful one. This essentially reflects the two-pronged test of (1) establishing an unlawful or improper (including discriminatory) motive for the prosecution; and (2) establishing that other similarly situated persons were not prosecuted.

The ICTY Prosecutor in *Celebici* emphasized the need to reassign available resources of the Prosecution that should not be considered as being significative of discriminatory intent, and that the evidence of discriminatory intent must be coupled with the evidence that the Prosecutor's policy had a discriminatory effect, so that other similarly situated individuals of other ethnic or religious backgrounds were not prosecuted. The ICTY Appeals Chamber took into consideration the 'unquestionably violent and extreme nature' of the crimes allegedly committed by the complainant and concluded that the decision to continue the trial against him was clearly consistent with the stated policy of the Prosecutor to 'focus on persons holding higher levels of responsibility, or on those who have been personally responsible for the exceptionally brutal or otherwise extremely serious offences'. Therefore, a decision by the Prosecutor, made in the context of a need to concentrate prosecutorial resources, to identify a person for prosecution on the basis that they were believed to have committed exceptionally brutal offences could in no way be described as a discriminatory or otherwise impermissible motive. Having reached the conclusion that the complainant was not the subject of a discriminatory selective prosecution, the Appeals Chamber founded it 'not strictly necessary to have reference to the additional question of whether there were other similarly situated persons who were not prosecuted or against whom prosecutions were discontinued'. It noted that the Prosecutor explicitly stated that accused in the same case against whom charges were withdrawn due to the constraints on the Prosecutor's resources could still be tried at a later stage by the ICTY or by national courts by virtue of the principle of concurrent jurisdiction.[68]

The Appeals Chamber concluded:

> Finally, even if in the hypothetical case that those against whom the indictments were withdrawn were identically situated to [the complainant], the Appeals Chamber cannot accept that the appropriate remedy would be to reverse the convictions of [complainant] for the serious offences with which he had been found guilty. Such a remedy would be an entirely disproportionate response to such a procedural breach. As noted by the Trial Chamber, it cannot be accepted that 'unless all potential indictees who are similarly situated are brought to justice, there should be no justice done in relation to a person who has been indicted and brought to trial'.[69]

In the case of the ICC, those opposing the surrender of persons to the ICC on the ground of discrimination by the Prosecutor and the ICC must discharge the burden of proving that this is so according to the standard postulated by the ICTY Appeals Chamber in *Celebici*, which has taken due account of the applicable standards in jurisprudence of national courts, with necessary adaptions for the purpose of international criminal justice. By the same token, the ICC Prosecutor, the ICC, and,

[68] *Celebici Case* §§609–19. [69] ibid §618.

where applicable, the UN Security Council must substantiate that they have not discriminated and do not discriminate against, for example, African offenders in the light of the relevant factors and circumstances explained by the ICTY Appeals Chamber in *Celebici*. Otherwise, prosecution by the ICC would not command trust, confidence, and/or credibility, and the third alternative to the obligation to extradite or prosecute would not be resorted to as often and regularly as it should.

II. Rome Statute of the ICC: Article 27 *versus* Article 98

In the context of the third alternative to the obligation to extradite or prosecute by surrendering an offender to an international criminal tribunal, a conflict between the obligation to surrender and other international legal obligations such as immunity of State officials may arise and has already arisen.

In the case of ad hoc international criminal tribunals established by the UN Security Council pursuant to Chapter VII of the UN Charter, the obligation to surrender the offender to such tribunals overrides the obligation to respect such immunity.[70] The same applies to hybrid courts; they do not recognize immunity since they are set up specifically to punish all persons who have committed crimes within their jurisdiction, including persons in official positions.[71]

In respect of the obligation to surrender to an international criminal tribunal set up by a treaty, such as the ICC, matters are much more complicated. Article 27 (Irrelevance of official capacity) of the ICC Statute stipulates:

1. This Statute shall apply equally to all persons without any distinction based on official capacity. In particular, official capacity as a Head of State or Government, a member of a Government or parliament, an elected representative or a government official shall in no case exempt a person from criminal responsibility under this Statute, nor shall it, in and of itself, constitute a ground for reduction of sentence.
2. Immunities or special procedural rules which may attach to the official capacity of a person, whether under national or international law, shall not bar the Court from exercising its jurisdiction over such a person.[72]

[70] *Prosecutor v Radovan Karadžić* (Decision on Accused's Second Motion for Inspection and Disclosure: Immunity Issue) IT-95-5/18-PT, ICTY T Ch (17 Dec 2008) §§17–18. One author (Dapo Akande, 'Immunity and International Criminal Tribunals' (*EJIL Talks!* (20 Dec 2008) <https://www.ejiltalk.org/immunity-and-international-criminal-tribunals/> accessed 21 November 2017), observes that Karadzic had no relevant immunities under customary international law, and at most he would merely have had functional immunities that would not apply in the cases of the serious international crimes he was charged with. However, the aforesaid ruling by the ICTY Trial Chamber would be relevant with regard to Milosevic, who at the time of his indictment was an incumbent Head of State with immunity *ratione personae*.

[71] See eg *Prosecutor v Charles Taylor* (Decision on Immunity from Jurisdiction) SCSL-2003-01-I, Special Ct for Sierra Leone App Ch (31 May 2004) §§44–53. Cf Sarah MH Nouwen, 'The Special Court for Sierra Leone and the Immunity of Taylor: The Arrest Warrant Case Continued' (2005) 18 Leiden JIL 645; Diane Orentlicher, 'Immunities and Amnesties' in Leila Nadya Sadat (ed), *Forging a Convention for Crimes Against Humanity* (CUP 2011) 202, 203–08.

[72] Cf Triffterer, *Commentary on the Rome Statute of the ICC* 779–93.

However, Article 98 (Cooperation with respect to waiver of immunity and consent to surrender) of the same Statute provides:

1. The Court may not proceed with a request for surrender or assistance which would require the requested State to act inconsistently with its obligations under international law with respect to the State or diplomatic immunity of a person or property of a third State, unless the Court can first obtain the cooperation of that third State for the waiver of the immunity.
2. The Court may not proceed with a request for surrender which would require the requested State to act inconsistently with its obligations under international agreements pursuant to which the consent of a sending State is required to surrender a person of that State to the Court, unless the Court can first obtain the cooperation of the sending State for the giving of consent for the surrender.[73]

It may be recalled that Article 13(b) of the ICC Statute authorizes the UN Security Council acting under Chapter VII of the UN Charter to refer a situation in which one or more of the crimes under the ICC Statute appears to have been committed to the ICC Prosecutor. Among States Parties to the ICC Statute, there is no conflict between Article 27 and Article 98 thereof. In relation to non-States Parties to the ICC Statute, the situation is more complex since a waiver of State or diplomatic immunity attaching to a person by reason of a connection with a particular non-State Party is required from that non-State Party.[74]

A. Article 98(1), ICC Statute

By becoming party to the ICC Statute, a State is deemed by virtue of Article 27 of the Statute to have implicitly waived any immunity under international law in

[73] ibid 1601–19.

[74] The distinction between States Parties and non-States Parties to the ICC Statute appears eg in the UK International Criminal Court Act 2001 (c 17) (Order 2001 (SI 2001/2169) (C 69)). S 23(1) and (2) of the Act stipulates that any State or diplomatic immunity attaching to a person by reason of a connection with a State Party to the ICC Statute does not prevent proceedings related to the arrest and surrender of that person to the ICC, whereas a waiver must be obtained from the non-State Party concerned for the arrest and surrender of such person to the ICC.

In contrast, Kenya's International Crimes Act of 2008 (Act no 16 of 2008, Laws of Kenya [Rev 2012]), implementing the ICC Statute, does not make such a distinction. Section 115 (Request involving conflict with other international obligations) provides that if the ICC requests for 'assistance concerning persons who, or information or property that, are subject to the control of another State or an international organization under an international agreement, the Attorney-General shall inform the ICC to enable it to direct its request to that other State or organization', and the minister responsible for matters relating to national security may postpone the request for assistance in such circumstances.

Article 24(6) of Uganda's Act 11 International Criminal Court Act of 2010 (*Uganda Gazette* no 39, vol ciii, 25 June 2010) provides that if the minister of justice considers that the circumstances set out in Art 98 of the ICC Statute apply to a request for provisional arrest, arrest, and surrender or other assistance, the minister shall consult with the ICC and request a determination as to whether Art 98 of that Statute applies.

See Christopher Gevers, 'Immunity and the Implementation Legislation of South Africa, Kenya, and Uganda' <https://papers.ssrn.com/sol3/papers.cfm?abstract_id=1975788>, accessed 29 November 2017.

proceedings before the ICC.[75] There have been at least three actual cases that have put Article 27 and Article 98(1) of the ICC Statute to the test. These cases have been extensively analysed in the legal literature; therefore only the pertinent arguments will be highlighted here, without going into factual details of the cases.

The first case relates to the prosecution of an incumbent President of Kenya, a State Party to the ICC Statute. Kenya's President Uhuru Muigai Kenyatta was accused of five counts of crimes against humanity in the context of the 2007–08 post-election violence in Kenya. When the ICC issued the summons to appear against him on 8 March 2011, he was Deputy Prime Minister and Minister of Finance. He became President of Kenya on 9 April 2013. His Deputy President William Ruto of Kenya was also accused before the ICC.

The second case concerns the ICC's arrest warrant for the incumbent President Al Bashir of Sudan, a non-State Party to the ICC Statute, after the UN Security Council had referred the situation in Darfur, Sudan, to the ICC Prosecutor pursuant to Article 13(b) of the ICC Statute in March 2005.[76] In March 2009, a Pre-Trial Chamber of the ICC authorized the issuance of an arrest warrant against Sudan's President Al Bashir for alleged war crimes and crimes against humanity in Darfur.[77] A second arrest warrant was issued in July 2010 to include charges of genocide.[78] These two arrest warrants list ten counts on the basis of his individual

[75] *Decision Pursuant to Article 87(7) of the Rome Statute on the Failure by the Republic of Malawi to Comply with the Cooperation Requests Issued by the Court with Respect to the Arrest and Surrender of Omar Hassan Al Bashir* ICC-02/05-01/09, Pre-Trial Ch I (12 Dec 2011) §§18, 41–47. This was followed on the following day with its *Decision Pursuant to Article 87(7) of the Rome Statute on the Failure by the Republic of Chad to Comply with the Cooperation Requests Issued by the Court with Respect to the Arrest and Surrender of Omar Hassan Al Bashir* ICC-02/05-01/09, Pre-Trial Ch I (13 Dec 2011). See also Dapo Akande, 'International Law Immunities and the International Criminal Court' (2004) 98 AJIL 407.

Contra: African Union Press Release no 002/2012 (9 Jan 2012), contending that the said Decision by the Pre-Trial Chamber of the ICC has the effect of: '(i) Purporting to change customary international law in relation to immunity *ratione personae*; (ii) Rendering Article 98 of the Rome Statute redundant, non-operational and meaningless; (iii) Making a decision *per incuriam* by referring to decisions of the African Union while grossly ignoring the provision of Article 23(2) of the Constitutive Act of the African Union, to which ... Malawi [is a State Party], and which obligates all AU Member States "*to comply with the decisions and policies of the Union*"' (emphasis original). Cf also Dapo Akande, 'ICC Issues Detailed Decision on Bashir's Immunity (... At Long Last ...) But Gets the Law Wrong' (*EJIL: Talk!* (15 Dec 2011) <https://www.ejiltalk.org/icc-issues-detailed-decision-on-bashir%E2%80%99s-immunity-at-long-last-but-gets-the-law-wrong/>, accessed 21 November 2017).

Malawi decided not to host the AU summit scheduled for July 2012 to avoid the dispute over what to do with President Al Bashir of Sudan. The summit was held instead at the headquarters of the AU in Addis Ababa, Ethiopia, a non-State Party to the ICC Statute.

[76] UNSC Res 1593.

[77] Pre-Trial Ch I, *Warrant of Arrest for Omar Hassan Ahmad Al Bashir* (4 Mar 20090. For criticisms, see Sarah Williams and Kena Sherif, 'The Arrest Warrant for President al-Bashir: Immunities of Incumbent Heads of States and the International Criminal Court' (2009) 14 J Conflict Security Law 71; Paola Gaeta, 'Does President Al Bashir Enjoy Immunity from Arrest?' (2009) 7 J Int'l Crim Justice 315; Michiel Blommestijn and Cedric Ryngaert, 'Exploring the Obligations for States to Act upon the ICC's Arrest Warrant for Omar Al-Bashir: A Legal Conflict between the Duty to Arrest and the Customary Status of Head of State Immunity' (2010) 5 Zeitschrift für Internationale Strafrechtsdogmatik 428.

[78] After the ICC Appeals Chamber unanimously reversed the ICC Pre-Trial Chamber I's decision not to issue a warrant for his arrest in respect of the crime of genocide. See *Decision on the Prosecutor's Application for a Warrant of Arrest against Omar Hassan Ahmad Al Bashir* (Judgment) ICC-02/05-01/09-OA, App Ch (3 Feb 2010). However, the issue of immunity was not raised or discussed.

criminal responsibility under Article 25(3)(a) of the ICC Statute. There are five counts of crimes against humanity: murder; extermination; forcible transfer; torture; and rape. There are two counts of war crimes: intentionally directing attacks against a civilian population as such or against individual civilians not taking part in hostilities; and pillaging. The three counts of genocide consist of genocide by killing; genocide by causing serious bodily or mental harm; and genocide by deliberately inflicting on each target group conditions of life calculated to bring about the group's physical destruction.

The third case was that of the arrest warrant issued by the ICC on 27 June 2011 for President Muammar Gaddafi of Libya, another non-State Party to the ICC Statute but the situation in whose State had been referred to the ICC Prosecutor by the UN Security Council.[79] The case against President Gaddafi was terminated on 22 November 2011 after his death.

The extraordinary session of the Assembly of the AU on 12 October 2013 reached the following outcome on Africa's relationship with the ICC. It reaffirmed the AU's 'strong conviction that the search for justice should be pursued in a way that does not impede or jeopardize efforts aimed at promoting lasting peace', while also reiterating its 'concern on the politicization and misuse of indictments against African leaders' especially when a sitting head of State and his deputy were being tried in an international court at the same time 'which could undermine the sovereignty, stability, and peace in that country and in other Member States as well as reconciliation and reconstruction and the normal functioning of constitutional institutions' including national and regional security affairs. Kenya was said to be a frontline State in the fight against terrorism at regional, continental, and international levels. Following the 2007 Post Election Violence (PEV), the mediation process in Kenya was initiated by the AU which led to the enactment of the National Accord and Reconciliation Act 2008[80] and the agreement establishing the coalition government, the implementation of which was under threat by the ICC's prosecution of the Kenyan leaders. The AU 'reaffirm[ed] the principles deriving from national laws and international customary law by which sitting Heads of State and other senior State officials [were] granted immunities during their tenure of office'. The AU decided, *inter alia*, that 'no charge shall be commenced or continued before any International Court or Tribunal against any serving AU Head of State or Government or anybody acting or entitled to act in such capacity during their term of office', and that 'the trials of President Uhuru Kenyatta and Deputy President William Samoei Ruto who [were] current serving leaders of the Republic of Kenya, should be suspended until they complete[d] their terms of office'. The AU also set up a Contact Group to consult the UN Security Council on all concerns of the AU on its relationship with the ICC, including the deferral, under Article 16 of the ICC Statute, of the Kenyan and Sudanese cases. The AU also decided that the Kenyan President would not appear

[79] UNSC Res 1970 (26 Feb 2011) UN Doc S/RES/1970 §§4–8; *Warrant of Arrest for Mohammed Abu Minyar Gaddafi*, ICC-01/11, Pre-Trial Ch I (27 June 2011), seeking his arrest for alleged commission of murder as a crime against humanity and persecution as a crime against humanity.

[80] Act no 4 of 2008, Laws of Kenya [Rev 2012].

before the ICC until such time as the concerns raised by the AU and its Member States had been adequately addressed by the Security Council and the ICC.[81]

Article 16 of the ICC Statute provides that no investigation or prosecution may be commenced or proceeded with under this Statute for a period of twelve months after the UN Security Council, in a resolution adopted under Chapter VII of the UN Charter, has requested the ICC to that effect; that request may be renewed by the Council under the same conditions. Pursuant to Article 27 of the Charter, decisions of the Council on all substantive matters shall be made by an affirmative vote of nine members including the concurring votes of the five permanent members. This stringent condition prevented the Council from adopting a resolution to request the ICC to defer the Kenyan and Sudanese cases.[82]

The charges against President Kenyatta were withdrawn by the Prosecution on 5 December 2014 due to lack of sufficient evidence, and the proceedings in this case were terminated and his summons to appear vacated by a Trial Chamber on 13 March 2015. The case is considered closed unless and until the Prosecution submits new evidence.[83] On 5 April 2016 another Trial Chamber of the ICC decided, by majority, that the charges against Deputy President Ruto was to be vacated without prejudice to his prosecution in the future.[84]

Where the UN Security Council refers the situation to the ICC pursuant to Article 13(b) of the ICC Statute, this entails the implementation of the ICC Statute as a whole, including Articles 27 and 98(1) thereof. A crucial question is whether Article 103 of the UN Charter overrides the rule of international customary law on immunities of State official from foreign criminal jurisdiction.

One argument is that any immunities are waived by the UN Security Council's referral.[85] As will be seen further, another argument posits that Article 103 of the UN Charter only prevails over 'other agreements', not customary international law including that of immunities.

Article 103 of the UN Charter, which appears in Chapter XVI under 'Miscellaneous Provisions', stipulates, '[i]n the event of a conflict between the

[81] Ext/Assembly/AU/Dec.1 (12 Oct 2013). See also Max du Plessis, Tiyanjana Maluwa, and Annie O'Reilly, *Africa and the International Criminal Court* (Chatham House 2013).

[82] See Lawrence Moss, 'The UN Security Council and the International Criminal Court: Towards a More Principled Relationship', *Friedrich Ebert Stiftung*, International Policy Analysis (Mar 2012) 7–8, 10–11.

[83] *Prosecutor v Uhuru Muigai Kenyatta* (Decision on the Withdrawal of Charges) ICC-01/09-02/11-1005, T Ch V(B) (13 Mar 2015). For analyses of the outcome of the case, see Chris Maina Peter, 'Fighting Impunity: African States and the International Criminal Court' in Evelyn A Ankumah (ed), *The International Criminal Court and Africa: One Decade On* (Intersentia 2016) 1, 21–40; Leila Nadya Sadat and Benjamin Cohen, 'Impunity Through Immunity: The Kenyan Situation and the International Criminal Court', ibid 101; George Kegoro, 'Looking Back, Looking Forward: The Implications of the Termination of the Kenyan case Before the ICC', ibid 199.

[84] *Prosecutor v Ruto and Sang* (Decision) ICC-01/09/01/11, T Ch V(A) (5 Apr 2016). On 6 April 2016, the ICC Prosecutor issued a statement clarifying that the Chamber declined to acquit the accused due to the special circumstances of this case which had been severely undermined by witness interference and politicalization of the judicial process at the ICC, and that the Prosecution may bring the case on the basis of the same charges in the future, or in a different form, in light of new evidence.

[85] See eg Max du Plessis, *The International Criminal Court that Africa Wants* (Institute for Security Studies 2010) 79.

obligations of the Members of the United Nations under the present Charter and their obligations under any other international agreement, their obligations under the present Charter shall prevail.' In the context of the UN Security Council resolution adopted under Chapter VII of the UN Charter referring the situation in Darfur, Sudan, to the ICC Prosecutor, two main questions arise. First, does the resolution create an obligation under the UN Charter? Secondly, if there is such an obligation under the Charter, can this obligation prevail over a rule of customary international law of immunity of the incumbent Head of State?

The first question can be answered in the positive. The ICJ held in *Lockerbie* that a UN Security Council resolution adopted under Chapter VII of the UN Charter is a decision imposing an obligation on Members of the UN to comply with in accordance with Article 25 of the Charter, and that, by virtue of Article 103 of the Charter this obligation prevails over their obligations under any other international agreement.[86] This means that the UN Charter obligations prevail over, for instance, the obligations of the Member States of the African Union pursuant to Article 23(2) of the Constitutive Act of the AU which obligates all AU Member States to 'comply with the decisions and policies of the Union', including the AU decisions asking its Member States not to cooperate with the ICC on the arrest and surrender of Sudanese President Al Bashir.[87]

With respect to the second question, the drafting history of Article 103 reveals that proposals to make the Article encompass all obligations under international law, and not just international agreements, which are in conflict with the obligations under the UN Charter did not succeed.[88] As ICJ Judge ad hoc Sir Elihu Lauterpacht has pointed out, Article 103 does not mean that 'the Security Council can act free of all legal controls'; a Security Council resolution cannot prevail over *jus cogens* that 'operates as a concept superior to both customary international law and treaty'.[89]

[86] *Question of Interpretation and Application of the 1971 Montreal Convention Arising from the Aerial Incident at Lockerbie (Libya v UK) (Libya v US) (Provisional Measures)* [1992] ICJ Rep 3 and 114, §§39 and 42 respectively.

[87] AU Decision on the Meeting of African States Parties to the Rome Statute of the International Criminal Court (ICC) Doc Assembly/AU/13(XIII) (3 July 2009) §10. For the argument that AU Member States have to abide by AU decisions, see eg AU Press Release no 118/2010 (29 Aug 2010) on the decision of the Pre-Trial Chamber of the ICC informing the UN Security Council and the Assembly of the States Parties to the Rome Statute about the Presence of President Omar Hassan Al Bashir of the Sudan in the Territories of the Republic of Chad and the Republic of Kenya; Diplomatic Note no MFA REL. 13/23A dated 29 Aug 2010 from the Ministry of Foreign Affairs of the Republic of Kenya addressed to all diplomatic missions and international organizations accredited to Kenya, circulating the document entitled 'Government response to the decision of the Pre-Trial Chamber of the International Criminal Court (ICC) to refer the matter of President Omar Al Bashir's presence in Kenya to the UN Security Council'; §5 of the AU Decision on the Implementation of the Decisions on the International Criminal Court Doc Ex.CL/639(XVIII) adopted by the 19th AU Summit, Assembly of the Union, 16th Ordinary Session, 30–31 Jan 2011 (Assembly/AU/Dec 334(XVI)).

[88] Rain Liivoja, 'The Scope of the Supremacy Clause of the United Nations Charter' (2008) 57 ICLQ 583, 602–05, 612; Martti Koskenniemi, 'Fragmentation of International Law: Difficulties Arising From the Diversification and Expansion of International Law', Report of the Study Group of the ILC, UN Doc A/CN.4/L.682 (13 Apr 2006), §§328–29, 344.

[89] Sep Op of Judge ad hoc Elihu Lauterpacht, *Case Concerning Application of the Convention on the Prevention and Punishment of the Crime of Genocide (Bosnia and Herzegovina v Yugoslavia (Montenegro)) (Further Request for the Indication of Provisional Measures)* Order of 13 Sept 1993 [1993] ICJ Rep 325, 439–40 §§99–100. The pertinent part of §100 of the Separate Opinion reads: 'The concept of *jus cogens*

The *jus cogens* norm in that case was the prohibition of genocide. As can be seen from Chapter 6, the customary international rule of immunity has not yet arisen to become a *jus cogens* norm. Nevertheless, the Report of the Study Group of the International Law Commission on 'Fragmentation of International Law: Difficulties Arising From the Diversification and Expansion of International Law' dated 13 April 2006 concludes in relation to the question of whether Article 103 'elevates the Charter above customary international law' as follows.

First, a literal interpretation renders a clear result. However expansively one interprets 'international agreements', it does not cover international custom. Second, however . . . as *lex generalis*, customary law normally yields to treaties as *leges specialis*—including, one would suppose, treaties establishing an international organization such as the United Nations. In any case, the practice of the Security Council has continuously been grounded on an understanding that Security Council resolutions override conflicting customary law. As the Security Council is a creation of the Charter, it would be odd if the prevailing effect of Security Council resolutions would not extend to the Charter itself. Therefore it seems sound to join the prevailing opinion that Article 103 should be read extensively—so as to affirm that Charter obligations prevail also over United Nations Member States' customary law obligations.[90]

The footnote accompanying the above quotation cites only the *obiter* of Judge ad hoc Elihu Lauterpacht in support of its contention, although that *obiter* does not actually go as far as the above conclusion of the Study Group.[91] In its subsequent report dated 18 July 2006, the Study Group states under the heading 'The scope of Article 103 of the Charter' that: 'Given the character of some Charter provisions, the constitutional character of the Charter and the established practice of States and United nations organs, Charter obligations may also prevail over inconsistent

operates as a concept superior to both customary international law and treaty. The relief which Article 103 of the Charter may give the Security Council in case of conflict between one of its decisions and an operative treaty obligation cannot—as a matter of simple hierarchy of norms—extend to a conflict between a Security Council resolution and *jus cogens*. Indeed, one only has to state the opposite proposition thus—that a Security Council resolution may even require participation in genocide—for its unacceptability to be apparent.'

[90] Koskenniemi, 'Fragmentation of International Law' §345.

[91] Strangely, while that footnote refers to Judge Lauterpacht's Sep Op, ICJ Rep 325, 440, it erroneously refers to §110 instead of §100 on that page. §110 appears on p 443 of that Sep Op and is irrelevant to the issue in question. §110 must be seen in its proper context. After referring, in §109 of his Sep Op, to the view that the Genocide Convention 'does no more than establishing for the Contracting States duties that are to be implemented by legislative action within their domestic legal spheres', Judge ad hoc Lauterpacht continues: '110. Any such narrow view must, however, be rejected. The statement in Article I that the Contracting Parties "undertake to prevent and to punish genocide" is comprehensive and unqualified. The undertaking establishes two distinct duties: the duty "to prevent" and the duty "to punish". Thus, a breach of duty can arise solely from failure to prevent or solely from failure to punish, and does not depend on there being a failure both to prevent and to punish. The confirmation in the same Article that genocide "is a crime under international law" does not change the position or restrict the application of the concept of genocide exclusively to individual criminality. The purpose of this latter provision is to permit parties, within the domestic legislation that they adopt, to assume universal jurisdiction over the crime of genocide—that is to say, even when the acts have been committed outside their respective territories by persons who are not their nationals.'

customary international law.'[92] No authority is cited to substantiate this statement, though. This latter statement is unchanged in the final version of the Report by the Study Group which was taken note of by the International Law Commission (ILC) which commended the conclusions therein to the attention of the UN General Assembly.[93] As already pointed out, the said *obiter* of Judge ad hoc Lauterpacht focuses on conflict between Article 103 of the UN Charter and *jus cogens* norms, not general international law, and this fact is actually and correctly recognized in the Report of the ILC's Study Group on Fragmentation of International Law dated 13 April 2006 when it deals with the relationship between Article 103 of the Charter and *jus cogens*.[94]

In an authoritative commentary on the UN Charter, while recognizing that the wording and the drafting history of Article 103 suggest that it only applies to treaties and other agreements, not to customary international law, 'the prevailing view supports a broad interpretation of Article 103 covering other sources, such as customary international law, as well'.[95] It cites the aforesaid *obiter* of Judge ad hoc Lauterpacht and the ILC's Study Group's Report and an opinion of one jurist.[96] The view is, in fact, not so 'prevailing' in the light of the contrary opinions also cited by the commentary that outnumber the 'prevailing view'.[97] The commentary then proceeds to assert: 'This understanding is in particular supported by those authors who consider the Charter as the "constitution of the international community" ... It can be justified by an extension of Art 103 *per analogiam* and by the universal acceptance of the prevalence of the Charter.'[98]

[92] UN Doc A/CN.4/L.702 (18 July 2006) §35. The report concludes that when a rule is in conflict with Art 103 of the UN Charter such rule becomes 'inapplicable as a result of such conflict and to the extent of such conflict' (ibid §41(*b*)).

[93] ILC, 'Report of the International Law Commission on the work of its 58th Session' (1 May–9 June and 3 July–11 Aug 2006) UN Doc A/61/10, 182–83 [35].

[94] Koskenniemi, 'Fragmentation of International Law' §§359–60, quoting the *obiter* of Judge Lauterpacht but, once again, erroneously referring to §110 (instead of the correct §100) of his Sep Op on p 440.

[95] Paulus and Leiß, 'Article 103', in Bruno Simma, Daniel-Erasmus Khan, Georg Nolte, and Andreas Paulus (eds), *The Charter of the United Nations* vol 2 (3rd edn, OUP 2012), 2110, 2132–33.

[96] Karl Zemanek, 'The Legal Foundation of the International System—General Course on Public International Law' (1997) 266 Recueil des Cours de l'Académie de Droit International 9, 232. The commentary also follows the ILC Study Group's erroneous reference to §110 instead of §100 on page 440 of Judge Lauterpacht's Sep Op, showing that the commentary merely copies verbatim the conclusion of the Study Group on this point. With respect to the arguments by two of the parties to the two cases before the Court of First Instance of the European Communities cited by the commentary, the Court did not specifically take a view on the matter of the prevalence of Art 103 of the Charter over customary international law, merely remarking that the UN Charter obligations binding upon UN Member States 'clearly prevail over every other obligation of domestic law and of international treaty law' (Case T-306/01 *Yusuf and Ali Barkaat Int'l Foundation v Council and Commission* [2005] ECR II-3533 §207; Case T-315/01 *Kadi v Council and Commission* [2005] ECR II-3649 §156).

[97] Paulus and Leiß, 'Article 103' 2133 [n 152].

[98] ibid 2133. The commentary cites two writings on the UN Charter as the 'constitution of the international community'; namely, Bardo Fassbender, 'The United Nations Charter as the Constitution of the International Community' (1998) 36 Colum J of Transnat'l L 529, 586; and R Bernhardt, 'Art 103', in Bruno Simma, Hermann Mosler, Albrecht Randelzhofer, Christian Tomuschat, Rüdiger Wolfrum, Andreas Paulus, and Eleni Chaitobu (eds), *The Charter of the United Nations* (2nd edn, OUP 2002) marginal no 21. It does not cite any source in support of the *per analogiam* extension of Art 103, though.

It is hereby submitted that the above conclusion that Article 103 of the UN Charter prevails over general customary international law is not substantiated by any judicial decision, State practice, or writings of publicists in general.[99]

As can be seen from Chapter 6 of this book, China and Russia, two of the five permanent members of the UN Security Council with the veto power, are firmly of the view that the 'trioka' of Heads of State, Heads of Government, and Ministers of Foreign Affairs have absolute immunity *ratione personae*. Arguably, therefore, it would be unlikely for these two permanent members of the UN Security Council to have adopted a Security Council resolution with intent to negate the personal immunity under customary international law of Sudan's President Al Bashir in disregard of Article 98 of the ICC Statute.

On the other hand, it could also be argued that, by urging 'all States and concerned regional and other international organizations to cooperate fully' with the ICC on the UN Security Council's referral of the situation in Darfur, Sudan, to the ICC,[100] the Council implicitly waived any immunity of the persons subjected to prosecution before the ICC.[101] That resolution was adopted with eleven votes in favour and four abstentions (Algeria, Brazil, China, and USA). Explaining its position regarding the resolution, China, one of the four abstaining States, would have preferred that the perpetrators stand trial in Sudanese courts and China did not favour the referral to the ICC without the consent of the Sudanese Government. Besides, China, a non-State Party to the ICC Statute, had major reservations regarding some of the provisions under the ICC Statute. The USA abstained because, as a non-State Party to the ICC Statute, it opposed the ICC's exercise of jurisdiction over nationals of non-States Parties. For Algeria, the AU was the best organization to bring peace and justice to Sudan. Brazil abstained because it was against the operative paragraph inserted at the instigation of the USA to exempt UN peacekeeping force members who are nationals of non-States Parties to the ICC Statute from the ICC's jurisdiction. Japan (then a non-State Party to the Statute), UK, Benin, Argentina, Greece, Denmark, Romania, and France cited accountability and the lack of impunity of those responsible for the atrocities in Darfur as their respective reasons for

[99] See further Asad G Kiyani, 'Al-Bashir & the ICC: The Problems of Head of State Immunity' (2013) 12 Chinese JIL 467.

[100] Operative §2 of UN Security Council Resolution 1533 (2005) '*Decides* that the Government of Sudan and all other parties to the conflict in Darfur shall cooperate fully with and provide any necessary assistance to the [ICC] and the Prosecutor pursuant to this resolution and, while recognizing that States not party to the Rome Statute have no obligation under the Statute, urges all States and concerned regional and other international organizations to cooperate fully.'

[101] Cf Claus Kreß and Kimberly Prost, 'Article 98 Cooperation with respect to waiver of immunity and consent to surrender' in Triffterer, *Commentary on the Rome Statute of the ICC* 1601, 1613, where the authors concede that customary international law 'has not yet taken a consolidated move' in the direction of denying immunity *ratione personae* before the ICC. However, the authors find the legal situation 'less problematic where the international proceedings against such a person [entitled to immunity *ratione personae*] have been triggered by a Security Council referral decided upon under Chapter VII of the UN Charter' because the Security Council 'may wish to decide explicitly or by implication that even immunities *ratione personae* do not constitute a bar to the cooperation of States in the execution of request made by the [ICC] for arrests and surrender'.

supporting the resolution. The Philippines and Tanzania emphasized the need to bring justice to the people of Sudan, particularly Darfur.

The word 'immunity' was only mentioned once in the explanation of the votes—by France and with reference to the operative paragraph on the 'exemption' opposed by Brazil. Interestingly, Russia, asserting that there be no impunity in the situation in Darfur, added that '[a]ll those responsible for grave crimes must be punished'. Must 'all' include the incumbent President of the Sudan, who must be brought to justice before the ICC without the shield of immunity *ratione personae*? As recently as November 2016, the Russian position in the Sixth Committee of the UN General Assembly, commenting on the ILC Special Rapporteur's proposal on exceptions to immunity of the troika, is that:

> [The Russian] delegation could not support such an approach. First, it did not agree that the proposed draft article on exceptions to immunity (draft article 7) reflected an established norm of customary international law. The Special Rapporteur had been unable to demonstrate convincingly the existence of such a norm, and the examples of practice presented in her report did not even demonstrate that such a norm was emerging. Furthermore, the proposed draft article could not be seen as progressive development when its provisions eroded one of the basic norms of international law and could give rise to new sources of tension in intergovernmental relations because of the inevitable increase in the number of attempts to prosecute officials of one State in another State.
>
> The question of violations of the immunity of the State and of State officials had been discussed many times in recent years by international courts, demonstrating the sensitivity of the issue. While ending impunity for serious international crimes was certainly an admirable goal, attempts to manipulate the norms of international law that underpinned contemporary international relations must be avoided. Immunity did not preclude responsibility and did not equate to impunity. State officials could be prosecuted for the most serious international crimes before international courts and tribunals; they could also be tried by the court of a foreign State if their own State decided to waive immunity, and of course there were no restrictions on the prosecution of officials in their own State. Thus, given that conventional means existed for holding accountable officials who committed serious crimes, the introduction of exceptions to immunity from foreign criminal jurisdiction would serve only as an additional means for some States to exert political pressure on others, using the need to avoid impunity as justification. In fact, there was no reason to believe that impunity would be reduced as a result, perhaps in part because there was a general lack of momentum among States to limit the immunity both of foreign officials and of their own officials.[102]

Similarly, Romania, at that same meeting, cautioned that 'more consideration should be given to identifying the emergence of international custom with regard to limitations and exceptions to immunity from the exercise of jurisdiction by other States, since the conclusion of the Special Rapporteur in that regard was not supported by sufficient State practice and *opinio juris*'.[103]

Of the States adopting the Security Council resolution referring the situation in Darfur to the ICC, Argentina has been the most unequivocal in asserting that

[102] *per* Ms Melikbekyan (Russia) UN Doc A/C.6/71/SR.28 (1 Nov 2016) §§11–12.
[103] ibid §21, *per* Mr Racovită (Romania).

commission of atrocity crimes 'might not be considered to be [an act] protected by immunity, whether *ratione personae* or *ratione materiae*'.[104]

In sum, the drafting history of this resolution leaves much room for interpretation regarding the 'implicit waiver of the immunity' of President Al Bashir by the UN Security Council.

Even if President Al Bashir, as an incumbent Head of State, does not have immunity *ratione personae*, it has been argued that he could still have immunity from arrest when attending UN meetings.[105] The basis for this is Article 105(2) of the UN Charter, stipulating that 'Representatives of the Members of the United Nations and officials of the Organization shall similarly enjoy such privileges and immunities as are necessary for the independent exercise of their functions in connexion with the Organization.' In addition, Articles 11–13 of the Headquarters Agreement between the USA and the UN[106] require the USA as the host State of the UN to not impose any impediments to representatives of UN Member States for the purpose of transit to or from the headquarters district on official business. This is irrespective of the relations existing between the US Government and the Governments of the persons in question. When visas are required for such persons, they shall be granted without charge and as promptly as possible.

President Al Bashir has also been charged with genocide. Article VI of the Genocide Convention, to which Sudan is party, provides that 'Persons charged with genocide or any of the other acts enumerated in Article III shall be tried by a competent tribunal of the State in the territory of which the act was committed, or by such international penal tribunal as may have jurisdiction with respect to those Contracting Parties which shall have accepted its jurisdiction.'

The ICJ has stated, *obiter*, in the *Bosnian Genocide Convention* case, that an 'international penal tribunal' within the meaning of Article VI must at least cover all international criminal courts created after the adoption of the Convention (at which date no such court existed) of potentially universal scope, and competent to try the perpetrators of genocide or any of the other acts enumerated in Article III. The nature of the legal instrument by which such a court is established is without importance in this respect. On the question whether Serbia and Montenegro was to be regarded as having 'accepted the jurisdiction' of the ICTY within the meaning of Article VI, the ICJ reformulated the question as follows: was Serbia and Montenegro obliged to accept the ICTY's jurisdiction, and to cooperate with it by virtue of the Security Council resolution which established the ICTY, or of some other rule of international law? If so, it would have to be concluded that, for Serbia and Montenegro, cooperation with the ICTY constituted both an obligation stemming from the resolution concerned and from the UN Charter, or from another norm of international law obliging Serbia and Montenegro to cooperate, and an obligation

104 UN Doc A/C.6/71/SR.29 (2 Nov 2016) §88, *per* Mr Fernández Valoni (Argentina).

105 Dapo Akande, 'The Legal Nature of Security Council's Referral s to the ICC and Its Impact on Al Bashir's Immunities' (2009) 7 J Int'l Crim Justice 333, 351–52.

106 (1948) 42 AJIL 445.

arising from its status as a party to the Genocide Convention, this last being the only one of direct relevance in the case at bar.[107]

Notwithstanding the requirement mentioned by the ICJ that the State concerned must have accepted the jurisdiction of the 'international penal tribunal' in question, it is arguable a teleological interpretation of the Genocide Convention would permit the use of that Convention as a basis for creating an obligation of cooperation for non-States Parties to the ICC Statute since they must be deemed to have accepted the jurisdiction of the ICC over the case, provided that there is a binding Security Council resolution conferring such jurisdiction. The argument would rely on the Genocide Convention as a basis for cooperation allowing ICC States Parties as well as non-States Parties to bypass immunities otherwise provided for in international law.[108] This line of contention is only valid if a UN Security Council resolution referring a situation to the ICC has the effect of depriving in the territory of a State which is *not party* to the ICC Statute any immunity of the persons sought by the ICC, be they incumbent Heads of State, Heads of Government, or Foreign Ministers. If the territorial State where, say, the incumbent Sudanese President is physically present is party to both the ICC Statute and the Genocide Convention, that State shall arrest and surrender him to the ICC pursuant to its obligations under both international instruments and owing to the fact that Sudan is also party to the Genocide Convention.[109] Otherwise, a possible avenue to deprive the persons entitled to immunity *ratione personae* derives from the prohibition of genocide as a norm of *jus cogens*. A crucial question is whether violation of a *jus cogens* norm has a consequence under customary international law of removing the immunity *ratione personae*. The Study Group of the ILC on Fragmentation of International Law argues that it does, citing the judgment of the UK House of Lords in *Pinochet (No 3)*,[110] where, according to the Study Group, the House of Lords 'denied immunity to a former head of State on the grounds that there cannot be any immunity against prosecution for

[107] *Application of the Convention on the Prevention and Punishment of the Crime of Genocide (Bosnia and Herzegovina v Serbia and Montenegro)* [2007] ICJ Rep 43, 227–28.

[108] Matthew Gillett, 'The Call of Justice: Obligations under the Genocide Convention to Cooperate with the International Criminal Court' (2012) 23 Crim L Forum 63, 68–96; Dapo Akande, 'The Impact of the Genocide Convention on the Obligation to Implement ICC Arrest Warrants' in Richard H Steinberg (ed), *Contemporary Issues Facing the International Criminal Court* (Brill Nijhoff 2016) 77–83. Goran Sluiter ('Using the Genocide Convention to Strengthen Cooperation with the ICC in the Al Bashir Case' (2010) 8 J Int'l Crim Justice 365) argues that the ICC is a competent international court envisaged by Art VI of the Genocide Convention. *Contra*: Paola Gaeta, 'Head of State Immunity as a Bar to Arrest' in Steinberg (ed), *Contemporary Issues Facing the International Criminal Court*, 84–111, and William Schabas, 'State Obligation in Implementing Arrest Warrants' (ibid 112ff). Gaeta points out that the preparatory work of the Genocide Convention (E/AC.25/SR.9 at 7) clearly indicated that it did not intend to impair the system of diplomatic immunity (which is a particular category of personal immunity). A fortiori, she argues, the same must be true for Heads of State, Heads of Governments, and Foreign Ministers who enjoy personal immunities under international law.

[109] Dapo Akande, 'Would the Addition of a Genocide Charge to the Bashir Arrest Warrant Change the Position on Immunity?' *EJIL Talk!* (24 Mar 2009 <https://www.ejiltalk.org/would-the-addition-of-a-genocide-charge-to-the-bashir-arrest-warrant-change-the-position-on-immunity/> accessed 15 August 2017).

[110] Koskenniemi, 'Fragmentation of International Law' §§370–71, citing *Regina v Bow Street Metropolitan Stipendiary Magistrate, ex parte Pinochet Ugarte (No 3)* 119 ILR 136.

breach of *jus cogens*'. On close scrutiny, however, there are nuances in the reasoning of the seven Law Lords in that case.

The main issue in *Pinochet (No 3)* was whether former President Pinochet of Chile could be extradited to Spain to stand trial for his alleged crimes, including torture, committed while he was in office. This involved the interpretation of the (now repealed) UK Extradition Act of 1989, which required, *inter alia*, that the conduct for which he was being sought for prosecution was also a crime under UK law at the time when the alleged offence was committed (ie the 'double criminality' requirement for extradition). A majority of five Law Lords held that English courts had no jurisdiction over torture offences committed by foreigners abroad until section 134 of the Criminal Justice Act 1988, which implemented the 1984 Torture Convention, came into effect on 29 September 1988; and that, accordingly, all the alleged offences of torture and conspiracy to torture were crimes for which Pinochet could not be extradited. By a majority of six to one, Lord Goff dissenting, it was held that a former Head of State had immunity from the criminal jurisdiction of the UK for acts done in his official capacity as head of State pursuant to section 20 of the State Immunity Act 1978 read in conjunction with Article 39(2) of Schedule 1 to the Diplomatic Privileges Act 1964; but that torture was an international crime against humanity in violation of *jus cogens* and after the entry into force of the 1984 Torture Convention, State Parties, including the UK, could not have intended that an immunity for former heads of State for acts of torture would survive their ratification of the Convention.[111] Only Lord Millett and Lord Phillips went as far as opining that the systematic torture was an international crime for which there could be no immunity even before the Genocide Convention entered into force; hence, no immunity under customary international law for Pinochet's torture-related offences.[112] The ILC's Study Group on Fragmentation of International Law opts to quote the following statement of Lord Millet, who was in the minority, in support of its conclusion that there is no immunity *ratione personae* for breach of *jus cogens*: 'International law cannot be supposed to have established a crime having the character of a *jus cogens* and at the same time to have provided an immunity which is co-extensive with the obligation it seeks to impose.'[113] The ILC Study Group concedes, however, that *jus cogens* does not necessarily 'provide automatic access to justice irrespective of procedural obstacles for punishing individuals or, for example, concerning relief in civil matters'.[114] It cites one case: *Al-Adsani* where the European Court of Human Rights held that international law as it then stood provided no basis for concluding that a State no longer enjoyed immunity from civil suits in the courts of another State where acts of torture, the prohibition of which had achieved the status of *jus cogens*, were alleged.[115]

[111] This is also the interpretation of the *ratio decidendi* of *Pinochet (No 3)* by the House of Lords in *Jones v Kingdom of Saudi Arabia* [2006] UKHL 26, *per* Lord Bingham of Cornhill (§19) and Lord Hoffmann (§§86–94), with whom the other three Law Lords concurred.

[112] For a detailed analysis of this judgment, see Andrea Bianchi, 'Immunity versus Human Rights: The Pinochet Case' (1999) 10 EJIL 237.

[113] 119 ILR 136, 153, quoted in Koskenniemi, 'Fragmentation of International Law' §370.

[114] Koskenniemi, ibid §§372–73.

[115] *Al-Adsani v the United Kingdom* [GC] no 35763/97, §§101–02, ECHR 2001-XI.

In 2016, the ILC Special Rapporteur on the topic 'Immunity of State officials from foreign criminal jurisdiction' proposed 'Draft Article 7 Crimes in respect of which immunity does not apply', paragraph 1(a) of which provides that immunity shall not apply in relation to genocide, crimes against humanity, war crimes, torture, and enforced disappearances. The official position of the UK, as stated in the Sixth Committee on 1 November 2016, is:

With regard to draft article 7, paragraph 1, [the UK delegation] recalled that a violation of a *jus cogens* norm pertaining to a criminal offence did not necessarily constitute an exception to immunity. As a matter of treaty law, States parties to the Convention against Torture and Other Cruel, Inhuman or Degrading Treatment or Punishment had implicitly waived the immunity of their officials in relation to torture, since that offence, as defined in the Convention, could only be committed by those acting on behalf of the State, and each State party had an express duty to establish jurisdiction over such offences whenever a suspect was present on its territory and not extradited. However, [the UK] delegation considered that an equivalent exception to immunity did not exist in respect of the other offences enumerated in draft article 7, paragraph 1(a), and would not be appropriate even as progressive development.[116]

Even the Netherlands, a staunch proponent of the obligation to extradite or prosecute as a rule of customary international law, adopts a nuanced position in relation to immunity. The Netherlands believed that the need to fight impunity, while important, did not justify an exception to the principle of immunity. The question of whether a State official enjoyed immunity from foreign domestic jurisdiction was one of forum and procedure. Many factors determined whether immunity would be granted before a domestic court, but the risk of impunity was not among them. Under normal circumstances, ample remedies would be available in the State for which the official performed his or her duties. Moreover, a decision to grant immunity expressly did not contain a pronouncement on whether the State official was guilty; it was merely a question of whether that particular forum was available. The Netherlands welcomed the trend in international criminal courts towards the prosecution of persons suspected of international crimes, and the non-availability of the plea of immunity. There was, however, an important difference between the jurisdiction of international courts and that of national courts. The former, including hybrid courts, derived their jurisdiction from the consent of the participating States. The exercise of such jurisdiction therefore did not infringe the sovereign equality of States or the principle that one sovereign power could not exercise jurisdiction over another (*par in parem non habet imperium*). The same could not be said of national courts: consent to jurisdiction of an international court or tribunal could not be taken to imply consent to the jurisdiction of a foreign domestic court. The Netherlands disagreed with the ILC Special Rapporteur's distinction between the immunity of State officials and the immunity of the State itself in relation to international crimes and *jus cogens*. In the Netherlands' opinion, the former was directly derived from the latter, and the two should be approached in the same way. The plea

[116] UN Doc A/C.6/71/SR.28 (1 Nov 2016) §29, *per* Mr Stephen.

of immunity *ratione materiae* was unavailable for international crimes, including violations of *jus cogens*, as such crimes could not be official acts. For State officials who enjoyed immunity *ratione personae*, on the other hand, the plea of immunity was available regardless of the accusation.[117]

Draft Article 7 was also opposed by Germany.[118] For the USA, '[i]t would be helpful to have a better idea of the conceptual basis for making immunity unavailable for certain crimes so as to be able to assess whether such exceptions were grounded in existing law.'[119] In Japan's opinion, the Special Rapporteur 'did not provide sufficient evidence that the three identified categories of exceptions to such immunity were already established'.[120] Greece agreed with the Special Rapporteur that 'it was not possible to identify a customary rule allowing for exceptions or limitations to immunity *ratione personae*, or even to identify a trend in favour of such a rule', although the developments in the previous twenty-five years 'constituted an ongoing paradigm shift concerning the issue of exceptions to immunity *ratione materiae* of State officials from foreign criminal jurisdiction in respect of such crimes as genocide, war crimes, crimes against humanity and torture'.[121] Only Slovenia went as far as to state broadly that exceptions to immunity could be established through the conclusion of an international treaty or inferred from a Security Council decision.[122]

The judgment of the Supreme Court of Appeal of South Africa on 15 March 2016 in *Minister of Justice and Constitutional Development v Southern African Litigation Centre*[123] analysed the relationship between Article 27 and Article 98 of the ICC Statute in relation to the immunity of visiting President Al Bashir of Sudan. It found 'a measure of consensus' that Article 98 of the Statute deals with requests for surrender or assistance in relation to nationals, including Heads of State, of non-States Parties to the ICC Statute such as Sudan. The Court continued:

> Beyond that there appear to be two views. The one, espoused by the AU,[124] is that it operates to protect Party States from the obligation to cooperate with requests from the ICC for arrest and surrender or assistance where that would involve their breaching their obligations to respect personal inviolability under customary international law towards non-Party States.[125] In other words it provides the justification for African States to refuse to arrest and surrender President Al Bashir, because he is entitled as the head of state of Sudan to immunity *ratione personae*.[126] The other view is that, as non-Party States and their nationals are ordinarily brought within the jurisdiction of the ICC by way of a Security Council reference under Article 13*(b)*, Article 27 is thereby made applicable to the non-Party State and therefore it

[117] UN Doc A/CN.6/71/SR.29 (2 Nov 2016) §§5–7, *per* Ms Lijnzaad.
[118] ibid §§12–15, *per* Ms Puerschel. [119] ibid §71, per Mr Townley.
[120] ibid §90, *per* Mr Hirotani. [121] ibid §§20, 22, *per* Ms Telalian.
[122] ibid §56, *per* Ms Horvat. [123] [2016] 2 All SA 365 (SCA).
[124] Citing Dapo Akande, 'The Effect of Security Council Resolutions and Domestic Proceedings on State Obligations to Cooperate with the ICC' (2012) 10 J Int'l Crim Justice 299, 301; ICC's *Decision Pursuant to Article 87(7) of the Rome Statute on the Failure by the Republic of Malawi to Comply with the Cooperation Requests issued by the Court with Respect to the Arrest and Surrender of Omar Hassan Ahmad Al Bashir* ICC-02/05-01/09 of 12 Dec 2011 (*Malawi*) §15.
[125] Citing Gaeta, 'Does President Al Bashir Enjoy Immunity from Arrest?' 327–29.
[126] Citing Blommestijn and Ryngaert, 'Exploring the Obligations for States to Act upon the ICC's Arrest Warrant for Omar Al-Bashir' 438–40.

is not open to it to rely on Article 98.[127] It is well-recognized that there is a tension between Articles 27 and 98 that has not as yet been authoritatively resolved.[128]

The South African Supreme Court of Appeal alluded to the ICC's decision in the *Democratic Republic of Congo* case concerning President Al Bashir[129] to the effect that, while the ICC itself recognized the customary international rule as propounded by the ICJ in *Arrest Warrant* of the immunity *ratione personae* of sitting Heads of State such as President Al Bashir, the ICC had concluded that President Al Bashir's immunity was removed by the UN Security Council's Resolution 1593 (2005). The Resolution decides that the Government of Sudan 'shall cooperate fully with and provide necessary assistance to the [ICC] and the Prosecutor pursuant to this resolution', thereby eliminating any impediment to the proceedings before the ICC, as this is also an implicit waiver by the UN Security Council of Al Bashir's immunities. The ICC had reiterated this justification in relation to President Al Bashir's visit to South Africa.[130] The Supreme Court of Appeal of South Africa concluded, however, that customary international law recognizes the personal immunity of Heads of State and other officials entitled to such personal immunity from arrest and prosecution or any inviolability while visiting a foreign State, and that customary international law as it currently stands does not recognize any exception to this immunity even in cases of acts of violation of *jus cogens* norms.[131] Section 4(1) of South Africa's Diplomatic Immunities and Privileges Act 37 of 2001 embodies this rule[132] and would apply to accord visiting Sudanese President Al Bashir immunity from arrest. That Act is, however, subject to the Implementation of the Rome Statute of the International Criminal Court Act 27 of 2002, enacted to implement South Africa's obligations under the ICC Statute. The latter Act removes a bar, including immunity, to the prosecution of international crimes in South Africa or to South Africa cooperating with the ICC by way of the arrest and surrender of persons charged with such crimes before the ICC, where an arrest warrant had been issued and a request for cooperation made.[133] The Court, therefore, held that the conduct of the Government of South Africa in failing to take steps to arrest and detain Sudan's President Al Bashir for surrender to the ICC, after his arrival in South Africa on 13 June 2015 to attend the 25th Assembly of the African Union, was

[127] Citing Dabo Akande, 'The Legal Nature of Security Council Referrals to the ICC and its Impact on Al Bashir's Immunities' (2009) 7 J Int'l Crim Justice 333, 342.

[128] *Minister of Justice and Constitutional Development v Southern African Litigation Centre* [2016] 2 All SA 365 (SCA). §60 of the majority opinion written by Wallis JA and concurred with by Shongwe JA and Majiedt JA.

[129] *Decision on the Cooperation of the Democratic Republic of the Congo Regarding Omar Al Bashir's Arrest and Surrender to the Court* ICC-02/05-01/09 9 April 2014 (*DRC*) §§25, 29.

[130] *Decision following the Prosecutor's request for an order further clarifying that the Republic of South Africa is under the obligation to immediately arrest and surrender Omar Al Bashir* ICC-02/05-01/09 13 June 2015 §9.

[131] §84 of the majority opinion.

[132] '(1) A head of state is immune from the criminal and civil jurisdiction of the Courts of the Republic, and enjoys such privileges as—*(a)* heads of state enjoy in accordance with the rules of customary international law . . .'

[133] §103 of the majority opinion.

inconsistent with South Africa's obligations in terms of the ICC Statute and section 10 of the Implementation Act, and was unlawful.[134]

In effect, what the South African Supreme Court of Appeal meant was that it had to implement South Africa's domestic law which, in the Court's opinion, was contrary to customary international law of personal immunity of the Head of State, and that South Africa had to bear State responsibility under international law for the breach of the said rule of customary international law.

On 6 July 2017, Pre-Trial Chamber II of the ICC issued its Decision under Article 87(7) of the ICC Statute on the non-compliance by South Africa with respect to the ICC's request for the arrest and surrender of Sudanese President Al Bashir.[135] The first substantive question for the Pre-Trial Chamber was whether South Africa was entitled not to comply with the request for arrest and surrender contrary to the provisions of the ICC Statute.

The Pre-Trial Chamber finds, by majority, that because the rights and obligations as provided for in the Statute, including Article 27(2), are applicable to Sudan (by imposition of the UN Security Council acting under Chapter VII of the UN Charter), the immunities of Al Bashir as Head of State do not bar States Parties to the Rome Statute from executing the ICC's request of his arrest and surrender for crimes under the ICC's jurisdiction allegedly committed in Darfur within the parameters of the Security Council referral. Article 98(1) of the Statute is held inapplicable to Al Bashir's situation, and States Parties to the Rome Statute are under the duty to execute the warrants of arrest issued by the ICC, and to implement the ICC's request for the arrest of Al Bashir and his surrender to the ICC. Besides, irrespective of whether South Africa considered itself obliged to respect his Head of State immunity under customary international law, it nevertheless had the duty under the ICC Statute to arrest him and surrender him to the ICC, as Article 98 of the Statute—even if applicable to the present situation—does not foresee the possibility for a requested State Party unilaterally to refuse compliance with an ICC's request for arrest and surrender.[136] As already explained, this reasoning has been disputed, especially by the AU, among others.

The Pre-Trial Chamber also touched, *obiter*, on the relevance of the Genocide Convention to which both South Africa and Sudan are party. The majority could not answer in the affirmative the question whether that Convention renders inapplicable, between South Africa and Sudan and with respect to implementation of the warrant for arrest for the alleged crime of genocide, Al Bashir's Head of State immunity. According to the majority, the Genocide Convention, unlike the ICC

[134] §113 of the majority opinion. The majority declined to express a view on the argument that the UN Security Council Resolution at issue implicitly waived Al Bashir's immunity and the argument that the second arrest warrant which included the charges of genocide overrode the immunity. For the majority, the first argument was 'hotly contested by the commentators', while 'the limited argument' they received on the Genocide Convention did not give them confidence that they should express a view on it (§106 of the majority opinion).

[135] ICC-02/05-01/09 §138.

[136] ibid §§107–08. Judge Brichambaut, dissenting, found the current state of the law to be unclear whether the UN Security Council resolution in question removes Al Bashir's immunities.

Statute in Article 27(2), does not mention immunities based on official capacity, and there is no convincing basis for a constructive interpretation of the provisions in the Convention such that would give rise to an implicit exclusion of immunities. Article IV of the Convention speaks of individual criminal responsibility of 'persons committing genocide'—which, as the ICJ has explained in *Arrest Warrant*, must not be confused with immunity from criminal jurisdiction—and can be effective even without reading into it an implicit exclusion of immunities based on official capacity. Article VI of the Convention is concerned with the allocation of competence among the national and international jurisdictions in trying 'persons charged with genocide' and does not bear upon immunities.[137]

Be that as it may, could it be argued that violation of *jus cogens* norms, such as the prohibition of genocide or torture, entails *non-recognition* of immunity as a procedural bar to prosecution of the perpetrators of crimes proscribed by *jus cogens*? For example, the ICJ in its Advisory Opinion in the *Wall* case, after finding Israel's violation of the right of the Palestinian people to self-determination as violation of an obligation *erga omnes*, opines:

> Given the character and the importance of the rights and obligations involved, the Court is of the view that all States are under an obligation not to recognize the illegal situation resulting from the construction of the wall in the Occupied Palestinian Territory, including in and around East Jerusalem. They are also under an obligation not to render aid or assistance in maintaining the situation created by such construction. It is also for all States, while respecting the United Nations Charter and international law, to see to it that any impediment, resulting from the construction of the wall, to the exercise by the Palestinian people of its right to self-determination is brought to an end.[138]

There is a view that the right to self-determination is a *jus cogens* norm.[139] This is especially so since 'respect for the principle of equal rights and self-determination of peoples' is enshrined in Article 1 under Chapter I (Purposes and Principles of the United Nations) of the UN Charter. If this is the case, can the cited reasoning by the ICJ in the *Wall* case apply *mutatis mutandis* to violation of the prohibition of genocide or torture and other *jus cogens* norms? As the High Court of Kenya has held in *Kenya Section of the International Commission of Jurists v Attorney General*, 'the duty to prosecute international crimes has developed into *jus cogens* and customary international law',[140] while the South African Constitutional Court has noted that that a 'State's duty to prevent impunity . . . is particularly pronounced with respect to those

[137] ibid §109. Judge Brichambaut, dissenting, concluded that the combined effect of a literal and contextual interpretation of Article IV of the Genocide Convention, in conjunction with an assessment of its object and purpose, means that Al Bashir does not enjoy personal immunity, having been 'charged' with genocide within the meaning of Article VI of the Genocide Convention.

[138] *Legal Consequences of the Construction of a Wall in the Occupied Palestinian Territory* [2004] ICJ Rep 136, 200 [159] (and cf 199 [155]).

[139] Sep Op of Vice-President Ammoun, *Legal Consequences for States of the Continued Presence of South Africa in Namibia (South West Africa) Notwithstanding Security Council Resolution 276 (1970)* [1971] ICJ Rep 16, 89ff.

[140] *Kenya Section of the International Commission of Jurists v Attorney General & Another*, Judgment of 28 Nov 2011 of the High Court of Kenya [2011] E-Kenyan Law Reports 14.

norms, such as the prohibition on torture, that are widely considered peremptory and therefore non-derogable'.[141]

Nevertheless, the ICJ has held in *Jurisdictional Immunities of the State (Germany v Italy: Greece Intervening)* that there is no conflict between a rule, or rules, of *jus cogens* and the rule of customary international law of State immunity because they address different matters. The rules of State immunity are procedural in character and are confined to determining whether or not the courts of one State may exercise jurisdiction in respect of another State; they do not bear upon the question whether or not the conduct in respect of which the proceedings are brought was lawful or unlawful.[142] Therefore,

> recognizing the immunity of a foreign State in accordance with customary international law does not amount to recognizing as lawful a situation created by the breach of a *jus cogens* rule, or rendering aid and assistance in maintaining that situation, and so cannot contravene the principle in Article 41 of the International Law Commission's Articles on State Responsibility.[143]

The ICJ continues:

> 95. To the extent that it is argued that no rule which is not of the status of *jus cogens* may be applied if to do so would hinder the enforcement of a *jus cogens* rule, even in the absence of a direct conflict, the Court sees no basis for such a proposition. A *jus cogens* rule is one from which no derogation is permitted but the rules which determine the scope and extent of jurisdiction and when that jurisdiction may be exercised do not derogate from those substantive rules which possess *jus cogens* status, nor is there anything inherent in the concept of *jus cogens* which would require their modification or would displace their application. The Court has taken that approach in two cases, notwithstanding that the effect was that a means by which a *jus cogens* rule might be enforced was rendered unavailable. In *Armed Activities*, it held that the fact that a rule has the status of *jus cogens* does not confer upon the Court a jurisdiction which it would not otherwise possess (*Armed Activities on the Territory of the Congo (New Application 2002) (Democratic Republic of the Congo* v *Rwanda), Jurisdiction and Admissibility, Judgment, I.C.J. Reports 2006*, p. 32, §64, and p. 52, §125). In *Arrest Warrant*, the Court held, albeit without express reference to the concept of *jus cogens*, that the fact that a Minister for Foreign Affairs was accused of criminal violations of rules which undoubtedly possess the character of *jus cogens* did

[141] *National Commissioner of the South African Police Service v the Southern African Human Rights Litigation Centre and Others*, Judgment of 30 Oct 2014 of the South African Constitutional Court, 2014 (12) BCLR 1428 (CC) §4.

[142] [2012] ICJ Rep 99, 140[93].

[143] ibid. Art 41 of the ILC's Articles on State Responsibility reads:

> *Article 41. Particular consequences of a serious breach of an obligation under this chapter*
> 1. States shall cooperate to bring to an end through lawful means any serious breach [of an obligation arising under a peremptory norm of general international law in the sense of involving a gross or systematic failure by the responsible State to fulfil the obligation].
> 2. No State shall recognize as lawful a situation created by a serious breach within the meaning of article 40, nor render aid or assistance in maintaining that situation.
> 3. This article is without prejudice to the other consequences referred to in this Part and to such further consequences that a breach to which this chapter applies may entail under international law.

not deprive the Democratic Republic of the Congo of the entitlement which it possessed as a matter of customary international law to demand immunity on his behalf (*Arrest Warrant of 11 April 2000 (Democratic Republic of the Congo* v *Belgium), Judgment, I.C.J. Reports 2002*, p. 24, §58, and p. 33, §78). The Court considers that the same reasoning is applicable to the application of the customary international law regarding the immunity of one State from proceedings in the courts of another.

96. In addition, this argument about the effect of *jus cogens* displacing the law of State immunity has been rejected by the national courts of the United Kingdom (*Jones* v *Saudi Arabia*, House of Lords, [2007] 1 *AC* 270; *ILR*, Vol. 129, p. 629), Canada (*Bouzari* v *Islamic Republic of Iran*, Court of Appeal of Ontario, *DLR*, 4th Series, Vol. 243, p. 406; *ILR*, Vol. 128, p. 586), Poland (*Natoniewski*, Supreme Court, *Polish Yearbook of International Law*, Vol. XXX, 2010, p. 299), Slovenia (case No. Up-13/99, Constitutional Court of Slovenia), New Zealand (*Fang* v *Jiang*, High Court, [2007] *NZAR*, p. 420; *ILR*, Vol. 141, p. 702) and Greece (*Margel-los*, Special Supreme Court, *ILR*, Vol. 129, p. 525), as well as by the European Court of Human Rights in *Al-Adsani* v *United Kingdom* and *Kalogeropoulou and Others* v *Greece and Germany* ... in each case after careful consideration. The Court does not consider the judgment of the French *Cour de cassation* of 9 March 2011 in *La Reunion aérienne* v *Libyan Arab Jamahiriya* (case No. 09-14743, 9 March 2011, *Bull. civ*, March 2011, No. 49, p. 49) as supporting a different conclusion. The *Cour de cassation* in that case stated only that, even if a *jus cogens* norm could constitute a legitimate restriction on State immunity, such a restriction could not be justified on the facts of that case. It follows, therefore, that the judgments of the Italian courts which are the subject of the present proceedings are the only decisions of national courts to have accepted the reasoning on which this part of Italy's second argument is based. Moreover, none of the national legislation on State immunity considered in paragraphs 70–71 ... has limited immunity in cases where violations of *jus cogens* are alleged.[144]

As immunity of State officials from foreign jurisdiction emanates from State immunity, it could be suggested that the ICJ's reasoning above applies *mutatis mutandis* to immunity of State officials.

In conclusion, even Article 103 of the UN Charter cannot override the customary international law on immunities accorded to nationals of non-States Parties to the ICC Statute who qualify for such immunities.

It may be recalled that in October 2013 the AU adopted the Decision on Africa's Relationship with the International Criminal Court[145] stating, *inter alia*, that the search for justice should not be pursued in such a way as to impede or jeopardize efforts aimed at promoting lasting peace. The indictments of and proceedings against the incumbent President and Deputy President of Kenya could allegedly undermine the sovereignty, stability, and peace of Kenya and of other AU Member States as well as reconciliation, reconstruction, and the normal functioning of constitutional institutions in Kenya through the mediation process forged by the AU in

[144] See also European Court of Human Rights' decision in *Stichting Mothers of Sbrebrenica and Others v the Netherlands* (no 65542/12) §158, relying on the ICJ judgment in *Germany v Italy* to reach the conclusion that '[i]nternational law does not support the position that a civil claim should override immunity from suit for the sole reason that it is based on an allegation of a particularly grave violation of a norm of international law, even a norm of *ius cogens*.'

[145] Ext/Assembly/AU/Dec.1 (12 Oct 2013).

the aftermath of Kenya's 2007 post-election violence. The Decision also recognized Kenya as a frontline State in the regional, continental, and global fight against terrorism, and the ICC's proceedings against President Uhuru Kenyatta and Deputy President William Samoei Ruto of Kenya would distract and prevent them from fulfilling their duties. The Declaration decided that no charges were to be commenced or continued before any international court or tribunal against any serving AU Heads of State or Government or any person acting or entitled to act in such capacity during their term of office, and that the trials of the Kenyan President and Deputy President before the ICC 'should' be suspended until they completed their terms of office.

To alleviate the AU's concerns just mentioned, a compromise, albeit a weak one, between the interest of international criminal justice and the call of public duty may be found in ICJ's Judgment in *Certain Questions of Mutual Assistance in Criminal Matters (Djibouti v France)*.[146] This compromise should be applicable to both nationals of States Parties and non-States Parties to the ICC Statute. The ICJ in *Djibouti v France* referred to its Judgment in *Arrest Warrant* upholding the enjoyment of 'full immunity from criminal jurisdiction and inviolability … against any act of authority of another State which would hinder him or her in the performance of his or her duties'. The ICJ in *Djibouti v France* then concluded that the determining factor in assessing whether or not there has been an attack on the immunity of the Head of State lies in the subjection of the latter to a constraining act of authority. In *Djibouti v France*, the ICJ found the summons not to be associated with the measures of constraint as it was in fact merely an invitation to testify which the Djibouti President could freely accept or decline. Consequently, there was no attack by France on the immunities from criminal jurisdiction enjoyed by the Head of State. A similar summons could be issued against nationals of non-States Parties to the ICC Statute who enjoy immunities under customary international law.

In addition, for high-level office holders of States Parties to the ICC Statute whose presence is necessary in their home States, a practical middle ground may be reached to balance the interest of international criminal justice with the need of national duties at home. The ICC Appeals Chamber in *Ruto* has interpreted Article 63 of the ICC Statute, entitled 'Trial in the presence of the accused', in combination with the requirement of a fair and expeditious trial with full respect for the rights of the accused and due regard for the protection of victims and witnesses under Article 64(2) thereof, so as to ensure justice in each individual case. Article 63(1) stipulating that 'The accused shall be present during trial' does not operate as an absolute bar in all circumstances to the continuation of trial proceedings in the absence of the accused who has appeared before the ICC to answer his or her charges. While recognizing the central role of the accused person in proceedings and the wider significance of the accused for the administration of justice, the Appeals Chamber rules that the Trial Chamber has discretion to allow absence of the accused, provided that (1) the absence can only take place in exceptional circumstances and must not become

[146] [2008] ICJ Rep 177, 236–38 [170–74].

the rule; (2) the possibility of alternative measures must have been considered, including changes to the trial schedule or a short adjournment of the trial; (3) any absence must be limited to that which is strictly necessary; (4) the accused must have explicitly waived his or her right to be present at trial; (5) the rights of the accused must be fully ensured in his or her absence, in particular through representation by counsel; and (6) the decision as to whether the accused may be excused from attending part of his or her trial must be taken on a case-by-case basis, with due regard to the subject matter of the specific hearings that the accused would not attend during the periods for which excusal has been requested.[147]

Rules 134*bis, ter*, and *quater* of the Rules of Procedure and Evidence were adopted by the Assembly of States Parties to the ICC Statute in 2013. Rule 134*bis* allows the accused person to submit a written request to the Trial Chamber for his or her presence in the courtroom through the use of video technology during part or parts of his or her trial, and the Trial Chamber shall rule on the request on a case-by-case basis, with due regard to the subject matter of the specific hearings in question. Rule 134*ter* permits the accused person to submit a written request to the Trial Chamber for him or her to be excused and to be represented by counsel only during part or parts of his or her trial, and the Trial Chamber shall rule on the request on a case-by-case basis, with due regard to the subject matter of the specific hearings in question, provided that any absence must be limited to what is strictly necessary and must not become the rule. While most of these new Rules may be reconciled with the ruling of the Appeals Chamber in *Ruto* just mentioned, Rule 134*quater* seems to depart from it by allowing the accused person 'who is mandated to fulfil extraordinary public duties at the highest national level' to submit a request to the Trial Chamber to be allowed to be excused and to be presented by counsel only while also specifically waiving his or her right to be present at the trial. The Trial Chamber is required to consider the said request expeditiously 'and, if alternative measures are inadequate, shall grant the request where it determines that it is in the interest of justice and provided that the rights of the accused are fully ensured'. The decision of the Trial Chamber in this matter shall be taken with due regard to the subject matter of the specific hearings in question and is subject to review at any time. The Appeals Chamber in *Ruto* held that the Trial Chamber did not properly exercise its discretion to excuse Ruto's presence based on Ruto's performance of his duties as the Deputy President of Kenya and on his signing a waiver of his right to presence during trial.[148] The Appeals Chamber then set out the aforesaid six limitations on the discretion of the Trial Chamber to excuse an accused person from presence during trial, none of which relates to the status of the accused being a person 'mandated to fulfil extraordinary public duties at the highest national level'. Furthermore, unlike Rules 134*bis* and *ter*, Rule 134*quater* does not specifically impose temporal limits on the absence

[147] *Prosecution v William Samoei Ruto and Joshua Arap Sang* (Decision on Mr Ruto's Request for Excusal from Continuous Presence at Trial) ICC-01/11 OA 5, App Cham (25 Oct 2013) esp §§49–50, 61–62.

[148] ibid §§59–62.

of the accused and, thus, implies a possibility of general absence unless the Trial Chamber considers otherwise.[149]

On 31 January 2017 the AU Summit entrusted the Open-Ended Committee of Foreign Affairs Ministers to discuss with the UN Security Council on the previous decision for deferral of the ICC proceedings against Sudan's President Al Bashir and Kenyan Deputy President Ruto in accordance with Article 16 of the ICC Statute.[150] The Committee would then submit the ICC Action Plan for consideration by the AU Peace and Security Council to be approved by the AU summit in June 2017.[151] On 14–15 May 2017, Sudanese President Al Bashir attended the Doha Forum in Doha, Qatar, at the invitation of the Government of Qatar,[152] a non-State Party to the ICC Statute. Qatar has played a role in brokering peace agreements in Sudan and maintained a close relation with that State.

As of this writing, there has been no consensus among AU Member States to withdraw from the ICC Statute. Lesotho and those African States with confidence in the ICC consider the ICC to be invaluable in upholding justice and the rule of law in Africa. In their view, the African regional court exercising criminal jurisdiction over crimes within the ICC's jurisdiction as envisaged by the Malabo Protocol can, at the most, be a court of first instance (or second instance where a national court has competent jurisdiction over the crimes) in the overall context of complementarity vis-à-vis the ICC, but it cannot replace or be a substitute for the ICC. On 10 February 2017 the new Government in the Gambia rescinded its notification to withdraw from the ICC. On 7 March 2017 South Africa rescinded its notification to withdraw from the ICC following the decision of South Africa's High Court, Gauteng Division, Pretoria, ruling that, procedurally, the decision by the national executive to deliver the notice of withdrawal of South Africa from the ICC Statute without prior parliamentary approval is unconstitutional and invalid.[153] However, Burundi's withdrawal from the ICC Statute became effective on 27 October 2017.

Instead of taking a decision whether to withdraw from the ICC en bloc, the AU Summit held on 27 June to 4 July 2017 merely managed to organize, on 4 July 2017, the Seminar on Carrying Forward the Legacy of the Extraordinary African Chambers (EAC) in the Trial of Hissène Habré. The objectives of the Seminar were to engage African States, including their ministers of justice, national judiciaries,

[149] Kevin Jon Heller, 'Will the New RPE Provisions Survive Judicial Review? (Probably Not.)' *Opinio Juris* (28 Nov 2013) <http://opiniojuris.org/2013/11/28/will-new-rpe-134-provisions-survive-judicial-review/>, accessed 15 August 2017.

[150] 'No investigation or prosecution may be commenced or proceeded with under this Statute for a period of 12 months after the Security Council, in a resolution adopted under Chapter VII of the Charter of the United Nations, has requested the Court to that effect; that request may be renewed by the Council under the same conditions.'

[151] Cf du Plessis, 'Exploring Efforts to Resolve the Tension Between the AU and the ICC over the Bashir Saga' 245; Godfrey M Musila, 'The Role of the African Union in International Criminal Justice: Force for Good or Bad?' in Ankumah, *The International Criminal Court and Africa* 299.

[152] The other prominent guests at the Forum included the President of Mali, the Prime Ministers of Finland, Lebanon, and Somalia, respectively, as well as the foreign minister of Costa Rica, and that of Malaysia. The theme of the Doha Forum was 'Development, Stability, and Refugee Crisis'.

[153] *Democratic Alliance v Minister of International Relations and Cooperation and Others*, Case no 83145/2016 (22 Feb 2017).

public prosecutors, and the AU in dialogue on the progressive development of international criminal justice and build capacity for the African judiciary, public prosecutors, civil society, and legal fraternities on international criminal justice. The Seminar documented and highlighted the contribution of the EAC as 'the first universal jurisdiction case in Africa' in promoting accountability and ending impunity for gross human rights violations in Africa by prosecuting violators on African soil. The Seminar also considered, in the context of devising a framework for the exercise of international criminal justice, a victim-centred approach, emerging trends on complementarity, incorporating gender perspectives, reparations to victims, and engaging Africa's youth.

B. Article 98(2), ICC Statute

With respect to Article 98(2) of the ICC Statute, at the Preparatory Commission for the International Criminal Court (PCNICC) in 1999–2000, the US delegation proposed a rule of procedure that would require that, in order for the ICC to have custody of the persons accused of crimes within the ICC's jurisdiction, the State of nationality of these persons must consent under international agreements to their surrender to the ICC.[154] This proposal would render futile the rationale behind Article 12 of the ICC Statute which permits the ICC to exercise jurisdiction if the territorial State *or* the State of nationality of the accused is party to the ICC Statute or has accepted its jurisdiction. The compromise eventually achieved at the PCNICC is the current Rule 195 (Provision of information), second paragraph, under Section V (Cooperation under Article 98), stating:

> The Court may not proceed with a request for the surrender of a person without the consent of a sending State if, under article 98, paragraph 2, such a request would be inconsistent with obligations under an international agreement pursuant to which the consent of a sending State is required prior to the surrender of a person of that State to the Court.

To allay the concerns of several delegations that it was merely a redraft version of the US proposal, an understanding has been adopted and incorporated in the final report of the PCNICC: 'It is generally understood that [Rule 195(2)] should not be interpreted as requiring or in any way calling for the negotiation or provisions in any particular international agreement by the [ICC] or by any other international organization or State.'[155] Corridor consultations among delegations resulted in the abandonment of any effort to oppose, revise, or amend the said Rule during the last hours of the PCNICC, thanks to the provision of Article 51(5) of the ICC Statute, which stipulates unequivocally that in the event of conflict between the ICC Statute and the Rules of Procedure and Evidence, the Statute shall prevail.[156]

[154] According to the last US proposal in 2000, 'The Court shall proceed with a request for surrender or an acceptance of a person into the custody of the Court only in a manner consistent with international agreements applicable to the surrender of the person' (Doc. PCNICC/2000/WGRPE(9)/DP. 4, 13 June 2000).

[155] Doc PCNICC/2000/WGRPE(9)/RT.3, 29 June 2000.

[156] Kittichaisaree, *International Criminal Law* 284–86.

The USA, a non-State Party to the ICC Statute, has enacted the American Servicemembers' Protection Act (ASPA),[157] in force as of 2 August 2002, to ensure that no US national shall be surrendered to the ICC pursuant to Article 12(2) and (3) of the ICC Statute,[158] unless the USA consents to such surrender. By virtue of ASPA, the US President is empowered to use force to rescue US nationals detained by the ICC and prohibits US cooperation with the ICC unless the President determines that cooperation would be in the national interest.

After the entry into force of the ICC Statute on 1 July 2002, the USA threatened to pull out of UN peacekeeping operations in Bosnia unless the UN Security Council adopted a resolution preventing the ICC from commencing an investigation or prosecution in respect of all US personnel engaged in UN or UN-authorized operations. The UN Security Council Resolution 1422 was unanimously adopted on 12 July 2002 to meet the US demand. The pertinent operative paragraphs of Resolution 1422 read:

Acting under Chapter VII of the Charter of the United Nations,

1. *Requests*, consistent with the provisions of Article 16 of the Rome Statute, that the ICC, if a case arises involving current or former officials or personnel from a contributing State not a Party to the Rome Statute over acts or omissions relating to a United Nations established or authorized operation, shall for a twelve-month period starting 1 July 2002 not commence or proceed with investigation or prosecution of any such case, unless the Security Council decides otherwise;
2. *Expresses* the intention to renew the request in paragraph 1 under the same conditions each 1 July for further 12-month periods for as long as may be necessary;
3. *Decides* that Member States shall take no action inconsistent with paragraph 1 and with their international obligations . . .[159]

Also at the insistence of the USA, the UN Security Council passed resolution 1487 on 12 June 2003 under the heading 'United Nations Peacekeeping', with the pertinent operative paragraphs replicating those of Resolution 1422.[160]

After the Security Council declined to renew the one-year exemption in 2004, the USA has been pressing hard for the conclusion of 'bilateral immunity agreements'

[157] 22 USC §§7421–32.

[158] 2. In the case of [a State Party to the ICC Statute referring to the ICC Prosecutor a situation in which one or more crimes within the jurisdiction of the ICC appear to have been committed or the ICC Prosecutor initiates an investigation in respect of such a crime *propio motu* pursuant to] article 13, paragraph (a) or (c), the Court may exercise its jurisdiction if one or more of the following States are Parties to this Statute or have accepted the jurisdiction of the Court in accordance with paragraph 3:

(a) The State on the territory of which the conduct in question occurred or, if the crime was committed on board a vessel or aircraft, the State of registration of that vessel or aircraft;
(b) The State of which the person accused of the crime is a national.

3. If the acceptance of a State which is not a Party to this Statute is required under paragraph 2, that State may, by declaration lodged with the Registrar, accept the exercise of jurisdiction by the Court with respect to the crime in question. The accepting State shall cooperate with the Court without any delay or exception in accordance with Part 9.

[159] UNSC Res 1422 (12 July 2002) UN Doc S/RES/1422.

[160] UNSC Res 1487 (12 June 2003) UN Doc S/RES/1487.

('BIAs' or 'Article 98 Agreements') with States around the world not to surrender US nationals to the ICC. The BIAs provide, in essence, that persons of one Party present in the territory of the other shall not be surrendered or transferred to the ICC or any other entity or third State for the purpose of surrender to or transfer to the ICC. 'Persons' shall mean current or former government officials, employees (including contractors), or military personnel or nationals of one Party. When one Party extradites, surrenders, or otherwise transfers a person of the USA to a third State, that Party will not agree to the surrender or transfer of that person to the ICC by a third State.

The official position of the US Department of State is that US military forces, civilian personnel, and private citizens are active in peacekeeping and humanitarian missions in more than one hundred States, and that Article 98 Agreements that are permitted by the ICC Statute allow the US to remain engaged internationally with its friends and allies by providing US nationals with essential protection from the ICC's jurisdiction, 'particularly against politically motivated investigations and prosecutions'.[161] On 2 May 2005 Angola became the 100th State to sign such an agreement with the US. The latest available information indicates that as of 2006, there were more than 102 States that signed the BIAs with the US, 46 of whom were States Parties to the ICC Statute.[162]

In parallel, whenever the UN Security Council adopts a resolution to refer to the ICC Prosecutor a situation in a non-State Party to the ICC Statute, the USA has been successful in having a standard formula included in such resolution. According to this formula, nationals, current or former officials, or personnel from a contributing State that is not party to the ICC Statute shall be subject to the exclusive jurisdiction of that contributing State for all alleged acts or omissions arising out of or related to operations, established or authorized by the competent organization, in the State referred to the ICC by the Council. Such exclusive jurisdiction may be expressly waived by that contributing State itself.[163]

The BIAs have been subject to criticisms. The widely held position of human rights NGOs, including Human Rights First and the Coalition for the International Criminal Court, is that both the drafting history and the wording of Article 98(2) of the ICC Statute indicate that the provision was intended to cover Status of Force Agreements (SOFAs) and like agreements. Only this interpretation is consistent with the principle of complementarity that underlies the ICC Statute, according to which the ICC will only step in if national courts with jurisdiction to try the case are unable or unwilling to do so. Troops sent overseas are usually covered by SOFAs, such as the NATO SOFA. SOFAs typically cover members of the visiting armed forces (and accompanying civilian personnel and dependents). If a member of the visiting force commits a crime against the laws of their own State (the sending State)

[161] Press Statement by the Spokesman of the US Dept of State, 23 Sept 2003.

[162] Coalition for the International Criminal Court, 'Status of US Bilateral Immunity Agreements' <http://www.iccnow.org/documents/CICCFS_BIAstatus_current.pdf>, accessed 15 August 2017.

[163] §6, UNSC Res 1593 (31 Mar 2005) UN Doc S/RES/1593 regarding the situation in Darfur, Sudan, and §6, UNSC Res 1970 (26 Feb 2011) UN Doc S/RES/1970 regarding the situation in Libya.

SOFAs give jurisdiction to the sending State if the act is not also a crime under the laws of the foreign State (the receiving State). If a member of a visiting force commits a crime against the laws of both the sending and receiving States, SOFAs give the sending State primary jurisdiction if the offence was committed in the performance of their official duty—although the sending State is required to give 'sympathetic consideration' to a request from the receiving State for a 'waiver of its right' where the case is 'of particular importance'.

According to one commentary to the ICC Statute, the draftsmen of Article 98(1) of the Statute were concerned with eliminating any obstacle to ratification of the ICC Statute which could result from 'already existing treaty obligations', and not with providing States Parties to the Statute with 'a tool to subsequently limit the [ICC's] power to effectively exercise its jurisdiction'.[164]

On 30 September 2002 the European Union issued the *European Union's Guiding Principles* in relation to the US' approach for EU Member States to sign BIAs with the USA. EU Member States are required by the Guiding Principles to '[take] into account existing agreements, such as Status of Forces Agreements and agreements on legal cooperation on criminal matters, including extradition'. They are reminded that entering into BIAs with the USA would be inconsistent with ICC States Parties' obligations under the ICC Statute and, possibly, other international agreements. Any agreement reached must not result in impunity for those persons covered who are reasonably suspected of committing crimes within the ICC's jurisdiction. In this connection, there shall be an 'operative provision [ensuring] appropriate investigation and—where there is sufficient evidence—prosecution by national jurisdictions concerning persons requested by the ICC'. The agreements with the USA must not be reciprocal, that is, the EU States must not consent to the non-surrender of their own nationals or the nationals of any other ICC State Party. In relation to the scope of persons covered by any bilateral agreement, these persons must be 'persons present on the territory of a requested State because they have been sent by a sending State', and must not include 'current or former government officials, employees (including contractors), or military personnel or nationals', as proposed by the US. The EU also proposes that BIAs include a 'termination or revision clause' (sunset provision) providing a way for States to adjust to changing circumstances.

The EU's Guiding Principles are probably the best practicable efforts for a compromise between the requirement for EU Member States party to the ICC Statute to fulfil their obligations under that Statute, on the one hand, and the need to engage the USA in international peacekeeping and other international affairs that may expose US nationals to risks of prosecution before the ICC, although the USA is not party to the ICC Statute, on the other hand. Any State wishing to avail itself of the third alternative to the obligation to extradite or prosecute must understand this

[164] Kreß and Prost, 'Article 98 Cooperation with respect to waiver of immunity and consent to surrender' 1617–18. See also Luis Moreno Ocampo, 'The ICC's Afghanistan Investigation: The Missing Option', Lawfare (24 Apr 2017), where the first ICC Prosecutor argues that the USA might use a 'SOFA-based challenge' to the ICC's jurisdiction to investigate and prosecute those involved in US detention practices and alleged torture in Afghanistan <https://www.lawfareblog.com/iccs-afghanistan-investigation-missing-option>, accessed 21 November 2017.

delicate situation surrounding the interpretation of Article 98(2) of the ICC Statute as appears in the EU's Guiding Principles.

Can the BIAs supersede the obligation under Article 86 of the ICC Statute which imposes on its States Parties the general obligation to cooperate with the ICC in its investigation and prosecution of crimes within the ICC's jurisdiction? Pursuant to Article 97, where a State Party receives such a request in relation to which it identifies problems which may impede or prevent the execution of the request, that State shall consult with the ICC without delay in order to resolve the matter, including the fact that execution of the request in its current form would require the requested State to breach a pre-existing treaty obligation undertaken with respect to another State. The ICC has held that Article 97 is built on the implicit and realistic expectation that, due to practical reasons, straightforward cooperation may occasionally not be possible. Rule 195 of the Rules of Procedure and Evidence of the ICC stipulates that, when a requested State considers that a request for surrender or assistance raises a problem of execution in respect of article 98, it notifies the ICC and provides any information relevant to assist the ICC in the application of Article 98. Article 97 cannot override the duty vis-à-vis the ICC under Article 86, but merely allows interim remedial measures to be addressed through consultations between the ICC and the requested State. It is eventually for the ICC—considering all the information made available to it—to decide on the matter, and, effectively, either confirm or withdraw its request for cooperation to the State. It is not for any requested States to declare unilaterally that the ICC's request for arrest and surrender was suspended for any reason.[165]

Anyway, every State must bear in mind that accepting the legitimacy of such BIAs risks seriously undermining the equality under the law governing international criminal justice and, consequently, the credibility of the third alternative. If nationals of a global superpower are exempted from being surrendered to an international criminal tribunal, why cannot nationals of any State, such as an AU Member State, which is not party to the ICC Statute? The *Celebici* test postulated by the ICTY Appeals Chamber as explained in Section I above must not become a dead letter.

[165] *Decision under article 87(7) of the Rome Statute on the non-compliance by South Africa with the request by the Court for the arrest and surrender of Omar Al-Bashir*, ICC-02/05-01/09 Pre-Trial Ch II §§112–22. Although the Decision specifically addressed the difficulty South Africa had in relation to Art 98(1) of the ICC Statute, it is submitted that this reasoning applies equally to Art 98(2) of that Statute.

PART III

EPILOGUE AND REFLECTIONS

8
Conclusions and the Way Forward

The foregoing analysis on the obligation to extradite or prosecute attempts to elaborate the primary rules concerning the obligation. It does not deal with the secondary rule of the general international law of State responsibility where the obligation is not fulfilled.[1]

The obligation to extradite or prosecute operates within the parameters of the two-tier mechanism of international criminal justice.[2]

At the *vertical* level are international criminal tribunals set up by the UN Security Council acting under Chapter VII of the UN Charter, mixed/hybrid tribunals usually set up by agreements between the UN and the State concerned, and the International Criminal Court (ICC) set up under the 1998 Rome Statute of the ICC. Their jurisdiction is limited temporally, spatially, and materially. The ICTY and the ICTR set up by the Security Council have 'primacy' over national jurisdictions; both Tribunals are sometimes accused of dispensing 'selective justice'.[3] Mixed/hybrid tribunals depend on cooperation of parties to the relevant agreement. For example, States other than Sierra Leone have no obligation to cooperate with the Special Court for Sierra Leone set up by an agreement between the UN and the Government of Sierra Leone, and not pursuant to the UN Security Council acting under Chapter VII of the Charter. The trial of Charles Taylor, former President of Liberia, before the Court was possible thanks to the willingness of Nigeria, where he was living in exile, to surrender him to the Court. The ICC, set up by the 1998 Rome Statute of the ICC, lacks universality of States Parties and operates on the principle of complementarity to national jurisdictions.

At the *horizontal* level, the national court relies on treaties of judicial cooperation or voluntary inter-State cooperation to have the offender extradited to stand trial before it. Prosecution of the big fish in domestic courts of the territorial State is usually practicable only after a *regime change* in that State, as in the case of the late Libyan

[1] The secondary rule is analysed in Stoyan Minkov Panov, 'The Obligation *Aut Dedere Aut Judicare* ("Extradite or Prosecute") in International Law: Scope, Content, Sources and Applicability of the Obligation "Extradite or Prosecute"', PhD thesis (Birmingham, 2016) ch 5 'State Responsibility and *Aut Dedere Aut Judicare* Obligation'.

[2] *Prosecutor v Blaškić* (Judgment on the request of Croatia for Review of the Decision of Trial Chamber II of 18 July 1997) IT-95-14, ICTY App Ch (29 Oct 1997) §§47, 54.

[3] See eg the statements of the President of Bosnia and Herzegovina, President of Serbia and Montenegro, and Minister of Justice of Rwanda, respectively, at the High-Level Session of the UN General Assembly on the Role of International Criminal Justice in Reconciliation, 10 Apr 2013.

President Ghaddafi's son Saif al-Islam Ghaddafi, ex-President Pinochet in Chile, ex-President Mubarak in Egypt, and former President Ríos Montt in Guatemala.

The obligation to extradite or prosecute plays a crucial role in enabling national courts to prosecute crimes, especially where an ad hoc, mixed/hybrid, or permanent international tribunal is not in a position to prosecute the same.[4] States can either prosecute the offender or extradite him or her to another State willing and able to do so, or surrender the person to such international tribunal as the third alternative, where feasible.

Chapters 1 and 2 of this book explain the foundation for the obligation to extradite or prosecute under international law as well as the work of the International Law Commission (ILC) in this matter. Chapter 3 elucidates bases for the obligation to be a rule of customary international law for core crimes under international law. Chapter 4 then expounds how treaty provisions on the obligation are to be construed and the various formula(e) to be chosen by States to suit their respective objectives. Chapter 5 explains the operation of universal jurisdiction in the context of the obligation to extradite or prosecute as well as conditions to be met in avoiding potential abuses in the exercise of universal jurisdiction. The scope of the obligation to extradite or prosecute is elaborated further in Chapter 6, which also clarifies the procedural constraints of immunity of State officials from foreign criminal jurisdiction. Under customary international law, there is no exception to immunity *ratione personae*, whereas the list of exceptions to immunity *ratione materiae* keeps expanding as the international community strives for the end of impunity for atrocities perpetrated by State officials. In any case, States may conclude treaties to expressly negate such immunity, as in Article 27(2) of the ICC Statute[5] which provides that immunities or special procedural rules that may attach to the official capacity of a person, whether under national or international law, shall not bar the ICC from exercising its jurisdiction over such a person. Chapter 7 points out the major impediments to the third alternative of surrendering the offender to a competent non-national court.

There are, admittedly, gaps in the existing international conventions that will expressly and unequivocally remove any potential immunity and other hurdle impeding extradition or prosecution of perpetrators of serious crimes.

I. Efforts to Fill the Void

There are currently no global or regional conventions devoted exclusively to extradition of alleged perpetrators of crimes against humanity and war crimes committed in an armed conflict not of an international character. Furthermore, Article VII of the Genocide Convention[6] is rudimentary in nature, stipulating that the Contracting

[4] Hitomi Takemura, 'A Critical Analysis of Positive Complementarity' in Stefano Manacorda and Adán Nieto (eds), *Criminal Law between War and Peace: Justice and Cooperation in Criminal Matters in International Military Interventions* (Ediciones de la Universidad de Castilla-La Macha 2009) 601; Lionel Nichols, *The International Criminal Court and the End of Impunity in Kenya* (Springer 2015) ch 2 'The Strategy of Positive Complementarity'.

[5] 2187 ILM 90. [6] 78 UNTS 277.

Parties to the Genocide Convention 'pledge themselves in [the cases of genocide and related acts proscribed by the Genocide Convention] to grant extradition in accordance with their laws and treaties in force'. Even in relation to war crimes in international armed conflict, Article 88(2) of the 1977 Additional Protocol I to the four Geneva Convention of 1949[7] merely requires that 'when circumstances permit, the High Contracting Parties shall cooperate in the matter of extradition', giving 'due consideration to the request of the State in whose territory the alleged offence has occurred'.[8] Worse still, the draftsmen of Article 88(2) did not adopt a phrase in the draft designed to prevent grave breaches from being treated as political offences for the purpose of extradition, leaving the question to be resolved in each case on the basis of the national legislation and the relevant treaties.[9]

Argentina, Belgium, the Netherlands, and Slovenia have launched an initiative for the adoption of a new international instrument on mutual legal assistance and extradition for the effective investigation and prosecution of the most serious crimes of international concern, in particular, the crimes of genocide, crimes against humanity, and war crimes, by domestic jurisdictions, with a view to closing the existing gap in the conventional regime relating to, *inter alia*, the obligation to extradite or prosecute.[10] In the beginning, they explained that the most appropriate forum for a worldwide discussion of the initiative would be the UN Commission on Crime Prevention and Criminal Justice (CCPCJ), where multiple mutual legal assistance treaties were recently negotiated, and which has the necessary technical expertise on mutual legal assistance and extradition provisions.[11] These States presented the initiative at the 22nd Session of the CCPCJ in April 2013[12] and at the 12th Session of the

[7] Protocol Additional to the Geneva Conventions of 12 Aug 1949, and relating to the Protection of Victims of International Armed Conflicts (Protocol I) 1125 UNTS 3.

[8] These gaps were pointed out by Dire Tladi in his statement in the ILC Plenary on the third report of the ILC Special Rapporteur on the topic 'Crimes against humanity' on 1 May 2017.

[9] §3580 of the 1987 ICRC Commentary to Additional Protocol I. However, the commentary to Art 88(2) emphasizes 'the absolute need to punish those guilty of grave breaches, with or without extradition' (ibid).

[10] Statements in the Sixth Committee by the Netherlands on 29 Oct 2013 and by Slovenia on 1 Nov 2013; also the statement of Belgium during the Interactive Dialogue between the Sixth Committee and the International Law Commission on the topic 'Crimes against humanity', 30 Oct 2013.

[11] The background of this initiative is explained in a non-paper entitled 'Towards a Multilateral Treaty for Mutual Legal Assistance and Extradition for Domestic Prosecution of the Most Serious International Crimes', informally circulated by Argentina, Belgium, the Netherlands, and Slovenia at the Sixth Committee in Nov 2013.

[12] These States together with Austria, Chile, Hungary, and Luxembourg submitted a draft resolution entitled 'International cooperation in the fight against the crime of genocide, crimes against humanity and war crimes' (Doc E/CN.15/2013/L.5 (28 Mar 2013)). They also argued that the CCPCJ has a mandate entrusted by the Salvador Declaration on Comprehensive Strategies for Global Challenges: Crime Prevention and Criminal Justice Systems and Their Development in a Changing World, §21 of which reads: '*Aware* that gaps may exist in relation to international cooperation in criminal matters, we invite the [CCPCJ] to consider reviewing this issue and explore the need for various means of addressing gaps that are identified' (Report of the Twelfth UN Congress on Crime Prevention and Criminal Justice, 12–19 Apr 2010, Doc A/CONF.213/18 at 7). The draft resolution was subsequently co-sponsored by Andorra, Cyprus, Estonia, Georgia, Latvia, Liechtenstein, Lithuania, Mongolia, Norway, Peru, Poland, Romania, Slovakia, Sweden, and the former Yugoslav Republic of Macedonia. However, it was withdrawn after extensive debate in the Committee of the Whole, where several delegations raised serious concerns regarding the mandate of the CCPCJ in this matter. Pakistan, for instance, expressed its

Assembly of States Parties to the Rome Statute of the International Criminal Court in November 2013, among others. By the end of the latter meeting, the number of States co-sponsoring this initiative had increased to 38.[13] The supporters of the initiative would prefer the CCPCJ, a technical body, to draft such international instrument to be endorsed by the Economic and Social Council and forwarded to the Third [Social, Humanitarian, and Cultural] Committee of the UN General Assembly for further action. They tried to avoid starting the initiative in the UN General Assembly, including its Sixth Committee, for fear of possible politicization of the debate on the initiative. Nonetheless, the initiative's opponents are against it everywhere, since they are not party to the ICC Statute and their domestic law does not criminalize some or even all of the crimes covered by the initiative—thus being unable to prosecute or even extradite (due to the lack of double criminality) persons accused of such crimes.

In November 2013, a non-paper entitled 'Towards a Multilateral Treaty for Mutual Legal Assistance and Extradition for Domestic Prosecution of the Most Serious International Crimes'[14] was informally circulated in the Sixth Committee by Argentina, Belgium, the Netherlands, and Slovenia. The new international instrument on mutual legal assistance and extradition to close existing gaps in the conventional regime could be based on existing procedural provisions found in relatively recent treaties on mutual legal assistance dealing with international or transnational crimes, such as the UN Convention against Transnational Organized Crime of 2000[15] and the UN Convention against Corruption of 2003,[16] which would be adapted for cooperation in the investigation and prosecution of crimes of genocide, crimes against humanity, and war crimes.[17]

In June 2017, the Netherlands hosted an international meeting to consider the aforesaid initiative.[18] The initiative, open to all States—be they party to the ICC

concerns over the draft resolution 'due to certain procedural and technical complications, including the fact that the nature of the crime of genocide, crimes against humanity and war crimes went far beyond the mandate of the Commission, as it was a functional commission for the Economic and Social Council [whose resolution 1992/1 on the establishment of the CCPCJ and the other foundational documents] did not envision such crimes'. Pakistan suggested that the initiative be pursued 'in the relevant forums' (CCPCJ Report on the 22nd session (7 Dec 2012 and 22–26 Apr 2013) Official Records of the Economic and Social Council, 2013, Supp 10 (E/2013/30) §§64–66).

[13] At the 12th Session of the Assembly of States Parties to the Rome Statute of the ICC, the Joint Declaration on the initiative to start negotiations on a multilateral treaty on mutual legal assistance and extradition was co-sponsored by the following 38 States from all the regional groups: Albania, Andorra, Argentina, Austria, Belgium, Bulgaria, Chile, Costa Rica, Cyprus, Czech Republic, Finland, Georgia, Greece, Hungary, Ireland, Liechtenstein, Lithuania, Luxembourg, Malawi, Mongolia, Netherlands, Norway, Panama, Paraguay, Peru, Republic of Moldova, Samoa, Senegal, Serbia, Seychelles, Slovakia, Slovenia, South Africa, Suriname, Sweden, the former Yugoslav Republic of Macedonia, Trinidad and Tobago, and Uruguay. Official Records of the Assembly of States Parties to the Rome Statute of the ICC, 12th session, The Hague, 20–28 Nov 2013 (ICC-ASP/12/20) i, Annex VIII at 83.

[14] Since then this non-paper has been continually updated and presented at various forums.

[15] (2001) 40 ILM 335. [16] (2004) 43 ILM 37.

[17] See also Anne-Sophie Massa, 'Bridging the Legal Gap: The International Initiative for Opening Negotiation on a Multilateral Treaty for Mutual Legal Assistance and Extradition in the Domestic Prosecution of Atrocity Crimes' in Evelyn A Ankumah (ed) *The International Criminal Court and Africa: One Decade On* (Intersentia 2016) 663.

[18] The following information appears in a non-paper disseminated to States by the Netherlands, on file with the present author.

Statute or not, draws upon the UN General Assembly Resolution on Principles of International Cooperation in the Detection, Arrest, Extradition and Punishment of Persons Guilty of War Crimes and Crimes against Humanity,[19] which stipulates, *inter alia*, 'States shall cooperate with each other on a bilateral and multilateral basis with a view to halting and preventing war crimes and crimes against humanity, and shall take the domestic and international measures necessary for that purpose'. It is intended to complement the ICC Statute mechanism and fill gaps in existing treaty regimes for the prosecution of core crimes under international law as well as to enable States to prosecute crimes under the ICC Statute in the first instance according to the principle of complementarity, failing which the ICC may exercise jurisdiction over such crimes pursuant to its Statute where applicable.

The goal of the initiative is further explained as setting up 'a modern procedural multilateral treaty on mutual legal assistance and extradition', replacing 'incomplete and outdated' ones, which would facilitate better practical cooperation between States investigating and prosecuting genocide, crimes against humanity, and war crimes. The Genocide Convention and the four Geneva Conventions of 1949 contain only limited and largely outdated provisions on mutual legal assistance and extradition, if any, while those stipulated in the Convention against Torture apply only to the crime of torture whose legal definition does not match those of genocide, war crimes, or crimes against humanity. A multilateral system is believed to be more efficient than the ad hoc system of bilateral agreements and to emphasize better the significance accorded by the international community to the efficient prosecution of these core international crimes. It is also more expansive in its scope of coverage than the International Law Commission's work on 'Crimes against humanity'. Procedural provisions will encompass, among others, freezing of assets; seizure and confiscation; protection of witnesses; transfer of criminal proceedings; disposal of confiscated proceeds of crime or property; taking of evidence or statements from persons; service of judicial documents; searches and seizures; identification or tracing of proceeds of crime, property, instrumentalities, or other things of evidentiary purposes; facilitation of the voluntary appearance of persons in the requesting State Party; videoconference; assistance to and protection of victims; and training and technical assistance.

As of 14 February 2017, the initiative received support from fifty-three States. Forty-eight of them are States Parties to the ICC Statute; namely, Albania, Andorra, Argentina, Austria, Belgium, Bolivia, Bosnia and Herzegovina, Bulgaria, Chile, Costa Rica, Côte d'Ivoire, Cyprus, Czech Republic, Finland, Georgia, Greece, Guinea, Hungary, Ireland, Latvia, Liechtenstein, Lithuania, Luxembourg, Malawi, Mali, Moldova, Mongolia, Netherlands, Norway, Panama, Paraguay, Peru, Poland, Portugal, St Kitts and Nevis, Samoa, Senegal, Serbia, Seychelles, Slovakia, Slovenia, South Africa, Suriname, Sweden, Switzerland, the former Yugoslav Republic of Macedonia, Trinidad and Tobago, and Uruguay. The remaining five are not party

[19] UNGA Res 3074 (XXVIII) (3 Dec 1973).

to the Statute; namely, Kazakhstan, Rwanda, São Tomé and Principe, Ukraine, and Vietnam.

Despite the strong support from a number of States, this initiative is not yet formally taken up by the UN or any of its specialized agencies. The initiative's objective is highly commendable: it will ensure that when a perpetrator of a core crime is not surrendered to the ICC or any other competent non-national criminal tribunal, States would cooperate among themselves to deny impunity to the perpetrator. Yet, so far not all of the 123 States Parties to the ICC Statute have expressed their support for the initiative. Almost all of those States that are not yet party to the ICC Statute are probably unable and/or unwilling to prosecute perpetrators of the crimes under the ICC Statute in their respective domestic courts anyway.

There is a parallel, but less ambitious, movement to fill the void in the conventional regime by having an international convention on crimes against humanity—the only core crime not yet discretely regulated by any treaty.[20]

II. The ILC's Crimes against Humanity Topic

In 2014, the ILC placed the topic 'Crimes against humanity' in its long-term programme of work as part of the efforts to fill the gaps identified in Section I.

A number of delegations to the Sixth Committee welcomed this inclusion, hoping that the ILC's work on this topic would help to develop international criminal law and fill gaps in the international legal framework as well as reflect and build upon the ILC's prior work. It was cautioned, nevertheless, that the topic involved complex legal issues to be addressed carefully. Several delegations emphasized the topic's relationship with existing legal instruments, and in particular the 1998 Rome Statute of the ICC, which should not be undermined. According to some delegations, the ICC Statute and implementing domestic legislation sufficiently filled any lacunae in this area and they doubted the need for further work. Concern was expressed that a crime against humanity convention drafted by the ILC would offer an instrument that satisfied those States that had no intention to become party to the ICC Statute, and, as such, could have the undesirable effect of discouraging further ratifications of the Statute. On the other hand, an opposite opinion was expressed that it would be impractical to have one comprehensive convention on all core crimes under international law, and that having a convention on crimes against humanity would be better than none at all.

Some delegations preferred the ILC to focus on strengthening mutual legal cooperation, adequate domestic legislation and building capacity to prosecute crimes against humanity at the domestic level. In this connection, some delegations emphasized the need for the ILC to take into account the initiative by a group of States

[20] Leila Hadya Sadat (ed), *Forging a Convention for Crimes against Humanity* (CUP 2011), and the 'Crimes against Humanity Initiative: A Rule of Law Project' by the Whitney R Harris World Law Institute, Washington University School of Law.

on a new treaty for mutual legal assistance and extradition for domestic prosecution of core crimes, as discussed in Section I above.

The view was also expressed that the most important task consisted in defining the legal concept and scope of crimes against humanity. While some delegations considered that work on definition of such crimes should be avoided, several others stressed that the definition of crimes against humanity contained in Article 7 of the Rome Statute should be retained as the material basis for the ILC's work. Moreover, it was suggested that the ILC address the effects and consequences of categorizing an act as a crime against humanity; explore and articulate relevant responsibilities pertaining to the prevention of crimes against humanity and consider mechanisms to ensure its effective prevention; and address both international and non-international armed conflicts.

It was also suggested that the ILC address procedural and jurisdictional aspects of the topic, which were directly linked to the principle of universal jurisdiction and the obligation to extradite or prosecute. In this regard, it was considered beneficial to analyse how an extradite-or-prosecute regime in respect of crimes against humanity might operate. Furthermore, the view was expressed that issues such as civil jurisdiction and immunity should not be dealt with under this topic. It was also suggested that the ILC adopt a victim-oriented approach in its work. The ILC was also encouraged to draw from the jurisprudence of the various international criminal courts and tribunals.[21]

In 2017, the ILC adopted on first reading the following draft articles on Crimes against humanity[22] that related to universal jurisdiction and the obligation to extradite or prosecute, respectively.

Article 7 Establishment of national jurisdiction

1. Each State shall take the necessary measures to establish its jurisdiction over the offences covered by the present draft articles in the following cases:
   (a) when the offence is committed in any territory under its jurisdiction or on board a ship or aircraft registered in that State;
   (b) when the alleged offender is a national of that State or, if that State considers it appropriate, a stateless person who is habitually resident in that State's territory;
   (c) when the victim is a national of that State if that State considers it appropriate.
2. Each State shall also take the necessary measures to establish its jurisdiction over the offences covered by the present draft articles in cases where the alleged offender is present in any territory under its jurisdiction and it does not extradite or surrender the person in accordance with the present draft articles.
3. The present draft articles do not exclude the exercise of any criminal jurisdiction established by a State in accordance with its national law.

[21] ILC, 'Report of the International Law Commission on the work of its 66th Session': Topical summary of the discussion held in the Sixth Committee of the General Assembly during its 69th Session, prepared by the Secretariat, UN Doc A/CN.4/678 §§81–84.

[22] ILC, 'Report of ... its 69th Session' (1 May–2 June and 3 July–4 Aug 2017) UN Doc A/72/10, 37ff.

Article 10 ***Aut dedere aut judicare***

The State in the territory under whose jurisdiction the alleged offender is present shall submit the case to its competent authorities for the purpose of prosecution, unless it extradites or surrenders the person to another State or competent international criminal tribunal. Those authorities shall take their decision in the same manner as in the case of any other offence of a grave nature under the law of that State.

Article 13 Extradition

1. Each of the offences covered by the present draft articles shall be deemed to be included as an extraditable offence in any extradition treaty existing between States. States undertake to include such offences as extraditable offences in every extradition treaty to be concluded between them.
2. For the purposes of extradition between States, an offence covered by the present draft articles shall not be regarded as a political offence or as an offence connected with a political offence or as an offence inspired by political motives. Accordingly, a request for extradition based on such an offence may not be refused on these grounds alone.
3. If a State that makes extradition conditional on the existence of a treaty receives a request for extradition from another State with which it has no extradition treaty, it may consider the present draft articles as the legal basis for extradition in respect of any offence covered by the present draft articles.
4. A State that makes extradition conditional on the existence of a treaty shall, for any offence covered by the present draft articles:
   (a) inform the Secretary-General of the United Nations whether it will use the present draft articles as the legal basis for cooperation on extradition with other States; and
   (b) if it does not use the present draft articles as the legal basis for cooperation on extradition, seek, where appropriate, to conclude treaties on extradition with other States in order to implement this draft article.
5. States that do not make extradition conditional on the existence of a treaty shall recognize the offences covered by the present draft articles as extraditable offences between themselves.
6. Extradition shall be subject to the conditions provided for by the national law of the requested State or by applicable extradition treaties, including the grounds upon which the requested State may refuse extradition.
7. If necessary, the offences covered by the present draft articles shall be treated, for the purposes of extradition between States, as if they had been committed not only in the place in which they occurred but also in the territory of the States that have established jurisdiction in accordance with draft article 7, paragraph 1.
8. If extradition, sought for purposes of enforcing a sentence, is refused because the person sought is a national of the requested State, the requested State shall, if its national law so permits and in conformity with the requirements of such law, upon application of the requesting State, consider the enforcement of the sentence imposed under the national law of the requesting State or the remainder thereof.
9. Nothing in the present draft articles shall be interpreted as imposing an obligation to extradite if the requested State has substantial grounds for believing that the request has been made for the purpose of prosecuting or punishing a person on account of that person's gender, race, religion, nationality, ethnic origin, culture, membership of a particular social group, political opinions or other grounds that are universally recognized as impermissible under international law, or that compliance with the request would cause prejudice to that person's position for any of these reasons.

10. Before refusing extradition, the requested State shall, where appropriate, consult with the requesting State to provide it with ample opportunity to present its opinions and to provide information relevant to its allegation.

The ILC Drafting Committee prefers a detailed provision on extradition in Draft Article 13, emulating, with necessary modifications to suit the situation of crimes against humanity, Article 16 of the 2000 United Nations Convention against Transnational Organized Crime and Article 44 of the 2005 United Nations Convention against Corruption which are well understood by States. A detailed provision on extradition will provide useful guidance to all relevant rights, obligations, and procedures. Draft Article 13 is to be read in conjunction with the *aut dedere aut judicare* obligation in Draft Article 10. It should be noted that in 2016 the ILC decided to retain the Latin terminology *aut dedere aut judicare* since it had been used in the topic 'The obligation to extradite or prosecute (*aut dedere aut judicare*)' and there had been no objection in the Sixth Committee to the use of this terminology in the Final Report on that topic.

The Draft Articles omit a provision on immunity of State officials from foreign criminal jurisdiction. Draft Article 6 (Criminalization under national law) provides in paragraph 5 that each State Party shall take the necessary measures to ensure that, under its criminal law, the fact that an offence referred to in Draft Article 6 was committed by a person holding an official position is not a ground for excluding criminal responsibility. The accompanying commentary clarifies that paragraph 5 means that an alleged offender cannot raise the fact of his or her official position as a substantive defence so as to negate any criminal responsibility, but 'paragraph 5 has no effect on any procedural immunity that a foreign State official may enjoy before a national criminal jurisdiction, which continues to be governed by conventional and customary international law', and is without prejudice to the ILC's work on the topic 'Immunity of State officials from foreign criminal jurisdiction'.[23] This is regrettable.

A convention on crimes against humanity without a provision comparable to Article 27(2) of the ICC Statute removing immunities or special procedural rules attaching to the official capacity of a person, whether under national or international law, is not a valuable contribution to efforts to prevent and punish crimes against humanity. Draft Article 3 of the ILC's Draft Articles on Crimes against humanity copies Article 7 of the ICC Statute. Article 7(1) of the Statute defines a crime against humanity as an act committed as part of a widespread or systematic attack directed against any civilian population, with knowledge of the attack. Paragraph 2 of that Article defines 'attack directed against any civilian population' as 'a course of conduct involving the multiple commission of acts referred to in paragraph 1 against any civilian population, pursuant to or in furtherance of a State or organizational policy to commit such attack'. Therefore, State officials do have prominent roles in the commission of crimes against humanity under the ICC Statute and the ILC's Draft Articles. There is no reason why States may not join a new treaty on crimes against humanity while also expressly 'waiving' and/or denying any immunity attaching to

[23] ibid 100 [31].

State officials accused of perpetrating such crimes. Otherwise, there is no value being added to what we already have at present.

III. Positive Complementarity

Capacity building for the national judiciary and a regional judicial mechanism can help alleviate the burden of the International Criminal Court.

An example of the former is the Special Criminal Court (SCC) of the Central African Republic (CAR). CAR has self-referred to the ICC Prosecutor the alleged war crimes and crimes against humanity committed in the context of a conflict in CAR since 1 July 2002, and the alleged war crimes and crimes against humanity committed in the context of renewed violence starting in 2012. Since 2014, hundreds of civilians have been reportedly killed by armed groups, in particular Muslim Séléka and Christian anti-Balaka vigilantes. In June 2015, the interim government of CAR set up the SCC, comprising fourteen judges from CAR and thirteen foreign judges entrusted with prosecuting genocide, war crimes, and crimes against humanity committed in CAR since 2003. In February 2017, Toussaint Mukimapa, from the neighbouring Democratic Republic of the Congo, was appointed Prosecutor of the SCC.

The ongoing controversy between the ICC and the AU as pointed out in Chapter 7 has prevented the UN Security Council from referring to the ICC the situation in South Sudan where war crimes and crimes against humanity have been or are being committed. In June 2014, the AU adopted the Protocol (Malabo Protocol) on the Statute of the African Court of Justice and Human Rights (ACJHR), extending the jurisdiction of the ACJHR to cover the crimes of genocide, war crimes, and crimes against humanity, as well as several transnational crimes such as trafficking in persons and drugs, terrorism, piracy, and unconstitutional changes of government and corruption.[24] Article 46A*bis* of the Amended ACJHR Statute stipulates that '[n]o charges shall be commenced or continued against any serving African Union Head of State or Government, or anybody acting or entitled to act in such capacity, or other senior State officials based on their functions, during their tenure of office.' This provision is criticized as being contrary to Article 27 of the ICC Statute.[25] In addition, Kenya has proposed an amendment to the tenth preambular

[24] The Malabo Protocol is reproduced in Amnesty International, *Malabo Protocol: Legal and Institutional Implications of the Merged and Expanded African Court* (2016) 40–64. For a background discussion of the ACJHR's jurisdiction over these crimes, see Mark du Plessis, 'Implications of the AU Decision to Give the African Court Jurisdiction over International Crimes', Institute for Security Studies, Paper 235 (June 2012). On the Malabo Protocol, see Ademola Abass, 'Historical and Political Background to the Malabo Protocol' in G Werle and M Vormbaum (eds), *The African Criminal Court* (TMC Asser 2017) 11.

[25] Cf Manuel J Ventura and Amelia J Bleeker, 'Universal Jurisdiction, African Perceptions of the International Criminal Court and the New AU Protocol on Amendments to the Protocol on the Statute of the African Court of Justice and Human Rights' in Ankumah, *The International Criminal Court and Africa* 441; Jutta F Bertram-Nothnagel, 'A Seed for World Peace Growing in Africa: The Kampala Amendment on the Crime of Aggression and the Monsoon of Malabo', ibid 347, 359–93.

paragraph of the ICC Statute to read: '*Emphasizing* that the International Criminal Court ... shall be complementary to national and regional criminal jurisdictions'. This proposal has not progressed beyond the Assembly of States Parties to the ICC Statute's working group on amendments of the ICC Statute. The Malabo Protocol requires the ratification of fifteen States for it to enter into force. As of this writing, only ten African States—Benin, Chad, Congo, Ghana, Guinea-Bissau, Kenya, Mauritania, São Tome and Principe, Sierra Leone, and Uganda—have signed, but not yet ratified, the Malabo Protocol.

Even when the Malabo Protocol is in force, the ACJHR will be a regional judicial mechanism that is complementary to, but cannot replace or be a substitute for, the ICC. Article 17 of the ICC Statute allows the ICC to exercise its jurisdiction over a crime under its Statute where a 'State which has jurisdiction over it ... is unwilling or unable genuinely to carry out the investigation or prosecution'. Nowhere in the ICC Statute is there any mention of a regional court prosecuting the crime. An object and purpose of the ICC Statute, as evident from paragraph 2 of Article 17, is to prevent the State 'shielding the person concerned from criminal responsibility for crimes within the [ICC's] jurisdiction ... which in the circumstances is inconsistent with an intent to bring the person concerned to justice'. If such a State together with other like-minded States establish a regional court with the purpose and effect prohibited by Article 17 of the ICC Statute, each of these States individually still cannot circumvent its obligations under the ICC Statute binding on it as treaty law or by virtue of the UN Security Council referring the situation in the respective State to the ICC pursuant to Article 13(b) of the ICC Statute.

IV. National Peace/Reconciliation, International Peace/Stability, and Other Considerations against *aut dedere aut judicare*

International law, like municipal law, is based on the system of values of the society where the law operates. Law does not exist in a vacuum; hence, values must be taken into account in the formulation of rules. A vital question is, who has the competence to give effect to values of the international community? Sovereign States acting individually or an international organization such as the United Nations?

Customary international law, representing the putative collective will of sovereign States, generally recognizes the sovereign equality of States, including non-interference in domestic affairs of another State. In the case of the core crimes of genocide, crimes against humanity, serious war crimes, and torture, the political leadership is usually involved either directly or indirectly and these crimes are frequently committed by State agents as part of a State policy. As such, the perpetrators often operate with impunity. Arrest and prosecution of national leaders are rarer than they should be. If there is no regime change in the State where the crimes are committed, foreign domestic criminal courts and/or the ICC may be the only viable option(s) to bring the perpetrators to justice; hence, the interplay of universal jurisdiction, the obligation to extradite or prosecute, and the availability or non-availability of immunity under international law. Inter-State tensions, sometimes aggravated by retaliation or reciprocal measures, often ensue.

On the other hand, customary international law also recognizes *jus cogens* and *erga omnes* obligations to temper some of the harsh consequences of sovereignty and immunities that may entail impunity for perpetrators of atrocities and deprive their victims of redress. A conceptual debate arising from the clash between these two opposite sets of rules is whether there can be no peace or national reconciliation without justice *or* whether justice must play second fiddle to peace and national reconciliation and/or regional/international peace.

The African Union's opposition to the ICC prosecuting the incumbent Presidents of Kenya and of Sudan seems to be based on the consideration that national peace and regional peace are more important. Also, it could be contended that combating impunity must be in the context of the democratic system of government whereby a democratically elected government may, for the sake of national reconciliation, grant an amnesty to perpetrators of mass atrocities and eagerly assert immunity for the State officials concerned in foreign courts.

In July 2008, the Ministerial Meeting of the Non-Aligned Movement (NAM) issued a joint statement, a paragraph of which addresses the situation in Sudan. It reads:

> The Ministers *noted* with satisfaction the sustained efforts being made by the Government of The Sudan, the African Union, the League of Arab States and the UN to reactivate the political process leading to a lasting peace in Darfur. They *expressed* their conviction that no action should be taken that could jeopardize the delicate nature of the process underway in The Sudan. In that context, the Ministers *expressed* deep concern over the recent application by the ICC Prosecutor against the President of The Sudan [... which] could seriously undermine the ongoing efforts aimed at facilitating the early resolution of the conflict in Darfur and the promotion of long-lasting peace and reconciliation in The Sudan and could be conducive to greater destabilization with far reaching consequences for the country and the region. Therefore, they decided to support steps in the UN and elsewhere aimed at defusing this new and dangerous situation and preventing its recurrence.[26]

The AU Assembly of Heads of State and Government has likewise appealed to the UN Security Council to defer the criminal proceedings against Al Bashir 'for purposes of striking a balance between peace and justice over this delicate matter'. After this request has been ignored, the AU has decided that all its Member States shall not cooperate in the arrest and surrender of Al Bashir to the ICC.[27] Chad and Kenya, both of which are AU Member States, were the first two States Parties to the ICC Statute which Al Bashir visited after the ICC's issuing the arrest warrant for him. Kenya and Chad's political reason not to cooperate with the ICC on the arrest

[26] Joint Statement of the NAM Ministerial Meeting, 27–30 July 2008, Tehran, §205, on file with the author who was special envoy of the Prime Minister of Thailand and head of the Thai delegation to the meeting.

[27] Decision of the Meeting of African States Parties to the Rome Statute of the ICC, Doc Assembly/AU/13(XIII) adopted by the 13th Ordinary Session of the Assembly on 3 July 2009 (Doc Assembly/AU/Dec 245(XIII) Rev 1); AU Press Releases nos 118/2010 and 119/2010 29 Aug 2010.

and surrender of Al Bashir is that they are Sudan's neighbours with an interest in ensuring peace and stability in Sudan and in promoting peace, justice, and reconciliation in that State, which can only be achieved through continuous engagement with Sudan's elected government. In their opinion, States do this as a matter of survival as they bear the brunt of instability or insecurity in their neighbouring States. They support the AU's pursuit of the interconnected, mutually interdependent, and equally desirable objectives of peace, justice, and reconciliation in Sudan.[28]

In January 2011, the AU Summit adopted a decision to support and endorse Kenya's request for a deferral of the ICC investigations and prosecutions regarding the 2008 post-election violence in Kenya, so as to allow Kenya's national mechanism to investigate and prosecute the cases under a reformed judiciary provided for in the new constitutional dispensation. The Summit also requested the UN Security Council to accede to this request in support of the ongoing peace building and national reconciliation processes, in order to prevent the resumption of conflict and violence in Kenya.

Mere threats of prosecution, be it at home or abroad or by a competent international criminal tribunal, may give an incentive to incumbent despotic leaders not to relinquish their power. A clear example is President Bashar Assad of Syria's relentless clinging to power despite overwhelming international pressure for him to leave office. He is fighting to the bitter end probably in view of threats of punishment and denial of any immunity before a foreign or international court, thereby leading to disproportionately high casualties in Syria and the escalation of the armed conflict in Syria into not only internal armed conflict, but also international armed conflict through proxies. Some other States have avoided the situation of despotic or beleaguered leaders fighting to the death. For example, pursuant to an agreement brokered by the Gulf Cooperation Council (GCC) signed by the then President Saleh of Yemen in November 2011, Yemen's Parliament would enact a law granting an amnesty to Saleh and his aides in return for Saleh ceding all power by 21 February 2012. On 21 January 2012, Yemen's Parliament passed the law, granting a blanket amnesty to President Saleh for acts during his thirty-three-year rule in Yemen whereas his aides were granted immunity from prosecution for 'political offences' provided that they were not acts of terrorism. Is this kind of solution legitimate?

V. Alternatives to Prosecution: Transitional Justice et al

Retributive justice requires that there be proportionate punishment as a morally justifiable response to crime, so that the victim of the crime can find satisfaction and society be saved by the deterrence of further commission of crime. Restorative (or

[28] Note MFA REL 13/23A, dated 29 Aug 2010, from the Ministry of Foreign Affairs of Kenya addressed to all diplomatic missions and international organizations accredited to Kenya, enclosing the Kenyan Govt's official statement in response to the decision of Pre-Trial Chamber I of the ICC to inform the UN Security Council of Mr Al Bashir's presence in Kenya (Doc ICC-02/05-01/09 27 Aug 2010). Chad's reason was gleaned from various media reports at that time.

reparative) justice, on the other hand, places an emphasis on the needs of victims and perpetrators of crime, whereby the perpetrators are to acknowledge and take responsibility for their conduct by giving reparation to their victims after having dialogue with them.[29] Restorative justice, for example through truth commissions, has been utilized as a crucial part of a political process of transition when the previous oppressive regime transfers its government power to a new regime that better protects the human rights of those under its jurisdiction or control. The truth commissions are normally entrusted with investigating and documenting atrocities, identifying the perpetrators of atrocities and involving them in a process of public assumption of their individual responsibilities, providing redress to victims of mass atrocities, and making recommendations for reform and establishing a mechanism to ensure accountability for future atrocities. After the end of the apartheid regime in South Africa, prosecuting those involved in implementing the racially oppressive regime would involve hundreds of thousands of prosecution which would be costly, time-consuming, and disruptive to national reconciliation and harmony. The mechanism of a Truth and Reconciliation Commission was resorted to instead. The work of some truth commissions, such as the ones in Argentina, Chile, and Peru, facilitated national prosecution of perpetrators of crimes covered under their respective mandates. In any case, these national mechanisms cannot supersede the international criminal tribunals having jurisdiction over the crimes in question. Neither can they override the obligation to extradite or prosecute binding upon the State(s) concerned.[30]

After the serious violations of international human rights and international humanitarian law in Rwanda in 1994, including the commission of genocide, the ICTR was set up to render retributive justice despite the opposition of the Rwandan Government. Inside Rwanda, *gacaca* (grassroots or community) courts worked for restorative justice to achieve closure and national reconciliation between Tutsi and Hutu ethnic groups who had been enemies in 1994.[31] Judges of the *gacaca* courts were chosen from among 250,000 ordinary Rwandans elected by their neighbours to collect information on the atrocities in Rwanda in 1994, try, and sentence the perpetrators who were *not* 'the planners, organizers, instigators, supervisors of the genocide; the leaders at the national, provincial or district level, within political parties, army, religious denominations or militia; the well-known murderers and those who committed rape or acts of sexual torture' who were subject to prosecution by

[29] Kathleen Daly, 'Restorative Justice versus Retributive Justice' (2005) 60 Crim Justice Matters 28; Wesley Cragg, *The Practice of Punishment: Towards a Theory of Restorative Justice* (Routledge 1992) 15.

[30] Steven R Ratner, Jason S Abrams, and James L Bischoff, *Accountability for Human Rights Atrocities in International Law: Beyond the Nuremberg Legacy* (3rd edn, OUP 2009) 259–72; Ilias Bantekas and Susan Nash, *International Criminal Law* (3rd edn, Routledge-Cavendish 2007) 580–84; Adolfo Ceretti, 'Collective Violence and International Crimes' in Antonio Cassese (ed), *The Oxford Companion to International Criminal Justice* (OUP 2009) 5, 14.

[31] According to José E Alvarez ('Alternatives to International Criminal Justice' in Cassese, *Oxford Companion to International Criminal Justice* 25, 38), '[a] doctrinaire approach to the duty to prosecute all perpetrators of serious international crimes would require future Rwandas to undertake what no government has ever done and no government, however rich, is ever likely to do, namely conduct fair and speedy trials for one-third of its adult population.'

Rwandan formal criminal courts. The *gacaca* courts relied substantially on confession procedures and guilty pleas. Although they could impose prison sentences of up to thirty years, they might impose 'community service' as a means of compensating the surviving victims of the 1994 atrocities.[32]

The restorative, or reparative, justice used during the transitional phase is therefore also called transitional justice comprising the 'full range of processes and mechanisms associated with a society's attempts to come to terms with the legacy of large-scale abuses, in order to ensure accountability, serve justice, and achieve reconciliation'.[33] Transitional justice is subject to criticisms when it grants amnesties to perpetrators of crimes. The ILC Special Rapporteur on the topic 'Crimes against humanity' points out that there are conflicting views as to the permissibility of amnesties under international law. No international treaty explicitly prohibits amnesties; Article 6(5) of the Protocol Additional to the Geneva Conventions of 12 August 1949, and relating to the protection of victims of non-international armed conflicts,[34] even encourages amnesties at the end of internal armed conflicts.[35] A possibility of including a provision on amnesty was too controversial for the negotiations for both the ICC Statute and the 2006 International Convention for the Protection of All Persons from Enforced Disappearance[36] that the final Statute and Convention omit any such provision. Although ad hoc international or 'hybrid' criminal courts as well as the Inter-American Court of Human Rights and the African Commission on Human and Peoples' Rights do not recognize amnesties granted by the States concerned to persons being prosecuted by these courts,[37] State practice beyond that is far from universal. The European Court of Human Rights cautions, *obiter*, that while there is the 'growing tendency in international law' against amnesties to grave breaches of fundamental human rights as they are incompatible with the unanimously recognized obligation of States to prosecute and punish such crimes, amnesties may be possible in particular circumstances, such as a reconciliation process and/or as a form of compensation to victims.[38] Since the granting of an amnesty by one State has no direct effect on prosecutions in a different State with concurrent prescriptive jurisdiction over the crime(s) in question, the ILC suggests that account must be taken of various situation-specific factors, and any amnesty would have to be evaluated in the light of that State's obligations under, *inter alia*, the obligation to extradite or prosecute and under customary international law as it currently exists

[32] Cécile Aptel, 'Gacaca' in Cassese, ibid 329; cf also Vanessa Thalmann, 'Rwandan Genocide Cases', ibid 498.

[33] *The Rule of Law and Transitional Justice in Conflict and Post-Conflict Societies*, UN Doc S/2004/616 2 (3 Aug 2004) §8, quoted in Fannie Lafontaine, 'Transitional Justice' in Cassese, ibid 538, 539.

[34] 1125 UNTS 609.

[35] 'At the end of hostilities, the authorities in power shall endeavour to grant the broadest possible amnesty to persons who have participated in the armed conflict, or those deprived of their liberty for reasons related to the armed conflict, whether they are interned or detained.'

[36] 2716 UNTS 3.

[37] See eg *Prosecutor v Furundzija* (Judgment) IT-95-17/1-T (10 Dec 1998) §155; ILC, 'Report of… its 66th Session' A/CN.4/678 §§121–24, and cases cited in the accompanying footnote.

[38] European Court of Human Rights in *Marguš v Croatia* [GC], no 4455/10 §139, 27 May 2014.

or as it evolves in the future,[39] as well as fulfil its obligations in relation to victims and others.[40]

Blanket amnesties issued by those who themselves are alleged to have committed mass atrocities are self-serving efforts to evade the rule of law and should not be recognized.[41] However, as argued by one learned author, the ICC Statute provide three or four routes for amnesties: (1) by the UN Security Council exercising its authority to defer investigation or prosecution pursuant to Article 16 of the ICC Statute; (2) through prosecutorial discretion under Article 53 of the Statute to the effect that an investigation would not 'serve the interests of justice'; (3) through a decision pursuant to Article 17 of the Statute that complementarity has been satisfied because an investigation, for example by a truth and reconciliation commission, undertaken prior to the granting of an amnesty, constitutes a satisfactory investigation; or (4) through the State Party concerned pardoning a perpetrator after a trial which is not a mere sham in the sense of being intended to shield the perpetrator from criminal justice.[42]

An argument is frequently made that sovereign States and their respective legal systems should determine who should be given an amnesty (including immunity) under their domestic law and when such amnesty comes to an end.

The case of former Guatemalan President General Efrain Ríos Montt is illustrative. In 1982, Ríos Montt staged a *coup d'état* to overthrow the then Guatemalan Government, but he was subsequently toppled by another coup led by another army general in 1983. In 1986, the latter general granted an amnesty to Ríos Montt and his aides for their acts while in office. Ríos Montt also enjoyed immunity from prosecution while he served as a Guatemalan congressman for fifteen years until he lost his re-election bid late in 2011 and was put under house arrest. On 1 March 2012 a Guatemalan court ruled that the 1986 amnesty decree was invalidated by the provisions of the 1948 Convention on the Prevention and Punishment of the Crime of Genocide to which Guatemala had become a State Party in 1950 and which was implemented in Guatemala's domestic law in 1973. Therefore, Ríos Montt has no amnesty or immunity from prosecution for the charges, brought in January 2012, of ordering 1,771 murders, 1,400 human rights violations, including rapes and torture, and displacement of 29,000 indigenous Guatemalans in a 'scorched earth' campaign aimed at eliminating the support for a left-wing guerrilla movement during his regime in 1982–83. At the age of 90, in 2017 he faced a second trial for genocide, this time for the killing of some 200 persons during a massacre in 1982.

Another example is the peace accord between the Colombian Government and the insurgent or 'rebel' group called the Revolutionary Armed Forces of Colombia,

[39] Third report of the Special Rapporteur on the topic 'Crimes against humanity', UN Doc A/CN.4/704 §§285–97. See also Diane Orentlicher, 'Immunities and Amnesties' in Sadat, *Forging a Convention for Crimes against Humanity* 202, 217–22.

[40] §(11) of the commentary to Art 10 of the Draft Articles on Crimes against humanity (ILC, 'Report ... of its 66th session' A/CN.4/678, 21, 124).

[41] José E Alvarez, 'Alternatives to International Criminal Justice' in Cassese, *Oxford Companion to International Criminal Justice* 25, 36.

[42] ibid 37. Cf Roger O'Keefe, *International Criminal Law* (OUP 2015) 461–82.

or FARC. Both sides agreed in 2015 to end the internal armed conflict that had been ravaging Colombia since 1964, with more than 220,000 persons estimated to have been killed. The Integral System of Truth, Reparations, Justice and Non-repetition forms part of the peace accord, and is implemented by the Special Jurisdiction for Peace exercised by a new Tribunal for Peace so as to guarantee the rights to truth, reparations, justice, and non-repetition for victims of war crimes, crimes against humanity, serious human rights crimes, and similar crimes under Colombian law, committed during the internal armed conflict. While the Truth and Reconciliation Commission set up by South Africa's Government of National Unity after the end of the apartheid regime granted an amnesty to perpetrators of crimes who agreed to tell the truth, the Tribunal for Peace in Colombia will sentence those insurgents who fully and publicly disclose the truth about very serious crimes, and accept responsibility for them, to five to eight years of labour on projects to provide reparations to victims and 'effective restriction of liberty'. Prior to sentencing, the insurgents must propose a plan of work in consultation with victims in the affected area in order to hear their views and ascertain whether the victims accept the plan. After the Tribunal for Peace also hearing the victims' views, it will impose the sentence and order sanctions that may accept, reject, or modify the proposed plan of reparative labour. In contrast, those insurgents failing to disclose the truth or to accept responsibility will be sentenced by the Tribunal for Peace up to twenty years' imprisonment. The Integral System also includes a truth commission entrusted with examining the broader truth of what happened in the armed conflict, and why, beyond the facts and responsibilities of particular crimes. There will be no amnesty for crimes against humanity, war crimes, genocide, or serious international human rights crimes such as extrajudicial executions, forced disappearances, torture, sexual violence, forced displacements, taking civilian hostages, grave deprivations of liberty, and recruiting or using child soldiers, or for similar crimes under Colombian law. However, an amnesty may be granted for rebellion and related political crimes as well as other crimes inherent in the act of armed rebellion, but without prejudice to the victims' right for any damages caused by those crimes. Such amnesty is in accordance with the call of the Additional Protocol II of the 1949 Geneva Conventions for the 'broadest possible amnesty' at the end of hostilities in an internal armed conflict.[43] The Tribunal would comprise Colombian judges plus a few foreign judges, probably to lend credibility to them. The USA has sought the extradition from Colombia of a number of FARC members for crimes, such as murder and kidnapping, committed against US nationals as well as 'narco-terrorism', or drug trafficking to finance acts of terrorism. FARC certainly would not have agreed to the peace accord for their members to be extradited to stand trial in the USA.

The peace accord signed by the two sides on 24 August 2016 was narrowly rejected by the national referendum held in October that year, with 50.2 per cent voting against and 49.8 per cent in favour. The opponents of the deal were

[43] Douglass Cassel, 'Colombia's Integral System of Truth, Reparations, Justice and Non-repetition: FAQ (Frequently Asked Questions)' (27 Dec 2015) <http://humanrights.nd.edu/assets/177162/faq_drft_9.27.15.pdf>, accessed 22 November 2017.

concerned, among other things, that those who had committed atrocities would not be punished for their crimes, that it would legalize narco-trafficking, and that the insurgents would have a guaranteed representation in Congress. A revised peace deal of 24 November 2016, with fifty changes to the initial deal, was finally approved by Congress a few days later, without going through the process of referendum as previously. The most significant modification was probably that the peace accord would not be incorporated into the Colombian Constitution as previously agreed, thereby leaving open the possibility that it might be modified by Congress, the judiciary, or a new Colombian administration. The modification dropped the participation of foreign judges, permitting only Colombian judges to hear cases. The Tribunal would also consider new cases during its first two years and seek to conclude its work within a decade. The Colombian Supreme Court would have competence to review the Tribunal's decisions. In addition, FARC agreed to forfeit their assets, some of which derived from drug trafficking, to help compensate victims of the armed conflict. To address the concern regarding impunity, the revised accord clarifies that 'effective restrictions of liberty' referred to in the initial peace accord must be served in areas no larger than the rural hamlets designated for FARC's disarmament and demobilization and supervised by the Tribunal and verified by the UN Mission on Colombia and the UN Office of the High Commissioner for Human Rights. Nonetheless, the provision in the initial accord allowing FARC members convicted of serious human rights violations to participate in politics remained unchanged since the main goal of any peace negotiation with a domestic insurgent group is to convince it to lay down arms in return for participation in the political process and assimilation into society.

Since the situation in Colombia has been subject to the ICC Prosecutor's preliminary investigation, the ICC Prosecutor is monitoring the implementation of this peace accord, especially regarding the concrete and progressive investigative steps and prosecutorial activities undertaken with respect to the potential cases for prosecution before the ICC which the ICC Prosecutor has identified.

The Colombian experience could serve as a good model for granting a limited amnesty in comparable circumstances. Although it differs from South Africa's Truth and Reconciliation Commission, the broader amnesty offered by the latter was not *unilaterally* issued by those who themselves were alleged to have committed mass atrocities, but as an essential part of joint efforts by all stakeholders for the sake of national peace and unity. It is submitted that a blanket amnesty issued unilaterally by perpetrators of mass atrocities as self-serving efforts to evade the rule of law must not be recognized. This submission is in line with the Report of the UN Secretary General on 'Implementing the Responsibility to Protect: Accountability for Prevention'. The Report posits that the removal of statutory limitations, amnesties, or immunities that prevent prosecution of State officials and other individuals responsible for atrocities can help strengthen national legal frameworks for accountability. It also considers addressing past violations as a helpful measure to restore the dignity of victims, facilitate redress of violations, and enable national reconciliation. Therefore, States must ensure that those responsible for genocide, war crimes, or crimes against humanity in their territory are prosecuted, and if they fail to do so the international community should consider all legal options available to ensure justice for victims and to prevent recurrence.[44] It is encouraging that the international community is often willing to step in for worthy causes. For instance, the Extraordinary African Chambers set up within the Senegalese court system to try Hissène Habré had a budget of €7.4 million. It was reportedly funded by approximately €3 million in contribution from Chad, €2 million from the European Union, €1 million from the Netherlands, US$1 million from the African Union, another US$1 million from the USA, €500,000 from Germany, €300,000 from France, and €100,000 from Luxembourg.[45]

Any amnesty would have to be evaluated in the light of that State's obligations under, *inter alia*, the obligation to extradite or prosecute under customary international law and applicable treaty provisions.[46]

An interesting development is that of the Agreement on the Resolution of the Conflict in the Republic of South Sudan,[47] signed in August 2015 by the parties to the conflicts in South Sudan. This Agreement, mediated by Africa's Intergovernment Authority on Development, includes Chapter V ('Transitional Justice, Accountability, Reconciliation and Healing') which provides for three main mechanisms to be set up by legislation enacted by South Sudan's Transitional Government of National Unity (Transition Period) (TGoNU).

First, the Commission for Truth, Reconciliation and Healing (CTRH) will be established as a critical part of the peace building process in South Sudan, to spearhead efforts to address the legacy of conflicts, promote peace, national reconciliation, and healing.

Secondly, an independent hybrid judicial body called the Hybrid Court for South Sudan (HCSS) shall be established by the African Union Commission to investigate and prosecute individuals bearing the responsibility for violations of international law and/or applicable South Sudanese law, committed from 15 December 2013 to the end of the Transitional Period. The HCSS shall have jurisdiction with respect to the crimes of genocide, crimes against humanity, war crimes, and other serious crimes under international law and relevant laws of the Republic of South Sudan including gender-based crimes and sexual violence. The HCSS shall be independent and distinct from the national judiciary in its operations, and shall carry out its own investigations. It shall have primacy over any national courts of the Republic of South Sudan. A person who planned, instigated, ordered, committed, aided and abetted, conspired in, or participated in a joint criminal enterprise in the planning, preparation, or execution of a crime under the jurisdiction of the HCSS shall be

[44] The Report, submitted in August 2017, was the 9th such report on the responsibility to protect but the first one by UN Secretary General António Guterres. There is a summary by the Global Centre for Responsibility to Protect <http://www.globalr2p.org/media/files/2017-summary-of-the-secretary-generals-report-on-r2p.pdf>, accessed 22 November 2017.

[45] Human Rights Watch <http://www.hrw.org/news/2012/12/19/senegal-proceedings-against-hissene-habre-draw-near>, accessed 22 November 2017.

[46] Cf Third report of the Special Rapporteur on the topic 'Crimes against humanity', UN Doc A/CN.4/704 §297.

[47] <http://www.gurtong.net/LinkClick.aspx?fileticket=CytVwytJdyM%3D&tabid=124>, accessed 22 November 2017.

individually responsible for the crime. The HCSS may order the forfeiture of the property, proceeds, and any assets acquired unlawfully or by criminal conduct, and their return to their rightful owner or to the State of South Sudan. The HCSS shall also award appropriate remedies to victims, including but not limited to reparations and compensation. The HCSS shall not be impeded or constrained by any statutes of limitations or the granting of pardons, immunities, or amnesties. No one shall be exempted from criminal responsibility on account of their official capacity as a government official, an elected official, or claiming the defence of superior orders. Individuals indicted or convicted by the HCSS shall not be eligible for participation in the TGoNU, or in its successor government(s) for a period of time determined by law, or, if already participating in the TGoNU or in its successor government(s), they shall lose their position in government. If proved innocent, individuals indicted shall be entitled to compensation as shall be determined by law.

The third mechanism under the Agreement is the Compensation and Reparation Authority (CRA). The TGoNU shall, within six months of the signing of this Agreement, set up a Compensation and Reparation Fund (CRF) and CRA to administer the CRF.

Unfortunately, there has been no peace in South Sudan after the signing of the Agreement. Yet, Chapter V of the Agreement shows a trend in post-conflict transitional justice that duly takes into account the need for individual criminal responsibility. This formula could be emulated elsewhere.

VI. Ending Impunity: Syria and Beyond

Syria has become a failed State since the uprising against President Bashar Al-Assad in 2011 has led to a civil war between several sides and subsequent international interventions leading to 'proxy wars' between some of the world's major military powers. The Independent International Commission of Inquiry on the Syrian Arab Republic was set by the UN Human Rights Council in August 2011.[48] It is entrusted with investigating all alleged violations of international human rights law including crimes against humanity in Syria since March 2011 as well as establishing the facts and circumstances that may amount to such violations and of the crimes committed and, where possible, identifying those responsible in order to ensure that they be held accountable therefor.

On 10 September 2015, France's Foreign Minister asked French prosecutors to proceed with the investigation of mass torture allegedly committed by the Assad regime in Syria after authenticating tens of thousands of photographs taken by a defector, a former police photographer recruited by Syrian officials to take pictures of persons detained by the Syrian Government. The extent to which France can prosecute perpetrators of such atrocities depends on French criminal law, including

[48] A/HRC/S-17/1 (21 Aug 2011).

the requirement that there be a French victim and the presence of the accused in France.[49]

Since May 2016, Germany has commenced its war crimes trial over atrocities in Syria, after mass arrivals of refugees and asylum seekers have brought witnesses, victims, as well as suspects into Germany. Among other key war crimes suspects are Ibrahim Al F, a Syrian who was alleged to be a leader of an Islamist rebel group notorious for kidnapping and torturing civilians in Aleppo, Syria, and Suliman AS, a Syrian suspected of having kidnapped a UN soldier in 2013.[50] A landmark development occurred in March 2017, when nine Syrian torture survivors, invoking Germany's universal jurisdiction law enacted to implement Germany's obligations under the ICC Statute, filed a criminal complaint with the German federal public prosecutor against six high-ranking Syrian officials in the Syrian military intelligence service close to President Assad, accusing them of having committed war crimes and crimes against humanity by subjecting the complainants to systematic torture in three secret Damascus prisons between October 2011 and July 2015. The German federal prosecutor started hearing witness testimony in this case on 20 July 2017.

Unfortunately for victims and the prosecution, high-level officials or senior military commanders are unlikely to travel to States exercising universal jurisdiction, and if they sometimes do they must be certain the host State will accord them immunity from prosecution. Domestic prosecution units entrusted with serious crimes committed abroad on a mass scale more often than not do not have adequate human and financial resources to take on too many cases at the same time. Victim participation may also not be a norm at domestic criminal prosecution of core crimes of international concern.[51]

On 21 December 2016 the UN General Assembly adopted Resolution 248 on the 'International, Impartial and Independent Mechanism to Assist in the Investigation and Prosecution of Those Responsible for the Most Serious Crimes under International Law Committed in the Syrian Arab Republic since March 2011'.[52] The resolution notes with concern the impunity for serious violations of international law and violations and abuses of human rights law committed during the conflict in Syria, in particularly the likelihood that crimes against humanity and war crimes might have been committed. It emphasizes, among other things, the need to ensure accountability through appropriate, fair, and independent investigations and prosecutions at the domestic or international level. Operative paragraph 3

[49] Adam Nossiter, 'France Opens Criminal Investigation of Torture in Syria Under Assad' (NY Times 30 Sept 2015) <https://www.nytimes.com/2015/10/01/world/europe/france-investigates-syria-torture-bashar-assad.html> accessed 22 November 2017.

[50] 'Germany to start trials over Syrian war crimes, as refugee influx brings suspects into country' (*ABC News*, 1 May 2016) <http://www.abc.net.au/news/2016-05-01/refugee-influx-spurs-germany-to-tackle-syrian-war-crimes/7374152>, accessed 22 November 2017.

[51] Patrick Kroker and Alexandra Lily Kather, 'Justice for Syria? Opportunities and Limitations of Universal Jurisdiction Trials in Germany', *EJIL Talk!* (12 Aug 2016) <https://www.ejiltalk.org/justice-for-syria-opportunities-and-limitations-of-universal-jurisdiction-trials-in-germany/>, accessed 22 November 2017.

[52] UNGA Res 248 (2017) UN Doc A/RES/71/248 (11 Jan 2017) with 105 votes in favour to 15 against and 52 abstentions.

of the resolution welcomes the efforts by States to investigate and prosecute crimes within their jurisdiction committed in Syria, 'in accordance with their national legislation and international law, and encourages other States to do the same and to share relevant information to that end with other States'. Operative paragraph 4 decides to set up the International Impartial and Independent Mechanism (IIIM) to Assist in the Investigation and Prosecution of Those Responsible for the Most Serious Crimes under International Law Committed in the Syrian Arab Republic since March 2011 under the auspices of the UN to closely cooperate with the Independent International Commission of Inquiry on the Syrian Arab Republic 'to collect, consolidate, preserve and analyse evidence of violations of international humanitarian law and human rights violations and abuses and to prepare files in order to facilitate and expedite fair and independent criminal proceedings, in accordance with international law standards, in national, regional or international courts or tribunals that have or may in the future have jurisdiction over these crimes, in accordance with international law.' As of 1 August 2017, thirty-six States pledged financial contributions to the IIIM totalling approximately US$9 million,[53] some US$4 million short of the estimated budget for the first year of the IIIM's operation.

The establishment of the IIIM by the UN General Assembly is controversial as some UN Member States considered that the UN General Assembly has acted *ultra vires*, overstepping into the purview of the UN Security Council. If the UN Security Council is able to set up an international criminal tribunal to punish the said crimes committed in Syria through the exercise of the Council's prerogative under Chapter VII of the UN Charter, all States shall be bound to surrender the persons sought by the tribunal, as in the case of the ICTY and the ICTR. Here, the third alternative of the obligation to extradite or prosecute comes into play. However, if there is no such tribunal, what is the meaning of investigation and prosecution of these crimes within their jurisdiction committed in Syria 'in accordance with their national legislation and international law' and criminal proceedings in national courts that have jurisdiction over these crimes 'in accordance with international law'? Is this pursuant to treaty obligations and/or customary international law? Is universal jurisdiction acceptable for these crimes committed in Syria?

The support for the IIIM gained traction after the reported confirmation that chemical weapons had been used in Syria. However, when there was an optimistic prospect for achieving the all-inclusive political solution for Syria in mid-2017, bringing individual criminal responsibility to account—which might undermine the said prospect—seemed to lose its impetus and priority in the eyes of the States participating in the diplomatic negotiation. 'Prosecuting those engaged in the peace negotiation, in particular Assad and his aides, would derail the peace process and perpetuate the ongoing situations in Syria,' was a familiar refrain. Another reason for keeping Assad in power was believed to be the failure of the major world powers directly involved in the Syrian conflicts to find his replacement with undoubted loyalty to all of them—an improbable feat indeed. Former ICTY and ICTR Prosecutor Carla del Ponte, a

[53] Denmark, Netherlands, Germany, and Finland were the largest donors, contributing over US$1 million each.

member of the Commission of Inquiry on Syria, publically vented her frustration with the Commission as it was not backed by any political will and was powerless as long as the UN Security Council did nothing, including not referring the situation in Syria to the ICC even though the situation in Syria was much worse than the one in the former Yugoslavia and the one in Rwanda which had led to the establishment of the ICTY and the ICTR, respectively.[54] The Syrian tragedy is a case study of how criminal justice is held hostage to international strategic goals of certain powers that be with the veto power in the UN Security Council. Let's hope that if the Syrian conflicts ever come to an end, those responsible for atrocities in Syria will be held criminally responsible somehow, somewhere, and that justice will prevail at long last.

The situation surrounding members of the Islamic State of Iraq and the Levant (ISIL) is also interesting. They come from various States. ISIL members operating in one State, say, Syria, may be Syrians or non-Syrians. The crimes committed by them include crimes against humanity, war crimes, and probably genocide. ISIL members could be punished by an ad hoc international criminal tribunal to be set up, and by the ICC in so far as the States of nationality of the accused are party to the ICC Statute[55] or where the UN Security Council has referred the situation in the State where the crimes have been committed by ISIL members to the ICC pursuant to Article 13(b) of the ICC Statute.[56] Where an act of terrorism committed by ISIL members has an international element, they could be extradited or prosecuted under the relevant conventions against international terrorism, such as the 1997 International Convention for the Suppression of Terrorist Bombings,[57] Article 8(1) of which follows the 'Hague formula' on the obligation to extradite or prosecute.

VII. Future Prospects of *aut dedere aut judicare* in International Criminal Justice

The establishment of international criminal courts or tribunals—permanent, ad hoc, hybrid etc—have not deterred perpetration of serious crimes of international concern. Ad hoc courts/tribunals have been perceived as instruments for victors' justice, and being biased against a particular groups in a society.[58] The permanent

[54] 'Veteran prosecutor to quit UN Syria human rights probe', *Al Jazeera* (7 Aug 2017) <http://www.aljazeera.com/news/2017/08/veteran-prosecutor-quit-syria-human-rights-probe-170806211848125.html>, accessed 22 November 2017.

[55] Art 12(2), ICC Statute.

[56] That provision stipulates that the ICC may exercise its jurisdiction over the crimes under the ICC Statute if '[a] A situation in which one or more of such crimes appears to have been committed is referred to the Prosecutor by the Security Council acting under Chapter VII of the Charter of the United Nations'.

[57] 2149 UNTS 256.

[58] With respect to the ICTY, see the criticisms in Marko Milanovic, 'Courting Failure: Where Are International Criminal Courts Likely to be Believed by Local Audience?' in Kevin John Heller, Federic Meegret, Sarah Nouwen, Jens Ohlin, and Darryl Robinson (eds), *The Oxford Handbook of International Criminal Law* (OUP, forthcoming); Milanovic, 'The Impact of the ICTY on the Former Yugoslavia: An Anticipatory Post-Mortem' (2016) 110 AJIL 233, and 'Establishing the Facts about

ICC has not been functioning as expected. When perpetrators of such crimes also enjoy impunity in domestic courts, criminal justice fails because it ceases to deter future perpetrators from committing these crimes.

Do we have to live with 'imperfect justice'?

An in-depth research has found that between 1993 and 2016 a total number of 313 individuals were indicted before the ICTY, ICTR, Special Court for Sierra Leone, Khmer Rouge Tribunal, and ICC, 198 of whom were put on trial at the cost of more than US$6 billion. The commonly articulated goals for international criminal justice are: (1) preventing violations of international criminal law; (2) ending impunity for past violations; (3) maintaining and restoring international peace and security; (4) establishing a reliable historical record; (5) providing closure or redress for victims; (6) expressing condemnation of heinous crimes; (7) fostering post-conflict reconciliation; (8) developing international criminal law; and (9) retribution. International criminal courts are most likely to achieve retribution, assigning responsibility for violations of the law and punishing the offender. However, the author of that research considers the goal of preventing violations of international criminal law as the highest and that of maintaining and restoring international peace and security the second highest in the hierarchy of goals for international criminal justice. In his view, these two are valued the most in every society, whereas the other goals are merely mechanisms to attain the two top goals.[59] This present author concurs with the overall conclusion in that research, but would contend that preventing violations of international criminal law can only be attained by States extraditing or prosecuting the person who has committed a crime, or surrendering the person to a competent international tribunal. Or else, the world is not safe from monstrous criminals running amok among us.

If justice is *temporarily* suspended for the sake of international peace and security or a national peace/reconciliation, it must be 'reactivated' when the time is ripe—so that justice is done and seen to be done eventually. Therefore, it makes sense to follow the wisdom of the draftsmen of Article 29 of the ICC Statute in excluding the crimes within the ICC's jurisdiction from being subject to any statute of limitations. The same logic must apply to all core crimes proscribed by *jus cogens* subject to prosecution at either the horizontal or vertical level.

Mass Atrocities: Accounting for the Future of the ICTY to Persuade Target Audiences' (2016) 47 Georgetown JIL 1321. Regarding analyses of the ICTR's work, see André Klip, 'The Legacy of the International Criminal for Rwanda' in Ankumah, *The International Criminal Court and Africa* 509; Leo C Nwoye, 'Transitional Justice and the ICC: Lessons from Rwanda', ibid 549. The UN General Assembly organized a debate on the 'Role of International Criminal Justice in Reconciliation' on 10 and 11 April 2013. Both the President of Bosnia and Herzegovina and the President of Serbia strongly criticized the work of the ICTY as being biased, and with a double standard. The Minister of Justice of Rwanda opined that the ICTR had been facing a confidence crisis and had not achieved its mandate as intended. The Permanent Representative of Croatia to the United Nations stated that although Croatia was not satisfied with the ICTY's work, Croatia cooperated with the ICTY and respected its judgments. The representative of Cambodia made an exception by praising the Extraordinary Chambers in the Court of Cambodia (ECCC), or the Khmer Rouge Tribunal, as a success and being instrumental in helping to ensure peace and stability in Cambodia.

59 Stuart Ford, 'A Hierarchy of the Goals of International Criminal Court' (2017) 27 Minnesota JIL forthcoming.

APPENDIX

Final Report of the International Law Commission on the Topic 'The Obligation to Extradite or Prosecute (*aut dedere aut judicare*)'*

A. Introduction

57. The Commission, at its fifty-seventh session (2005), decided to include the topic 'The obligation to extradite or prosecute (*aut dedere aut judicare*)' in its programme of work and appointed Mr Zdzislaw Galicki as Special Rapporteur.[412]

58. The Special Rapporteur submitted four reports. The Commission received and considered the preliminary report at its fifty-eighth session (2006), the second report at its fifty-ninth session (2007), the third report at its sixtieth session (2008), and the fourth report at its sixty-third session (2011).[413]

59. At the sixty-first session (2009), an open-ended Working Group was established under the chairmanship of Mr Alain Pellet,[414] and from its discussions, a proposed general framework for consideration of the topic, specifying the issues to be addressed by the Special Rapporteur, was prepared.[415] At the sixty-second session (2010), the Working Group was reconstituted and, in the absence of its Chairman, was chaired by Mr Enrique Candioti.[416] The Working Group had before it the Survey of multilateral conventions which might be of relevance for the topic prepared by the Secretariat (A/CN.4/630).

60. At the sixty-fourth (2012) and sixty-fifth (2013) sessions, the Commission established an open-ended Working Group on the obligation to extradite or prosecute (*aut dedere aut*

* From ILC, 'Report of the International Law Commission on the work of its 66th Session' (5 May–6 June and 7 July–8 Aug 2014) UN Doc A/69/10, 139–65. Reproduced in accordance with the Guidelines on the Publication of Commission Documents (ILC, 'Report of the International Law Commission on the work of its 59th Session' (7 May–5 June and 9 July–10 Aug 2007) UN Doc A/62/10 §381).

412 At its 2865th meeting, 4 Aug 2005 (*Official Records of the General Assembly, Sixtieth Session, Supp 10* (A/60/10) para 500). The General Assembly, in para 5 of resolution 60/22 of 23 Nov 2005, endorsed the decision of the Commission to include the topic in its programme of work. The topic had been included in the long-term programme of work of the Commission at its fifty-sixth session (2004), on the basis of the proposal annexed to that year's report (*Official Records of the General Assembly, Fifty-ninth Session, Supp 10* (A/59/10) paras 362–63).

413 A/CN.4/571 (preliminary report); A/CN.4/585 and Corr 1 (2nd report); A/CN.4/603 (3rd report); and A/CN.4/648 (4th report).

414 During its sixtieth session, at its 2988th meeting, 31 July 2008, the Commission decided to establish a working group on the topic under the chairmanship of Mr Alain Pellet, with a mandate and membership to be determined at the sixty-first session (*Official Records of the General Assembly, Sixty-third Session, Supp 10* (A/63/10) para 315).

415 For the proposed general framework prepared by the Working Group, see ibid, *Sixty-fourth Session, Supp 10* (A/64/10) para 204.

416 At its 3071st meeting, 30 July 2010, the Commission took note of the oral report of the temporary Chairman of the Working Group (ibid *Sixty-fifth Session, Supp 10* (A/65/10) paras 337–40).

judicare), under the chairmanship of Mr Kriangsak Kittichaisaree, to undertake an evaluation of the progress of work on the topic in the Commission, particularly in the light of the judgment of the International Court of Justice in the *Questions relating to the Obligation to Prosecute or Extradite (Belgium v Senegal)* case, of 20 July 2012,[417] and to explore possible future options to be taken by the Commission.[418]

B. Consideration of the Topic at the Present Session

61. At the present session, the Commission constituted a Working Group on the obligation to extradite or prosecute (*aut dedere aut judicare*) under the chairmanship of Mr Kriangsak Kittichaisaree. The Working Group continued to evaluate work on this topic, particularly in the light of comments made in the Sixth Committee at the sixty-eighth session of the General Assembly on the 2013 report of the Working Group.[419] The Working Group held two meetings, on 6 May and 4 June 2014.

62. The Working Group considered several options for the Commission in deciding how to proceed with its remaining work on the topic. After careful consideration, the Working Group deemed it appropriate that the Commission expedite its work on the topic and produce an outcome that was of practical value to the international community. The 2013 report constituted the basis of the final report of the Working Group. The Working Group also discussed the issues that were partially or not covered by its 2013 report but were subsequently raised in the Sixth Committee during the sixty-eighth session of the General Assembly, namely: gaps in the existing conventional regime; the transfer of a suspect to an international or special court or tribunal as a potential third alternative to extradition or prosecution; the relationship between the obligation to extradite or prosecute and *erga omnes* obligations or *jus cogens* norms; the customary international law status of the obligation to extradite or prosecute; and other matters of continued relevance in the 2009 General Framework. The Working Group's consideration of the above issues exhausted all the issues remaining to be analysed in relation to the topic.

63. At its 3217th meeting, on 7 July 2014, the Commission took note of report of the Working Group (A/CN.4/L.844), which, *inter alia*, contained the recommendation that the Commission: (1) adopt the 2013 and 2014 reports, which provide useful guidance for States; and (2) conclude its consideration of the topic 'Obligation to extradite or prosecute (*aut dedere aut judicare*)'.

64. At its 3242nd meeting, on 7 August 2014, the Commission adopted the final report on the topic, 'Obligation to extradite or prosecute (*aut dedere aut judicare*)' (see Sect. C below) and decided to conclude its consideration of the topic. It also expressed its deep appreciation to the Chairman of the Working Group, Mr Kriangsak Kittichaisaree, for his very valuable contribution and the work done in an efficient and expeditious manner. The

[417] *Questions relating to the Obligation to Prosecute or Extradite (Belgium v Senegal), Judgment, ICJ Reports 2012*, 422.

[418] At its 3152nd meeting, 30 July 2012, the Commission took note of the oral report of the Chairman of the Working Group (*Official Records of the General Assembly, Sixty-seventh Session, Supp 10* (A/67/10) paras 208–21) and at its 3189th meeting, 31 July 2013, the Commission took note of the report of the Working Group (*Official Records of the General Assembly, Sixty-eighth Session, Supp 10* (A/68/10) para 149).

[419] ibid *Sixty-eighth Session Supp 10* (A/68/10) annex A.

Commission also recalled, with gratitude, the work of the former Special Rapporteur on the topic, Mr Zdzislaw Galicki.

C. Final Report on the Topic

65. This report is intended to summarize and to highlight particular aspects of the work of the Commission on the topic 'The obligation to extradite or prosecute (*aut dedere aut judicare*)', in order to assist States in this matter.

1. Obligation to fight impunity in accordance with the rule of law

(1) The Commission notes that States have expressed their desire to cooperate among themselves, and with competent international tribunals, in the fight against impunity for crimes, in particular offences of international concern,[420] and in accordance with the rule of law.[421] In the Declaration of the High-level Meeting of the General Assembly on the Rule of Law at the National and International Levels, the Heads of State and Government and heads of delegation attending the meeting on 24 September 2012 committed themselves to 'ensuring that impunity is not tolerated for genocide, war crimes, crimes against humanity and for violations of international humanitarian law and gross violations of human rights law, and that such violations are properly investigated and appropriately sanctioned, including by bringing the perpetrators of any crimes to justice, through national mechanisms or, where appropriate, regional or international mechanisms, in accordance with international law'.[422] The obligation to cooperate in combating such impunity is given effect in numerous conventions, *inter alia*, through the obligation to extradite or prosecute.[423] The view that the obligation to extradite or prosecute plays a crucial role in the fight against

[420] See eg General Assembly resolution 2840 (XXVI) of 18 Dec 1971 entitled 'Question of the punishment of war criminals and of persons who have committed crimes against humanity'; General Assembly resolution 3074 (XXVIII) of 3 Dec 1973 on the 'Principles of international cooperation in the detection, arrest, extradition and punishment of persons guilty of war crimes and crimes against humanity'; and principle 18 of Economic and Social Council resolution 1989/65 of 24 May 1989 entitled 'Effective prevention and investigation of extra-legal, arbitrary and summary executions'.

[421] General Assembly resolution 67/1 of 24 Sept 2012.

[422] ibid para 22.

[423] See Part 3 below. In the case concerning *Questions relating to the Obligation to Prosecute or Extradite (Belgium v Senegal)*, the International Court of Justice states: 'Extradition and prosecution are alternative ways to combat impunity in accordance with Art. 7, para 1 [of the Convention against Torture and Other Cruel, Inhuman or Degrading Treatment or Punishment of 1984].' (*Questions relating to the Obligation to Prosecute or Extradite (Belgium v Senegal)*, Judgment, *ICJ Reports 2012*, 422, at 443 para 50). The Court adds that the States Parties to the Convention against Torture have 'a common interest to ensure, in view of their shared values, that acts of torture are prevented and that, if they occur, their authors do not enjoy impunity' (ibid 449 para 68). The Court reiterates that the object and purpose of the Convention are 'to make more effective the struggle against torture by avoiding impunity for the perpetrators of such acts' (ibid 451 para 74 and cf also para 75). Special Rapporteur Zdzislaw Galicki's fourth report dealt at length with the issue of the duty to cooperate in the fight against impunity. He cited the following examples of international instruments that provide a legal basis for the duty to cooperate: Art 1(3) of the Charter of the United Nations, the Declaration on Principles of International Law concerning Friendly Relations and Cooperation among States in accordance with the Charter of the United Nations, the preamble to the 1998 Rome Statute of the International Criminal Court, and guideline XII of the Guidelines of the Committee of Ministers of the Council of Europe on eradicating impunity for serious human rights violations, adopted by the Committee of Ministers, 30 Mar 2011, A/CN.4/648 paras 26–33.

impunity is widely shared by States;[424] the obligation applies in respect of a wide range of crimes of serious concern to the international community and has been included in all sectoral conventions against international terrorism concluded since 1970.

(2) The role the obligation to extradite or prosecute plays in supporting international co-operation to fight impunity has been recognized at least since the time of Hugo Grotius, who postulated the principle of *aut dedere aut punire* (either extradite or punish): 'When appealed to, a State should either punish the guilty person as he deserves, or it should entrust him to the discretion of the party making the appeal.'[425] The modern terminology replaces 'punishment' with 'prosecution' as the alternative to extradition in order to reflect better the possibility that an alleged offender may be found not guilty.

2. The importance of the obligation to extradite or prosecute in the work of the International Law Commission

(3) The topic 'The obligation to extradite or prosecute (*aut dedere aut judicare*)' may be viewed as having been encompassed by the topic 'Jurisdiction with regard to crimes committed outside national territory' which was on the provisional list of fourteen topics at the first session of the Commission in 1949.[426] It is also addressed in articles 8 (Establishment of jurisdiction) and 9 (Obligation to extradite or prosecute) of the 1996 Draft code of crimes against the peace and security of mankind. Article 9 of the Draft code stipulates an obligation to extradite or prosecute for genocide, crimes against humanity, crimes against United Nations and associated personnel, and war crimes.[427] The principle *aut dedere aut judicare* is said to have derived from 'a number of multilateral conventions'[428] that contain the obligation. An analysis of the draft code's history suggests that draft article 9 is driven by the need for an effective system of criminalization and prosecution of the said core crimes, rather than actual State practice and *opinio juris*.[429] The article is justified on the basis of the grave nature of the crimes involved and the desire to combat impunity for individuals who commit these crimes.[430] While the draft code's focus is on core crimes,[431] the material scope

[424] eg Belgium (A/CN.4/612 para 33); Denmark, Finland, Iceland, Norway, and Sweden (A/C.6/66/SR.26 para 10); Switzerland (ibid para 18); El Salvador (ibid para 24); Italy (ibid para 42); Peru (ibid para 64); Belarus (A/C.6/66/SR.27 para 41); Russian Federation (ibid para 64); and India (ibid para 81).

[425] Hugo Grotius, *De Jure Belli ac Pacis*, Bk II ch XXI sect IV (Francis W Kelsey Eng tr, Oxford/London: Clarendon/Humphrey Milford, 1925) 527–29 at 527).

[426] United Nations, *The Work of the International Law Commission*, vol 1 (8th edn (United Nations 2012) 37.

[427] 'Without prejudice to the jurisdiction of an international criminal court, the State Party in the territory of which an individual alleged to have committed a crime set out in article 17 [genocide], 18 [crimes against humanity], 19 [crimes against United Nations and associated personnel] or 20 [war crimes] is found shall extradite or prosecute that individual'. See also the Commission's commentary on this article (*Official Records of the General Assembly, Fifty-first Session Supp 10* (A/51/10) ch II).

[428] Draft code of crimes against the peace and security of mankind, art 8 para (3) (ibid).

[429] *Official Records of the General Assembly, Forty-ninth Session, Supp 10* (A/49/10) 80 para 142.

[430] Draft code of crimes against the peace and security of mankind, art 8 paras (3), (4) and (8) and art 9 para (2) (ibid *Fifty-first Session, Supp 10* (A/51/10)).

[431] At the first reading in 1991, the draft code comprised the following 12 crimes: aggression; threat of aggression; intervention; colonial domination and other forms of alien domination; genocide; apartheid; systematic or mass violations of human rights; exceptionally serious war crimes; recruitment, financing and training of mercenaries; international terrorism; illicit traffic in narcotic drugs; and wilful and severe damage to the environment. At its sessions in 1995 and 1996, the Commission reduced the number of crimes in the final draft code to four crimes: aggression; genocide; war crimes; and crimes

of the obligation to extradite or prosecute covers most crimes of international concern, as mentioned in (1) above.

3. Summary of work

(4) The following summarizes several key aspects of the Commission's work on this topic. In the past, some members of the Commission, including Special Rapporteur Zdzislaw Galicki, doubted the use of the Latin formula '*aut dedere aut judicare*', especially in relation to the term '*judicare*', which they considered as not reflecting precisely the scope of the term 'prosecute'. However, the Special Rapporteur considered it premature at that time to focus on the precise definition of terms, leaving them to be defined in a future draft article on 'Use of terms'.[432] The report of the Commission decided to proceed on the understanding that whether the mandatory nature of 'extradition' or that of 'prosecution' has priority over the other depends on the context and applicable legal regime in particular situations.

(5) The Commission considered useful to its work a wide range of materials, particularly: the Survey of multilateral conventions which may be of relevance for the Commission's work on the topic 'The obligation to extradite or prosecute (*aut dedere aut judicare*)' conducted by the Secretariat[433] (hereinafter 'Secretariat's Survey (2010)'), which identified multilateral instruments at the universal and regional levels that contain provisions combining extradition and prosecution as alternatives for the punishment of offenders; and the Judgment of 20 July 2012 of the International Court of Justice in the case concerning *Questions relating to the Obligation to Prosecute or Extradite (Belgium v Senegal).*

(a) Typology of provisions in multilateral instruments

(6) The Secretariat's Survey (2010) proposed a description and a typology of the relevant instruments in the light of these provisions, and examined the preparatory work of certain key conventions that had served as models in the field. For some provisions, it also reviewed any reservations made. It pointed out the differences and similarities between the reviewed provisions in different conventions and their evolution, and offered overall conclusions as to: (a) the relationship between extradition and prosecution in the relevant provisions; (b) the conditions

against humanity, adhering to the Nuremberg legacy as the criterion for the choice of the crimes covered by the draft code. The primary reason for this approach appeared to have been the unfavourable comments by 24 Governments to the list of 12 crimes proposed in 1991. A fifth crime, crimes against United Nations and associated personnel, was added at the last moment on the basis of its magnitude, the seriousness of the problem of attacks on such personnel and 'its centrality to the maintenance of international peace and security' (A/CN.4/448 and Add.1).

The crime of aggression was not subject to the provision of art 9 of the draft code. In the Commission's opinion, '[t]he determination by a national court of one State of the question of whether another State had committed aggression would be contrary to the fundamental principle of international law *par in parem imperium non habet*. … [and] the exercise of jurisdiction by the national court of a State which entails consideration of the commission of aggression by another State would have serious implications for international relations and international peace and security.' (Draft code of crimes against the peace and security of mankind, *Official Records of the General Assembly, Fifty-first Session, Supp 10* (A/51/10) 30 para 14).

[432] A/CN.4/603 paras 36–37. In his preliminary report, the Special Rapporteur discussed various Latin formulas relevant to this topic; namely: *aut dedere aut punire; judicare aut dedere; aut dedere aut prosequi; aut dedere, aut judicare, aut tergiversari*; and *aut dedere aut poenam persequi* (A/CN.4/571, paras 5–8). See also: Raphäel van Steenberghe, 'The Obligation to Extradite or Prosecute: Clarifying its Nature', *Journal of International Criminal Justice*, vol 9 (2011), 1089 at 1107–08, on the formulas *aut dedere aut punire, aut dedere aut prosequi*, and *aut dedere aut judicare.*

[433] A/CN.4/630.

applicable to extradition under the various conventions; and (c) the conditions applicable to prosecution under the various conventions. The Survey classified conventions that included such provisions into four categories: (a) the 1929 Convention for the Suppression of Counterfeiting Currency and other conventions that have followed the same model; (b) regional conventions on extradition; (c) the 1949 Geneva Conventions and the 1977 Additional Protocol I; and (d) the 1970 Hague Convention for the Suppression of Unlawful Seizure of Aircraft and other conventions that have followed the same model.

(7) The 1929 Convention for the Suppression of Counterfeiting Currency and other conventions that have followed the same model[434] typically: (a) criminalize the relevant offence, which the States Parties undertake to make punishable under their domestic laws; (b) make provision for prosecution and extradition which take into account the divergent views of States with regard to the extradition of nationals and the exercise of extraterritorial jurisdiction, the latter being permissive rather than compulsory; (c) contain provisions which impose an obligation to extradite, with prosecution coming into play once there is a refusal of extradition; (d) establish an extradition regime by which States undertake, under certain conditions, to consider the offence as extraditable; (e) contain a provision providing that a State's attitude on the general issue of criminal jurisdiction as a question of international law was not affected by its participation in the Convention; and (f) contain a non-prejudice clause with regard to each State's criminal legislation and administration. While some of the instruments under this model contain terminological differences of an editorial nature, others modify the substance of the obligations undertaken by States Parties.

(8) Numerous regional conventions and arrangements on extradition also contain provisions that combine options of extradition and prosecution,[435] although those instruments typically emphasize the obligation to extradite (which is regulated in detail) and only contemplate submission to prosecution as an alternative to avoid impunity in the context of that cooperation. Under that model, extradition is a means to ensure the effectiveness of criminal jurisdiction. States Parties have a general duty to extradite unless the request fits within a condition or exception, including mandatory and discretionary grounds for refusal. For instance, extradition of nationals could be prohibited or subject to specific safeguards. Provisions in subsequent agreements and arrangements have been subject to modification and adjustment over time, particularly in respect of conditions and exceptions.[436]

[434] eg. (a) 1936 Convention for the Suppression of the Illicit Traffic in Dangerous Drugs; (b) the 1937 Convention for the Prevention and Punishment of Terrorism; (c) the 1950 Convention for the Suppression of the Traffic in Persons and of the Exploitation of the Prostitution of Others; (d) the 1961 Single Convention on Narcotic Drugs; and (e) the 1971 Convention on Psychotropic Substances.

[435] These instruments include: (a) the 1928 Convention on Private International Law, also known as the 'Bustamante Code', under Book IV (International Law of Procedure), Title III (Extradition); (b) the 1933 Convention on Extradition; (c) the 1981 Inter-American Convention on Extradition; (d) the 1957 European Convention on Extradition; (e) the 1961 General Convention on Judicial Cooperation (*Convention générale de coopération en matière de justice*); (f) the 1994 Economic Community of West African States (ECOWAS) Convention on Extradition; and (g) the London Scheme for Extradition within the Commonwealth.

[436] It may also be recalled that General Assembly has adopted the Model Treaty on Extradition (resolution 45/116, annex) and the Model Treaty on Mutual Assistance in Criminal Matters (resolution 45/117). See also the 2004 *Model Law on Extradition* prepared by the United Nations Office on Drugs and Crime, Available at <http://www.unodc.org/pdf/model_law_extradition.pdf>. See also Revised Manuals on the Model Treaty on Extradition and on the Model Treaty on Mutual Assistance in Criminal Matters, available at: <http://www.unodc.org/pdf/model_treaty_extradition_revised_manual.pdf>, (visited on 3 June 2014).

(9) The four Geneva Conventions of 1949 contain the same provision whereby each High Contracting Party is obligated to search for persons alleged to have committed, or to have ordered to be committed, grave breaches, and to bring such persons, regardless of their nationality, before its own courts. However, it may also, if it prefers, and in accordance with its domestic legislation, hand such persons over for trial to another High Contracting Party concerned, provided that the latter has established a prima facie case.[437] Therefore, under that model, the obligation to search for and submit to prosecution an alleged offender is not conditional on any jurisdictional consideration and that obligation exists irrespective of any request for extradition by another party.[438] Nonetheless, extradition is an available option subject to a condition that the prosecuting State has established a prima facie case. That mechanism is made applicable to Additional Protocol I of 1977 by renvoi.[439]

(10) The 1970 Hague Convention for the Suppression of Unlawful Seizure of Aircraft stipulates in article 7 that '[t]he Contracting State in the territory of which the alleged offender is found shall, if it does not extradite him, be obliged without exception whatsoever and whether or not the offence was committed in its territory, to submit the case to its competent authorities for the purpose of prosecution.' This 'Hague formula' is a variation of the Geneva Conventions formula and has served as a model for several subsequent conventions aimed at the suppression of specific offences, principally in the fight against terrorism, but also in many other areas (including torture, mercenarism, crimes against United Nations and associated personnel, transnational crime, corruption, and enforced disappearance).[440]

[437] Arts 49, 50, 129, and 146, respectively, of the First, Second, Third, and Fourth Geneva Conventions. The reason these Geneva Conventions use the term 'hand over' instead of 'extradite' is explained in the Secretariat's Survey (2010) at para 54. According to Claus Kreβ ('Reflection on the *Iudicare* Limb of the Grave Breaches Regime' *Journal of International Criminal Justice* 7 (2009) 789), what the *judicare* limb of the grave breaches regime actually entails is a duty to investigate and, where so warranted, to prosecute and convict.

[438] See Jean S Pictet (ed), *The Geneva Conventions of 12 August 1949: Commentary*, vol 4 (International Committee of the Red Cross 1958) 593.

[439] Art 85(1), (3) and Art 88(2) of Additional Protocol I of 1977.

[440] These include, *inter alia*: (a) the 1971 Organization of American States (OAS) Convention to Prevent and Punish the Acts of Terrorism Taking the Form of Crimes Against Persons and Related Extortion that are of International Significance; (b) the 1971 Convention for the Suppression of Unlawful Acts against the Safety of Civil Aviation; (c) the 1973 Convention on the Prevention and Punishment of Crimes against Internationally Protected Persons, including Diplomatic Agents; (d) the 1977 European Convention on the Suppression of Terrorism; (e) 1977 Organization of African Unity Convention for the Elimination of Mercenarism in Africa; (f) the 1979 International Convention against the Taking of Hostages; (g) the 1979 Convention on the Physical Protection of Nuclear Material; (h) the 1984 Convention against Torture and Other Cruel, Inhuman or Degrading Treatment or Punishment; (i) the 1985 Inter-American Convention to Prevent and Punish Torture; (j) the 1987 South Asian Association for Regional Cooperation (SAARC) Regional Convention on Suppression of Terrorism and the 2004 Additional Protocol thereto; (k) the 1988 Protocol for the Suppression of Unlawful Acts of Violence at Airports Serving International Civil Aviation, Supplementary to the Convention for the Suppression of Unlawful Acts against the Safety of Civil Aviation; (l) the 1988 Convention for the Suppression of Unlawful Acts against the Safety of Maritime Navigation; (m) the 1988 United Nations Convention against Illicit Traffic in Narcotic Drugs and Psychotropic Substances; (n) the 1989 International Convention Against the Recruitment, Use, Financing and Training of Mercenaries; (o) the 1994 Inter-American Convention on the Forced Disappearance of Persons; (p) the 1994 Convention on the Safety of United Nations and Associated Personnel and its 2005 Optional Protocol; (q) the 1996 Inter-American Convention against Corruption; (r) the 1997 Inter-American Convention against the Illicit Manufacturing of and Trafficking in Firearms, Ammunition, Explosives, and Other Related Materials; (s) the 1997 Organization for Economic Cooperation and Development (OECD) Convention on Combating Bribery of Foreign Public Officials in International Business Transactions; (t) the 1997 International Convention for the Suppression of Terrorist Bombings;

However, many of those subsequent instruments have modified the original terminology which sometimes affect the substance of the obligations contained in the Hague formula.

(11) In his Separate Opinion in the Judgment of 20 July 2012 of the International Court of Justice in the case concerning *Questions relating to the Obligation to Prosecute or Extradite (Belgium v Senegal)*, Judge Yusuf also addressed the typology of 'treaties containing the formula *aut dedere aut judicare*' and divided them into two broad categories.[441] The first category of international conventions contained clauses which impose an obligation to extradite, and in which submission to prosecution becomes an obligation only after the refusal of extradition. Those conventions are structured in such a way that gives priority to extradition to the State in whose territory the crime is committed.The majority of those conventions do not impose any general obligation on States Parties to submit to prosecution the alleged offender, and such submission by the State on whose territory the alleged offender is present becomes an obligation only if a request for extradition has been refused, or some factors such as nationality of the alleged offender exist. Examples of the first category are article 9, paragraph 22 of the 1929 International Convention for the Suppression of Counterfeiting Currency, article 15 of the African Union Convention on Preventing and Combating Corruption, and article 5 of the Optional Protocol to the Convention on the Rights of the Child on the sale of children, child prostitution, and child pornography. The second category of international category of international conventions contains clauses which impose an obligation to submit to prosecution, with extradition being an available option, as well as clauses which impose an obligation to submit to prosecution, with extradition becoming an obligation if the State fails to do so. Such clauses in that category can be found in, for example, the relevant provisions of the four Geneva Conventions of 1949, article 7 paragraph 1 of the 1970 Hague Convention for the Suppression of Unlawful Seizure of Aircraft, and article 7 paragraph 1 of the Convention against Torture.

(12) In light of the above, the Commission considers that when drafting treaties, States can decide for themselves which conventional formula on the obligation to extradite or prosecute best suits their objective in a particular circumstance. Owing to the great diversity in the formulation, content, and scope of the obligation to extradite or prosecute in conventional

(u) the 1998 Convention on the Protection of the Environment through Criminal Law; (v) the 1999 Criminal Law Convention on Corruption; (w) the 1999 Second Protocol to the Convention for the Protection of Cultural Property in the Event of Armed Conflict; (x) the 1999 International Convention for the Suppression of the Financing of Terrorism; (y) the 2000 Optional Protocol to the Convention on the Rights of the Child on the sale of children, child prostitution and child pornography; (z) the 2000 United Nations Convention against Transnational Organized Crime and its Protocols; (aa) the 2001 Council of Europe Convention on Cybercrime; (bb) the 2003 African Union Convention on Preventing and Combating Corruption; (cc) the 2003 United Nations Convention against Corruption; (dd) the 2005 International Convention for the Suppression of Acts of Nuclear Terrorism; (ee) the 2005 Council of Europe Convention on the Prevention of Terrorism; (ff) the 2006 International Convention for the Protection of All Persons from Enforced Disappearance; (gg) the 2007 Association of South East Asian Nations (ASEAN) Convention on Counter-Terrorism; (hh) 2010 Protocol Supplementary to the Convention for the Suppression of Unlawful Seizure of Aircraft; and (ii) the 2010 Convention on the Suppression of Unlawful Acts Relating to International Civil Aviation.

[441] Sep Op of Judge Yusuf in the case concerning *Questions relating to the Obligation to Prosecute or Extradite (Belgium v Senegal)*, Judgment, *ICJ Reports 2012*, 422 at 567–68 paras 19–22. See also Secretariat survey (2010) para 126. Cf also Belgium's comments submitted to the Commission in 2009, where Belgium identified two types of treaties: (a) treaties that contain an *aut dedere aut judicare* clause with the obligation to prosecute conditional on refusal of a request for extradition of the alleged perpetrator of an offence; and (b) treaties that contain a *judicare vel dedere* clause with the obligation on States to exercise universal jurisdiction over perpetrators of the offences under the treaties, without making this obligation conditional on refusal to honour a prior extradition request (A/CN.4/612 para 15), quoted by Special Rapporteur Galicki in his fourth report (A/CN.4/648 para 85 and n 56).

practice, it would be futile for the Commission to engage in harmonizing the various treaty clauses on the obligation to extradite or prosecute.[442]

(13) Although the Commission finds that the scope of the obligation to extradite or prosecute under the relevant conventions should be analysed on a case-by-case basis, it acknowledges that there may be some general trends and common features in the more recent conventions containing the obligation to extradite or prosecute. One of the most relevant trends appears to be the use of the Hague formula that serves 'as a model for most of the contemporary conventions for the suppression of specific offences'.[443] Of the conventions drafted on or after 1970, approximately three-quarters follow the Hague formula. In those post-1970 conventions, there is a common trend that the custodial State shall, without exception, submit the case of the alleged offender to a competent authority if it does not extradite. Such obligation is supplemented by additional provisions that require States Parties: (a) to criminalize the relevant offence under its domestic laws; (b) to establish jurisdiction over the offence when there is a link to the crime or when the alleged offender is present on their territory and is not extradited; (c) to make provisions to ensure that the alleged offender is under custody and there is a preliminary enquiry; and (d) to treat the offence as extraditable.[444] In particular, under the prosecution limb of the obligation, the conventions only emphasize that the case be submitted to a competent authority for the purpose of prosecution. To a lesser extent, there is also a trend of stipulating that, absent prosecution by the custodial State, the alleged offender must be extradited without exception whatsoever.

(14) The Commission observes that there are important gaps in the present conventional regime governing the obligation to extradite or prosecute which may need to be closed. Notably, there is a lack of international conventions with this obligation in relation to most crimes against humanity,[445] war crimes other than grave breaches, and war crimes in non-international armed conflict.[446] In relation to genocide, the international cooperation

[442] As the Secretariat's Survey (2010) concludes (A/CN.4/630 para 153), 'The examination of conventional practice in this field shows that the degree of specificity of the various conventions in regulating these issues varies considerably, and that there exist very few conventions that adopt identical mechanisms for the punishment of offenders (including with respect to the relationship between extradition and prosecution). The variation in the provisions relating to prosecution and extradition appears to be determined by several factors, including the geographical, institutional and thematic framework in which each convention is negotiated ... and the development of related areas of international law, such as human rights and criminal justice. It follows that, while it is possible to identify some general trends and common features in the relevant provisions, conclusive findings regarding the precise scope of each provision need to be made on a case-by-case basis, taking into account the formulation of the provision, the general economy of the treaty in which it is contained and the relevant preparatory works.'

[443] ibid para 91. [444] ibid para 109.

[445] The 2006 International Convention for the Protection of All Persons from Enforced Disappearance follows the Hague formula, and refers to the 'extreme seriousness' of the offence, which it qualifies, when widespread or systematic, as a crime against humanity. However, outside of this, there appears to be a lack of international conventions with the obligation to extradite or prosecute in relation to crimes against humanity.

[446] The underlying principle of the four Geneva Conventions of 1949 is the establishment of universal jurisdiction over grave breaches of the Conventions. Each Convention contains an article describing what acts constitute grave breaches that follows immediately after the extradite-or-prosecute provision. For the First and Second Geneva Conventions, this article is identical (arts 50 and 51, respectively): 'Grave breaches to which the preceding Article relates shall be those involving any of the following acts, if committed against persons or property protected by the Convention: wilful killing, torture or inhuman treatment, including biological experiments, wilfully causing great suffering or serious injury to body or health, and extensive destruction and appropriation of property, not justified by military necessity and carried out unlawfully and wantonly.' Article 130 of the Third Geneva Convention stipulates, 'Grave breaches to which the preceding Article relates shall be those involving any of the following acts, if

regime could be strengthened beyond the rudimentary regime under the Convention for the Prevention and Punishment of the Crime of Genocide of 1948. As explained by the International Court of Justice in the case concerning *Application of the Convention on the Prevention and Punishment of the Crime of Genocide (Bosnia and Herzegovina v Serbia and Montenegro)*, article VI of the Genocide Convention only obligates Contracting Parties to institute and exercise territorial criminal jurisdiction as well as to cooperate with an 'international penal tribunal' under certain circumstances.[447]

(b) Implementation of the obligation to extradite or prosecute

(15) *The Hague formula.* The Commission views the Judgment of the International Court of Justice in the case concerning *Questions relating to the Obligation to Prosecute or Extradite (Belgium v Senegal)* to be helpful in elucidating some aspects relevant to the implementation of the obligation to extradite or prosecute. The Judgment confines itself to an analysis of the mechanism to combat impunity under the Convention against Torture. In particular, the Judgment focuses on the relationship between the different articles on the establishment of jurisdiction (article 5), the obligation to engage in a preliminary inquiry (article 6), and the obligation to prosecute or extradite (article 7).[448] While the Court's reasoning relates to the specific implementation and application of issues surrounding that Convention, since the relevant prosecute-or-extradite provisions of the Convention against Torture are modelled upon those of the Hague formula, the Court's ruling may also help to elucidate the meaning of the prosecute-or-extradite regime under the 1970 Hague Convention and other conventions which have followed the same formula.[449] As the Court also holds that

committed against persons or property protected by the Convention: wilful killing, torture or inhuman treatment, including biological experiments, wilfully causing great suffering or serious injury to body or health, compelling a prisoner of war to serve in the forces of the hostile Power, or wilfully depriving a prisoner of war of the rights of fair and regular trial prescribed in this Convention.' Article 147 of the Fourth Geneva Convention provides: 'Grave breaches to which the preceding Article relates shall be those involving any of the following acts, if committed against persons or property protected by the present Convention: wilful killing, torture or inhuman treatment, including biological experiments, wilfully causing great suffering or serious injury to body or health, unlawful deportation or transfer or unlawful confinement of a protected person, compelling a protected person to serve in the forces of a hostile Power, or wilfully depriving a protected person of the rights of fair and regular trial prescribed in the present Convention, taking of hostages and extensive destruction and appropriation of property, not justified by military necessity and carried out unlawfully and wantonly.' The four Conventions and the Additional Protocol I of 1977 do not establish an obligation to extradite or prosecute outside of grave breaches. No other international instruments relating to war crimes have this obligation, either.

[447] *ICJ Reports 2007*, 43 at 226–27 and 229 paras 442, 449. Article VI reads: 'Persons charged with genocide or any of the other acts enumerated in article III shall be tried by a competent tribunal of the State in the territory of which the act was committed, or by such international penal tribunal as may have jurisdiction with respect to those Contracting Parties which shall have accepted its jurisdiction.' The Court at para 442 did not exclude other bases when it observed that 'Article VI only obliges the Contracting Parties to institute and exercise territorial criminal jurisdiction; while it certainly does not prohibit States, with respect to genocide, from conferring jurisdiction on their criminal courts based on criteria other than where the crime was committed which are compatible with international law, in particular the nationality of the accused, it does not oblige them to do so.'

[448] *Questions relating to the Obligation to Prosecute or Extradite (Belgium v Senegal)*, Judgment, *ICJ Reports 2012*,422 at 450–61 paras 71–121.

[449] The Court notes that art 7(1) of the Convention against Torture is based on a similar provision contained in the 1970 Hague Convention (ibid para 90). As Judge Donoghue puts it, 'The dispositive paragraphs of today's Judgment bind only the Parties. Nonetheless, the Court's interpretation of a multilateral treaty (or of customary international law) can have implications for other States. The far-reaching nature of the legal issues presented by this case is revealed by the number of questions posed by Members

the prohibition of torture is a peremptory norm (*jus cogens*),[450] the prosecute-or-extradite formula under the Convention against Torture could serve as a model for new prosecute-or-extradite regimes governing prohibitions covered by peremptory norms (*jus cogens*), such as genocide, crimes against humanity, and serious war crimes.

(16) The Court determines that States Parties to the Convention against Torture have obligations to criminalize torture, establish their jurisdiction over the crime of torture so as to equip themselves with the necessary legal tool to prosecute that offence, and make an inquiry into the facts immediately from the time the suspect is present in their respective territories. The Court declares: 'These obligations, taken as a whole, might be regarded as elements of a single conventional mechanism aimed at preventing suspects from escaping the consequences of their criminal responsibility, if proven.'[451] The obligation under article 7 paragraph 1, 'to submit the case to the competent authorities for the purpose of prosecution', which the Court calls the 'obligation to prosecute', arises regardless of the existence of a prior request for the extradition of the suspect. However, national authorities are left to decide whether to initiate proceedings in the light of the evidence before them and the relevant rules of criminal procedure.[452] In particular, the Court rules that '[e]xtradition is an option offered to the State by the Convention, whereas prosecution is an international obligation under the Convention, the violation of which is a wrongful act engaging the responsibility of the State.'[453] The Court also notes that both the 1970 Hague Convention and the Convention against Torture emphasize 'that the authorities shall take their decision in the same manner as in the case of any ordinary offence of a serious nature under the law of the State concerned'.[454]

(17) *Basic elements of the obligation to extradite or prosecute to be included in national legislation.* The effective fulfilment of the obligation to extradite or prosecute requires undertaking necessary national measures to criminalize the relevant offences, establishing jurisdiction over the offences and the person present in the territory of the State, investigating or undertaking primary inquiry, apprehending the suspect, and submitting the case to the prosecuting authorities (which may or may not result in the institution of proceedings) or extraditing, if an extradition request is made by another State with the necessary jurisdiction and capability to prosecute the suspect.

(18) *Establishment of the necessary jurisdiction.* Establishing jurisdiction is 'a logical prior step' to the implementation of an obligation to extradite or prosecute an alleged offender present in the territory of a State.[455] For the purposes of the present topic, when the crime was allegedly committed abroad with no nexus to the forum State, the obligation to extradite or prosecute would necessarily reflect an exercise of universal jurisdiction,[456] which is 'the

of the Court during oral proceedings.' (Declaration of Judge Donoghue in *Questions relating to the Obligation to Prosecute or Extradite (Belgium v Senegal)*, Judgment, *ICJ Reports 2012*, 422 at 590 para 21.)

[450] ibid 422 at 457 para 99.

[451] ibid 455 para 91. See also 451–52 and 456, paras 74–75, 78, 94.

[452] ibid 454–56 paras 90, 94.

[453] ibid 456 para 95.

[454] Art 7 para 2 of the Convention against Torture and art 7 of the Hague Convention of 1970, ibid para 90.

[455] Report of the AU-EU Technical ad hoc Expert Group on the Principle of Universal Jurisdiction (8672/1/09/ Rev1), annex para 11. The International Court of Justice in the case concerning *Questions relating to the Obligation to Prosecute or Extradite (Belgium v Senegal)* holds that the performance by States Parties to the Convention against Torture of their obligation to establish universal jurisdiction of their courts is a necessary condition for enabling a preliminary inquiry and for submitting the case to their competent authorities for the purpose of prosecution (*Questions relating to the Obligation to Prosecute or Extradite (Belgium v Senegal)*, Judgment, *ICJ Reports 2012*, 422 at 451 para 74).

[456] According to one author, 'The principle of *aut dedere aut judicare* overlaps with universal jurisdiction when a State has no other nexus to the alleged crime or to the suspect other than the

jurisdiction to establish a territorial jurisdiction over persons for extraterritorial events'[457] where neither the victims nor alleged offenders are nationals of the forum State and no harm was allegedly caused to the forum State's own national interests. However, the obligation to extradite or prosecute can also reflect an exercise of jurisdiction under other bases. Thus, if a State can exercise jurisdiction on another basis, universal jurisdiction may not necessarily be invoked in the fulfilment of the obligation to extradite or prosecute.

Universal jurisdiction is a crucial component for prosecuting alleged perpetrators of crimes of international concern, particularly when the alleged perpetrator is not prosecuted in the territory where the crime was committed.[458] Several international instruments, such as the very widely ratified four Geneva Conventions of 1949 and the Convention against Torture, require the exercise of universal jurisdiction over the offences covered by these instruments, or, alternatively to extradite alleged offenders to another State for the purpose of prosecution.

(19) *Delay in enacting legislation*. According to the Court in the case concerning *Questions relating to the Obligation to Prosecute or Extradite (Belgium v Senegal)*, delay in enacting necessary legislation in order to prosecute suspects adversely affects the State Party's implementation of the obligations to conduct a preliminary inquiry and to submit the case to its competent authorities for the purposes of prosecution.[459] The State's obligation extends beyond merely enacting national legislation. The State must also actually exercise its jurisdiction over a suspect, starting by establishing the facts.[460]

(20) *Obligation to investigate*. According to the Court in the case concerning *Questions relating to the Obligation to Prosecute or Extradite (Belgium v Senegal)*, the obligation to investigate consists of several elements.

As a general rule, the obligation to investigate must be interpreted in light of the object and purpose of the applicable treaty, which is to make more effective the fight against impunity.[461]

The obligation is intended to corroborate the suspicions regarding the person in question.[462] The starting point is the establishment of the relevant facts, which is an essential stage in the process of the fight against impunity.[463]

As soon as the authorities have reason to suspect that a person present in their territory may be responsible for acts subject to the obligation to extradite or prosecute, they must investigate. The preliminary inquiry must immediately be initiated. This point is reached, at the latest, when the first complaint is filed against the person,[464] at which stage the establishment of the facts becomes imperative.[465]

mere presence of the person within its territory' (Mitsue Inazumi, *Universal Jurisdiction in Modern International Law: Expansion of National Jurisdiction for Prosecuting Serious Crimes under International Law* (Intersentia 2005) 122).

[457] *Arrest Warrant of 11 April 2000 (Democratic Republic of the Congo v Belgium) ICJ Reports 2002*, 3, Joint Sep Op of Judges Higgins, Kooijmans, and Buergenthal, 75 para 42.

[458] It should be recalled that the 'Obligation to extradite or prosecute' in art 9 of the 1996 draft code is closely related to the 'Establishment of jurisdiction' under art 8 of the draft code, which requires each State Party thereto to take such measures as may be necessary to establish its jurisdiction over genocide, crimes against humanity, crimes against United Nations and associated personnel, and war crimes, irrespective of where or by whom those crimes were committed. The Commission's commentary to Art 8 makes it clear that universal jurisdiction is envisaged (*Official Record of the General Assembly, Fifty-first Session, Supp 10* (A/51/10) para 7).

[459] *Questions relating to the Obligation to Prosecute or Extradite (Belgium v Senegal)*, Judgment, *ICJ Reports 2012*, 422 at 451–52 paras 76, 77.

[460] ibid 453 para 84. [461] ibid 454 para 86. [462] ibid 453 para 83.

[463] ibid 453–54 paras 85–86. [464] ibid 454 para 88. [465] ibid 454 para 86.

However, simply questioning the suspect in order to establish his or her identity and inform him or her of the charges cannot be regarded as performance of the obligation to conduct a preliminary inquiry.[466]

The inquiry is to be conducted by the authorities who have the task of drawing up a case file and collecting facts and evidence (for example, documents and witness statements relating to the events at issue and to the suspect's possible involvement). These authorities are those of the State where the alleged crime was committed or of any other State where complaints have been filed in relation to the case. In order to fulfil its obligation to conduct a preliminary inquiry, the State in whose territory the suspect is present should seek the cooperation of the authorities of the aforementioned States.[467]

An inquiry taking place on the basis of universal jurisdiction must be conducted according to the same standards in terms of evidence as when the State has jurisdiction by virtue of a link with the case in question.[468]

(21) *Obligation to prosecute*. According to the Court in the case concerning *Questions relating to the Obligation to Prosecute or Extradite (Belgium v Senegal)*, the obligation to prosecute consists of certain elements.

The obligation to prosecute is actually an obligation to submit the case to the prosecuting authorities; it does not involve an obligation to initiate a prosecution. Indeed, in light of the evidence, fulfilment of the obligation may or may not result in the institution of proceedings.[469] The competent authorities decide whether to initiate proceedings, in the same manner as they would for any alleged offence of a serious nature under the law of the State concerned.[470]

Proceedings relating to the implementation of the obligation to prosecute should be undertaken without delay, as soon as possible, in particular once the first complaint has been filed against the suspect.[471]

The timeliness of the prosecution must be such that it does not lead to injustice; hence, necessary actions must be undertaken within a reasonable time limit.[472]

(22) *Obligation to extradite*. With respect to the obligation to extradite:

Extradition may only be to a State that has jurisdiction in some capacity to prosecute and try the alleged offender pursuant to an international legal obligation binding on the State in whose territory the person is present.[473]

466 ibid 453–54 para 85. 467 ibid 453 para 83. 468 ibid 453 para 84.

469 Cf also *Chili Komitee Nederland v Pinochet*, Court of Appeal of Amsterdam, 4 Jan 1995 *Netherlands Yearbook of International Law*, vol 28 (1997), 363–65, in which the Court of Appeal held that the Dutch Public Prosecutor did not err in refusing to prosecute former Chilean President Pinochet while visiting Amsterdam because Pinochet might be entitled to immunity from prosecution and any necessary evidence to substantiate his prosecution would be in Chile with which the Netherlands had no cooperative arrangements regarding criminal proceedings. See Kimberley N Trapp, *State Responsibility for International Terrorism* (OUP 2011) 88 n 132.

470 *Questions relating to the Obligation to Prosecute or Extradite (Belgium v Senegal)*, Judgment, *ICJ Reports 2012*, 422 at 454 and 456 paras 90, 94.

471 ibid paras 115, 117.

472 ibid paras 114, 115. Cf Sep Op of Judge Cançado Trindade in that case at 546–48 paras 148, 151–53; Dis Op of Judge ad hoc Sur in the same case at 620 para 50; and Dis Op of Judge Xue at 578 para 28.

473 ibid 422 at 461 para 120.

Fulfilling the obligation to extradite cannot be substituted by deportation, extraordinary rendition, or other informal forms of dispatching the suspect to another State.[474] Formal extradition requests entail important human rights protections which may be absent from informal forms of dispatching the suspect to another State, such as extraordinary renditions. Under extradition law of most, if not all, States, the necessary requirements to be satisfied include double criminality, *ne bis in idem, nullem crimen sine lege*, speciality, and non-extradition of the suspect to stand trial on the grounds of ethnic origin, religion, nationality, or political views.

(23) *Compliance with object and purpose.* The steps to be taken by a State must be interpreted in the light of the object and purpose of the relevant international instrument or other sources of international obligation binding on that State, rendering the fight against impunity more effective.[475] It is also worth recalling that, by virtue of article 27 of the Vienna Convention on the Law of Treaties, which reflects customary international law, a State Party to a treaty may not invoke the provisions of its internal law as justification for its failure to perform a treaty.[476] Besides, the steps taken must be in accordance with the rule of law.

(24) In cases of serious crimes of international concern, the purpose of the obligation to extradite or prosecute is to prevent alleged perpetrators from going unpunished by ensuring that they cannot find refuge in any State.[477]

(25) *Temporal scope of the obligation.* The obligation to extradite or prosecute under a treaty applies only to facts having occurred after the entry into force of the said treaty for the State concerned, 'unless a different intention appears from the treaty or is otherwise established'.[478] After a State becomes party to a treaty containing the obligation to extradite or prosecute, it is entitled, with effect from the date of its becoming party to the treaty, to request another State Party's compliance with the obligation to extradite or prosecute.[479]

Thus, the obligation to criminalize and establish necessary jurisdiction over acts proscribed by a treaty containing the obligation to extradite or prosecute is to be implemented as soon as the State is bound by that treaty.[480] However, nothing prevents the State from investigating or prosecuting acts committed before the entry into force of the treaty for that State.[481]

[474] Cf Draft art 12 of the draft articles on the expulsion of aliens adopted by the Commission on second reading in 2014, see *Official Records of the General Assembly, Sixty-ninth Session, Supp 10* (A/69/10) ch IV and European Court of Human Rights, *Bozano v France*, Judgment of 18 Dec 1986, Application 9990/82 paras 52–60, where the European Court of Human Rights has held that extradition, disguised as deportation in order to circumvent the requirements of extradition, is illegal and incompatible with the right to security of person guaranteed under art 5 of the European Convention on Human Rights.

[475] See the reasoning in the case concerning *Questions relating to the Obligation to Prosecute or Extradite (Belgium v Senegal)*, Judgment, ICJ Reports 2012, 422 at 453–54 paras 85–86. Therefore, the Court rules that financial difficulties do not justify Senegal's failure to comply with the obligations under the Convention against Torture (ibid para 112). Likewise, seeking guidance from the African Union does not justify Senegal's delay in complying with its obligation under the Convention (ibid).

[476] ibid para 113.

[477] ibid 422 at 461 para 120. As also explained by Judge Cançado Trindade, 'The conduct of the State ought to be one which is conducive to compliance with the obligations of result (in the *cas d'espèce*, the proscription of torture). The State cannot allege that, despite its good conduct, insufficiencies or difficulties of domestic law rendered it impossible the full compliance with its obligation (to outlaw torture and to prosecute perpetrators of it); and the Court cannot consider a case terminated, given the allegedly "good conduct" of the State concerned.' (Sep Op of Judge Cançado Trindade, ibid 422 at 508 para 50 and see also his full reasoning at 505–08 paras 44–51.)

[478] ibid 422 at 457–58 paras 100–02, citing art 28 of the Vienna Convention on the Law of Treaties, which reflects customary international law.

[479] ibid 458 paras 103–05. [480] ibid 451 para 75. [481] ibid 458 paras 102, 105.

(26) *Consequences of non-compliance with the obligation to extradite or prosecute*. In *Belgium v Senegal*, the Court found that the violation of an international obligation under the Convention against Torture is a wrongful act engaging the responsibility of the State.[482]

As long as all measures necessary for the implementation of the obligation have not been taken, the State remains in breach of its obligation.[483] The Commission's articles on responsibility of States for internationally wrongful acts stipulate that the commission of an internationally wrongful act attributable to a State involves legal consequences, including cessation and non-repetition of the act (art 30), reparation (arts 31, 34–39), and countermeasures (arts 49–54).

(27) *Relationship between the obligation and the 'third alternative'*. With the establishment of the International Criminal Court and various ad hoc international criminal tribunals, there is now the possibility that a State faced with an obligation to extradite or prosecute an accused person might have recourse to a third alternative—that of surrendering the suspect to a competent international criminal tribunal.[484] This third alternative is stipulated, for example, in article 11 paragraph 1 of the International Convention for the Protection of All Persons from Enforced Disappearance, 2006.[485]

(28) In her Dissenting Opinion in the case concerning *Questions relating to the Obligation to Prosecute or Extradite (Belgium v Senegal)*, Judge Xue opines that had Senegal surrendered the alleged offender to an international tribunal constituted by the African Union to try him, they would not have breached their obligation to prosecute under art 7 of the Convention against Torture, because such a tribunal would have been created to fulfil the purpose of the Convention, and this is not prohibited by the Convention itself or by State practice.[486] Of course, if 'a different intention appears from the treaty or is otherwise established'[487] so as not to permit the surrender of an alleged offender to an international criminal tribunal, such surrender would not discharge the obligation of the States Parties to the treaty to extradite or prosecute the person under their respective domestic legal systems.

(29) It is suggested that in light of the increasing significance of international criminal tribunals, new treaty provisions on the obligation to extradite or prosecute should include this third alternative, as should national legislation.

(30) *Additional observation*. A State might also wish to fulfil both parts of the obligation to extradite or prosecute, for example, by prosecuting, trying, and sentencing an offender and then extraditing or surrendering the offender to another State for the purpose of enforcing the judgment.[488]

[482] ibid 456 para 95. [483] ibid 460–61 para 117.

[484] Article 9 of the 1996 Draft code of Crimes against the Peace of Mankind stipulates that the obligation to extradite or prosecute under that article is '[w]ithout prejudice to the jurisdiction of an international criminal court'.

[485] 'The State party in the territory under whose jurisdiction a person alleged to have committed an offence of enforced disappearance is found shall, if it does not extradite that person or surrender him or her to another State in accordance with its international obligations or surrender him or her to an international criminal tribunal whose jurisdiction it has recognized, submit the case to its competent authorities for the purpose of prosecution.'

[486] Dis Op of Judge Xue, at 582 para 42 (dissenting on other points).

[487] Article 28 of the Vienna Convention on the Law of Treaties.

[488] This possibility was raised by Special Rapporteur Galicki in his preliminary report (A/CN.4/571) paras 49–50.

(c) Gaps in the existing conventional regime and the 'third alternative'

(31) As noted in paragraph (14) above, the Commission reiterates that there are important gaps in the present conventional regime governing the obligation to extradite or prosecute, notably in relation to most crimes against humanity, war crimes other than grave breaches, and war crimes in non-international armed conflict. It also notes that it had placed on its programme of work in 2014 the topic 'Crimes against humanity', which would include as one element of a new treaty an obligation to extradite or prosecute for those crimes.[489] It further suggested that, in relation to genocide, the international cooperation regime could be strengthened beyond the one that exists under the 1948 Convention on the Prevention and Punishment of the Crime of Genocide.[490]

(32) Instead of drafting a set of model provisions to close the gaps in the existing conventional regime regarding the obligation to extradite or prosecute, the Commission recalls that an obligation to extradite or prosecute for, *inter alia*, genocide, crimes against humanity, and war crimes is already stipulated in article 9 of the 1996 Draft Code, which reads:

> Without prejudice to the jurisdiction of an international criminal court, the State Party in the territory of which an individual alleged to have committed a crime set out in article 17 [genocide], 18 [crimes against humanity], 19 [crimes against United Nations and associated personnel] or 20 [war crimes] is found shall extradite or prosecute that individual.[491]

(33) The Commission also refers to the 'Hague formula', quoted in paragraph (10) above. As noted in that paragraph, the 'Hague formula' has served as a model for most contemporary conventions containing the obligation to extradite or prosecute,[492] including the United Nations Convention against Transnational Organized Crime and the United Nations Convention against Corruption which have been mentioned by several delegations in the Sixth Committee in 2013 as a possible model to close the gaps in the conventional regime. In addition, the Judgment of the International Court of Justice in the case concerning *Questions relating to the Obligation to Prosecute or Extradite (Belgium v Senegal)* is helpful in construing the Hague formula.[493] The Commission recommends that States consider the Hague formula in undertaking to close any gaps in the existing conventional regime.

(34) The Commission further acknowledges that some States[494] have inquired about the link between the obligation to extradite or prosecute and the transfer of a suspect to an international or special court or tribunal, whereas other States[495] treat such a transfer differently from extradition. As pointed out in paragraph (27) above, the obligation to extradite or

[489] *Official Records of the General Assembly, Sixty-eighth Session, Supp 10* (A/68/10) Annex B.

[490] ibid Annex A para 20. A study by Chatham House suggested that the Commission's future work on this topic should concentrate on drafting a treaty obligation to extradite or prosecute in respect of core international crimes and emulate the extradite-or-prosecute mechanism developed in art 7 of the 1970 Hague Convention for the Suppression of Unlawful Seizure of Aircraft and incorporated in the 1984 UN Convention against Torture and Other Cruel, Inhuman or Degrading Treatment and Punishment, and, most recently, in the 2006 International Convention for the Protection of All Persons from Enforced Disappearance. See Miša Zgonec-Rožej and Joanne Foakes, 'International criminals: Extradite or Prosecute?' Chatham House Briefing Paper, Doc IL BP 2013/01, July 2013.

[491] See also the Commission's commentary on this article in *Official Records of the General Assembly, Fifty-first Session, Supp 10* (A/51/10) ch II.

[492] *Official Records of the General Assembly, Sixty-eighth Session, Supp 10* (A/68/10) Annex A para 16 and accompanying n 28.

[493] ibid paras 21–22.

[494] 494 Chile, France, and Thailand.

[495] Canada and the United Kingdom of Great Britain and Northern Ireland.

prosecute may be satisfied by surrendering the alleged offender to a competent international criminal tribunal.[496] A provision to this effect appears in article 11 paragraph 1, of the 2006 International Convention for the Protection of All Persons from Enforced Disappearance, which reads:

> The State party in the territory under whose jurisdiction a person alleged to have committed [an act of genocide/a crime against humanity/a war crime] is found shall, if it does not extradite that person or surrender him or her to another State in accordance with its international obligations or surrender him or her to a competent international criminal tribunal or any other competent court whose jurisdiction it has recognized, submit the case to its competent authorities for the purpose of prosecution.

(35) Under such a provision, the obligation to extradite or prosecute may be satisfied by a 'third alternative', which would consist of the State surrendering the alleged offender to a competent international criminal tribunal or a competent court whose jurisdiction the State concerned has recognized. The competent tribunal or court may take a form similar in nature to the Extraordinary African Chambers, set up within the Senegalese court system by an agreement dated 22 August 2012 between Senegal and the African Union, to try Mr Habré in the wake of the Judgment in the case concerning *Questions relating to the Obligation to Prosecute or Extradite (Belgium v Senegal)*.[497] This kind of 'internationalization' within a national court system is not unique. As a court established by the agreement between Senegal and the African Union, with the participation of national and foreign judges in these Chambers, the Extraordinary African Chambers follow the examples of the Extraordinary Chambers in the Courts of Cambodia, the Special Court for Sierra Leone, and the Special Tribunal for Lebanon.

(36) The above examples highlight the essential elements of a provision containing the obligation to extradite or prosecute, and may assist States in choosing the formula that they consider to be most appropriate for a particular context.

(d) The priority between the obligation to prosecute and the obligation to extradite, and the scope of the obligation to prosecute

(37) The Commission takes note of the suggestion made by one delegation[498] to the Sixth Committee in 2013 to analyse these two aspects of the topic. It also notes the suggestions of other delegations[499] that the Commission establish a general framework of extraditable offences or guiding principles on the implementation of the obligation to extradite or prosecute. It wishes to draw attention to the Secretariat Survey (2010) and paragraphs (6)–(13) above, which have addressed these issues.

[496] See also the Council of Europe, *Extradition, European Standards: Explanatory notes on the Council of Europe convention and protocol and minimum standards protecting persons subject to transnational criminal proceedings* (Council of Europe Publishing 2006), where it is stated that: 'In the era of international criminal tribunals, the principle [*aut dedere aut judicare*] may be interpreted *lato sensu* to include the duty of the state to transfer the person to the jurisdiction of an international organ, such as the International Criminal Court' (ibid 119, footnote omitted).

[497] The Extraordinary African Chambers have jurisdiction to try the person or persons most responsible for international crimes committed in Chad between 7 June 1982 and 1 Dec 1990. The Trial Chamber and the Appeals Chamber are each composed of two Senegalese judges and one non-Senegalese judge, who presides over the proceedings. The Trial Chamber and the Appeals Chamber are each composed of two Senegalese judges and one non-Senegalese judge, who presides over the proceedings; see *Statute of the Extraordinary African Chambers*, arts 3 and 11, *International Legal Materials* 52 (2013) 1020–36.

[498] Mexico. [499] Cuba and Belarus, respectively.

(38) To recapitulate, beyond the basic common features, provisions containing the obligation to extradite or prosecute in multilateral conventions vary considerably in their formulation, content, and scope. This is particularly so in terms of the conditions imposed on States with respect to extradition and prosecution and the relationship between these two courses of action. Although the relationship between the obligation to extradite and the obligation to prosecute is not identical, the relevant provisions seem to fall into two main categories; namely, (a) those clauses pursuant to which the obligation to prosecute is only triggered by a refusal to surrender the alleged offender following a request for extradition; and (b) those imposing an obligation to prosecute *ipso facto* when the alleged offender is present in the territory of the State, which the latter may be liberated from by granting extradition.

(39) Instruments containing clauses in the first category impose on States Parties (at least those that do not have a special link with the offence) an obligation to prosecute only when extradition has been requested and not granted, as opposed to an obligation *ipso facto* to prosecute the alleged offender present in their territory. They recognize the possibility that a State may refuse to grant a request for extradition of an individual on grounds stipulated either in the instrument or in national legislation. However, in the event of refusal of extradition, the State is obliged to prosecute the individual. In other words, these instruments primarily focus on the option of extradition and provide the alternative of prosecution as a safeguard against impunity.[500] In addition, instruments in this category may adopt very different mechanisms for the punishment of offenders, which may affect the interaction between extradition and prosecution. In some instances, there are detailed provisions concerning the prosecution of offences that are the subject of the instrument, while in other cases, the process of extradition is regulated in greater detail. The 1929 International Convention for the Suppression of Counterfeiting Currency and subsequent conventions inspired by it[501] belong to this first category.[502] Multilateral conventions on extradition also fall into this category.[503]

[500] Secretariat Survey (2010) para 132. In effect, these conventions appear to follow what was originally foreseen by Hugo Grotius when he referred to the principle *aut dedere aut punire.* Hugo Grotius, *De Jure Belli ac Pacis,* Bk II ch XXI sect IV (Eng tr Francis W Kelsey, Clarendon/Humphrey Milford 1925) 527–29 at 527.

[501] eg the 1936 *Convention for the Suppression of the Illicit Traffic in Dangerous Drugs*; the 1937 *Convention for the Prevention and Punishment of Terrorism*; the 1950 *Convention for the Suppression of the Traffic in Persons and of the Exploitation of the Prostitution of Others*; the 1961 *Single Convention on Narcotic Drugs*; and the 1971 *Convention on Psychotropic Substances*. See also Secretariat Survey (2010) para 29.

[502] The overall structure of the mechanism for the punishment of offenders in these conventions is based on the idea that the State in whose territory the crime was committed will request the extradition of the offender who has fled to another State and that extradition should, in principle, be granted. These conventions, however, recognize that States may be unable to extradite in some cases (most notably when the individual is their national or when they have granted asylum to him or her) and provide for the obligation to prosecute as an alternative. Secretariat Survey (2010) para 133 and n 327 citing Marc Henzelin, *Le Principe de l'universalité en droit penal international: Droit et obligation pour les États de poursuivre et de juger selon le principe de l'universalité* (Basel 2000) 286, who qualifies the system as *primo dedere secundo prosequi.*

[503] eg the 1981 *Inter-American Convention on Extradition*; the 1957 *European Convention on Extradition*; the 1961 *General Convention on Judicial Cooperation (Convention générale de coopération en matière de justice)*; the 1994 *Economic Community of West African States (ECOWAS) Convention on Extradition*; and the *London Scheme for Extradition within the Commonwealth*. These conventions are based on the general undertaking by States Parties to surrender to one another all persons against whom the competent authorities of the requesting Party are proceeding for an offence or who are wanted for the carrying out of a sentence or detention order. However, the obligation to extradite is subject to a number of conditions and exceptions, including when the request involves the national of the requested State. When extradition is refused, the conventions impose an alternative obligation to prosecute the alleged offender as a mechanism to avoid impunity. See also Secretariat Survey (2010) para 134.

(40) Clauses in the second category impose upon States an obligation to prosecute *ipso facto* in that it arises as soon as the presence of the alleged offender in the territory of the State concerned is ascertained, regardless of any request for extradition. Only in the event that a request for extradition is made does the State concerned have the discretion to choose between extradition and prosecution.[504] The clearest example of such clauses is the relevant common article of the 1949 Geneva Conventions, which provides that each State Party 'shall bring' persons alleged to have committed, or to have ordered to be committed, grave breaches to those Conventions, regardless of their nationality, before its own courts, but 'may also, if it prefers', hand such persons over for trial to another State Party concerned.[505] As for the Hague formula, its text does not unequivocally resolve the question of whether the obligation to prosecute arises *ipso facto* or only once a request for extradition is submitted and not granted.[506] In this regard, the findings of the Committee against Torture and the International Court of Justice in the case concerning *Questions relating to the Obligation to Prosecute or Extradite (Belgium v Senegal)*, in relation to a similar provision contained in article 7 of the 1984 Convention against Torture,[507] are instructive. The Committee against Torture has explained that:

> the obligation to prosecute the alleged perpetrator of acts of torture does not depend on the prior existence of a request for his extradition. The alternative available to the State party under article 7 of the Convention exists only when a request for extradition has been made and puts the State party in the position of having to choose between (a) proceeding with extradition or (b) submitting the case to its

[504] Secretariat Survey (2010) para 127 and n 307. Those opining that the accused must be present in the territory of the State concerned as a precondition of the assertion of universal jurisdiction include Judges Higgins, Kooijmans, and Buergenthal (Joint Sep Op in *Arrest Warrant of 11 April 2000 (Democratic Republic of the Congo v Belgium), ICJ Reports 2002*, 80 para 57). See also Sep Op of Judge Guillaume, ibid para 9 and Gilbert Guillaume, 'Terrorisme et droit international', *Recueil des cours de l'Académie de droit international* 215 (1990) 368–69. However, Marc Henzelin (*Le Principe de l'universalité en droit penal international*, 354) argues that the presence of the alleged offender in the territory of the State is not required for prosecution under the relevant provision of the 1949 *Geneva Conventions*.

[505] While this provision appears to give a certain priority to prosecution by the custodial State, it also recognizes that this State has the discretion to opt for extradition, provided that the requesting State has made out a prima facie case. Secretariat Survey (2010) para 128, citing Declan Costello, 'International Terrorism and the Development of the Principle *Aut Dedere Aut Judicare*', *Journal of International Law and Economics* 10 (1975) 486; M Cherif Bassiouni and Edward M Wise, *Aut Dedere Aut Judicare: The Duty to Extradite or Prosecute in International Law* (Dordrecht 1995) 15; and Christian Maierhöfer, '*Aut dedere—aut judicare*': *Herkunft, Rechtsgrundlagen und Inhalt des völkerrechtlichen Gebotes zur Strafverfolgung oder Auslieferung* (Berlin 2006) 75–76. Authors who emphasize the priority attributed to prosecution in the 1949 Geneva Conventions are said to include Luigi Condorelli, 'Il sistemadella repression dei crimini di Guerra nelle Convenzioni di Ginevra del 1949 e nel primo protocollo addizionale del 1977', in P Lamberti Zanardi and G Venturini (eds), *Crimini di guerra e competenza delle giurisdizioni nazionali: Atti del Convegno, Milano, 15–17 maggio 1997* (Milan 1998) 35–36; and Henzelin, *Le Principe de l'universalité en droit penal international*, 353 (who qualifies the model of the 1949 Geneva Conventions as *primo prosequi secundo dedere*). *Cf* also Art 88(2) of *Additional Protocol I* to the 1949 Geneva Conventions, which calls on States Parties to 'give due consideration to the request of the State in whose territory the alleged offence has occurred', thus implying that prosecution by the latter State would be preferable.

[506] Art 7 of the 1970 Hague Convention for the Suppression of Unlawful Seizure of Aircraft provides that '[t]he Contracting State in the territory of which the alleged offender is found shall, if it does not extradite him, be obliged ... to submit the case to its competent authorities for the purpose of prosecution.'

[507] Art 7 states: 'The State Party in the territory under whose jurisdiction a person alleged to have committed any offence referred to in article 4 is found shall in the cases contemplated in article 5, if it does not extradite him, submit the case to its competent authorities for the purpose of prosecution.'

own judicial authorities for the institution of criminal proceedings, the objective of the provision being to prevent any act of torture from going unpunished.[508]

(41) Likewise, in the case concerning *Questions relating to the Obligation to Prosecute or Extradite (Belgium v Senegal)*, the International Court of Justice considered art 7(1) of the Convention against Torture as requiring:

> the State concerned to submit the case to its competent authorities for the purpose of prosecution, irrespective of the existence of a prior request for the extradition of the suspect. That is why Article 6, paragraph 2, obliges the State to make a preliminary inquiry immediately from the time that the suspect is present in its territory. The obligation to submit the case to the competent authorities, under Article 7, paragraph 1, may or may not result in the institution of proceedings, in the light of the evidence before them, relating to the charges against the suspect. However, if the State in whose territory the suspect is present has received a request for extradition in any of the cases envisaged in the provisions of the Convention, it can relieve itself of its obligation to prosecute by acceding to that request.[509]

(42) Accordingly, it follows that the choice between extradition and submission for prosecution under the Convention did not mean that the two alternatives enjoyed the same weight. Extradition was an option offered to the State by the Convention while prosecution was an obligation under the Convention, the violation of which was a wrongful act resulting in State responsibility.[510]

(43) With respect to the Commission's 1996 Draft Code, art 9 provides that the State Party in whose territory an individual alleged to have committed these crimes is found 'shall extradite or prosecute that individual'. The commentary to art 9 clarifies that the obligation to prosecute arises independently from any request for extradition.[511]

(44) The scope of the obligation to prosecute has already been elaborated in paragraphs (21) to (26) above.

(e) *The relationship of the obligation to extradite or prosecute with* erga omnes *obligations or* jus cogens *norms*

(45) The Commission notes that one delegation[512] to the Sixth Committee in 2013 raised the issue of the impact of the *aut dedere aut judicare* principle on international responsibility when it relates to *erga omnes* obligations or *jus cogens* norms, such as the prohibition of torture. The delegation suggested an analysis of the following questions: (a) in respect of whom the obligation exists; (b) who can request extradition; and (c) who has a legal interest in invoking the international responsibility of a State for being in breach of its 'obligation to prosecute or extradite'.

[508] *Guengueng* et al *v Senegal*, Merits, Decision of the Committee Against Torture under Art 22 of the Convention against Torture and Other Cruel, Inhuman or Degrading Treatment or Punishment, 36th Sess, Doc CAT/C/36/D/181/2001, 19 May 2006 para 9.7.

[509] In *Questions relating to the Obligation to Prosecute or Extradite (Belgium v Senegal)*, Judgment, *ICJ Reports 2012*, 422 at 456 paras 94–95.

[510] ibid 456 para 95.

[511] The custodial State has an obligation 'to take action to ensure that such an individual is prosecuted either by the national authorities of that State or by another State which indicated that it was willing to prosecute the case by requesting extradition'. Para 3 of the commentary to art 9, *Yearbook of the International Law Commission 1996*, vol 2 (Part Two) 31. Reference should also be made to the commentary to art 8 (whereby each State party 'shall take such measures as may be necessary to establish its jurisdiction' over the crimes set out in the Draft Code 'irrespective of where or by whom those crimes were committed').

[512] Mexico.

(46) Several members of the Commission pointed out that this area was likely to concern the interpretation of conventional norms. The statements of the International Court of Justice in this regard in the case concerning *Questions relating to the Obligation to Prosecute or Extradite (Belgium v Senegal)* must be read within the specific context of that particular case. There, the Court interpreted the object and purpose of the Convention against Torture as giving rise to 'obligations *erga omnes partes*', whereby each State Party had a 'common interest' in compliance with such obligations and, consequently, each State Party was entitled to make a claim concerning the cessation of an alleged breach by another State Party.[513] The issue of *jus cogens* was not central to this point. In the understanding of the Commission, the Court was saying that insofar as States were parties to the Convention against Torture, they had a common interest to prevent acts of torture and to ensure that, if they occurred, those responsible did not enjoy impunity.

(47) Other treaties, even if they may not involve *jus cogens* norms, may lead to *erga omnes* obligations as well. In other words, all States Parties may have a legal interest in invoking the international responsibility of a State Party for being in breach of its obligation to extradite or prosecute.

(48) The State that can request extradition normally will be a State Party to the relevant convention or have a reciprocal extradition undertaking/arrangement with the requested State, having jurisdiction over the offence, being willing and able to prosecute the alleged offender, and respecting applicable international norms protecting the human rights of the accused.[514]

(f) The customary international law status of the obligation to extradite or prosecute

(49) The Commission notes that some delegations to the Sixth Committee opined that there was no obligation to extradite or prosecute under customary international law, whereas others were of the view that the customary international law status of the obligation merited further consideration by the Commission.[515]

(50) It may be recalled that in 2011 the then Special Rapporteur Galicki, in his Fourth Report, proposed a draft article on international custom as a source of the obligation *aut dedere aut judicare*.[516]

[513] *Questions relating to the Obligation to Prosecute or Extradite (Belgium v Senegal)*, Judgment, *ICJ Reports 2012*, 422 at 449–50 paras 67–70. See also Sep Op of Judge Cançado Trindade, 527–29 paras 104–08, and Declaration of Judge Donoghue, 586–89, paras 9–17. Cf Dis Op of Judge Xue, 571–77 paras 2–23, and Dis Op of Judge ad hoc Sur, 608 and 610–11 paras 13, 19–20. Cf also the Sep Op of Judge Skotnikov, 482–85 paras 9–22.

[514] See eg Council of Europe, *Extradition, European Standards*, ch 4, 'Material human rights guarantees as limitations to extradition'; Danai Azaria, *Code of Minimum Standards of Protection to Individuals Involved in Transnational Proceedings*, Report to the Committee of Experts on Transnational Criminal Justice, European Committee on Crime Problems, Council of Europe, [PC-TJ/Docs 2005/PCTJ (2005) 07 E. Azaria], Strasbourg, 16 Sept 2005.

[515] A/CN.4/666 para 60.

[516] A/CN.4/648 para 95. The draft article reads:

Article 4
International custom as a source of the obligation *aut dedere aut judicare*

1. Each State is obliged either to extradite or to prosecute an alleged offender if such an obligation is deriving from the customary norm of international law.
2. Such an obligation may derive, in particular, from customary norms of international law concerning [serious violations of international humanitarian law, genocide, crimes against humanity and war crimes].
3. The obligation to extradite or prosecute shall derive from the peremptory norm of general international law accepted and recognized by the international community of States

(51) However, the draft article was not well received either in the Commission[517] or the Sixth Committee.[518] There was general disagreement with the conclusion that the customary nature of the obligation to extradite or prosecute could be inferred from the existence of customary rules proscribing specific international crimes.

(52) Determining whether the obligation to extradite or prosecute has become or is becoming a rule of customary international law, or at least a regional customary law, may help indicate whether a draft article proposed by the Commission codifies or is progressive development of international law. However, since the Commission has decided not to have the outcome of the Commission's work on this topic take the form of draft articles, it has found it unnecessary to come up with alternative formulas to the one proposed by Mr Galicki.

(53) The Commission wishes to make clear that the foregoing should not be construed as implying that it has found that the obligation to extradite or prosecute has not become or is not yet crystallizing into a rule of customary international law, be it a general or regional one.

(54) When the Commission adopted the Draft Code in 1996, the provision on the obligation to extradite or prosecute thereunder represented progressive development of international law, as explained in paragraph (3) above. Since the completion of the Draft Code, there may have been further developments in international law that reflect State practice and *opinio juris* in this respect.

(55) The Commission notes that in 2012 the International Court of Justice in the case concerning *Questions relating to the Obligation to Prosecute or Extradite (Belgium v Senegal)* ruled that it had no jurisdiction to entertain Belgium's claims relating to Senegal's alleged breaches of obligations under customary international law because at the date of Belgium's filing of the Application the dispute between Belgium and Senegal did not relate to breaches of obligations under customary international law.[519] Thus, an opportunity has yet to arise for the Court to determine the customary international law status or otherwise of the obligation to extradite or prosecute.[520]

(*jus cogens*), either in the form of international treaty or international custom, criminalizing any one of acts listed in paragraph 2.

517 *Official Records of* the *General Assembly, Sixty-sixth Session, Supp 10* (A/66/10) paras 320–26.

518 In particular, some States disagreed with the conclusion that the customary nature of the obligation to extradite or prosecute could necessarily be inferred from the existence of customary rules proscribing specific international crimes. *Topical summary of the discussion held in the Sixth Committee of the General Assembly during its Sixty-sixth Session, prepared by the Secretariat* (A/CN.4/650) para 48.

See also the positions of Argentina, in A/C.6/62/SR.22 para 58 and the Russian Federation, in A/CN.4/599 para 54, respectively.

519 *Judgment, ICJ Reports 2012*, 422 paras 53–55, 122(2), with Judge Abraham and Judge ad hoc Sur dissenting on this point (ibid, Sep Op of Judge Abraham, 471–76 paras 3–20; Dis Op of Judge ad hoc Sur, 610 para 17).

520 Judge Abraham and Judge ad hoc Sur concluded that the Court, if it had found jurisdiction, would not have upheld Belgium's claim of the existence of the customary international law obligation to prosecute or extradite. In his Separate Opinion, Judge Abraham considered there was insufficient evidence, based on State practice and *opinio juris*, of a customary obligation for States to prosecute before their domestic courts individuals suspected of war crimes or crimes against humanity on the basis of universal jurisdiction, even when limited to the case where the suspect was present in the territory of the forum State (ibid, Sep Op of Judge Abraham, 611–17 paras 21, 24–25, 31–39). In his Dissenting Opinion, Judge ad hoc Sur said that despite the silence of the Court, or perhaps because of such silence, 'it seems clear that the existence of a customary obligation to prosecute or extradite, or even simply to prosecute, cannot be established in positive law' (ibid, Dis Op of Judge ad hoc Sur, 610 para 18). By contrast, the Separate Opinions of Judge Cançado Trindade (ibid, Sep Op of Judge Cançado Trindade, 544 para 143) and of Judge Sebutinde (ibid, Sep Op of Judge Sebutinde, 604 paras 41–42) both stressed that the Court only

(g) Other matters of continued relevance in the 2009 General Framework

(56) The Commission observes that the 2009 General Framework[521] continued to be

found that it had no jurisdiction to address the merits of the customary international law issues given the facts presented in the case. In any case, any reference to the existence or non-existence of the customary law obligation in the case concerning *Questions relating to the Obligation to Prosecute or Extradite (Belgium v Senegal)*, was to the obligation in the cases of crimes against humanity and war crimes in internal armed conflicts. It did not touch upon such obligation in the context of genocide, war crimes in international armed conflicts, or other crimes of international concern such as acts of terrorism.

[521] For ease of reference, the 2009 General Framework is reproduced here. It reads as follows:

List of questions/issues to be addressed

(a) **The legal bases of the obligation to extradite or prosecute**

(i) The obligation to extradite or prosecute and the duty to cooperate in the fight against impunity;

(ii) The obligation to extradite or prosecute in existing treaties: Typology of treaty provisions; differences and similarities between those provisions, and their evolution (cf conventions on terrorism);

(iii) Whether and to what extent the obligation to extradite or prosecute has a basis in customary international law;*

(iv) Whether the obligation to extradite or prosecute is inextricably linked with certain particular 'customary crimes' (eg piracy);*

(v) Whether regional principles relating to the obligation to extradite or prosecute may be identified.*

(b) **The material scope of the obligation to extradite or prosecute**
Identification of the categories of crimes (eg crimes under international law; crimes against the peace and security of mankind; crimes of international concern; other serious crimes) covered by the obligation to extradite or prosecute according to conventional and/or customary international law:

(i) Whether the recognition of an offence as an international crime is a sufficient basis for the existence of an obligation to extradite or prosecute under customary international law;*

(ii) If not, what is/are the distinctive criterion/criteria? Relevance of the *jus cogens* character of a rule criminalizing certain conduct?*

(iii) Whether and to what extent the obligation also exists in relation to crimes under domestic law?

(c) **The content of the obligation to extradite or prosecute**

(i) Definition of the two elements; meaning of the obligation to prosecute; steps that need to be taken in order for prosecution to be considered 'sufficient'; question of timeliness of prosecution;

(ii) Whether the order of the two elements matters;

(iii) Whether one element has priority over the other—power of free appreciation (*pouvoir discrétionnaire*) of the requested State?

(d) **Relationship between the obligation to extradite or prosecute and other principles**

(i) The obligation to extradite or prosecute and the principle of universal jurisdiction (does one necessarily imply the other?);

(ii) The obligation to extradite or prosecute and the general question of 'titles' to exercise jurisdiction (territoriality, nationality);

(iii) The obligation to extradite or prosecute and the principles of *nullum crimen sine lege* and *nulla poena sine lege*;**

(iv) The obligation to extradite or prosecute and the principle *non bis in idem* (double jeopardy);**

(v) The obligation to extradite or prosecute and the principle of non-extradition of nationals;**

mentioned in the Sixth Committee[522] as relevant to the Commission's work on the topic.

(57) The 2009 General Framework raised several issues in relation to the obligation to extradite or prosecute that are covered in the preceding paragraphs, but some issues have not, namely: the obligation's relationship with the principles of *nullum crimen sine lege* and *nulla poena sine lege* and the principle *non bis in idem* (double jeopardy); the implications of a conflict between various principles (eg non-extradition of nationals versus no indictment in national law; obstacles to prosecution versus risks for the accused to be tortured or lack of due process in the State to which extradition is envisaged); constitutional limitations; circumstances excluding the operation of the obligation (eg political offences or political nature of a request for extradition; emergency situations; immunities); the problem of multiple requests for extradition; guarantees in case of extradition; and other issues related to extradition in general.

(vi) What happens in case of conflicting principles (eg non-extradition of nationals *v* no indictment in national law? obstacles to prosecute *v* risks for the accused to be tortured or lack of due process in the State to which extradition is envisaged?); constitutional limitations.**

(e) **Conditions for the triggering of the obligation to extradite or prosecute**

(i) Presence of the alleged offender in the territory of the State;

(ii) State's jurisdiction over the crime concerned;

(iii) Existence of a request for extradition (degree of formalism required); Relations with the right to expel foreigners;

(iv) Existence/consequences of a previous request for extradition that had been rejected;

(v) Standard of proof (to what extent must the request for extradition be substantiated?);

(vi) Existence of circumstances that might exclude the operation of the obligation (eg political offences or political nature of a request for extradition; emergency situations; immunities).

(f) **The implementation of the obligation to extradite or prosecute**

(i) Respective roles of the judiciary and the executive;

(ii) How to reconcile the obligation to extradite or prosecute with the discretion of the prosecuting authorities;

(iii) Whether the availability of evidence affects the operation of the obligation;

(iv) How to deal with multiple requests for extradition;

(v) Guarantees in case of extradition;

(vi) Whether the alleged offender should be kept in custody awaiting a decision on his or her extradition or prosecution; or possibilities of other restrictions to freedom?;

(vii) Control of the implementation of the obligation;

(viii) Consequences of non-compliance with the obligation to extradite or prosecute.

(g) **The relationship between the obligation to extradite or prosecute and the surrender of the alleged offender to a competent international criminal tribunal (the 'third alternative')**

To what extent the 'third' alternative has an impact on the other two.

[*It might be that a final determination on these questions will only be possible at a later stage, in particular after a careful analysis of the scope and content of the obligation to extradite or prosecute under existing treaty regimes. It might also be advisable to examine the customary nature of the obligation in relation to specific crimes.

** This issue might need to be addressed also in relation to the implementation of the obligation to extradite or prosecute (f).]

522 At the Sixth Committee debate in 2012, Austria, the Netherlands, and Vietnam considered the 2009 General Framework a valuable supplement to the work of the Commission. In the opinion of the Netherlands, the work of the Commission should eventually result in presenting draft articles based on that General Framework. At the Sixth Committee debate in 2013, Austria reiterated the usefulness of the 2009 General Framework to the work of the present Working Group.

(58) The Commission notes that the United Nations Office on Drugs and Crime has prepared the 2004 Model Law on Extradition, which addresses most of these issues.[523] The Secretariat Survey (2010) has also explained that multilateral conventions on extradition usually stipulate the conditions applicable to the extradition process.[524] Nearly all such conventions subject extradition to the conditions provided by the law of the requested State. There may be grounds of refusal that are connected to the offence (eg the expiry of the statute of limitations, the failure to satisfy requirements of double criminality, specialty, *nullum crimen sine lege* and *nulla poena sine lege* or *non bis in idem*, or the fact that the crime is subject to the death penalty in the requesting State) or not so connected (eg the granting of political asylum to the individual or the existence of humanitarian reasons to deny extradition). The degree of specificity of the conditions applicable to extradition varies depending on factors such as the specific concerns expressed during the course of negotiations (eg non-extradition of nationals, application or non-application of the political exception or fiscal exception clauses), the particular nature of the offence (eg the risk of refusal of extradition based on the political character of the offence appears to be more acute with respect to certain crimes), and drafting changes to take into account problems that may have been overlooked in the past (eg the possible triviality of the request for extradition or the protection of the rights of the alleged offender) or to take into account new developments or a changed environment.[525]

(59) The relationship between the obligation to extradite or prosecute and other principles as enumerated in the 2009 General Framework belongs not only to international law, but also to the constitutional law and domestic law of the States concerned. Whatever the conditions under domestic law or a treaty pertaining to extradition, they must not be applied in bad faith, with the effect of shielding an alleged offender from prosecution in or extradition to an appropriate criminal jurisdiction. In the case of core crimes, the object and purpose of the relevant domestic law and/or applicable treaty is to ensure that perpetrators of such crimes do not enjoy impunity, implying that such crimes can never be considered political offences and be exempted from extradition.[526]

[523] Available at <http://www.unodc.org/pdf/model_law_extradition.pdf>. See also Revised Manuals on the Model Treaty on Extradition and on the Model Treaty on Mutual Assistance in Criminal Matters, available at: <http://www.unodc.org/pdf/model_treaty_extradition_revised_manual.pdf> (visited on 3 June 2014).

[524] Secretariat Survey (2010) para 139.

[525] ibid para 142.

[526] A good example is Art 1 of the Additional Protocol, dated 15 Oct 1975, to the 1957 European Convention on Extradition, which reads:

> For the application of Article 3 [on political offences] of the Convention, political offences shall not be considered to include the following:
> (a) the crimes against humanity specified in the Convention on the Prevention and Punishment of the Crime of Genocide adopted on 9 December 1948 by the General Assembly of the United Nations;
> (b) the violations specified in Article 50 of the 1949 Geneva Convention for the Amelioration of the Condition of the Wounded and Sick in Armed Forces in the Field, Article 51 of the 1949 Geneva Convention for the Amelioration of the Condition of Wounded, Sick and Shipwrecked members of Armed Forces at Sea, Article 130 of the 1949 Geneva Convention relative to the Treatment of Prisoners of War and Article 147 of the 1949 Geneva Convention relative to the Protection of Civilian Persons in Time of War;
> (c) any comparable violations of the laws of war having effect at the time when this Protocol enters into force and of customs of war existing at that time, which are not already provided for in the above-mentioned provisions of the Geneva Conventions (*Council of Europe Treaty Series No 086*).

Index